FINANCING CANADIAN FEDERATION: 5

Local Government Finance in Canada

Harry M. Kitchen

THE UNIVERSITY OF WESTERN ONTARIO

Andrew Sancton
Director
Local Government Program
& Associate Professor of Political Science

Social Science Centre
London, Canada N6A 5C2
Telephone: (519) 661-3266 Ext. 5162
        or: (519) 661-3657

Canadian Tax Foundation
L'Association Canadienne
d'Études Fiscales

Canadian Cataloguing in Publication Data

Kitchen, Harry M.
    Local government finance in Canada

(Financing Canadian federation, ISSN 0225-5103 ; 5)

Includes index.
ISBN 0-88808-020-4

1. Local finance—Canada.
2. Finance, Public—Canada.
I. Canadian Tax Foundation.   II. Title.   III. Series.

HJ9350.K58   1984   336'.014'71   C84-098877-X

©1984, Canadian Tax Foundation
Printed in Canada   4M   7-84

Foreword

The expenditures and revenues of local governments play a major role in Canadian life. In recent years, the wide range of essential community services provided by Canada's nearly 5,000 municipalities accounted for over 8 per cent of total GNP. Despite the significant impact of local governments on economic activity, relatively little research effort has been directed at the examination and analysis of their finances in a comprehensive way. Most studies have focussed either on the financial problems of specific cities or metropolitan areas or on particular services such as education and transportation. There has never been a thorough comparative analysis of municipal finances across Canada. In the light of increasing urbanization and mounting demands for services that seem greater than the revenue resources available to satisfy them, such a comprehensive examination is long overdue.

This volume is intended to fill that need. The author begins with an historical overview of the development of the local government sector and a review of the trends in organization reform that have emerged over the last several years. He then analyzes the expenditure and revenue patterns of local governments and continues with a discussion of the dilemmas facing them today in the areas of employment and compensation, pensions, accounting and budgeting, and productivity. He concludes with suggestions of ways in which the local sector can work toward greater economic efficiency.

Harry M. Kitchen is Professor of Economics at Trent University. He has written extensively in the area of local government finance and is the co-author (with Robin W. Boadway) of another Foundation monograph, *Canadian Tax Policy* (second edition, 1984).

This is the fifth volume in the Foundation's series on Financing Canadian Federation and was supported in part with funds provided by the Aluminum Company of Canada Limited, Canadian General Electric Company Limited, Du Pont of Canada Limited, Imperial Oil Limited, The Molson Companies Limited, Noranda Mines Limited, Southam Inc., and The Steel Company of Canada, Limited.

Paula Pike edited the manuscript and prepared the index. Martha Warnes verified references and assisted with proofreading.

The views expressed in this volume are those of the author and should not be attributed to the organizations that helped finance the project or to the Foundation and its members.

Douglas J. Sherbaniuk
Director
July 1984

Contents

CONTENTS

List of Tables

Preface

One of the most neglected areas in the field of public finance is the municipal sector. While this was understandable at a time when municipal budgets were relatively small and municipal services somewhat limited, it is surprising that the significant growth in budgets and services provided by local governments over the past three decades has not inspired a corresponding increase in the empirical research devoted to municipal issues. Clearly, such research is needed if governments are to make intelligent and informed decisions about the many issues that affect their revenues and expenditures, and hence, improve the allocation of society's resources. This book is intended to fill a portion of this void. It is a reasonably detailed account of local government expenditures and revenues along with an overview of their economic effects. Hopefully, the material in this book will provide the reader with a better understanding of the municipal financial scene and assist in subsequent evaluations of local expenditure and revenue issues. In addition, it is hoped that this book will raise enough questions and generate enough concerns to prompt some much needed research into many issues that currently affect the local level financial picture.

This book is divided into four parts. Part I presents an overview of the municipal financial scene in Canada. In this part, Chapter 1 briefly reviews the development of the municipal financial system up to and beyond Confederation. It then devotes some attention to the various reforms proposed for reorganizing local governments in order to provide their services more efficiently. Chapter 2 combines the provincial and municipal sectors so as to provide a comparative basis for discussing a number of financial implications. The reason for this aggregation is rather obvious but, perhaps, needs stating. A simple comparison of municipal revenue and expenditure figures in municipalities in different provinces may be meaningless because of the different provincial/municipal allocation of responsibilities in each of the provinces. This combination of municipal and provincial sectors eliminates most of these difficulties and, in turn, provides this author with a basis for making some useful comparative comments on a number of fiscal indicators.

In some ways, Part II follows the format of the early part of the preceding chapter. However, a different data base is used. In Chapter 2, local and provincial expenditures were aggregated so as to facilitate interprovincial comparisons. In this section of the book, local expenditures alone will be considered, thus providing the basis for commenting on and assessing the municipal sector as it has developed and is currently functioning in the different provinces. Briefly, Chapter 3 begins with a comparative assessment of the relative importance of the local sector in the provincial economies. This is followed by an interprovincial comparison of the growth of local expenditures and, more specifically, operating expenditures financed from local revenues for the period 1968 to 1978. This chapter concludes with a discussion of the level of government responsible for providing local public services (in total) along with the absolute level of these operating expenditures by province and size of municipality for 1978.

Chapters 4 and 5 separate local operating expenditures into two classifications: major (Chapter 4) and minor (Chapter 5). The discussion in these two chapters concentrates on an interprovincial comparison and description of each functional expenditure under the following three headings: local government responsibility for funding each function from its own sources of revenue, per capita municipal operating expenditures by province, and per capita local operating expenditures by size and location of municipality.

Chapter 6 addresses a number of issues relating to both capital expenditure levels and budgeting methods and the financing of the corresponding capital projects.

Part III consists of four chapters. Chapter 7 reviews the local revenue patterns across the provinces and outlines the changing levels and relative dependence on this source over the past few years. Chapters 8, 9, and 10 review and evaluate a number of issues involving local property taxes, intergovernmental transfers, and other revenue sources (primarily user charges) respectively.

Part IV covers a number of topics of particular importance to municipal governments. Chapter 11 discusses local government employment and compensations issues, while Chapter 12 deals with the increasingly important and topical area of local public-sector pensions. Chapter 13 reviews the many facets of local government accounting and budgeting. Chapter 14 covers additional expenditure-related issues including local government productivity; cash managment policies; purchasing and pooling arrangements; boards, commissions, and special-purpose bodies; provincial/municipal funding arrangements; and forecasting. Chapter 15 concentrates on the future of municipal finance with specific emphasis placed on ways in which local governments may improve their ability to meet their required expenditures. Among the alternatives considered in Chapter 15 are an expansion in the use of existing revenue sources, a transferral of expenditure responsibility from the local to the provincial government, and the possibility of tapping into income or sales tax revenues.

There are a few points that must be taken into account when reading this book. First, the terms "local government" and "municipal government" are used interchangeably, and refer to all activities of local governments. This usage differs from the standard Statistics Canada treatment of municipal versus local; where the former refers to services undertaken by the incorporated municipality itself and the latter includes these services as well as those provided by other local public organizations such as elementary and secondary school boards (when this is defined as a local rather than provincial responsibility); municipal hospitals; homes for the aged; and separate boards, commissions, and special-purpose bodies.

Second, the book's intertemporal analysis runs from 1968 to 1978 except where more recent data are available. Since published data were not available on a consistent and uniform basis prior to 1968, this year was chosen as the initial year of the analysis. With the exception of some instances, where more recent data are available, 1978 is the last year for which data were available at the time of writing.

Third, unless otherwise stated and in order to achieve uniformity and consistency across provinces and over time, the data base employed in this study is that which was collected and compiled by the Local Government Section of the Public Finance Division of Statistics Canada. This differs from the data base published by some provincial governments. For a discussion of these statistical differences, the reader is referred to the Introduction of the Canadian Tax Foundation's *Provincial and Municipal Finances, 1981*.

Fourth, local governments in the Yukon and Northwest Territories are excluded from this discussion. Reference, then, is confined to local governments in the 10 provinces.

Fifth, in a book of this scope, it is impossible to be completely exhaustive or entirely up to date and, therefore, the reader may observe some discrepancies between the operation of a particular municipality on a specific function and the operation described in the following chapters. For this, the author apologizes. The discussions and analyses contained in this book, however, both describe the situation that tends to exist in most municipalities and make suggestions as to what should exist if greater efficiency is to be achieved in the provision of local services.

In writing this book, I have received assistance from many people and organizations, not the least of which include the Canadian Tax Foundation and its Director, Douglas Sherbaniuk. Karen Sheppard provided invaluable research assistance in collecting and compiling most of the data and in writing selected portions of this book. The typing and repeated typing of the various drafts were patiently and competently handled by Grace Dyer and Carol Wood of Trent University and Karin Treff and Pat Hunt of the Tax Foundation's staff. In addition, special thanks go to David Perry of the Canadian Tax Foundation for allowing me to tap his thorough knowledge of the institutional and descriptive features of the local finance scene in Canada. Similar thanks go to government officials at all levels, but most of all to Graham Marr of Statistics Canada who provided me with numerous pages of unpublished and extremely useful data. Finally, my greatest thanks go to Richard Bird of the University of Toronto and Melville McMillan of the University of Alberta for their incisive and detailed comments on the entire manscript. Without these comments, this book would have been substantially inferior in its final form.

Harry Kitchen
Department of Economics
Trent University

Part I

An Overview

1
Historical Development
of the Local Government Sector

INTRODUCTION

While municipal or local government finances have long had a direct impact on the Canadian way of life, municipalities are not free to control solely their own financial destinies. Their powers and expenditure responsibilities, along with their revenue sources, are dictated by provincial statutes. In turn, these provincial statutes are defined by the powers of the Constitution Act. This Act has brought about the establishment of local governments that are legally subordinate to their respective provincial governments. As such, municipalities have been and are particularly limited in their ability to control their own sources of revenue. This has led to a situation where most of a municipality's current revenue is obtained from a mixture of real property taxation, licences, fees or user charges, and provincial transfers.

Before launching into a presentation and assessment of the municipal finance scene in Canada, this chapter will briefly review the development of the municipal sector from pre-Confederation days to the present. In addition, some space is devoted to the current structure and recent reforms of local government that have taken place across the country over the past two decades.

DEVELOPMENT OF THE LOCAL SECTOR

PRE-CONFEDERATION GROWTH
OF THE MUNICIPAL SECTOR[1]

During the period leading up to Confederation, Upper Canada (which was later to become the Province of Ontario) had developed a more extensive system of local government than that which existed in either Lower Canada or Atlantic Canada. By the beginning of the nineteenth century, such concerns as sanitation, streets, education, welfare, and local law enforcement were becoming sufficiently important (especially in the urban areas) to warrant their provision by local governments. In 1841, the District Councils Act was passed in Upper Canada. This provided for an elected district council to take over the administrative responsibilities previously exercised by the Courts of Quarter Sessions[2]

---

[1]For a more detailed development of this topic, see among others, John Harvey Perry, *Taxes, Tariffs and Subsidies* (Toronto: University of Toronto Press, 1955) and G.P. de T. Glazebrook, "The Origins of Local Government," in Frederick Henry Armstrong, H.A. Stevenson, and J.D. Wilson, eds., *Aspects of Nineteenth Century Ontario* (Toronto: University of Toronto Press, 1974).

[2]Government by session involved the meeting of justices of the peace for each county in regular session once a year in January and if a second session was needed they would meet again in early summer. At these so-called quarter sessions, besides hearing all legal cases, the justices conducted all the necessary business of local government. At each session the justices had a grand jury to assist them. The grand jury had no executive powers. For further information see Donald C. Rowat, *Your Local Government: A Sketch of the Municipal System in Canada,* 2nd ed. (Toronto: Macmillan, 1975), 2-3.

in rural areas. This Act allowed rural districts to establish a system of local government similar to that already enjoyed by the urban municipalities. While the district councils were given responsibility for roads, municipal offices, taxation, justice, education, and welfare, their most important functions were constructing and maintaining roads and bridges and laying out and creating school districts.

This expansion in the provision of local services generated a number of problems, not the least of which was the method of financing these additional services. Unfortunately, from the municipalities' perspective, sufficient revenues were not forthcoming from the provincial and federal levels of government. Consequently, rural municipalities were left with the necessity of increasing their own sources of revenue. To achieve this, they expanded their tax base from a simple levy on selected forms of property, as outlined in the Assessment Act of 1793, to include a more fully developed tax based on personal and real property as well as a tax on personal income.

During the same period, the Municipal Corporation Act (1849) was passed. Instead of creating a new system of municipal government, its chief objective was to consolidate all of the existing municipal legislation and establish villages, towns, and cities as the basic urban municipal unit. Although considerably amended, the Municipal Corporation Act is still the basis for municipal government in Ontario today. Thus, by 1867, Upper Canada developed an extensive system of local government. This system established a reasonable basis for providing municipal services and generated the subsequent revenues necessary to supply them.

Although Lower Canada faced many of the same political and economic pressures as Upper Canada, little progress was made in the early establishment of local government. In 1840, an ordinance was passed that provided for a system of local government that was similar in many ways to the district councils established in 1841 in Upper Canada. Even though these newly created municipal units were given the power of taxation, most of the real power remained with the British-appointed governor. With the exception of customs duties, the burden of taxation was previously unknown to the people of Lower Canada and, to say the least, the suggestion of a new tax system did not meet with a favourable response. By 1855, the Lower Canada Municipal and Road Act was passed. This legislation became the foundation of Quebec's municipal institutions and remained in effect, with minor changes, until the turn of the century. Under this Act, incorporated municipalities were authorized to tax personal income, profits of businesses and professions, and real property.[3]

Municipal organization in Atlantic Canada prior to 1867 was, by comparison, quite underdeveloped. For example, only a few parts of New Brunswick were organized into municipalities and no municipal organization existed in Nova Scotia. Early local government in New Brunswick was conducted by the Courts of Quarter Sessions and a grand jury, while similar governmental responsibilities were undertaken by the Courts of Quarter Sessions in Nova Scotia. However, this was altered in 1851 when New Brunswick passed legislation providing for the establishment of municipal institutions. During this

---

[3]Perry, supra footnote 1, at 578.

time, the few municipalities that did exist made use of poll taxes and direct property taxes. Property included income and real and personal property.

Various reasons have been suggested for the slow development of local government in eastern Canada. Perhaps the most likely reasons included the general indifference of the people, the great compactness of the area involved, which made it easier to retain centralized control, and the lack of urgency to provide roads in a region where people could rely on water-borne transportation.

GROWTH OF THE MUNICIPAL SECTOR— CONFEDERATION TO WORLD WAR II

By Confederation, both Ontario and Quebec had relatively well-established municipal governments and financial systems. In fact, Ontario's municipal financial responsibilities and revenue sources had developed to the point where they are essentially the same today, with the only major changes being "the substitution of a business tax for the personal property tax in 1904 and the repeal of the income tax in 1935."[4] To give some indication of the proportion of total tax revenue that was derived from each of the revenue sources in Ontario municipalities, Toronto may be cited as an example. In the fiscal year 1878-79, 81 per cent of taxation revenue was derived from taxes on real estate, 15 per cent from taxes on personal property, and 4 per cent from taxes on income. By the fiscal year 1892-93, the corresponding percentages were 89 per cent, 7 per cent and 4 per cent respectively.

When Quebec entered Confederation, incorporated municipalities were allowed to impose their own tax on incomes. This was soon changed, however, and in 1870 the Quebec government repealed the right of towns, villages, and counties to levy income taxes. At the same time, the authority to levy income taxes was retained for some Quebec cities. In fact, this situation remained unchanged until the wartime tax agreements between Quebec and the federal government were enacted during the second world war.

In comparison with Ontario and Quebec, municipal governments in both Atlantic and western Canada were either lacking or considerably underdeveloped in 1867. For instance, it was not until 1877 that a municipalities act creating a system of municipal government was enacted in New Brunswick. At the same time, Nova Scotia waited until 1879 before it created a municipal system for all non-urban areas and until 1888 before it approved legislation providing for town or city government with an elected mayor and council. These municipal governments, and the corresponding municipal expenditures, required revenue sources previously untapped.

Municipalities in Nova Scotia, prior to the 1900s, used poll taxes, land taxes, personal property taxes, and income taxes to raise revenue. The poll tax, which did not account for more than one-quarter of total municipal revenue after 1888, was, nevertheless, a significant revenue source for this province, as were property taxes. Income tax revenue was relatively unimportant.

---

[4]Perry, supra footnote 1, at 34.

By way of contrast, income tax was an important revenue source in New Brunswick. In Fredericton, for example, it represented about one-third of the revenues obtained from the property tax. In the last quarter of the nineteenth century, New Brunswick revised its municipal financial system so that five-sixths of its municipal tax revenue would be derived from levies on real and personal property and income (all assessed at full value) and one-sixth would be derived from a poll tax on male persons age 21 or over.

Only two municipalities, Charlottetown and Summerside, existed in Prince Edward Island before 1890 and their revenue was derived almost entirely from poll and real and personal property taxes.

Turning to western Canada, it was in 1870 that Manitoba, formerly a part of the Northwest Territories, became a province. Three years later the first Municipal Act, providing for the establishment of local municipalities, was passed. British Columbia entered as a province in 1871 and in 1872 the provincial legislature passed an act allowing municipalities to incorporate. Throughout the latter part of the nineteenth century, land and personal property formed the basis for taxation in Manitoba, and British Columbia derived municipal revenue from real property taxes. These two provinces were unique in that their municipalities did not at any time impose taxes on income.

The municipalities in territories that were later to become Saskatchewan and Alberta were governed by the Northwest Territories' Ordinance Respecting Municipalities of 1883. This Act provided for the taxation of real and personal property, as well as income in excess of $500; the real propery tax, however, was the only tax seriously imposed.

By the 1900s, municipalities in every province in Canada levied a tax of some form on real property. At the same time, there was growing dissatisfaction with the personal property tax in all of the provincial municipalities that imposed it. The inequalities and inconsistencies that resulted from the taxation of less visible property led to considerable agitation for its abolition. Municipalities in Quebec had never implemented a tax on personal property. Ontario municipalities, on the other hand, subsequently abolished this tax in 1904. Similar action was taken by municipalities in Saskatchewan (1908) and Manitoba and Alberta (early 1900s). The municipalities in British Columbia had never availed themselves of this tax since the taxation of personal property was considered to be in the provincial domain. With the exception of Halifax, however, the remaining municipalities in Atlantic Canada showed no signs of abandoning personal property taxation until after World War I.

During the time personal property taxation was facing widespread opposition and subsequent abolition, the provinces introduced a municipal business tax to fill part of the resulting revenue shortfall. The introduction of this tax at the municipal level began in Quebec when the City of Montreal had been granted the right to impose the tax as early as 1876. Shortly thereafter other Quebec cities were granted access to the business tax and by the mid-1900s, a business tax in one form or another was authorized in virtually every municipality in Canada.

During this same period, real property taxes became the most widely used revenue source across Canada and accounted for 82 per cent of total municipal revenues in 1913, 82 per cent in 1921, and 81 per cent in 1930.[5] Although this was true for municipalities right across Canada, the bases upon which the real property tax was levied were quite diverse (see Chapter 8).

Up until 1913, this heavy reliance on the real property tax posed no difficulties for municipalities. Speculation and the general boom conditions, which were particularly apparent in the western provinces, ensured that the property tax would yield substantial revenues and that individuals would have no difficulty meeting their tax obligations. When land and income values began to plummet in 1913, however, the municipalities found their financial positions seriously jeopardized. This state of affairs was exacerbated in most of the provinces by the imposition of provincial property taxes that tended to limit municipal use of the tax and render collections more difficult. It was during this period that the western municipalities beat a hasty retreat from the use of the "single tax" principle and began to include improvements to land in their tax bases. Only in the rural municipalities of Saskatchewan and Alberta was the practice of taxing land only retained.

Municipalities were becoming increasingly dependent on revenues generated by the real property tax, and were simultaneously depending less on the yield from the municipal personal income tax. By the 1920s, municipal income taxation existed in only four provinces: Nova Scotia, New Brunswick, Ontario, and Saskatchewan. In fact, municipal income taxation had never been enthusiastically received and it played a significant role only in New Brunswick. In 1907, for example, the ratio of taxable income assessed to realty assessment in New Brunswick reached 34 per cent while the corresponding figure in Ontario for the same year was 4 per cent.[6] By the 1930s, however, municipal income tax was the object of growing discontent. Municipalities eventually vacated this field in 1941 by federal-provincial agreement.

GROWTH OF THE MUNICIPAL SECTOR—
WORLD WAR II TO THE PRESENT

Although there has always been some variation in the level of, and responsibility for, municipal expenditures in the different provinces, the expenditure patterns were virtually established by the end of World War II. In most instances, local governments in Ontario provided the same services as they did in Nova Scotia or, indeed, any other province. Regardless of the locality, post-World War II municipalities began to face increasing pressures for more involvement in the lives of citizens. The trend toward greater urbanization, rapid technological advances, and the concentration of industrial production in urban areas led to increasing demands being placed on local governments. In 1947, the local government sector in aggregate accounted for 4.4 per cent of the Gross National Expenditure (GNE). At the same time, the federal and provincial governments' contribution totalled 14.1 per cent and 5.2 per cent of GNE respectively (Appendix Table A.1).

---

[5] Perry, supra footnote 1, at 128.

[6] Solomon Vineburg, *Provincial and Local Taxation in Canada* (New York: AMS Press, 1968), 69 and 72.

During the three decades following 1947, the growth of the municipal sector continued significantly. Increases in personal disposable income and tensions created by an expanding industrial society generated demands for better local services, including police protection, roads, street lighting, sewers, and water. At the same time, local governments increased significantly the provision of local services such as education and recreational facilities. In most instances, these services were previously lacking or were supplied on a relatively modest scale. By 1980, the contribution of the local sector in aggregate to total GNE had almost doubled, from 4.4 per cent to 8.6 per cent. During this same time, the federal government's involvement had increased modestly from 14.1 per cent to 16.7 per cent of GNE while the increase at the provincial level had been the most significant, rising from 5.2 per cent to 12.5 per cent of GNE (Appendix Table A.1).

To gain a slightly different perspective, although one that still supports the figures presented above, it is useful to note that per capita local government expenditures rose from $46.40 in 1947 to $1,035.59 (current dollars) in 1980 for an increase of 2,132 per cent (Table 1.1). Similar increases can be noted for the federal (1,263 per cent) and provincial (2,660 per cent) governments. Overall, the government sector, in current dollars, rose at a rate that was significantly higher than the rate of increase in the private sector.

While these figures indicate the importance of each level of government, they must be interpreted somewhat cautiously. For example, increases due to increased population have been eliminated by presenting the figures in per capita terms, but illusory increases in the form of increased prices still remain. Hence it is useful to adjust for these inflationary increases and to reassess the relative importance of the government sector. The results suggest that the rate of increase in the cost of providing a standard set of goods and services in the public sector exceeds similar cost figures in the private sector. To be more precise, the increase in constant per capita dollars in the entire public sector amounted to 127 per cent, with the local (148 per cent) and provincial (203 per cent) sector increases outstripping the federal (52 per cent) increase. Indeed, the real increase in the local and provincial sectors, taken separately, exceeded that of the private sector (143 per cent), thus illustrating the increasing role that is being assumed by this sector of the economy.

Table 1.1   Per Capita Increase in GNE (Current and Constant Dollars), Excluding the Government Sector, 1947-80

	Increase in current dollars 1947-80	Increase in constant dollars 1947-80
	per cent	
Total GNE..................................	1,053	137
Total GNE excluding the government sector	775	143
Federal government expenditures	1,263	52
Provincial government expenditures	2,660	203
Local government expenditures	2,132	148
Total government sector	1,944	127

Source: Calculated from Appendix Table A.2.

Throughout the past three decades, rapid increases in expenditures by local and provincial governments have created many problems related to the revenue available for funding these expenditures. The property tax, the longtime backbone of municipal finance, has come under severe criticism from a number of groups, including the general public, politicians, and academics. Despite these criticisms, this tax retains an important role at the local level. In 1947, real and personal property taxes accounted for 51.5 per cent of all local government revenue while transfers from other governments amounted to 17.2 per cent, and other sources, including amusement taxes, business taxes, licences, and fees generated the remaining 31.3 per cent (Appendix Table A.3). By 1978, the pendulum had swung so that real and personal property taxes in aggregate accounted for only 37 per cent of total municipal revenue, with transfers covering 47.6 per cent and other revenue contributing 15.4 per cent. While these figures reflect both ends of the 32-year period extending from 1947 to 1978, the municipal finance scene as a whole has been characterized by a declining percentage of revenues coming from its own sources and an increasingly larger portion coming from transfers primarily from provincial governments.

Throughout this period, the structure and imposition of the property tax did change. These changes were slow and were made only after considerable deliberation and cautious assessment of their implications. Of interest here are a few events that should be noted. For instance, when Newfoundland entered the Dominion of Canada in 1949, the property tax had not been used there to any great extent except in the city of St. John's. By 1952, this situation changed and the property tax replaced the poll tax as the most important revenue source in almost every municipality. In Quebec, municipalities had been authorized to levy a property tax on Catholic property owners for the construction and maintenance of Roman Catholic buildings. This tax was used therefore "as the means of providing a formal and systematic contribution to the construction and maintenance of religious buildings."[7]

During the 1960s and 1970s, the real property tax continued as the main tax source for local governments. Personal property taxes and poll taxes declined in importance until they had virtually disappeared by the early 1970s. As well, during these two decades, a number of reports[8] that deal to a greater or lesser extent with municipal financial problems were published. As a result of these reports, a number of suggestions have been implemented—for example, (1) the transfer of some expenditure functions from the municipal to the provincial level; (2) the reduction or elimination of a number of property exemptions; (3) improvements in assessment techniques, and more importantly, the introduction of equalized assessment; (4) the adoption of property tax credits; and (5) improvements in the administrative machinery.

---

[7]Perry, supra footnote 1, at 458.

[8]For a review of the eight provincial reports, see Joe Martin, "Real Property Taxation: Stirrings of Reform" (September-October 1972), 20 *Canadian Tax Journal* 437-52. Newfoundland and British Columbia were the only two provincial governments not to publish a report, although in the latter case, a joint provincial-municipal study was undertaken, but aborted before completion. More recently, at least two studies have been completed on municipalities; one on Metropolitan Toronto and one on the Regional Municipality of Waterloo. See Ontario, *Report of the Royal Commission on Metropolitan Toronto,* 2 Vols. (Toronto: the Commission, June 1977); and Ontario, *Report of the Waterloo Region Review Commission* (Waterloo: the Commission, March 1979).

THE PRESENT STRUCTURE OF LOCAL GOVERNMENT

By the beginning of the twentieth century, most provinces had in place or were about to establish a system of municipal institutions. The province of Quebec received local government somewhat less warmly than did Ontario. In the Atlantic region, the introduction of local government was strongly opposed because of a fear of property taxation. In the west, conversely, local government was viewed favourably, since many settlers wished to maintain the organized systems that they had left in Upper Canada.[9] In any case, a system of local government evolved across Canada, with perhaps the most salient feature being the complexity of their structures.[10] Because they were designated as "creatures" of their provinces, there existed the potential for 10 distinct systems of municipal organization. Despite the legislative freedom awarded by the Constitution, provincial governments have developed municipal systems that appear similar to the casual observer but very different to students of organizational structure.

The following section describes the present structure of local government in each province, outlining their historical perspective where relevant and describing recent reform measures where applicable. It may be useful to begin this description with a brief overview of the Canadian municipal system as a whole.

Overview[11]

Until recently, the various systems of local government in Canada displayed an organization according to municipal type that had not changed for many years (Table 1.2). Although the basic system allows for only four classes of municipalities—cities, towns, villages, and rural districts—there are notable exceptions. Several provinces in the East make no use of the rural system of local government, and over the period 1968-78, several other provinces underwent considerable reorganization of their larger (urban) municipal governments. Table 1.2 suggests that over the decade, every province underwent some form of change in municipal organization, be it expansion or consolidation, in response to either population growth or royal commission recommendations. In short, specific differences have emerged across the country, and a brief review from east to west will illustrate these.

With the exception of Nova Scotia, the provinces in Atlantic Canada have never provided for a system of rural municipalities. Conversely, in the balance of the provinces, isolated northern areas are minimally organized into local

---

[9]C.R. Tindal and S. Nobes Tindal, *Local Government in Canada: An Introduction* (Toronto: McGraw-Hill Ryerson, 1979), 17.

[10]Paul Hickey, "The Changing Structure of Municipal Government in Canada," in Canadian Institute of Chartered Accountants, *Municipal Finance and Administration in Canada,* rev. ed. (Toronto: the Institute, 1972), 6.

[11]Most of the information contained in this section has been compiled from a variety of well-established books on the subject including: Canadian Tax Foundation, *Provincial and Municipal Finances, 1981* (Toronto: the Foundation, 1981), Chapter 8; Margot J. Fawcett and C.E. (Ted) Clarke, eds., *The 1982 Corpus Almanac of Canada,* Vol. 2 (Toronto: Corpus, 1982), Chapter 17; David Siegel, "Provincial-Municipal Relations in Canada: An Overview" (Summer 1980), 23 *Canadian Public Administration* 282-88; supra footnote 9, at Chapter 4; and Donald J.H. Higgins, *Urban Canada: Its Government and Politics* (Toronto: Macmillan, 1977), Chapters 1 and 4.

Table 1.2   Municipalities by Type by Province, 1968 and 1978

| | Regional municipality | | | | Unitary municipalities | | | | | | | | Quasi-municipalities and local improvement districts c | | Total | |
| | Metropolitan and regional municipality a | | Counties and regional districts | | Cities | | Towns | | Villages | | Rural municipalities b | | | | | |
Province	1968	1978	1968	1978	1968	1978	1968	1978	1968	1978	1968	1978	1968	1978	1968	1978
Nfld.	—	—	—	—	2	2	63	131	80d	—	4	—	10e	174	159	307
P.E.I.	—	—	—	—	1	1	7	8	22	28	—	—	—	—	30	37
N.S.	—	—	—	—	3	3	39	38	—f	—	24	24	—	—	66	65
N.B.	—	—	—	—	6	6	21	21	87	85	—	—	—	—	114	112
Que.	1	3	74	72	66	66	84	192	302	240	1,099	1,004	18	13	1,726	1,577
Ont.	1	12	38	27	38	45g	152	144	155	120	562	476	18	17	964	837
Man.	1	—	—	—	9	5	36	35	40	40	110	105	10	—	214	202
Sask.	—	—	—	—	11	11	130	135	358	346	294	299	—	—	803	791
Alta.	—	—	—	—	10	10	100	104	167	168	49	48	46	21	366	351
B.C.	—	—	25	28	31	33	13	11	56	58	40	38	—	269	65	437
All prov.	3	15	137	127	177	182	745	819	1,267	1,085	2,182	1,994	102	494	4,613	4,716

aIncludes urban communities in Quebec and Metro Toronto and regional municipalities in Ontario. bIncludes municipalities in Nova Scotia parishes, townships in Quebec, townships in Ontario, rural municipalities in Manitoba, Saskatchewan, and municipal districts in Alberta. cIncludes local government communities, local government improvement districts in Newfoundland, improvement districts in Ontario, Alberta and Saskatchewan, and government districts in Manitoba. dLocal government communities with limited power. eIn 1968 these districts were nonself-governing. fExcludes village service commission with limited functions. gIncludes five boroughs in Metro Toronto.

Source: The data for 1968 were taken from Donald C. Rowat, *The Canadian Municipal System: Essays on the Improvement of Local Government* (Toronto: McClelland and Stewart, 1969), viii and the data for 1978 from Statistics Canada, *Canada Year Book 1980-1981*, Catalogue no. CS11-402E.

improvement or provincial government districts if they are organized at all. In the country as a whole, over the period from 1968-78, there has been a doubling of the number of these quasi-municipalities. The two-tiered municipal systems in Quebec, Ontario and British Columbia differ from the rest of the provinces but even this difference has changed recently. In 1968, the second tier of government was the county. Its governing unit consisted of representatives from the various unitary municipalities with the exception of cities, which were governed separately. By 1978, the county concept was replaced in several of the larger metropolitan areas by regional governments. In Ontario, a single regional municipality (Metro Toronto) was expanded to 12 separate regional governments. In Quebec, two regional governments now operate in addition to the original metropolitan area of Montreal. British Columbia was the only western province to establish similar second-tier governing bodies (regional districts). Manitoba and Saskatchewan, understandably, have a larger number of rural municipalities, while Alberta has fewer but larger rural units because of early rural consolidation. Their relative magnitudes have remained roughly the same over the 1968–78 period. Before 1968, British Columbia had no towns, and assigned the status of city to all urban areas. Because these cities are under the jurisdiction of the larger regional districts (unlike Ontario and Quebec), however, the discrepancy between status and population is inconsequential.

Newfoundland

As mentioned previously, local government came later to Newfoundland than elsewhere in the country. This late development was a result of a highly centralized population that could be adequately serviced by the provincial government.[12] In 1980, there were 315 incorporated areas in the province encompassing less than 1 per cent of its area, but containing more than 80 per cent of its total population.[13] For the rest of the province, local service districts under the aegis of appointed trustees have been established to provide specific services.

Table 1.2 indicates that there are only two cities—Corner Brook and St. John's—and this number has not changed since 1968. St. John's can, however, be considered to have a very limited form of regional government since the inception of a metropolitan area board. Newfoundland has recently embarked on a general scheme of municipal reorganization arising from the Whalen Royal Commission, which, as of 1980, provided for a complete consolidation and revision of municipal legislation, including provision for regional government and greater local autonomy.[14]

Prince Edward Island

Municipal governments have never been strong in Prince Edward Island, and there are a total of only three incorporated districts on the Island. The scattered nature of populated communities to be served over a rather ubiquitous, flat

---

[12]The first town did not appear until 1888, with the incorporation of St. John's. Fawcett and Clarke, supra footnote 11, at 17-19.

[13]Canadian Tax Foundation, supra footnote 11, at 200.

[14]Fawcett and Clarke, supra footnote 11, at 17-19.

plain, has left most service responsibilities with the provincial government. There is only one city, Charlottetown, and it is not regionally organized, and much of the Island has not been municipally incorporated.[15] There are, however, five regional administrative units that provide elementary and secondary education for the Island, with individual boards elected by residents of the units. Table 1.2 indicates that the small municipal system that is in place is relatively stable, and it seems likely to remain that way.

Nova Scotia

Nova Scotia is one of the few provinces that is municipally organized over its entire area. As of 1980, the province was divided into 24 rural municipalities with 3 cities and 39 towns located within these rural jurisdictions but administered separately. In addition, several other organizations, such as school boards, village and local commissioners, rural fire districts, and special purpose bodies, operate within the rural municipalities.[16] Halifax–Dartmouth is at present the only collective metropolitan authority, despite recommendations for sweeping reforms of local government organization by a 1974 royal commission.

New Brunswick

As a result of the Byrne Commission,[17] which identified and outlined many inequities in the provision and financing of local services in New Brunswick, the system of local government was radically restructured in 1967. Many functions that had traditionally been the responsibility of local governments were transferred to the province. In addition, the existence of a large number of unincorporated local service districts that are not municipal organizations were designed to provide local services under the direct jurisdiction of the provincial Department of Municipal Affairs.[18] At the same time, the old county system was replaced by cities, towns, villages, and local service districts. Table 1.2 indicates that this organization has not changed since that time.

Quebec

Quebec has, by far, the most extensive system of counties and rural municipalities. Table 1.2 indicates that there are presently over 1,500 municipalities, down somewhat from the 1968 figure as a result of limited provincial efforts to encourage consolidation.[19] The organized area of the province is divided into 3 metropolitan and regional municipalities, and 72 municipal counties, administered by a county corporation. Cities and towns are exempt politically and administratively from this county system, but all unorganized territory falls under it. There are presently three two-tiered governments (two—Outaouias and Quebec City—were formed recently, but the Montreal

[15]Higgins, supra footnote 11, at 23.

[16]Fawcett and Clarke, supra footnote 11, at 17-23.

[17]New Brunswick, *Report of the Royal Commission on Finance and Municipal Taxation in New Brunswick* (Fredericton: Queen's Printer, 1963).

[18]Fawcett and Clarke, supra footnote 11, at 7-17.

[19]Siegel, supra footnote 11, at 284.

Urban Community has existed since 1968), with each regional government set up to alleviate the problems of planning for the provision of local services and to meet local capital requirements.[20] The province is currently undergoing significant municipal financial reform, and this should alter the organization of much of the power within all the municipalities.[21]

Ontario

Over 95 per cent of the province's population is municipally organized on less than 10 per cent of its land. The Ontario Municipal Act, which was amended in 1980, allows for a change in the status or boundaries of municipalities as population or local conditions warrant it. Regional government, which led to the amalgamation of many political units, was introduced because of the difficulties encountered in long-term planning, the provision of local services, and the financing of capital projects, especially in the highly commercial and industrial urban areas of the province.[22]

Before the development of regional government, which began in Metropolitan Toronto in 1954, southern Ontario was divided into counties containing cities, towns, rural villages, and townships. At the same time, the more heavily populated areas of northern Ontario contained similar local structures while the less populated areas were organized as districts and administered by the provincial government. Since 1969, 12 additional two-tiered regional governments encompassing some 101 cities, towns, villages, townships, and improvement districts have been created. Even though each of these regional governments has its own act, a number of similarities exist. They all have an upper-tier council drawn from the lower-tier municipalities within the region. In each instance, specific legislation has established the number of constituent municipalities, their boundaries, representation at the upper tier, and responsibility for the provision of various local services. With few exceptions, distribution of water, sewage treatment, arterial roads, health, welfare, police protection, planning and capital borrowing are the responsibility of the upper tier.[23] Street maintenance, street lighting, fire protection, garbage collection, parks and recreation, and libraries, have been left to the lower-tier municipalities.

Manitoba

With the exception of the northern part of Manitoba, which is organized into 17 local government districts and administered by the provincial government, the rest of the province is divided into rural municipalities. These contain some incorporated cities, towns, and villages and each is politically independent of the rural municipal council.

Table 1.2 records the organization of the 202 municipalities in the province. The only notable attempt at reform has been the 1972 conversion of Winnipeg's two-tiered system into a unitary system.[24]

---

[20]Fawcett and Clarke, supra footnote 11, at 17-39.

[21]François Vaillancourt, "Financing Local Authorities in Quebec—The Reform of Bill 57" (May-June 1980), 28 *Canadian Tax Journal* 274-88.

[22]Fawcett and Clarke, supra footnote 11, at 17-27.

[23]Canadian Tax Foundation, supra footnote 11, at 209.

[24]Supra footnote 9, at 28.

Saskatchewan

With the exception of a small number of organized communities with elected councils, the northern part of Saskatchewan is municipally unorganized. Responsibility for the provision of municipal services in the unorganized area rests with the provincial government through the Department of Northern Saskatchewan. All of southern Saskatchewan is divided into rural municipalities, villages, towns, and cities.[25]

Table 1.2 shows that within the 299 rural areas, some alterations have occurred in the number of cities, towns, and villages since 1968. Much of this has arisen because of annexation, the province's equivalent to a two-tiered organization.

Alberta

As a result of a number of successive reorganizations, the system of local government in Alberta is rather complex. The entire province is organized into counties, municipal districts, improvement districts, and special areas within which incorporated cities, towns, and villages operate independently.[26] Counties were established in 1951 to reorganize local boundaries so that one centralized local government would be responsible for providing all local services with the exception of hospitals. Municipal districts, which are primarily located in the southern part of the province, are units of rural local government and are responsible for the provision of police services, welfare, health, public works, and roads.

Improvement districts, many of which are very large, exist in the entire northern half of the province and in isolated areas of the southern part. In these areas, the provincial government is entirely responsible for administering local services and collecting necessary revenues. Finally, three special areas in the southeastern part of the province are entirely administered by the provincial government.

British Columbia

Only a very small portion of the total area (0.5 per cent) of British Columbia has been municipally organized. This area covers more than 80 per cent of the population.[27] Since 1965, regional districts have been in operation, and these cover the administration of the entire province. The districts bring together all organized and unorganized areas in a combination of two-tiered and unitary governments. Aside from statutory administration and land use, however, each regional government carries out only those functions that its members think necessary. These regional governments are much weaker than their counterparts in Quebec and Ontario, and British Columbia depends to a greater degree on lower tiers for the provision of services.

---

[25]Canadian Tax Foundation, supra footnote 11, at 214.

[26]Ibid., at 217.

[27]Siegel, supra footnote 11, at 287.

REFORM OF THE LOCAL SECTOR

An avalanche of public inquiries over the past several decades has turned local governments inside out in virtually every region of this country and produced a profusion of reforms: annexations, consolidations, provincial advisory bodies, two-tiered federated structures, special-purpose bodies, transfers of service between provincial and local governments, and even the elimination of some municipal institutions. Before questions regarding the need for and direction of these reforms can be properly addressed,[28] however, it is necessary to identify the traditional roles and objectives of local governments.

THE TRADITIONAL ROLE OF LOCAL GOVERNMENT

Many experts have written about the traditional roles of local governments.[29] It is customary when discussing Canadian local government to define the prerequisites of municipal systems by emphasizing the subordinate institutional position of the municipality. No attempt will be made here to justify local government, nor to question what constitutes a municipal organization. Rather, this discussion will centre on the original and current responsibilities of local governments and the evolution and adaptation of these structures. Reasons why today's local government systems may fall short of exhibiting what many feel to be ideal characteristics, might be revealed by examining their original objectives and their present responsibilities. The latter is the task of Chapters 4 and 5, which consider existing expenditure responsibility levels in the light of a set of criteria designed to provide a sound rationale for the assignment of a service to a specific level of government. The former, that of defining the traditional role of local government, is the task of this section.

Because local governments are what is now commonly referred to as "purely creatures of their provinces," they possess only those responsibilities assigned to them by each province. Municipal governments were originally established and are still intended to facilitate the allocation of certain responsibilities to a third, and more local, level of operation. Thus, it is argued that local governments have two basic roles: administration and representation, more commonly known as service and access.[30] This combination of roles suggests that local governments exist to provide services in accordance with the needs and preferences of their citizens.[31] Frequently, however, these roles are in conflict with one another.

---

[28]While there have been extensive internal reforms and restructuring within local governments, this discussion will focus on external structural changes, such as division of responsibility between municipalities and provinces. For a discussion of the former, with both theory and empirical evidence, the interested reader is directed to Katherine A. Graham, "Organizational Change in Urban Local Governments: A Perspective," in Lionel D. Feldman, ed., *Politics and Government of Urban Canada, Selected Readings,* 4th ed. (Toronto: Methuen, 1981), 291-316.

[29]Thomas J. Plunkett, *Urban Canada and Its Government: A Study of Municipal Organization* (Toronto: Macmillan, 1968), 6; L.J. Sharpe, "Theories of Local Government," in Feldman, ibid., at 28; C.R. Tindal, *Local Government Reform in Canada* (Toronto: Institute of Public Administration, 1977), 2-4; and, for example, see Kenneth Grant Crawford, *Canadian Municipal Government* (Toronto: University of Toronto Press, 1954).

[30]Tindal, supra, at 2.

[31]These two roles are described in some detail in Ontario, *The Ontario Committee on Taxation Report* (Toronto: Queen's Printer, 1967).

By the 1960s the very simple system of cities, towns, villages, and counties that existed in most provinces could often not provide effectively the services that were initially assigned to them. Certainly, as the next section will show, they were not large enough, either administratively or financially, and could not cope effectively with the widespread industrialization and urbanization that was to occur.

THE IMPACT OF URBANIZATION ON LOCAL GOVERNMENT

When the Canadian municipal system was initiated, only one person in every three lived in urban areas. Today this proportion has grown to three out of four.[32] Further, it is expected that by the year 2001, Canada's population will be over 90 per cent urban, residing primarily in 12 major centres.[33] Since 1931, the total national population has more than doubled, but the urban population has more than tripled.[34] The social, economic, and political consequences of this transformation to essentially an industrial-urban economy posed fundamental problems for local government systems developed at a time when an agricultural-rural economy prevailed. The impact of both urbanization and industrialization on the Canadian way of life has been well documented and is discussed with considerable expertise elsewhere.[35] To the extent that the accommodation to these changes required a much more sophisticated and organized but still local unit of control, however, some discussion is warranted.

The rapid rate of urbanization during the past half-century raised serious issues for municipal governments charged with providing local services. Few governments were equipped to keep up with the pace and scale of the migration from rural to urban communities. In fact, the traditional role of local governments underwent fundamental changes in response to the complexities introduced by urbanization, and these cannot simply be considered extensions of traditional "service" functions—roads, water, and environment. In many cases, the multiplicity of problems associated with the rapid rate of urbanization placed greater emphasis on a new or expanded set of social and development services never before required—for example, the provision of recreation and cultural facilities, the need for health and welfare programs, the control and

[32]M. O. Dickerson, S. Drabek, and J. T. Woods, eds., *Problems of Change in Urban Government* (Waterloo: Wilfrid Laurier University Press, 1980), 1.

[33]Paul Hickey, "The Changing Structure of Municipal Government in Canada," in Canadian Institute of Chartered Accountants, *Municipal Finance and Administration in Canada* (Toronto: the Institute, 1967), 3.

[34]Institute of Local Government, Queen's University, *Urban Population Growth and Municipal Organization*, Local Government Reference Paper no. 1 (Kingston, Ontario: the Institute, February 1973), 1.

[35]See for example, T. J. Plunkett and G. M. Betts, *The Management of Canadian Urban Government: A Basic Text For a Course in Urban Management* (Kingston, Ontario: Queen's University Press, 1978), 21-31; Feldman, supra footnote 28, in general; supra footnote 9, at Chapter 3. By urbanization here is meant a process in which the territorial units of organization become more specialized, and therefore more interdependent, and in which the social system becomes more complex. George A. Nader, *Cities of Canada*, Vol. 7 (Toronto: Macmillan, 1975), 2. For a rather detailed definition of urbanization, with respect to the three approaches (demographic, economic, and sociological) the interested reader is directed to Higgins, supra footnote 11, at 2-8.

regulation of planning and development, and the provision of public housing.[36] This growth in new services has increased the strain on local government budgets working with limited sources of revenue such as the property tax. It has also raised serious questions about how authority, service delivery, and financial responsibility should be distributed among the differing and often competing levels of government. In addition, considerable doubt has been cast on the property tax as an appropriate source of revenue, simply because most of the newer services such as social welfare programs, parks, and recreational facilities are related more to people than to property. This position, however, differs from that which states that "hard services" (water, roads, sewers, etc.) should be financed from taxes levied on real property (Chapter 8).

Since local taxes have not been sufficient to support local services, this growing shortfall of local revenue has been met with higher grants from provincial or federal authorities. Chapter 9, which deals with grants, indicates that such transfers have allowed local governments to meet their expenditure requirements. This has put considerable strain on provincial-municipal relations and has reduced local autonomy. It thus becomes obvious that the magnitude and scope of municipal services concomitant with urban growth have created noticeable pressures on both the structure and nature of traditional local government.

LOCAL GOVERNMENT REFORM

The response to such rapid urbanization has, of course, varied from municipality to municipality and from province to province. Nonetheless, since the 1950s, every province except Prince Edward Island has subjected its local governments either in total or piecemeal to reviews of their structures and responsibilities. While the literature is full, if not replete, with accounts of how[37] and why[38] municipal government came to Canada, it does little to provide proper justification for either continuing or altering the inherent structure of local government. Sorting out the question of what municipal government is, however, is not new to intergovernmental inquiry, for it has been one of the main pre-occupations of royal commissions for at least the last quarter century. But while specific provincial decisions have varied, certain dominant themes emerge. Among the most recurrent themes that pervade virtually all the instances of urban municipal reform is that accelerated urbanization severely strains the capabilities of any existing level of government to respond effectively to new needs and conditions.[39]

---

[36]Plunkett and Betts, supra, at 25-31. For a good description of these and other growth pressures and service demands, the interested reader is directed to Leonard O. Girtler and Ronald W. Crowley, *Changing Canadian Cities: the Next 25 Years* (Toronto: McClelland and Stewart, 1977); and Lloyd Axworthy and James M. Gillies, *The City: Canada's Prospects, Canada's Problems* (Toronto: Butterworth, 1973).

[37]Higgins, supra footnote 11, at 155.

[38]David M. Cameron, "Provincial Responsibilities for Municipal Government" (Summer 1980), 23 *Canadian Public Administration* 222-35.

[39]See for example, in general: Crawford, supra footnote 29; Higgins, supra footnote 11; and supra footnote 9.

Recognition of the difficulties inherent in attempting to service a rapidly expanding population came first to Ontario. With virtually all growth in the suburbs, it became evident rather quickly that existing local governments would be hard pressed to continue providing a minimum level of essential services, to say nothing of fulfilling expanding education, health, and welfare needs. In response, a new structure of municipal organization was proposed and regional government born.[40]

Various other provinces, studying Ontario's approach, showed remarkable consistency in recommending the structure of a regional government to deliver needed public services. Unfortunately, none of the seven provinces that undertook reform made a serious effort to determine what a proper region was, relying on the assumption that traditional county boundaries would serve adequately. Coincident with this trend was the conviction that local government should remain essentially a local delivery corporation, with its real aim being the achievement of efficiency and effectiveness in service delivery. Thus, structural reform in all but one of the participating provinces concentrated on reform as a geographical realignment of local government boundaries in an effort to improve efficiency and enhance responsiveness. The exception was in New Brunswick, where the redistributive goal of minimizing inequities between municipal governments led to the transfer of many basic functions to the provincial government.

The mainstream of local reform produced two additional positions: one that believed efficient restructuring required a reduction in the number of municipalities and the other that felt such consolidation should be carried out in conjunction with the transfer of some responsibilities from local governments to their respective provinces or regional units. Both positions were aimed at improving service and access, the traditionally defined roles of local government. While the essence of local government is that it is local, however, almost all reformist pressure over the past 20 years seems to have translated into something beyond this.[41] To make local government systems better suited to meeting the perceived needs of an increasingly urbanized society, most provinces have turned to reducing the number of units, to realigning boundaries, and to redistributing functions. Out of this has arisen a number of regional governments in Ontario: metropolitan government in Toronto; regional districts in British Columbia; urban communities in Quebec; a unitary system, for a brief time, in Manitoba; numerous reforms in Alberta and Nova Scotia; and a general overhaul in New Brunswick.[42]

---

[40]Explicit details can be found in a number of sources including: Frank Smallwood, *Metro-Toronto: A Decade Later* (Toronto: Bureau of Municipal Research, 1963); Frank Smallwood, "Reshaping Local Government Abroad: Anglo-Canadian Experiments" (September-October 1970), 30 *Public Administration Review* 521-30; and Higgins, supra footnote 11, at 138.

[41]L. J. Sharpe, "The Failure of L. G. Modification in Britain: A Critique of Functionalism," in Feldman, supra footnote 28, at 323.

[42]Specifics are far too detailed for the purposes of this chapter and the interested reader is directed to: Higgins, supra footnote 11, at Chapter 4; supra footnote 9, at Chapter 4; Feldman, supra footnote 28, at Part V; and T. J. Plunkett, "Structural Reform of Local Government in Canada," in L. D. Feldman and Michael D. Goldrick, eds., *Politics and Government of Urban Canada: Selected Readings*, 3rd ed. (Toronto: Methuen, 1976), Chapter 20.

While the scale of structural change in municipal government represents the response of provincial governments to some of the requirements of an increasingly urbanized society, many of these changes have not been confined to urban areas alone. A number of reforms have affected the organization and provision of services to rural municipalities. For example, the increased centralization of police and fire protection plus the consolidation of numerous small elementary and secondary schools into larger institutions, illustrates the substantial impact that urban-initiated reform has had on rural communities. Regardless of whether the local government is urban or rural, provincial governments have become increasingly involved with a wide range of new as well as traditional services, either through a direct arm in the case of conditional grants or an indirect arm in the case of regional and district governments. Whatever the reform, it is certain that local governments will continue to evolve in a way that is so complex that the traditional role of days past will seem distant and archaic.

SUMMARY

The historical evolution of the municipal financial scene has undergone a number of important and significant changes. At one point, municipalities received very little revenue in the form of intergovernmental grants. At the same time, they relied on revenue from personal and real property taxes, poll taxes, and to a lesser or greater extent depending on the specific province, revenue from municipal income taxes. Throughout the twentieth century, a number of changes have occurred including the elimination or virtual elimination of personal property taxation, poll taxes, and municipal income taxes. Greater reliance on intergovernmental transfers has replaced many of the previous taxes and has reduced the dependence on real property tax as a major generator. Over this same period, municipal expenditures have shown a steady increase with some temporary interruptions. Local government expenditure pressures have been particularly acute since the end of World War II. This partly occurred because construction of the public plant and equipment was postponed and maintenance deferred during the depression and war years. At the same time, a rapidly expanding population required educational facilities, welfare services, hospitals, and largely expanded municipal services such as roads, water, and sanitary facilities. Municipal governments, virtually dependent on a single source of revenue (the real property tax), have resorted to vociferous appeals to provincial governments for financial aid in the face of ever-increasing expenditure pressures.

Over the past 15 years, this concern with meeting local expenditure commitments led to the formation of a number of commissions charged with the responsibility for reforming local governments. In essence, most of the reforms were intended to improve the efficiency and effectiveness of delivering local services. These improvements have created a situation where local governments have had an easier time meeting their expenditure commitments.

With this brief historical and institutional background behind us, the remainder of this book will concentrate on recent developments (the past decade or two) and important issues concerning local government expenditures and revenues.

2

The Provincial/Local
Financial Scene

INTRODUCTION

The variations in the responsibilities of municipal or local levels of government in Canada are significant. In New Brunswick, for example, minimum levels of elementary and secondary education and social assistance are financially supported by the provincial government; whereas in Ontario, minimum levels of the same services are funded by both the provincial government and municipal governments. Such diversity in the responsibility for and funding of local services makes it difficult to undertake any comparative assessment of municipal expenditure and revenue levels on an interprovincial basis. To overcome this problem and to facilitate an interprovincial comparison, this chapter will integrate the provincial and municipal financial sectors and attempt to assess their interprovincial similarities and differences. This will be accomplished by drawing on a number of fiscal indicators including provincial per capita levels of expenditure and revenue; by assessing the variation in the aggregated expenditure functions and revenue sources by province; by measuring the revenue effort in the ten provinces of Canada; and by reviewing the patterns of tax preference and utilization over the past few years.

PROVINCIAL/LOCAL EXPENDITURE PATTERNS

PROVINCIAL/LOCAL EXPENDITURES
BY PROVINCE, 1968-78

From 1968[1] to 1978 Canadians witnessed a significant expansion in the level of provincial and local expenditures. Measured as a share of gross domestic product (GDP), the combined current and capital expenditures rose from 21.8 per cent in 1968 to 29.2 per cent in 1978 (Table 2.1). In current dollars this growth in total expenditures increased by a factor of 4.4. At the same time, GDP in Canada increased by a factor of only 3.2. To be more precise and to assess the importance of this increase on a regional basis, Table 2.1 illustrates consolidated provincial and local expenditures combined as a percentage of gross domestic provincial product (GDPP). For example, in each of the years studied, combined provincial and local expenditures in Atlantic Canada and more specifically in Newfoundland and Prince Edward Island accounted for the largest percentage of GDPP. By comparison, the same aggregated government sectors accounted for the smallest percentage of GDPP in Ontario, British Columbia, and more recently Alberta. Figures for the remaining provinces fell between these extremes.

---

[1]The year 1968 was chosen as the base year in the historical development because it was the first year for presentation of the revised data on a consistent basis.

Table 2.1   Consolidated Provincial/Local Expenditures as a Percentage
of Gross Domestic Provincial Product (GDPP) for Selected Years[a]

| | 1968 | | 1978 | |
Province	Total expenditures	Total expenditures as a percentage of GDPP	Total expenditures	Total expenditures as a percentage of GDPP
	($000,000)	*per cent*	*($000,000)*	*per cent*
Newfoundland	329.7	37.4	1,548.2	54.6
Prince Edward Island.	60.5	33.1	306.1	49.1
Nova Scotia.	454.5	27.8	1,934.5	37.2
New Brunswick.	367.3	29.8	1,462.2	35.8
Quebec	3,965.1	25.0	17,960.0	37.1
Ontario	5,166.7	19.5	20,183.9	25.4
Manitoba	582.3	20.0	2,399.3	28.9
Saskatchewan	627.4	24.2	2,455.6	27.6
Alberta	1,164.8	21.5	6,303.8	23.6
British Columbia	1,269.9	18.0	6,529.8	26.3
All provinces.	13,988.1	21.8	61,083.4	29.2

[a]Excludes intergovernmental grants.

Source: Total provincial/local expenditure figures were obtained from Statistics Canada, *Consolidated Government Finance, 1968* and *Consolidated Government Finance, 1978*, Catalogue no. 68-202. GDPP figures were obtained from The Conference Board of Canada, *The Provincial Economies, 1961-1980 Data* (Ottawa: the Board, 1981).

Although the pattern of variation between provinces remained fairly constant in each of the years observed (Table 2.1), combined provincial/local government expenditures increased substantially in each of the provinces over the period from 1968 to 1978. The greatest increases in provincial/local expenditures (in total current dollars) occurred in Prince Edward Island, British Columbia, and Alberta where they were more than 5 times larger in 1978 than in 1968 (Table 2.2). Ontario and Saskatchewan recorded the smallest increase (1978 expenditures were 3.9 times greater than those in 1968), while the 1978 average over all provinces was 4.4 times the 1968 average. In part, these increases can be attributed to a high income elasticity of demand for some services (education) and to substantial price increases in some of the labour-intensive services. A number of government services including police and fire protection, education, social services, and refuse collection are labour intensive. In most of these activities, it is felt that productivity growth has been substantially lower than in either the manufacturing or agricultural sector. Since approximate wage parity has been maintained between the service, manufacturing, and agricultural sectors, the cost of providing a given level of public goods or services has risen.[2] It is highly unlikely that this trend will change over the next decade or two.

---

[2]Some explanations for the increase in local expenditures will be discussed more extensively in Chapters 3, 4, 5, and 6.

**Table 2.2 1978 Provincial/Local Expenditures as a
Multiple of 1968 Provincial/Local Expenditures**

Province	Factor
Newfoundland	4.7
Prince Edward Island	5.1
Nova Scotia	4.3
New Brunswick	4.0
Quebec	4.5
Ontario	3.9
Manitoba	4.1
Saskatchewan	3.9
Alberta	5.4
British Columbia	5.1
All provinces	4.4

Source: Calculated from the data in Table 2.1.

While the growth in total expenditures outlined above allows one to make some useful observations on the rate of increase and the significance of this sector in the provincial economy over time, it is quite misleading to use these same totals in making any province-by-province comparisons of provincial and local expenditure levels and the inherent services that these expenditures support. The use of per capita figures, although fraught with certain difficulties,[3] does facilitate a reasonably reliable comparison of expenditure levels. Such figures eliminate expenditure differentials that can be attributed to differences in population size alone. Further presentation of per capita expenditure figures in constant dollars eliminates differences due to price increases—increases that do not reflect real changes in the level of services supplied.

Table 2.3 provides data on constant and current per capita expenditure levels in the provincial/local sector for each of the years 1968 and 1978. Of interest here is the substantial variation in both the absolute levels of expenditures in each of the years observed and the rate of increase in per capita expenditures over the period 1968 to 1978. For example, the 1968 per capita differential (in current dollars) between the highest-spending province (Alberta) and lowest-spending province (Prince Edward Island) amounted to $214 or almost 32 per cent of the average for all of the provinces in Canada, (column 1, Table 2.3). By 1978, the differential between the highest (Alberta) and lowest (New Brunswick) amounted to $1,122 or almost 43 per cent of the Canadian average (column 3, Table 2.3). In addition, current per capita dollar expenditures in all provinces increased by about 285 per cent with the province of Prince Edward Island leading the way at 446 per cent. At the other extreme, Ontario exhibited the

---

[3]The limitation of per capita figures arises because population is an inadequate proxy for expenditure needs. Some groups, such as dependent children and the aged, require extra public funds. To the extent that some provinces have a larger share of these specific groups suggests that these provinces must face heavier expenditure per capita levels. In addition, quality differences in the provision of a service may be completely disguised when using per capita figures. In spite of these misgivings, it appears to be the best measure one can use in making interprovincial comparisons.

slowest increase at 234 per cent. One observation, which can generally be made from Table 2.3, is that provinces with per capita provincial/local current expenditure levels in 1968 lower (higher) than the average for all provinces exhibited an expenditure growth rate higher (lower)than the average for all provinces. All provinces with the exception of New Brunswick, which had lower than average per capita expenditures in 1968, displayed faster than average growth rates over the eleven-year period. While Ontario and Alberta each had higher than average per capita expenditures in 1968, the growth rates over the period differed. Alberta's rate of growth in per capita expenditures was faster than the Canadian average, while Ontario's growth rate was slower.

Although per capita current expenditure figures facilitate a province-by-province comparison of expenditure levels, they do not in their unadjusted form account for regional differences that may be attributed to differences in the cost of supplying their services nor do they facilitate an assessment of the real increase in these expenditures over time. In order to achieve both of these objectives, it is necessary to deflate current per capita expenditure levels using the implicit price index for government current expenditures on goods and services adjusted for regional differences.[4] This was done in columns 2 and 4 of Table 2.3. Not surprisingly, the elimination of inflationary increases in per capita provincial/local expenditures reveals a pattern similar to that of current dollar expenditures with the basic differences being that the absolute variation between the provincial figures was smaller and the rate of increase was lower. For instance, New Brunswick (approximately $825) exhibited the lowest per capita level of constant dollar expenditures in 1978 while Alberta (approximately $1,263) displayed, by far, the highest level.

Perhaps of equal interest here is the relatively low rate of increase in constant per capita expenditures and the substantial variation that arose in the increase in these expenditures. For instance, all but 51 of the 285 percentage-point increase in per capita provincial/local expenditures for all provinces can be attributed to inflation. Similar province-by-province observations can be made. Thus, Ontario and New Brunswick displayed the lowest per capita increase in real expenditures (32 per cent and 40 per cent respectively) while Prince Edward Island had the highest increase (80 per cent). Given that there are many variables that might cause this variation (including differences in the interprovincial levels of income and hence differences in the demand for local or provincial services), the following section will assess the relative importance of three general factors: increases in expenditures due to inflation, increases due to volume of service, and increases due to greater levels of service.

---

[4]To obtain constant dollar figures, current figures were deflated by adjusting the implicit price index on current government expenditures on goods and services to reflect provincial differences. Construction of a provincial index for current government expenditures on goods and services was obtained in two steps. First, the percentage by which the consumer price index for Canada differed from that for each province (obtained by taking a simple average of all cities in each province for which a city consumer price index was available) was calculated. Second, this percentage differential was applied to the implicit price index for current government expenditures on goods and services in order to obtain a government expenditure index for each province. The assumption underlying this approach is that the relative differences between provinces in the government expenditure index will be identical to the relative differences in the consumer price index.

Table 2.3 Per Capita Provincial and Local Consolidated Expenditures Aggregated in Current and Constant[a] (1968) Dollars for Selected Years

Province	1968		1978		Rate of growth, 1968-1978	
	(1) Current	(2) Constant	(3) Current	(4) Constant	(5) Current	(6) Constant
	dollars				per cent	
Newfoundland	651.58	651.58	2,720.91	1,020.98	317.6	56.7
Prince Edward Island ...	550.00	550.00	2,509.02	991.71	446.2	80.3
Nova Scotia	592.57	592.57	2,300.24	916.80	288.2	54.7
New Brunswick	587.68	587.68	2,103.88	824.73	258.0	40.3
Quebec	668.88	668.88	2,863.06	1,137.04	328.0	70.0
Ontario	711.47	711.47	2,373.74	935.28	233.6	31.5
Manitoba	599.69	599.69	2,320.41	901.83	286.9	50.4
Saskatchewan	653.54	653.54	2,590.30	1,023.03	296.3	56.5
Alberta	764.30	764.30	3,226.10	1,262.66	322.1	65.2
British Columbia	634.00	634.00	2,580.95	998.05	307.1	57.4
All provinces	677.19	677.19	2,608.40	1,021.30	285.2	50.8

[a]To obtain constant dollar figures, the current dollar figures were deflated by adjusting the implicit price index on current government expenditures on goods and services to reflect provincial differences. See infra footnote 4 of the text.

Source: Calculated from the data in Table 2.1 and from Statistics Canada, Consumer Prices and Price Indexes, 1979, Catalogue no. 62-010.

GENERAL FACTORS AFFECTING
EXPENDITURE INCREASES

The variation in per capita constant dollar expenditures as presented in Table 2.3 may lead to a quick generalization that different levels of service were being supplied to the respective provincial populations. In fact, this is likely true. An accurate measure of whether service levels were truly different, however, requires a considerable amount of nonfinancial data such as the number of police employed per 1,000 population, the number of firemen employed per residential and commerical buildings, or the frequency of garbage collection per week. None of these data was available on a consistent country-wide basis. Additional variations in expenditure levels may also be attributed to the population base being served. To the extent that some services cater to specific groups (such as dependent children or the aged) and given that some provinces have a disproportionate share of these groups in their populations, expenditure levels will differ simply because of the necessity of servicing these special groups.

In spite of the limitations outlined in the previous paragraph and lacking the more sophisticated nonfinancial data[5] necessary to measure accurately both the volume and level of services supplied by the combined provincial/local sector, this section will employ a crude but nonetheless useful method of disaggregating the total growth in provincial/local expenditures (from 1968 to 1978) into the three components of inflation, volume of services, and level of services.

Inflationary increases reflect the increases in the cost of supplying public goods and services that have not been offset by productivity increases. Increases in the volume of service supplied refer to increases attributed solely to population growth in a serviced area. In this latter case, both inflationary increases and increases in the service levels have been eliminated. Finally, increases in the total level of service were calculated by multiplying the increase in per capita constant dollars from 1968 to 1978 times the total population serviced in 1978.[6] The sum of these three components must equal the increase in total current expenditures over the period studied.

---

[5]The Ministry of Treasury, Economics and Intergovernmental Affairs, Municipal Finance Branch, of the Ontario Government originally developed this in selected years for certain municipalities. For more discussion on this, see Ontario, *The Classification of Expenditure: A Guide for Municipal Treasurers and Auditors* (Toronto: Ministry of Treasury, Economics and Intergovernmental Affairs, Municipal Finance Branch, 1974). Since that publication, the Municipal Finance Branch in the Ontario Government has been developing nonfinancial reporting requirements for a number of municipal services.

[6]To measure the importance of each of these components, the following steps were taken: First, the increase in total expenditures attributed to inflation was determined. This was obtained by subtracting the total increase in constant dollars (column 2, Appendix Table A.4) from the total increase in current dollars (column 1, Appendix Table A.4). Second, the increase attributed to the volume of service was measured by holding service levels (per capita expenditures) and inflation constant at 1968 levels (column 2, Table 2.3), and by estimating the total cost of servicing the increased population from 1968 to 1978 (column 4, Appendix Table A.4) at the level of service (expenditure per capita) existing in 1968. The resultant figures (column 5, Appendix Table A.4) were taken as a percentage of the total increase in constant dollars (column 2, Appendix Table A.4) in order to estimate the proportion of constant dollar expenditures arising from increases in the volume of service (column 6, Appendix Table A.4). In order to estimate the percentage of total current expenditures attributed to volume increases, the figures calculated in the preceding sentence were taken as
(Continued on next page.)

Table 2.4 Percentage of Total Provincial/Local Expenditure Increases Attributed to Inflation, Volume of Service, and Level of Service, 1968-1978[a]

Province	Inflation	Volume of service	Level of service
		per cent	
Newfoundland	79.4	3.4	17.2
Prince Edward Island	75.4	2.7	21.9
Nova Scotia	78.6	3.0	18.4
New Brunswick	81.2	3.8	15.0
Quebec	77.4	1.6	21.0
Ontario	81.4	5.6	12.6
Manitoba	80.7	2.1	17.2
Saskatchewan	81.3	− 0.4	19.1
Alberta	74.7	6.4	18.9
British Columbia	76.1	6.4	17.5
All provinces	78.9	4.0	17.1

[a]For a discussion of the methodology employed in calculating these figures see footnote 6 of this chapter. A minus figure indicates a decrease.

Source: Calculated from data in Appendix Table A.4.

Table 2.4 displays the relative importance of each of the three components in accounting for the increase in total provincial/local expenditures from 1968 to 1978. More than three-quarters of the increase in all provinces combined (78.9 per cent) was due to inflation. In each of the individual provinces, inflation was responsible for something between 81.4 per cent of the increase in Ontario (the highest) and 74.7 per cent in Alberta (the lowest). Similar interprovincial patterns can be observed for the increases attributed to both volume and level of service. Expansion in the volume of service was responsible for 4.0 per cent of the overall total increase. The range, however, for this component was more noticeable. It extended from a high of 6.4 per cent in Alberta and British Columbia to a low of 0.4 per cent in Saskatchewan. Ontario (5.6 per cent) was the only other province to show a volume increase in excess of the overall average. This final component, level of service, accounted for the remaining expenditure increase. In this instance, Prince Edward Island exhibited the largest increase (21.9 per cent) while Ontario displayed the lowest (12.6 per cent). The combined provincial average was 17.1 per cent.

In short, inflation has been the most significant contributing factor in the rise of provincial and local expenditures on goods and services, accounting for almost 79 per cent (depending on the province) of the total increase. Service level

---

[6]Continued

a percentage of the total percentage increase in current expenditures. The results are reported in column 7, Appendix Table A.4. Third, total increases in the levels of service were calculated by multiplying the per capita increase in constant dollars (column 8, Appendix Table A.4) by the 1978 population level and taking the resultant totals (column 9, Appendix Table A.4) as a percentage of the total increase in constant dollars (column 2, Appendix Table A.4). These results (column 10, Appendix Table A.4) were then taken as a per cent of the percentage increase in total non-inflationary expenditures in order to ascertain the increase in total expenditures attributed to rising service levels (column 11, Appendix Table A.4).

improvements (including the expansion of existing services or the introduction of new services) grew significantly. This growth contributed to somewhere between 13 per cent and 22 per cent of the expenditure increase in most provinces. The volume of service was the smallest contributor to expenditure increases and in one province, Saskatchewan, reduced expenditures in this area were implied.

LOCAL EXPENDITURES AS A PERCENTAGE OF PROVINCIAL/LOCAL EXPENDITURES, 1968-1978

It is useful, at this time, to review briefly the importance of the local sector in terms of its relative financial impact on the provincial/local scene in each of the Canadian provinces. Before launching into this, however, one is cautioned about the meaning and interpretation of the numbers presented in this section. An interprovincial comparison of local government expenditures at any given time must be treated with care. In a number of instances, provincial governments perform functions that in other jurisdictions are the responsibility of the local sector. Similarly, local responsibilities within any province may change over time and hence any intertemporal comparisons of local expenditures must be handled carefully.

With these concerns in mind, Table 2.5 lists the proportion of combined provincial/local expenditures that were absorbed by the local sector in each province for two specific years—1968 and 1978. In general, the local sectors in all provinces accounted for a smaller proportion of aggregated expenditures in 1978 as compared with 1968. The one exception was New Brunswick where a marginal increase in the overall importance of the local sector can be seen. The fact that local expenditures were more significant in the late 1960s may support the view that local governments then had greater access to revenues and hence expanded the size of their operations. By the middle 1970s and into the 1980s, however, revenue constraints, whether actual or assumed, led to a partial restriction in the funds available for local expenditures. In addition, in some provinces, functions that were formerly under the control of local governments were transferred to the province, thus reducing the proportionate size of these local sectors.

Three of the provinces in Atlantic Canada displayed a much greater degree of centralization in their provision of a number of the provincial and local functions. For example, Newfoundland had at the time studied, and still has, a relatively small local sector. A partial explanation for this rests on the fact that local governments here had little opportunity to become entrenched and a greater proportion of the combined provincial/local activities were centralized at the provincial level. A greater degree of centralization also existed, and exists, in New Brunswick and Prince Edward Island although this occurred for different reasons. Briefly, the local sectors in these two provinces displayed less relative importance as a direct result of each respective provincial government's action in assuming the financial responsibility for providing many local services. In these three named provinces, the local sector accounted for 7.4 per cent to 26.7 per cent of the aggregated provincial/local sector expenditures (1978). By comparison, these percentages were significantly lower in the rest of Canada. Indeed, when all provinces were averaged together, the entire local sector accounted for roughly 38 per cent of the provincial/local total in 1978. In the same year, Alberta and Ontario exhibited the greatest reliance on the local sec-

Table 2.5   Local Expenditures as a Percentage of Total Provincial and Local Expenditures,[a] 1968 and 1978

Province	1968	1978
Newfoundland	9.3	7.4
Prince Edward Island	30.6	26.2
Nova Scotia	34.8	33.5
New Brunswick	11.4	12.4
Quebec	44.9	35.5
Ontario	53.4	43.3
Manitoba	46.6	38.5
Saskatchewan	46.7	38.2
Alberta	49.9	42.5
British Columbia	49.4	36.5
All provinces	46.9	37.8

[a]Excludes intergovernmental transfers.

Source: Calculated from data in Appendix Tables A.5, A.6, and A.7.

tor at 42.5 per cent and 43.3 per cent of the aggregated expenditures respectively. Local sectors in the remaining provinces fell within 3 percentage points of the national average.

Before leaving this section it is worth noting that the relative composition of the local expenditure pattern changed significantly over the 1968 to 1978 period. In every province the absolute level of local capital expenditures increased, although at a rate lower (with the exception of New Brunswick) than the rate of increase in noncapital expenditures. In essence, municipalities are now devoting a greater proportion of their total budgets to goods and services that are of a noncapital nature. For example, the amounts expended on the construction and expansion of schools and roads have declined relative to operating expenditures for municipal services. Two exceptions to this are in the provinces of New Brunswick and Prince Edward Island where local fixed capital expenditures absorbed a higher share of total budgetary expenditures in 1978 than in 1968 (Table 2.6).

Table 2.6   Local Fixed Capital Expenditures as a Percentage of Total Local Expenditures, 1968 and 1978

Province	1968	1978
Newfoundland	46.2	31.4
Prince Edward Island	16.7	32.1
Nova Scotia	20.1	12.1
New Brunswick	25.4	31.9
Quebec	28.2	16.3
Ontario	25.5	15.3
Manitoba	17.4	13.9
Saskatchewan	19.7	18.7
Alberta	26.1	23.7
British Columbia	20.2	17.0
All provinces	25.1	17.0

Source: Appendix Table A.5.

Municipal capital expenditures declined overall as a proportion of budgetary allocations (from 25.1 per cent to 17.0 per cent) from 1968 to 1978. The greatest decline in the relative importance of these expenditures occurred in municipalities (in aggregate) in Newfoundland, Ontario, and Quebec, while municipalities in British Columbia, Manitoba, Saskatchewan, and Alberta displayed the slowest rate of decrease.

PROVINCIAL/LOCAL EXPENDITURE PATTERNS BY FUNCTION

PROVINCIAL AGGREGATES

Although provincial/local expenditures have increased rather noticeably over time, a more significant and perhaps enlightening review includes some observations on the changing composition of total expenditures over the period 1968-1978 along with a brief presentation of the relative importance of each of the expenditure functions in the 10 different provinces. To accommodate the first interest, Table 2.7 presents the proportion of total provincial/local expenditures absorbed by each of the expenditure functions both including (columns 1 and 3) and excluding (columns 2 and 4) federal grants. The figures including federal grants represent the proportion of total provincial/local expenditures (all provinces combined) absorbed by each function regardless of the source of revenue; whereas, the figures excluding federal grants represent the importance of the different functions in terms of their command over the revenue raised by the provincial and local governments combined. The distributional pattern in each of the years is similar in both cases. Such similarity, however, does not exist over time; for example, from 1968 to 1978 a significant reduction occurred in the proportion of total expenditures absorbed by each of education and transportation and communication. To be more specific, education, which accounted for roughly 33 per cent of all provincial/local expenditures in 1968 (regardless of whether federal grants were included or excluded), accounted for approximately 24 per cent in 1978, a decline of some 9 percentage points. A reduction of roughly 4 percentage points was recorded in the expenditure function "transportation and communication." This, however, should not suggest that the costs of education or the amounts of public money spent by provincial and local governments on transportation and communication has decreased. On the contrary, per capita costs (excluding federal grants)[7] on education have increased rather significantly from $189.28 in 1968 to $521.85 in 1978 (Tables A.6 and A.7) with the post-secondary sector accounting for a greater percentage increase than expenditures on primary and secondary education.[8] This trend reflects the increased proportion of the population

---

[7] In the remainder of this chapter, all expenditure figures, unless otherwise cited, will refer to expenditures excluding federal grants. This is analytically more important for our purposes since these expenditure figures will refer to expenditures that must be financed by local and provincial governments from their own sources of revenue.

[8] The per capita increase in education expenditures from 1971 to 1977 amounted to 74.3 per cent. This consisted of a per capita increase on primary and secondary education and post-secondary education of 70.9 per cent and 82.9 per cent respectively. Figures calculated from Statistics Canada, *Consolidated Government Finance: Revenue, Expenditure, Assets and Liabilities: Fiscal Year Ended Nearest to December 31, 1971;* and the same for 1976, Catalogue no. 68-202.

Table 2.7 Provincial/Local Expenditures by Function as a Percentage
of Provincial/Local Expenditures in All Provinces in Canada,
1968 and 1978

| | 1968 | | 1978 | |
| | (1) Including federal grants | (2) Excluding federal grants | (3) Including federal grants | (4) Excluding federal grants |
Function				
	per cent			
Education	33.0	33.7	23.9	24.1
Health	17.9	14.8	19.2	15.3
Transportation and communication	13.1	14.0	8.9	9.7
Social services	8.0	6.6	12.0	11.0
Debt charges	5.0	5.6	8.4	9.6
General government	4.6	5.1	6.7	7.6
Protection of persons and property	6.0	6.7	5.4	6.0
Environment	3.9	4.3	3.9	4.2
Recreation and culture	2.5	2.8	3.3	3.6
Resource conservation and industrial development	3.6	3.6	4.7	4.8
Housing, regional planning and development	0.4	0.4	1.8	1.9
Other	1.9	2.1	1.9	2.1

Source: Appendix Tables A.6 and A.7.

attending universities and the decreased proportion enrolling in elementary and secondary institutions over the past few years. A similar picture exists in the case of transportation and communication. In this instance, the increase in per capita expenditures from $78.45 to $209.95 was substantially a result of escalating expenditures on roads alone.

Other functions that have declined as a percentage of total expenditures are protection to persons and property (police, firefighting, regulatory and correctional services, along with expenditures on courts of law), and resource conservation (fish and game, forests, mines, oil and gas, and water). The remaining functions increased in relative importance—with social services and debt charges leading the way (Table 2.7).

While this review illustrates the changing impact of each of the many expenditure functions on the total of all provincial and local budgets, it does not indicate the increases in each of these functions nor the individual contribution of each function to the overall increase in expenditures from 1968 to 1978. To overcome this deficiency, Table 2.8 displays the absolute increase in per capita expenditures (excluding federal grants) by function for the 1968 to 1978 period. Per capita total expenditures increased from $560.67 to $2,162.88 (Table 2.8) or by a factor of 3.9. However, much of this increase was illusory, and can be attributed to an increase in the prices of goods and services purchased by provincial and local governments. Deflation of this expenditure increase by the appropriate implicit price index for government expenditure on goods and services

Table 2.8   Increase in Per Capita Provincial/Local Expenditures
Excluding Federal Grants by Function for All Provinces,
1968-1978

Function	(1) 1968 level	(2) 1978 level	(3) Absolute dollar increase	(4) Percentage of total expenditure increase[a]
	dollars			*per cent*
General government	28.87	164.23	135.36	8.4
Protection of persons and property	37.84	130.50	92.66	5.8
Transportation and communication	78.45	209.95	131.50	8.2
Health	83.21	331.05	247.84	15.5
Social services	37.02	238.29	201.27	12.6
Education	189.28	521.85	332.57	20.8
Resource conservation and industrial development...	20.42	103.74	83.32	5.2
Environment	24.15	91.50	67.35	4.2
Recreation and culture....................	15.64	78.64	63.00	3.9
Housing, regional planning and development ...	2.40	40.86	38.46	2.4
Debt charges	31.59	207.15	175.56	11.0
Other	11.80	45.11	33.31	2.1
Total......................	560.67	2,162.88	1,602.21	100.0

[a]This column may not add to 100 due to rounding.

Source: Calculated from data in Appendix Tables A.6 and A.7.

suggests that real per capita expenditures rose from $560.67 to $846.85 or by a factor of 1.5 rather than by 3.9.

Of some importance to this discussion is the proportion of the total increase attributed to increases in each of the individual functions.[9] Education, while declining in terms of the proportion of budgetary expenditures absorbed by it, accounted for over one-fifth (20.8 per cent) of the entire increase over the decade under study. When combined with health (15.5 per cent) and social services (12.6 per cent), these three functions together accounted for almost 50 per cent of the per capita expenditure increase. In terms of importance, the next four functions including debt charges (11.0 per cent), transportation and communication (8.2 per cent), general government (8.4 per cent), and protection (5.8 per cent) accounted for a further 33 per cent of the increase. The rest of the functions as listed in Table 2.8 absorbed the remainder of the overall increase.

One conclusion evident from these observations is that the bulk of the increase in provincial/local per capita expenditures can be largely attributed to increases in the costs of providing services for people who are deemed to be worthy of support because of the specific circumstances in which they happen

[9]The percentage figures presented here and in column 4 of Table 2.7 are the same regardless of whether current dollars or constant dollars are employed in the presentation.

to find themselves. For example, primary and secondary education accounted for most of the increase in educational expenditures; hospital and medical care accounted for nearly all of the increase in health expenditures; and expanded assistance for the unemployed, financially needy, and the handicapped accounted for virtually the entire increase in expenditures on social services. Expenditures on these so-called "soft-services" are not likely to subside although funds for these services may grow slower as governments at all levels attempt to restrict the growth of their respective expenditures.

A simple assessment of the increase in aggregate provincial/local expenditures disguises an important element of the provincial/local expenditure scene, namely that there is diversity among provinces in per capita expenditures in almost all of the major functions. Part of this variation can be explained by differences in the composition or traits of the population being served; for example, higher than average provincial per capita expenditures on education may be a result of a greater proportion of the provincial population being in the elementary and secondary school-age category, or higher per capita expenditures on health or social services might arise from a disproportionate share of the provincial population being old, sick, or otherwise incapacitated and consequently in need of publicly financed services. These characteristics, however, fail to explain the major portion of the diversity. It is impossible to precisely pinpoint the factors accounting for these differences, but tradition and even political philosophy have some bearing on the patterns and levels of service that have arisen over time. The notion that the public sector ought not to be deeply involved in providing certain services or levels of service still exists and appears to prevail in some provinces more than in others. This notion is generally more prevalent in rural than in urban areas in all provinces. Perhaps the only statistically significant relationship that can be found as an explanation for the considerable range in average per capita expenditures in the provinces is the one between per capita income and per capita expenditures (excluding federal grants). Even this relationship, it can be argued, is not as significant as one may think. For example, a simple rank correlation between per capita expenditures and per capita income for 1968 and 1978 generated values of .79 and .78 respectively.[10] Although significant at the 5 per cent level, there is still considerable room for other factors beside per capita income to explain the extant diversity.

Recognizing the existence of many factors that might explain the differences, Table 2.9 (columns 1 and 4) lists the average per capita expenditures by function for all provinces[11] for 1968 and 1978. In addition, the standard deviation (columns 2 and 5) and coefficient of variation (columns 3 and 6) are reported. The standard deviation is a measure of absolute variation around the average. If there is substantial variation in the average (as indeed exists in Table 2.9) then

---

[10]Rank correlation coefficients were calculated from data in The Conference Board of Canada, *The Provincial Economies, 1961-1978 Data: A Supplement to the Quarterly Provincial Forecast* (Ottawa: the Board, 1979) and Appendix Tables A.6 and A.7.

[11]The average per capita expenditure figures are not weighted. Instead, they merely reflect the average of the 10 provincial averages. These figures differ from those that are weighted by population and presented under the "All provinces" category in Appendix Tables A.6 and A.7. These unweighted figures are employed in the determination of the coefficient of variation since we are really interested in analyzing the diversity in the levels on a province-by-province basis.

a measure of absolute variation is not particularly useful. The coefficient of variation, by comparison, is a measure of relative variation and here facilitates a comparison of variation across expenditure functions where averages are noticeably different. A low value for this coefficient suggests that there is relatively little variation in the average per capita expenditures on an inter-provincial basis.

A review of Table 2.9 reveals some interesting results. First, on an inter-provincial basis, a large variation in per capita average expenditures can be seen for every function. In fact, a 30 per cent or 40 per cent variation was frequently the norm and in no case, in either year, was the variation below 23 per cent. Second, with the exception of transportation and communication expenditures, the lack of consistency in the coefficient of variation for any function over the decade should be noted. For some expenditures such as education, health, social services, debt, environment, recreation and culture, and protection, the variation declined. For others including general government, resource conservation, and industrial development (natural resources and agriculture), it increased. Overall, the variation in all expenditures combined remained constant at 28 per cent. Third, the functions with the greatest degree of variation tended to be those with the lowest average per capita expenditure for all provinces.

While the emphasis in this chapter, and indeed, in most of this book, is on expenditures financed from own-source revenues, one must be reminded constantly that such expenditure levels and their variations do *not* represent the actual levels or variations in the actual level of services supplied. Actual service levels are reflected in expenditure figures funded by both federal grants and own-source revenues. Indeed, when one observes per capita expenditures financed from all revenue sources, one notes the significant levelling effect that federal grants have played. To illustrate, Table 2.10 records average per capita expenditures by function for all provinces along with their respective standard deviations and coefficients of variation. In every instance, the variation in per capita expenditures was smaller and in most cases considerably smaller than the variation in expenditures financed from own-source revenues (Table 2.9).

PROVINCIAL VARIATION

As was evident in the last section, a review of aggregate provincial expenditure figures disguises most of the interprovincial variation; a variation that may yield significant insights into the levels and types of government services supplied in the different provinces in Canada. To summarize the interprovincial differences, Table 2.11 records the variation in the proportion of total expenditures attributed to the major functions.

When the average of the 10 provinces is taken, regardless of the year chosen, education accounted for the largest proportion of combined provincial/local expenditures. In 1968, this figure amounted to 34.2 per cent (Table 2.11) and was roughly 2.3 times the second highest expenditure function (transportation and communication). By 1978, this percentage had dropped by more than 10 points to a level of 23.6 per cent of all provincial/local expenditures from own-source revenues. At the same time, the importance of this function had declined so that it was only 1.6 times the second-highest expenditure function (health). Over the 11-year period under observation, significant decreases in the

Table 2.9   Variation in Provincial/Local Per Capita Expenditures (Excluding Federal Grants) by Major Function for All of Canada, 1968 and 1978

	1968			1978		
Function	(1) Average for all provinces[a]	(2) Standard deviation[b]	(3) Coefficient of variation[c]	(4) Average for all provinces[a]	(5) Standard deviation[b]	(6) Coefficient of variation[c]
	dollars			*dollars*		
General government	23.89	6.10	.26	140.94	62.98	.45
Protection of persons and property	28.50	12.94	.45	108.27	39.14	.36
Transportation and communication	70.13	20.80	.30	206.25	62.36	.30
Health	62.52	23.40	.37	279.97	90.35	.32
Social services	27.38	14.17	.52	182.89	75.06	.41
Education	160.26	53.33	.33	443.72	110.54	.25
Resource conservation and industrial development	20.95	5.39	.26	141.64	116.41	.82
Environment	17.20	9.58	.56	72.86	39.74	.55
Recreation and culture	13.15	7.10	.54	64.92	31.91	.49
Debt charges	26.68	11.35	.43	191.43	47.66	.25
Total	464.75	130.77	.28	1,905.33	525.59	.28

[a]Unweighted average for all provinces. See footnote 11 in the text for a discussion of this point. [b]A measure of absolute variation. Roughly interpreted, this is an average of the deviations of the individual observations about the average. [c]A measure of relative variation. It is obtained by dividing the standard deviation by the average.

Source: Calculated from data in Appendix Tables A.6 and A.7.

Table 2.10   Variations in Provincial/Local Per Capita Expenditures (Financed from All Revenue Sources Including Federal Grants) for All of Canada, 1968 and 1978

Function	1968			1978		
	(1) Average of all provinces[a]	(2) Standard deviation[b]	(3) Coefficient of variation[c]	(4) Average of all provinces[a]	(5) Standard deviation[b]	(6) Coefficient of variation[c]
	dollars			*dollars*		
General government	27.92	3.89	.14	160.09	56.41	.35
Protection of persons and property	32.29	11.52	.36	123.17	29.82	.24
Transportation and communication	96.69	15.25	.16	258.83	45.74	.18
Health	113.78	20.36	.18	471.73	56.91	.12
Social services	52.18	18.04	.35	274.42	63.45	.23
Education	203.89	41.05	.20	589.27	77.50	.13
Resource conservation and industrial development	28.92	6.55	.23	199.91	156.33	.78
Environment	21.08	8.26	.39	86.73	34.02	.39
Recreation and culture	14.97	6.83	.46	74.96	25.89	.35
Total	641.40	63.58	.10	2,560.49	320.95	.13

aUnweighted average for all provinces.   bA measure of absolute variation.   cA measure of relative variation.

Source: Calculated from data in Appendix Tables A.6 and A.7.

proportion of provincial/local budgets devoted to education occurred in each and every province (Appendix Tables A.6 and A.7).

Table 2.11 suggests that the interprovincial variation in the proportion of combined municipal and provincial expenditures tended to be smaller for education than for any other function. Nevertheless, some variation did exist and is worth noting. In 1968, Alberta and Ontario ranked at the top in the proportion of total provincial/local expenditures devoted to education (38.5 per cent—Appendix Table A.6). By 1978, this had changed with Alberta devoting 21.3 per cent (Appendix Table A.7) of its combined expenditures to this function, a figure which was 2.3 percentage points below the province-by-province average. The two extremes were recorded by Newfoundland and Prince Edward Island, which devoted 20.4 per cent and 28.6 per cent respectively of all their combined provincial/local "own-funded" expenditures to education.

Transportation and communication, the other major function exhibiting a significant decrease in the proportion of aggregated provincial/local expenditures, declined by 4.2 percentage points from a provincial average of 15.2 per cent of expenditures in 1968 to 11.0 per cent in 1978 (Table 2.11). When ranked by province, the variation in the proportion of provincial/local budgets absorbed by transportation and communication expenditures yielded some noticeable differences. For example in 1968, Saskatchewan (the highest) spent almost one-fifth of its combined provincial/local budget (excluding federal grants) on this

Table 2.11   Variation in the Percentage of Total Provincial/Local
Expenditures (Excluding Federal Grants) Attributed to Major
Functions, 1968 and 1978

	1968			1978		
	(1)	(2)	(3)	(4)	(5)	(6)
Function	Average[a]	Standard deviation	Coefficient of variation[b]	Average[a]	Standard deviation	Coefficient of variation[b]
	per cent			*per cent*		
General government	5.2	.8	.16	7.2	1.8	.25
Protection..........	5.8	1.3	.23	5.6	1.0	.17
Transportation and communication	15.2	2.2	.14	11.0	2.2	.20
Health	13.5	2.1	.15	14.6	2.1	.14
Social services	6.2	2.8	.45	9.5	2.5	.26
Education	34.2	3.4	.10	23.6	2.5	.11
Resource conservation and industrial development	4.7	.9	.20	7.5	5.9	.78
Environment	3.4	1.5	.44	3.6	1.0	.29
Recreation and culture	2.6	1.0	.39	2.9	1.1	.39
Debt charges........	6.7	4.1	.61	10.4	2.8	.27

[a]Unweighted average of total provincial/local expenditures attributed to the major functions.
[b]Obtained by dividing the average by the standard deviation.

Source: Calculated from data in Appendix Tables A.6 and A.7.

function, while Newfoundland and Quebec (the lowest) spent less than 12 per cent on this service (Appendix Table A.6). By 1978, the proportion had fallen in every single province with New Brunswick spending relatively more than any other province on this item (15.2 per cent). On the other hand, Newfoundland, Ontario, and Quebec were the only provinces spending less than 9 per cent of their budgetary totals on transportation and communication services (Table A.7).

Health, the third function to absorb a substantial share of provincial/local budgets, accounted for a provincial average of almost 14 per cent in 1968, and almost 15 per cent in 1978. This modest increase of 1 percentage point overall arose because the combined provincial/local sectors in six provinces (Prince Edward Island, Nova Scotia, New Brunswick, Ontario, Manitoba, and British Columbia) increased the proportion of their budgets devoted to this function, while the rest exhibited a decrease. As was true for educational expenditures discussed above, the degree of provincial variation (in terms of the proportion of total provincial and local expenditures attributed to this function) showed considerable consistency; the coefficient of variation was .15 in 1968 and .14 in 1978 (Table 2.11).

With respect to expenditures on health itself, there was some interprovincial variation in the relative importance of this function. In 1978, for instance, Manitoba and British Columbia spent over 17 per cent of their aggregated budgets on this service, while Newfoundland spent 10 per cent on similar services. In the remaining provinces, between 14 per cent and 16 per cent of all expenditures were attributed to health services.

Together, these three functions accounted for 63 per cent of all provincial and local government expenditures in 1968 and almost 50 per cent in 1978. While this decrease of some 13 percentage points was a combination of a decrease in the proportion devoted to education (10.6 percentage points) and transportation and communication (4.2 percentage points) and an increase in health (1.1 percentage points), it is worth noting that a number of financially less significant but nevertheless important functions increased in importance. For example, the proportion of provincial and local budgets (on average) devoted to social services, debt charges, general government, and resource conservation and industrial development increased by 3.3, 3.7, 2.0, and 2.8 percentage points respectively (Table 2.11). Although not as large as the previously listed functions, they tended to exhibit a greater degree of province-by-province variation. The coefficients of variation in 1978 here ranged from .25 for general government to .78 for resource conservation and industrial development.

On a regional basis, a casual perusal of the figures in Appendix Table A.7 suggests that the proportion of total expenditures devoted to social services in 1978 tended to be highest in Quebec (13.5 per cent) and lowest in Alberta (6.0 per cent) and Atlantic Canada (between 6 per cent and 9 per cent depending on the province). The remaining western provinces and Ontario devoted roughly 11 per cent of their total expenditures to this function. Similar inferences on a regional basis cannot be made about the expenditures on servicing the debt or financing general government. In each of these instances, neighbouring provinces often displayed significant variations in the extent to which each of these functions absorbed provincial/local budgetary expenditures.

Finally, protection, environment, and recreation and culture, the least important absorbers of provincial/local budgets, displayed notable variations on a province-by-province basis. In these three functions, with a few exceptions, regional differences can be observed. The provinces of Atlantic Canada generally contributed a smaller proportion of their total expenditures to each of these services.

In every province in 1978, over 82 per cent of total local and provincial expenditures were devoted to seven functions. These included education, health, transportation and communication, social services, debt charges, general government, and protection to persons and property. While the relative expenditure levels of these seven functions varied on an interprovincial basis, education absorbed the largest percentage in every province. With two exceptions (Newfoundland, where it ranked fourth, and New Brunswick where it ranked third), health absorbed the second-largest proportion. At the other extreme, general government and protection tended to be closer to the bottom in terms of importance, thus leaving transportation and communication, social services, and debt charges in the middle in terms of importance.

To obtain a clearer picture of the combined provincial/municipal sector on an interprovincial basis, it is useful to review per capita expenditure levels and rates of growth as they pertain to different functions in different provinces. Table 2.12 lists 1968 and 1978 per capita expenditures excluding the portion funded by federal grants. Alberta had the highest level ($654.81 in 1968 and $2,853.63 in 1978) in each of the two years, while Newfoundland had the lowest in 1968 ($280.51) and New Brunswick in 1978 ($1,226.60). The figures of per capita provincial/local expenditures can be compared more readily by assigning the value of 100 to the average of all provinces ($464.75 in 1968 and $1,905.33 in 1978) and computing relative numbers that express how much each province spends in relation to the national average. Once again, Alberta had an expenditure relative of 140.9 in 1968 and 149.8 in 1978, thus indicating that the combined provincial/local sector in Alberta spent 41 per cent and 50 per cent respectively, more than the national average from its own revenue sources. At the other extreme, the four provinces in Atlantic Canada had expenditure relatives ranging from 60.4 to 77.1 in 1968 and from 64.4 to 87.4 in 1978. This indicates that out of their own funds, each of these provinces spent less than the national average. Manitoba was the only other province to display expenditures that were less than the province-by-province average.

The largest increase in per capita expenditures occurred in the two provinces displaying the lowest expenditure levels in 1968 (Newfoundland and Prince Edward Island). On the other hand, the slowest rate of growth occurred in Ontario (239 per cent), which ranked fifth in per capita expenditure in 1978 as compared to second in 1968. By 1978, three of the four western provinces (Manitoba excluded) and Quebec displayed the largest per capita provincial/local expenditures from own-source revenues. To be more specific and depending on the province, these per capita figures were between $300 and $1,300 more than similar totals for the provinces in eastern Canada (Table 2.12).

Efforts have been made to discover and measure the significant variables that explain these provincial expenditure diversities. The most important variable appears to be the tax base since this variable is generally employed as a measure

Table 2.12   Growth of Per Capita Provincial/Local Expenditures (Excluding Federal Grants) by Province, 1968-1978

	1968 per capita	1968 expenditure relative[a]	1978 per capita	1978 expenditure relative[a]	Per capita increase	Percentage increase
	$	%	$	%	$	%
Newfoundland	280.51	60.4	1,664.47	87.4	1,383.96	493.4
Prince Edward Island ...	286.62	61.7	1,261.30	66.2	974.68	340.1
Nova Scotia	358.26	77.1	1,453.34	76.3	1,095.08	305.7
New Brunswick	347.70	74.8	1,226.60	64.4	878.90	252.8
Quebec	560.22	120.5	2,336.11	122.6	1,775.89	317.0
Ontario	619.82	133.4	2,098.49	110.1	1,478.67	238.6
Manitoba	462.70	99.6	1,728.28	90.7	1,265.58	273.5
Saskatchewan	530.84	114.2	2,180.11	114.4	1,649.27	310.7
Alberta	654.81	140.9	2,853.63	149.8	2,198.82	335.8
British Columbia	546.04	117.5	2,250.92	118.1	1,704.88	312.2
Provincial average[b] ...	464.75	100.0	1,905.33	100.0	1,440.58	310.0

aExpenditure relatives are obtained by dividing the provincial per capita value by the average for all provinces and multiplying by 100. The resultant figure illustrates whether the individual provincial figure is greater or less than the average for all provinces.

bUnweighted average.

Source: Calculated from data in Appendix Tables A.6 and A.7.

Table 2.13   Index[a] Reflecting the Relationship Between Per Capita Provincial/Local Expenditure Relative and Per Capita GDP Relative by Province, 1968 and 1978

Province	1968	1978
	per cent	
Newfoundland	91.8	140.7
Prince Edward Island	98.3	103.8
Nova Scotia	95.8	99.0
New Brunswick	100.5	83.3
Quebec	119.2	127.3
Ontario	96.9	93.9
Manitoba	91.1	90.5
Saskatchewan	112.1	97.7
Alberta	105.2	87.9
British Columbia	88.6	96.4

[a]Per capita expenditure relative divided by per capita GDPP relative, with the resulting figure being multiplied by 100.

Source: Calculated from data in Table 2.12 and from The Conference Board of Canada, *The Provincial Economies, 1961-1980 Data* (Ottawa: the Board, 1981).

of the demand for public services and as an indication of the willingness (or lack of willingness) of the general public to accept certain expenditure levels. An index reflecting the province-by-province relationship between per capita GDPP and per capita provincial/local government expenditures is presented in Table 2.13 for 1968 and 1978. This index is calculated by dividing the expenditure relative for each province by the per capita GDPP[12] relative for the same province. A figure of 100 suggests that the relationship between a province's per capita provincial/local expenditures excluding federal grants and the average of all provinces is identical to the relationship between the same province's per capita GDP. If a province's per capita expenditures from its own funds is at a level that is 75 per cent of the national average and if its per capita GDPP is also 75 per cent of the national average, then it can be argued that the provincial/local government sector in this province is funding its own expenditures at a rate equal to the national average.

In 1978, all but three of the provinces' own provincial/local expenditures, relative to their tax bases as measured by GDPP, were below average. Only Newfoundland, Prince Edward Island (the two provinces with the lowest per capita tax bases) and Quebec with the fifth-lowest per capita tax base) used their revenue bases more heavily than the national average. By comparison, Ontario and the four western provinces displayed higher revenue bases and higher absolute expenditure levels but relatively smaller burdens.

A further and potentially more revealing division of this expenditure analysis in each of years 1968 and 1978 is summarized in Table 2.14 and presented in greater detail in Appendix Tables A.6 and A.7. Here, an interprovincial com-

---

[12]Per capita GDPP relatives are obtained by dividing the average per capita figure in each province by the average of all provinces and multiplying this by 100.

parison of functional per capita expenditures can be seen. Not surprisingly, education, although declining as a proportion of total local budgets in all provinces during the decade running from the late 1960s to the late 1970s, displayed the largest absolute per capita dollar increase of any of the expenditure functions. The range in per capita provincial expenditures was extreme; for example, expenditures on education ranged from a low of $88.15 (Newfoundland) to a high of $253.75 (Alberta) in 1968 and from a low of $289.21 (New Brunswick) to a high of $607.87 (Alberta) in 1978 (Table 2.14). In each of these years, the range between the highest and lowest province was $165.60 and $318.66 respectively. These figures exceeded the value for the province with the lowest per capita expenditure on that function. Indeed, in both years the four provinces in Atlantic Canada and Manitoba recorded average per capita expenditures (funded from own-source revenue) that were lower than the average (unweighted) for all provinces.

Table 2.14   Range of Per Capita Expenditures (Excluding Federal Grants) by Major Function, 1968 and 1978

	1968			1978		
Function	Lowest value	Highest value	Provincial average[a]	Lowest value	Highest value	Provincial average[a]
			dollars			
General government	15.44 (Nfld.)	33.18 (B.C.)	23.89	77.11 (Nfld.)	239.94 (Alta.)	140.94
Protection of persons and property......	9.83 (P.E.I.)	47.69 (Ont.)	28.50	56.29 (P.E.I.)	165.74 (Alta.)	108.27
Transportation and communication ...	32.72 (Nfld.)	104.85 (Sask.)	70.13	135.77 (Nfld.)	325.82 (Alta.)	206.25
Health	25.42 (P.E.I.)	96.88 (Que.)	64.41	172.65 (Nfld.)	397.03 (B.C.)	279.97
Social services	16.04 (N.S.)	67.27 (Que.)	27.38	95.18 (P.E.I.)	314.86 (Que.)	182.89
Education	88.15 (Nfld.)	253.75 (Alta.)	160.26	289.21 (N.B.)	607.87 (Alta.)	443.72
Resource conservation and industrial development......	15.24 (N.B.)	32.80 (Alta.)	20.95	51.64 (Man.)	365.41 (Nfld.)	141.64
Environment	1.30 (Nfld.)	26.50 (Alta.)	17.20	27.56 (P.E.I.)	160.49 (Alta.)	72.86
Recreation and culture...........	3.63 (Nfld.)	23.11 (Sask.)	13.25	29.46 (N.B.)	124.54 (Alta.)	64.92
Debt charges	11.54 (B.C.)	43.00 (Que.)	26.68	119.64 (P.E.I.)	276.57 (Nfld.)	191.43
Total.............	280.52 (Nfld.)	654.81 (Alta.)	464.75	1,226.60 (N.B.)	2,853.63 (Alta.)	1,905.33

[a]Unweighted average.

Source: Appendix Tables A.6 and A.7.

Similar observations and comments can be made about the other functions. By 1978, health had clearly become entrenched as the second most important provincial/local expenditure function in almost every province. Once again, the four Atlantic provinces displayed own-source funded expenditures that were lower than the national average.

Rather than reviewing each of the remaining functions in detail, a summary of the more salient features will be presented leaving the reader to collect the details from the data supplied (see Table 2.14, Appendix Tables A.6 and A.7). With few exceptions, the combined provincial/local sectors in the provinces in Atlantic Canada incurred expenditures that on a per capita functional basis tended to be lower than the average of all the Canadian provinces. As well, particularly for 1978, the same sectors in Quebec, Saskatchewan, Alberta, and British Columbia almost always spent more than the overall average on each of the functions. For the remaining provinces, the pattern was slightly more erratic: Ontario spent less than the average on transportation and communication, general government, and resource conservation and industrial development, while Manitoba spent less on these three functions in addition to education and environment.

REVENUE PATTERNS

RELATIVE IMPORTANCE OF AGGREGATED PROVINCIAL/ LOCAL REVENUE SOURCES

The rapid rise in provincial/local expenditures from the late 1960s to the late 1970s necessitated significant increases in the funds required for financing the existing and new services supplied by this combined government sector. At the same time, a noticeable and important change occurred in the relative importance of the individual revenue sources. For example, in 1968, revenue from total taxation accounted for over 60 per cent of the total provincial/local revenue; whereas, by 1978, this same source accounted for slightly less than 49 per cent (Tables 2.15, Appendix Tables A.8 and A.9). This decrease of over 11 percentage points was attributed to a decrease in the importance of property taxation (8.4 percentage points), corporate income taxation (.6 of 1 percentage point), consumption taxes (7.1 percentage points), and other taxes (.5 of 1 percentage point). This decrease was partially offset by an increase in the role of personal income taxes (5 percentage points). In fact, property and related taxes, which generated the largest sum of revenue in 1968 (21.8 per cent of the total), declined (13.4 per cent of the total revenue) so that they were just below consumption taxes (11.8 per cent) and noticeably below the personal income tax (17.9 per cent) as a revenue generator in 1978.[13]

As the relative importance of total taxes declined, the importance of conditional and unconditional grants remained constant. In 1968, the sum of these grants accounted for nearly 17.5 per cent of total revenue, while in 1978 this figure increased marginally to 17.6 per cent (Table 2.15).

---

[13]The category of other revenues exceeded property tax revenue in 1978 but this includes many small and diverse revenue sources and as such has been excluded from our discussion of comparative individual revenue sources.

**Table 2.15   Percentage of Total Consolidated Provincial/Local
Revenues Obtained from Each Revenue Source, 1968 and 1978**

Revenue source	1968	1978
	per cent	
Taxes		
Personal income	12.9	17.9
Corporation income	4.8	4.2
Real and personal property	21.8	13.4
Consumption	18.9	11.8
Other...	2.1	1.6
Total taxes	60.5	48.9
Grants		
Conditional	11.0	12.3
Unconditional	6.5	5.3
Miscellaneous		
Sale of goods and services.............................	3.8	5.0
Privileges, licences and permits	3.9	2.5
Natural resource revenue	4.4	9.0
Payments in-lieu-of taxes	0.2	0.3
Others..	9.9	16.6

Source: Appendix Tables A.8 and A.9.

Revenues from privileges, licences, and permits decreased marginally in relative importance, falling from 3.9 per cent of total revenue in 1968 to 2.5 per cent in 1978 (Table 2.15). While this decline is not terribly significant, the category of natural resource revenue rose substantially both in absolute and in relative importance. By 1978, it accounted for 9.0 per cent of aggregrated provincial/local revenue, a figure that was 4.6 percentage points higher than in 1968. The growing dependence on natural resource revenue occurred at the same time the provincial/local sector displayed greater dependence on revenue from the sales of goods and services (rising from 3.8 per cent to 5.0 per cent of total revenue over the 11-year period).

Other revenue includes: return on investments (accounting for 49 per cent of this source in 1978), health and social insurance levies (accounting for 40 per cent), and miscellaneous other minor revenue sources such as contributions to government-operated pension plans, bullion and coinage revenue, and fines and penalties. The total of these revenue sources exhibited a rather dramatic increase rising by 6.7 percentage points from a level generating 9.9 per cent of provincial/local revenue in 1968 to a level of 16.6 per cent of the same total in 1978. The bulk of this increase can be attributed to the increased revenue obtained from health and social insurance levies and to a lesser extent from returns on investments.

LEVEL AND GROWTH OF TOTAL AND
PER CAPITA REVENUE SOURCES

As in the case of the earlier expenditure analysis, the existence of a relative decrease in the importance of a few revenue functions (especially property and related taxes) does not suggest that they have fallen in absolute terms. Indeed, the opposite is the case. Property taxes on a per capita basis increased by 138 per cent over the period under study.[14] By comparison, all other taxes in current dollars increased by a significantly larger percentage with per capita personal income taxes leading the way at 441 per cent. This was followed by corporate taxes at 239 per cent, consumption taxes at 144 per cent, and other taxes at 214 per cent. Overall current per capita provincial/local taxes rose by something in excess of 215 per cent. Substantial increases in conditional grants (336 per cent), unconditional grants (218 per cent), and other revenue sources (297 per cent) also contributed rather significantly to the total per capita current dollar increases of 289 per cent (calculated from Table 2.16).

Although percentage increases, as presented in the previous paragraph, are useful in terms of illustrating the growth in each function, they may be deceiving in terms of clearly illustrating the impact of each of these sources on the general public. For example, a large percentage increase may be a direct result of an extremely small value in the initial year and an absolute dollar increase that is neither very large nor significant. A case in point is the current dollar revenue source entitled "payments in-lieu-of taxes." This source increased by more than 697 per cent from 1968 to 1978 or from a dollar impact of $1.03 to $8.21 (Table 2.16). Obviously, this source had little impact on the overall increase in revenue (0.4 per cent of total revenue increase).

To evaluate more accurately the importance of each of these revenue sources in contributing to the increase in per capita provincial/local revenues from 1968 to 1978, Table 2.16 supplies data on the absolute per capita current and constant dollar values of the more important revenue sources in each of two years, along with the per capita absolute increase for each source and the percentage that each contributed to the total increase over the period studied.

All provincial/local taxes in current dollars accounted for slightly less than 45 per cent of the per capita increase with personal income taxes responsibile for almost 20 percentage points of this increase. This was followed by property and related taxes (10.4 per cent), consumption taxes (9.4 per cent), corporate income taxes (4.0 per cent), and other taxes (1.5 per cent). A further 37.4 per cent of the overall current dollar increase resulted from the remaining provincial and local revenue sources with slightly more than half of this increase attributed to the "other revenue" category (18.9 per cent). Natural resource revenue (10.6 per cent) and revenue from sales of goods and services (5.4 per cent) contributed significantly to the growth in provincial/local revenue. Finally in 1978, total grants accounted for 17.7 per cent of all revenues with conditional grants (12.8 per cent) being more than twice as important as unconditional grants (4.9 per cent).

Although current dollar revenue figures suggest some interesting changes and illustrate significant shifts in the relative importance of many of the revenue sources, they should not be interpreted as reflecting the total increase in the real burden on taxpayers or on consumers of goods and services. Part of this increase in the taxpayers' capacity can be attributed to inflationary increases in property values, personal incomes, or prices of goods and services. The elimina-

---

[14]Calculated from the data in columns 1 and 4, Table 2.16.

Table 2.16   Per Capita Revenue Sources in Current and Constant (1968) Dollars[a] for All Provinces, 1968 and 1978

Revenue source	(1) 1968 dollars	(2) 1978 current dollars	(3) 1978 constant dollars	(4) Current dollar increase, 1968-1978	(5) Per cent of total current dollar increase, 1968-1978	(6) Constant dollar increase, 1968-1978	(7) Per cent of total constant dollar increase, 1968-1978
	dollars				per cent	dollars	per cent
1. Personal income tax	85.41	462.38	237.61	376.97	19.6	152.20	22.9
2. Corporate income tax	31.97	108.48	55.75	76.51	4.0	23.78	3.6
3. Property taxes	144.96	345.50	177.54	200.54	10.4	32.58	4.9
4. Consumption taxes	125.61	306.01	157.25	180.40	9.4	31.64	4.8
5. Other taxes	13.61	42.67	21.93	29.06	1.5	8.32	1.3
6. Total taxes	401.56	1,265.05	650.08	863.49	44.9	248.52	37.4
7. Sale of goods and services	24.99	129.52	66.56	104.53	5.4	41.57	6.3
8. Privileges, licences, and permits	25.80	65.70	33.76	39.90	2.1	7.96	1.2
9. Natural resource revenue	28.85	232.60	119.53	203.75	10.6	90.68	13.6
10. Payments-in-lieu of taxes[b]	1.03	8.21	4.22	7.18	0.4	3.19	0.5
11. Other revenue	65.65	428.74	220.32	363.09	18.9	154.67	23.3
12. Total own-source revenue	547.88	2,129.81	1,094.46	1,581.93	82.3	546.58	82.2
13. Federal unconditional grants	43.21	137.55	70.68	94.34	4.9	27.47	4.1
14. Federal conditional grants	73.19	318.79	163.82	245.60	12.8	90.63	13.6
15. Total revenue[c]	664.28	2,586.15	1,328.96	1,921.87	100.0	664.68	100.0

[a]Deflated by consumer price index. [b]Included in own-source revenue since this property could have been taxed if payments-in-lieu of taxes had not applied.

[c]Add rows 12, 13, and 14 to obtain column totals.

Source: Appendix Tables A.8 and A.9.

tion of such price increases reflects the changing real burden on provincial/local taxpayers. Table 2.16 (columns 6 and 7) illustrates both the constant dollar increase in the major revenue sources and the proportion of the total increase contributed by each. Clearly, constant absolute dollar increases are substantially lower than current dollar increases. The percentage of the total constant dollar increase contributed by each revenue source, however, shows greater variation than was evidenced in the corresponding current dollar figures. Personal income taxes on a per capita basis grew by almost 23 per cent and accounted for over 61 per cent of the increase in per capita total taxes. Property and related taxes, consumption-based taxes, and the corporate (provincial) income tax accounted for a much lower percentage of the overall increase at 4.9 per cent, 4.8 per cent and 3.6 per cent respectively. By comparison, the real per capita increase in grants amounted to over 17 per cent of the total increase, while other revenue (23.3 per cent), natural resource revenue (13.6 per cent), and sales of goods and services (6.3 per cent) accounted for most of the remaining increase.

INTERPROVINCIAL VARIATION IN THE DEPENDENCE ON REVENUE SOURCES

In the earlier discussion of provincial/local expenditure patterns, regional variations in both the per capita levels and the proportion of provincial/local budgets devoted to each function were observed frequently. Similar differences, on a regional basis, can be noted in the relative dependence that the combined provincial/local sector places on the various revenue sources. Clearly, a great deal of this variation can be explained by differences in industrial structures and natural resource bases, both of which distinctly affect the fiscal capacity of the different regions.

Table 2.17 lists the relative variations, on a provincial basis, in the proportion of consolidated provincial/local revenues on which this combined government sector was dependent for the years 1968 and 1978. Once again, a low value for the coefficient of variation suggests that there is very little variation in the proportion of total revenues supported by a specific revenue source across the country. On the other hand, a relatively high value suggests considerable interprovincial variation. While substantial variation exists in the individually listed revenue sources, less variation appears to prevail in total taxes and total own-source revenue.[15] Indeed, it is interesting to note the consistency of these figures over the period studied. In the case of taxes in total, the coefficients of variation were .26 and .28 in 1968 and 1978 respectively; whereas for total own-source revenue, the same coefficients were .22 and .23 for the same years.

---

[15]It has been suggested that data on personal income taxes, total taxes, total own-source revenue, and conditional grants be presented so as to exclude the province of Quebec. The rationale for this arises out of the different federal/provincial financial arrangement between this province and the federal government. Briefly, in lieu of participating in certain joint shared-cost programs, Quebec receives equivalent compensation by way of additional tax points, equalization payments, and adjustment payments from the federal government. While the rationale for excluding Quebec is plausible, the Quebec data have been included throughout this chapter, precisely because of the interest in comparing provincial levels of income taxation, own-source revenue, unconditional grants, etc. across provinces even if there are different financial arrangements in existence.

Table 2.17   **Variation in the Proportion of Consolidated Provincial/Local Revenues Contributed by Major Revenue Functions, 1968 and 1978**

Revenue source	1968			1978		
	(1) Average[a]	(2) Standard deviation	(3) Coefficient of variation	(4) Average[a]	(5) Standard deviation	(6) Coefficient of variation
	per cent			*per cent*		
1. Personal income tax	9.3	3.9	.42	15.0	4.8	.32
2. Corporate income tax	3.6	1.1	.30	3.4	1.6	.47
3. Property taxes	16.9	6.7	.40	10.9	5.1	.47
4. Consumption taxes	17.9	4.4	.25	12.3	4.4	.36
5. Other taxes	1.2	2.2	1.81	1.2	.8	.66
6. Total taxes	48.8	12.6	.26	42.7	11.9	.28
7. Sale of goods and services	4.8	1.7	.35	4.9	1.0	.21
8. Privileges, licences and permits	3.4	.4	.13	2.0	.7	.35
9. Natural resource revenue	4.7	7.4	1.58	8.1	14.8	1.82
10. Other revenue	9.9	3.9	.39	13.7	3.7	.27
11. Total own-source revenue	71.7	15.5	.22	71.6	16.8	.23
12. Federal unconditional grants	12.7	10.7	.84	12.4	11.4	.92
13. Federal conditional grants	15.6	5.6	.36	16.0	6.0	.37

aUnweighted provincial average.

Source: Calculated from data in Appendix Tables A.8 and A.9.

On average, total own-source revenue accounted for more than 71 per cent of total revenue in each of the years studied. At the same time, the range between the province placing the greatest reliance on own-source revenue and that placing the least virtually remained unchanged. In each of the years, own-source revenue in the Atlantic provinces accounted for somewhere between 45 per cent and 59 per cent of total provincial/local revenue, while the same figures for the remaining provinces ranged between 73 per cent and 92 per cent (Appendix Tables A.8 and A.9). Obviously, federal conditional and unconditional grants accounted for the remainder. Clearly, Atlantic Canada was much more dependent on federal funds than was the rest of Canada. This is explained, in large part, by the differing fiscal capacities of each of the regions. Overall, federal conditional and unconditional grants contributed approximately 16 per cent and 12 per cent of total provincial/local revenues in each of the years observed (Table 2.17). This remarkable consistency in the average contribution of both types of grants in total, is not observed when the provinces are viewed separately; for example, Newfoundland's and Alberta's dependence on grants declined by the greatest amount or by 6.8 and 5.6 percentage points respectively from 1968 to 1978, while Prince Edward Island's and Manitoba's dependence increased by 8.3 and 4.7 percentage points respectively. All other provinces displayed increases or decreases of a lesser magnitude (Appendix Tables A.8 and A.9).

A review of the variation in individual tax sources suggests that in 1978, as compared with 1968, less variation existed in the reliance on personal income taxes. In fact, if Quebec with its different federal/provincial fiscal arrangements had been excluded from the interprovincial analysis, the coefficients of variation for personal income taxes would have fallen to .34 and .27 in 1968 and 1978 respectively. This illustrates a greater revenue reliance on provincial personal income tax in the province of Quebec. Overall, the dependence on personal income taxes increased from 9 per cent of total revenue in 1968 to 15 per cent in 1978.

With the exception of "other taxes," property and related taxes displayed a considerable degree of variation, while at the same time declining in relative importance from 1968 to 1978. In 1968, property taxes accounted for almost 17 per cent of all provincial/local revenue (on average); whereas, by 1978 this source contributed less than 11 per cent. As the coefficients of variation suggest, the interprovincial range in the dependence on this item increased over the period. In fact, in 1968, property taxes accounted for between 3 per cent (Newfoundland) and 15 per cent (Nova Scotia) of all revenue in Atlantic Canada and between 19 per cent (Alberta) and 26 per cent (Ontario) in the rest of the provinces. By 1978, the range in Atlantic Canada had narrowed so that the provincial/local sector's dependence varied from slightly more than 3 per cent (Newfoundland) to almost 10 per cent (Nova Scotia). Excluding Alberta (7.9 per cent), the remaining provinces recorded a dependence ranging from over 11 per cent (Quebec) to almost 18 per cent (Ontario) of aggregated provincial/local revenues. The relative decline in the importance of this revenue source was evident in every province with the exception of Newfoundland where it remained constant at 3.1 per cent of total revenues with Alberta, Quebec, and Saskatchewan displaying the greatest decrease (10.9 per cent, 9.9 per cent, and 9.6 per cent respectively) (Appendix Tables A.8 and A.9.)

Similar comments can be drawn from the data on consumption-based taxes. While more important than property taxes[16] as a revenue generator at the combined provincial/local level, they too illustrated an average decline of 5.6 percentage points in terms of revenue contributions (Table 2.17). It must be mentioned, however, that during the period studied provincial retail sales tax rates varied from province-to-province and that Alberta has never introduced a retail sales tax. With this in mind, if Alberta is excluded from the comparison of consumption-based taxes, the coefficient of variation as presented in Table 2.17 would be .11 for 1968 and .13 for 1978, thus suggesting that the degree of variation in the relative dependence on this revenue component among the nine provinces with a retail sales tax is not great. To be more specific, no distinct regional variation was observed in the utilization of consumption-based taxes. Over nine provinces, the range extended from almost 11 per cent of all revenue in Saskatchewan in 1978 (lowest) to almost 17 per cent in Newfoundland (highest).

The proportion of revenues raised from corporate and other miscellaneous taxes, remained fairly constant at slightly more than 3 per cent and 1 per cent respectively in each of the years observed. Although not terribly significant as a revenue generator, considerable interprovincial variation did exist in each of these revenue sources as reflected in their coefficients of variation (Table 2.17).

The greatest degree of variation can be seen in the use of natural resource revenue. The extremely heavy dependence on this revenue source by the con- solidated provincial/local sectors in Alberta (46 per cent of all revenue in 1978 and 25.4 per cent in 1968), Saskatchewan (20.5 per cent and 5.8 per cent in 1978 and 1968 respectively), and British Columbia (8.5 per cent and 9.1 per cent in 1978 and 1968 respectively) combined with virtually no dependence (less than 2 per cent) in the remaining provinces generated the large coefficients of variation.

By 1978, relatively little interprovincial variation can be seen in revenues obtained by local and provincial governments from sales of goods and services. The dependence, on average, of this revenue source remained fairly constant over the decade under study.

Finally, other revenue (consisting of a multitude of miscellaneous nontax sources) constituted by far the largest percentage of nontax own-source revenue in 1968 and 1978. As well, the interprovincial variation (reflected by the coefficient of variation) in the dependence on this revenue source declined over this period.

VARIATION IN PROVINCIAL PER CAPITA REVENUE LEVELS BY SOURCE

The substantial variation in the proportion of provincial/local total revenue supported by the different revenue functions is also evident in the per capita levels of combined provincial/local revenues attributed to the different revenue

---

[16]Property-related taxes are primarily, although not exclusively a local revenue source (see Chapter 8 on property taxation), while consumption-based taxes, particularly the sales taxes, tend to be provincial taxes.

sources. Table 2.18 records the average per capita level of the different revenue functions in all provinces in Canada along with the provinces displaying the highest and lowest per capita values from each revenue source. Table 2.19 notes the relative inteprovincial variation in the absolute per capita yield of each of the revenue sources. Obviously, the interprovincial variation in per capita revenue is more extreme for some functions than for others, but nevertheless, is quite extreme for all functions.[17]

On a province-by-province comparison, Alberta, which had the highest per capita revenue levels both in terms of total and own-source revenue in each of 1968 and 1978, also exhibited the greatest percentage increase—almost 500 per cent. By comparison, Ontario, which ranked second in per capita total revenue in 1968 ($695) and eighth in 1978 ($2,203), displayed the slowest growth (less than 220 per cent) in per capita total revenues (see Appendix Tables A.8 and A.9). The four provinces in Atlantic Canada displayed the lowest per capita levels of revenue in 1968; however, by 1978, Prince Edward Island and Newfoundland climbed to fifth and sixth place respectively. Clearly, revenue patterns tend to follow expenditure patterns. Thus, higher levels of provincial/local revenues have emerged in three of the western provinces (Manitoba excluded) and Quebec. This may be attributed in part to higher tax rates and in part to growing tax bases.

While the 1978 interprovincial variation in total per capita revenue was comparatively low (the coefficient of variation was .28—Table 2.19), the variation was substantially higher for provincial/local own-source revenues. The explanation for this greater province-by-province variation is quite straightforward but needs mentioning. This difference can be attributed directly to conditional and unconditional grants.

Of all the *major* revenue sources employed in all provinces, revenues from unconditional grants displayed the greatest variation on both total and per capita bases in each of 1968 and 1978 (Table 2.19). By far the highest per capita levels were recorded in Atlantic Canada in each of these years. These levels should not be surprising since such grants are distributed for the purpose of funding provincial and local government expenditures in areas where the taxpaying capacity of the residents is deemed to be below an accepted standard. Federal conditional grants,[18] on the other hand, are given for specific purposes or projects. From 1968 to 1978, on a provincial per capita average, these funds increased by a factor of 4.4, whereas unconditional grant funds grew by a factor of 3.2 (calculated from Appendix Tables A.8 and A.9). The interprovincial variation in conditional grants was considerably less than that of unconditional grants. Once again the Atlantic provinces ranked at the top of the list in each of the years observed.

---

[17]Note the different values for the average columns in Table 2.17 and 2.18. In the former, the average has been weighted by population to reflect the average for all of the Canadian provinces; whereas, the latter is simply the average of all of the provincial averages not weighted by population. Use of the unweighted average provides for an analysis of interprovincial variation in the use of the different revenue sources.

[18]For a thorough discussion of federal grants, see Robin W. Boadway, *Intergovernmental Transfers in Canada* (Toronto: Canadian Tax Foundation, 1980).

Over the decade studied the greatest interprovincial variation occurred in natural resource revenue. In both years, Alberta recorded the highest per capita level with British Columbia and Saskatchewan also listing significant sums. The remaining provinces placed little reliance on this source for generating revenue. Specifically, the per capita differential between the highest ranking province (Alberta at $2,074) and lowest (Prince Edward Island at $4) in 1978 amounted

Table 2.18   **Range of Per Capita Consolidated Provincial/Local Revenue by Major Source, 1968 and 1978**

Revenue source	1968			1978		
	Average for all provinces[a]	Highest province	Lowest province	Average for all provinces	Highest province[a]	Lowest province
			dollars			
Personal income tax	85.41	117.57 (Que.)	24.25 (P.E.I.)	462.38	652.84 (Que.)	238.89 (P.E.I.)
Corporate income tax ..	31.97	41.96 (Ont.)	9.58 (P.E.I.)	108.48	271.15 (Alta.)	29.76 (P.E.I.)
Property taxes.........	144.96	177.45 (Ont.)	17.01 (Nfld.)	345.50	446.05 (B.C.)	71.26 (Nfld.)
Consumption taxes	125.61	148.92 (Que.)	47.04 (Alta.)	306.01	382.39 (Nfld.)	22.44 (Alta.)
Other taxes	13.61	19.95 (Que.)	2.18 (N.B.)	42.67	62.80 (Ont.)	. 7.66 (Nfld.)
Total taxes............	401.56	451.93 (Que.)	181.73 (Nfld.)	1,265.05	703.69 (P.E.I.)	1,431.12 (B.C.)
Sale of goods and services	24.99	48.75 (P.E.I.)	15.85 (Que.)	129.52	230.40 (Alta.)	68.18 (N.B.)
Privileges, licences, and permits	25.80	30.40 (Ont.)	14.32 (P.E.I.)	65.70	93.76 (Que.)	25.40 (P.E.I.)
Natural resource revenue	28.85	193.15 (Alta.)	.43 (P.E.I.)	232.60	2,074.08 (Alta.)	3.56 (P.E.I.)
Payments-in-lieu of taxes	1.03	3.58 (N.S.)	0.00 (N.B.)	8.21	13.08 (N.S.)	.25 (P.E.I.)
Other revenue	65.65	113.99 (Sask.)	20.63 (Que.)	428.74	744.22 (Alta.)	177.78 (N.B.)
Total own-source revenue	547.88	653.13 (Alta.)	262.61 (P.E.I.)	2,129.81	4,132.03 (Alta.)	1,069.40 (P.E.I.)
Unconditional grants ...	43.21	164.48 (Nfld.)	2.15 (B.C.)	137.55	614.52 (P.E.I.)	13.34 (Ont.)
Conditional grants	73.19	128.80 (Nfld.)	30.17 (Que.)	318.79	677.86 (P.E.I.)	285.05 (Ont.)
Total revenue	664.28	759.36 (Alta.)	535.85 (N.B.)	2,586.15	4,509.04 (Alta.)	2,016.20 (N.B.)

[a]Weighted provincial average.

Source: Calculated from data in Appendix Tables A.8 and A.9.

to $2,070 (Appendix Table A.9). The remaining nontax own-source revenues exhibited considerably less variation in the extent to which they were used by the different aggregated provincial/local governments.

Including the province of Quebec, where different fiscal arrangements have been implemented between the province and the federal government, the absolute dollar value of provincial taxes collected varied considerably: from a per capita high of $1,431 and $1,430 in British Columbia and Quebec respectively to a low of $704 per capita in Prince Edward Island with the remaining Atlantic provinces recording levels substantially lower than the national average (Appendix Table A.9). With the exception of consumption-based taxes, Atlantic Canada collected significantly lower revenues (per capita and total) from the different major taxes at its disposal. Since the property tax is the most important tax source for local governments and since local governments are the central focus in this book, it is necessary to review the interprovincial difference that existed and to a large extent, still exists. The variation in average per capita provincial property taxes remained constant from 1968 to 1978 (Table 2.19), while the revenue from this tax, on average, increased by a factor of 2.5. By 1978, British Columbia led all provinces in the per capita absolute level of this tax with a value of $446. This exceeded the per capita level for Newfoundland

Table 2.19   Interprovincial Variation in Consolidated Provincial/Local Per Capita Revenues by Revenue Source, 1968 and 1978

	1968			1978		
	(1)	(2)	(3)	(4)	(5)	(6)
		Standard	Coefficient of		Standard	Coefficient of
Revenue source	Average[a]	deviation	variation	Average[a]	deviation	variation
	dollars			*dollars*		
Personal income tax	59.60	28.21	.47	369.79	19.30	.32
Corporate income tax . .	22.94	9.64	.42	93.67	70.74	76
Property taxes	109.87	50.73	.46	275.60	126.87	.46
Consumption taxes	111.21	27.49	.25	288.53	102.10	.35
Other taxes	7.71	5.61	.73	29.06	17.40	.60
Total taxes	311.33	99.29	.32	1,058.01	270.27	.26
Sale of goods and services	30.23	10.43	.35	127.79	45.56	.36
Privileges, licences, and permits	21.43	5.26	.25	50.50	18.93	.37
Natural resource revenue	33.85	56.39	1.67	297.12	647.54	2.18
Total own-source revenue	462.29	144.05	.31	1,903.02	917.43	.48
Unconditional grants . . .	72.69	58.00	.80	280.69	248.81	.89
Conditional grants	95.36	27.04	.28	387.73	112.68	.29
Total revenue	630.44	73.22	.12	2,571.44	721.96	.28

[a]Unweighted provincial average.

Source: Calculated from data in Appendix Tables A.8 and A.9.

(which was the lowest at $71) by some $375. In fact, for the same year the remaining Maritime provinces had values ranging from $125 (Prince Edward Island) to $197 (Nova Scotia); whereas the rest of Canada ranged from $306 in Quebec to $394 in Ontario (Appendix Table A.9).

An analysis of the extent to which local governments depend on property tax as a revenue source is of equal importance here. While total local and provincial taxes, on average, increased by a factor of 3.2 over the period studied, Newfoundland was the only province that listed an increase in per capita property tax revenue (by a factor of 4.2) in excess of this figure. This can be attributed directly to the extremely low level of per capita property taxes that this province collected in 1968. The increase in the other nine provinces ranged from a factor of 2.9 (highest) in New Brunswick and British Columbia to a low of 2.0 in Saskatchewan and Ontario (calculated from Appendix Tables A.8 and A.9).

LOCAL OWN-SOURCE REVENUE AS A PROPORTION OF CONSOLIDATED PROVINCIAL/LOCAL OWN-SOURCE REVENUE

The revenue analysis thus far has concentrated on consolidated own-source revenues received by the provincial/local government sector. The remaining discussion will focus on the local sector alone. By way of introduction then, Table 2.20 presents data on the proportion of total provincial and local revenues arising solely from the local sector in each of the provinces for the years 1968 and 1978. One must be cautious in making interprovincial comparisons when reviewing these figures because the provision of local services and the subsequent funding of these services differ accross Canada. A good example of this arose in the province of New Brunswick where the provincial government in the middle to late sixties assumed the major responsibility for funding a number of services that had previously been in the domain of local governments. As a result, local revenues (own source) that accounted for 31 per cent of the provincial/local sector combined in 1968, only accounted for 10.9 per cent in 1978 (Table 2.20). A similar decrease in the local sector's revenue yield occurred in Prince Edward Island over the same period (from 21.3 per cent of the combined provincial/local sector in 1968 to 8.1 per cent in 1978). By comparison, the proportion of provincial/local own-source revenue attributed to the local sector alone for all the provinces decreased from 31.4 per cent (1968) to 22.5 per cent (1978) of the total (a decrease of 28 per cent). Larger than average decreases occurred in Alberta (52 per cent), Newfoundland (40 per cent), Quebec (33 per cent), and Saskatchewan (36 per cent), while smaller than average decreases existed in British Columbia (15 per cent), Manitoba (5 per cent), Ontario (17 per cent), and Nova Scotia (24 per cent) (calculated from Table 2.20).

As in the case of the earlier expenditure analysis, the percentages in Table 2.20 provide some indication of the relative importance of revenues at the local level in the 10 provinces. With the exception of Nova Scotia, Atlantic Canada generally relies less heavily on local governments to raise revenue from their own sources. By contrast, the aggregated provincial/local sectors in Manitoba, Ontario, and British Columbia collect proportionately more revenue from their local sectors.

Table 2.20   Percentage of Consolidated Provincial/Local Own-Source
Revenue Attributed to Local Sources, 1968 and 1978[a]

Province	1968	1978
	per cent	
Newfoundland..	14.1	8.5
Prince Edward Island	21.3	8.1
Nova Scotia	31.4	24.0
New Brunswick	11.1	10.9
Quebec	29.7	19.9
Ontario...	34.3	28.4
Manitoba	34.5	32.8
Saskatchewan	33.2	21.3
Alberta	30.2	14.4
British Columbia.......................................	29.3	24.9
All provinces	31.4	22.5

[a]Local own-source revenue excludes all grants.

Source: Calculated from Statistics Canada, *Local Government Finance, 1968* and *Local Government Finance, 1978,* Catalogue no. 68-204, and from Appendix Tables A.8 and A.9.

FISCAL CAPACITY

"Fiscal capacity" is a measure of the ability of the provincial/local sector to obtain revenues from its own revenue sources. While one may use different measures of tax capacity, the most appropriate for the purposes of this book is that used in Table 2.21.[19] Relative fiscal capacity is obtained by estimating the per capita yield in each province arising from a standardized tax system (that is, by applying a uniform tax rate for each tax source to a uniform tax base for that source). Once the totals have been derived for each province, the average for all provinces is calculated and set equal to 100. Finally, the separate provincial/local figures are then recorded as a percentage of the national average, thus generating an interprovincial index reflecting the relative position of each of the 10 provinces.

As Table 2.21 suggests, there is considerable variation in provincial relative fiscal capacity.[20] Alberta recorded an index for all own-soruce revenues that was 127 per cent above the national average and virtually double that of the next closest province, British Columbia (column 3 of Table 2.21). Column 2, referring to natural resource revenue only, provides most of the basis for the variation in overall fiscal capacities. This column indicates that six provinces have a fiscal capacity that is 10 per cent or less of the national average, while Alberta

---

[19]For a description of the measure of revenue capacity and tax effort, see Canada, Department of Finance, *Federal-Provincial Fiscal Arrangements in the Eighties: A Submission to the Parliamentary Task Force on the Federal-Provincial Fiscal Arrangements* (Ottawa: the Department, 1981), 43-49.

[20]The choice of 1977 rather than 1978 indices represents the latest year for which published data are available. In addition, it can be safely assumed that an interprovincial comparison of revenue capacity would, in 1978, be similar to that in 1977. Hence, the 1977 figures can act as a proxy for 1978.

Table 2.21   Indices of Provincial/Local Fiscal Capacity from
Own-Source Revenues,[a] 1977[b]

Province	(1) Nonresource revenue	(2) Resource revenue	(3) All revenue
Newfoundland	62	38	59
Prince Edward Island	63	0	55
Nova Scotia	72	5	64
New Brunswick	72	10	65
Quebec	89	9	79
Ontario	107	8	95
Manitoba	89	9	79
Saskatchewan	92	146	99
Alberta	134	892	227
British Columbia	113	130	115
All provinces	100	100	100

[a]Based on total provincial and local revenues from own sources, subject to exclusions for interest revenues of provincial governments and all nontax revenues of local governments. [b]Fiscal year ending nearest December 31, 1977.

Source: Canada, *Federal-Provincial Fiscal Arrangements in the Eighties: A Submission to the Parliamentary Task Force on the Federal-Provincial Fiscal Arrangements* (Ottawa: Department of Finance, 1981), 44.

is almost 800 per cent above the national average. The index reflecting nonresource revenue (column 1) also displays some modest variation with Alberta reigning at the top, some 34 per cent above the national average and the four Atlantic provinces lying at the bottom (from 62 per cent to 72 per cent of the national average).

TAX EFFORT

Tax effort is a measure of the extent to which a province uses its own revenue sources. In doing so, it takes into account the fiscal capacity of the provincial/local sector to raise revenue from its own sources, regardless of whether these taxes are imposed on individuals or business enterprises. The interprovincial indices reflecting tax efforts for 1977 are presented in Table 2.22.[21] These indices compare the actual revenues collected in each province with the revenues that could have been collected had the national average tax rate been applied to the estimated fiscal capacities for each province. Column 1 of Table 2.22 records the indices for actual revenues collected. Column 2 shows the indices after each province's actual provincial/local own-source revenues have been adjusted to take into account provincial surplus or deficit positions.[22] In this latter instance, the levels of tax effort are those that would have arisen if total revenues had been sufficient to give them a standardized (average per capita) level of deficit or surplus. If a province had a deficit that exceeded the national average per capita deficit, this adjustment would raise that province's index of tax effort because its tax effort would have to rise in order to finance the deficit. On the other

[21]These indices could be used as a proxy for 1978. See supra footnote 20 for an explanation.

[22]For a discussion of this, see supra footnote 19, at 46-48.

Table 2.22   Indices of Provincial/Local Tax Effort,[a] 1977[b]

Province	(1) Actual revenues	(2) Actual revenues adjusted for surpluses and deficits
Newfoundland	101	104
Prince Edward Island	95	111
Nova Scotia	95	109
New Brunswick	84	97
Quebec	120	122
Ontario	100	110
Manitoba	99	116
Saskatchewan	105	105
Alberta	80	54
British Columbia	98	94
All provinces	100	100

[a]Based on provincial and local government revenues from own sources, subject to exclusion for interest revenues of provincial governments and all nontax revenues of local governments. [b]Fiscal year ending nearest to December 31, 1977.

Source: Canada, *Federal-Provincial Fiscal Arrangements in the Eighties: A Submission to the Parliamentary Task Force on the Federal-Provincial Fiscal Arrangements* (Ottawa: Department of Finance, 1981), 47.

hand, if the per capita deficit was lower than the national average or if the province had a surplus, the adjusted tax effort would decline because the province was in a position to reduce its tax effort in order to incur an average per capita deficit or surplus.[23]

While four provinces displayed tax efforts from actual revenues equal to or greater than the national average (column 1), seven provinces displayed tax efforts, when adjusted to account for revenues and surpluses, higher than the national average. The data suggest that provinces that display relatively low fiscal capacities for their combined provincial/local sectors also display relatively high tax efforts.

COMPARISON OF REVENUE CAPACITY, TAX EFFORT, AND EXPENDITURE LEVELS

A number of implications emerge from the comparative data in Table 2.23. First, the combined provincial/local sectors in Alberta and British Columbia recorded higher than average expenditure levels and fiscal capacities and lower than average tax efforts. Second, three of the provinces in Atlantic Canada (Newfoundland, Prince Edward Island, and Nova Scotia) and Manitoba had lower than average fiscal capacities and expenditure levels and higher than average tax efforts. Third, New Brunswick displayed lower than average figures for fiscal capacity and expenditure level but a close to average tax effort. Fourth, some provinces (Quebec, Ontario, and Saskatchewan) had lower than average fiscal capacities and higher than average tax efforts and expenditure levels.

---

[23]Supra footnote 19, at 46-47.

Table 2.23   Comparison of Fiscal Capacity, Tax Effort,
and Expenditure Levels, 1978[a]

Province	Index for fiscal capacity[b]	Index for tax effort[c]	Index for expenditure level[d]
Newfoundland	59	104	87
Prince Edward Island......	55	111	66
Nova Scotia..............	64	109	76
New Brunswick...........	65	97	64
Quebec	79	122	123
Ontario	95	110	110
Manitoba	79	116	91
Saskatchewan	99	105	114
Alberta	227	54	150
British Columbia	115	94	118

[a]The 1977 indices for fiscal capacity and tax effort are used as proxy measures for the year 1978.
[b]Obtained from column 3 of Table 2.18. [c]Obtained from column 2 of Table 2.19. [d]Obtained from Table 2.11.

SUMMARY

As was suggested at the outset, a comprehensive interprovincial assessment of the Canadian local financial situation is fraught with problems. In some provinces the responsibility for specific functions such as education and health and welfare rests with the provincial government, while in other provinces these functions are the responsibility of local governments (see Chapters 4 and 5). To avoid the pitfalls associated with an interprovincial comparison of the different municipal responsibilities and to provide a framework for assessing municipal finance in each of the individual provinces, this chapter has aggregated provincial and local expenditures and revenues.

On the basis of the material covered in this chapter, there are a number of salient features that should be highlighted. First, the bulk of the increase in provincial/local expenditures financed from own-source revenues can be attributed to inflation, a component over which the provincial/local sector has limited control. Second, over the 11-year period under observation, the increase in expenditures on the "soft" services of education, health and social services accounted for almost 50 per cent of the entire increase in per capita expenditures at the provincial/local level. Third, substantial variation in per capita expenditures and revenues, both including and excluding federal grants, continues to exist. Fourth, substantial variation in the extent to which local governments are responsible for providing local services can be witnessed by the difference in the proportion of provincial/local per capita expenditures attributed to the local sector alone. Fifth, regional trends are apparent in both levels of per capita expenditure financed from own-source revenue and per capita levels of revenue actually collected. Finally, noticeable differences in the fiscal capacities existing in each of the 10 provinces are largely responsible for dictating the levels of expenditure and extent to which provincial/local tax sources are used.

Part II

Expenditure Analysis

3
Local Government Expenditures

INTRODUCTION

The removal of provincial data from the expenditure figures means that inter-provincial comparisons of the remaining municipal data must be treated cautiously. Such interprovincial comparisons for a number of purposes may be meaningless; meaningless because some functions (such as the provision of education, welfare, and the administration of justice) are provided by the province in some provinces but are the direct responsibility of local governments in others. Such a comparative assessment, however, does provide a useful means of making interprovincial assessments of such things as the relative sizes of local sectors, the specific expenditure responsibilities at the municipal level, and the levels of service supplied at this level. In addition, this sort of comparison provides a basis for illustrating and commenting on existing provincial differences and the ways in which the local sector in some provinces may be altered to provide more effectively local services or to finance specific expenditures. Consideration of municipal expenditures financed from own-source revenues, moreover, forms part of the framework for outlining and assessing the financial problems facing many local governments.

RELATIVE IMPORTANCE OF LOCAL EXPENDITURES, 1968 AND 1978

While the combined provincial/local expenditures as a proportion of the gross domestic provincial product (GDPP) increased from 1968 to 1978 (Table 2.1), a similar increase was not observed in the local sector alone (Table 3.1). Specifically, local government expenditures funded from own-source revenues (when aggregated over all provinces) amounted to slightly more than 6 per cent of gross national product (GNP) in each of the years observed. This supports the contention that the local sector's relative importance remained fairly constant from 1968 to 1978. Obviously, there were changes in the importance of the local sector in a number of individual provinces, but in no case was this change very noticeable (Table 3.1). Part of the explanation for a marginal shift in the relative importance of some local sectors lies in the changes that occurred in both the levels and volumes of service supplied (discussed below). Where the change was more noticeable, however, the data generally reflected a change in expenditure responsibilities of these local governments.

In Atlantic Canada, municipal expenditures when calculated as a percentage of GDPP generated percentages that were lower than the corresponding figures in each of the remaining provinces, regardless of the year selected (Table 3.1). Corresponding figures for the remaining provinces tended to fluctuate around the Canadian average.

A comparison of the data in Tables 2.1 and 3.1 generates some interesting observations. As indicated in Chapter 2, Table 2.1, the aggregated provin-

Table 3.1   Local "Own-Source Funded" Expenditures, by Province,
as a Proportion of GDPP, 1968 and 1978

	1968		1978	
Province	Total local expenditures	Per cent of GDPP	Total local expenditures	Per cent of GDPP
	millions of dollars	*per cent*	*millions of dollars*	*per cent*
Newfoundland	25.1	2.9	72.2	2.5
Prince Edward Island . .	7.5	4.1	32.0	5.1
Nova Scotia	85.6	5.2	275.9	5.3
New Brunswick	25.9	2.1	110.3	2.7
Quebec	1,096.4	6.9	3,147.7	6.5
Ontario	1,717.6	6.5	4,948.2	6.2
Manitoba	159.5	5.7	559.5	6.7
Saskatchewan	173.9	6.7	501.4	5.6
Alberta	329.4	6.1	1,549.5	5.8
British Columbia	407.0	5.8	1,670.3	6.7
All provinces	4,027.9	6.3	12,854.8	6.1

Source: Appendix Tables B.1 and B.2, and The Conference Board of Canada, *The Provincial Economies, 1961-1980 Data* (Ottawa: the Board, 1981).

cial/local expenditures for the provinces in Atlantic Canada and to a lesser extent Quebec, accounted for a larger proportion of GDPP than was seen in the rest of Canada. This tendency for eastern Canada to display relatively larger combined provincial/local expenditures when calculated as a proportion of GDPP is not observed when the local expenditures are viewed separately (Table 3.1). In fact, Newfoundland, Prince Edward Island, New Brunswick, and to a lesser extent Nova Scotia, all displayed relatively small local expenditures from own-source revenues, thus necessitating the comment that local governments in these provinces have generally assumed a less important role in funding local expenditures than is true in the rest of Canada. This can be attributed to the greater importance of federal grants in the Atlantic region. These grants are authorized because the area is poor, but they are given to the provincial rather than to the local governments. These provincial governments, therefore, generally have assumed a greater role in supporting, and in some cases directly supplying, a number of local services. Considerable attention will be devoted to a discussion of the different governmental responsibilities for supplying the various services across Canada in Chapters 4 and 5.

GROWTH OF LOCAL GOVERNMENT EXPENDITURES FINANCED FROM OWN-SOURCE REVENUES, 1968 TO 1978

In 1978, local expenditures in Newfoundland and New Brunswick were the lowest (23 per cent and 29 per cent respectively) of the Canadian per capita average of $549. Nova Scotia, which was the highest in this region, recorded a figure of 60 per cent (Table 3.2). By comparison, the average municipality in each of the remaining provinces ranged from a low of 91 per cent in Quebec to

Table 3.2   Growth of Per Capita Local Expenditures Funded from Own-Source Revenues, 1968 to 1978

Province	1968	1978		Growth 1968 to 1978		Ratio of growth of local expenditures to consolidated provincial/local expenditures	
	(1) Current dollars	(2) Current dollars	(3) Constant dollars	(4) Current dollars	(5) Constant dollars	(6) Current dollars	(7) Constant dollars
	dollars			*per cent*			
Newfoundland	49.54	126.83	50.96	156.0	2.9	.32	.02
Prince Edward Island	69.07	262.41	117.09	280.0	69.5	.82	.94
Nova Scotia	122.36	328.11	135.85	168.2	11.0	.55	.18
New Brunswick	41.60	158.68	66.83	281.4	60.6	1.11	1.58
Quebec	184.98	501.79	209.29	171.3	13.1	.54	.20
Ontario	243.98	586.00	239.69	140.2	−1.8	.59	−.05
Manitoba	176.00	541.08	208.70	207.4	18.6	.76	.41
Saskatchewan	206.32	528.93	219.95	156.4	6.6	.50	.11
Alberta	239.09	793.01	331.50	231.7	38.7	.69	.55
British Columbia	204.69	660.21	265.21	222.5	29.6	.71	.50
All provinces	200.89	548.93	223.97	173.2	11.5	.61	.23

Source: Recorded or calculated from data in Appendix Tables A.6, A.7, and B.4.

a high of 145 per cent in Alberta. Such variations were not observed in the growth of local expenditures. For example, New Brunswick and Prince Edward Island displayed the highest growth rate (280 per cent in current per capita expenditures), a rate that was significantly above that for any other province.

It must be pointed out that the large percentage increase can be attributed to the relatively low per capita expenditure level that existed in New Brunswick in 1968 and to a very large one-shot capital expenditure on education in Prince Edward Island in 1978 (see Appendix Table B.2). In fact, the absolute per capita dollar increase in local expenditures in these two provinces exceeded only those of Newfoundland. Most of the explanation for the lower increase in Newfoundland rests in the fact that some of the local functions were shifted away from the local sector and onto the provincial level of government over the period under study. As for the remaining provinces, the rate of increase in per capita current dollars ranged from a low of 140 per cent in Ontario to a high of 232 per cent in Alberta, a notable range in the growth of municipal expenditures (Table 3.2).

When compared with the above figures, the changes in constant per capita local expenditures were relatively modest. These ranged from a slight decrease of almost 2 per cent in Ontario to a high of almost 70 per cent and 61 per cent in Prince Edward Island and New Brunswick (column 5 of Table 3.2) respectively. With the exception of the aggregated local governments in New Brunswick, the growth in locally funded expenditures on a per capita basis in the other provinces fell substantially below the growth in the consolidated provincial/local expenditures financed from their own revenue sources over the period under study. Indeed, in observing the ratio of the growth in local to the growth in consolidated provincial/local expenditures (column 6, Table 3.2), one notes that the growth in the local sector, in most provinces, was less than 70 per cent of the growth in the consolidated provincial/local level.

LOCAL GOVERNMENT OPERATING EXPENDITURES AGGREGATED BY PROVINCE, 1968 TO 1978

Table 3.3 records the levels of per capita local operating expenditures funded from own-source revenues along with a comparative analysis of the relative percentage increase in each province from 1968 to 1978. Although the evidence extracted from Table 3.3 does not suggest any clear-cut pattern or relationship between the level of operating expenditures vis-à-vis capital expenditures, it does, when compared with Appendix Tables B.1 and B.2, indicate that local operating expenditures almost always exceed local capital expenditures. The erratic nature of capital expenditures suggests that any distinct trend or analysis based on rates of growth over time is highly questionable. For this reason and because a large proportion of capital expenditure is financed from borrowing and, therefore, does not reflect direct yearly claims on local budgets (other than through annual interest and repayment charges), the rest of this chapter and Chapters 4 and 5 will be devoted to a discussion of operating expenditures that must be financed from own-source revenues. Capital expenditures and the problems associated with their financing will be addressed in Chapter 6.

Local per capita operating expenditures in Atlantic Canada ranged between 17 per cent (Newfoundland) and 65 per cent (Nova Scotia) of the Canadian

Table 3.3   Per Capita Local Operating Expenditures (in Current Dollars)
Funded from Own-Source Revenues, 1968 and 1978

Province	1968		1978		Increase 1968 to 1978	
	dollars	per cent[a]	dollars	per cent[a]	dollars	per cent[a]
Newfoundland	23.71	16.9	79.93	19.1	56.22	20.2
Prince Edward Island..	66.00	47.0	82.28	19.7	16.28	5.9
Nova Scotia..........	90.72	64.6	260.00	62.2	169.28	60.9
New Brunswick.......	26.47	18.8	96.33	23.0	69.86	25.2
Quebec	124.09	88.4	369.58	88.4	245.49	88.4
Ontario	170.21	121.2	469.39	112.2	299.18	107.7
Manitoba	150.47	107.1	453.87	108.5	303.40	109.2
Saskatchewan	157.33	112.0	381.04	91.1	223.71	80.5
Alberta	153.08	109.0	514.82	123.1	361.74	130.2
British Columbia	153.40	109.2	524.98	125.5	371.58	133.8
All provinces.........	140.43	100.0	418.18	100.0	277.75	100.0

aPer cent of all province average.

Source: Appendix Tables B.1 and B.2.

average in 1968 and between 19 per cent (Newfoundland) and 62 per cent (Nova Scotia) in 1978. These levels were considerably lower than the aggregated local government expenditures in the remaining provinces in these years. Specifically, by 1978, Ontario and three of the western provinces (with the exception of Saskatchewan) emerged as being well above the Canadian average with per capita levels in localities in these provinces being some 9 per cent to 26 per cent above the average for all provinces. A comparison of the relative increase in local per capita operating expenditures (last column of Table 3.3) across provinces displays a regional pattern with the five provinces in eastern Canada and Saskatchewan all exhibiting increases that were lower than the Canadian average.

LOCALLY FUNDED EXPENDITURES AND LEVEL OF RESPONSIBILITY

In order to facilitate a meaningful interprovincial comparison of the level of local government expenditures, it is essential to examine systematically the various provincial/local own-source responsibility arrangements. It is meaningless to claim in isolation that a specific level of expenditure in absolute dollars is spent, on average, by municipalities in a given province or that this expenditure is higher or lower by a certain amount or percentage than a corresponding figure for another province. This sort of claim indicates virtually nothing about differences that may be attributed to service levels or costs nor does it indicate anything about the differences that may occur because certain expenditures in some provinces are the responsibility of local governments, while the same services in other provinces are financially supported by provincial governments. It is possible, however, to measure the proportion of total expenditures that may be assigned to different responsibilities assumed by different levels of government. The following two tables (and those presented in Chapters 4 and 5 dealing with separate expenditure functions) attempt to illustrate this very point for 1978.

In each of Tables 3.4 and 3.5, the first column lists all local expenditures (total or functional depending on the table) as a per cent of total provincial/local expenditures. The second column displays the proportion of the total local sector's expenditures (functional or total) that is financed from own-source revenues (excluding grants). These figures yield a rough estimate of the extent to which the aggregated local sector in each province is responsible for raising its own revenue in order to meet its expenditure requirements. The third column measures the proportion of local expenditures that are financed from own-source revenues as a per cent of provincial and local expenditures combined. While there may be some weaknesses in constructing an index of this sort, there is one advantage in basing it on the aggregated provincial/local sector rather than on the local sector alone. Roughly the same services are supplied in each province, but the level of government (local or provincial) responsible for providing and funding these diverse services frequently differs among provinces. By excluding direct provincial funding (grants) or provincial provision of services and programs provided for local residents, one is able to measure the extent to which the local sector is dependent on locally raised revenue in financially supporting the total of all services and programs supplied to local residents. After all, it is this claim on local funds, required to support a relatively uniform (interprovincially) level and range of local services and programs, that is of prime importance to local politicians and administrators.

Columns 4 and 6 display local government own-source expenditures on a per capita basis: column 4 with respect to total expenditures and column 6 with respect to operating expenditures only. On average, across all provinces, local governments devoted approximately three-quarters (76.2 per cent—calculated from Table 3.4) of their total own-source expenditure budgets to operating costs and one-quarter to capital costs in 1978. Clearly, it is operating expenses rather than capital expenses that bear most heavily on local governments. In four of the ten major expenditure categories (general government, protection, education, and social services), over 85 per cent of own-source expenditures were devoted to operating expenses (Table 3.5). Similar figures were 74 per cent in recreation and culture, 69 per cent in health, and 56 per cent in regional development and housing (calculated from Table 3.5). In only three functions (transportation, environment, and resource conservation) was a larger portion of the total own-source expenditure budget devoted to capital rather than operating expenses. Consequently, in all expenditure categories (with the exception of those mentioned in the previous sentence) the removal of capital expenses from total expenditures leaves the relative ranking of operating to total expenditures virtually unchanged. This observation is verified by columns 5 and 7 (Table 3.5) that record the percentage that each per capita expenditure function represents of total expenditures. With the exception of those functions that display high capital costs, these proportions are comparable.

An additional task of this section and the next two chapters is to identify and account for any variation in the local expenditure levels of urban regions as compared to non-urban municipalities in each province. (See Tables 3.4 and

Table 3.4   Total Expenditures, 1978

	Local government responsibility			Local government own-source expenditures[a]					
	(1)	(2)	(3)	(4)	(5)	(6)	(7)	(8)	(9)
Province	Local expenditures as a per cent of provincial/local expenditures	Local expenditures financed by own-source revenue as a per cent of total local expenditures	Local expenditures financed by own-source revenue as a per cent of provincial/local expenditures	Per capita expenditures—all local governments	Per cent of total local government expenditures	Per capita operating expenditures—all local governments	Per cent of total local government expenditures	Per capita expenditures—all urban regions[b]	Per cent of total local government expenditures
	per cent	per cent		dollars	per cent	dollars	per cent	dollars	per cent
Nfld.	7.4	63.0	4.7	126.83	23.1	79.93	19.1	311.97	52.0
P.E.I.	26.2	39.9	10.5	262.41	47.8	82.28	19.7	—	—
N.S.	33.5	42.5	14.2	328.12	59.8	260.00	62.2	729.71	121.5
N.B.	12.4	60.7	7.5	158.68	28.9	96.33	23.0	313.61	52.2
Que.	35.5	49.4	17.5	501.79	91.4	369.58	88.4	590.42	98.3
Ont.	43.3	56.5	24.5	586.08	106.8	469.39	112.2	522.73	87.1
Man.	38.5	60.5	23.3	541.07	98.6	453.87	108.5	689.40	114.8
Sask.	38.2	53.3	20.4	528.93	96.4	381.04	91.1	661.35	110.1
Alta.	42.5	57.7	24.5	793.01	144.5	514.82	123.1	891.58	148.5
B.C.	36.5	70.1	25.6	660.21	120.3	524.98	125.5	693.09	115.4
All prov.	37.8	55.7	21.1	548.90	100.0	418.18	100.0	600.43	100.0

[a]Excludes both conditional and unconditional grants. [b]Capital and operating expenditures are not available on a separate basis.

Source: Calculated from Appendix Table B.2 and from Statistics Canada, *Local Government Finance, Preliminary 1978—Estimates 1979*, Catalogue no. 68-203.

Table 3.5   Local Government Functional Expenditures, All Provinces, 1978

Function	Local government responsibility			Local government own-source expenditures[a]					
	(1)	(2)	(3)	(4)	(5)	(6)	(7)	(8)	(9)
	Local expenditures as a per cent of provincial/local expenditures	Local expenditures financed by own-source revenue as a per cent of total local expenditures	Local expenditures financed by own-source revenue as a per cent of provincial/local expenditures	Per capita expenditures—all local governments	Per cent of total local government expenditures	Per capita operating expenditures—all local governments	Per cent total local government expenditures	Per capita expenditures—all urban regions[b]	Per cent of total local government expenditures
	per cent			*dollars*	*per cent*	*dollars*	*per cent*	*dollars*	*per cent*
General government ...	25.9	83.0	21.5	37.60	6.9	35.96	8.6	41.29	7.2
Protection	53.0	86.8	46.0	64.28	11.7	60.64	14.5	83.40	13.9
Transportation ..	49.1	69.9	34.3	79.83	14.5	35.93	8.6	93.41	15.5
Health	9.7	13.9	1.3	6.68	1.2	4.60	1.1	1.30	1.0
Social services ...	9.3	43.2	4.0	12.55	2.3	10.87	2.6	8.59	1.3
Education	66.6	34.6	23.0	143.74	26.3	128.38	30.7	136.35	20.7
Resource conservation and Industrial Development	6.7	95.1	6.4	7.77	1.4	3.35	.8	3.72	.6
Environment.....	83.4	83.2	69.4	70.28	12.8	28.85	6.9	71.90	13.6
Recreation and culture	68.9	79.0	54.4	46.27	8.4	34.29	8.2	49.25	9.2
Housing and regional development	27.0	81.7	22.1	10.47	1.9	5.85	1.4	17.02	3.1
Other	35.5	72.7	25.8	69.43	12.6	69.43	16.6	83.07	13.9
Total	37.8	55.7	21.1	548.90	100.0	418.15	100.0	600.43	100.0

[a]Excludes both conditional and unconditional grants. [b]Capital and operating expenditures are not available on a separate basis.

Source: Calculated from Appendix Table B.2 and from Statistics Canada, *Local Government Finance, Preliminary 1978—Estimates 1979*, Catalogue no. 68-203.

3.5, column 8.) A case can be made to support the hypothesis that expenditures, by size and function, will be different for local governments in urban regions as opposed to other areas. There exists a body of literature that documents the variations in densities, urban agglomerations, and scale economies and their effects on both the demand and efficiency of supplying locally provided services. This hypothesis is tested here with the aid of data published for urban regions in the *Local Government Finance* series,[1] Statistics Canada, and in various provincial statistical reports on municipal expenditures. Unfortunately, the collection of urban region data is a relatively new exercise for Statistics Canada (introduced in 1976) and as such, presents two major obstacles to this analysis. First, the data are available only in preliminary and estimate form; consequently, their degree of accuracy for urban regions is not as precise as those obtained from municipal aggregates. This, therefore, reduces the validity of the comparative analysis. The figures in Tables 3.4 and 3.5, however, do give some indication of the variation of expenditures by size of municipality. Second, the data published for urban regions are not separated into operating and capital expenditures, nor are such data readily available. Hence, a valid comparison can be made only on the basis of total expenditure figures. Support for the hypothesis of varying urban expenditure levels is found if the relevant data for urban regions vary substantially from that of all local governments combined. This comparative exercise is made possible through an examination of the per capita expenditure levels found in columns 4 and 8 and the percentages of total expenditures they represent in columns 5 and 9 of Tables 3.4 and 3.5.

TOTAL LOCAL EXPENDITURES AGGREGATED BY PROVINCE

The data in Table 3.4 compare the relative importance of the local sector in each province. They suggest that local governments in three of the Atlantic Provinces

---

[1]Following is a breakdown of the urban region and per cent of the provincial population residing in each urban area as reported in Statistics Canada, *Local Government Finance, Preliminary 1978—Estimates 1979,* Catalogue no. 68-203, 17-22.

Newfoundland—St. John's	15.5%		Ontario—Durham	3.0	
			—Haldimand-Norfolk	1.1	
Nova Scotia—Halifax-Dartmouth	22.1%		—Haldimand-Wentworth	5.0	
New Brunswick—Saint John	12.7%		—Halton	2.8	
Quebec—Montreal	33.9		—London	2.9	
—Outaouis	3.0	44.0%	—Niagara	4.4	
—Quebec	7.1		—Ottawa-Carleton	6.3	67.4%
Manitoba—Winnipeg	54.9%		—Peel	4.6	
Saskatchewan—Regina	16.2	30.8%	—Sudbury	2.0	
—Saskatoon	14.5		—Thunder Bay	1.4	
Alberta—Calgary	25.6	50.7%	—Toronto	25.7	
—Edmonton	25.1		—Waterloo	3.5	
British Columbia —Vancouver	43.7	51.3%	—Windsor	2.4	
—Victoria	7.6		—York	2.5	

No urban region exists in Prince Edward Island.

(Nova Scotia is the exception) are relatively less important (they spent between 7 per cent and 26 per cent of combined provincial/local expenditures) than the remaining provinces when it comes to assuming responsibility for delivering local programs and services to their residents. By comparison, municipalities in Ontario and Alberta accounted for 43 per cent of similarly aggregated totals, while the remaining provinces displayed proportionate responsibilities ranging from 34 per cent to 39 per cent in 1978 (column 1, Table 3.4).

Although the percentages in the preceding paragraph reflect the relative importance of total local expenditures vis-à-vis the provincial government in each of the provinces, they do not in themselves reflect the claim that these expenditures have on local revenue sources, since the bulk of total government expenditures may be financed by grants from the provincial governments or alternatively they may be financed from local revenues. To assess the relative impact of each of these, column 2 of Table 3.4 lists the proportion of all local expenditures financed from own-source revenues. One might expect to observe a pattern of relatively large grants accruing to municipalities with relatively large municipal sectors (the assumption being that municipalities with greater involvement in the provision of services would likely receive greater assistance in the form of grants). This pattern, however, is not evident. In fact, a simple rank correlation between the relative size of the local sector and the proportion of local total expenditures covered by grants was insignificant in 1978. Local governments in all provinces but Prince Edward Island and Nova Scotia, moreover, were required to finance 50 per cent or more of all local expenditures from their own sources of revenue. The balance was covered by grants. Local governments in British Columbia appear to have received the least provincial assistance, since only 40 per cent of their total expenditures were financed by grants.

Recognizing that these different provincial/local responsibilities exist in the provision of a number of local services, a clearer picture of the relative impact on the local tax base (on an interprovincial basis) can be obtained from a comparison of the proportions of all provincial/local expenditures funded from local revenue sources. In this instance, the four provinces in Atlantic Canada and especially Newfoundland and New Brunswick were responsible for funding a smaller proportion of combined provincial/local expenditures than the rest. In fact in 1978, local governments in this region accounted for under 15 per cent of total provincial/local expenditures. Elsewhere, municipal sectors (except Quebec) were responsible for raising from own-source revenues between one-quarter and one-fifth of the funds required for meeting their aggregated expenditure commitments.

Per Capita Operating Expenditures

A simple ranking of the total per capita expenditures by local governments (column 4, Table 3.4) and own-source responsibilities (column 3, Table 3.4) displays considerable consistency. The municipal sectors in Alberta and British Columbia recorded the highest per capita expenditures ($793 and $660 respectively) and ranked second (tied with Ontario) and first respectively in terms of provinces in which the municipal sector was responsible for funding its own expenditures in 1978. After eliminating capital expenditures (as outlined under debt charges in Chapter 6), the operating costs in these two provinces are still higher than the corresponding sectors in the rest of Canada. In fact, British Columbia and Alberta recorded operating expenditures funded from own-source revenues at levels exceeding the Canadian average by 26 per cent and 23 per cent respectively (column 6, Table 3.4). By way of comparison, only the local sectors in Ontario and Manitoba exhibited per capita expenditures on operating functions higher than the overall average. The levels of responsibility for funding all services provided to local citizens in Atlantic-region communities were the lowest and correspondingly, their actual outlays were well below the Canadian average (columns 3, 6, and 7, Table 3.4).

In summary, the variation in the figures presented reflects differences in the level of government responsible for delivering and financing local services. A further discussion of this variation can be found in Chapters 4 and 5.

Per Capita Expenditures by Size of Municipality

With the exception of Ontario,[2] Table 3.4 clearly illustrates that average per capita expenditures in urban regions exceeded the average for all municipalities in 1978. The differential, in some cases, was more than 100 per cent; for example, the City of St. John's, Newfoundland, spent $312 per capita (column 8) whereas the corresponding figure for all local sectors combined in the same province was $127 (in 1978). A similar pattern can be observed for Nova Scotia and New Brunswick. In the remaining provinces, the differences were not as large, although expenditures in urban regions were higher. Prince Edward Island was excluded as it had no "urban area" in 1978 as defined by Statistics Canada.

On average, spending by local governments in urban areas exceeded provincial averages by about $50 per person, thus reflecting a host of factors unique to the service and delivery of municipal functions in urban but not rural areas. The cost of service delivery and expenditure levels, generally, were higher for most services in most urban regions. Explanations of the differentials for each respective function will be attempted in Chapters 4 and 5.

FUNCTIONAL ALLOCATION OF
TOTAL EXPENDITURES

Without engaging in a detailed review of individual functions in the various provinces, there is some merit in drawing out some of the more salient features as they apply to all local governments on a national basis. Table 3.5 illustrates (1) the wide variation that exists in local government expenditures as a percentage of combined provincial/local expenditures by function (column 1); (2) the extent to which local governments are responsible for funding their own expenditures (column 2); and (3) actual own-source responsibilities as a share of provincial/local expenditures (column 3).

Responsibility for local expenditures (including that portion funded by grants) as a proportion of provincial/local expenditures combined ranged from

---

[2]This may exist because a proportionately larger percentage of the population in Ontario lives in urban regions.

a high of 83 per cent for environmental services to a low of 7 per cent for resource conservation and industrial development (column 1). Similarly, the degree of provincial assistance that local governments received in the form of grants varied from a high of 86 per cent for health expenditures to a low of 5 per cent for resource conservation and industrial development (calculated by substracting the figures in column 2 from 100 per cent). Therefore, own-source responsibility, although considerably reduced by the removal of grants, exhibited a similar variation on a functional basis. In the area of health expenditures, actual own-source responsibility was reduced to only 1 per cent; whereas roughly 69 per cent of all environmental expenditures were financed by local revenues. The remaining functions ranged between these two extremes (column 3).

When considering all local services, municipalities across Canada, on average, were responsible for just under 40 per cent of combined provincial/local services (column 1), but received almost half the necessary funds in the form of provincial grants (column 2). The main point to note here is that locally generated funds were required to finance only 21 per cent of total provincial/local expenditures (column 3). A cursory examination of the data contained in provincial government publications of local government data, however, reveals considerable variation in the per capita expenditure levels of local government within and across provinces. Differences in provincial/municipal grant structures, local circumstances, and provincial systems account for the bulk of this variation.

In order to facilitate the investigation of this local "flavour" of municipal expenditure patterns, it is necessary to assess the degree to which per capita expenditures correspond to the level of responsibility that each local government possesses. When this exercise is performed on a functional basis, significant trends emerge. In particular, a simple rank correlation between responsibility levels and own-source expenditures reveals that the five functions ranked as exhibiting the highest per capita expenditure also exhibited the highest percentage of own-source responsibility.[3] In the provision of environmental services, for example, local governments are required, on average, to finance the highest proportion of combined provincial/local expenditures (69 per cent) and this function accordingly, displayed the second highest local per capita expenditure level ($70 per person). Similarly, all local governments supplied 54 per cent (second highest) of all local expenditures on recreational services at a level of $46 per capita (fourth highest absolute level when education and other expenditures are excluded). The protection and transportation functions also exhibited both high absolute levels and a large degree of own-source responsibility. From these data one observes that higher local responsibility tends to be associated with those functions providing considerable local benefits and lower responsibility with those having large external or redistributive effects.

Municipal expenditures displayed significant variations according to the size of the municipality and its regional location (a northern versus a southern loca-

---

[3]Because the absolute level of education expenditures is considerably higher than any other expenditure category, and the "other" category represents a varying number of miscellaneous functions, these two categories were removed for the purposes of this statistical test.

tion in the province). These patterns differed from the provincial patterns and warrant some investigation. In 1978, it was estimated that per capita expenditures in towns amounted to approximately 80 per cent of similar city expenditures, while village expenditures were slightly less than 60 per cent of the city levels.[4] The obvious question to ask is—why did such variation exist? Not unlike the experience with provincial trends, the answer reflects the presence of distinct local preferences, priorities, and cost differentials. A local government finance report in Ontario for example, found that urban expenditure levels were higher than rural levels because in rural areas many services were either not provided by municipalities or were provided at a much lower standard.[5] This same report revealed that urban areas spent relatively more on salaries, wages, and benefits, while rural areas apportioned larger amounts to materials, services, and financial expenses. The difference, it is argued, reflects the mix of services provided in each. In rural areas the emphasis is more often on road construction and maintenance. These services frequently involve higher material costs than many urban services such as police protection.[6] The major difference in cost, however, is likely due to the quality and quantity of services provided in these areas.

Local government expenditures also vary according to regional location within each province. In Ontario, for example, a distinction can be made between rural north and rural south and between urban north and urban south. Higher expenditures are evident in all northern communities and reflect, at least in part, the costs associated with isolation, severity of winters, and the more scattered nature of settlements, be they rural or urban.[7] Data from similar provincial departments of municipal affairs reports reveal this is also true of local governments operating in the northern regions of British Columbia, Alberta, Saskatchewan, and Quebec. A much larger portion of the increased expenditure levels can be tied directly to a conscious effort on the part of governments to reduce the disparities between service levels in northern and southern regions. Neither rural nor urban communities in the north of these provinces have experienced the same level of population and household growth as in southern regions, but they have been expanding and improving services. These increases

---

[4]These percentages are based on calculations drawn from provincial municipal reports. Data considered appropriate for the comparative analysis was only available for the following five provinces, and since at least one province from each major region in Canada was included and remarkable consistency emerged, this sample was considered adequate for the purpose of identifying city size expenditure trends on a national basis. Manitoba, *1978 Statistical Information Respecting the Municipalities of the Province of Manitoba* (Winnipeg: Department of Municipal Affairs, 1980). Nova Scotia, *Department of Municipal Affairs Annual Report of Municipal Statistics For the Year 1978* (Halifax: Queen's Printer, 1981). Ontario, Ministry of Intergovernmental Affairs, *1978 Municipal Financial Information* (Toronto: the Ministry, 1980). Prince Edward Island, *Annual Report 1978: Department of Municipal Affairs* (Charlottetown: the Department, 1979). Saskatchewan, *Annual Report of the Department of Municipal Affairs and of the Municipal Road Assistance Authority of the Province of Saskatchewan for the Fiscal Year 1978-79* (Regina: Queen's Printer, 1980).

[5]Ontario, *Local Government Finance in Ontario, 1978* (Toronto: Municipal Finance Branch, Ministry of Treasury and Economics, 1979), 8.

[6]Ibid., at 9.

[7]Ontario, *Local Government Finance in Ontario, 1975 and 1976* (Toronto: Municipal Finance Branch, Ministry of Treasury, Economics and Intergovernmental Affairs, 1977), 25.

in levels of service have been described as a means of "catching-up," particularly with respect to such services as roads, sewers, and water.[8] In many cases, conditional grants from senior levels of government have initiated the improvement of such services, but a substantial portion of these expenditures must be borne by locally raised revenues.

SUMMARY

To describe the variation in local government expenditure levels across provinces is a relatively easy exercise. A number of regional trends emerge, almost all of which separate Atlantic Canada from the rest of the country. For example, own-source-funded expenditures as a percentage of GDPP were lower in Atlantic Canada. At the same time, both absolute expenditure levels funded from locally raised revenues and those expenditures as a percentage of aggregated provincial/local figures were lower in this region of Canada. It is not surprising to note, therefore, that local governments here tend to have less responsibility for raising local revenues to finance services provided by the combined provincial/local sectors.

Further variations in expenditure levels can be observed for urban regions within and across provinces vis-à-vis similar expenditures for the average of all municipalities within and across provinces. By and large, expenditures by function and in total tend to be higher in the more heavily populated areas. As well, some evidence suggests that a municipality located in the northern part of a province tends to incur higher costs for providing services similar to those received by residents in the southern and more heavily populated part of the same province.

While this chapter has provided a brief outline of the patterns and levels of municipal expenditures in Canada, it has not set out, with any intensity or rigour, the relative importance of the historical, traditional, political, and economic factors that shape these variations and absolute levels. Indeed, this task would be a large and difficult one. Instead, this chapter has provided the background for a further and more detailed description of the individual expenditure functions that will be completed in Chapters 4 and 5.

---

[8]Ontario, *Local Government Finance in Ontario, 1977* (Toronto: Municipal Finance Branch, Ministry of Treasury and Economics, 1978), 22.

4
Expenditures on Major Services

INTRODUCTION

The division of local expenditure functions into major and minor services is neither a clear-cut nor an easy task. Indeed, the range of activities included under each of the functional expenditure headings listed in this and the next chapter consists of services that have been supplied at the local level for years plus new services that have recently fallen into the local domain. The selection of major services to be discussed in this chapter, therefore, reflects the view of the author. Given this, this chapter concentrates on a description of general government, environment, transportation, protection of persons and property, and education. Chapter 5 discusses health, social services, recreation and culture, resource conservation and industrial development, and planning, development and housing. The discussion of each of these functions is separated into an interprovincial comparison of three features associated with municipal expenditures: (1) the extent of local government responsibility in providing local services, (2) per capita levels of operating expenditure, and (3) variations in per capita expenditures by size and regional location of the municipality.

The category of local expenditures entitled "other" is excluded from the discussion in this chapter and the next. The bulk of the expenditures under this grouping is made up of debt servicing charges and is discussed in Chapter 6. As for the many and sundry small remaining items in the "other" function, the relative size and varied nature of these individual items suggest that a discussion of them, when aggregated, would be rather meaningless.

PROPORTION OF ALL LOCALLY FUNDED EXPENDITURES ABSORBED BY MAJOR FUNCTIONS, 1968 AND 1978

While it is difficult to compare accurately local sectors across provinces because of the differing local fiscal structures (outlined below), it may be useful to illustrate the proportionate distribution of locally funded budgets (aggregated by province) among the diverse expenditure functions for which local governments are responsible in the different provinces. Table 4.1 records the proportion of locally funded expenditures absorbed by the five major functions listed in the introduction to this chapter.

Overall, the relative importance of these expenditures when combined fell by almost 5 percentage points (from almost 74 per cent to slightly more than 69 per cent of total locally funded expenditures) from 1968 to 1978. On a province-by-province basis, larger decreases were observed in six of the provinces (Prince Edward Island, Nova Scotia, New Brunswick, Ontario, Saskatchewan, and Alberta). Three of the provinces (Manitoba, British Columbia, and Newfoundland) spent roughly the same proportion of their locally funded budgets on the total of these services, while Quebec spent proportionately more in the latter years of the period under study.

Educational expenditures funded from own-source revenues declined by 4 percentage points over all the provinces with the greatest decline occurring in Prince Edward Island (where the responsibility was shifted from the provincial to the local sector in the early 1970s), Alberta, and Saskatchewan. At the same time, local responsibility for funding education in New Brunswick disappeared completely. In fact, every province recorded a decrease in local responsibility with the exception of Newfoundland.

The remarkable consistency in the proportion of local budgets absorbed by expenditures on general government in each of the years 1968 and 1978 is not displayed for all provinces when individually examined. For example, excluding Prince Edward Island where the elimination of funding for educational purposes increased the relative importance of all other functions over the period under observation, the proportion of local budgets absorbed by the general government function rose by 4.0 percentage points in Newfoundland and 3.1 percentage points in Quebec. Noticeable decreases occurred in British Columbia (2.6 percentage points), Manitoba (1.9 percentage points), and Nova Scotia (1.0 percentage points), while the rest of the provinces displayed local figures that remained constant or changed only marginally.

Transportation and communication expenditures displayed wide variations in the relative share of locally funded budgets they absorbed, even though the overall average was fairly consistent (8.7 per cent and 8.6 per cent respectively in 1968 and 1978) over the 11-year period. New Brunswick (6.4 percentage points) and British Columbia (7.1 percentage points) exhibited the. largest relative increase in this service, while Newfoundland (12.0 percentage points) and Ontario (3.6 percentage points) recorded the greatest proportionate decrease (Table 4.1).

Overall, expenditures from local revenue sources on environmental services declined by slightly more than 1 percentage point over the same period with the direction and magnitude of the change displaying no consistency on a regional basis. For example, two of the western provinces recorded relative increases in expenditures on this function (Manitoba and Saskatchewan), while two recorded relative decreases (Alberta and British Columbia). Similarly, one of the provinces in Atlantic Canada increased its relative expenditure (Prince Edward Island for reasons provided above), while the remaining provinces exhibited relative decreases (Table 4.1).

Finally, average municipal expenditures on protection services absorbed a slightly larger proportion of the average local budget in 1978 when compared with 1968 (Table 4.1). This occurred because of a slight increase in the relative importance of this function at the local level in eight of the ten provinces. A slight decrease was noted in New Brunswick and Alberta.

GENERAL GOVERNMENT

LOCAL OWN-SOURCE RESPONSIBILITY

General government services are provided by most municipalities across the country, with the exception of those few local improvement districts and unincorporated communities in Atlantic Canada and the West that receive services

Table 4.1   Proportional Distribution of
Locally Funded Operating Expenditures on Major Services Aggregated by Province, 1968 and 1978

Province	General government		Environment		Transportation		Protection		Education		Total	
	1968	1978	1968	1978	1968	1978	1968	1978	1968	1978	1968	1978
					per cent							
Newfoundland	14.9	18.9	8.2	1.5	23.6	11.6	9.4	10.2	5.1	16.5	61.2	58.7
Prince Edward Island	4.7	12.8	7.5	21.1	6.9	14.0	8.2	16.9	46.7	3.2	74.0	68.0
Nova Scotia	8.5	7.5	8.8	5.0	4.8	7.2	11.8	13.5	41.5	33.6	75.4	66.8
New Brunswick	8.7	8.1	20.9	11.5	16.6	23.0	26.9	26.7	4.4	0	77.5	69.3
Quebec	11.3	14.5	6.7	6.0	9.9	10.5	14.7	16.1	27.0	24.6	69.6	71.7
Ontario	7.1	7.0	8.9	8.3	8.9	5.3	13.5	14.8	37.5	33.4	75.9	68.8
Manitoba	7.6	5.7	8.1	8.4	10.1	11.3	12.7	13.7	35.5	34.8	74.0	73.9
Saskatchewan	7.2	8.2	6.5	8.2	12.0	11.9	9.8	11.8	43.8	31.8	79.3	71.9
Alberta	6.5	6.5	9.2	6.7	11.7	15.0	13.7	11.9	34.6	21.0	75.7	61.1
British Columbia	7.0	4.4	7.3	4.0	0	7.1	14.0	12.6	41.7	42.7	70.0	70.8
All provinces	8.4	8.6	8.2	6.9	8.7	8.6	13.8	14.5	34.8	30.7	73.9	69.3

Source: Appendix Tables B.1 and B.2.

from rural jurisdictions.[1] On average across Canada, local governments accounted for almost 26 per cent of combined provincial and local government expenditures on this service. This figure fluctuated from province to province, (see Table 4.2). Although local governments when compared with provincial governments were responsible for providing a smaller proportion of general government services, they were largely dependent on raising their own revenues in order to meet these financial commitments. Conditional grants tended to play a minor role in supporting general government services. In virtually every province, conditional grants for this function totalled less than 5 per cent of all conditional grants (Appendix Table C.3) received by local governments and in some provinces, specific grants for this purpose were non-existent.

Table 4.2 (column 2) illustrates the extent to which local governments were responsible for raising their own revenues to finance local government services. The range extended from a high of 93 per cent in Manitoba to a low of 60 per cent in New Brunswick with the overall average being 83 per cent. Obviously, these figures do not by themselves provide a clear insight into the impact on local revenue sources. One needs to observe both the proportions and absolute levels of all provincial and local government expenditures on this function that are the responsibility of local governments themselves. When this is done, the impact on local governments in some provinces, such as Prince Edward Island, is not nearly as serious as previously noted. In this instance, the bulk of general government expenditures is undertaken by the provincial government and as a result, local governments are required to fund only 6.4 per cent of the combined provincial and local expenditures on this function. The appropriate figures for local sectors in other provinces ranged from almost 8 per cent in New Brunswick to just under 30 per cent in Saskatchewan with the average for all of Canada resting at 21.5 per cent.

PER CAPITA OPERATING EXPENDITURES BY PROVINCE

Virtually all expenditures on general government services cover operating costs, since the major expense in this function is the salaries and wages of council, general administration, and the finance department. A minimum level of expenditure is therefore required and it can be expected that the number of elected and appointed officials will increase with population size.[2] A very small part of these operating costs is offset by grants, usually provided by the provincial government, for the support of employing students in the administration and planning departments of local government offices. Once this minimum level of expenditure is made on wages and salaries, however, other expenses— such as the cost of temporary borrowing and provisions for reserve funds— cause per capita expenditures to vary without consistency.[3]

A wide variation in expenditures on these services is indeed evident when per capita operating expenditures are assessed across the country. In Quebec, the

---

[1] Alberta, *Report of the Provincial-Municipal Finance Council on the Responsibilities and Financing of Local Government in Alberta* (Edmonton: the Council, 1979), 20.

[2] Ontario, *Local Government Finance in Ontario, 1977* (Toronto: Municipal Finance Branch, Ministry of Treasury and Economics, 1978), 38.

[3] Ibid., at 38-39.

Table 4.2   General Government Expenditures, 1978

Province	Local government responsibility			Local government own-source expenditures[a]					
	(1)	(2)	(3)	(4)	(5)	(6)	(7)	(8)	(9)
	Local expenditures as a per cent of provincial/local expenditures	Local expenditures financed by own-source revenue as a per cent of total local expenditures	Local expenditures financed by own-source revenue as a per cent of provincial/local expenditures	Per capita expenditures—all local governments	Per cent of total local government expenditures	Per capita operating expenditures—all local governments	Per cent of total local government expenditures	Per capita expenditures—all urban regions[b]	Per cent of total local government expenditures
	per cent			*dollars*	*per cent*	*dollars*	*per cent*	*dollars*	*per cent*
Nfld.	19.1	87.5	16.7	17.85	14.1	15.22	18.9	32.84	10.2
P.E.I.[c] ...	7.7	83.2	6.4	10.57	4.0	10.55	12.8	—	—
N.S.	27.1	75.9	20.6	23.21	7.1	19.48	7.5	40.46	5.8
N.B.	13.1	60.2	7.9	9.28	5.8	7.80	8.2	17.53	5.6
Que.	28.7	80.1	23.0	55.93	11.1	53.61	14.5	65.81	11.1
Ont.	32.6	88.7	28.9	35.37	6.0	32.86	7.0	33.08	6.0
Man.	28.3	92.8	26.3	26.83	5.0	25.87	5.7	56.19	8.2
Sask.	33.6	87.6	29.4	32.80	6.2	31.25	6.1	41.57	6.5
Alta.	17.4	77.6	13.5	33.46	4.2	33.46	6.5	41.14	4.7
B.C.	16.5	76.8	12.7	26.34	4.0	23.10	4.4	42.97	6.3
All prov. ..	25.9	83.0	21.5	37.60	6.9	35.96	8.6	41.29[d]	7.2

[a]Excludes both conditional and unconditional grants. [b]Capital and operating expenditures are not available on a separate basis. [c]No urban regions listed in the Statistics Canada publication. [d]Average of nine provinces listed.

Source: Calculated from Appendix Table B.2 and from Statistics Canada, *Local Government Finance, Preliminary 1978—Estimates 1979*, Catalogue no. 68-203.

relevant per capita own-source expenditure averaged $53.61 in 1978, while the comparable figure for New Brunswick was only $7.80 per person (column 6, Table 4.2). This wide range is significant, since the all-provinces figure is quite high at $35.96 per person. Some of this variation can be explained by differences in responsibilities in the various provinces. In Quebec, for example, the per capita operating expenditure on this function was substantially higher than for any other province. It must be noted, however, that a large portion of Quebec's general government allocation was actually devoted to education.[4] Comparison of Quebec's figures with those for the other provinces, therefore, must be treated with caution.

In other provinces, the allocation of general government expenditure into its various components was essentially the same. At least three-quarters of each municipal general government's budget was devoted to administrative costs. Only a slight deviation from this pattern was exhibited in Prince Edward Island and Newfoundland where the comparable figures represented just under half the budget. Both provinces were made up of small-sized municipalities, so the required number of elected officials was reduced considerably. In Ontario and British Columbia, by comparison, complex two- and three-tiered local government structures necessitated that the bulk of general government expenses be devoted to administration costs. As for the balance of general government expenditures, neither the executive function nor miscellaneous items accounted for more than 10 per cent of total general government operating expenditures. It should be noted, however, that the administration of general government services did not place an onerous demand on locally raised funds, since on average, the cost of such services absorbed less than 9 per cent of total operating expenditures.

PER CAPITA EXPENDITURES BY MUNICIPALITY SIZE AND REGION

Examination of Table 4.2 reveals that, on average, expenditures in urban regions on general government services are only slightly higher than for all local governments combined, but there exists substantial deviation from this average across the country. In the provinces of New Brunswick, Quebec, Saskatchewan, and Alberta general government expenditures in urban regions are only $8 to $10 per capita higher than those for all local governments in each respective province. The comparable figure for urban regions in Manitoba, Nova Scotia, and Newfoundland is approximately two times that of each respective provincial total. In British Columbia, the difference is $17, while in Ontario per capita expenditures in urban regions are actually $2 lower than the average for all municipalities within that province.

This marked difference may be due, at least in part, to the various stages of urban development in which the various provinces find themselves. For example, in Atlantic Canada and especially Nova Scotia and Newfoundland (many municipal services in New Brunswick are funded by the provincial government),

---

[4]See the figure listed under "other" in Statistics Canada, *Local Government Finance: Revenue and Expenditure, 1977,* Catalogue no. 68-204, 11.

the lack of many large urban regions and the fact that those that do exist are relatively new and unorganized, suggest that general government costs may be higher here. In some instances, the amalgamation of small towns into larger units effectively has raised the expenditures in urban regions far above the average for local governments in the province, and this differential is not expected to be reduced in the near future.[5] In Newfoundland, general government expenditures in the St. John's urban region averaged almost $33 per person in 1978, while the provincial average rested at nearly $18 per person. Similarly, in Nova Scotia, the region of Halifax-Dartmouth spent roughly $40 per person on these administrative services, significantly above the provincial average of slightly more than $23 per person. By comparison, urban regions in the rest of Canada tended to face a more revenue-elastic revenue base. When combined with a demand for local services and programs, which is frequently higher in large urban than in smaller urban and rural communities, the result was a higher level of expenditures in large urban municipalities.

In addition to regional variances, the expenditures on general government services also vary by municipality size and location within each province. Analysis of departments of municipal affairs' data reveals that the cost of general government services in small centres, especially in rural settings, is extremely low. The expenditure levels of villages in Prince Edward Island, Nova Scotia, and Saskatchewan, for example, are less than half of those in cities and these differences can be attributed directly to the provision of only limited services that do not require as complex a hierarchy of administrative staff. Local governments in the northern parts of Ontario, Quebec, Manitoba, Alberta, and British Columbia, however, face an additional set of factors that have recently increased general government organization and expenditure. It appears that in most cases, the "catching-up" process earlier referred to has created additional costs for the administration of newly improved services. Most northern communities in fact, in both the urban and rural areas of these provinces, have had to bear general government organizational and clerical costs substantially higher than their respective southern counterparts in order to support these improved service levels.

ENVIRONMENT

LOCAL GOVERNMENT OWN-SOURCE RESPONSIBILITY

Expenditures supporting physical services—water and sewer systems, land drainage, and garbage collection and disposal—are considered among the most basic and fundamental of local government responsibilities. Traditionally, both the delivery and financing of these hard services have always been under the direct jurisdiction of local authorities, and they continue to absorb a significant

---

[5]Municipal officials in Newfoundland, for example, reported that since the amalgamation of several districts into incorporated cities, the size, and nature of general administrative procedures have enlarged considerably. It was also noted in conversations that such significant reorganization was not without the need for additional financial support. A large portion of the necessary funds were generated by increases in taxes, which have been causing for several years significant migration to surrounding villages and outports, where local taxes are minimal or, in a few cases, almost entirely absent.

proportion of provincial and local expenditures. In 1978, local governments on average accounted for more than 83 per cent of combined provincial/municipal expenditures on this function. Although there was considerable interprovincial variation in this figure, municipalities in all provinces tended to play a larger part in providing these services than did provincial governments.

Once again, grants played a varied but nevertheless important role in aiding local governments in their financing of these services. With the exception of Prince Edward Island, municipalities in the Atlantic provinces benefitted more from grants than did municipalities in other regions of the country. This is reflected in the figures in Table 4.3 (column 2).

The more important statistic is generally thought to be the one that reflects the proportion of combined provincial and local expenditures financed from revenues raised solely by the municipality itself. In this instance, one observes considerable variation in the own-source responsibility levels across the provinces. At one extreme are three of the Atlantic provinces (Prince Edward Island is the exception) each of which financed less than 55 per cent of all environmental expenditures (column 3, Table 4.3) At the other extreme are the remaining provinces. These generated between 62 per cent and 85 per cent of the necessary revenues in 1978. Despite this variation, environmental services continue to represent one of the more truly local functions in terms of delivery and financial responsibility.

PER CAPITA OPERATING EXPENDITURES BY PROVINCE

The very high local responsibility levels identified above translate into very high per capita expenditures. After education and protection, environmental expenditures represent the third most significant claim on local budgets, consuming, on average, almost 13 per cent. This outlay is not, however, considered an undue hardship on local governments. To the extent that environmental services are so basic and essential to municipal existence and development, it is only logical that each municipality have a reasonably high degree of responsibility for their provision, administration, maintenance, and operation.[6]

Most of the costs incurred on environmental services are in the form of capital expenditures, particularly in light of the complex sewage collection and disposal plants, storm sewers, water plants and lines, and waste disposal sites that must first be set in place. Fortunately, most sewer systems have a long life and are replaced infrequently. For areas constructing new systems, however, the debt component is very high and the resulting capital costs substantial. There are, of course, high operating costs associated with the administration of these services and the recent introduction of pollution control requirements has only served to exacerbate these costs. Many municipalities now frequently combine to establish joint authorities in order to circumvent the costs of operating some of the more expensive types of facilities.[7]

---

[6]Supra footnote 1, at 295.

[7]David Siegel, "Provincial-Municipal Relations in Canada: An Overview" (Summer 1980), 23 *Canadian Public Administration* 294.

Table 4.3 Environment Expenditures, 1978

Province	Local government responsibility			Local government own-source expenditures[a]					
	(1)	(2)	(3)	(4)	(5)	(6)	(7)	(8)	(9)
	Local expenditures as a per cent of provincial/local expenditures	Local expenditures financed by own-source revenue as a per cent of total local expenditures	Local expenditures financed by own-source revenue as a per cent of provincial/local expenditures	Per capita expenditures—all local governments	Per cent of total local government expenditures	Per capita operating expenditures—all local governments	Per cent of total local government expenditures	Per capita expenditures—all urban regions[b]	Per cent of total local government expenditures
	per cent	per cent	per cent	dollars	per cent	dollars	per cent	dollars	per cent
Nfld.	73.2	49.0	35.9	28.30	22.3	1.22	1.5	56.37	17.8
P.E.I.[c]	71.5	90.1	64.4	31.76	12.1	17.40	21.1	—	—
N.S.	86.0	63.1	54.3	36.34	11.1	12.99	5.0	49.90	7.1
N.B.	92.7	57.2	53.0	32.03	20.2	11.08	11.5	52.49	16.7
Que.	96.8	87.0	84.2	81.08	16.2	22.18	6.0	110.30	17.3
Ont.	73.9	84.6	62.5	66.30	11.3	38.96	8.3	63.93	20.0
Man.	91.5	92.9	84.8	56.34	10.4	38.12	8.4	66.01	9.6
Sask.	87.9	83.5	73.4	54.83	10.4	31.25	8.2	73.38	11.5
Alta.	84.1	86.6	72.8	73.27	9.2	34.49	6.7	103.48	11.7
B.C.	80.3	77.4	62.2	63.21	9.6	21.00	4.0	71.20	10.5
All prov. . .	83.3	83.2	69.3	70.28	12.8	28.85	6.9	71.90[d]	13.6

[a]Excludes both conditional and unconditional grants. [b]Capital and operating expenditures are not available on a separate basis. [c]No urban regions listed in the Statistics Canada publication. [d]Average of nine provinces.

Source: Calculated from Appendix Table B.2 and from Statistics Canada, *Local Government Finance, Preliminary 1978—Estimates 1979*, Catalogue no. 68-203.

Generally, less expensive services such as the water supply, are operated by local governments as separate self-supporting utilities. Where this service is not provided directly, the municipality makes contractual arrangements with either private distributors or adjacent municipalities. Because the efficient operation of some environmental services, such as sewage treatment, is often dictated by a host of demographic, engineering, and economic factors unrelated to municipal boundaries, provision through private contractors is as frequently utilized as public provision.[8]

Across the provinces, environmental operating costs appear to have two distinct patterns. In the Atlantic provinces, such costs are generally below the all-province average of almost $29 per capita, but this is not inconsistent with lower than average own-source responsibility levels. Conversely, municipalities in the rest of the country all support expenditure levels near or above the all-province average, and this accords closely with what would be expected from the high responsibility levels evident.

In virtually all provinces, departments of environment or their equivalents impose some type of environmental quality act that sets provincial standards for the protection of community public health. While such measures help to ensure that environmental deterioration does not occur, the costs of complying with this legislation have forced many municipalities into large, long-term debts.[9] Most provincial government policy, however, is designed to ensure that environmental operations are conducted effectively and economically, and are based on the "polluter-pays" principle. Any municipality violating regulations designed to maintain environmental quality as a direct desire of citizen demands is, therefore, justifiably subject to pay the related costs. It is not reasonable to view health and environmental regulations as an infringement on municipal autonomy, since local governments have a responsibility to recognize that they do not exist in isolation from either other local governments or from the province itself. These regulations, in conjunction with the local delivery and financing of environmental services, result in a reasonably efficient and effective provision of service that is responsive to public accountability. This in turn leads to greater pressures to reduce costs, and/or to justify further expenditure increases.[10]

PER CAPITA EXPENDITURES BY MUNICIPALITY SIZE AND REGION

Urban development places new demands on a municipality's existing physical services infrastructure. Generally, the more urbanized the municipality the more extensive and important are these services that are so basic and essential to municipal existence and development.[11] Therefore, environmental expenditures vary significantly according to municipality size and location.

---

[8]Ontario, *Report of the Waterloo Region Review Commission* (Waterloo: the Commission, March 1979), 188.

[9]Supra footnote 1, at 299.

[10]Supra footnote 1, at 298.

[11]Supra footnote 1, at 293.

In many rural areas the sparsity of settlement makes the cost of communal services, such as water treatment and waste disposal, prohibitive. Many individual households, therefore, have their own services privately supplied at a cost that is substantially lower than if similar services were provided through the public sector at a level and quality similar to those of urban residents.[12] Some larger rural districts do have communal sewer and water systems. These systems are often owned by ministries of the environment, and most of the costs therefore are borne by the ministry involved.[13] Few rural areas can or need to support treatment plants and waste disposal sites of a size required in large municipal areas, so costs are again reduced. This is not to imply that similar provincial environmental quality standards do not apply here, but rather that services are often amalgamated in rural districts. Most provinces recognize, for example, that such simple items as proper sanitary landfill operations are beyond the financial reach of most small rural local governments and, therefore, provide extensive financial support where the investment in capital equipment and operating costs are justified. As a long-term perspective, it would be useful to consider the coordination of rural site operations with multiregional resource recovery systems located near major urban centres.[14]

Clearly, the quantity of environmental services, such as water, waste disposal, and sewer systems is directly related to population size. In urban areas the presence of commercial and industrial land-use sites places additional demands on traditional infrastructures. Rapid urbanization and residential growth have led to substantial infrastructure expansions and their accompanying up front outlays. Increased storm-water runoff arising from rapid growth in urban sectors has led to flooding and increased soil erosion. To overcome this problem, considerable strain has thus been placed on sewerage and sewage treatment plants.[15] These pressures appear to be greatest for urban regions in Alberta and Saskatchewan and can be related directly to the growth occurring in each of these areas. The excessive demand on existing infrastructure here necessitates new facilities and expenditures that are far above other urban regions. Elsewhere across the country, however, urban region expenditures (with the exception of Ontario) exceeded each respective provincial average (column 8, Table 4.3). This reflects, in part, the increased costs associated with servicing complex urban systems.

In many urban regions, the central local government acts as the wholesaler—providing the major facilities for water, sewage, drainage, and garbage—while area municipalities do the retailing and provide the local connectors.[16] With the provision of water, for example, Metro Toronto owns

---

[12]This was found to be the case in Ontario. See Ontario, *Local Government Finance in Ontario, 1975 and 1976* (Toronto: Municipal Finance Branch, Ministry of Treasury, Economics and Intergovernmental Affairs, 1977), 20.

[13]Ontario, *Local Government Finance in Ontario, 1978* (Toronto: Municipal Finance Branch, Ministry of Treasury and Economics, 1979), 23.

[14]Supra footnote 1, at 304.

[15]See Ontario, *Report of the Royal Commission on Metropolitan Toronto,* Vol. 2 (Toronto: the Commission, 1977), 257.

[16]Ibid., at 260.

and operates all water treatment plants and area municipalities in turn purchase water from Metro to sell to customers within their boundaries. Similarly in Quebec, municipalities in the Outaouais Regional Community and the St. Charles River Watershed are members of special joint boards charged with the provision of water and sewage services over the urban areas of their watersheds. In Prince Edward Island, distribution systems have been designed in Summerside and Charlottetown to serve regional areas. In each of these cases, substantial provincial grants supplied the funds necessary to initiate the required capital-intensive facilities.

Some environmental services, such as solid waste disposal facilities, are labour intensive. In many urban areas such services are subject to high wage settlements, and substantial efforts have been made to limit costs and increase productivity through a variety of means. These include: contracting out garbage collection, reducing the number of collections per week, and requiring medium- and high-density developments to pay for the services they require. Such schemes have been moderately helpful in the alleviation of exorbitant environmental service costs, but reduce only a portion of the rising costs incurred at the local level.

The capital intensive nature of most environmental services suggests that local governments must engage in a careful evaluation of the situation. This should include detailed cost-benefit analyses of the implications of expanding their facilities in order to accommodate continued growth in the size of their municipalities. To this end, it is not unreasonable that municipalities continue to aim for the most efficient delivery of services, be it by contractual arrangements that are closely tied to interregional planning processes or under the administration of local departments.

TRANSPORTATION

LOCAL OWN-SOURCE RESPONSIBILITY

Although transportation represents one of the traditional local services, responsibility for its provision is not easily and readily separated between the local and provincial levels of government. Because of the nature of most transportation services, both financial and service-delivery responsibilities require the coordinated involvement of all levels of government including federal. Provincial governments, in general, are responsible for intercity road systems, roads in unorganized territories, and major arterial roads running through organized areas.[17] This leaves local roads the sole responsibility of municipalities. But because such roads often give rise to general rather than purely local benefits, usually this responsibility is subsidized by the province.[18] This is particularly true in the Atlantic provinces where a greater proportion of combined provincial and local transportation services is placed in the hands of each provincial government. Accordingly, local governments in these provinces were required

---

[17]Supra footnote 7.

[18]According to Richard M. Bird, in *Charging for Public Services: A New Look at an Old Idea* (Toronto: Canadian Tax Foundation, 1976), the federal government also contributes substantial financial support for water, rail, road, and air transportation.

to fund only between 8 per cent (Prince Edward Island) and 26 per cent (New Brunswick) of combined provincial and local transportation expenditures in 1978 (column 1, Table 4.4). Similarly, a lower-than-average proportion of combined transport costs was financed by local sectors in British Columbia (32 per cent), Saskatchewan (45 per cent), and Quebec (32 per cent). Only the provinces of Ontario, Alberta, and Manitoba exceeded the national average of 49 per cent.

On average, the proportion of these expenditures financed purely from own-source revenue was quite high at almost 70 per cent, leaving the smaller balance of local transport costs to be covered through upper-tier subsidies. The value of these grants varied from the funding of slightly more than one-tenth of the associated costs in British Columbia to as much as one-half in Ontario. In fact, the receipt of grants was most significant in municipalities in Ontario, Newfoundland, and Prince Edward Island (covering between 52 per cent and 47 per cent of all local expenditures).[19] Grants for this service are provided in most provinces in a manner that represents provincial financial aid in fulfilling a local responsibility with broader (nonlocal) benefits, rather than a transfer of responsibility to each province.

One must again compare the proportion of all provincial and local expenditures on this function that must be financed by local revenue sources in order to get a clear picture of local responsibility. Ultimately, it is the impact on local taxes and user charges and fees that is of foremost concern to local politicians and administrators. In this instance, almost one-half of all transportation and communication expenditures conducted by both levels of government in both Manitoba and Alberta are financed by municipal governments, while corresponding figures at the other end of the spectrum range from 4.3 per cent in Prince Edward Island to 18.0 per cent in New Brunswick. Local sectors in the remaining provinces (Saskatchewan, Quebec, Ontario, and British Columbia), conversely, had higher responsibility levels, ranging between 20 per cent and 40 per cent of aggregated provincial and local expenditures. Whether these values represent the provision of services that are both quantitatively and qualitatively different in the various regions across the country depends on the responsibilities assigned to the local government sectors in each province, the associated per capita operating costs, and the subsequent allocation of each municipal transport budget.

PER CAPITA OPERATING EXPENDITURES
BY PROVINCE

In many cases, roads of a purely local nature are not easily distinguishable. The division of financial responsibility is, therefore, somewhat arbitrary, since local traffic often uses provincial highways and traffic bound to or from provincial highways must invariably use local roads to reach them. Consequently, there are considerable variations in local per capita operating expenditures due, in part, to different provincial allocations of local responsibilities. In the Atlantic

---

[19]For a qualitative discussion of the complex provincial road grant systems, the interested reader is directed to Canadian Tax Foundation, *Provincial and Municipal Finances, 1981* (Toronto: the Foundation, 1981), Chapter 11.

Table 4.4   Transportation Expenditures, 1978

Province	(1) Local expenditures as a per cent of provincial/local expenditures	Local government responsibility			Local government own-source expenditures[a]				
		(2) Local expenditures financed by own-source revenue as a per cent of total local expenditures	(3) Local expenditures financed by own-source revenue as a per cent of provincial/local expenditures	(4) Per capita expenditures—all local governments	(5) Per cent of total local government expenditures	(6) Per capita operating expenditures—all local governments	(7) Per cent of total local government expenditures	(8) Per capita expenditures—all urban regions[b]	(9) Per cent of total local government expenditures
		per cent		*dollars*	*per cent*	*dollars*	*per cent*	*dollars*	*per cent*
Nfld.	17.1	50.8	8.7	22.03	17.3	9.34	11.6	70.32	22.6
P.E.I.[c] . .	8.0	53.2	4.3	11.54	4.4	11.54	14.0	—	—
N.S.	21.1	60.8	12.8	29.87	9.1	18.70	7.2	154.09	18.7
N.B.	26.4	68.2	18.0	52.50	33.1	22.16	23.0	84.65	27.0
Que.	31.9	83.6	26.7	94.72	18.9	38.22	10.5	88.90	14.8
Ont.	64.5	48.6	31.4	58.37	10.0	24.88	5.3	59.08	11.6
Man.	51.9	83.0	43.1	90.57	16.7	51.29	11.3	97.06	14.1
Sask.	44.6	79.4	35.4	108.90	20.6	45.34	11.9	79.00	12.4
Alta.	56.7	82.0	46.5	156.88	19.8	77.22	15.0	136.95	13.1
B.C.	31.8	89.9	28.6	75.05	11.4	37.27	7.1	70.67	5.4
All prov. .	49.1	69.9	34.3	79.83	14.5	35.93	8.6	93.41[d]	15.5

[a]Excludes both conditional and unconditional grants. [b]Capital and operating expenditures are not available on a separate basis. [c]No urban regions listed in the Statistics Canada publication. [d]Average of nine provinces.

Source: Calculated from Appendix Table B.2 and from Statistics Canada, *Local Government Finance, Preliminary 1978—Estimates 1979*, Catalogue no. 68-203.

region, provincial governments are wholly responsible for all highways located outside cities, towns, and local improvement districts. They often enter agreements, however, with local governments to contribute a minimum of 50 per cent of the maintenance costs of highways that approach or run through municipalities (Nova Scotia and New Brunswick) or directly pay the costs for the main highways that run through all incorporated districts (Newfoundland). The operating costs that municipalities in these provinces must finance, therefore, are far below the national average, which was $35.93 per capita in 1978 (Table 4.4). On the other hand, the provincial governments of Alberta, Saskatchewan, and Quebec have charged their cities with the responsibility of servicing all principal and secondary highways within their boundaries, and these additional costs are reflected directly in higher-than-average per capita operating expenditures (column 6, Table 4.4).

A very large proportion of each municipality's transportation budget is devoted to road and road-related services (on average, over 90 per cent) and with only a few exceptions (Ontario, Quebec, British Columbia, and New Brunswick), very little is allocated to other expenditures, such as public transit or common services. Local transportation facilities, however, are one of the few municipal responsibilities that require higher capital outlays than operating expenditures (environmental services and resource conservation being the others). Because capital costs vary directly with both the quantitative and qualitative extensiveness of each provincial transportation system, it can be assumed that the associated operating and maintenance costs, which must be borne locally, will also vary according to the extensiveness of each municipal highway system contained within the boundary of each province. Given that in the provinces of Alberta, Saskatchewan, Manitoba, Quebec, and Ontario decidedly higher proportions of municipal road mileage are maintained than in the rest of Canada, it is not surprising to find higher-than-average per capita operating expenditures. The local systems in the Prairies, for example, are among the most extensive in the country and require three of the highest operating budgets to maintain them. Local governments in Ontario and Quebec maintain qualitatively expensive road systems (a greater proportion of paved roads) and accordingly, face expenditures of a different, but only slightly less costly nature (Table 4.5).

Climatic and geographic conditions varying substantially on a regional and provincial basis also influence local transportation construction and maintenance costs. Engineering expenses occupy a large proportion of local government budgets in British Columbia and Newfoundland and these are representative of the costs associated with a unique terrain. Similarly, snow and ice removal expenditures are extraordinarily high in Quebec, and these reflect the seasonal variation in costs that climatic factors induce. Here, as well as in Newfoundland and Nova Scotia, special winter maintenance grants subsidize the costs associated with severe winters. Finally, contrasting topography in eastern and western Canada have given rise to distinct land-use settlement patterns to which local public transportation systems must adapt and, therefore, costs accordingly escalate.

In the prairie provinces extensive rural road systems are based on a grid-road pattern that provides major farm-to-market access. Because of the high

Table 4.5   **Municipal Highway Road Distance,[a] 1976**

| Province | Paved | Road type | | Total |
		Other surfaced	Earth	
		thousands of kilometres		
Newfoundland	1.4	1.3	.3	3.0
Prince Edward Island....	.2	—	—	.2
Nova Scotia............	1.7	.2	—	2.0
New Brunswick.........	2.1	.5	.1	2.7
Quebec	23.3	14.1	3.2	40.6
Ontario	48.9	74.3	5.0	128.2
Manitoba	4.0	38.8	17.7	60.5
Saskatchewan	4.3	96.8	78.8[b]	179.9
Alberta	17.5	84.0	40.2	141.7
British Columbia	12.7	3.5	.3	16.5
Total	116.1	313.6	145.6	575.3

[a]Includes county, township, city, town and village roads. [b]Includes extensive lengths of road allowances.

Source: Canadian Tax Foundation, *Provincial and Municipal Finances, 1979* (Toronto: the Foundation, 1979), 234.

maintenance costs associated with these extensive systems, provincial financial assistance is provided to most rural areas in Manitoba, Saskatchewan, and Alberta. Similarly, access roads to oilfields, industrial sites, resorts, and regional parks, because of their economic value to the province as a whole, are also highly subsidized by provincial funding in both Saskatchewan and Alberta. These grants reduce maintenance costs somewhat, but still leave some of the highest transportation operating budgets to be financed from local revenues.

Urban transportation connector services have been developed to accommodate the high volume of traffic found in the more densely populated regions of Ontario and Quebec. These give rise to quite a different set of transportation costs, and provincial assistance is available to local sectors according to measured need and fiscal capacity.[20] In most instances, approved roads, bridges, and public transit systems, receive funding to ensure and promote the coordination of municipal transportation systems for maximum service and efficiency. Because of the magnitude of this assistance, the proportion of operating costs that must be locally borne is considerably lower than that in the western provinces, but still higher than that required to maintain the less-complex systems in the Atlantic provinces (Table 4.4).

---

[20]The Ministry of Transportation and Communications in Ontario, for example, subsidizes municipal roads according to the form of municipal organization, so that communities receive funding in direct relation to the category in which each falls. For exact details of the subsidies provided to the categories of (1) townships, (2) towns and villages, (3) cities and segregated towns, and (4) regions and categories, the interested reader is further directed. See ibid.

PER CAPITA EXPENDITURES BY MUNICIPALITY SIZE AND REGION

Because each local transportation network is primarily the responsibility of each local government, its cost will be a direct function of the size of the municipality that it is intended to service. Very large centres, of course, because of their high volume of traffic, give rise to very complex transportation systems. Large municipal governments, consequently, find themselves financially responsible for building roads and expressways, operating buses, streetcars and subways, planning port facilities, and even regulating trucking and the taxi industry. On the other hand, very small centres need rarely contend with such elaborate networks and often avoid maintaining even a basic transit system (such as a bus) simply because the nature of their settlement neither requires nor can support it. Yet, the per capita costs in these rural or small communities may be higher because of the scattered population that is served by road construction and maintenance.

The difference in costs between urban and rural regions is particularly pronounced in the Atlantic region, where urban transportation expenditures are considerably higher than the national provincial average. In these provinces, the few urban transportation networks that do exist are considerably more elaborate than the single roads or island ferries that service the majority of outlying communities. In Ontario the differential is virtually non-existent. In Quebec, Saskatchewan, Alberta, and British Columbia, per capita expenditures in urban regions are lower than for the average of the aggregated provincial/local sector. The reasons for this are slightly different in Quebec than in the prairie provinces. In Quebec the growth in population in the large urban areas has been virtually zero. As a result, there has been little, if any, demand for an expansion of the urban transportation system. The bulk of urban transportation costs, therefore, has been spent on maintaining the existing system. In the West, by comparison, there has been an increase in urban expenditures but this has been outweighed (in some cases, substantially outweighed) by the expansion, improvement, and maintenance of the many miles of rural roads (columns 4 and 8, Table 4.4).

Transportation is one function on which smaller centres and rural areas frequently spend more on roads than do many towns or cities. Higher transportation costs in densely populated rural areas are essential for the maintenance of a well-serviced road system. In sparsely populated and northern areas, the scarcity of settlements and the expense of maintaining roads in regions with severe climatic conditions also generate higher costs than exist in more densely populated areas.

Some towns, most cities, and all urban regions in most of the provinces across the country maintain some form of public transit system. It appears the more urban the municipality, as reflected by population size, the greater the need for transit as a method of transportation to move large numbers of people in and out of city cores.[21] Public transit systems are generally the responsibility of local governments. This allocation is appropriate given that the benefac-

---

[21]This was found to be the case in the city size analysis performed for supra footnote 2, at 46.

tors of the system are for the most part local residents and that the planning of this service must be coordinated in each municipality with overall plans for residential growth, sewer and water extensions, school and community facilities, and commercial development.[22] The current policy whereby provincial governments provide large grants for these transportation services may be challenged. To the extent that these services benefit local residents, then local residents could be expected to pay for them. To the extent that benefits accrue to nonresidents, however, it can be argued that provincial grants should be paid to the local government to cover the value of these external benefits.

Current policy on funding public transit costs indicates that a number of provincial governments including Ontario, Quebec, and British Columbia have been providing increasing levels of assistance for the operation of public transit systems.[23] Part of this increased assistance has been tied directly to the policy of encouraging greater transit use through the adoption of fare prices that do not generate sufficient revenue to cover all of the operating costs. For instance, recent changes in the funding arrangements in Metro Toronto now base the provincial subsidy on cost rather than on the size of the operating debt.[24] Under municipal reform in Quebec, a new financing formula has shifted the basis of support from debt service to a proportion of total operating revenue and capital expenditure.[25] Instead of either of these approaches, the province of Alberta moved to a flat per capita grant for support of public transit costs. In some instances the province has chosen to assume complete responsibility for transit systems. B.C. Hydro operated transit systems in a number of areas until recently when they were transferred to a new provincial Crown agency—the Urban Transit Authority. Similarly, Ontario has contracted VIA Rail to provide a commuter rail service between Toronto and its suburbs (Go Transit).

In regions where provincial assistance is much lower, but still available, municipally organized special-purpose bodies comprised of locally and provincially appointed members are sometimes established to operate a transit system. Conversely, in cities such as Winnipeg, Regina, and Saskatoon, the transit function is carried out directly by a city department. Other cities, such as Moncton, provide subsidies to contractors who privately supply transit services. It appears that public transit expenditures are gaining importance in most urban municipal transportation budgets across the country, and given present trends, they can be expected to become a financial priority of local governments in the future.

PROTECTION OF PERSONS AND PROPERTY

LOCAL OWN-SOURCE RESPONSIBILITY

An important and necessary service supplied jointly by provincial and local governments is the protection of citizens and their property. At present, the

---

[22]A view expressed by supra footnote 1, at 273.

[23]Supra footnote 12 refers to the increased municipal transit costs that reflect in large part increased provincial grants favouring public transportation.

[24]Supra footnote 15, at 249.

[25]Kenneth D. Cameron, "Tenth National Seminar: Summary of Discussions" (Summer 1980), 23 *Canadian Public Administration* 201.

responsibility for protective services is allocated on the basis of municipality size and location, but there tends to be a remarkable similarity of treatment across the country. In every province, provincial governments are responsible for policing services in unorganized and smaller but organized territories, either through a contract with the RCMP, or through provincial police forces (Ontario and Quebec). In those provinces with larger organized regions, the local government is responsible for policing, either through municipal police forces or a contract with the RCMP or provincial force. Fire protection is a local government responsibility in every province. Whether it is municipally or voluntarily provided, however, is usually a direct function of municipality size.[26] Consequently in 1978, local expenditures in almost all provinces, as a percentage of aggregated provincial and local expenditures, hovered near the national average of 53.0 per cent. Only Newfoundland (11.3 per cent) and Prince Edward Island (24.4 per cent) deviated significantly from this norm, since in both these provinces, municipalities had no responsibility for the administration of justice (column 1, Table 4.6). Police services here were and still are provided by the RCMP except in St. John's (Newfoundland) where the province provides the local police force. In the remaining provinces, municipalities are responsible for providing the bulk of the revenue necessary to fund these expenditures. In fact, of all the major services provided by local governments in 1978, only resource conservation required a larger proportion of financing from own-source revenues. In Manitoba, British Columbia, Newfoundland, and Ontario grants, which normally reduce the amount of local funds that must be allocated to protection services, were very small. In Quebec, Alberta, and Saskatchewan, they were slightly higher. Only in Prince Edward Island, Nova Scotia, and New Brunswick, did conditional grants, most of which went to police rather than fire, display a noticeable impact in 1978. Here, they accounted for between 26 per cent and 40 per cent of total local expenditures on protective services (calculated from column 2, Table 4.6).

Column 3 (Table 4.6) illustrates the actual proportion of aggregated provincial and local protection expenditures that were financed from own-source revenues. This proportion was considerably lower than the grant figures alone suggest. In fact, responsibility for protection at 46 per cent of all provincial/local expenditures on this function, ranks third, falling noticeably behind environment (69 per cent—Table 4.3) and recreation and culture (55 per cent—Table 5.4). Given that municipalities were and still are responsible for providing almost half of all expenditures on protection, this function does have an important impact on local budgets.

PER CAPITA OPERATING EXPENDITURES BY PROVINCE

The high own-source responsibility levels identified above translate into equally high per capita expenditures. In absolute terms, the $60.64 (Table 4.6) spent per person on protective services represents one of the highest operating expenses in local government budgets (14.5 per cent), surpassed only by education and

---

[26]This information is based on a summary of the various provincial arrangements provided by supra footnote 7, at 293.

Table 4.6   Protection Expenditures, 1978

Province	Local government responsibility			Local government own-source expenditures[a]					
	(1) Local expenditures as a per cent of provincial/local expenditures	(2) Local expenditures financed by own-source revenue as a per cent of total local expenditures	(3) Local expenditures financed by own-source revenue as a per cent of provincial/local expenditures	(4) Per capita expenditures—all local governments	(5) Per cent of total local government expenditures	(6) Per capita operating expenditures—all local governments	(7) Per cent of total local government expenditures	(8) Per capita expenditures—all urban regions[b]	(9) Per cent of total local government expenditures
	per cent	per cent	per cent	dollars	per cent	dollars	per cent	dollars	per cent
Nfld.	11.3	86.3	9.7	8.22	6.5	8.22	10.2	7.59	2.5
P.E.I.[c] ..	24.4	74.0	18.0	14.79	5.6	13.93	16.9	—	—
N.S.	49.6	64.9	32.2	35.91	10.9	35.07	13.5	86.03	12.3
N.B.	53.7	60.1	32.3	29.58	18.6	25.72	26.8	81.05	25.8
Que.	52.0	82.1	42.7	61.53	12.3	59.23	16.1	87.66	14.5
Ont.	75.2	89.8	67.5	73.65	12.6	69.47	14.8	74.54	13.3
Man.	53.0	93.9	49.7	66.58	12.3	62.18	13.7	91.22	13.2
Sask.	48.7	83.6	40.7	50.29	9.5	44.96	8.8	119.97	17.5
Alta.	47.5	82.1	39.0	65.84	8.3	61.26	11.9	107.63	12.3
B.C.	51.2	91.7	47.0	71.28	10.8	66.15	12.6	94.90	13.8
All prov. ...	53.0	86.8	46.0	64.28	11.7	60.64	14.5	83.40[d]	13.9

aExcludes both conditional and unconditional grants. bCapital and operating expenditures are not available on a separate basis. cNo urban regions listed in the Statistics Canada publication. dAverage of nine provinces.

Source: Calculated from Appendix Table B.2 and from Statistics Canada, *Local Government Finance, Preliminary 1978—Estimates 1979*, Catalogue no. 68-203.

debt charges.[27] There is, however, noticeable deviation from the average operating expense on both a provincial and regional basis. Per capita expenditures ranged from a high of $69 in Ontario to a low of only $8 in Newfoundland. In general, per capita expenditures were lowest in Atlantic Canada and highest in the western provinces. This variation appears to indicate the delivery of quite a wide range of protective services across the provinces. A large part of the apparent difference between service levels, however, can be explained through a more detailed analysis of the various provincial-municipal arrangements and the allocation of each local budget.

The key point to remember about protection services is that they do not consist of a single public good. Rather, they range from such items as police and fire protection to courts, emergency, and regulatory services. The bulk of most local budgets is devoted to police and fire expenditures and these are very municipal in nature.[28] Most provinces, therefore, have allocated the larger part of this responsibility to local governments, and only the actual method of servicing varies. In Ontario, British Columbia, Quebec, and Nova Scotia, each city and major town is responsible for maintaining a municipal police force, while in Manitoba, Alberta, and New Brunswick, the RCMP are contracted to police villages and unorganized parts of the provinces. In Alberta, a law enforcement transfer (grant) has been established to ease the burden of these RCMP municipal contracts. Allocated on a block grant basis, it enables the province to provide financial assistance to municipalities, while allowing the municipalities sufficient autonomy and flexibility in setting local priorities.[29] Unique to Ontario and Quebec are provincial police forces, charged with maintaining peace, order, and public safety in all those parts of each province not within an organized municipality. In both Newfoundland and Prince Edward Island, however, small, unorganized, and often isolated communities do not warrant many services other than those of the RCMP. Per capita expenditures, however, are slightly higher in Prince Edward Island than in Newfoundland because the cities of Charlottetown and Summerside have chosen to operate their own local police forces. In any case, it appears that all provincial-municipal arrangements are directed toward the attainment of a minimum set of standards, guaranteeing adequate and efficient police services to meet the needs of all areas in each province.

A similar provision of service is expected for fire protection, which absorbs approximately one-third of each local protection budget. In every province it is

---

[27]This excludes the "other" category, which consists of a number of miscellaneous items not related to any one particular function supplied by local governments.

[28]Bird, for example, lists the numerous services supplied by a police force. They range from control and reduction of crime (patrols and investigations), maintenance of public order (policing public events and controlling minor disturbances), and traffic control (patrols and radar units) to community support and other services, such as locating missing persons and providing aid in emergencies. Supra footnote 18, at 129-30.

[29]Other asssitance programs in Alberta include the RCMP and Municipal Policing Contract, which are five-year phase-in grants made available to those urban centres whose population rises to the level where the municipality becomes financially responsible for police services. Supra footnote 1, at 239 and 250-51. A similar form of assistance is available in most provinces. In Ontario, this takes the form of a per capita grant, awarded to those municipalities that maintain their own police forces; however, the funds received need not be spent on police protection.

primarily a municipal responsibility for both finance and service delivery, and most large towns and cities are equipped with full-time departments operating under a fire marshalls act. Fire protection is, in fact, one of the few services provided directly by municipal councils and not governed by compulsory provincial standards and levels of firefighting services.[30] In a few cases, small unconditional grants are supplied, and in complex municipal systems (those in Ontario and British Columbia) this aid is supplemented by upper-tier municipalities (counties and districts) that provide a fire coordination service for the benefit of lower-tier communities.[31] The only other sources of outside financing are occasional payments by individual provinces for the protection of Crown land.

The rest of the protection budget is devoted to courts of law, correction, rehabilitation, and regulatory measures. In no province, however, is this expense very large, as local governments are only responsible for overnight lockups. Most judicial districts, buildings, jails, and reformatories outside the federal penitentiary system are constructed and maintained by the provinces, and the operation of probation services for all courts of criminal and family jurisdictions are also the responsibility of each province. The only exception occurs in Nova Scotia where municipalities frequently combine in order to construct and maintain correctional facilities as well as lockups.[32] Sizeable provincial grants are also awarded in most cases to offset the operating costs of regional and county jails, and the salaries of a number of public officers such as coroners, sheriffs, court clerks, judges, and registrars.[33]

PER CAPITA EXPENDITURES BY MUNICIPALITY SIZE AND REGION

The nature of most protective services varies directly with the size of the municipality being serviced. Large urban municipalities require specialized and complex police services. These are largely unnecessary in small rural

---

[30]Because fire protection is a service that is supplied in response to the needs and preferences of residents, directly reflecting local interests and benefits, most finance councils have argued it is one public service that can and should remain solely a local government responsibility for both delivery and financing. Supra footnotre 15, at 281-83; and supra footnote 1, at 257-59.

[31]The Fire Marshall of Ontario, for example, is responsible for directing, coordinating and advising on all aspects of fire prevention, firefighting, and fire investigation within the province. See Canadian Tax Foundation, *Provincial and Municipal Finances, 1977* (Toronto: the Foundation, 1977), 190. Supra footnote 1, at 256, states that fire protection services involve not only activities related to the suppression of fires, but also activities related to fire prevention. At the present time, all municipalities in Alberta spend a proportionately large sum of money on activities related to fire suppression and a small sum on those related to fire protection. Based on extensive research, especially in the U.S., it has been demonstrated that municipalities that devote more time and money to fire prevention programs, in the long run reduce both the capital and operating costs of fire departments by reducing the need for fire suppression. It is argued that when more emphasis is placed on fire inspections to enforce provincial regulations and to inform the public on fire prevention safeguards to be observed, the occurrence of fires and the need for municipalities to invest heavily in fire suppression equipment is substantially reduced.

[32]Supra footnote 7.

[33]This information is based on the summary provided for each province in supra footnote 19, at Chapter 8.

communities. Densely populated areas need highly organized fire protection services, while adequate service can be delivered voluntarily in low-density areas. Consequently, with the exception of St. John's, Newfoundland and urban communities in Ontario where urban expenditures on this function are almost equal to the average over the entire province, the data reveal that urban regions incur larger expenditures than for the average over the province. Table 4.6 suggests that urban regions spend between 1.5 (Quebec and Manitoba) and 3.0 times (Nova Scotia and New Brunswick) as much as the average over all municipalities in each respective province.

In metropolitan centres such as Toronto, Montreal, and Vancouver, extraordinarily high per capita expenditures can be attributed in part to the additional costs and services required to accommodate daytime population increases associated with commuters. This daily increase in required service levels is evident, but to a much lesser extent, in most major urban centres serving suburbs.[34] Once again, because these expenditures absorb essentially the same proportion of total local budgets, the higher per capita figures, where they exist, fequently represent a wider and more complex service-delivery in urban than in rural settings.

In very small centres, be they rural or urban, the nature of protection services takes on a very different meaning. An examination of municipal populations reveals that for those communities not experiencing enough growth to warrant or to enable them to cover the costs of policing, the assumption of any responsibility often creates undue financial hardships. Consequently, in the very small towns of Newfoundland, Prince Edward Island, and most western provinces, provincial governments or the RCMP assume a large portion of the financial responsibility and local governments are required only to fund small per capita outlays to employ local peace officers for the enforcement of township bylaws. It may appear that the provision of these services at provincial expense in rural and small urban municipalities is inequitable when compared to larger urban centres that are required to pay for the service they receive. There are, however, a couple of reasons why police services are financed this way.[35] First, it is unreasonable to require small centres, be they rural or urban, to finance, even in part, those services over which they have virtually no control simply because they lack the ability that larger centres possess to influence the service to suit local needs. Second, it is difficult to allocate the costs of RCMP services equitably between rural and small urban communities since a large portion of the costs associated with such items as highway patrol cannot be rationally apportioned on an assessment or population basis. It is reasonable, therefore, that own-source expenditure levels in villages and small towns will tend to be very low, ranging from one-third of all expenditures by cities in Nova Scotia to only one-fifth of similar expenditures by cities in Prince Edward Island and Manitoba. These expenditures reflect both a lower level of service, and one that is largely provincially subsidized.

---

[34]Supra footnote 2, at 45.

[35]The arguments presented here are based on those formulated by the Alberta Provincial-Municipal Finance Council when it addressed the question of which level of government should assume the financial and delivery responsibility for police protection services. Supra footnote 1, at 243-44.

In rural areas the costs of fire protection are also kept to a minimum, largely due to the existence of local volunteer fire departments that service these lower-populated regions at a much lower wage rate than do professional firefighters.[36] Often rural municipalities have cost-sharing agreements with nearby towns and small urban centres for the provision of fire protection services on a regional basis. Both capital and operating costs are reduced considerably when this type of intermunicipal cooperation exists. In fact, regional arrangements make good economic sense and are found in most rural areas across the country.[37] They allow for the development of a broad range of service in which both the benefits and costs are shared by several municipalities.

EDUCATION

LOCAL GOVERNMENT OWN-SOURCE RESPONSIBILITY

The British North America Act charged every province with the responsibility for its own education system, so there exists in Canada 10 distinct provincial systems of elementary and secondary education, each with its own separate policies and programs.[38] In most provinces local school boards levy property taxes to facilitate delivery responsibility, but provincial governments provide the funding for major capital expenditures. Because the benefits of providing and maintaining a basic level of education extend beyond the boundaries of any one local jurisidiction, the province is viewed as an appropriate level of government from which to enact education legislation and to finance the associated costs. Consequently, within the 10 provincial education systems there are some characteristics that vary considerably, while others are fairly similar.[39]

In most provinces the administration of elementary and secondary education is the responsibility of locally elected or appointed school boards. In only two provinces, Prince Edward Island and New Brunswick, is education directly a provincial responsibility. Local school boards here have limited taxing and decision-making responsibilities in providing programs not financed by the

---

[36]While capital expenditures for fire fighting equipment may be quite high, operating costs are relatively low. Supra footnote 1, at 251, argues that a large part of the operating expenditures can be attributed to manpower costs, which can be reduced if municipalities are willing to include voluntary labour to augment a small full-time force.

[37]The major expenses for smaller municipalities involve capital expenditures in facilities and equipment, and there is no doubt that substantial savings occur when municipalities voluntarily cooperate with each other for the use of their resources. In Alberta, these agreements are drawn up for a specified period of time between a town, which agrees to provide the fire protection services within a designated area, and the rural municipality, which agrees to pay the town a sum of money and/or share the costs of acquisition and maintenance of fire fighting equipment. Supra footnote 1, at 254 and 258.

[38]Because this chapter is concerned with locally-administered services that have an impact on local government finances, only elementary and secondary school systems are discussed here. Any post-secondary services such as universities, colleges, trade and vocational institutions, because they are the complete financial responsibility of each provincial government, are not examined in this chapter.

[39]All the details of these systems, and the other provinces to follow, are simply too complicated to describe here. The interested reader is directed to each Provincial Summary of supra footnote 19, at 237-52, or individual provincial reports that address various questions related to the school systems, such as supra footnote 15, at 307-38, or supra footnote 1, at 338-51.

province. Newfoundland's system is unique because all of its school boards are denominational in character with approximately one-third of the members elected and the rest appointed on the advice of religious denominations.[40] In Nova Scotia, district school boards have a membership that is one-third municipally appointed, one-third provincially appointed, and one-third elected at large. In Ontario, Manitoba, Saskatchewan, British Columbia, and Quebec, school boards are autonomous bodies elected completely separate from municipal councils. Alberta follows this pattern in cities, but in the counties education is the responsibility of school committees of the county councils.

It is obvious that the most complex of all intergovernmental relationships involves the provision of primary and secondary education. The financial arrangements in providing this service perhaps illustrate one of the best examples of the impossibility of separating provincial and municipal roles and of determining which level of government is accountable for the provision of this public service. Only in Prince Edward Island and New Brunswick is the relationship relatively straightforward because here the provincial governments have assumed complete responsibility for the collection of taxes, construction of schools, employment of teachers, and decisions about curricula.

In all other provinces education costs represent the most significant claim on local revenues, although there are considerable variations in the allocation of financial responsibility across Canada (Table 4.7). Regardless of financial commitment at the local level, there is substantial provincial involvement in the education systems in all provinces. Typically, provincial governments provide large conditional grants, specify courses of instruction and course content, and establish minimum standards for teacher qualification and physical facilities.[41] This leaves, of course, relatively little room for school boards to exert local autonomy.

Table 4.8 illustrates the total and per capita levels of education grants. These grants payable to elementary and secondary school boards are generally provided for operating expenditures (day-to-day operational costs such as salaries, maintenance, and repairs) and extraordinary expenditures (long-term debt charges and transportation of pupils). Table 4.7 shows that with the exception of Newfoundland, where local expenditures are extremely small, grants provided the largest portion of required funds—ranging from a high of 81 per cent in Quebec to a low of 43 per cent in British Columbia. Local governments in British Columbia relied the most heavily on locally raised revenue (57 per cent), while similar governments in Quebec were the least dependent on locally raised funds (19 per cent) with municipalities in the other provinces falling in between. This is further witnessed in the figures recorded in Table 4.8, where in 1978 the highest per pupil grant of $1,933 was given in Quebec and the lowest of $833 in British Columbia. Generally speaking, in 1978 per pupil grants from donor governments for educational purposes were, on average, at least twice those contributed by recipient governments from own-source funds (see Tables 4.7 and 4.8).

---

[40]The following provincial-municipal arrangements are based on the summary provided by supra footnote 7, at 297-98. Some school boards in other provinces, for example, are also denominational.

[41]Supra footnote 7, at 298.

Table 4.7 Education Expenditures, 1978

	Local government responsibility			Local government own-source expenditures[a]					
	(1)	(2)	(3)	(4)	(5)	(6)	(7)	(8)	(9)
Province	Local expenditures as a per cent of provincial/local expenditures	Local expenditures financed by own-source revenue as a per cent of total local expenditures	Local expenditures financed by own-source revenue as a per cent of provincial/local expenditures	Per capita expenditures—all local governments	Per cent of total local government expenditures	Per capita operating expenditures—all local governments	Per cent of total local government expenditures	Per capita expenditures—all urban regions[b]	Per cent of total local government expenditures
	per cent	*per cent*		*dollars*	*per cent*	*dollars*	*per cent*	*dollars*	*per cent*
Nfld.	2.8	86.8	2.4	13.31	10.5	13.31	16.5	42.52	13.7
P.E.I.[c] . .	70.2	27.8	19.5	133.08	50.7	2.64	3.2	—	—
N.S.	67.5	30.1	20.3	112.20	34.2	87.28	33.6	216.79	31.0
N.B.	—	—	—	—	—	—	—	—	—
Que.	10.0	18.9	1.9	90.96	18.1	90.96	24.6	86.70	15.0
Ont.	70.1	41.6	29.2	177.60	30.7	156.78	33.4	151.55	30.0
Man.	73.6	44.0	32.4	168.00	31.0	157.94	34.8	205.17	29.8
Sask.	72.2	37.3	26.9	151.30	28.6	121.17	31.8	166.38	26.1
Alta.	62.6	31.0	19.4	129.36	16.3	108.11	21.0	143.92	16.4
B.C.	79.2	57.1	45.2	250.43	37.9	224.17	42.7	214.09	31.0
All prov. . .	66.6	34.6	23.1	143.74	26.3	128.38	30.7	136.35[d]	20.7

[a]Excludes both conditional and unconditional grants. [b]Capital and operating expenditures are not available on a separate basis. [c]No urban regions listed in the Statistics Canada publication. [d]Average of eight provinces.

Source: Calculated from Appendix Table B.2 and from Statistics Canada, *Local Government Finance, Preliminary 1978—Estimates 1979*, Catalogue no. 68-203.

Table 4.8   Specific Purpose Intergovernmental Transfers for Education, 1978

Province	Transfers from federal government to provincial governments		Transfer from provincial governments to local governments	
	($000)	dollars per pupil	($000)	dollars per pupil
Newfoundland..............	39,528	258.06	—	—
Prince Edward Island	11,043	397.33	42,056	1,513.19
Nova Scotia	59,981	309.12	196,838	1,014.43
New Brunswick	60,619	380.14	—	—
Quebec	453,789	375.34	2,337,420	1,933.36
Ontario....................	572,625	299.94	1,951,783	1,022.33
Manitoba	78,286	363.00	214,397	994.13
Saskatchewan	76,093	359.60	226,560	1,070.67
Alberta....................	109,705	251.01	547,806	1,253.38
British Columbia	154,511	298.41	431,302	832.97
All provinces	1,616,180	321.01	5,948,162	1,181.43

Source: Canadian Tax Foundation, *Provincial and Municipal Finances, 1981* (Toronto: the Foundation, 1981), 238.

Once the impact of grants and the proportion of provincial and local expenditures for which municipal governments are responsible are known, then actual own-source responsibility can be determined (see column 3, Table 4.7). In this area there is some consistency across the country, although there are four exceptions. In most provinces local governments contributed between 20 per cent and 30 per cent of total expenditures, except in New Brunswick where education is solely a provincial responsibility; in Newfoundland and Quebec where the provinces have assumed a great deal of responsibility; and in British Columbia where there appears to be less provincial support (Table 4.7).

PER CAPITA OPERATING EXPENDITURES BY PROVINCE

Education expenditures, on a per capita basis, represent by far the largest single claim on local revenues. The associated operating expenses use, on average, over one-third of local operating budgets, and in per capita terms, are approximately twice the amount spent on the next two most costly items (debt and protection expenditures).

There exists, however, significant deviation from this average operating expenditure and it can be partially explained by the variation in local responsibility levels earlier identified. Consequently, per capita expenditures accord quite well with local responsibility and explain some, but not all, of the variation in education expenditures across the provinces. Because education is almost entirely funded by provincial grants in Prince Edward Island, for example, it is not surprising that local government operating expenditures amounted to $2.64 per capita in 1978. There is, of course, no allocation for education expenses in the local budgets of New Brunswick because education is entirely a provincial responsibility there. Similarly, very low operating budgets are required for educational purposes by the local governments of Newfoundland and Quebec because they are responsible for supplying less than 3 per cent of the necessary funds. At the other end of the spectrum, local education operating expenditures are very high in British Columbia ($224.17 per capita) but are in line with the high responsibility level placed on municipal budgets in that province. The remaining provinces tend to be very close to the Canadian average, which rests at $128.38 per capita.

The collection of local education funds generally takes one of two forms. In Ontario, Manitoba, Saskatchewan, and British Columbia , there are provisions for tax-supported public and private schools and school boards use the same tax bases as municipalities. The dual school system in Quebec (Protestant and Roman Catholic) operated under very similar arrangements until recent municipal reform refused local boards access to property tax revenues. Education funds in this province are currently provided by provincial grants only, but this is viewed as an interim step until proposed regional governments subsume all education responsibilities.[42]

A foundation program for financing school expenditures is employed in several provinces (Prince Edward Island, Manitoba, Saskatchewan, and Alberta). Here, municipal contributions are required annually, related to equalized assessment, and usually collected in the form of a standard levy.[43] Under the various foundation programs and in accordance with provincial education acts, certain nonshareable expenditures are borne entirely by local governments. Such is the case in Nova Scotia and in Manitoba, where approximately 20 per cent of total standard costs are provided from municipal levies. In Alberta, the county unit collects the required taxes assessed by the school committee. In British Columbia, the cost of a complicated operating budget (it is based on the cost of an equitable but basic per pupil education level) is shared by the provincial government and each school district. Shareable municipal costs for education are usually related to the assessed value of property subject to local taxation. Costs of any additionally budgeted educational services must be borne entirely by school districts, as is the case for local school boards in Nova Scotia an Prince Edward Island.

PER CAPITA EXPENDITURES BY MUNICIPALITY SIZE AND REGION

While the average number of school years completed in the elementary and secondary systems varies from province to province (11 in Newfoundland and Quebec, 13 in Ontario for the time being and Nova Scotia, and 12 years in all others), no province deviates significantly from having one-fifth to one-quarter of their total population enrolled in the public school system (see column 2,

---

[42]Supra footnote 7, at 297. See also François Vaillancourt, "Financing Local Authorities in Quebec—The Reform of Bill 57" (May-June 1980), 28 *Canadian Tax Journal* 277-78, for details of the school board reform.

[43]The legitimacy of the School Foundation Program Fund was questioned in supra footnote 1, at 342-46, in light of its declining financial support in real dollar terms and is addressed in a review article by Melville L. McMillan, "Local Fiscal Reform in Alberta?—A Review and Assessment of the Report of Alberta's Provincial-Municipal Finance Council" (March-April 1980), 28 *Canadian Tax Journal* 170-71.

Table 4.9). Per pupil municipally financed operating expenditures vary of course from province to province, but in some cases this variation is greater than in other cases or this variation is greater than that which can be explained by the interprovincial variation in local responsibilities.

The provincial governments, for example in Ontario, Nova Scotia, Manitoba, and Saskatchewan, each require local school boards to raise approximately 30 per cent of the necessary education funds through municipal taxation. If the school systems are quantitatively and qualitatively the same, per pupil operating expenditures should be essentially the same in each province. This is true for Ontario and Manitoba, but Saskatchewan and Nova Scotia display considerably lower per pupil expenditures. Similar comparisons can be made in the remaining provinces with the degree of local responsibility for funding education expenditures being reflected in the absolute per pupil level of expenditure (Table 4.9).

With a few exceptions (Ontario, Quebec, and British Columbia) expenditure levels are higher for school systems operating in urban regions. This may be attributed to higher wage and salary settlements plus quality differences reflected in such things as the training of teachers. This differential ranges from as much as three times greater in St. John's ($43) than in rural Newfoundland ($13) to being only slightly higher comparing urban and rural regions in Saskatchewan and Alberta. In those provinces where the provincial average exceeds the urban average (Ontario, Quebec, and British Columbia), the difference might reflect the higher costs of transporting students, materials, and supplies throughout the province rather than the provision of a lower standard of education in urban areas.

Table 4.9   Public School Enrollment and Per Pupil Operating Expenditures, by Province, 1978

Province	Enrollment	Proportion of provincial population[a]	Per pupil municipal own-source operating expenditures[b]
		per cent	*dollars*
Newfoundland	153,174	26.9	51.82
Prince Edward Island....	27,793	22.8	13.12
Nova Scotia............	194,038	23.1	389.60
New Brunswick.........	159,467	22.9	—
Quebec	1,208,994	19.2	494.85
Ontario	1,909,145	22.6	707.84
Manitoba	215,663	20.9	761.69
Saskatchewan	211,606	22.3	560.36
Alberta	437,063	22.4	493.33
British Columbia	517,786	20.5	1,175.42
All provinces..........	5,034,729	21.5	615.23

[a]Calculated from 1978 population figures contained in Canada, Department of Finance, *Economic Review: A Perspective on the Decade, April 1980* (Ottawa: Department of Supply and Services, 1980). [b]Calculated from column 6 of Table 4.7 and column 1 of Table 4.9.

Source: Statistics Canada, *Education in Canada, a Statistical Review for 1978-79,* Catalogue no. 81-229, 84-85.

SUMMARY

While interprovincial, and quite often intraprovincial, variations exist in virtually every issue raised in this chapter, a number of the more salient features should be mentioned. First, over the entire country, the combined total of locally funded expenditures on education, transportation, protection, environment, and general government accounted for approximately 70 per cent of all expenditures financed from locally generated revenues.

Second, excluding those provinces where elementary and secondary education is primarily the responsibility of provincial governments, less than half of the local expenditures on this service are funded by monies raised locally. British Columbia is the lone exception. As for the other services over all provinces, more than two-thirds, and sometimes as much as four-fifths, of all local expenditures are covered by locally raised revenue.

Third, of all combined provincial/local expenditures, the local sector, in aggregate, tended to be responsible for funding approximately two-thirds of all expenditures on environmental services and almost one-half of protection expenditures, roughly one-third of transportation costs, and between one-quarter and one-fifth of education and general government expenditures.

Fourth, the overall per capita level of locally funded expenditures on each of the services ranged from a high of $144 for education to $80 for transportation, $70 for environmental services, $64 for protection, and $38 for general government. By comparison, similar expenditures in urban areas were noticeably higher for protection and transportation services, marginally higher for environmental and general government functions, and slightly lower for education.

Fifth, regional variation was noted in some of the indicators used for the intermunicipal variations; for example, per capita local expenditures for each province suggested that the absolute levels were lower in Atlantic Canada for most of the services. Similarly, the percentage of local expenditures financed from local revenues and the responsibility for financing all provincial and local expenditures on environmental, protection, and transportation services were lower in Atlantic Canada. A similar pattern was not observed for general government and education.

Finally, the per capita level of expenditures in urban areas was lower than the provincial average in some instances and higher in others, with no clearly defined pattern observable. Out of all the provinces, urban regions in Ontario recorded per capita expenditure figures that more frequently than elsewhere tended to be below the provincial average.

5
Expenditures on Minor Services

INTRODUCTION

The minor services are: health, social services, recreation and culture, resource conservation and industrial development, and housing, regional planning and development. Throughout this chapter, each of these services will be discussed separately using the organization and approach adopted in the last chapter. The discussion will concentrate on interprovincial variations in own-source responsibility, per capita expenditure levels across the country, and comparisons of expenditure levels in urban regions with similar figures for all municipalities within each province.

PROPORTIONAL DISTRIBUTION OF MINOR SERVICES FINANCED FROM OWN-SOURCE REVENUES, 1968 AND 1978

Of the group of services discussed in this chapter, expenditures on recreation and culture were the only ones of significance, accounting for 8.2 of the total of 14.1 percentage points (Table 5.1). Locally funded expenditures on this function rose in importance from 1968 to 1978 in every province except Newfoundland, with the overall average increasing by 2.4 percentage points. Prince Edward Island, Ontario, and Alberta exhibited growth rates in excess of the Canadian average, while the other provinces displayed rates of increase equal to or slightly below this average. By 1978, expenditures on recreation and culture tended to approach those on the major functions discussed in Chapter 4.

The remaining functions including health, social services, resource conservation and industrial development, and housing, regional planning and development were and still are almost entirely funded by provincial governments and hence none of them represent significant claims on local budgets. Absolute expenditures on these services, however, are expanding and together with the levels identified earlier (Chapter 4), indicate a trend in local expenditures toward a larger proportion of local budgets being allocated to "soft services" (protection and social services) and a smaller proportion toward "hard services" (transportation and environment). With respect to this trend, it is useful to note that most of these soft services are labour intensive, and given the rising relative cost of labour, their allocations in local budgets are likely to continue to increase in the future.

HEALTH SERVICES

LOCAL GOVERNMENT OWN-SOURCE RESPONSIBILITY

In the past several decades the responsibility for health services has shifted among the three levels of government more than any other municipal service. The introduction of universal hospital and medical insurance plans and fundamental changes in the scope of federal and provincial health programs has

Table 5.1   Percentage Distribution of Locally Funded Operating Expenditures on Nontraditional Services Aggregated by Province, 1968 and 1978

Province	Health		Social services		Recreation and culture		Resource conservation and industrial development		Housing, regional planning, and development		Total	
	1968	1978	1968	1978	1968	1978	1968	1978	1968	1978	1968	1978
					per cent							
Newfoundland	0	0	0	0	5.3	3.1	0	.3	0	0	5.3	3.4
Prince Edward Island...	0	.1	.6	.1	2.5	11.7	0	0	0	1.8	3.1	13.7
Nova Scotia...........	0	2.3	5.0	11.1	3.1	5.1	0	.4	0	.8	8.1	19.7
New Brunswick	.2	0	.1	0	7.2	9.7	0	1.1	0	1.3	7.5	12.1
Quebec	1.0	.3	.7	.6	5.5	7.9	0	.4	0	1.5	7.2	10.7
Ontario	0	1.4	3.2	4.3	5.3	8.4	0	1.2	0	1.2	8.5	16.5
Manitoba	0	1.0	1.4	.4	5.8	7.4	0	.7	0	1.8	7.2	11.3
Saskatchewan	0	3.1	1.2	.9	4.8	7.1	0	.3	0	.3	6.0	11.7
Alberta	0	2.0	1.8	1.6	6.5	10.0	0	1.1	0	2.5	8.3	17.2
British Columbia	1.2	.8	4.8	1.9	6.9	7.8	0	.3	0	1.2	12.9	12.0
All provinces	0	1.1	2.4	2.6	5.8	8.2	0	.8	0	1.4	8.2	14.1

Source: Appendix Tables B.1 and B.2.

largely subsumed the role local governments once played in health care.[1] This is clearly evident in Table 5.2, which illustrates the rather insignificant role of local expenditures in the combined provincial/local health scene. Local health expenditures, on average, represented only 9.7 per cent of total provincial/local expenditures on this function in 1978. Of all the major functions, health is one of two (the other being social services) that is primarily the responsibility of provincial governments. Essentially, provincial departments of health across the country are organized in much the same manner. They all provide approximately the same range of public health programs through which they discharge quite similar responsibilities.[2] Some interprovincial differences do exist, however, in the financial allocation of these services. In eastern Canada, with the exception of Nova Scotia (that is, Newfoundland, Prince Edward Island, New Brunswick, and Quebec) provincial governments exercise virtually complete financial control over this service, since in no province do local health expenditures account for more than 0.2 per cent of total provincial/municipal expenditures. Conversely, local governments in Alberta and Saskatchewan are charged with the greatest degree of municipal financial responsibility (37.0 per cent and 30 per cent respectively of combined expenditures in 1978, column 1, Table 5.2). In the remaining provinces, the municipal sectors in Manitoba, Ontario, and Nova Scotia were each responsible for almost 16 per cent, 11 per cent, and 9 per cent respectively of their total health expenditures in 1978. In British Columbia, the corresponding figure was less than 2 per cent.

A new provincial health service financing scheme was put in place in 1977. Briefly, this scheme consists of both a transfer of tax points and cash payments. The federal government has reduced its share of personal and corporate income tax points by 13.5 and 1 percentage points respectively. This reduction allows the provinces to increase their corresponding tax rates by equivalent amounts. To assist those provinces whose tax bases are felt to be deficient, these tax points are equalized to a per capita national average. The cash payment component of the scheme is made up of a closed-ended block grant that has a few qualifications over its use (primarily the maintenance of minimum health standards). These grants are calculated on the basis of a complex formula[3] that includes a base year's expenditures, a growth factor, an equalization basis, and transitional adjustments.

The health expenditures actually incurred by local governments themselves, therefore, are minimal—averaging slightly less than 14 per cent of the combined health total (column 2, Table 5.2). This translates into a relatively insignificant demand on local revenues, because those few expenditures that are made at the local level are financed largely through upper-tier grants and subsidies. By com-

---

[1]For a more descriptive discussion of the various provincial hospital plans and medical programs than is possible here, the interested reader is directed to Canadian Tax Foundation, *Provincial and Municipal Finances, 1981* (Toronto: the Foundation, 1981), Chapter 9.

[2]According to ibid., at 225, these include ". . .mental health, public health nursing, public health engineering, occupational health, industrial hygiene, epidemiology (communicable diseases, venereal disease, and food control), tuberculosis control, cancer treatment, maternal and child health care, dental services, diagnostic laboratory services, and medical statistics." Rehabilitation services are also provided in all provinces to help the disabled, the tuberculous, and the mentally ill, but these are sometimes administered or augmented through a provincial department of welfare.

[3]Ibid., at 222, for details.

Table 5.2   Health Expenditures, 1978

Province	Local government responsibility			Local government own-source expenditures[a]					
	(1) Local expenditures as a per cent of provincial local expenditures	(2) Local expenditures financed by own-source revenue as a per cent of total local expenditures	(3) Local expenditures financed by own-source revenue as a percent of provincial local expenditures	(4) Per capita expenditures—all local governments	(5) Per cent of total local government expenditures	(6) Per capita operating expenditures—all local governments	(7) Per cent of total local government expenditures	(8) Per capita expenditures—all urban regions[b]	(9) Per cent of total local government expenditures
	per cent	*per cent*		*dollars*	*per cent*	*dollars*	*per cent*	*dollars*	*per cent*
Nfld.	—	—	—	—	—	—	—	—	—
P.E.I.[c]	—	—	—	—	—	—	—	—	—
N.S.	8.7	16.6	1.4	6.49	2.0	5.97	2.3	5.28	.8
N.B.	—	—	—	—	—	—	—	.37	.1
Que.	.2	93.3	.2	1.11	.2	1.11	.3	.14	.2
Ont.	10.7	13.6	1.5	7.38	1.3	6.57	1.4	5.49	.9
Man.	15.8	11.2	1.8	8.89	1.6	4.54	1.0	2.25	.3
Sask.	30.0	8.8	2.6	11.81	2.2	11.81	3.1	19.30	3.0
Alta.	37.0	14.5	5.4	29.69	3.7	10.30	2.0	26.29	2.9
B.C.	1.5	52.4	.8	4.43	.7	4.20	.8	6.57	.9
All prov.	9.7	13.9	1.3	6.68	1.2	4.60	1.1	7.30	1.0

[a]Excludes both conditional and unconditional grants. [b]Capital and operating expenditures are not available on a separate basis. [c]No urban region recorded in Statistics Canada data.

Source: Calculated from Appendix Table B.2 and from Statistics Canada, *Local Government Finance, Preliminary 1978—Estimates 1979*, Catalogue no. 68-203.

parison, for those provinces where local governments fund some health expenditures, Alberta's municipalities tend to be more dependent on local revenue sources (5.9 per cent in 1978) than any other province. Quebec, on the other hand, shows the least amount of dependence on local revenues (.2 per cent in 1978). Similarly, in none of the remaining provinces do local health expenditures represent a significant claim on local revenues, since their own-source contributions hover closely around the national average (1.3 per cent of total health expenditures in the year under study).

PER CAPITA OERATING EXPENSES BY PROVINCE

Health expenditures at the local level are allocated primarily to the general field known as "public health" and to the support of health units and boards of health.

Preventive health services, such as inoculations, check-up clinics, and health inspections are usually administered through local health units. To the extent that effective preventive care reduces the required amount of curative care, such services are considered an integral part of the total health care system. It is felt that these services are best administered at the local level of government because this level responds directly to local conditions.

The traditional scope of municipal public health services, however, has been rapidly expanding for some time. The consequence of this expansion to broader "community" health services has been a major increase in health expenditures[4] and these are no longer the sole responsibility of local governments. Most provinces, in fact, play a dominant role in the planning, coordination, and control of both the delivery and financing of these publicly financed health services.

In Ontario,[5] for example, these services are provided under the auspices of autonomous boards of health (established under the Public Health Act). Seventy-five per cent of all operating costs of the 31 district and 7 county health units is covered by provincial grants. For the cities and boroughs that make up Metropolitan Toronto, 33⅓ per cent of all operating costs is covered by provincial grants and the rest is funded from municipal revenues.[6] Ambulance services

---

[4]This was also found to be the case in a study carried out in the United States on the growth and nature of health services. Aside from price increases, which of course accounted for the largest share of rising health costs (57.5 per cent), changes in the health care system itself were identified as being responsible for just over one-third of health cost increases. Since improvements have been made in public health programs and the hospital system, demand has risen to absorb the greater quantity and quality of available services. See Richard H. Leftwich and Ansel M. Sharp, *Economics of Social Issues*, 4th ed. (Dallas, Texas: Business Publications, 1980), 205-30. It is also reported, in Ontario, *Local Government Finance in Ontario, 1975 and 1976* (Toronto: Municipal Finance Branch, Ministry of Treasury, Economics, and Intergovernmental Affairs, 1977), 22, that high growth in health expenditures is the result of several factors: major wage increases for public health nurses, municipal responses to increasing public concern about environmental health, increased municipal contributions to new hospitals, and the establishment of medical centres in communities without medical practitioners.

[5]For further detail on this section, see supra footnote 1.

[6]According to Ontario, *Report of the Royal Commission on Metropolitan Toronto,* Vol. 2 (Toronto: the Commission, 1977), 342, back in 1967 the province sought to encourage the establishment of district health units with these 75 per cent subsidies. County health units that did not amalgamate with others continued to receive a 50 per cent provincial subsidy, while local health boards received only 25 per cent in the form of grants.

are funded almost entirely by the province, although they are privately as well as municipally supplied and psychiatric hospitals are owned and operated directly by the province. Consequently, locally financed operating costs (in Ontario) were very low at $6.57 per capita in 1978 absorbing less than 2 per cent of local budgets (column 6, Table 5.2).

In Saskatchewan, preventive health services are decentralized into 10 health regions and a northern health district with the cost of the administered health programs being divided roughly in the proportion of 94 per cent provincial and 6 per cent municipal. Consequently, local operating expenditures are slightly higher here than in most provinces. In 1978, they were $11.81 per capita. This municipal contribution should decrease, however, because of a newly imposed provincial ceiling on local contributions. The two main cities, Regina and Saskatoon, operate autonomous health departments, but these too are funded largely with provincial per capita operating grants.

Since 1973, Alberta's provincial government has assumed 100-per cent responsibility for the operating expenses of the 25 local health units and 2 local boards of health in Edmonton and Calgary. Mental health clinics and hospitals are maintained by the province, but apart from a provincially operated air ambulance service, ambulance services are privately operated. Consequently, local government health expenditures at $10.50 per capita in 1978 were above the average for Canada, but this figure represented only 2 per cent of total local budgets.

The residents of British Columbia are served by 17 health districts and 5 municipal health departments (Vancouver, Richmond, Burnaby, the North Shore, and the Capital Regional District), the former of which is provincially staffed and the latter, municipally staffed. Health units other than those in metropolitan areas are financed by a small local levy, but the major portion of operating costs is borne by the province. Here, as in the other provinces, the local government contribution to health expenditures was quite low at $4.20 per person in 1978, absorbing less than 1 per cent of total local operating budgets (columns 5 and 6, Table 5.2).

Except for the inner part of the city of Winnipeg and the Indian reserves, community health services in Manitoba are financed by the provincial government and delivered through eight regional units. In the city of Winnipeg, the health department and hospitals are municipally operated and financed by a block grant from the province to the city. The relatively low per capita expenditure of $4.54 in 1978 for all municipalities provided the remainder of the funds needed. This expenditure did not represent a significant burden on local budgets as it amounted to less than 2 per cent of the average municipal budget.

In Nova Scotia, health services, including community nursing, prevention and promotion programs, and nutrition services, are provided through eight health units covering the entire province. These units are funded by the provincial government. A number of public hospitals (14 out of 48) are owned by municipal governments. Once again, the locally raised operating expenditure of $6 per capita only accounted for 2 per cent of local budgets in 1978.

In the remaining provinces (New Brunswick, Prince Edward Island, Newfoundland), locally funded health expenditures are virtually insignificant, if not entirely absent. In each case, local municipalities are required to make little or no contribution to health services and almost all public health units are provincially planned, coordinated, controlled, and financed.

Finally, almost all provincial governments provide free (at no direct charge to municipalities) public health officers, technical advice, consultant services, central laboratory services, and cancer clinics, as well as extended home care programs, and comprehensive community health services. Given the wide range of these provincially funded services, it appears as if most health expenditures are being absorbed by the provinces.[7] Hence, it is not surprising that local health expenditures comprise roughly 1 per cent of local operating budgets.

PER CAPITA EXPENDITURES BY MUNICIPALITY SIZE AND REGION

Since health services are generally administered from decentralized health units, boards, or regions, little or no responsibility, and therefore variation in expenditure, exists on a municipal basis. For the few autonomous municipal health boards that do operate, the expenditures are highly subsidized. Provincial governments have assumed responsibility for health insurance programs leaving municipalities with the responsibility for funding hospitals and preventive care.

Per capita health expenditures by urban regions generally approximate the average for the province whenever municipal contributions are required (see column 8, Table 5.2). Only the cities of Regina and Saskatoon significantly exceeded average local expenditures in their province in 1978.

SOCIAL SERVICES

LOCAL GOVERNMENT OWN-SOURCE RESPONSIBILITY

As with health services, both the federal and provincial levels of government have assumed a major role in the design, delivery, control, and financing of social services. Even though the social service system has become an accepted function of government today, social welfare at the time of Confederation was considered to be of such little importance that it was not even included in the British North America Act.

Post-Confederation industrialization, depression, and war, however, quickly modified the expectations of society and this resulted in a growing range of publicly provided social services. While the provision of welfare payments is the largest and best-known element of the social service system, the scope of these services now goes beyond this singular function to include a wide range of public pension and old-age payments, subsidies for job creation and manpower training, and a host of other direct services.[8] The provision of these services has

---

[7]For a very strong argument why public health should remain a lower-tier responsibility, the interested reader is directed to ibid., at 343.

[8]According to supra footnote 6, at 354, there has never been a true consensus of the most appropriate overall mix of public and private responsibility for individual well-being. The report argues that the present ". . .result can hardly be called a social services system; it is rather a collection of programs aimed at a variety of wants and needs."

come to be considered primarily a provincial and federal responsibility, while the provision of the more locally based programs is now delegated to municipal authorities.

Cooperative programs between all three levels of government are not uncommon, but there is usually a distinction made between federal-provincial and provincial-municipal arrangements. The Canada Assistance Plan provides the basis for coordinating the various public welfare programs among all the provinces and the federal government.[9] Each province in turn provides a variety of exclusively provincial programs and usually engages in some form of shared provincial/local responsibility with the local governments being responsible for administering or managing most of them. Typically, recipients of social assistance are divided so that some deal with their provincial government and some with their local governments. Programs covering extended periods of time are generally administered by the province. Short-term programs are administered by local governments, with the assistance of substantial provincial grants. The main programs falling under local jurisdiction are: general welfare, assistance to the needy, child care, and aid to the elderly.

As with health services, the cost of welfare programs at the local level represents only a minor part of the total cost of programs over which the various provinces have given municipalities some responsibility. Table 5.3 clearly illustrates that local expenditures in 1978 averaged only slightly more than 9 per cent of combined provincial and local social service expenditures, and that grants covered almost three-fifths of this responsibility leaving, on average, 43 per cent of total local expenditures to be funded from local revenue sources (column 2, Table 5.3). Specific provincial-local arrangements, of course, vary across the country, but local own-source responsibility is generally quite low. In Newfoundland, Prince Edward Island, and New Brunswick, social services are entirely financed by provincial governments. Local expenditures in Quebec amounted to less than 1 per cent of all combined provincial/local expenditures on this service in 1978, while similar governments in Manitoba, Saskatchewan, British Columbia, and Alberta contributed between 3 per cent and 6 per cent of all expenditures on social services. Municipalities in Nova Scotia and Ontario incurred greater expenditures at 36 per cent and 22 per cent respectively of all expenditures on this function (column 1, Table 5.3).

Of the social service expenditures incurred at the local level, provincial grants generally financed a large proportion. In essence, 4 per cent of aggregated provincial/local expenditures across the country was financed from locally raised revenues in 1978. Only in Nova Scotia and Ontario were these percentages noticeable at almost 14 per cent and 9 per cent respectively. Elsewhere, the percentages ranged from 0.5 per cent in Quebec to 3.5 per cent in Alberta (column 3, Table 5.3).

---

[9]The categorical shared-cost assistance programs include old age assistance, blind person's allowances, disabled person's allowances, and unemployment assistance—see supra footnote 1, at 262, for details. Exclusively federal programs, such as old age security, family allowance and unemployment insurance, are described in Canadian Tax Foundation, *The National Finances, 1981-82* (Toronto: the Foundation, 1982), Chapter 7.

Table 5.3   Social Services Expenditures, 1978

	Local government responsibility			Local government own-source expenditures[a]					
	(1)	(2)	(3)	(4)	(5)	(6)	(7)	(8)	(9)
Province	Local expenditures as a per cent of provincial/local expenditures	Local expenditures financed by own-source revenue as a per cent of total local expenditures	Local expenditures financed by own-source revenue as a percent of provincial/local expenditures	Per capita expenditures—all local governments	Per cent of total local government expenditures	Per capita operating expenditures—all local governments	Per cent of total local government expenditures	Per capita expenditures—all urban regions[b]	Per cent of total local government expenditures
	per cent			dollars	per cent	dollars	per cent	dollars	per cent
Nfld.	—	—	—	—	—	—	—	—	—
P.E.I.[c]	—	—	—	—	—	—	—	—	—
N.S.	35.5	38.8	13.8	28.87	8.8	28.83	11.1	20.74	3.0
N.B.	—	—	—	—	—	—	—	—	—
Que.	.6	83.8	.5	2.22	.4	2.22	.6	3.29	.5
Ont.	22.1	39.9	8.8	24.94	4.3	20.18	4.3	21.17	4.1
Man.	3.6	18.5	.7	1.96	.4	1.82	.4	6.18	.9
Sask.	2.7	43.3	1.2	3.55	.7	3.43	.9	5.12	.8
Alta.	5.8	59.6	3.5	8.24	1.0	8.24	1.6	8.87	1.0
B.C.	3.4	89.0	3.0	10.04	1.5	9.97	1.9	11.98	1.7
All prov.	9.3	43.2	4.0	12.55	2.3	10.87	2.6	8.59	1.3

[a]Excludes both conditional and unconditional grants. [b]Capital and operating expenditures are not available on a separate basis. [c]No urban region recorded in Statistics Canada data.

Source: Calculated from Appendix Table B.2 and from Statistics Canada, *Local Government Finance, Preliminary 1978—Estimates 1979*, Catalogue no. 68-203.

PER CAPITA OPERATING
EXPENDITURES BY PROVINCE

Social services in Canada have grown in both magnitude and scope with sufficient impact to have made it financially impossible for local governments to
raise sufficient revenues to cover all of the necessary expenditures. As with the
provision of health services, federal and provincial governments have emerged
to assume an important role.

Per capita locally funded operating expenditures showed a reasonable degree
of variation in 1978 with the highest levels being recorded in Nova Scotia ($29)
and Ontario ($20), and the lowest in Manitoba ($2), Quebec ($2), and Saskat-
chewan ($3). The two remaining provinces, Alberta ($8) and British Columbia
($10), recorded levels below the Canadian average of $11 (column 6, Table 5.3).
This variation in local expenditure levels is directly related to the variation in the
provision and funding of local services. The Social Aid Act in Quebec, for
example, provides almost all of the funding necessary to provide required social
services. Similarly, the Manitoba Social Services Act makes the province almost
entirely responsible for funding social services. Only a very small portion of
local operating expenditures are covered out of locally raised funds. The Social
Development Act of Alberta and the Saskatchewan Assistance Act offer essentially the same comprehensive social assistance programs and provide funding
that covers up to 90 per cent of operating costs. In British Columbia the
Ministry of Human Resources absorbs, by far, the largest portion of all the
costs of municipally provided services, so that local governments incur expenditures at a level below the national average.

Expenditure levels are noticeably higher only for municipal governments in
Nova Scotia and Ontario. In these provinces the greater percentages of program
expenditures financed by local governments and, hence, the higher absolute
expenditure levels, are attributed directly to numerous provincial/local programs that stipulate that municipalities must play a greater role in funding the
various services. Given the relatively low per capita expenditure levels, it is not
surprising to note that this function absorbed a very small proportion of own-
source revenues in every province except Nova Scotia (where it accounted for 11
per cent). In Ontario (the next highest province), the same service absorbed
slightly more than 4 per cent of local funds, while on average across Canada, it
accounted for only 2.6 per cent of locally raised revenues in 1978 (column 7,
Table 5.3).

PER CAPITA EXPENDITURES BY MUNICIPALITY
SIZE AND REGION

The funding and provision of many social services may depend on the size of the
municipality. Some services, such as day care and family counselling, cannot be
provided feasibly in rural areas, villages, or small towns even though the need
may be just as great as in the larger urban areas.

In comparing per capita expenditures in urban areas with those for the
average of the entire province (column 8 versus column 4, Table 5.3), consistent
patterns do not emerge. In two provinces, Ontario and Nova Scotia, urban
expenditure levels are less than the provincial averages, while in Quebec and the
four western provinces, exactly the opposite prevails. An obvious explanation

for these differences does not exist. For some services, urban expenditures are higher simply because these services are provided in urban areas alone. For other services, the recipients of social assistance are concentrated more heavily in communities away from the large urban centres. The outcome in terms of per capita expenditure levels, therefore, depends on the relative impact of these two influences.

Finally, urban areas in Ontario and Nova Scotia spent respectively only 4 per cent and 3 per cent of their locally raised revenues on social service programs in 1978. For the remaining provinces, the similar figure hovered around 1 per cent (column 9, Table 5.3).

RECREATION AND CULTURE

LOCAL GOVERNMENT OWN-SOURCE RESPONSIBILITY

In the combined fields of recreation and culture, municipal governments are responsible for the operation of parks, recreational facilities, and cultural attractions (such as libraries and museums) that have a local importance. Because such services generally benefit the local citizenry, it is reasonable that local governments bear the larger (if not total) portion of the costs of financing these services.[10]

In all provinces, locally administered recreation and culture facilities depend almost entirely on locally raised revenues. On average, local government revenues funded amost 70 per cent of the expenditures made at the combined provincial/local level in 1978 (column 1, Table 5.4). While provincial grants for locally administered recreation and cultural services were typically not large, they did contribute to some provincial variation in the average level of all combined provincial/local expenditures financed strictly from local revenues. When compared with the rest of Canada, local governments in the four provinces in Atlantic Canada were more dependent on grants and, therefore, less dependent on local revenues for funding recreation and culture expenditures (column 2, Table 5.4). As a result, regional variation emerged in the proportion of all provincial and local expenditures financed from municipal revenue sources alone (column 3, Table 5.4). Municipalities in Atlantic Canada displayed the lowest responsibility levels with local governments in Prince Edward Island and Newfoundland funding (on average) less than 20 per cent; those in Nova Scotia and New Brunswick less than 35 per cent; and those in the rest of Canada funding more than 50 per cent of all provincial/local totals on this function.

PER CAPITA OPERATING EXPENDITURES
BY PROVINCE

Regional variation in local government responsibility levels also surfaced in the comparison of locally raised per capita operating expenditures for recreation

---

[10]Rapid increases in recreation and culture expenditures have been identified in a number of studies. Two sources that indicate the magnitude and nature of the increases are: N. H. Lithwick, A. M. Maslove, and E. Swimmer, *Ottawa-Carleton Competitive Position: A Competitive Economic Analysis* (Ottawa: Finance department, Regional Municipality of Ottawa-Carleton, 1979), 10; and Ontario, *Local Government Finance in Ontario, 1977* (Toronto: Municipal Finance Branch, Ministry of Treasury and Economics, 1978), 10.

Table 5.4   Recreation and Culture Expenditures, 1978

	Local government responsibility			Local government own-source expenditures[a]					
	(1)	(2)	(3)	(4)	(5)	(6)	(7)	(8)	(9)
Province	Local expenditures as a per cent of provincial/local expenditures	Local expenditures financed by own-source revenue as a per cent of total local expenditures	Local expenditures financed by own-source revenue as a percent of provincial/local expenditures	Per capita expenditures—all local governments	Per cent of total local government expenditures	Per capita operating expenditures—all local governments	Per cent of total local government expenditures	Per capita expenditures—all urban regions[b]	Per cent of total local government expenditures
	per cent	*per cent*		*dollars*	*per cent*	*dollars*	*per cent*	*dollars*	*per cent*
Nfld.	29.3	64.2	18.8	10.02	7.6	6.17	7.3	23.91	7.6
P.E.I.[c]	29.6	61.5	18.2	11.59	4.4	9.65	11.7	–	–
N.S.	57.1	60.2	34.4	14.64	4.5	13.25	5.1	40.12	5.7
N.B.	62.1	53.9	33.4	14.17	8.9	9.34	9.7	23.17	7.4
Que.	64.9	78.8	51.2	40.21	8.0	29.21	7.9	45.79	7.8
Ont.	72.0	79.5	57.2	51.11	8.7	39.42	8.4	38.76	6.6
Man.	63.7	86.2	54.9	40.80	7.9	33.58	7.4	50.42	7.3
Sask.	74.0	74.7	55.3	46.55	8.8	27.06	7.1	52.64	8.2
Alta.	71.2	80.5	57.3	73.27	9.2	51.48	10.0	98.80	11.3
B.C.	74.3	82.0	60.9	54.84	8.2	40.95	7.8	69.66	10.2
All prov.	68.9	79.0	54.5	46.27	8.4	34.29	8.2	49.25[d]	9.2

[a]Excludes both conditional and unconditional grants. [b]Capital and operating expenditures are not available on a separate basis. [c]No urban region recorded in Statistics Canada data. [d]Average for nine provinces only.

Source: Calculated from Appendix Table B.2 and from Statistics Canada, *Local Government Finance, Preliminary 1978—Estimates 1979*, Catalogue no. 68-203.

and culture in 1978. Operating expenditures, on average, amounted to $34 per capita, and ranged from a high of $51 in Alberta to a low of $6 in New-foundland. In between these extremes, the remaing provinces in Atlantic Canada recorded figures from $9 to $13 per capita, while similar totals for Quebec, Ontario, and the West ranged from $27 to $41 (column 6, Table 5.4).

Expenditures for these services are among the fastest growing in the municipal budget. In 1978 they absorbed, on average, 8 per cent of locally raised funds (column 7, Table 5.4) and there is every reason to expect that this per-centage will increase over time. Part of the increase, of course, can be attributed to the recurring costs associated with new facilities constructed in earlier years.[11] A more subtle but nonetheless influencing factor is a new-found willingness on the part of local ratepayers to pay for these soft services as a result of their increased real incomes. This trend has created a growing need for more for-malized recreation programs, library facilities, and cultural activities, although the exact magnitude of the expenditures undertaken varies directly with the financial resources of a given community. While the demand may be present, the high costs of recreation programs often place undue hardships on the finan-cial resources of many local governments, since a number of municipalities have been drawn into various programs with large capital subsidies from the provin-cial governments and then have been left to bear the operating costs.

To offset the deterrent effect of high costs, many provinces (particularly in the East) provide limited conditional assistance. This includes specific grants to cover in part the operating costs of libraries, recreational facilities, and for the preservation of historic sites. Most municipalities, however, reserve the right to pass bylaws respecting recreation and community services and retain ultimate responsibility for both the provision and the financing of these facilities. When this happens, provincial requirements apply only to those municipalities that accept direct provincial financial assistance.[12]

PER CAPITA EXPENDITURES BY MUNICIPALITY SIZE AND REGION

Greater urbanization and high density dwellings place higher-than-normal demands on existing recreation and cultural services and facilities and create a demand for services that otherwise would not exist. Larger concentrations of people, however, mean that economies of scale can be realized through the pro-vision of a number of facilities and hence these services can be made affordable to larger numbers of people. Unquestionably, each municipality must decide for itself what resources to devote and what activities to emphasize with respect to the provision of all types of recreation and community services. Certain fac-tors related to municipal size may, however, determine the nature and feasibility of services offered.

Primarily because of the high costs of many recreation programs and cultural facilities, many medium- to small-sized towns find it financially impossible to support most community facilities in an efficient manner. In many provinces,

[11]This was found to be the case for local governments in Ontario—see Ontario, supra footnote 4, at 23.

[12]Alberta, *Report of the Provincial-Municipal Finance Council on the Responsibilities and Financing of Local Government in Alberta* (Edmonton: the Council, 1979), 279-80.

affected towns and villages join surrounding municipalities to circumvent this problem and to participate in the joint operation of various programs and facilities. In most cases (particularly in Ontario and the West) community leagues, voluntarily staffed and financed by user charges, provide recreation programs and maintain small community facilities. The operation and finance of more complex facilities, such as swimming pools and arenas, are usually the direct responsibility of larger area municipalities.[13]

With the exception of Ontario, locally funded expenditures on recreation and cultural services tend to be higher in urban areas than elsewhere and in some provinces (Nova Scotia and Alberta, for example), substantially higher. Although the explanation for this different pattern is neither obvious nor clear cut, it tends to be dependent directly on the relative weight assigned to the following factors: first, in a number of urban areas and particularly in Ontario, the relatively high concentration of population has led to an expansion in the number of privately sponsored recreational facilities and hence, less pressure to have services provided through the public sector. Where this has happened, per capita expenditures by local governments have been lower than elsewhere. Second, the desire to provide some minimal level of many recreation (swimming pools, tennis courts, and arenas) and cultural services (public libraries and community centres) in scattered non-urban settlements, suggests that per capita expenditure levels could be higher in rural areas. For example, there is some evidence suggesting that in Ontario, the harshness of winters and the relative lack of privately provided facilities and clubs have created a growing demand for and the subsequent provision of many recreational and cultural services in the rural and more isolated regions of this province.[14] In these instances, the per capita costs of providing services, even though of lower quantity and quality, have been higher in non-urban areas.

RESOURCE CONSERVATION AND INDUSTRIAL DEVELOPMENT

LOCAL GOVERNMENT OWN-SOURCE RESPONSIBILITY

These functions, although important to the economy of the province as a whole, do not, as a rule, represent a significant burden on local budgets. In fact, most of the services included in this category, such as natural resources, agriculture, tourism, trade, and industry, are almost exclusively the responsibility of the various provincial governments.[15] Natural resources, for example, are entirely a provincial responsibility in all provinces but Ontario and the West. In these two regions, however, municipalities account for an extremely small proportion of total local and provincial expenditures. To the extent that a province considers its natural resources to be significant to its economy, each provides assistance to agriculture, fisheries, forestry, and mineral resources. In the western regions, provincial assistance in the form of technical advice and train-

---

[13]Ibid., at 276.

[14]Ontario, supra footnote 4, at 25.

[15]For a complete description of both the federal and provincial roles in natural resources and industry, see supra footnote 1, at Chapter 13.

ing is particularly critical to the agriculture industry. Because the economic benefits from this resource accrue to areas generally larger than one particular municipality, local contributions usually are not required for this service. They occasionally are made, however, in some of the prairie provinces. In the Province of Alberta, for example, agricultural service boards are financed by a combination of municipal revenues and a number of conditional grants.

In provinces with commercial fishing industries, the provincial governments assume a role similar to those with agriculture industries. In this instance, municipalities are generally relieved of the expenditures associated with storage facilities, research and development, or marketing techniques.

In the area of trade and industry, provinces have been accepting a greater role in the development of manufacturing and service industries. Because there is a need to coordinate and balance the income and employment fluctuations that affect economies heavily dependent on the production and export of foodstuffs and raw materials, the province and not the municipality is considered the appropriate level of government from which to initiate new programs.[16] Ontario and Alberta are the only provinces with local governments that engage in expenditures for the benefit of local trade and industry. These expenditures do not, however, represent a significant drain on local revenue sources.

Given the relatively high profile of provincial governments in funding these services, it is not surprising to note that less than 7 per cent of all provincial/local expenditures combined were made by local governments in 1978 (column 1, Table 5.5). Of particular interest here, is the substantial deviation witnessed in Ontario where 24 per cent of all combined expenditures were made by local governments. For the remaining provinces, municipalities in Alberta (on average) contributed proportionally more (of the combined total) than the Canadian average. Manitoba was slightly below the Canadian average, while expenditures by municipalities in the remaining provinces were either non-existent or extremely small.

With the exception of New Brunswick (65 per cent) and Quebec (88 per cent), expenditures financed by own-source revenues in the remaining provinces amounted to 90 per cent or more of all local expenditures (column 2, Table 5.5). Obviously, grants were virtually non-existent for the support of this function at the local level. In spite of this low dependence on grants, the proportion of aggregated provincial/local expenditures financed from own-source revenues averaged only 6 per cent over the entire country (column 3, Table 5.5). Local governments in Ontario displayed proportionately higher expenditures at almost 23 per cent of the total. Municipalites in Alberta and Manitoba, by comparison, were the next highest recording percentages of 7 per cent and 5 per cent respectively in 1978. Local governments in the remaining provinces financed 2 per cent or less of all aggregated sums spent on this function.

PER CAPITA OPERATING EXPENSES BY PROVINCE

The low level of operating expenditures devoted to the group of locally funded services listed under this function is exhibited in the locally funded per capita

---

[16]Ibid., at 281.

Table 5.5 Resource Conservation and Industrial Development Expenditures, 1978

	Local government responsibility			Local government own-source expenditures[a]					
	(1)	(2)	(3)	(4)	(5)	(6)	(7)	(8)	(9)
Province	Local expenditures as a per cent of provincial/local expenditures	Local expenditures financed by own-source revenue as a per cent of total local expenditures	Local expenditures financed by own-source revenue as a percent of provincial/local expenditures	Per capita expenditures—all local governments	Per cent of total local government expenditures	Per capita operating expenditures—all local governments	Per cent of total local government expenditures	Per capita expenditures—all urban regions[b]	Per cent of total local government expenditures
	per cent			*dollars*	*per cent*	*dollars*	*per cent*	*dollars*	*per cent*
Nfld.	—	—	—	.41	.3	.23	.3	.56	0
P.E.I.[c] . . .	—	—	—	—	—	—	—	—	—
N.S.	1.2	90.5	1.1	1.52	.5	1.04	.4	7.01	1.0
N.B.	1.9	64.9	1.2	1.44	.9	1.06	1.1	5.60	1.8
Que.	1.7	87.6	1.5	1.48	.3	1.48	.4	1.63	.2
Ont.	24.0	93.6	22.5	12.37	2.1	5.63	1.2	3.13	.5
Man.	5.4	91.7	5.0	3.75	.7	3.17	.7	2.42	.4
Sask.	.9	98.9	.9	1.88	.4	1.14	.3	2.90	.4
Alta.	7.2	99.2	7.1	27.76	3.5	5.67	1.1	9.79	1.2
B.C.	2.3	96.7	2.2	2.06	.3	1.57	.3	.46	.3
All prov. . .	6.7	95.1	6.4	7.77	1.4	3.35	.8	3.72[d]	.6

[a]Excludes both conditional and unconditional grants. [b]Capital and operating expenditures are not available on a separate basis. [c]No urban region recorded in Statistics Canada data. [d]Average for nine provinces only.

Source: Calculated from Appendix Table B.2 and from Statistics Canada, *Local Government Finance, Preliminary 1978—Estimates 1979*, Catalogue no. 68-203.

figures (column 6, Table 5.5). The average for Canada was marginally above $3, with municipalities in Ontario and Alberta recording expenditures of almost $6 (the highest) and those in Newfoundland recording a figure of less than $1 per capita (the lowest) in 1978.

As a per cent of budgeted expenditures financed from local revenue sources, these expenditures absorbed more than 1 per cent of municipal expenditures only in New Brunswick, Ontario, and Alberta (column 3, Table 5.5). The average for Canada was less than 1 per cent, suggesting that these expenditures do not exert a significant claim on local revenues.

PER CAPITA EXPENDITURES BY MUNICIPALITY SIZE AND REGION

Local own-source expenditures for agriculture, trade, tourism, and industry (services subsumed under this category) are not always higher in urban areas. Urban areas, in fact, displayed per capita expenditure levels above the provincial average (operating plus capital) in Newfoundland, Nova Scotia, New Brunswick, Quebec, and Saskatchewan and lower per capita levels in Ontario, Manitoba, Alberta, and British Columbia (columns 4 and 8, Table 5.5). This random pattern exists because of the relative importance assigned to the separate components of this function. In some provinces, locally funded expenditures on industrial development in urban areas may increase the relative weight of this component in the overall expenditure figures; whereas, in other areas, concentrated expenditures (locally funded) may be directed to improvements in expenditures on tourism, agriculture, or in a few instances, on natural resources in the non-urban areas. Obviously, higher or lower expenditure levels in urban areas will depend on the relative importance assigned to the individual services provided by municipal governments.

PLANNING, DEVELOPMENT, AND HOUSING

LOCAL GOVERNMENT OWN-SOURCE RESPONSIBILITY

Efficient and effective planning is perhaps the most administratively complex of all municipal services.[17] Although originally designed to guide physical development, local government planning mechanisms have today grown, in response to increasingly complex municipal organizations, to encompass the administration of the more broadly based field of community development and housing. By virtue of its original purpose—promoting the most effective physical development of the community—the planning function always has been the responsibility of local governments. Today, however, the economic, social, and physical factors affecting development often extend beyond municipal boundaries. All provinces have retained a degree of supervisory power over the planning activities of their local governments. Although the technicalities are complicated and varied, supervisory powers are generally vested in either a minister, a cabinet, or a separate agency such as the Saskatchewan Provincial Planning Appeals Board or the Ontario Municipal Board.[18] In

---

[17]Ontario, *Report of the Waterloo Region Review Commission* (Waterloo: the Commission, March 1979), 228.

[18]Because the exact details of the various provincial arrangements are too complex to list here, the interested reader is directed to supra footnote 1, at Chapter 8.

Newfoundland, all municipal plans are prepared locally but must be approved by the provincial minister according to the Urban and Regional Planning Act. Similarly, in Nova Scotia, New Brunswick, Prince Edward Island, Ontario, and Manitoba, provincial planning acts provide for the appointments of provincial advisory boards. These boards integrate the municipal and regional planning function.

Three exceptions to this rule of close supervision exist. In Quebec, until 1979 (prior to the adoption of Loi sur l'aménagement et l'urbanisme) the absence of provincial controls encouraged a permissive municipal planning sector. Since 1979, however, new laws have given the provincial Ministry of Municipal Affairs (Ministre des Affaires Municipales) specific supervisory powers over local planning decisions. Both Alberta and British Columbia, however, continue to place almost complete supervisory responsibility for this function within the local sector. In Alberta, regional plans are prepared by regional planning commissions composed of representatives from affected municipalities. Municipalities are then free to adopt any plan that conforms to the region plan.[19] In British Columbia provincial controls of municipal planning activities were not established until 1978 when the Minister of Municipal Affairs was given the power to approve official community plans. These broad powers, however, have yet to be used to modify a municipal decision.

Most reports investigating the planning function argue that the primary responsibility for detailed land-use planning, zoning, development control, housing standards, and maintenance and occupancy standards should rest within area municipalities.[20] Most of the present supervisory systems— primarily provincial ministries of housing—were more appropriate when local governments did not have sufficient political or technical sophistication to provide an adequate standard of planning. Given that many local services—public works, schools, libraries and recreation facilities—must be coordinated with planning policies, it is only appropriate that municipalities also have responsibility for regulating the physical evolution of their communities and neighbourhoods.

Local government can, for example, effectively encourage or inhibit the construction of housing through its local planning policies, development controls, and zoning bylaws. Although the vast majority of Canada's housing stock will continue to be privately supplied, all levels of government are gaining importance in influencing density and form, and in facilitating housing production. Local governments, for example, can play an active role in the provision of low-income housing: today many rental accommodations are built and/or managed by municipalities.[21] Federal and provincial funds usually finance the capital

---

[19]Graham Murchie, David Stuart, and Neil Taylor, *Planning in Alberta: A Guide and Directory* (Edmonton: Department of Municipal Affairs, 1978), 15-29.

[20]See for example, supra footnote 6, at 207-26; supra footnote 17, at 229; and supra footnote 12.

[21]For a comprehensive description of the role of government in the housing field, see Canadian Council on Social Development, *A Review of Canadian Social Housing Policy* (Ottawa: the Council, 1977), and Central Mortgage and Housing Commission, *Federal Housing Action Program* (Ottawa: the Commission, 1975), as well as Klein & Sears, *The Provision and Conservation of Housing in Metropolitan Toronto*, a Report prepared for The Royal Commission on Metropolitan Toronto (Toronto: Klein & Sears, 1975).

costs of public accommodation, while the municipality bears any operating losses. Direct federal and provincial provision of rental units, because it often opposes local development plans, has in most cases, however, been replaced or at least supplemented by a series of grant programs and low-cost loans that recognize the municipal role. Community planning branches operate in some provinces (Saskatchewan and Quebec) and nonprofit housing corporations exist in others (Manitoba, British Columbia, and Ontario). All use upper-tier funding based on a more recent approach to housing that emphasizes conservation and rehabilitation in light of a growing housing shortage and high mortgage rates.

While there is a great deal of provincial involvement in expenditures on this function, there are considerable administrative responsibilities placed on municipal governments to ensure compliance with commercial, industrial, and residential development as set out in municipal plans. A wide variation exists in the associated financial responsibilities required by each local government in the various provinces. Local expenditures, for example, as a percent of the combined provincial/local total on this function varied from a low of almost 10 per cent in Newfoundland to a high of almost 78 per cent in Prince Edward Island in 1978. The average Canadian municipality for the same year accounted for 30 per cent of the same total (column 1, Table 5.6). These values may be misleading, however, because each province provides a varying degree of financial support to its municipal planning sector through grants or special programs. This support ranges from a large amount of grant support in Newfoundland and Nova Scotia to almost no grant support and, therefore, the necessity to raise proportionately larger local funds to support this function in Quebec, Alberta, and Prince Edward Island (column 2, Table 5.6).

The level of responsibility assigned to the municipal governments is directly related to the dependence or lack of dependence on local revenue. In those provinces displaying significant municipal responsibility, well over one-half of local planning and development expenditures tend to be funded from local revenue sources. Where municipal responsibility was low (Newfoundland, Nova Scotia, and New Brunswick), provincial governments took an active role with the specific intention of encouraging the provision of necessary services, while simultaneously alleviating the associated local financial burden. A great many local governments also relied on federally supplied funds and programs to initiate development and housing services that otherwise would have been financially prohibitive. The effective utilization of these programs depended, however, on municipal needs and priorities.[22]

---

[22]The now defunct federal Neighbourhood Improvement Program, for example, allocated funds and designed qualified improvement areas according to specified criteria on the basis of an annual agreement with the federal government and each provincial government. Federal assistance in the form of both loans and grants was made available for the improvement of hard services (sewers, road repair) and soft services (recreational) on a shared basis: 50 per cent federal, 25 per cent provincial, and 25 per cent municipal. Utilization of the funds varied substantially from province to province. Ontario and Quebec were by far the most active participants in this program because their local sectors had strong financial positions and the ability to provide the required municipal contribution. See K. J. Sheppard, *The Canadian Inner City: Case Study of Decline and Policy Response in Peterborough, Ontario* (unpublished thesis, Trent University, Peterborough, April 1980), 39-47.

Table 5.6 Planning, Development, and Housing Expenditures, 1978

Province	Local government responsibility			Local government own-source expenditures[a]					
	(1) Local expenditures as a per cent of provincial/local expenditures	(2) Local expenditures financed by own-source revenue as a per cent of total local expenditures	(3) Local expenditures financed by own-source revenue as a percent of provincial/local expenditures	(4) Per capita expenditures—all local governments	(5) Per cent of total local government expenditures	(6) Per capita operating expenditures—all local governments	(7) Per cent of total local government expenditures	(8) Per capita expenditures—all urban regions[b]	(9) Per cent of total local government expenditures
	per cent	*per cent*		*dollars*	*per cent*	*dollars*	*per cent*	*dollars*	*per cent*
Nfld.	9.8	17.4	1.7	.41	.9	0	0	21.00	6.7
P.E.I.[c]	77.7	89.8	69.8	33.99	13.0	1.48	1.8	—	—
N.S.	12.3	36.4	4.5	2.72	.8	2.08	.8	21.56	3.1
N.B.	20.5	59.1	12.1	1.50	.9	1.25	1.3	15.58	5.0
Que.	20.5	96.4	19.8	6.74	1.3	5.55	1.5	12.47	2.1
Ont.	20.3	75.9	15.4	9.91	1.7	5.63	1.2	7.63	1.3
Man.	40.7	65.7	26.8	8.17	1.5	8.17	1.8	11.16	1.6
Sask.	20.5	60.4	12.4	4.53	.9	1.14	.3	13.84	2.2
Alta.	57.3	93.6	53.6	34.51	4.4	12.87	2.5	37.29	4.4
B.C.	50.3	80.5	40.5	12.33	1.9	6.30	1.2	12.68	1.8
All prov.	30.0	81.7	24.5	10.47	1.9	5.85	1.4	17.02[d]	3.1

[a]Excludes both conditional and unconditional grants. [b]Capital and operating expenditures are not available on a separate basis. [c]No urban region recorded in Statistics Canada data. [d]Average for nine provinces only.

Source: Calculated from Appendix Table B.2 and from Statistics Canada, *Local Government Finance, Preliminary 1978—Estimates 1979*, Catalogue no. 68-203.

Perhaps a better indication of the role of local governments in planning and development lies in an interprovincial comparison of the relative importance of the local sector in funding combined provincial and municipal expenditures. Local government revenues funded, on average, less than one-quarter of total development expenditures in 1978, but this figure ranged from a high of 70 per cent in Prince Edward Island, and 54 per cent in Alberta to less than 2 per cent in Newfoundland.

PER CAPITA OPERATING EXPENDITURES
BY PROVINCE

Although planning and development is a relatively minor function as identified above, spending on this function has, in dollar terms, risen dramatically in most provinces since the early 1970s to accommodate surges in housing needs and urbanization.[23] Per capita operating expenditures on this function are still among the lowest of the municipal services, but this is directly attributable to substantial provincial financial support. Local governments (in 1978) were required to fund directly out of own-source revenues, on average, less than $6 per capita for the support of this service. The relatively high responsibility levels associated with the municipal role in some provinces, such as Prince Edward Island and Alberta, were not translated into noticeable operating expenditures financed from local revenues. Municipalities in Alberta recorded expenditures of almost $13 per person in 1978, some $7 above the national average (column 6, Table 5.6). Lower per capita locally funded expenditures in the range of $1 to $2 were recorded in Prince Edward Island, Nova Scotia, New Brunswick, and Saskatchewan. Alberta was the only province in which these expenditures absorbed more than 2 per cent of locally raised revenues in 1978 (column 7, Table 5.6).

PER CAPITA EXPENDITURES BY
MUNICIPALITY SIZE AND REGION

As urban Canada has grown, so too has its need for an increasingly sophisticated planning sector. If municipalities are to plan effective land-use schemes, transportation networks, industrial parks, and public facilities near the borders of neighbouring communities, then a certain degree of area-wide planning is needed. In short, local planning policies must be conducted in conjunction with area-wide objectives and standards, rather than in direct opposition to the efforts of surrounding communities. As populations and densities continue to rise in urban areas, regional planning offers a viable means of conducting economic development and providing major transportation links.

In most provinces, provincial planning acts provide for a system of integrated municipal planning to direct general economic and community development in a manner beneficial to large intermunicipal jurisdictions.[24] Unique to Ontario and British Columbia are two-tiered regional planning systems to coordinate and control the planning functions. A regional planning process also operates in the more urbanized sectors of most other provinces (such as in Montreal and Quebec City), but its operation is not as formal as is

[23]For example, see Ontario, supra footnote 4, at 23.

[24]Supra footnote 1, at Chapter 8.

found in the regional governments of Ontario or the regional districts of British Columbia. There are, for example, no two-tiered governments in Alberta, although the need to coordinate community development across the jurisdictions of neighbouring municipalities is recognized and implemented wherever urban structure warrants it. In such areas, regional planning is recognized as one of the most effective and impartial ways of dealing with contentious issues, such as the competition between municipalities for land-use developments that produce large property tax revenues.[25] A certain degree of area-wide coordination is also required to regulate the increasing involvement of urban municipalities in landbanking for both residential and commercial purposes.

The scope of the planning process, and its associated costs, therefore, will necessarily be a function of municipality size and structure. Per capita expenditures in large urban areas were, on average, 70 per cent higher than the national average ($17 per capita compared with $10) in 1978. In every province, with the exception of Ontario, expenditures on this function in urban regions exceeded those for the rest of the province. In fact, in the urban areas of Newfoundland, Nova Scotia, and New Brunswick, the expenditures were up to 10 times higher than similar expenditures for the rest of the province. Much of this differential can be attributed to expenditures designed to meet new upgrading and development standards in each of the respective provinces. In Saskatchewan, where the urban expenditure was three times the provincial average, urban areas have been taking advantage of provincial assistance for major improvements in the basic municipal infrastructure necessary to accommodate the increasing population associated with the location of industries in or near urban areas.[26] A similar program exists in Alberta. In Quebec, Manitoba, Alberta, and British Columbia, in 1978, the differential in urban and provincial totals ranged from a high of almost 100 per cent (Quebec) to virtually nothing (British Columbia) (columns 4 and 8, Table 5.6).

The planning needs tend to be different in non-urban areas. While these expenditures are lower in every province except Ontario, they are extremely important to the development of cohesive rural districts. Many rural municipalities in Ontario, for example, have increased their participation in the upgrading of rural land through the Provincial Drainage Program.[27] In Saskatchewan, the Agricultural Service Centre Program provides assistance to rural and urban communities suffering water supply shortages. Also in operation is the Prairie Farm Rehabilitation Administration for environmental upgrading and land purchases.[28] Recent emphasis has also been placed on reconciling industrial and urban land-use expansion with rural environment protection. As densities in city cores increase, unrestrained new commercial development will continue to gravitate toward the rural-urban fringe. Most rural communities now recognize the need to insist that such development be in accordance with local community plans and objectives.

---

[25]Supra footnote 12, at 316.

[26]Saskatchewan, *Annual Report 1978-79, Saskatchewan Municipal Affairs* (Regina: Department of Municipal Affairs, 1980), 30.

[27]Ontario, supra footnote 10.

[28]Supra footnote 26.

SUMMARY

Of the five expenditure functions discussed in this chapter, recreation and culture is the only one reflecting significant expenditure levels and modest drains on local budgets. The rest tend to be smaller in magnitude or more heavily financed by provincial governments. While these expenditure levels, in total, are much smaller in dollar values than the functions discussed in Chapter 4, their importance in terms of funding local services is, nevertheless, important and often vital in the provision of an adequate quantity and quality of local services. Many of the patterns and regional variations observed for the major expenditures discussed in the previous chapter were also observed for the expenditures discussed here.

6
Capital Expenditures and Financing

INTRODUCTION

One of the important issues facing local governments is the budgeting for and financing of capital expenditures. As municipalities expand and grow older, attention must be devoted to the expansion or replacement of their capital stock. Water plants and sewage treatment facilities must be expanded or replaced. Cultural and recreational facilities need to be renewed or created. Transportation and communications facilities must be updated and extended. While capital expenditures have increased, they have, however, grown slower than operating expenditures.

The nature of capital expenditures is such that their budgeting and financing have generated problems that are, in some cases, different from those associated with operating expenditures. First, capital expansion tends to be lumpy in nature. Large expenditures in one year may preclude similar expenditures in subsequent years with little, if any, consistent trend or pattern emerging. Second, the financing of capital expenditures frequently differs from that of operating expenditures. Operating expenditures are financed from locally raised revenues or grants, while capital expenditures may be funded from these sources in addition to monies generated from special assessments, reserve funds, and borrowing. The utilization of these other revenue sources generates issues, concerns, and problems unique to the funding of capital projects.

After a brief presentation of the level and relative importance of capital expenditures, this chapter will address a number of issues revolving around the choice of the correct decision-making rule; the various ways in which local capital budgets are controlled; and the implications for financing capital expenditures out of available alternative revenue sources.

LOCAL CAPITAL EXPENDITURES

It is difficult, for a number of reasons, to compare local capital expenditures on an interprovincial basis in any specific year or over time. An important reason for this difficulty is the increased emphasis that has been placed on shifting the responsibility for capital outlays on to developers via planning requirements. This has led to a reduction in the local government's responsibility for financing specific capital projects. In Ontario, for example, the Ontario Planning Act requires developers of new subdivisions to set aside land for parks and playgrounds (5 per cent of the area to be developed or up to 1 acre for every 120 dwelling units). In lieu of this, the developer may enter into an agreement with the local government officials to transfer a sum of money equivalent to the market value of the stipulated amount of land. Similarly, some municipalities make greater use of lot levies and special assessments (these are discussed below) to finance capital projects. This suggests that differences do exist, however, in the extent to which these municipalities are attempting to finance some of their capital projects through charges placed directly on the beneficiaries of the services provided by the capital projects. Intermunicipal variation in the application of special levies to finance capital projects may make interprovincial and intertemporal comparisons somewhat suspect. The inherent lumpiness of financing many capital projects suggests, moreover, that any intertemporal comparison of local capital expenditures must be undertaken with caution, for expenditures in one year may be considerably higher than those in preceding or subsequent years.

In spite of these qualifications, some general trends have emerged over the past few years and are worth noting. If one observes the overall expenditure averages for 1968 and 1978, one notes that local capital expenditures on the four most important functions (education, transportation and communications, environment, and recreation and culture) accounted for over 85 per cent of all local capital expenditures in each year (calculated from Table 6.1). None of the remaining functions tended to be very significant in terms of the relative impact that each had on the level of capital expenditures.

In reviewing the four functions accounting for the bulk of capital expenditures, it is not surprising to note that expenditures on education, which had accounted for over 43 per cent of all capital expenditures by local governments in 1968 and exceeded all other functions, actually declined so that by 1978 they accounted for slightly less than 15 per cent of all capital expenditures. In this latter year, these expenditures ranked behind those for transportation and communications (34 per cent of the total) and environment (28 per cent of the total) in importance. (Calculated from data in Table 6.1.)

Financial support for education expenditures comes from grants, current operating revenues, lot levies, special assessments, and borrowings. In total, conditional grants tended to finance less than one-quarter of all capital expenditures in each of the years observed. Education, which received the highest grant in 1968, was the only function on which per capita grants declined in absolute terms from 1968 to 1978 (Table 6.1). This shift merely reflects a change in the demand for capital assets. The rapid expansion of schools in the mid-1960s followed by a decline in the school-aged population in the 1970s accounted for this decline in grant funding for this function. At the same time, increasing urbanization and growing population densities led to a demand for better means of transportation, improved environmental conditions, and greater recreational and cultural facilities. An interprovincial comparison of capital expenditures by function, therefore, does not seem to reveal any noticeable trends other than those associated with changes in the demographic or industrial base of the individual municipality or province.

Rising incomes and the greater availability of leisure time have contributed to an increased demand for local capital expenditures on recreation and cultural facilities with the greatest demand occurring in urban as opposed to rural areas. Per capita capital expenditures, which were almost non-existent in every province in 1968, increased significantly by 1978 with generally higher levels of expenditure occurring in Ontario and the four western provinces (Appendix Tables B.1 and B.2). The bulk of the funds for these expenditures, regardless of the province in which the municipality is located, was contributed by the municipalities themselves.

Table 6.1   Local Per Capita Expenditures by Major Function,[a] 1968 and 1978

Function	1968				1978			
	Conditional grants for capital expenditures		Funded from other revenue		Conditional grants for capital expenditures		Funded from other revenue	
	dollars	*% of total*	*dollars*	*% of total*	*dollars*	*% of total*	*dollars*	*% of total*
General government ...	.02	.1	2.46	4.1	1.24	3.2	1.64	1.3
Protection	.02	.1	.92	1.5	.22	.6	3.64	2.8
Transportation and communications.....	5.46	28.6	12.77	21.1	13.82	36.0	43.90	33.6
Health	.05	.3	1.72	2.8	1.31	3.4	2.08	1.6
Social services	.01	.1	.47	.8	.12	.3	1.68	1.3
Education	12.01	62.9	22.53	37.3	9.85	25.6	15.36	11.8
Environment	1.01	5.3	12.02	19.9	5.45	14.2	41.43	31.7
Recreation and culture .	.03	.2	3.23	5.3	3.29	8.6	11.98	9.2
Housing, regional planning and development	—	—	—	—	1.03	2.7	4.62	3.5
Other	.49	2.6	4.34	7.2	2.11	5.5	4.38	3.4
Total...............	19.10	100.0	60.46	100.0	38.44	100.0	130.71	100.0

[a]These figures reflect the average for all Canadian municipalities.

Source: Calculated from data in Appendix Tables B.1 and B.2.

Increased income, urbanization, and population densities have been the primary causes behind the increased demands for better transportation and communications facilities and for noticeable improvements in the levels of environmental facilities for local residents. Over the past 15 years, housing booms and rapid expansions of many urban areas created significant demands on local infrastructures (streets, roads, street lighting, and public transit). In addition to these demands came a growing interest in an improved environment and thus pressures increased to improve or replace sewage disposal systems, garbage collection and disposal facilities, water purification and distribution plants, and general pollution controls.

While considerable interprovincial variation can be noted in per capita expenditures on each of these two functions (Appendix Tables B.1 and B.2), higher expenditures almost always exist in those areas with higher concentrations of people and/or higher per capita levels of income. At the same time and with very few exceptions, the bulk of these expenditures tend to be financed by local governments through revenues generated from operating funds, borrowing, reserves, and special assessments.

Changing demographic patterns have led to reduced expenditures on educational facilities in some provinces and to increases in others (Appendix Tables B.1 and B.2). Where reductions in the school-aged population have been more noticeable, virtually no new capital construction has taken place and very little replacement of run-down capital stock has occurred. Responsibility for funding capital construction expenditures is wide-ranging. In some provinces, these projects are funded directly by the provincial government. In others, grants are provided to school boards or local governments to cover the construction costs. In still others, school boards or local governments borrow the necessary funds but, where this occurs, the provincial government subsequently provides grants to the local governments to cover the costs of servicing the debt. Regardless of the approach followed, every provincial government essentially assumes the financing responsibility. Comparisons of the relative importance of local funds versus grants are, therefore, somewhat meaningless in the case of funding educational facilities.

While the explanation for the existing differentials and the explanation for the rate of increase in the functions listed here has been attributed primarily to demand factors, one must not be left with the impression that these are the only relevant variables. For example, the extent to which local governments have been able to use their own sources of revenue in supporting many local capital expenditures (supply constraint) has been undoubtedly an important factor in undertaking a number of expenditures. Finally, other factors such as tradition, political considerations, and provincial government regulations, have also exerted their influence.

THE CAPITAL EXPENDITURE DECISION

Local policy makers must decide which capital expenditures to undertake before they consider the capital budgeting process and the various means of capital financing available to them. The determination of justifiable capital projects is, theoretically, straightforward. A project is desirable if the net present value arising from its implementation is greater than zero, that is, if the discounted value of the stream of current and future benefits exceeds the discounted value of the stream of current and future costs.[1] When this happens,

---

[1]More specifically, the present value of the costs and benefits of a capital project in any year is calculated by multiplying each respective cost or benefit by the discount factor written as $\frac{1}{(1+r)^i}$ where r is the rate of discount and i is the index for the year concerned. The discounted values of benefits and costs for all years are then totalled to yield the present value of benefits and costs as follows. The present value of benefits where B_0, B_1 . . . B_n reflect the benefits in each year is obtained from the following expression:

$$\frac{B_0}{(1+r)^0} + \frac{B_1}{(1+r)^1} + \frac{B_2}{(1+r)^2} \cdots \frac{B_n}{(1+r)^n} = \sum_{i=0}^{n} \frac{B_i}{(1+r)^i}$$

The present value of costs, where C_0, C_1, ... C_n represent the costs in each year, is calculated in the following manner.

$$\frac{C_0}{(1+r)^0} + \frac{C_1}{(1+r)^1} + \frac{C_2}{(1+r)^2} \cdots \frac{C_n}{(1+r)^n} = \sum_{i=0}^{n} \frac{C_i}{(1+r)^i}$$

Finally, the net present value (NPV) of a capital project is obtained by subtracting the discounted costs from the discounted benefits.

$$NPV = \sum_{i=0}^{n} \frac{B_i}{(1+r)^i} - \sum_{i=0}^{n} \frac{C_i}{(1+r)^i}$$

(Continued on next page.)

the completion of a project will generate benefits to society that are greater than the cost of the project.

Although simple in theory, capital expenditure decisions are far from simple in practice, since it is difficult to identify and quantify the relevant benefits and costs. In the public sector, for instance, most benefits are of an intangible nature and not amenable to easy or obvious quantification. How does one place a value on the benefits accruing to users of a facility (recreation area, street, or bridge), when the users are not required to pay a fee or price each time the facility is used? Further difficulties are encountered in attempting to place a value on the neighbourhood or spillover effects (benefits accruing to non-users) arising from the completion of a capital project. In spite of such measurement problems, attempts should be made to include estimates of the benefits generated. Where similar facilities exist in the private sector, the calculation of benefits to the direct users may be based on the amount individuals pay for similar services in the private sector. The calculation of benefits to the non-users (spillover effect) is considerably more complex and may require the use of some rather crude estimations.

In addition to the problems of estimating benefits, the calculation of projected costs is often less than complete. Not only are the initial construction costs to be considered, but all future costs (maintenance and operating) and nonmarket costs must be included in a benefit-cost analysis. The limited available evidence[2] suggests that many municipalities ignore future and nonmarket costs in their assessments of the true costs of a capital project. It appears as if some of the larger urban governments, in fact, are the only ones to consider all cost components. The rest simply ignore many of the relevant and important recurring costs.

Considerable improvement could be achieved, therefore, in the capital expenditure decision-making process if a more careful and precise benefit-cost analysis were undertaken prior to the initiation of a capital project. This might prevent the undertaking of questionable projects (those promised by local politicians in the heat of a political campaign or those for which only partial grant support is available from provincial or federal governments).

CONTROL OF CAPITAL BUDGETING

The scant literature on capital budgeting by local governments[3] tends to be non-analytical, fragmented, and generally anecdotal. Most of the material is instructional and includes manuals, guides, or handbooks outlining the step-by-step procedures to follow in preparing and submitting capital budgets to local

---

[1]Continued

Whenever the net present value of a capital project exceeds zero, its completion will generate benefits to society that are greater than the cost of the project. For a thorough and excellent discussion of the benefit/cost technique and its implications, see Canada, Treasury Board Secretariat, Planning Branch, *Benefit-Cost Analysis Guide* (Ottawa: Information Canada, 1976).

[2]See Garnet Garven and Richard J. Long, "Capital Budget Decision-Making Processes in Canadian Urban Municipalities" (Winter 1981), 24 *Canadian Public Administration* 634-40.

[3]Almost all of the Canadian literature appears in the form of memoranda or instructions drafted by either city administrators or provincially supported organizations and sent to local committees responsible for undertaking capital expenditures.

councils or provincially backed organizations[4] responsible for the control and the approval of all such expenditures. In addition to outlining budgetary procedures, this material frequently includes forms and reports, descriptions of what is and what is not a capital expenditure, calendar dates that must be adhered to for expenditure approval, guidelines for estimating costs, and any financial laws or regulations to be followed.

Control over local capital budgets and subsequent borrowing by local governments is exercised by municipal boards or commissions appointed by the different provincial governments or by the appropriate minister responsible for municipal affairs. The primary purpose of these supervisory bodies is to ensure that capital expenditures and borrowing costs never reach a level where they will push local governments into a financially insolvent state.

While some form of control exists in every province, the extent to which local governments are required to meet certain budgetary conditions and borrowing restrictions varies. For example, capital budgets detailing anticipated capital expenditures and sources of financing over a five-year period, are required by legislation in Nova Scotia, Manitoba, British Columbia, and Regina in Saskatchewan. In Quebec, the Montreal Charter requires the preparation of a three-year capital budget. For other provinces, although not required by legislation, capital budgets are prepared often.[5]

Limitations on long-term borrowing for the financing of capital projects exist everywhere. These limitations vary, however, in a number of ways. First, the authority responsible for approving the loan and/or its terms ranges from ministerial approval in Newfoundland, Nova Scotia, and Quebec to approval by the Inspector of Municipalities in British Columbia to approval by boards or commissions elsewhere. Second, the maximum term of the loan tends to correspond with the length of the life of the asset up to a maximum limit ranging from 40 years in Newfoundland, Prince Edward Island, Nova Scotia, Quebec, and Saskatchewan to 30 years in municipalities in New Brunswick, Ontario, Manitoba, and British Columbia. The maximum length of time is 25 years in Alberta. Third, a limitation on the amount of money borrowed is fixed by statute in Prince Edward Island where it cannot exceed a fixed percentage of taxes levied and in New Brunswick, Saskatchewan, and British Columbia where total borrowings must be less than a prescribed percentage of local property and business assessment. In Newfoundland and Alberta, there are no statutory limitations on total borrowings; however, in these two provinces and in Nova Scotia, Quebec, Ontario, and Manitoba, total local borrowing is controlled by the provincial body or minister (referred to above) responsible for approving all loans for capital projects. Fourth, the methods of raising revenue (including the establishment of sinking funds and/or the issuance of debentures) is closely controlled in some provinces and not in others. The method of this control frequently coincides with the approval for borrowing in all provinces with the

---

[4]For a summary of the various provincially supported commissions or boards, see Canadian Tax Foundation, *Provincial and Municipal Finances, 1981* (Toronto: the Foundation, 1981), Chapter 8.

[5]See A. Beedle, *Accounting for Local Government in Canada, The State of the Art* (Vancouver: The Canadian Certified General Accountants' Research Foundation, 1981), 215. For more detail on this point and those in the following paragraph of the text, see supra footnote 4.

exception of Prince Edward Island and Manitoba where there are no restrictions on the types of debentures that can be issued. Fifth, while all long-term borrowing must be approved by the relevant provincially supported body responsible for overseeing all loans, the local electorate must also approve such borrowing in Quebec and in some instances, British Columbia (local residents must approve all projects unless the debt is incurred for local improvements, water and sewerage projects, public utilities, or facilities shared or constructed by the provincial or federal government). In other provinces (Prince Edward Island, Nova Scotia, Manitoba, and Saskatchewan), specific consent of the people is not required unless the minister or council dictates that it need be. No approval is required by the electorate in Alberta, Ontario, and New Brunswick as long as loans are contained within their statutory limits (where they exist) and as long as they cover the generally accepted capital expenditures associated with the local infrastructure necessary for any municipal operation. To the extent that a debt must be incurred for any capital structure not essential to the municipal operation (for example, large auditorium, theatre, or arena complex), local resident approval may be required in each and every province. Sixth, in every single province, local governments receive assistance for raising revenue for capital projects either through the opportunity of borrowing directly from a specific commission or the provincial government or through assistance in marketing their local debentures.

DIFFICULTIES WITH THE CAPITAL BUDGETING PROCESS

The most obvious constraint on municipal capital spending is the requirement that the bulk of capital expenditures must be approved[6] by a governing body superior to local councils and their related boards and commissions. The extent to which these governing bodies oversee local capital spending and/or their financing varies from province to province. In some provinces, such as Ontario, control is fairly extensive and includes an annual review of all capital projects along with a five-year capital budget. A request for approval to undertake capital expenditures must also include a detailed description of the projects along with detailed specifications and drawings for these projects. Finally, the means of financing the impending capital projects must be outlined and must include a presentation of the way in which the money is to be raised, the types and terms of the borrowing to be undertaken, and the length of time over which the borrowing may last. In other provinces, such as Prince Edward Island, control over capital spending is less stringent. Capital budgets need not be submitted to higher governing bodies and municipalities are not required to outline details of the specific types of financing to be undertaken. Instead, the governing agency is interested only in the total request for capital projects and the subsequent borrowing which is required for financing these projects. Their primary concern is, clearly, that of ensuring financial solvency and this objective cannot be criticized as some municipalities do not have levels of management expertise sufficient to assess fully and carefully the impact of these expenditure programs on their local budgets and hence their local community.

---

[6]Capital expenditures financed from current revenue as opposed to borrowing need not always be approved by the governing body.

A number of issues arise and must be carefully addressed in exercising control over local capital budgets. For example, is the control too stringent or too relaxed and does it adequately and effectively achieve the objective it is designed to achieve? Are capital budgets comprehensively and carefully integrated into growth management programs? Is the impact of capital expenditures on local operating budgets fully and accurately considered? Do grants for capital projects distort local budgetary decisions? These, along with other issues, will be discussed in the following few paragraphs.

In some provinces, a number of criticisms have been levied against the strict requirements imposed by the provincial government or its agent regarding capital budgeting.[7] It is generally considered that provincial authorization and review of total borrowings are advantageous. Whether such authorization and control should reasonably be extended to include detailed drawings and descriptions of the capital project to be undertaken, however, is questioned frequently. In the case of sewers, for instance, it may be the case that the approving body must be told the size of the sewers, their exact locations, and numerous other matters of a highly technical nature in addition to the total borrowings for which the municipality is applying. From the point of view of the municipality, these details appear to be matters for which provincial controls are neither necessary or desirable. If the rationale for a body approving all local capital projects is the maintenance of financial solvency, then this body ought to be concerned with controlling total borrowing and not specific projects. On the other hand, if this agency is to be used as a device for controlling the specific capital projects to be undertaken, it is likely to involve an unnecessary duplication of work and to be more time-consuming than alternative schemes such as the distribution of capital grants to local governments for projects deemed by the provincial government to be desirable.

Additional criticism has been levied against the length of time it takes to seek provincial approval for the implementation of a specific project. In some instances, the approval period stretches into several months with the consequence that neither the call for tenders nor the beginning of the project may be conducted at the ideal time of year.[8]

Unfortunately, the effects of capital budgeting with the consequent expenditures on future operating and maintenance costs are frequently ignored or casually projected. Concern about this issue was recently expressed by the Association of Municipalities of Ontario. This organization agreed that provincial grants for local capital expenditures on recreation and cultural facilities must be made only after a careful assessment of all on-going operating and

---

[7] For example, section 64 of the Ontario Municipal Board Act states that a municipality in Ontario shall not authorize, proceed with, or provide money for "any undertaking, work, project, scheme, act, matter or thing," where the cost or any portion of the cost is to be raised in subsequent years or provided for by debentures "until the approval of the Board has first been obtained." It is significant that under this section the Board is required not only to approve the expenditure, but also to approve the proposed project.

[8] For a detailed assessment of the various stages of capital budgeting, and some possible suggestions for improvements as it applied to Metropolitan Toronto, see S.M. Makuch and K.D. Jaffary, *Local Decision-Making and Administration*, A Study for the Royal Commission on Metropolitan Toronto (Toronto: the Commission, June 1977), 55-63. Many of these comments apply to capital budgeting at the local level in all provinces.

programming costs was undertaken.[9] Clearly, the intent here is to protect local governments from costly burdens in the future. There is, unfortunately, little evidence of municipalities accurately and seriously estimating the future financial impact of current local capital expenditures.

A recent survey of Canadian urban municipalities (48 respondents with populations in excess of 75,000 people) indicated that an alarmingly large proportion failed to consider many of the costs that will have an impact on future budgets. It was observed, for example, that most municipalities (83 per cent) considered debt costs but considerably fewer considered annual maintenance and operating costs (54 per cent), contributions from current revenues (48 per cent), opportunity costs (4 per cent), and other miscellaneous costs (2 per cent).[10] Without the inclusion of all major cost components, the use of cost estimates is of limited value and potentially misleading. A further and equally disturbing finding suggested that in those cases where costs were calculated effectively, the information was often not made available to decision makers or else it was presented too late and/or in a format that prevented decision makers from recognizing the importance of the material and using it effectively in their decision-making processes.[11] Finally, the survey results suggested the existence of a direct and positive correlation between the size of the muncipality and the comprehensiveness of the costs considered. Larger urban or regional areas tend to have the resources required to undertake reasonably sophisticated and detailed financial impact studies;[12] whereas smaller municipalities lack both the technical expertise and specialized personnel to conduct such detailed studies and as a result, much of their assessments of future impacts tend to be more judgmental and frequently less accurate. These local governments can receive from provincial governments, on request, assistance for such studies; unfortunately, such requests are seldom made.

A further and frequent criticism of local capital budgeting practices revolves around the claim that local governments frequently undertake projects for which grants contribute a large proportion of total construction costs. Examples abound and are prevalent in every province; a few will suffice in support of this claim. Historically, bridges and roads have been subsidized in different proportions. In Ontario, the purchase of parkland in river valleys qualifies for provincial grants from the conservation authority, while similar purchases elsewhere attract no subsidy. The construction of sanitary sewers and sewage treatment plants attracts federal subsidies but sewage separation projects, designed to forestall the need for new treatment facilities, do not qualify for a subsidy.[13] These are a few examples of situations where provincial and federal programs induce municipalities to spend in ways that may not accurately reflect

---

[9]The Association of Municipalities of Ontario, *Capital Funding for Cultural and Recreational Facilities*, AMO Reports, no. 41 (Toronto: the Association, September 1980).

[10]Supra footnote 2.

[11]Ibid.

[12]For evidence on one city, specifically Toronto, see Harry M. Kitchen, *Public Finance in Metropolitan Toronto*, A Study for the Royal Commission on Metropolitan Toronto (Toronto: the Commission, 1977), 74-5.

[13]Supra footnote 8, at 61.

municipal priorities. This practice has led, moreover, to inefficiencies in the allocation of local resources.

A stated policy objective of local policy makers and administrators has been to integrate capital programs and growth management objectives.[14] The available evidence suggests, unfortunately, that this integration has been and is considerably less than espoused. First, capital programs and budgets have often been drawn up or altered without the consent or involvement of all local departments or officials. This lack of coordination between local departments has created situations where capital maintenance or construction of a specific project may not be coordinated with other capital projects in the same or following years. For example, one frequently observes the construction or maintenance of sidewalks or roadways and shortly afterward the tearing up of these facilities to construct or replace sewers or water mains. Such uncoordinated efforts prove to be costly and difficult to justify. Second, further problems abound because capital projects often represent political compromises and compliances with legal approval dates (calendar) rather than well-thought-out plans for community improvement. The notion that capital projects flow smoothly from well-organized community plans to implementation simply has not been borne out. Among the reasons for this is the likelihood that a number of development or management decisions are made in a public forum. For example, as was indicated earlier, the electorate is involved in approving capital projects in some municipalities. However, these forums are never able to cover all aspects of community planning such as the maintenance, renewal, and construction of new projects. While the overall policy may include an integrated approach to capital programs and growth management objectives, this objective can be paid only lip-service. The sheer numbers of people involved and their interest in only selected aspects of the overall plan place constraints on the actual achievement of this objective.

A final issue in the capital budgeting process is that the largest proportion of capital expenditures, in general, tends to be devoted to rehabilitation and renewal projects—projects that are basically short term in nature. This emphasis on short-term projects has arisen because of (1) the reluctance of local decision makers or advisers to become locked into long-term projects without guarantees of future funding and (2) concern about the impact of future annual interest and debt repayment charges on local budgets. While municipalities may be required to raise only a small portion of the initial total capital cost, a substantial financial burden may still arise from debt financing in subsequent years.

FINANCING CAPITAL EXPENDITURES

It is possible for a municipality to pay for capital expenditures out of current operating revenues, special assessments, lot levies, grants from provincial and/or federal governments and their agents, reserves and reserve funds, borrowing, or from a number of smaller sources including the proceeds from sales

---

[14]For a summary of the limited U.S. evidence on this topic, see Michael J. White, "Capital Budgeting," in John E. Petersen and Catherine Lavigne Spain, eds., *Essays in Public Finance and Financial Management: State and Local Perspectives* (Chatham, New Jersey: Chatham House, 1978).

of fixed assets, prepaid special charges, income from investments, donations, and miscellaneous revenue. Even though the use of these smaller sources represents very small sums of revenue, they do allow municipalities to avoid the use of revenue from the other more significant categories.

Given that municipalities in every province have a choice of financing capital expenditures from the above alternatives, the choice may vary from province to province and may be subject to certain statutory or nonstatutory restrictions. Statutory or regulatory restrictions are imposed in all provinces by the provincially supported body responsible for overseeing local solvency. Restrictions of a nonstatutory or nonregulatory nature may also apply from time to time in all provinces. Examples of these restrictions follow:

1) When the cost of a particular project is extremely high in relation to the operating budget, the financing of this project from current revenues often creates severe increases in a municipality's mill rate, increases that may not be justified especially if the benefits from this asset are to be spread out over future years and future users. In this instance, long-term borrowing may be an appropriate device for raising capital funds.

2) A further restriction on the type of financing (and one which may dictate greater use of own-source revenues as opposed to borrowing) may arise in instances where some boards or commissions—particularly school boards—engage in capital borrowings that are substantial enough to absorb virtually the entire borrowing capacity (as defined by the regulatory bodies) of a particular jurisdiction. The consequences of this action would prevent the municipality in question from undertaking additional borrowing, hence forcing this local area into alternative funding if capital expenditures were to be incurred.

3) Problems might arise in instances where regional governments exist. For example, if the upper-tier government is responsible for raising capital funds through borrowing for both itself and the lower-tier municipalities (as it is in Ontario), then the allowable debt capacity may be absorbed entirely by one level of government, thus preventing other governments in the same jurisdiction from borrowing activities. Fortunately, there is currently no evidence in Ontario to suggest that this has been a problem.[15] There is, however, nothing to indicate that it may not be a problem in the future.

While the specific choice of the revenue source for financing capital projects may be dictated by situations similar to those outlined above, this is not likely to be true for the majority of municipalities. Authorities, instead, will be faced with the alternatives of paying for the project directly out of current operating funds; using revenues from special assessments or lot levies; financing it by using reserves and reserve funds; or borrowing on a short-term or long-term basis. The choice of the appropriate alternative may not be an easy one and may vary depending on the location and size of the borrowing community, its credit rating, its fiscal capacity for meeting capital expenditures out of current revenues, and its anticipated future expenditures.

---

[15]For information supporting this, see Ontario, *Local Government Finance in Ontario, 1978* (Toronto: Municipal Finance Branch, Ministry of Treasury and Economics, 1979), 74.

FUNDING FROM OPERATING REVENUES

In principle, the financing of capital projects out of current revenues may be desirable if the benefits from the projects accrue to the users in the immediate period. However, capital expenditures seldom generate benefits of such a short-term nature and if the benefits do accrue solely in the short run, there is a practical argument against financing the project out of current operating revenues; this may result in an immediate heavy property tax burden on local residents.

Regardless of the rationale for the use or non-use of current operating revenues, some evidence exists on the extent to which municipalities use these as a means of financing capital expenditures (Tables 6.2 to 6.7 provide data for the only provinces that record it in the form required for the purposes of this discussion). Rural municipalities including villages, smaller towns, and some districts or regions tend to finance larger proportions of their capital expenditures from current operating revenues. This is due, in part, to the greater difficulty that these municipalities encounter vis-à-vis larger urban areas in borrowing for capital projects and to the prevalence in smaller centres of paying for all expenditures (whether capital or operating) out of local operating revenues.

The type of financing used also pertains to the nature of the capital expenditure. For assets with a short life expectancy (such as police cars and possibly fire engines) or expenditures of a recurrent nature (such as the annual maintenance and upgrading of sidewalks, roads, street lighting, and parks), there is a greater tendency to finance from current operating funds. For expenditures of a nonrecurrent nature (libraries, museums, buildings, and larger fixed assets) or with a longer life expectancy (sewer lines and water works), there is a greater tendency to utilize other sources of revenue—primarily long-term loans.

Whether or not operating revenue funds are used depends on the level of capital assistance obtained in the form of grants from the federal and/or provincial authorities. If grants account for a large percentage of total expenditures, then the net cost to the municipality may be low enough to allow the municipal share to be financed from current revenues. Indeed, the available evidence, both in tabular form displayed in this section and in written documentation elsewhere,[16] supports this contention.

Finally, the tendency to depend on operating revenue funds as a means of financing capital expenditures is greater in Ontario and the western provinces than in the East. This can be attributed partially to (1) the lower levels of capital expenditures taking place in the East as a result of reasonably stable local populations and (2) previously developed municipal infrastructures. Moreover, the provincial governments in Atlantic Canada tend to be more responsible for direct engagement in or financial support of local capital projects.

Revenues drawn from operating funds are occasionally generated by a "capital levy." While this type of levy may be misnamed (in the sense that it is not designated as a separate levy on the tax bill), its use involves the addition of a few mills (for example, 4 mills in Hamilton) to the mill rate employed for

---

[16]Ibid., at 85, for evidence in Ontario.

Table 6.2   Composition of Municipal Capital Financing by Size of Municipality in Nova Scotia, 1978

Size of municipality	Borrowing			Reserves	Revenue fund	Grants	Other revenue	Unapplied from previous period
	Debentures	Short-term	Total					
				per cent				
Cities..........	25.4	42.9	68.3	1.3	1.8	12.5	5.8	10.4
Towns..........	21.5	38.7	60.2	1.9	13.4	10.9	1.7	12.1

Source: Calculated from data in Nova Scotia, *Department of Municipal Affairs Annual Report of Municipal Statistics for the Year 1978* (Halifax: Queen's Printer, 1981).

Table 6.3   Composition of Municipal Capital Financing by Size of Municipality in New Brunswick, 1979

Size of municipality	Borrowing				Reserves	Revenue fund	Grants	Other revenue	Unapplied from previous period
	Debentures	Other term[a]	Short-term	Total					
					per cent				
Cities	17.5	5.3	42.7	65.5	.1	2.7	15.2	3.7	13.0
Towns	19.1	5.1	41.0	65.2	.7	2.1	15.0	1.9	15.2
Villages	23.4	10.5	28.2	62.1	.4	4.9	21.6	2.4	8.8

[a]These borrowings were from agencies such as the Central Mortgage and Housing Corporation or Department of Regional and Economic Expansion or from banks, credit unions, or Winter Capital Project Loans.

Source: Calculated from data in New Brunswick, Department of Municipal Affairs, *1979 Annual Report of Municipal Statistics* (Fredericton: the Department, 1980).

Table 6.4   Composition of Municipal Capital Financing by Size of
Municipality in Ontario, 1978

Size of municipality	Borrowing	Reserves and reserve fund	Revenue fund	Other revenues
		per cent		
Metro Toronto				
Upper-tier	44.5	1.5	31.1	22.9
Lower-tier	20.5	37.2	20.4	21.9
Regions				
Upper-tiers....................	6.5	3.7	89.1	0.8
Lower-tiers				
100,000 plus	50.2	16.0	13.8	20.0
50,000-99,999	45.9	10.4	29.5	14.3
25,000-49,999	46.1	14.2	27.2	12.5
10,000-24,999	28.7	23.9	33.9	13.5
5,000-9,999	12.0	20.3	48.9	18.7
2,500-4,999	16.5	8.1	49.1	26.3
1,000-2,499	11.2	4.5	51.4	32.9
under 1,000	7.9	7.3	50.6	34.2
Districts				
Lower tiers				
100,000 plus	41.9	22.8	18.3	17.0
50,000-99,999	66.6	4.1	20.8	8.4
25,000-49,999	15.3	43.8	11.6	29.3
10,000-24,999	2.8	11.4	24.7	61.0
5,000-9,999	18.3	16.4	39.2	26.0
2,500-4,999	0.5	15.6	51.6	32.2
1,000-2,499	6.9	14.5	54.9	23.7
under 1,000	9.0	11.4	48.1	31.5

Source: Ontario, *Local Government Finance in Ontario, 1978* (Toronto: Municipal Finance Branch, Ministry of Treasury and Economics, 1979), 87.

financing operating expenditures. Revenues generated by this levy are transferred from the operating revenue fund to reserves or the reserve fund for future capital projects or used in the current year to finance current capital expenditures. In general, such a levy tends to be used by larger municipalities who have ongoing capital expenditures.

SPECIAL ASSESSMENTS

Capital projects have been financed by using special assessments[17] for many years in many Canadian municipalities. In essence, a special assessment is a specific charge or levy imposed on residential and/or commercial/industrial properties to pay for additional or improved capital facilities that border on these local properties. Examples of such projects include the construction or reconstruction of sidewalks, the initial paving or repaving of streets, and the installment or replacement of water mains, sanitary and storm sewers. In each instance, the abutting property is presumed to benefit from the local improvement and, therefore, expected to bear a portion or all of the capital costs.

[17]Special assessments are levies on existing property and differ from lots levies or development charges, which are imposed on new property developments.

Table 6.5   Composition of Municipal Capital Financing by Size of Municipality in Manitoba, 1979

Size of municipality	Borrowing				Prepayments	Reserves	Revenue fund	Grants	Other	Unexpended
	Debentures	Bank	Other	Total						
					per cent					
Cities...............	28.6	17.6	13.2	59.4	.1	6.0	4.2	12.4	12.0	6.1
Towns...............	20.2	3.1	25.0	48.3	2.9	7.8	26.1	3.3	6.1	5.6
Villages.............	—	6.6	9.3	15.9	—	6.5	61.9	—	13.7	2.1
Local government districts..	—	—	—	—	—	7.1	80.0	—	.9	12.1
Rurals..............	7.8	—	.7	8.5	.1	39.0	32.1	1.2	17.4	1.7

Source: Calculated from data in Manitoba, *1979 Statistical Information Respecting the Municipalities of the Province of Manitoba* (Winnipeg: Department of Municipal Affairs, 1980).

Table 6.6   Composition of Municipal Capital Financing by Size of Municipality in Alberta, 1979

Size of municipality	Long-term debt	Transfers[a]	Other[b]	Unexpended funds
		per cent		
Cities	41.4	43.2	6.3	9.2
Towns	35.2	39.1	16.0	9.7
Villages	33.1	45.8	11.1	10.0
Counties	24.7	54.7	11.2	9.4
Municipal districts	7.7	77.0	7.1	8.2
Improvement districts	7.3	85.7	4.4	2.6

[a]Includes grants, transfers from reserves, reserve funds, and revenue funds. [b]Includes short-term borrowing.

Source: Calculated from data in Alberta, *Municipal Statistics Including Improvement Districts and Special Areas for the Year Ended December 31, 1979* (Edmonton: Alberta Municipal Affairs, 1981).

In apportioning the local charge on the benefiting properties, a number of bases can be used including: (1) foot frontage, (2) area (size) of lot, (3) assessed value of benefiting properties, (4) zone within the benefiting area (that is, all properties located in the benefiting area are levied a charge), and (5) direct benefits as measured by the increase in property values.[18] The foot frontage basis is by far the most commonly used in apportioning charges (Table 6.8).

Table 6.8 displays the variation in the extent to which special assessments are used in different municipalities. While there is considerable variation in the proportion of any local improvement project financed by abutting properties both within the same province and across provinces, there is less variation in the bases used in apportioning the costs. The foot frontage basis is employed in most instances. Municipalities in Quebec (Table 7.1) rely more on special assessment charges than do those in other provinces. As well, their assessment bases tend to display greater variety than those used elsewhere. Paving costs in Quebec are assigned on the basis of foot frontage, while levies for road construction may assume foot frontage or land values. In addition, general revenue may be used to finance these expenditures. Similar variations in financing local improvement charges are evident for other local projects.

Although special assessments tend not to contribute significant sums of revenue to local budgets, they are, nevertheless, an important means of financing local improvement projects. They provide a useful method of allocating costs according to benefits and so answer the demand for publicly provided facilities. This allocation of costs on the basis of benefits received does not suggest that income distribution issues are unimportant; rather it indicates that income distribution policies are more properly a function of either the provincial governments or federal government.[19] Indeed, the primary objective at the

[18]For a description of these, see Tax Foundation, Inc., *Special Assessments and Service Charges in Municipal Finance* (New York: the Foundation, 1970), 11-12; and Richard M. Bird, *Charging for Public Services: A New Look at an Old Idea* (Toronto: Canadian Tax Foundation, 1976), 107-9.

[19]For a strong defence of the efficiency model as a basis for funding local expenditures, wherever possible, see George F. Break, *Financing Government in a Federal System* (Washington, D.C.: Brookings Institution, 1980), Chapter 5.

Table 6.7   Composition of Municipal Capital Financing by Size of Municipality in British Columbia, 1979

Size of municipality	Borrowing			Reserves	Revenue fund	Grants	Other	Unapplied from previous period
	Long-term	Short-term	Total					
				per cent				
Cities............	11.7	21.8	33.5	10.2	10.8	6.4	6.7	32.2
Districts.........	23.4	15.1	38.5	9.5	20.0	9.3	10.0	13.1
Towns...........	23.6	28.1	51.7	2.4	24.6	6.8	2.1	12.4
Villages.........	22.9	27.7	50.6	3.7	18.2	10.6	4.6	12.3

Source: Calculated from data in British Columbia, *Municipal Statistics, Including Regional Districts, for the Year Ended December 31, 1978* (Victoria: The Ministry of Municipal Affairs, 1983).

Table 6.8   Special Capital Levies, Ontario Municipalities, 1971

Municipality	Special capital levies as per cent of total revenue[b]	Amount and basis of levy[a]					
		Sidewalks	Pavement[c]	Water main	Sanitary sewer	Storm sewer	Off-street parking
Borough							
Scarborough	1.28	50%; FF[d]	100%; FF	$5/FF (max.)	$10/FF (residential), $24/FF (commercial)	0	0
Cities							
Hamilton	n.a.	40%	40% cost	0	$8.50/FF	0	0
Sault Ste. Marie	0.33	25%; $2.50-4/FF	25%; $5-6/FF	0	90%; $6.50/FF	30%; $3.00/FF	0
Kingston	3.03	40%	40%	80%	80%	15%	100%
Sarnia	3.62	80%; $4.89/FF	80%; $4.89/FF	50%; $7.77/FF	50%; $7.77/FF	5%; $7.66/FF	0
Peterborough	2.70	60%	60%	100%	100%	100%	0
Cornwall	2.02	60%	60%	100%	100%	100%	0
Waterloo	2.61	40-75%	40-75%	50-75%	50-75%	30-60%	50%
Barrie	1.16[e]	100%; FF	100%; FF	100%; FF	100%; FF	0	0
Towns							
Oakville	1.66	0	0	60%; $7/FF	60%; $7/FF	0	0[f]
Richmond Hill	1.12	0	0	100%	100%	25%	0
Timmins	0.70[g]	50%	0	0	100%	0	0
Kapuskasing	2.65	0	0	66⅔%	66⅔%	0	0
Ajax	0.0	0	0	0	0	0	0
Orangeville	n.a.	100%	100%	0	0	0	0
Picton	0.0	0	0	0	0	0	0
Vaughan	1.42	FF	FF	FF	FF	0	0
Townships							
Pickering	n.a.	h	h	100%; FF	100%; FF	0	0

aPercentages refer to per cent of cost to be covered by special levy. bSix-year average (1965-70) except where otherwise indicated. cPavements constructed as local improvements. dFront footage basis. eTwo years only. fPaid out of parking revenue. gThree years only. hAlthough streets, sidewalks, etc., are paid for out of general revenues, street lighting is paid for by a special rate on the assessed value of properties within defined street-light areas.

Source: Richard M. Bird, *Charging for Public Services: A New Look at an Old Idea* (Toronto: Canadian Tax Foundation, 1976), 110.

local level ought to be a concern with the adoption of an efficient pricing policy for the provision of local public goods.

In principle, the imposition of special assessments must be supported as a means of financing those projects whose benefits can be assigned to specific properties.[20] For those projects whose benefits are more widespread or incapable of being assigned to specific properties, funding from general revenue sources is clearly more justified. The principle of user pricing as applied to local improvements is clearly an ideal policy to accept. The accurate apportionment of these costs to abutting properties is, however, somewhat more difficult to achieve.

Difficulties in apportioning these costs to abutting properties arise in the attempt to measure accurately the value of benefits that will accrue to local properties, and hence, in assessing the proper charge to be imposed on the neighbouring land and buildings. For example, a common approach to financing the capital costs of sidewalk construction or replacement is to charge the bordering properties between 40 per cent and 60 per cent of the total construction costs, leaving the municipality with the responsibility for raising the rest of the funds. Similar policies exist for other local improvement projects. Whether or not the percentage assigned to abutting properties is correct (in that it truly measures the additional benefits to local properties) is a matter of some conjecture. Obviously, attempts to measure these extra benefits are neither easy nor precise and, at best, local authorities must frequently resort to crude calculations of the additional benefits. The argument that municipalities can improve their estimation techniques and thus charge more accurately may be legitimate; however, the important point is that local governments are clearly operating on the right principles by assigning some, but not all, of the costs of most local improvements to abutting properties.

Further difficulties arise in correctly selecting the basis for apportioning the costs to individual properties. Foot frontage tends to be the most commonly used basis and this seems particularly appropriate for financing projects such as water distribution and sewage collection lines where the cost per connection increases with the number of feet of pipe between connections. Charges for any local improvement whose cost per piece of property is directly related to the width of the lot can be justified on this basis. For projects such as neighbourhood parks whose benefits tend to accrue to particular areas or blocks within a community, the zone method of assessment may be best in allocating a portion of the total cost to properties within the serviced area.

The argument that the three remaining methods of allocating costs (lot size, property value increase, and assessment value increase) are justifiable implies that they are superior to either foot frontage or zone assessment. Clearly, this is difficult to justify in principle and/or in practice. Lot size has been suggested as a proxy for the depth of lot where the distance of the house from the street affects the cost of the service. Lot size, however, is neither a close proxy for lot depth nor does it necessarily bear a close relationship to the actual costs of constructing or replacing local services as they pass through or by abutting properties. Where it is necessary to run the service from the street to the house, a more

---

[20]For a fuller justification of this principle, see Bird, supra footnote 18, at 106-7.

accurate reflection of the costs would involve the use of foot frontage charges plus connection fees.

In theory, a rational and optimal charging policy dictates that properties benefiting from local improvement projects should contribute toward their costs in accordance with the value of the additional benefits received by each piece of property as reflected in increased property values. Although this policy seems like a sound approach, such an allocation initially requires extensive checking and record keeping to calculate the increase in property values and also requires assurances that the increase or a specific portion thereof is solely a result of the work completed. Obviously, such accuracy in estimating the benefits and hence the appropriate charge to be levied is difficult, if not impossible, to calculate.

The assignment of charges according to assessed values or increases in assessed values of properties abutting the local improvement project is also fraught with difficulties. There is no sound reason, other than ease of administration, to indicate that assessed values should be adopted, since assessed values are unlikely to be highly or directly correlated with increases in values attributed to the specific project.[21] In addition, increases in assessed values may arise from factors other than the local improvements undertaken and thus capture more than the increase due to the public works themselves.

DEVELOPMENT CHARGES

Virtually all municipalities in Canada are entitled to impose development charges on properties benefiting from local improvements or additional capital facilities. Generally, these charges, which are a relatively new phenomenon, can be separated into cash imposts and lot or unit levies. Cash imposts are usually referred to as additional lump-sum charges levied on certain buildings, the erection or enlargement of which may necessitate a larger water or sewer system than would otherwise be required. Lot or unit levies usually apply to new urban developments and are justified on the basis of covering the cost of providing services specifically designed for the use of the occupiers or future occupiers of the land within the subdivision or to meet expenditures incurred by reason of the subdivision. The imposition of these imposts or levies involves an agreement between the developer and the municipality, whereby the developer is required to pay a levy to the municipality to finance specific services.

Revenues collected from lot or unit levies, such as water and sewage impost charges, are generally kept in a special fund. While water and sewage charges must cover only the expenditures for which they are assigned, surpluses from lot levies or any contributions that are not required for the purpose for which they are levied can frequently be spent on other purposes.

A comparison of the magnitude of lot levies is difficult for at least two reasons. First, not all municipalities levy such charges for the provision of services. Instead, they require developers to provide services that would otherwise be furnished through special charges. Second, it is difficult to obtain data on a comparative basis within one province let alone all of Canada. One recent study

---

[21]Ibid., at 108-9.

based on standardized lots for 12 cities in Ontario in 1978, displayed this existing variation. During that year, a single-family unit levy ranged from $250 per lot (lowest) in one city to $2,328 per lot in another city (highest). Similarly, multiple unit levies based on standardized lots ranged from $100 per unit (lowest) to $1,500 per unit (highest).[22] In a second study based on individual municipalities within five adjacent regions including and surrounding Metropolitan Toronto, reported total lot levies (local plus regional) ranged from $0 to $4,610 per single-family detached units in 1979.[23]

If the objective is to charge property owners for services specifically accruing to their property, then the imposition of development charges is more economically efficient than a general tax levy imposed on all property owners regardless of whether the services apply to the property or not. In addition, these charges are easy to administer and inexpensive to collect.

If, as is generally the case, revenues collected from water and sewer imposts are applied specifically to the costs associated with enlarging or expanding these services, then economic efficiency is improved. On the other hand, if the revenue from lot levies is either too high in comparison with the actual costs of development or if it is expended on projects not directly related to the development, as may be the case, then new homeowners end up subsidizing existing property owners.

Additional distortions arise when lot levies vary on identical properties among municipalities. This may be an incentive for some developers to build in specific areas in order to avoid the charges. While this is unlikely to be a serious problem in most parts of the country, it is noticeable in large metropolitan or regional areas with different political jurisdictions.

Because municipalities tend to treat residential property differently from commercial/industrial property, a further distortion is created. The majority of municipalities in Ontario do not impose development charges on commercial and industrial property, whereas many of these same municipalities impose such charges on residential property.[24] The imposition of development charges on property owners (residential and commercial/industrial) affects property prices, although it is not yet entirely clear to what extent this happens. Accurate charges for specific services applied to all properties using the services have different effects than do variable charges on different types of properties (that is, residential or commercial) in different geographical locations.

Since both lot levies and special assessments are used for financing similar municipal projects, a brief comparison of a few of the implications arising from each is useful. While each of these may be considered as a method of capturing the benefits from a specific project, special assessments are often superior to lot levies. Part of this advantage lies in the formula adopted for allocating the costs of the service installed. Special assessments are applied after the project has been initiated or completed, whereas lot levies are imposed, in most instances,

---

[22] *Planning Administration and Development Control in the Region of Waterloo* (Waterloo: Waterloo Region Review Commission, 1978), 348.

[23] David P. Amborski, "Lot Levies: Service Pricing to Finance Urban Growth" (mimeograph, Ryerson Polytechnical Institute, Toronto, January 1980), 32.

[24] Supra footnote 22, at 372-74.

before the development begins. The determination of special assessment charges is potentially fairer (on the benefits received criterion) and more efficient because it is designed to capture the actual costs incurred. Lot levies, on the other hand, are paid in advance with their values being determined by a pre-arranged formula. Unfortunately, this application of lot levies is frequently inefficient and unfair for each development faces its own peculiarities and hence, different costs. What is needed is an individually designed levy for each development, and this has occurred in a few instances, only after sufficient pressure has been applied to alter the prescribed levy. This outcome of "arbitrary rules with the possibility of individual adjustment has often been to maximize political conflict in the process, and inequity and inefficiency in the results."[25]

The application of lot levies also shifts more of the financing costs onto developers with the consequent tendency of blocking development and creating inefficiencies in the allocation of resources. Special assessments, on the other hand, tend not to distort the allocation of resources in this way.[26] With a persistent decline in new development, the imposition of lot levies is likely to diminish. During these conditions, special assessments will increase in importance as a means of financing the improvement or replacement of existing capital projects.

RESERVES AND RESERVE FUNDS

Financing capital projects through the use of reserves and reserve funds[27] is, essentially, the reverse of financing via borrowing. Instead of borrowing to finance capital expenditures and repaying this debt in the future, reserves or reserve funds reverse that timetable. A portion of current revenue is annually set aside in a special account and allowed to accumulate until it is eventually withdrawn and used to finance or partially finance a specific capital project or projects. These reserves, while they are accumulating, are deposited in interest-earning accounts.

When aggregated by province, most municipalities, regardless of size, tend to place proportionately less reliance on reserves and reserve funds than on current revenues as a means of financing capital expenditures. In some instances, this difference is very large and often larger for smaller towns, villages, and rural areas than for larger urban areas (Tables 6.2 to 6.7).

Although the use of this revenue source is similar in distributional pattern to that observed for current revenues, (that is, it is employed to a greater degree in Ontario and the West than in Atlantic Canada), the precise explanation for this pattern is neither consistent nor obvious in all municipalities. Some available evidence does indicate, however, that local officials frequently do not plan their capital projects with the number of years or foresight required to establish a

---

[25]Richard M. Bird and Enid Slack, "Urban Finance and User Charges," rev. 1981, a paper presented at the Conference on State and Local Finance of the Committee on Taxation, Resources, and Economic Development (Cambridge, Massachusetts: the Committee, September 27, 1980), 16.

[26]Ibid.

[27]Reserve funds include funds for specific projects. Reserves include funds that are collected for nonspecific projects but that may be used for various capital projects. For a description of these, see Ontario, *Reserves, Reserve Funds, Allowances and Other Special Funds*, Financial Procedures Bulletin no. 5 (Toronto: Ministry of Intergovernmental Affairs, 1979).

reserve fund into which current revenues can accumulate until the project is to be initiated. Undoubtedly, part of this explanation is due to very little planning on the need for future capital projects, but occasionally, it is a direct result of the duration of time (one, two, or three years) for which representatives are elected to local office. Short terms of office lead to the introduction of a number of capital projects that are intended to maximize the possibilities of the re-election of local representatives. However, while lack of planning and office duration do affect the use of reserves, the expected or unexpected availability of local operating revenues or the availability of provincial and federal grants dictate the timing of many capital projects.

GRANTS

Local capital expenditures are frequently subsidized by both federal and provincial grants with the bulk of these grants coming from provincial sources (see Chapter 9). The rationale for specific (conditional) grants is generally clear cut. They are frequently offered to cover capital projects that the grantor feels are an important, if not an essential, component of the local scene or to cover the costs of projects generating spillover benefits (to other than the receiving community). The actual impact of these grants, however, occasionally leaves the local community with consequences that are not always desirable, necessary, or warranted. Local officials or administrators, all too frequently, select their capital projects on the basis of available grants. Projects for which a proportionately larger share of the total capital cost is borne by grants often take precedence over projects with less grant support even though the latter group may be more desirable or necessary to accommodate the true preferences or needs of the local residents. Although this distortion of local priorities is difficult to quantify, conversations with municipal officials suggest that it happens more frequently than is desirable. In order to avoid this distortion and to meet more effectively the demands of the local residents a greater use of unconditional grants is required. With this requirement met, it is alleged, local governments will be more inclined to spend their funds on projects that more accurately reflect the desires or demands of the local citizens. Of course, the other side of this argument arises when spillover or neighbourhood effects occur. In these instances, it might not be prudent or efficient to allow local governments to make decisions on the basis of their constituents' interests alone for such parochial decisions are unlikely to reflect the benefits or costs accruing to nonresidents.

The extent to which grants are utilized in financing local capital expenditures varies from province to province and from year to year. As was pointed out earlier in this chapter, the largest proportion of all grant revenue is devoted to the four major functions of education, environment, transportation and communications, and recreation and culture. Even though interprovincial and intertemporal consistency in local capital grant support is difficult to find, some comments can be made. The function education displays the most noticeable differences in grant support (Appendix Tables B.1 and B.2). The explanation for this, however, does not rest in differing local responsibilities for the ultimate assumption of these costs but rather in the timing of provincial assistance. For example, there are two ways in which provincial capital assistance can be provided to school boards or local governments: (1) provincial authorities may provide a grant to cover the entire capital expenditure prior to construction or (2) local governments or school boards may be required to borrow the funds to cover the expenditure and at a later date receive a grant from the province to cover the ensuing debt charges.[28] While this latter method was popular in the 1960s and early 1970s when education facilities were expanding, the former method has been more popular in recent years (Table 6.1), primarily because of the reduction in the demand for educational facilities and hence, a reduction in the requirement for funds.

Variation in grant support for local capital expenditures on transportation and communication facilities is recorded in Appendix Tables B.1 and B.2. The fact that local governments in some provinces have received relatively more grant support than those in others indicates changes in the population and industrial bases, along with the different emphases provincial governments place on expenditures of this nature. Clearly, expenditures on improving or extending transportation systems are highly visible. At election time, both provincial and local incumbents seeking re-election can point to a fairly extensive and relatively high-quality system as being a direct result of their political influence.

The changing importance of grant support for environmental, recreation and cultural facilities was noted earlier and need not be repeated here. (See Chapters 4 and 5.)

Whereas reserves, reserve funds, and operating revenues used in financing capital projects display some regional variations, they tend to conform to similar patterns when ranked by size of municipality regardless of the region of the country in which the municipality is located. Such consistency, however, is not evident in the dependence on grants. In New Brunswick (Table 6.3) and British Columbia (Table 6.7), villages or rural areas as opposed to large urban centres seem to place greater reliance on grants as a means of financing capital expenditures; whereas the opposite appears to be the case for municipalities in Nova Scotia (Table 6.2) and Manitoba (Table 6.5). In these latter provinces, grants seem to be more important for projects in larger urban areas than they are for ones in smaller rural or urban centres.

OTHER LOCALLY RAISED REVENUE

This category includes a number of unrelated revenue sources, such as revenue held over from previous periods; proceeds from the sale of fixed assets; investment income; private donations for specific capital projects; prepaid special charges or contributions made by landowners for projects benefiting them; and a number of smaller, miscellaneous items. The volatile nature of most of these items contributes to the impossibility of drawing any pattern based on regions or size of municipality. In some instances, larger urban areas exhibit greater dependence on these sources, while the opposite is apparent in other areas. Perhaps the only significant conclusion one can draw from the available data is that the total of all sources constituting this category account for a reasonable portion of capital funds. In fact with very few exceptions, this category supplied more than 15 per cent of all capital funds in 1978 and 1979 (Tables 6.2 to 6.7).

---

[28]Supra footnote 4, at 237-39.

BORROWING

Short-term borrowing at the local level may be used to finance capital expenditures or to cover an unexpected deficit in a municipality's operating budget. In this latter instance, the deficit must be eliminated by budgeting for sufficient revenue in the ensuing year. Long-term borrowing, on the other hand, is restricted to the financing of capital expenditures alone. Ideally, borrowing for capital projects can be justified as long as the benefits from the project are expected to fall on future users. The project is financed by borrowed funds and the principal and interest charges are repaid out of future operating revenues. Such a policy attempts to match up future beneficiaries with those who bear the costs.

Short-Term Borrowing

Short-term local government borrowing takes many forms including bank loans and/or the issuance of bills, certificates, or notes sold to banks or other investors. Short-term capital borrowing is used to finance some capital projects whose life expectancy is rather short. More importantly though, frequently it is used for the purpose of financing a series of smaller projects until these projects can be consolidated and refinanced through longer-term debt. Market conditions frequently dictate the type of financing to be undertaken. When interest rates are high, municipalities will defer long-term borrowing in anticipation of lower interest rates in the future. Such a policy leads to a greater dependence on short-term borrowing and current operating revenues as a means of financing capital projects.[29] Finally, the timing of forthcoming capital grants may necessitate a greater reliance on short-term borrowing. If receipt of the capital grant is dependent on the completion or partial completion of the capital project, then the municipality may be required to borrow in order to bridge the gap between payments for construction of the project or purchase of the asset and the actual receipt of the grant.

Regardless of the rationale for short-term borrowing, it is used extensively in all provinces and in most municipalities when arranged by size (Tables 6.2 to 6.7). In fact, where the data are available, the dependence on short-term borrowing as a means of financing capital projects almost always exceeds long-term borrowing and in some cases is more than twice as important as long-term borrowing (Tables 6.2 and 6.3). In the past two or three years with comparatively high long-term interest rates, this differential in the dependence on short- versus long-term borrowing has been increasing.

Long-Term Borrowing

Long-term borrowing tends to be closely scrutinized and in some cases restricted by the provincial department or agency responsible for overseeing the activities of local governments. Municipalities borrow directly from private lenders, from other governments, or from departments, agencies or provincial corporations designed to assist in providing funds for specific projects. For example, a number of housing-related projects are financed partially by funds borrowed from Canada Mortgage and Housing Corporation and/or from provincial

---

[29]Supra footnote 15, at 85.

ministries or departments responsible for housing services. In addition, the Ministry of the Environment frequently provides loans for municipal sewer and water projects. Provinces offer specific loans for projects deemed to be important within their specific political jurisdiction. These include, for example, loans for tile drainage and shore line assistance in Ontario and for capital projects undertaken in the winter in New Brunswick. Low-interest loans to municipalities are also provided through various provincial corporations in Ontario including the Universities Capital Aid Corporation (for which the rate of interest is lower than the market rate and the funds are allocated for specific projects) and the Municipal Improvement Corporation, (acts as a lender of last resort and accepts lower than market interest rates on loans to municipalities with populations less than 20,000, the proceeds of which may be used for general municipal purposes).

Other types of provincial loan assistance range from nothing more than a general commitment by the provincial government to formal guarantees on loan repayments for money borrowed by local governments for all capital projects in Prince Edward Island (under the Town and Village Debenture Guarantee Act) to an arrangement whereby a provincial agent or body such as the Municipal Finance Authority in British Columbia[30] and the Municipal Finance Corporation in Nova Scotia[31] lend the required capital funds to the requesting municipality in their own province. In these latter two provinces, the authority or corporation acts by issuing debentures on itself and lending the proceeds to the requesting municipality. A number of approaches lie between these extremes. In New Brunswick, the provincial government (under the Clean Environment Act) defrays part of the cost of preventing pollution and establishing water works by guaranteeing repayment of loans and by paying all or part of the interest costs on the borrowed funds. In Quebec the Department of Municipal Affairs and the Quebec Municipal Commission supervise the marketing of local debentures, while the Municipal Budgets and Finance Branch of the Department of Municipal and Urban Affairs in Manitoba undertakes the preparation of local debentures for all local capital requests. In Saskatchewan and Newfoundland the Municipal Finance Corporation purchases a portion of municipal debentures. And finally in Alberta, the Alberta Municipal Financing Corporation assists local governments by purchasing and selling municipal debentures.

The Ontario financing scene is perhaps the most complicated, unstable, and inefficient. In this province, regional governments have been charged with the responsibility of raising capital funds for all area municipalities within their boundaries. At the same time, even the smallest municipalities outside of regional governments have debt issuing powers. Given that the size of the municipality tends to be negatively correlated with the interest attached to debt instruments, smaller communities outside of regional governments generally pay higher servicing costs than similarly sized municipalities within regional

---

[30]Vancouver may raise its own revenue if it chooses; otherwise, all other municipalities must borrow for long-term projects from the Municipal Finance Authority. School and hospital facilities are not financed by debenture sales through the Municipal Finance Authority.

[31]Halifax can decide whether to borrow from the Municipal Finance Corporation or to borrow on its own.

governments. The scene is complicated further by the fact that school boards have the power to issue their own debt instruments, thus creating a situation where two bodies from the same locality may be competing simultaneously for the same pool of funds.

A significant source of long-term borrowing in most provinces is the public market where municipalities issue serial debentures and/or sinking fund debentures. Serial debentures[32] are issued for a given number of years with a certain number reaching maturity and being redeemed by the municipality each year. Serial debentures may take different forms including annuity serials, straight serials, and irregular serials.

Annuity serials are similar to home mortgages in that the total interest and principal repayment is roughly the same throughout the life of the security. In the early years, the interest portion of the payment is higher and in later years the principal portion is higher. Straight serials require annual principal payments of approximately equal amounts. Interest payments are higher in the early years and decline as the securities approach maturity. Irregular serials involve a "balloon maturity" date, that is, a significant portion of the principal is postponed until the full term of the issue is reached. While this type of debenture is disallowed in all provinces except Ontario and Quebec, its use in these two provinces is not that extensive. In fact, it is not used in Ontario at all.

In choosing a particular type of serial debenture, a number of considerations must be weighed. Annuity serials may be favoured in instances where capital projects must be built with a capacity large enough to service additional users in the future. Examples of municipal projects that may be financed in this way include water and sewage plants, schools, fire stations, and police stations, all of which are constructed on the basis of meeting a current and potentially expanding population base. Under this financial arrangement, a municipality is able to avoid heavy debt service charges in the early years of the project and to redistribute the costs in a more equitable and manageable manner.

Straight serial debentures carry heavier debt charges in earlier years than in later years (see Table 6.9 for a comparison of debt charges on straight versus annuity serials). From a municipality's point of view, this has the advantage of lowering the interest charge and thus freeing the municipality for future borrowing without increasing the annual debt servicing charges. For most capital projects, however, this method of financing may violate the rationale of equating those who receive the benefits from the capital project with those who bear the cost. Indeed, acceptance of this criterion provides a stronger basis for utilizing annuity rather than straight serials for most capital projects, yet most municipalities prefer to adopt straight serial debentures rather than annuity debentures. In fact, a highly accurate equating of individuals who receive benefits from capital projects with those who carry the costs is not at the heart of a municipality's decision once it has decided to borrow through serial debentures. Instead, simplicity and ease of marketing along with minimizing the debt servicing charge are of prime importance. To meet these objectives, straight

---

[32]For a detailed discussion of serial bonds, their advantages, disadvantages, and use in the United States, see Alan Walter Steiss, *Local Government Finance* (Lexington, Massachusetts: D.C. Heath, 1975), 113-16.

Table 6.9   A Comparison of Debt Service Charges on One Million Dollars over Ten Years Using Straight and Annuity Serial Debenture Financing

Payable at end of year	Straight serial debentures				Annuity serial debentures			
	Outstanding principal	Principal repayment	Interest payment[a]	Total debt charges	Outstanding principal	Principal repayment	Interest payment[a]	Total debt charges[b]
	dollars							
1	1,000,000	100,000	150,000	250,000	1,000,000	49,252	150,000	199,252
2	900,000	100,000	135,000	235,000	950,748	56,640	142,612	199,252
3	800,000	100,000	120,000	220,000	894,108	65,136	134,116	199,252
4	700,000	100,000	105,000	205,000	828,972	74,906	124,346	199,252
5	600,000	100,000	90,000	190,000	754,066	86,142	113,110	199,252
6	500,000	100,000	75,000	175,000	667,924	99,063	100,189	199,252
7	400,000	100,000	60,000	160,000	568,861	113,923	85,329	199,252
8	300,000	100,000	45,000	145,000	454,938	131,011	68,241	199,252
9	200,000	100,000	30,000	130,000	323,927	150,663	48,589	199,252
10	100,000	100,000	15,000	115,000	173,264	173,264	25,988	199,252
Total	—	1,000,000	825,000	1,825,000	—	1,000,000	992,520	1,992,520

[a]15 per cent of outstanding principal. [b]Total debt charges $= \text{Principal } \dfrac{i(1+i)^n}{(1+i)^n - 1}$ where i = interest rate and n = number of years.

serial debentures have a simpler maturity schedule, are easier to understand, and quicker to market than annuity serials. As well, the nature of the money market may dictate that straight serials rather than annuity serials be issued if debt service charges are to be minimized. For example, the interest rate on straight serials may vary with their maturity dates. If longer-term interest rates are noticeably lower than shorter-term interest rates, then the issuance of straight serial debentures provides a means of lowering interest charges by bringing a larger proportion of the principal under the lower interest rate. On the other hand, if the demand for short-term money is abnormally high, there is little advantage in competing for it, unless of course, the municipality assumes that interest rates are going to rise in the future in which case it may wish to finance through borrowing now rather than later. This uncertainty about the effect of inflation on interest rates has substantially reduced the availability of long-term money. As a result, many municipalities are opting for greater dependence on current revenues, reserves and reserve funds, and where essential, limited borrowing.

Irregular serials known as "balloon issues" can be used in financing capital projects where there is some uncertainty as to the amounts that will be available for servicing the debt after the construction costs have been met. When combined with the creation of reserve funds, these serials can be justified as an adequate basis for funding certain local capital projects. By comparison, sinking-fund debentures are issued to mature at a fixed future date. Each year the municipality pays an agreed sum of money to a trustee who, in turn, invests the portion that is not immediately applied toward paying the debt or discharging the obligation. The funds invested by the trustee must be used to purchase a somewhat restricted list of securities including: (1) those directly issued by or guaranteed by the federal, provincial, or municipal governments themselves; (2) securities stipulated in the Trustee Act of the province in which the municipality is located; and (3) occasional investments in chartered banks, public corporations, and countries where the municipality has outstanding debentures payable in that country's currency.

The bylaws authorizing the existence of sinking fund debentures provide for annual contributions by the municipality in amounts necessary to provide a sinking fund sufficient to retire the principal amount of each issue of debentures at maturity. In calculating the interest income from securities purchased by the sinking fund, legislation dictates that an interest rate of no more than 5 per cent per annum can be employed in estimating the dollar value of the sinking fund. Since virtually every security being purchased by the sinking fund generates interest income of more than 5 per cent, surpluses are earned. These surpluses, with the permission of the trustee, may be used to make up tax arrears, to compensate for any discount on the issuance of debentures, to meet foreign exchange losses on debenture principal and interest, to redeem debentures in advance of maturity where this is allowed, and to meet deficiencies that may exist in other sinking funds.

For a few yet significant reasons, local governments and their borrowing agencies tend to place a greater reliance on serial rather than sinking-fund debentures. Sinking funds are more expensive and more difficult to administer because they require expert advice on the investment of funds along with frequent actuarial computations to ensure that adequate funds will be available to cover the principal payment at maturity. As well, the types of securities that can be held in sinking funds are closely restricted and they frequently generate less revenue than is obtainable from other safe securities. The inflexible maturity dates of sinking-fund debentures seem to create more difficulties in marketing these securities when compared with serial debentures.

Sinking funds, on the other hand, provide at least one benefit for the municipality and that is the opportunity of selling their own securities to the sinking fund. This is especially advantageous when market conditions do not favour the public issuance of new debentures; however, it appears that this advantage is not sufficient to outweigh the substantial administrative costs associated with the operation of sinking funds.

Large municipalities, with access to larger markets and better credit ratings, tend to place a greater dependence on the issuance of debentures as a means of financing capital expenditures. Smaller municipalities are more likely to borrow on a long-term basis from various federal or provincial departments or agencies that lend money for specific capital projects.

The relatively high interest rates in the past few years have caused municipalities to decrease their dependence on public debentures as a means of financing capital projects. Instead, there has been an increasing reliance placed on short-term borrowing, reserves, operating revenues, and even deferment of a number of capital projects. Deferment of long-term borrowing in anticipation of comparatively lower long-term interest rates can lead to substantially lower debt costs for any particular municipality. For example, a small decline in long-term interest rates can much more than compensate for the higher short-term costs in holding back an issue. The ability of a municipality to alter the time for issuing public debentures suggests that annual capital expenditures need not follow the same pattern as annual debenture borrowing.

Distribution of Debenture Debt

Table 6.10 sheds light on the level and distribution of debenture debt issued by municipalities for general purposes or on behalf of their enterprises. The level of per capita debenture debt outstanding in 1978 was almost $300 in Saskatchewan and between $300 and $400 in each of the provinces in Atlantic Canada. By comparison, Ontario and Manitoba recorded debenture debt levels of slightly less than $600 per capita. Figures for the provinces of British Columbia ($947), Quebec ($1,034), and Alberta ($1,162)[33] were above the Canadian municipal average of $708.

Regardless of the province cited, the bulk of these debentures was issued for general capital projects. More specifically, over 73 per cent of all debentures for all municipalities combined was issued for general capital purposes with school facilities absorbing another 21 per cent and utilities slightly more than 5 per cent. With the exception of local governments in Newfoundland, New Brunswick, and Quebec, where the proportion of debentures issued for general

Table 6.10 Distribution of Per Capita Debenture Debt Outstanding for Local Governments and Their Enterprises by Purpose and Province, 1978

Purpose	Nfld. $[a]	Nfld. %[b]	P.E.I. $	P.E.I. %	N.S. $	N.S. %	N.B. $	N.B. %	Que. $	Que. %	Ont. $	Ont. %	Man. $	Man. %	Sask. $	Sask. %	Alta. $	Alta. %	B.C. $	B.C. %	All prov. $	All prov. %
General																						
Serial	303	84.7	155	39.9	231	59.2	316	95.1	732	70.8	366	62.8	130	21.8	113	38.1	692	59.5	251	26.5	449	63.4
Sinking fund	55	15.3	66	17.0	10	2.6	7	2.0	79	7.6	n.a.	n.a.	220	37.0	65	21.9	10	.9	323	34.2	71	10.1
Schools																						
Serial	N.A.	N.A.	136	35.0	145	37.2	N.A.	N.A.	222	21.4	165	28.3	182	30.6	99	33.3	188	16.2	13	1.3	103	14.5
Sinking fund	N.A.	N.A.	24	6.1	2	.5	N.A.	N.A.	n.a.	n.a.	19	3.3	6	.9	16	5.3	n.a.	n.a.	360	38.0	47	6.6
Utilities																						
Serial	—	—	8	2.0	1	.3	9	2.8	—	—	32	5.6	4	.8	0	0	259	22.3	0	0	34	4.9
Sinking fund	—	—	—	—	1	.3	0	0	—	—	—	—	53	9.0	4	1.3	14	1.2	—	—	4	.5
Total																						
Serial	303	84.7	299	76.9	378	96.7	325	97.9	956	92.4	564	96.7	317	53.2	212	71.5	1139	98.0	264	27.8	586	82.8
Sinking fund	55	15.3	90	23.1	13	3.3	7	2.1	79	7.6	19	3.3	279	46.8	85	28.5	24	2.0	683	72.2	122	17.2
Total debenture debt	357	100.0	389	100.0	391	100.0	332	100.0	1034	100.0	583	100.0	596	100.0	297	100.0	1162	100.0	947	100.0	708	100.0

[a]All $ figures are per capita. [b]All per cents are a percentage of the total.

N.A.—not applicable. n.a.—not available. —nothing borrowed.

0—very small sums borrowed.

Source: Calculated or recorded from data in Appendix Table B.3.

capital purposes was considerably higher than the national average, general capital debt accounted for approximately 60 per cent of outstanding debenture debt in the remaining provinces.

Debenture debt issued for school facilities displayed as much variation as for general capital projects with Newfoundland and New Brunswick's local governments carrying no debt at all for this purpose. At the other extreme was Prince Edward Island, Nova Scotia, Saskatchewan, and British Columbia, where school debenture debt amounted to roughly 40 per cent of outstanding long-term debt (Table 6.10).

The issuance of similar debt instruments by local governments to cover utility construction was either non-existent or accounted for an extremely small proportion of total debenture debt issued in every province except for Manitoba (10 per cent of total debt) and Alberta (22 per cent of total debt).

Of all the long-term debt issued, serial debentures were utilized far more extensively than sinking-fund debentures in every province with the exception of Manitoba (53 per cent in serial versus 47 per cent in sinking-fund debentures) and British Columbia (28 per cent in serials versus 72 per cent in sinking funds). While the overall proportion of serial to sinking-fund debentures was 83 per cent versus 17 per cent, serial debentures accounted for almost 100 per cent of outstanding long-term debt instruments in many of the provinces (Table 6.10).

The largest proportion of long-term debt instruments issued by municipalities for their own purposes or on behalf of their own enterprises was issued in Canada. In fact, almost 83 per cent of all outstanding municipal debentures in 1978 were distributed in the domestic market. On an interprovincial basis, the four provinces in Atlantic Canada, Saskatchewan, and Alberta concentrated their issues almost entirely in Canada (Table 6.11). Local governments in the remaining provinces marketed a significant proportion (between 14 per cent and 22 per cent of the total) of their debentures in the U.S. market with smaller offerings being made in European money markets.

Concentration in the domestic market has arisen for various reasons. Relatively higher bond ratings (discussed below) in Canada than elsewhere have caused local governments in Atlantic Canada to market their securities domestically. The willingness of provincial governments to purchase the securities of local governments and their enterprises has been a major factor in the extent to which local governments have marketed bonds in Canada. When compared with the other provinces, the provincial governments in Newfoundland, Prince Edward Island, and Alberta hold proportionately larger amounts of local government securities. The existence of the Alberta Heritage Trust Fund has created a large agency, which in the past, has purchased large sums of securities from various governments in Canada. As of March 1982, however, this policy has changed with the Alberta Heritage Trust Fund now concentrating on securities from Alberta-based governments alone. Pension funds, insurance companies, financial institutions, and the general public have all played a major role in purchasing debentures from local governments.

The rise of foreign money markets, as a source of capital funds, exists for large urban municipalities or municipal financing authorities or corporations who are seeking large sums of money and are able, because of their size, to secure these funds with lower debt servicing costs.

Table 6.11   Distribution of Outstanding Debenture Debt Classified by Place of Payment and Province, 1978

Payable in	Newfoundland	Prince Edward Island	Nova Scotia	New Brunswick	Quebec	Ontario	Manitoba	Saskatchewan	Alberta	British Columbia	All provinces
						per cent					
Canada only	100.0	99.8	100.0	99.3	73.1	86.5	76.9	94.8	98.3	81.8	82.9
England only	—	—	—	—	0.0	—	—	—	—	0.0	0.0
United States only	—	0.2	—	0.7	21.8	13.5	22.1	5.2	1.7	14.5	14.7
United States and Canada	—	—	—	—	—	—	—	—	—	0.4	0.1
England, United States, and Canada	—	—	—	—	0.0	—	—	—	—	0.0	0.0
Switzerland	—	—	—	—	2.4	—	—	—	—	0.5	1.0
Germany	—	—	—	—	2.6	—	1.1	—	—	2.8	1.4

—   nothing borrowed.   0.0—very small sums borrowed.

Source: Calculated from data in Statistics Canada, *Local Government Finance, 1978*, Cat. no. 68-204, Table 17.

Impact of Annual Debenture Debt Charges

One of the major concerns facing local officials is the impact of annual debt charges on local budgets. Unfortunately, much of this concern is ex post, that is, the concern is expressed after the debt charges have been incurred, not prior to the initiation of capital projects that create the debt servicing charges.

Table 6.12 records per capita local debenture debt charges, separated into interest charges, serial principal payments, and sinking-fund requirements for 1978. In every province with the exception of Saskatchewan (46 per cent), interest charges absorbed close to 60 per cent or more of total debenture debt charges (calculated from Table 6.12). At the same time, the range in per capita values extended from a low of $36.32 in Newfoundland to a high of $145.73 in Alberta. Regionally, per capita debenture debt charges tend to be lower in Atlantic Canada than elsewhere.

When compared interprovincially, local governments (in aggregate) in those provinces displaying the lowest per capita debenture levels (Newfoundland, Prince Edward Island, and New Brunswick) tended to devote the highest proportion of own-source revenues and unconditional grants to servicing this debt (Table 6.13). To be more precise, almost 44 per cent of these revenues in Prince Edward Island were required for meeting debenture debt charges in 1978. Similar figures for Newfoundland and New Brunswick were 31 per cent and 24 per cent respectively. At the other extreme in absolute per capita debenture debt levels, were local governments in Quebec, Alberta, and British Columbia (Table 6.12) — the only provinces with average per capita debt levels above the national average. At the same time, local debt servicing commitments in each of these provinces absorbed about 21 per cent to 27 per cent of local own-source revenues and unconditional grants. This figure was above the national average for 1978 (Table 6.13). While absolute per capita debenture debt levels in the remaining provinces (Nova Scotia, Ontario, Manitoba, and Saskatchewan) fell

Table 6.12   Per Capita Local Debenture Debt Charges[a] by Province, 1978

Province	Interest charge	Serial principal	Sinking-fund requirement	Total
		dollars		
Newfoundland	27.54	6.80	1.98	36.32
Prince Edward Island	27.66	14.45	2.73	44.84
Nova Scotia	34.47	28.42	b	62.89
New Brunswick	26.70	19.85	.04	46.59
Quebec	83.41	45.18	4.3	133.24
Ontario	46.64	36.88	b	83.52
Manitoba	49.48	32.95	1.85	84.26
Saskatchewan	22.87	23.24	3.69	49.80
Alberta	87.37	58.36	—	145.73
British Columbia	87.04	26.20	15.73	128.97
All provinces	61.89	37.35	3.15	102.40

[a]Includes debenture debt issued by local governments for general and school purposes or by local government enterprises (utilities). [b]Sinking-fund requirements included with serial principal. —nil.

Source: Calculated from data in Statistics Canada, *Local Government Finance, 1978,*Cat. no. 68-204, Table 10.

Table 6.13   Debenture Debt Charges as a Per Cent of Own-Source Revenue plus Unconditional Grants,[a] by Purpose and Province, 1978

Purpose	Nfld.	P.E.I.	N.S.	N.B.	Que.	Ont.	Man.	Sask.	Alta.	B.C.	All prov.
					per cent						
General											
Interest	23.3	13.0	5.6	13.5	12.6	5.2	5.3	2.4	7.7	9.6	7.9
Serial principal	5.4	6.2	4.1	9.9	6.5	3.7	3.8	2.4	4.7	4.0	4.6
Sinking-fund requirement	1.7	1.9	b	0.0	.9	b	—	.5	—	.6	.3
Total general	30.4	21.1	9.7	23.4	20.2	8.9	9.0	5.3	12.4	14.2	12.9
Schools											
Interest	—	13.3	3.5	n.a.	4.0	2.3	2.8	1.8	2.7	4.6	3.1
Serial principal	—	7.2	3.5	n.a.	2.2	2.0	2.0	1.9	2.2	.2	1.9
Sinking-fund requirement	—	.7	b	n.a.	—	b	—	.2	—	1.6	.2
Total schools	—	21.2	7.0	n.a.	6.2	4.3	4.8	3.9	4.9	6.4	5.1
Utilities											
Interest	.1	.8	.1	.4	.1	.4	.8	0.0	3.4	0.0	.5
Serial principal	.3	.7	.1	.4	.1	.5	.2	0.0	2.4	0.0	.5
Sinking-fund requirement	—	—	b	b	—	b	.3	0.0	—	.4	.1
Total utilities	.4	1.4	.2	.8	.1	.8	1.4	.1	5.8	.4	1.1
Total interest	23.3	27.0	9.3	13.9	16.6	7.8	8.9	4.3	13.9	14.2	11.5
Total serial principal	5.8	14.1	7.6	10.3	9.0	6.2	5.9	4.4	9.3	4.3	7.0
Total sinking-fund requirement	1.7	2.7	b	0.0	.9	b	.3	.7	—	2.6	.6
Total debt charges	30.8	43.8	16.9	24.2	26.5	14.0	15.2	9.3	23.1	21.0	19.1

Totals may not add precisely due to rounding.   [a]Unconditional grant revenue is included, as municipalities may use this revenue to pay debt charges.   [b]Sinking-fund requirements included with serial principal.   0.0—signifies very small amount.   —nil.   n.a.—not applicable.

Source: Calculated from data in Statistics Canada, *Local Government Finance, 1978*, Cat. no. 68-204, Tables 1 and 10.

between the extremes cited above, the annual service charges associated with this debt absorbed a smaller proportion of own-source revenues and unconditional grants.

With only one exception (Prince Edward Island), the bulk of local debenture debt service charges applied to the financing of capital projects for general purposes with schools accounting for most of the remainder. Total general debenture debt servicing charges, overall, exceeded those for schools by a factor of 2.5. Interprovincially, the range in this differential was more extreme with local governments in Newfoundland and New Brunswick displaying zero charges for schools, while those in Prince Edward Island incurred debt service charges that were equal for both school and general purposes. Utilities, by comparison, accounted for an insignificant proportion of total debenture debt servicing charges in all but one province (Alberta).

While the amounts incurred on debenture debt servicing charges are large enough to absorb a significant proportion of budgetary revenues, these amounts are not the only debt servicing charges that are incurred for funding capital expenditures. Additional interest charges arise from other long-term borrowings and some short-term borrowings. To provide an indication of the relative importance of each of these sources of revenue, Table 6.14 records interest charges as a percentage of own-source revenue and unconditional grants. In essence, neither of these charges is very significant, yet each of them does increase the total interest charges that must be financed out of local revenue in each of the provinces.

Characteristics of Debenture Debt

While securities issued as serial or sinking-fund debentures may take different forms, they generally come under the heading of general obligation bonds or special tax revenue or assessment bonds, or some combination of the two. General obligation debentures are issued for specific projects such as libraries and schools and frequently are viewed by investors as the safest type of municipal bond. They are fully backed by municipalities and because municipalities are creatures of the province, they are ultimately backed by the provincial governments themselves. Obviously, the bond rating (see below) and hence interest rate payable on the securities are functions of the economic base of the municipality and therefore reflect its ability to redeem the security at maturity.

Special tax, revenue or assessment debentures are quite common and are issued for a number of projects including arenas or community centres, water and sewer facilities, curbs, sidewalks, and roads. As distinct from general obligation debentures, these debentures are repaid or partially repaid from proceeds derived from special taxes or charges or from a special assessment levied against the users (or property) who directly benefit from the facilities constructed. To facilitate the marketability of these securities, most municipalities have pledged to guarantee them fully in the event that the revenue from the special tax, charge, or assessment is insufficient to meet the redemption value.

If one accepts the criterion of charging the beneficiaries for the cost of constructing the projects, then one must favour the issuance of special tax, revenue,

Table 6.14   All Interest Charges as a Percentage of Own-Source Revenue
plus Unconditional Grants,[a] 1978

Province	Interest on debenture debt	Interest on other long-term borrowing	Short-term borrowing	total
	per cent			
Newfoundland.........................	23.3	2.0	.4	25.7
Prince Edward Island	27.0	.6	1.4	29.0
Nova Scotia	9.3	.5	1.4	11.2
New Brunswick	13.9	.1	.9	14.9
Quebec...............................	16.6	.4	2.9	19.9
Ontario..............................	7.8	0.0	.2	8.0
Manitoba	8.9	—	.8	9.7
Saskatchewan	4.3	.1	1.6	6.0
Alberta...............................	13.9	.2	.2	14.3
British Columbia......................	14.2	.2	.7	15.1
All provinces	11.5	.2	1.0	12.7

[a]See note a in Table 6.13.   0.0—signifies very small amount.   —nil.

Source: Calculated from data in Statistics Canada, *Local Government Finance, 1978*, Cat. no. 68-204, Tables 1 and 10.

or assessment bonds in instances where the benefits from capital projects can be specifically assigned to individuals or property. If on the other hand, the benefits from capital projects are widely dispersed or if it is impossible to assign benefits to specific individuals or property, a case can be made for utilizing general obligation bonds. In most cases, municipalities attempt to follow this criterion in issuing debentures.

A number of municipalities have added a "callable" feature to their debentures. In essence, this gives the municipality the right to purchase back the debenture either at any time prior to maturity or after a stipulated number of years. If the bonds are called in before maturity, it is stated that the issuer will pay the holder a specified premium which is an amount added to the face value of the debenture.

The "callable" provision offers a number of distinct advantages for the issuing municipality over fixed-term securities. Depending on its financial circumstances, the municipality has a period of time in which it can exercise its option to redeem the securities prior to maturity. This may be desirable if the local government's saving in interest cost is greater than the premium which it must pay on early redemption. It may also be desirable in instances where the objective is to convert old debt into new debt or where the wish is to smooth out the debt retirement operation. The major disadvantage of the "callable" provision is that it injects an element of uncertainty into the security issued. This uncertainty may be manifested in slightly higher interest rates than would otherwise be paid and/or premium payments for early retirement.

Municipalities in their quest for capital funds have discovered a need for some flexibility in the terms and conditions assigned to their securities if they are to appeal to the changing desires of potential investors. Two features have been added (over the past few years) as a sweetener in attempting to market local bonds; these are: extendability and retractability. Extendable debentures are issued currently by municipalities only in the provinces of Ontario and Manitoba. In essence, this feature allows the holder to continue holding the security for a period of a further five years at the interest rate stipulated on the original debenture. Obviously, the prime advantage of this security rests with the holder, who may exercise his option to continue receiving higher interest rates at a time when rates on comparable securities elsewhere have fallen. Similarly, retractable debentures are designed to attract potential investors. This feature, which is used more extensively than in the case of extendables, allows an investor to dispose of the debenture prior to the maturity date, a situation that would likely arise if interest rates on alternative securities were higher than on the outstanding debentures. The main advantage for the municipality of features such as these is that local governments are able to make their securities more marketable and thus attract investors who want to ensure a certain level of financial security at a time of uncertain inflation rates.

Bond Rating

Perhaps the most important factor involved in long-term borrowing is the interest rate attached to the securities to be marketed, for it is this rate that plays a major role in determining the timing and type of financing to be undertaken and hence, the burden on the borrower. Municipalities, therefore, are extremely concerned about their bond rating for it is this rating that largely dictates the rate of interest (and other special features) necessary to make the bonds marketable.

For municipalities not faced with the prospect of raising revenue through debenture issues, ratings are unnecessary and almost never undertaken. If a municipality is, however, interested in marketing its debentures beyond the local community, the establishment of a bond rating is virtually a prerequisite before the major investors will become involved. A rating is established by a major rating service (the best-known include Moody's Investors Service and Standard and Poor's Corporation)[34] either at the request of the municipality or voluntarily if the bond issue is extremely large. This rating involves a rather detailed and current assessment of a municipality's capacity to bear debt and its capacity to raise revenue under normal and depressed economic circumstances. A municipality's bond issue is rated only in terms of its credit risk and not in terms of its investment merits.

Designed to meet investors' needs of objective and uniform quality differentiation among a vast universe of fixed-income securities, the bond rating system has both absolute and relative characteristics. The system is absolute in

---

[34]In the past few years, the Canadian Bond Rating Service has ventured into bond rating services for Canadian municipalities. While still relatively new, this agency presented ratings for the City of Saskatoon and the Regional Municipality of Sudbury in 1980-81. A fundamental difference exists between the approach taken by U.S. agencies (Moody's or Standard and Poor's) and that taken by the Canadian Bond Rating Service. The American agencies rate an individual issue (and not the municipality itself) and then monitor conditions for this issue during its lifetime. This is important to note, as the specific terms and provisions of an issue can alter its rating. The Canadian agency, by comparison, appears to be rating the overall strength of the municipality itself and then monitoring (for an annual fee) the financial status of the municipality.

distinguishing between solid grade and speculative grade issues. Solid grade issues are those whose risks are deemed to be minimal or moderate and are very likely to return principal and interest. Such issues carry ratings of either triple A, double A, A, or triple B. If there are significant risks that a bond issue will not pay interest and principal, such an issue would be considered speculative and assigned a rating of a double B, B, triple C, double C, or C.

The system is relative in that within the two broad categories—solid and speculative—the ratings must rely on value judgments as to the safeness of each particular issue. It must also be noted that these ratings are not buy or sell recommendations, nor are they an indication of marketability or price of the security in question, nor are they an evaluation of performance quality. Instead, they address only credit quality or risk. Table 6.15 summarizes the general characteristics involved in the assignment of specific ratings for different bond issues. Obviously, all municipalities would prefer to have a triple A rating for this would lead to lower interest rates. While specific differentials in interest rates assigned to the different ratings are neither consistent among municipalities nor over time, it appears as if the difference between a triple A and a double A is in the order of one-half of a percentage point. For each consecutive lower rating, the differential rises by roughly one-quarter of a percentage point. In fact, if one assumes the differential is one-half of a percentage point and returns to Table 6.9 and recalculates the debt charges on the basis of 14.5 per cent, a 10-year savings of $27,500 arises under serial debentures, while the total 10-year debt charge under the annuity serial would be lower by $37,830. This may not seem like much but most municipalities only consider long-term borrowing in national and international markets if the total to be borrowed is not one million but many millions (for example, Winnipeg issued $35,000,000 in long-term debentures in 1977, the Municipal Finance Authority of British Columbia issued $98,000,000 in debentures in 1980). These savings, therefore, can be significant. For example, if $50 million is to be borrowed, this differential would lead to a savings of almost $1.4 million dollars in interest payments over 10 years under straight serials and almost $1.9 million under annuity serials.

Table 6.16 provides a listing of bond ratings on United States issues of Canadian municipal bonds by two rating agencies. All municipalities listed recorded a rating of triple B or better. This is not surprising for these municipalities have a fairly solid economic base and are relatively large communities. Smaller communities or communities with a poor rating are not likely to engage in international marketing. Either they will finance their capital projects by other than issuing long-term debentures or else they will sell their debentures locally. In fact, in virtually every province, local authorities in smaller centres or economically depressed areas are encouraged to sell their debentures locally rather than in distant markets.

The inaccessibility to national and international capital markets faced by smaller municipalities in Canada or the generally lower credit ratings of these communities individually along with the lower rating for some larger urban areas suggests that all municipalities ought to give serious consideration to the formation of organizations such as the Municipal Finance Authority in British Columbia or the Municipal Finance Corporation in Nova Scotia. Clearly, the

Table 6.15   Comparison of Municipal Bond Rating Systems

Moody's Investor Service	Symbol	Symbol	Standard and Poor's Corporation
Best quality, carrying smallest degree of investment risk; referred to as "gilt edge"	Aaa	AAA	Prime; obligation of highest quality and lowest probability of default; quality management and low debt structure
High quality; rated lower than Aaa because margins of protection not as large	Aa	AA	High grade; only slightly less secure than prime; second lowest probability of default
Higher medium grade, many favorable investment attributes; some element of future risk evident	A	A	Upper medium grade; safe investment; weakness in local economic base, debt burden, or fiscal balance
Lower medium grade; neither highly protected nor poorly secured; may be unreliable over any great length of time	Baa	BBB	Medium grade; lowest investment security rating; may show more than one fundamental weakness; higher default probability
Judged to have speculative elements; not well safeguarded as to interest and principal	Ba	BB	Lower medium grade; speculative non-investment grade obligation; relatively high risk and uncertainty
Lacks characteristics of desirable investment	B	B	Low grade; investment characteristics virtually non-existent
Poor standing; issues may be in default	Caa	CCC	
Speculative in high degree; marked shortcomings	Ca	CC	Defaults
Lowest rated class; extremely poor prospects of ever attaining any real investment standing	C	C	

Source: Alan Walter Steiss, *Local Government Finance* (Lexington, Massachusetts: D.C. Heath, 1975), 137.

Table 6.16   Bond Ratings for Selected Canadian Municipalities

| Municipality | Bond ratings on U.S. issues of Canadian securities | | Canadian ratings of Canadian securities |
	Standard and Poor	Moody's	Canadian Bond Rating Service
Municipal Finance Authority of British Columbia	AAA	Aaa	—
Vancouver (B.C.)	AA	Aaa	—
Calgary (Alta.)	BBB[a]	—	—
Edmonton (Alta.)	AA[a]	A1	—
Regina (Sask.)	BBB[a]	—	—
Saskatoon (Sask.)	BBB[a]	—	AA
Winnipeg (Man.)	AA	Aa	—
Brantford (Ont.)	A[a]	—	—
Durham[b] (Ont.)	AA	Aaa	—
Hamilton-Wentworth[b] (Ont.)	AA	Aa	—
London (Ont.)	AAA	Aaa	—
Ottawa-Carleton[b] (Ont.)	AA	Aaa	—
Peel[b] (Ont.)	AA +	Aaa	—
Sudbury[b] (Ont.)	—	—	A
Metro Toronto (Ont.)	AAA	Aaa	—
Windsor (Ont.)	BBB	—	—
Metro Montreal (Que.)	A	A	—
Communauté Urbaine de Montréal (Que.)	A[a]	A[a]	—
Quebec City (Que.)	—	A	—
Saint John (N.B.)	A[a]	A[a]	—
Halifax (N.S.)	BBB[a]	—	—

[a]Not recently rated. [b]Regional municipality. —no rating reported.

Source: Wood Gundy Limited, *Financial Statistics: Canadian Provinces and Selected Municipalities,* 1981 ed. (Toronto: Wood Gundy, 1981), 12a.

advantages are immense. Local authorities simply apply for funds from the finance authority who in turn totals up all the requests for local funds and issues long-term debentures against the authority itself. When the proceeds are received from the sale of these debentures, the funds are dispersed to the requesting communities. In this way, the credit risk of the aggregation of all municipalities, which is of course backed by the province, is almost always less than that for each individual municipality—witness the credit rating (triple A) for the Municipal Finance Authority in British Columbia. An authority or agency acting for all municipalities has quick access to the necessary administrative machinery, qualified expertise, and best possible deal. In fact, the advantages are such that it is difficult to understand why organizations identical or similar to those in British Columbia and Nova Scotia have not been established in provinces whose municipalities are engaging in borrowing for capital projects.

Selection of Long-Term Debt

In earlier sections of this chapter, mention was made of situations in which municipalities used operating revenues, grants, reserves or reserve funds, or other revenue sources as opposed to borrowing in financing local capital projects. Borrowing, however, is favoured and used in a number of instances as follows:

1) Municipalities undertaking large capital projects are frequently unable to raise enough revenue from local sources without imposing prohibitively high mill rates or levies on the local residents.

2) Long-term borrowing tends to finance a proportionately greater share of capital expenditures in municipalities with higher population growth rates[35] since it is believed that future beneficiaries ought to pay the cost.

3) Borrowing is utilized more heavily in situations where there are specific beneficiaries but the local improvement costs would be too onerous to carry in one year.

4) Debenture borrowing is more prevalent in larger centres than in smaller centres and in municipalities with higher bond ratings than in those with lower bond ratings.

5) For projects with proportionately large grant support there is a greater tendency to finance the balance of the project with current revenues and/or reserves than with borrowing. If the support is relatively low, then the tendency to issue debentures to cover the balance increases.[36]

However, significant and recent increases in long-term interest rates have encouraged many municipalities to defer capital projects, to use own-source revenues more extensively, or to concentrate more heavily on short-term borrowing as a means of financing capital expenditures. Many of these actions, of course, are undertaken with the expectation of lower long-term rates in the future when long-term debentures may be issued.

SUMMARY

Changing demographic and population patterns have led to shifts in the locations and types of capital expenditures that have been undertaken. For example, the relative decline in the school-aged population has led to relatively lower expenditures on educational facilities. Population shifts from rural to urban centres have created demands for relatively higher expenditures on local public transportation and communication systems.

Higher incomes have created stronger demands for recreational and cultural facilities everywhere. The shift in economic activities away from eastern and central Canada to western Canada has created relatively higher demands for capital expenditures in the latter area and thus lower demands in the former areas.

Decisions as to whether capital projects should be completed are based, all too often, on incomplete or insufficient information. Seldom is full coverage of all current and future costs adequately considered in any decision on the

---

[35]For statistical evidence supporting this in Ontario, see supra footnote 15, at 83.

[36]Indeed, some limited evidence suggests that a number of municipalities, whose size or tax base is so small as to prohibit any borrowing, incur only those capital expenditures for which grant support is extremely high. In this case, it may be argued that grants exist partially because of a municipality's inability to undertake long-term borrowing. See supra footnote 15, at 86, for evidence on this.

feasibility of a particular project. Incomplete inclusion of future interst costs, for instance, has had a noticeable impact on future budgetary revenues.

Provincial control of capital budgets is designed to protect municipalities and their enterprises from engaging in capital expenditures that may be damaging to their future financial health or solvency. This control ranges from being relatively strict and detailed in some provinces to being relatively relaxed in others.

Undoubtedly, the financing of capital expenditures is one of the most important issues facing local authorities. Funds for these expenditures may be drawn from operating revenues, special assessments, lot levies, grants, reserves and reserve funds, short- and long-term borrowing, and a number of miscellaneous and relatively insignificant sources. While the choice among these different alternatives may be a complex matter, it tends to depend on one or more of the following factors: the interest cost of borrowing money; the availability of grants for capital projects; the acceptance of current tax increases to finance capital expenditures; the desire to tie the payment for capital expenditures to the beneficiaries of these expenditures; and a number of other political and/or economic factors. Of particular interest in the recent past has been the impact that inflation has had on the decision to incur capital expenditures. Many capital projects have been postponed indefinitely, while many others have been postponed until sufficient funds have been collected in reserves or reserve funds. For those projects for which postponement is impossible, recent borrowing through debentures has necessitated the addition of a number of "sweeteners" including extendable or retractable features in order to make these securities more appealing to potential investors.

Part III
Revenue Analysis

7
Local Government Revenue Patterns by Province, 1968-1978

INTRODUCTION

Local governments in Canada derive all of their powers from provincial legislation and as such, they are more confined than either the provincial governments or federal government in terms of their access to and control over revenue sources. Local governments are, for example, prevented from gaining direct access to the more elastic revenue sources of personal and corporate income taxation. Instead, they have been left with the real property tax as their only tax of any consequence and it is the allegedly inelastic base associated with this tax that has generated many of the revenue problems currently facing a large number of local governments. While revenue issues and alternative means of raising funds to cover these shortages are important considerations, it is not the purpose of this chapter to engage in such discussions. A full discussion of property taxes (Chapter 8), grants (Chapter 9), and other revenues (Chapter 10) and the implications arising from the usage of these various revenue sources will be covered later. By way of introduction to the various revenue sources, this chapter contains an outline and a discussion of the changes in the dependence of municipalities (aggregrated by province) on the different sources of revenue from 1968 to 1978.

In assessing the local revenue figures, at least four specific issues will be reviewed and commented upon. First, an interprovincial comparison of local revenue levels and the relative importance of the different revenue sources that make up the totals will be assessed. Clearly, substantial caution must be exercised in making these interprovincial comparisons because the absolute revenue levels will largely be dictated by whether or not the local government is responsible for providing certain services. In spite of this note of caution, it is useful to observe the actual revenue burden directly imposed by local governments on their residents. The availability of data for two specific years,[1] 1968 and 1978, (the first and last year for which data are available on an intertemporally and interprovincially consistent basis) provides a basis for making comments on the rate of increase and changing importance of these revenue sources for municipalities in Canada. Second, the deflation of current dollar revenue increases provides a base for comparing the real increase in local revenue sources. Third, the construction of an index reflecting per capita local revenues (aggregated across all municipalities) as a percentage of per capita gross domestic provincial product (GDPP) generates a common base against which

---

[1]It must be pointed out that limiting the time period ignores some significant shifts that occurred earlier in the post-war period. Data limitations, nevertheless, do not allow for an inclusion of the earlier years.

one can compare the significance of local revenue demands on real resources in the different provinces. Fourth, separation of revenue figures for urban areas provides the basis for a discussion of revenue sources by size of municipality.

AN INTERPROVINCIAL COMPARISON OF LOCAL REVENUE SOURCES IN CURRENT DOLLARS

From 1968 to 1978, the average increase in per capita revenues for all Canadian municipalities approached 220 per cent—rising from a low of $288 in 1968 to a high of $919 in 1978 (Table 7.1). In each of these years, municipalities in Atlantic Canada, on average, received revenues consistently and considerably lower than the national average. Clearly, much of this differential can be explained by the fact that municipalities in the Atlantic region do not have the same legislative responsibility for supplying local services as do local levels of government in the rest of Canada. For example, local governments in New-foundland and New Brunswick are not responsible for providing and funding the elementary and secondary education systems. Similarly, municipalities in these two provinces and in Prince Edward Island bear no responsibility for health and social welfare expenditures. Because of reduced expenditure com-mitments, therefore, the average municipality in Newfoundland (lowest) in 1978, collected $183 per capita, followed by New Brunswick ($224), Prince Edward Island ($585), and Nova Scotia ($739). By way of comparison, average per capita local revenues in the remaining provinces ranged from $848 in British Columbia (lowest of remaining provinces) to a high of $1,193 in Alberta (Appendix Table C.2).

Throughout this period, a number of significant trends began to emerge on the revenue side of the local finance picture. Own-source local revenues per capita (revenues collected from local taxes, user charges, grants-in-lieu of taxes, privileges, licences, permits, returns on investments, and miscellaneous other revenue) in absolute current dollar terms, more than doubled in every province except for Prince Edward Island where the increase was a relatively modest 21 per cent. At the same time, the relative importance of own-source revenues declined, with the average for all municipalities in Canada falling from slightly more than 64 per cent of all local revenues in 1968 to slightly more than 52 per cent of total local revenues in 1978 (calculated from Table 7.1). This decline of 12 percentage points in the relative contribution of own-source revenues was caused by greater than average declines in municipalities in Newfoundland, Prince Edward Island, Nova Scotia, New Brunswick, Quebec, Saskatchewan, and Alberta. Decreases in the dependence on own-source revenues, which were less than the national average, occurred in Ontario and Manitoba, while local governments in British Columbia averaged an increase in the utilization of own-source revenues by 5 percentage points (column 4, Table 7.2).

In reviewing the composition of own-source revenues, it is useful to note that the largest portion of the decline in the importance of this revenue source can be attributed to a decline in the dependence on local taxes and more specifically, on real property taxes. After all, it is the real property tax that has attracted most of the attention in discussions of local government finance. It is this tax that is highly visible and thus open to criticism. Property tax increases have been challenged in the courts, questioned in the press, and maligned by the public.

Table 7.1   Per Capita Local Revenues by Source, 1968 and 1978

Revenue source	1968			1978		
	Highest	Lowest	Average	Highest	Lowest	Average
			dollars			
Taxes						
Property.......	151 (Ont.)	12 (Nfld.)	121	406 (B.C.)	45 (P.E.I.)	296
Special assessment ...	23 (Que.)	0 (Nfld., P.E.I., N.B.)	11	27 (Que.)	0 (N.B.)	13
Business	20 (Ont.)	— (N.B.)	11	51 (Ont.)	— (P.E.I., N.B.)	32
Other	4 (Sask., Nfld., N.S.)	— (Ont., N.B.)	1	21 (Man.)	— (P.E.I., N.B., Alta.)	7
Total taxes	176 (Ont.)	18 (N.B.)	144	432 (B.C.)	46 (P.E.I.)	348
Grants in-lieu- of taxes	23 (Que., N.B., Alta.)	2 (B.C., Sask.)	14	43 (Man.)	— (P.E.I., N.B.)	19
Sales of goods and services......	21 (Alta.)	4 (Nfld.)	12	143 (Alta.)	19 (Nfld.)	77
Other own- source revenue ...	33 (Alta.)	3 (N.B.)	15	81 (Alta.)	4 (Nfld.)	36
Total own- source revenue ...	220 (Alta.)	42 (Nfld.)	185	593 (Alta.)	86 (P.E.I.)	480
Unconditional grants	4 (N.S.)	0 (Nfld., N.B., P.E.I., Que.)	1	77 (Que., N.S.)	13 (Nfld.)	56
Conditional grants	124 (Ont.)	2 (N.B.)	102	526 (Alta.)	32 (N.B.)	382
Total revenue......	341 (Ont.)	48 (Nfld.)	288	1,192 (Alta.)	183 (Nfld.)	919

0—indicates less than $1 per capita. —nil, or non-existent.

Source: Recorded from Appendix Tables C.1 and C.2.

Indeed, it has been the increasing reference to property taxation which has led to requests for reform and to provinces for local tax relief for municipalities in most of Canada. Overall, real property taxes accounted for 42 per cent of local revenues in 1968 and slightly more than 32 per cent in 1978 (calculated from data in Table 7.1), a decline of almost 10 percentage points[2] (column 1, Table 7.2). In most provinces, the relative importance of property taxes as a municipal revenue source declined, with the greatest decline occurring in municipalities in Prince Edward Island (22 percentage points). In fact, this is the only province in which per capita municipal property taxes declined in absolute value as well (from $50 per capita to $45 per capita), thus reflecting the noted shift in expenditure responsibility. On average, the revenue dependence on local property taxes fell by 18 percentage points in municipalities in Nova Scotia, 15 percentage points in Saskatchewan, 12 percentage points in Alberta, 11 percentage points in Quebec, 10 percentage points in Ontario, and 4 percentage points in Manitoba. By contrast, municipalities, on average, in New Brunswick, Newfoundland, and British Columbia exhibited marginal increases (5, 4, and 3 percentage points respectively) in their dependence on local property taxes as a source of revenue (column 1, Table 7.2).

It is essential to note, however, that per capita local property taxes in Newfoundland and New Brunswick (Appendix Table C.1) were extremely low in 1968 (10 per cent and 14 per cent of the average for all provinces) and the second and third lowest in 1978 (behind Prince Edward Island) at levels of 15 per cent and 27 per cent of the national average respectively (Appendix Table C.2). While the relative dependence on this source of revenue increased in these two provinces, the actual per capita levels of property taxes collected by their local governments were considerably lower than in all other provinces except for New Brunswick (in 1978). By comparison, local governments in British Columbia recorded per capita property tax levels higher than the overall average in each of the years[3] (Appendix Tables C.1 and C.2), thus reflecting a fairly heavy dependence on this revenue source. For local governments in Nova Scotia, Quebec, Ontario, and three of the western provinces (British Columbia excluded), the decline in the relative importance of property taxes as a revenue generator occurred at the same time as the absolute per capita dollar level rose by somewhere between 115 per cent and 150 per cent, depending on the province selected (calculated from Appendix Tables C.1 and C.2).

The changing importance of all local taxes closely approximates the changes recorded for real property taxes (column 2 versus column 1, Table 7.2). In addition, the decline in the relative dependence on the total of all local taxes in most provinces (Nova Scotia, New Brunswick, and British Columbia excepted)

---

[2]In the 1950s and early 1960s, property taxes accounted for over 50 per cent of all local revenues—see Melville L. McMillan, *Local Intergovernmental Fiscal Relations in Australia and Canada,* Occasional Paper no. 23 (Canberra: Centre for Research on Federal Financial Relations, Australian National University, 1981). During this period, the extensive use of property taxes (which rose faster than incomes) led to a number of complaints that resulted during the late 1960s and 1970s in a greater emphasis on grants and thus less on property taxes.

[3]For a discussion of the extent to which property taxes have been over or under utilized, see Harry M. Kitchen, "Property Taxation: Overutilized or Underutilized?" (July-August 1982), 30 *Canadian Tax Journal* 610-17.

Table 7.2 Changing Importance of Major Per Capita Local Revenue Sources,[a] 1968-1978

Province	(1) Property taxes	(2) Total taxes	(3) Other own-source revenue	(4) Total own-source revenue	(5) Unconditional grants	(6) Conditional grants
Newfoundland	+4.3	−1.5	−28.3	−29.7	+6.9	+22.8
Prince Edward Island	−22.4	−25.2	−2.7	−27.9	+2.8	+25.2
Nova Scotia	−17.6	−17.3	+1.3	−16.0	+8.4	+7.7
New Brunswick	+5.4	+5.4	−47.9	−42.4	+31.7	+10.7
Quebec	−10.7	−17.0	−3.6	−20.6	+8.1	+12.4
Ontario	−10.2	−11.0	+2.3	−8.8	+5.2	+3.6
Manitoba	−4.0	−4.9	+1.8	−3.0	+.9	+2.1
Saskatchewan	−15.1	−18.4	+2.7	−15.6	+4.3	+11.3
Alberta	−12.4	−13.4	−3.0	−16.5	+2.8	+13.8
British Columbia	+2.5	0	+4.8	+4.8	+5.3	−10.2
All provinces	−9.7	−12.2	+0.3	−11.9	+5.8	+6.2

[a]This measures the percentage point change, being the change in the relative importance of the various revenue sources from 1968 to 1978. The sum of the changes in all revenue sources added together for each province must equal zero.

+ Increase.   − Decrease.

Source: Calculated from data in Appendix Tables C.1 and C.2.

was greater than the corresponding decline in the dependence on local property taxes alone. The explanation for this is very simple but perhaps needs stating: special assessments, business taxes, and other local taxes displayed a decline in their relative importance as revenue generators from 1968 to 1978.

On average, nontax own-source revenues (grants in-lieu-of taxes, sales of goods and services, privileges, licences and permits, return on investments, and other) grew from a per capita level of $41 in 1968 to $132 in 1978 (Table 7.1). The bulk of this increase can be attributed to a greater reliance on revenues generated from user charges and fees. Overall, the own-source revenue component displayed a marginal increase in terms of its importance as a revenue generator (less than 1 percentage point—column 3, Table 7.2). In Ontario, Nova Scotia, and the western provinces (except for Alberta), the relative dependence on nontax own-source revenue rose between 1 and 5 percentage points. For the remaining provinces, the decrease ranged from 3 to 48 percentage points.

The decline in the relative dependence on all own-source revenues as a means of financing local expenditures, coincided with an increase in the dependence on conditional and unconditional grants. On average, for all Canadian municipalities, unconditional grants provided 6 per cent of all local revenue in 1978, up from .3 per cent in 1968, while conditional grants supplied almost 42 per cent, an increase from 35 per cent in 1968. Over this period, the average growth rate of both types of grants combined, for all municipalities, exceeded 325 per cent (calculated from Table 7.1), a growth rate substantially higher than for any other local revenue source. On a province-by-province basis, similar increases in the importance of this local revenue source were observed with municipalities in all provinces (with the exception of Ontario, Manitoba, and British Columbia) exhibiting an increase in the dependence on grants considerably higher than the national average (columns 5 and 6, Table 7.2).

Before leaving this section it should be noted that data on per capita property tax levels presented above refer to the level of per capita property taxes collected by local governments alone and not to the total of all property taxes (provincial plus local) collected. As such, these data cannot be used for any interprovincial comparison of property tax levels. To correct for this, Table 7.3 aggregates provincial and local per capita property taxes for 1968 and 1978 and compares these levels with those for local property taxes alone. In most provinces, the per capita levels of local property taxation equal the per capita levels for local plus provincial property taxes. This arises either because the provincial governments do not collect property taxes (Newfoundland, Quebec, and Alberta) or because the levels collected, from unorganized territories, for example, are so small in per capita terms that they do not alter the overall per capita levels (Nova Scotia, Ontario, and Manitoba). The only instances where collections from unorganized territories are large enough to affect per capita levels occurred in Saskatchewan in 1978 and British Columbia in 1968 and 1978. As for the provinces of Prince Edward Island and New Brunswick, the provincial governments assume an active role in collecting property tax revenues. Much of this revenue is used to finance a number of services under provincial jurisdiction in these provinces but within the domain of local governments in the remaining provinces.

Table 7.3   Property Tax Levels by Province, 1968 and 1978

	1968		1978	
	(1) Local per capita property	(2) Local & provincial per capita	(3) Local per capita property	(4) Local & provincial per capita
Province	taxes[a]	property taxes[b]	taxes[a]	property taxes[b]
		dollars		
Newfoundland	12	12	53	53
Prince Edward Island .	50	50	45	124
Nova Scotia	78	78[c]	168	168[c]
New Brunswick	18	60	81	163
Quebec	103	103	256	256
Ontario	151	151[c]	338	338[c]
Manitoba	116	116	336	336[c]
Saskatchewan	133	133[c]	297	298
Alberta	125	125	302	302
British Columbia	132	137	406	420
All provinces ;	121	123	296	301

[a]Recorded from Table 7.1. [b]The sum of figures in Table 7.1 and figures calculated from data in Statistics Canada, *Provincial Government Finance: Revenue and Expenditure, Fiscal Year Ended March 31, 1969*, and the same for *Fiscal Year Ended March 31, 1979*, Catalogue no. 68-207. [c]Provincial property taxes that are so small that they do not raise provincial and local per capita property taxes above the level for local governments alone.

While the differential in absolute per capita property tax levels across the provinces was extremely large (columns 2 and 4, Table 7.3), the relative variation in per capita provincial/local levels did not change throughout the period under observation (the coefficient of variation for this revenue source was .47 for each of 1968 and 1978—calculated from columns 2 and 4 in Table 7.3).

Finally, it must not be assumed that the per capita property tax figures in Table 7.3 reflect the true property tax burden. The final burden can be obtained only after the appropriate deduction of the various tax relief schemes, including property tax credits applied against provincial income taxes in Ontario and Manitoba or home-owner grants in Saskatchewan and British Columbia. (For a discussion of the various property tax relief schemes available, see Chapter 8.)

AN INTERPROVINCIAL COMPARISON OF LOCAL REVENUES IN CONSTANT DOLLARS

The rapid increase in per capita current dollar local revenues (and expenditures) has been and still is the source of considerable criticism and unease among many local taxpayers. While some of this criticism may have been warranted, much of it has been unjustified, particularly since this increase has not generated a larger role for local governments. Clearly, a review of the data (Table 7.4) suggests that the largest part of the current dollar increase in per capita revenues during this period has been attributed directly and solely to inflation and not to additional or greater levels of service.

Table 7.4   Current and Constant Per Capita Dollar Increase (Decrease) in Local Revenues by Major Source and Province, 1968-1978

Revenue source	Newfoundland	Prince Edward Island	Nova Scotia	New Brunswick	Quebec	Ontario	Manitoba	Saskatchewan	Alberta	British Columbia	All provinces
					dollars						
Property taxes											
Current	39	(5)	90	63	153	187	220	164	177	274	175
Constant	8	(32)	(11)	14	(1)	(18)	15	(16)	(7)	25	(5)
Total taxes											
Current	56	(9)	116	63	178	226	249	181	211	284	204
Constant	8	(37)	(5)	14	(12)	(18)	16	(22)	(4)	19	(8)
Total own-source revenue											
Current	64	15	187	64	247	324	361	294	373	387	295
Constant	2	(37)	10	(9)	(10)	(3)	33	1	12	39	3
Grants											
Unconditional											
Current	13	16	73	71	77	53	15	46	36	47	55
Constant	5	6	27	28	31	20	4	17	13	18	21
Conditional											
Current	58	387	285	30	345	272	237	324	451	124	280
Constant	15	96	65	13	81	32	32	71	109	(20)	48
Total revenue											
Current	135	419	546	166	669	649	613	664	860	557	631
Constant	21	65	102	30	102	49	68	89	135	37	72

Source: Current dollar increases calculated from data in Appendix Tables C.1 and C.2. Constant dollar figures deflated by the implicit price index for government current expenditures on goods and services adjusted for regional differences. See footnote 4, Chapter 2, for an explanation of this adjustment. Figures in brackets indicate a decrease.

By converting current per capita dollar increases into constant dollars,[4] one is able to observe the real increase in the per capita revenues generated by the different sources of revenue for local governments over the period 1968 to 1978. Of considerable interest is the real increase in local revenues. For the average Canadian municipality, the current dollar increase of $631 per capita actually amounted to only $72 in real terms. Interprovincially, the greatest increase in local real per capita revenues occurred in Alberta ($135), Nova Scotia ($102), and Quebec ($102), with municipalities in Newfoundland and New Brunswick recording the lowest increase at $21 and $30 respectively (Table 7.4).

For the average Canadian municipality from 1968 to 1978, the real per capita increase in local revenues of $72 was attributed, almost entirely, to a real increase in the level of per capita grants. In fact, $69 out of this total was due to conditional ($48) and unconditional ($21) grants leaving the remaining $3 to local own-source revenues. Except for a modest decrease of $2 in the real value of per capita grants in British Columbia, grants received by local governments rose in all of the remaining provinces. Alberta, Quebec, and Prince Edward Island recorded the highest levels, exhibiting per capita increases of more than $100, while Newfoundland and Manitoba were at the other extreme with increases of $20 and $36 respectively.

While the overall real per capita increase in own-source revenues amounted to $3, the average municipality in four provinces actually recorded a decrease for this same figure (Prince Edward Island $37, Quebec $10, New Brunswick $9, and Ontario $3). Marginal increases were recorded for similar municipalities in four provinces (Newfoundland $2, Saskatchewan $1, Nova Scotia $10, and Alberta $12), while modest increases were noted in only two provinces (British Columbia $39 and Manitoba $33).

For all provinces, the bulk of local own-source revenues was made up of local taxes and, more specifically, real property taxes. In real terms, the per capita increase in property taxes has not generated noticeably increased revenues for local governments. On average, the real value of per capita property tax revenues fell by $5 from 1968 to 1978 (Table 7.4). This same rate of decrease was not evident for the average municipality in each of the provinces, although it was not significantly different. For example, real per capita local property tax revenues fell in 6 of the 10 provinces (Prince Edward Island $32, Ontario $18, Saskatchewan $16, Nova Scotia $11, Alberta $7, and Quebec $1) and rose in the remaining provinces (Newfoundland $8, New Brunswick $14, Manitoba $15, and British Columbia $25).

From 1968 to 1978, municipal nontax own-source revenues displayed an increase in real terms of $11 per capita across the country. This average was a

---

[4]Constant per capita dollar figures were obtained by deflating current per capita dollar figures by the implicit price index for government current expenditures on goods and services adjusted for regional differences. For an explanation of this adjustment, see footnote 4 in Chapter 2. The rationale for deflating the current figures by this index follows from the bulk of own-source revenue being used to finance current government expenditures and not capital expenditures. Since our objective is to observe what the government buys with its money, this index is then suitable. If our objective, on the other hand, had been to measure the real resources extracted from the private sector, the deflation index would have measured what the private sector gave up (personal consumption index).

combination of (1) a higher-than-average increase in Nova Scotia, Ontario, and the four western provinces, (2) a lower-than-average increase in Quebec, (3) no change in Prince Edward Island, and (4) a decrease in Newfoundland and New Brunswick.

LOCAL GOVERNMENT DEMAND ON SOCIETY'S RESOURCES

While the previous figures display the importance of local revenues and significant trends in their composition, they do not adequately support or reject the contention that local governments have absorbed a greater share of society's resources. Clearly, one needs a common denominator against which to measure the importance of the local sector's revenues. In this instance, GDPP per capita serves as this common denominator. When per capita local revenues by source are taken as a percentage of per capita GDPP, an index indicating whether the various revenue sources have been absorbing an increasing share of provincial resources is obtained.

One notes from Table 7.5 that a modest increase (1 percentage point) in society's resources went to the average local sector in Canada from 1968 to 1978 (from 9.3 per cent to 10.3 per cent of GDPP). Indeed, this modest increase was evident for the average municipality in all provinces with the exception of Saskatchewan and Alberta (where modest decreases were observed) and British Columbia (where the proportion of provincial resources going to local governments was unchanged) (final row, Table 7.5). This overall average municipal increase of 1 percentage point was obtained by summing the decrease of .6 of 1 per cent in own-source revenue with a more than offsetting increase in conditional and unconditional grants of 1.6 per cent.

In every province, with the exception of British Columbia, grants absorbed a larger percentage of GDPP in 1978 than in 1968, while in only two provinces (Manitoba and British Columbia) did own-source revenues absorb a larger proportion of GDPP in the more recent year. Clearly, the decline in the proportion of provincial resources absorbed by local own-source revenues was largely attributed to a decline in the importance of property taxation. Municipalities, on average, in Newfoundland, New Brunswick, and British Columbia were the only ones displaying increases in the relative importance of property taxes, and in these cases, the increases were marginal.

Finally, with some minor interprovincial variations, nontax own-source revenues overall, absorbed approximately the same percentage of GDP in each year (1.4 per cent in 1968 and 1.5 per cent in 1978).

While it may be argued that individual municipalities in any province deviate from the provincial averages used in this chapter, it does appear as if local sectors, on average, have marginally increased the proportion of provincial resources they now command. This increase in the relative importance has, however, generally resulted from a shift away from a dependence on local revenues and toward an increase in the reliance on grants.

Table 7.5   Per Capita Local Revenue by Major Source as a Per Cent of Per Capita GDPP, 1968 and 1978

Major revenue source	Nfld.		P.E.I.		N.S.		N.B.		Que.		Ont.		Man.		Sask.		Alta.		B.C.		All provinces	
	1968	1978	1968	1978	1968	1978	1968	1978	1968	1978	1968	1978	1968	1978	1968	1978	1968	1978	1968	1978	1968	1978
									per cent													
Property taxes	.7	1.1	3.0	.9	3.7	2.7	.9	1.4	4.5	3.3	4.2	3.6	4.0	4.2	4.9	3.2	3.4	2.2	3.9	4.1	3.9	3.3
Total taxes	1.2	1.5	3.3	.9	4.1	3.3	.9	1.4	6.0	4.1	4.8	4.3	4.6	4.8	5.7	3.6	3.9	2.6	4.4	4.4	4.6	3.9
Other own-source revenue	1.2	.6	1.0	.8	1.0	1.5	1.9	.6	1.9	1.4	1.1	1.4	1.5	1.9	1.3	1.6	2.1	1.7	.9	1.4	1.4	1.5
Total own-source revenue	2.4	2.1	4.3	1.7	5.1	4.8	2.8	2.0	7.9	5.5	5.9	5.7	6.1	6.7	7.0	5.2	6.0	4.3	5.3	5.8	6.0	5.4
Unconditional grants	0	.3	0	.3	.2	1.2	0	1.2	0	1.0	0	.6	.1	.2	.1	.5	0	.3	0	.5	0	.6
Conditional grants	.3	1.3	5.7	9.4	3.8	5.9	.1	.5	4.1	5.7	3.4	4.2	3.4	4.2	3.5	4.4	3.0	4.1	3.2	2.4	3.3	4.3
Total revenue	2.7	3.7	10.0	11.4	9.1	12.0	2.9	3.8	12.0	12.2	9.4	10.5	9.6	11.1	10.5	10.1	9.1	8.7	8.6	8.6	9.3	10.3

Source: Local per capita revenue figures were obtained from Appendix Tables C.1 and C.2. Per capita GDPP figures were obtained from The Conference Board of Canada, *The Provincial Economies, 1961-1980 Data* (Ottawa: the Board, 1981).

MUNICIPAL REVENUE PATTERNS BY
SIZE OF MUNICIPALITY

Given that per capita expenditures on services provided by larger urban governments tend to be higher than per capita expenditures on similar services provided in smaller communities (see Chapters 4 and 5), it is not surprising to
observe similarly higher levels of revenue being received by these larger
municipalities. To be more specific, in 1978, own-source per capita revenues in
the average urban region, were approximately $120 higher ($600 per capita)
than the same figure for the average of all municipalities in the 10 provinces. In
each province, the same trend was observed, with the per capita average revenue
levels in urban regions exceeding the average for all municipalities within the
province by somewhere between $275 per capita (Nova Scotia displaying the
largest differential) and $53 per capita (Ontario recording the smallest differ-
ential). At the same time and across the same municipalities, the proportion of
local revenues generated from own-revenue sources was higher for the larger as
opposed to smaller communities. Similar patterns were recorded in both the
absolute per capita level and the proportion which each revenue source contributed to total revenues for the remaining sources over which the
municipalities have specific control.

Offsetting the differential in the extent to which different-sized
municipalities are dependent on own-source revenues is the dependence on
grants. Since larger units of government tend to be relatively more dependent on
own-source revenues, they must be relatively less dependent on grants. This
need not imply, however, that the absolute value of per capita grants is less for
urban regions than for other areas. In fact, figures for 1978 indicate that per
capita grants (on average) for all Canadian municipalities totalled $438, while
those for all urban regions totalled $439 (Table 7.6). On a province by province
comparison, the differential between per capita grants for urban regions and
those for all municipalities is more noticeable, with three provinces recording
higher levels in urban regions (Nova Scotia, New Brunswick, and Quebec) and
the remaining provinces recording lower levels.

Regardless of the province under consideration, the combination of own-
source revenues and grants tends to be higher in larger urban areas than in
smaller urban or rural areas.

SUMMARY

While this chapter has not attempted to provide an analysis of the different
taxes or sources of revenue available to local governments, it has suggested a
number of the more salient features arising from the level and pattern of local
revenues, both interprovincially and intertemporally. First, per capita local
revenues (in total or from own-source revenues alone) are lower in the provinces
in Atlantic Canada, especially Newfoundland and New Brunswick, than
elsewhere. As suggested, this can be attributed to the different provincial/local
expenditure responsibilities for local services. Second, while per capita revenues
from own-sources increased in every province, these sources, in total, contributed a relatively smaller proportion of all revenues for the average
municipality in each province over the period from 1968 to 1978. At the same

Table 7.6 Comparison of Major Per Capita Municipal Revenue Sources by Size of Municipality, by Province,[a] 1978

Revenue source	Nfld.				N.S.				N.B.				Que.				Ont.			
	All municipalities		Urban regions		All municipalities		Urban regions		All municipalities		Urban regions		All municipalities		Urban regions		All municipalities		Urban regions	
	$[b]	%[c]	$	%	$	%	$	%	$	%	$	%	$	%	$	%	$	%	$	%
Property tax	53	29.3	174	58.7	168	22.8	354	32.6	81	36.4	198	42.0	256	27.2	319	30.1	338	34.1	378	37.2
Business tax	16	8.9	41	13.9	25	3.4	43	3.9	n.a.	n.a.	n.a.	n.a.	22	2.4	10	.9	51	5.2	76	7.5
Total taxes	77	42.3	241	81.0	202	27.3	420	38.6	82	36.5	198	42.0	315	33.4	400	37.7	402	40.6	456	44.9
Other own-source revenue	29	15.5	34	11.6	90	12.7	150	13.8	103	17.7	76	16.1	111	11.9	134	12.6	138	13.9	137	13.5
Total own-source revenue	106	57.8	275	92.6	295	40.0	570	52.4	121	54.2	274	58.1	426	45.3	534	50.3	540	54.5	593	58.4
Unconditional grants	13	6.9	0	0	77	10.5	125	11.5	71	31.7	159	33.8	77	8.1	99	9.3	54	5.5	53	5.2
Conditional grants	64	35.3	21	7.2	366	49.6	392	36.1	32	14.1	38	8.2	438	46.6	429	40.4	396	40.0	369	36.4
Total revenue	183	100.0	297	100.0	739	100.0	1088	100.0	224	100.0	472	100.0	941	100.0	1061	100.0	990	100.0	1015	100.0

(Table concluded on next page.)

Table 7.6 Concluded

Revenue source	Man.				Sask.				Alta.				B.C.				All prov.			
	All municipalities		Urban regions		All municipalities		Urban regions		All municipalities		Urban regions		All municipalities		Urban regions		All municipalities		Urban regions	
	$b	%c	$	%	$	%	$	%	$	%	$	%	$	%	$	%	$	%	$	%
Property tax	336	37.7	399	40.4	297	31.2	345	34.5	302	25.3	309	25.5	406	47.9	443	50.0	296	32.3	370	35.6
Business tax	21	2.4	35	3.5	20	2.1	13	1.3	39	3.3	72	5.9	10	1.2	17	1.9	32	3.5	58	5.6
Total taxes	382	42.9	462	46.8	335	35.2	380	38.0	354	29.7	399	32.9	432	50.9	483	54.5	348	37.8	451	43.4
Other own-source revenue	155	17.4	196	19.9	150	15.8	194	19.3	239	20.1	290	23.9	135	15.9	139	15.7	132	14.5	149	14.3
Total own-source revenue	537	60.3	658	66.7	485	51.0	574	57.3	593	49.8	689	56.8	567	66.8	622	70.2	480	52.3	600	57.7
Unconditional grants	18	2.0	19	2.0	48	5.0	56	5.6	37	3.1	26	2.1	48	5.6	52	5.9	56	6.1	62	6.0
Conditional grants	336	37.7	309	31.4	418	44.0	371	37.1	562	47.2	497	41.0	234	27.8	212	23.9	382	41.6	377	36.3
Total revenue	891	100.0	986	100.0	951	100.0	1001	100.0	1192	100.0	1212	100.0	848	100.0	886	100.0	919	100.0	1039	100.0

Totals may not add precisely, due to rounding. aPrince Edward Island is excluded from the comparison as figures are not available for urban regions. bDollar figures are per capita. cPer cents are of totals. n.a.—not applicable.

Source: Data for all municipalities are recorded from Appendix Tables C.1 and C.2. Data for urban regions are calculated from Statistics Canada, *Local Government Finance, Preliminary 1978—Estimates 1979*, Catalogue no. 68-203, Table 9.

time, grants became absolutely and relatively more important as a contributor of local revenues. Third, in the recent past, property taxes have assumed relatively less importance as a source of local revenues in municipalities in most provinces in Canada. Fourth, in real per capita terms, own-source revenues and particularly property taxes increased by insignificantly small amounts over the period under observation. Fifth, contrary to popular belief, the taxes and charges adopted by local governments over the period 1968 to 1978 did not lead to significantly higher levels of private sector resources being diverted into the local public sector. Sixth, with a few exceptions, per capita revenue levels tend to be higher for larger urban municipalities. Similarly, the relative dependence on own-source revenue tends to be greater for large municipalities, while the relative dependence on grants from the federal and provincial governments tends to be greater for smaller communities.

8
Local Property Taxation[1]

INTRODUCTION

A local government's major source of tax revenue comes from real property taxation with significantly less amounts arising from local taxes on business and special assessments (see Chapter 7). Additional taxes, which include the yields from poll taxes and other local levies, are extremely small in terms of their capacity to generate revenue.

As was illustrated in Table 7.2, local property taxation has declined in relative importance in most provinces both in terms of the contribution this tax makes to local revenue sources and in terms of the proportion of personal provincial income it now absorbs.[2] The relative decline in the importance of this tax has, however, neither prevented nor deterred increasing amounts of criticism being levied against it as a source of revenue for local governments. Critics have attacked it on a number of fronts: (1) it has been argued that it imposes a heavy tax burden on low-income individuals; (2) it has been attacked because it is an inelastic source of revenue; and (3) it has been criticized because of its inability to measure a taxpayer's ability to pay. In spite of these criticisms, the durability and importance of this tax is witnessed by the fact that it is and has been the major source of tax revenue for local governments for years. In the last two decades, mounting criticism of this form of taxation led to a number of reports dealing in part with suggestions for property tax reform. In fact, during the 1960s, eight provincial governments[3] commissioned or undertook specific reviews of their local property tax systems. Further concern in the 1970s led to additional reports or studies evaluating the municipal financial situation and more specifically the use of the property tax in a number of provinces and municipalities. As a result of these reports and their findings, certain suggestions have been implemented. These include the reduction or elimination of a number of exemptions, the introduction of equalized assessment in some provinces, the adoption of tax relief programs, and improvements in administrative machinery.

Before proceeding with an evaluation of property taxation, this chapter will outline briefly the structure of local property taxation in Canada placing specific emphasis on assessment practices and policies, the tax base, and regressivity. The various forms of property tax relief will also be presented and discussed.

---

[1]Certain portions of this chapter follow rather closely material in Robin W. Boadway and Harry M. Kitchen, *Canadian Tax Policy*, second edition (Toronto: Canadian Tax Foundation, forthcoming), Chapter 4.

[2]An interprovincial comparison of local property taxes does not give a truly adequate picture of the burden of property taxes on local residents in the various provinces. See Chapter 7 of this text.

[3]Newfoundland and British Columbia were the only two provincial governments not publishing reports although, in the latter case, a joint provincial/municipal study was started but discontinued before completion. For a review of the provincial reports, see Joe Martin, "Real Property Taxation: Stirrings of Reform" (September-October 1972), 20 *Canadian Tax Journal* 437-52.

THE REAL PROPERTY TAX

STRUCTURE

The structure of the real property tax as it applies to both residential and nonresidential property displays more variability than any other major tax in Canada. The major explanation for this variability rests with the level of government responsible for administering the tax. Property taxes are, by and large, administered by local governments,[4] while other taxes such as personal and corporate income taxes, manufacturing, and retail sales taxes are controlled by either the federal or provincial governments. Clearly, the level of administration will dictate the degree of uniformity prevalent in establishing the tax base and tax rates. In the case of property taxation, uniformity seldom exists among municipalities within the same region or metropolitan area. Adjacent municipalities frequently tax identical properties at different rates. This is true for both residential and nonresidential property and especially noticeable in the larger metropolitan areas or regional governments with different municipal tax jurisdictions.[5]

The yield generated by the property tax is directly dependent on the tax rate and the tax base. Real property taxes are imposed on land and buildings: items that are nonmovable. Personal property taxes, on the other hand, include taxes on goods and chattels, movable items or objects that are not affixed to land. With the exception of municipalities in Nova Scotia, Manitoba, and British Columbia, where municipalities are authorized to tax personal property in a restricted manner, problems of discovery and valuation of all forms of personal property have caused this form of taxation to become discarded as a separate tax in the remaining provinces. Vestiges of personal property taxation used, however, can still be found in Canada, where items like machinery, fixtures, and similar things are included in the real property tax base in Newfoundland, Nova Scotia, Ontario, Alberta, and British Columbia. In Prince Edward Island, New Brunswick, and Quebec, only machinery, equipment, and fixtures that provide services to buildings are subject to property taxes. In Saskatchewan, machinery in general is not assessable and is taxed only when used in mines, gravel pits, and oil and gas wells. In Manitoba, machinery is part of the personal property tax base rather than the real property tax base.[6]

Recent developments in property taxation have occurred in municipalities in Quebec where the property tax continues to be imposed on land and buildings,

---

[4]In certain instances, provincial governments have collected property taxes primarily in unorganized areas where municipal taxation is non-existent. Prince Edward Island and New Brunswick, however, are two provinces that have established a province-wide system of property taxation administered provincially.

[5]For evidence supporting this statement in the Regional Government of the Municipality of Waterloo, see Harry Kitchen, *Issues in Municipal Finance* (Waterloo, Ontario: Waterloo Region Review Commission, 1978); and in Metropolitan Toronto, see Harry M. Kitchen, *Public Finance in Metropolitan Toronto,* a Study for The Royal Commission on Metropolitan Toronto (Toronto: the Commission, 1977). For additional evidence in other large cities in Canada, see F. H. Finnis, "The Weight of Property Taxation in Canada—Single-Family Dwellings and Light Industrial Property" (May-June 1980), 28 *Canadian Tax Journal* 289-325.

[6]Canadian Tax Foundation, *Provincial and Municipal Finances, 1981* (Toronto: the Foundation, 1981), 135-37.

but has been expanded to include a new form of compensation in lieu of property taxation on the production and distribution systems of telecommunication, electricity and gas companies. This form of taxation is dependent on gross revenues and the taxes raised are distributed to municipalities according to the weighted share of the population residing in the recipient municipality. In no case will a municipality receive less revenue than under the former method of taxation.[7] In Ontario, the Blair Commission recommended that the definition of real property be altered to follow the New Brunswick legislation and include only machinery serving a functional operation of the building or making it more habitable.[8] Such a change, however, has not been implemented. Finally, the situation in British Columbia is difficult to outline briefly,[9] but generally, the value of machinery and fixtures in excess of $1,500 is included in the tax base in the province. The assessed value on which taxes are imposed also varies, with the variation depending on the purpose for which taxes are levied (that is, school and hospital versus general purpose). Moreover, as of January 1, 1980, 50 per cent of the assessed value of all agricultural land became exempt from the tax base used for school and hospital purposes.

Intermunicipal variations in property tax bases also exist in the following instances: the tax treatment of mobile homes; the special statutory assessment rules on "farm lands and/or buildings, forest and wooded lands, public and private utilities, pipelines, and railways"[10]; and the total or partial exemptions, whether mandatory and/or discretionary, granted to a number of organizations, including various industries, schools, churches, Crown lands, public properties, homes for the aged, charitable organizations, and cemeteries.[11] Not only will variations in the special concessions produce differentials[12] in the tax bases among municipalities and substantial reductions in the tax base in any one locality, but also the tax base in any specific community may change continually as "land is placed into use or changes use through development and building, or as values attached to existing assessment are revised."[13]

---

[7]For more specific information, see ibid., at 116-17, and François Vaillancourt, "Financing Local Authorities in Québec—The Reform of Bill 57" (May-June 1980), 28 *Canadian Tax Journal* 274-88, at 282.

[8]Ontario, *Report of The Commission on the Reform of Property Taxation in Ontario* (Toronto: the Commission, 1977).

[9]For more detail, see Frederic H. Finnis, *Property Assessment in Canada*, Canadian Tax Papers no. 62 (Toronto: Canadian Tax Foundation, 1979), Chapter 11, and supra footnote 6, at 136.

[10]Supra footnote 6, at 137.

[11]For more detailed information on these points, see Finnis, supra footnote 9, and supra footnote 6, at 136-37.

[12]This is not to imply that differentials are now intended, as they are often deliberately established. For example, the prevalence of exempt or partially exempt property creates noticeable differentials in the assessment base. In addition, the existence of a split mill rate in Ontario favours residential property vis-à-vis commercial and industrial property; that is, the property tax rate levied on commercial and industrial assessment must be 15 per cent (10 per cent for school taxes) above that on residential and farm assessment. This differential was originally justified on the grounds that commercial and industrial property owners could deduct their property taxes as a business expense, while homeowners could not. Homeowners, of course, are not taxed on the imputed income from their property either.

[13]Supra footnote 8, at 1.

The tax rate that is applied to the tax base is determined by dividing the required funds of a municipality by its total taxable assessment in each municipality and by expressing the result as a mill rate or as a percentage.[14] Multiplication of the tax rate by the tax base (taxable assessed value of a specific property) yields the tax liability of the property owner.

In spite of increasing criticism and concern, real property taxes continue to be the major source of tax revenues for local governments. Recently there have been numerous attempts to reform this form of taxation with the objective of eliminating a number of its undesirable characteristics. These include the distortions and inequities created by the variations in assessment procedures, less than comprehensive tax bases along with differential treatment of different properties, and the traditionally assumed regressivity of residential property taxes. While some suggestions for improvement have been implemented, others have not. Nevertheless, these three areas of criticism have been the focus of most of the recent work on property taxation and deserve detailed discussion.

Assessment

Perhaps the most publicized and serious administrative fault of the real property tax has been, and to a lesser extent still is, inaccurate assessment. This criticism is founded on the observation that "the ratio of assessed value to market value shows a large amount of variation both within and among localities."[15] Undervaluation in itself is not inequitable for if all property were assessed at the same uniform percentage of true value, the result would be simply a higher rate of tax.

While the differences in assessment may be attributed to a number of factors, they can generally be grouped in two categories: intentional and unintentional. Intentional variations have existed in order "to accomplish objectives like increasing grants from provincial or state governments, encouraging industry to locate in a municipality, and to placate a large number of potentially vocal taxpayers—home owners."[16] Unintentional variations have arisen because of infrequent sales of certain properties and hence, the ensuing difficulty of establishing accurate market values or the tendency of assessors to evaluate similar properties at different rates. For instance, newly constructed homes are almost always assessed at a higher percentage of market value than older homes.[17]

---

[14] $\dfrac{\text{Total tax revenue required}}{\text{Total taxable assessment}} \times 1,000$ yields the mill rate.

Real property taxes are generally levied at rates expressed in mills per dollar of the assessed value of property, except for some municipalities in Atlantic Canada where the rate is expressed as a percentage.

[15] J. A. Johnson, "Municipal Tax Reform—Alternatives to the Real Property Tax" (Supplement 1976), 2 *Canadian Public Policy* 335-46, at 337.

[16] Ibid.

[17] In support of this statement, within the residential single-family housing sector in Mississauga, Ontario, it was found in 1970 that older houses, especially those with substantial land, were noticeably undervalued for assessment purposes when compared with newer houses. See Bureau of Municipal Research, *Market Value Assessment* (Toronto: the Bureau, 1970).

Regardless of the cause of these variations, uneven assessment practices have been observed in, at least, two ways: first, real property within a municipality is frequently not assessed at a uniform percentage of market value (see Table 8.1); and second, wide variation often exists between assessment values on virtually identical properties located in different municipalities (Table 8.2). Table 8.1 illustrates the extreme variation that existed in the ratio of market to assessed value of single-family residential properties in 1977 in each of the areas that were amalgamated into the new City of Cambridge (1973) in southern Ontario. In Galt, for example, the ratio ranged from a factor of 3.52 to 55.45 with a median value of 10.00. In percentage terms, this means that houses were assessed at somewhere between 28.4 per cent and 1.8 per cent of market value in the same year. Similar patterns were observed for each of the remaining areas, although the median value was much lower for Hespeler and Preston, where reassessment of all property had actually been completed on the basis of the 1969 tax year. The other municipalities were operating on assessment procedures established in 1940 or earlier.

While Table 8.1 illustrates the considerable variation existing within and among municipalities in one rather small geographic area, it represents a pattern that is likely to exist in most areas in Canada. An earlier study in Ontario[18] covering 22 geographically scattered municipalities displayed a similar variation in the assessment-sales ratios both within and among municipalities. In addition, this latter study observed higher assessment-sales ratios for apartments compared to non-apartments and generally lower ratios on land than on buildings. Continuing support for these last two points is available in two recent studies. First, the *Report of the Commission on the Reform of Property Taxation in Ontario* noted that in Metro Toronto single-family residences on average were assessed at 8.9 per cent of market value while multi-unit dwellings (more than six residences) were assessed at 21.7 per cent of market value.[19] Second, it was found that land (as distinct from buildings) in the region of Niagara[20] (southern Ontario) was substantially undervalued for assessment purposes. In fact, a move to market value assessment with unchanged property tax rates would result in noticeable increases in tax revenues from this particular form of real property. The results of a more recent study on property assessment in Brandon, Manitoba[21] supported the hypothesis that land is undervalued relative to buildings, but it rejected the generally accepted hypothesis that single-family dwellings are undervalued relative to other types of dwellings. Because this is the first piece of Canadian evidence generating such results, it must not be assumed that similar results occur frequently. Indeed, what it really supports is the necessity of acquiring more evidence before making conclusive statements on this issue.

---

[18]Ontario, "Assessment Inequities Throughout Ontario," in *The Ontario Committee on Taxation Report,* Vol. 2 (Toronto: Queen's Printer, 1967), 246-61. This report covered 22 Ontario municipalities from 1961 to 1963, including Metropolitan Toronto.

[19]Supra footnote 8, at 24.

[20]Ibid., at 140.

[21]James M. Dean, "Assessment Bias by Property Class in Brandon" (September-October 1980), 28 *Canadian Tax Journal* 600-606.

Table 8.1   Assessed Residential Property as a Ratio and Percentage
of Market Value in the City of Cambridge for 1977[a]

Merged area	Ratio of market value to assessed value	Median of market to assessed value	Assessed value as a per cent of market value	Median of assessed value as a per cent of market value
			per cent	*per cent*
Galt	3.52 to 55.45	10.00	28.41 to 1.80	9.97
Hespeler	1.34 to 12.44	2.56	74.63 to 8.04	39.06
Preston	1.31 to 58.51	2.38	76.34 to 1.71	40.49
North Dumfries	8.28 to 62.34	13.01	12.08 to 1.60	7.44
Waterloo Township....	.34 to 47.66	13.03	294.12 to 2.10	6.67

[a]This does not include multi-unit dwellings.

Source: Harry Kitchen, *Issues in Municipal Finance* (Waterloo, Ontario: Waterloo Region Review Commission, 1978), 36.

Similar variation in the ratio of assessed to market value can be observed in the comparison of nearly identical residential properties in selected cities across Canada. For example, the results obtained from a study conducted by the provincial directors of assessment in Canada are highlighted in Table 8.2. It is apparent from this study that residential dwellings in Atlantic Canada are the only ones where taxable assessment approaches market value. But this in itself should not suggest that assessed values in the remainder of Canada are not based on up-to-date market values. In British Columbia, for example, the survey shows the ratio to be about 13 per cent. Recent changes in this province's legislation have established the upper limit at 11 per cent. This has been done in the hope of restraining the increase in property taxes. Additional evidence supporting this pattern of assessed to market value ratios is available in a study completed by F. H. Finnis for the Canadian Tax Foundation and reproduced in the residential column of Table 8.3. Although the characteristics of the hypothetical property (a specified two-story average home generally found across Canada) on which Finnis collected information including assessed and market values and the location of the cities chosen were occasionally different than in the provincial assessors' review, his results are consistent with the results recorded in Table 8.2.

Similar variations have been observed for some time in industrial and commercial assessments. For example, in the mid-1960s *The Report of the Ontario Committee on Taxation* cited differences in the ratio of assessed to market value of industrial and commercial properties over the period 1961-63 among and within 22 Ontario municipalities including Metro Toronto.[22] Further evidence suggesting that Ontario municipalities overassessed commercial and industrial property vis-à-vis residential property was provided in two separate studies conducted in the early to middle 1970s.[23] The most recent evidence covering a

[22]See supra footnote 18, at 250-59.

[23]See supra footnote 17, and supra footnote 8.

Table 8.2   Assessed Value as a Ratio of Market Value for Residential Property in Selected Cities for Two Properties, 1978

Province and municipality	Property 1[a]	Property 2[b]
Newfoundland		
St. John's	1.08	.79
Corner Brook	.93	.90
Prince Edward Island		
Charlottetown	.92	.91
Nova Scotia		
Halifax	.81	.92
Sydney	.70	.82
New Brunswick		
Fredericton	.78	.79
Quebec		
Neufchatel (Quebec City)	.78	.79
Ontario		
Etobicoke (Metro Toronto)	.08	.08
Manitoba		
Portage La Prairie	.20	.17
Saskatchewan		
Regina	.10	.09
Alberta		
Fort Saskatchewan	.45	.47
Edmonton	.13	.15
British Columbia		
Victoria	.13	.13

[a]Property 1: 1½ storey, inexpensive construction, ground floor area 500-850 square feet.
[b]Property 2: 1 storey, average construction, ground floor area about 1,000 square feet.

Source: Calculated from data in Association of Provincial Directors of Assessment, "Tax Incidence Review" (mimeograph, 1978).

number of cities in Canada[24] indicates that the pattern in the ratio of assessed to market value for industrial property (industrial column in Table 8.3) is similar to that for residential property, that is, higher in Atlantic Canada and Quebec than in the rest of Canada.

Although the evidence is limited (Table 8.3), the earlier cited claim that commercial and industrial property is overassessed when compared with residential property appears to be more noticeable in municipalities in British Columbia and Ontario. Indeed, the earlier studies making this claim were based on municipalities in Ontario alone. While uneven assessment to market value ratios for industrial/commercial and residential property appears to exist, overassessment of industrial property does not, by itself, imply higher taxes for this sector. Clearly, the burden of taxation on each type of property will depend upon the tax rate as well as the assessment base. (A low tax rate on a high assessment base may generate the same tax burden as a high tax rate on a smaller assessment base.) Knowledge of the level of taxes is required before one can make a conclusive statement on whether the overassessment of industrial property in some provinces ultimately generates a heavier tax burden on this category

---

[24]The hypothetical properties on which assessors were asked to place valuations are described in Finnis, supra footnote 5, at 297.

**Table 8.3 Ratio of Assessed to Market Value for Residential and
Light Industrial Property in Selected Cities, 1978**

Province and municipality	Residential	Industrial
Newfoundland		
St. John's................................	na[a]	na[a]
Prince Edward Island		
Charlottetown...........................	1.00	1.00
Nova Scotia		
Halifax................................	.91	.75
Dartmouth.............................	.87	.87
New Brunswick		
Saint John	.99	.86
Quebec		
Montreal		
Pierrefonds	.94	—
Dollard des Ormeaux	.86	
Point Claire	—	.95
Quebec City[b]	.54	.59
Ontario		
Metro Toronto		
Scarborough	.09	.14
Manitoba		
Winnipeg	.14	.15
Saskatchewan		
Regina	.10	.06
Alberta		
Calgary...............................	.14	.15
Edmonton	.15	.14
British Columbia		
Vancouver (Burnaby)...................	.15	.30
Victoria (Saanich).....................	.13	.25

[a]Assessment based on rental value. [b]Residential property is in Sillery.

Source: F.H. Finnis, "The Weight of Property Taxation in Canada—Single-Family Dwellings and Light Industrial Property" (May-June 1980), 28 *Canadian Tax Journal* 311, Table 9.

of property. Indeed, this issue of tax burden for industrial versus residential property will be addressed later in this chapter.

While there are many interprovincial and intraprovincial assessment variations at the local level, and while the kinds of variation may differ from province to province, it is generally felt that the bulk of the existing inconsistencies and discriminating features can be included in one or more of the following five points:

1) Residential property is frequently underassessed relative to commercial and industrial property. This is apparently more obvious in some provinces (Ontario and British Columbia) than others.

2) Apartment buildings tend (although not always) to be assessed at a higher proportion of market value than single-family dwellings.

3) Land values, when compared with building values, appear to be underassessed in virtually every province.

4) Older buildings are often underassessed vis-à-vis newer buildings.

5) Some evidence, especially in the United States, illustrates the overassessment of low-value rental units (whether apartments or houses) relative to high-value units.[25]

This prevalence of uneven assessment has generated criticism in almost every municipality in Canada. The culmination of this concern has been reflected in a number of recent changes in assessment procedures.[26] In the eyes of at least one expert, for instance, it has been suggested that "the basic criteria for an assessment system are comprehensiveness, uniformity, and 'openness'."[27] To satisfy these criteria:

1) all real property must be assessed whether taxable or not;

2) all real property must be assessed at current market value;

3) assessments should be made by trained experienced personnel working for a central agency which has direct and complete responsibility for all assessment within a province;

4) the assessment function must be organized in such a way that assessors become very familiar with local real estate markets; and

5) property owners must be given ready access to pertinent assessment information and appeal bodies.[28]

The extent to which these objectives have been achieved varies considerably among the provinces. Most provinces have argued in favour of market value as the fairest basis for property assessments, but not every province can agree on what constitutes market value in the absence of sales information.[29] One general exception arises in the treatment of farm land where virtually all provinces assess farm land according to its market value as farm land and not as its actual value on the open market.

The centralization of assessment administration varies from complete provincial responsibility in Prince Edward Island, Nova Scotia, New Brunswick, Ontario, Saskatchewan, and British Columbia (where an independent provincial agency exists) to local responsibility in Quebec where the municipality's only involvement with the provincial government is its use of a provincially prepared manual. In Newfoundland and Manitoba, the province assumes the responsibility for assessment in all but one or two of the larger cities in each of the provinces (St. John's and Corner Brook are excluded in Newfoundland; Winnipeg is excluded in Manitoba). Finally in Alberta, assessment is a local responsibility under the guidelines established in the provincial assessment

---

[25]See R. M. Bird and N. E. Slack, *Residential Property Tax Relief in Ontario,* Ontario Economic Council Research Studies (Toronto: University of Toronto Press, 1978), 14. This study suggests that all of these points, with the exception of point 5, account for most of the inequities in Ontario.

[26]For a thorough and extensive review of the provincial assessment picture, see Finnis, supra footnote 9.

[27]F. A. Clayton, "Real Property Tax Assessment Practices in Canada," in supra footnote 15, 347-62, at 348.

[28]Ibid., at 349.

[29]The methods for determining market value in this instance include the comparative sales approach, the depreciated replacement cost approach, and the income capitalization approach. For the method used in each province, see ibid.

manual. Local governments, however, may and do request the province to undertake the assessment task.

While all provinces require an annual preparation of the assessment roll, not all property is revalued or revisited each year. In Newfoundland, the property must be reassessed, at least once in every five years. For Prince Edward Island, revaluation must occur once in every three to five years. For Nova Scotia, the time period is once every three years, while New Brunswick plans to produce annual valuations that reflect a one-year lag in market values. In this instance, however, each property will be inspected every third year. Once reassessment on the basis of market value is completed in Quebec (probably by 1983), municipalities will be expected to update their assessments annually by means of an adjustment factor.

By contrast, the province of Ontario was in the process of assessing all property on the basis of market value, when in June 1978, the provincial government suddenly announced that it was no longer pursuing market value assessment across the province. At the same time, it stated that it would undertake market value assessment in any municipality that specifically requested it to do so, and at the end 1983, some had made this request.[30] Manitoba, Saskatchewan and Alberta are in the process of reassessment, with Manitoba requiring a revaluation at least once in every five years. In Saskatchewan, the reassessment is on the basis of 1961 to 1970 average values with cities and towns being legally required to reassess every 8 years and other municipalities every 12 years. Generally, reassessments are conducted on a seven-year cycle in Alberta. An independent assessing authority in British Columbia inspects all properties every four years and updates their values annually. In the latter province, all properties were assessed at current values beginning in 1978.[31]

At this point, it is worth noting that assessment totals for land and buildings (improvements) are listed separately on assessment roles in Newfoundland, Quebec, and the four western provinces. Elsewhere, similar assessment figures record the total assessed value as one figure.[32]

One area in which there has been noticeable improvement in the assessment function over the past two decades has been in the quality of assessment. Much of this can be attributed to fairly extensive training programs and to the more rigorous educational requirements now being imposed on property tax assessors.

Finally, the extent to which taxpayers are made aware of the assessment procedures, the relationship of their assessment to other similar properties, and the appeals procedure differ noticeably among provinces. Quebec and Ontario appear to be much more secretive and defensive about their position than the provinces of New Brunswick, Prince Edward Island, and the four western provinces.[33]

---

[30]For reference to Ontario's chequered history on market value assessment, see Richard M. Bird and Enid Slack, "Can Property Taxes be Reformed?—Reflections on the Ontario Experience" (Fall 1981), 24 *Canadian Public Administration* 469-85.

[31]For more detail, see Finnis, supra footnote 9.

[32]Ibid.

[33]Supra footnote 27, at 361.

Tax Base

Taxation of real property continues to be the dominant form of taxation available to municipalities in Canada. Newfoundland is the only Canadian province that has not made the real property tax a mandatory local tax. Instead local councils decide whether or not this tax is to be levied. Only 34 out of 306 municipalities in this province have opted to tax real property. St. John's is also the only Canadian city not using capital value (it uses rental value instead) as a basis for assessment, although it is in the process of reassessing on the basis of capital value.

Critics of the general property tax have argued that this tax is unfair and discriminating since it taxes housing, while leaving other forms of consumer spending untouched. Although it has been alleged that this tax inequity is greater in Canada than in the United States because homeowners in the latter country can deduct property taxes from personal income taxes, it has also been suggested that this claim should not be exaggerated since most of this revenue is used to finance municipal expenditures. As such, the property tax has been viewed as the tax price paid for consuming municipal services and, therefore, may be considered a neutral or nondistorting benefit-based tax.[34] This claim, unfortunately, is difficult to support since the residential property tax is tied to the consumption of housing services and not to the consumption of benefits received from public services. The tax can be a sound benefit-based tax only if the two are highly correlated across households and there is really no solid evidence suggesting that a high degree of correlation exists in Canadian municipalities.

The residential property tax, furthermore, may not discriminate against housing expenditures because the tax is unlikely to be sufficiently large to offset the favourable effects afforded housing services under the personal income tax. The exclusion from the personal income tax base of capital gains on principal residences and the omission of imputed rent on owner-occupied dwellings[35] both lead to a bias in favour of increasing housing expenditures. Unless the property tax is sufficiently large to more than offset these favourable distortions, its imposition may actually lead to an improvement rather than a further distortion in the allocation of capital resources.

Even if one accepts the argument that the property tax could be justified as a benefit-based tax, a uniform rate applied evenly throughout a specific municipality would very likely overtax certain properties in specific parts of the municipality.[36] Clearly, what is required on benefit grounds is a series of different effective tax rates across various classes of property with each rate reflecting a measurement of the benefits accruing to each class of property. In this way, greater equity and efficiency would be achieved in the provision of many of the property-related municipal services (snow removal, street lighting,

---

[34]D.A.L. Auld and F. C. Miller, *Principles of Public Finance: A Canadian Text* (Toronto: Methuen, 1975), 170.

[35]For a discussion of these, see supra footnote 1, at 71-77 and 83-85.

[36]For a more extensive elaboration on the points made in this paragraph, see John Bossons, "Property Tax Reform: What is Desirable?" in John Bossons, Michael Denny, and Enid Slack,
(Continued on next page.)

etc.). For the people-related services (education, welfare, etc.) provided by local governments, ability-to-pay criteria should be adopted and in this instance, the burden of property taxation imposed for financing these services could be partially alleviated by the use of provincial income tax credits.

Since the real property tax applies to improvements as well as to land, it is also claimed by critics that the tax discriminates against improvements and therefore may encourage slum housing. A partial solution to this problem may rest in the use of site value taxation (discussed later in this chapter), which would tax land according to its economic potential. However useful site value taxation may be, nearly all provinces have embarked on market value assessment systems based on land and improvements, and major changes in this base seem at present unlikely.

A general criticism is that property tax discriminates against some land-intensive industries like railways and favours more capital-intensive industries such as trucking, air transportation, and shipping. To alleviate this distortion, some provinces assess land-intensive industries on a different basis other than property. On the other hand, it has been suggested that agriculture is one land-intensive industry that is favourably treated.

A further argument against the real property tax is that allowable exemptions have substantially reduced the tax base and thus have created a number of serious problems. For example, in Ontario in 1973 (the latest year for which tax exempt assessment figures were published), tax-exempt property, in total, amounted to almost 17 per cent of local taxable assessment. The inclusion of these properties in the tax base in that year could have reduced property taxes by roughly $100 per household, while holding local tax revenues constant.[37] Similar statements can be made about tax-exempt property in the other provinces. Full exemptions have generally been given to property "owned by upper-tiered governments, charitable, religious and education institutions, and partial exemptions are often given to farmers, homeowners and selected industries."[38] Tax exemptions on upper-tiered government properties have been the result of constitutional considerations, while tax exemptions are given to charitable institutions on the assumption that they generate positive externalities (benefits to society for which society does not pay directly) that should be encouraged.[39]

---

[36]Continued

Municipal Fiscal Reform in Ontario: Property Taxes and Provincial Grants (Toronto: Ontario Economic Council, 1981), 9-88.

[37]Calculated from data in Ontario, Ministry of Treasury, Economics and Intergovernmental Affairs, *1973 Municipal Financial Information* (Toronto: the Ministry, 1975). The suggestion that including exempt property in the tax base and taxing it would increase property tax revenue by about $100 per household does not imply that municipal revenues would rise by $100. Indeed, on some of this exempt property, local governments received grants in lieu of taxes. Clearly, full taxation of exempt property would lead to decreases in the grants received, thus generating municipal revenue increases of less than $100 per household.

[38]Supra footnote 15, at 341.

[39]Ibid.

The exemption of certain properties discriminates in favour of tax-exempt organizations leading to a mix of land use that may be different from that which might exist under equal treatment of all properties. A continuation of this policy granting tax-exempt status is difficult to support. If a sound case can be made for preferential treatment, then selected organizations should be rewarded directly in the form of grants rather than on the basis of their property holdings. This kind of subsidization would be established openly and would be subject to review and amendment by elected representatives according to their interpretation of the public interest.

However frequent the claims for the elimination of tax exemptions have been, public pressure and the prospect of losing a number of municipal services supplied by the tax-exempt organizations generally have resulted in recommendations suggesting only some, but not extensive, inclusion in the tax base. For instance, the most recent report on the reform of property taxation[40] recommended continued exemption for cemeteries, church property used as a place of worship, certain charitable organizations depending on their activities, and land held in trust for a band of Indians. The same report, on the other hand, recommended the removal of tax-exempt status for some charitable organizations and private schools. Finally, in virtually all suggestions for reform, it has been recommended that exempt property be assessed and in most instances, grants in-lieu-of taxes be paid in amounts equivalent to the value of taxes that could be collected under a truly comprehensive property tax.

Regressivity

Probably the strongest and longest standing criticism of the real property tax has been directed against its alleged regressivity; that is, it has traditionally been claimed that the tax absorbs a greater percentage of the income of low-income earners than of high-income earners. In fact, the limited Canadian empirical evidence in Canada supports this claim.[41] However, recent critics[42] have attacked this empirical evidence and the assumptions underlying it. To be specific, their criticism is that there is no reliable data supporting regressivity: these are simply numbers that depend entirely on the underlying assumptions. These attacks on traditional incidence theory among academic economists and some municipal administrators will be outlined in the discussion following.

---

[40]Supra footnote 8, at 70-83.

[41]See F. A. Clayton, "Distribution of Urban Residential Property Tax Burdens and Expenditure Benefits in Canada" (unpublished Ph.D. dissertation, Queen's University, 1966); W. Irwin Gillespie, *The Incidence of Taxes and Public Expenditures in the Canadian Economy,* Studies of the Royal Commission on Taxation, no. 2 (Ottawa: Queen's Printer, 1966); W. Irwin Gillespie, "On the Redistribution of Income in Canada" (July-August 1976), 24 *Canadian Tax Journal* 417-50; Irving Jay Goffman, *The Burden of Canadian Taxation: Allocation of Federal, Provincial and Local Taxes Among Income Classes,* Canadian Tax Papers, no. 29 (Toronto: Canadian Tax Foundation, 1962); and Allan M. Maslove, *The Pattern of Taxation in Canada* (Ottawa: Information Canada, 1972).

[42]For a thorough and extensive critique of the "so called" regressivity of property taxes, see supra footnote 25, at Chapters 4 and 5.

The Traditional View[43]

The traditional approach to regressivity assumes that the property tax is separable into two components: a tax on land and a tax on structures. Supporters of this view assume that land is fixed in supply, and as such, any tax on land must be borne by the owner. It cannot be shifted to others through changing the supply of land. Taxes, therefore, are capitalized into the price of land with the consequent effect that land prices will fall.

On the other hand, this approach assumes that the supply of structures can be altered through capital expansion projects, and as such, any tax on buildings can be shifted forward to the consumers of the services provided by the buildings. Since the supporters of this view assume that the supply of structures is infinitely elastic in the long run[44] (that is, any quantity will be provided at a specific rate of return), it further follows that the entire amount of the tax will be passed on. In the case of rental residential property, for example, the tax can be shifted forward to the tenants and in the case of nonresidential property, it can be shifted to consumers of the goods and services produced by commerce and industry. Similarly, for owner-occupied residences, the tax on structures is borne by the owners in proportion to their imputed housing expenditures.

Since much of the existing empirical work on the incidence of property taxation in Canada has been based on these assumptions, their results must be treated with considerable caution. To assume, in any tax jurisdiction, that land is in fixed supply and that any quantity of buildings will be supplied at a given rate of return is highly questionable. Land is not in fixed supply. It can be created through land-fill operations or an expansion of municipal boundaries. In this case, a tax on land will tend to affect the quantity supplied and may not be borne entirely by the owners.

Although the advocates of the traditional theory have claimed that taxes on structures are fully shifted, this occurs, if at all, only in the long run. Nevertheless, the incidence studies have apparently assumed that full shifting takes place immediately, a result that arises only if the demand for housing is perfectly inelastic (fixed). Knowledge of the housing market does not support this claim. To apply the conventional incidence assumptions requires a great deal of empirical information on the nature of the housing market in each area studied, information that has not been built into the studies cited. In fact, the distinct lack of specific characteristics reflecting the local situation and the general acceptance of broad and sweeping assumptions based on somewhat questionable observations make the results of the existing studies highly suspect.

A further criticism revolves around the use of annual income as a basis for measuring the incidence of this tax. Housing expenditures (including property taxes), it is claimed, are more directly related to some concept of permanent or

---

[43]This review of the traditional approach and the next section on the new approach follow very closely (but in a substantially condensed form) the material in Richard M. Bird, "The Incidence of the Property Tax: Old Wine in New Bottles?" in supra footnote 15, at 323-34, and supra footnote 25, at Chapter 3. For a fuller discussion on this material, refer to Henry J. Aaron, *Who Pays the Property Tax: A New View*, Studies of Government Finance (Washington, D.C.: Brookings Institution, 1975).

[44]The same conclusion would exist if the demand for structures were completely inelastic.

LOCAL GOVERNMENT FINANCE IN CANADA

normal income.[45] In one comparison undertaken in the United States, the property tax, when measured against normal income (defined as average income over a five-year period), was slightly regressive for tenants, slightly progressive for owners, and overall, roughly proportional even under the traditional shifting assumptions.[46]

Although the evaluation presented here has been highly critical of the traditional approach, one must realize that given the proper specification of the relevant functions and variables, this approach may provide us with useful information on a number of local policy issues. These include the short-run impact on local housing prices resulting from a change in municipal taxes and the long-run incidence arising from a marginal change in local taxes.

The New View

As distinct from the conventional view, which suggests that the incidence of property taxation on structures (with the exception of owner-occupiers) rests on tenants and consumers of the services of these structures, the new view states that the burden falls on property owners. This difference arises because of the ways in which the tax is viewed. The earlier approach dealt with incidence in a specific municipality, whereas the new approach assesses the incidence over the entire country. In this latter case, the proponents have simply borrowed a model of corporate tax incidence and applied it to an analysis of property taxes.[47]

In this model, the following assumptions are made: (1) the total supply of labour and capital is fixed; (2) product and factor markets are perfectly competitive with factors receiving the value of their marginal product; and (3) capital is perfectly mobile between industries and regions. Given these assumptions, it is argued that a uniform (nationwide) tax on all types of property will not change the price of housing or other goods but will, instead, lower the profits and rents of profit-earners and landlords. In other words, the tax is borne by the owners of these assets and since this ownership is assumed to be more concentrated among high-income than low-income earners, the incidence of the tax will be progressive.

Although this may be a theoretically interesting analysis, the advocates of this approach realize that the property tax is not imposed at a uniform rate on all types of property. Some properties are exempt and there are wide variations in the effective rates of tax among localities and types of properties. These variations generate a number of effects (called "excise tax effects") that may be analyzed using the traditional method discussed above.

Since land is assumed to be fixed in supply, the portion of the tax imposed on land will be borne by the owners and capitalized in land values. Differential taxes on reproducible capital (structures), on the other hand, will lead to movements of capital from high- to low-taxed areas or industries. Because of the assumed property of diminishing marginal returns to capital, the return will fall in the lower-taxed sector and rise in the higher-taxed sector. The reallocation

For further discussion see Aaron, supra footnote 43, at Chapter 3.

[46]Ibid., at 36-38.

[47]For a lengthier discussion of this, see supra footnote 1, at 126-31.

of capital will continue until a new equilibrium is reached where the net (after tax) returns to capital are identical in the lower- and higher-taxed areas (industries). In this way, the burden of the property tax in the higher-taxed sector will be partially passed on to capital returns in the lower-taxed area. This analysis assumes that the total amount of capital is fixed and that the less than uniform application of the property tax or less than uniform application of increases in the property tax will generate a reallocation of capital among industries or geographical areas. Hence, the burden of property taxes is eventually felt as a reduction in the net return to capital in all sectors.

Part of the tax may also be shifted to labour and consumers. When capital leaves the higher-taxed area and moves into the lower-taxed area, labour requirements will be reduced in the former and increased in the latter. If the lower-taxed area employs relatively large amounts of capital relative to labour when compared with the higher-taxed area, more labour will be released than can be absorbed in the lower-taxed area at the going wage rate. This excess supply of labour will tend to depress wage rates in order to absorb the labour. In this way, part of the burden of the tax will be borne by labour. Conversely, if the higher-taxed area were relatively capital intensive, the wage rate for labour would tend to rise.

At the same time, the imposition of a less than uniform property tax or a less than uniform increase in property taxes across the country will cause the relative prices of goods purchased in the higher-taxed areas or industries to rise when compared with goods from lower-taxed areas or industries. Persons devoting relatively larger proportions of their incomes to purchasing goods produced in the higher-taxed sectors will bear a relatively heavier tax burden.

The overall incidence of the tax will be determined by the combined effect of the tax on capital, labour, and consumers. The exact sharing of the burden will depend on the ease with which capital may be substituted for labour between the higher- and lower-taxed areas, the relative capital intensities of the two sectors, and the elasticities of demand for the goods produced in the two sectors.

As with the conventional approach, there is no doubt that the conclusions drawn in the new view follow from the assumptions made. The serious question, however, is whether or not the assumptions accord with reality. For example, in the new view, it is assumed that the supply of capital is perfectly inelastic. Such a claim may be difficult to support in Canada because the Canadian economy is very small and relatively open. Capital is highly mobile across national borders and among provinces signifying that the rate of return in Canada or in each of the different provinces is, in some measure, determined by that in the United States or the other provinces. Furthermore, differentials in effective property tax rates among the different provinces or between Canada and the United States may affect the volume of capital stock in each of the provinces or in Canada vis-à-vis the United States. A recent study by Ballentine and Thirsk,[48] however, has suggested that Canada's connection to world capital markets may be more complicated than outlined in this paragraph. Briefly, their position is that the existence of international tax treaties creates a more complex

---

[48]J. Gregory Ballentine and Wayne R. Thirsk, *The Fiscal Incidence of Some Experiments in Fiscal Federalism: Technical Report* (Ottawa: Supply and Services Canada, 1979).

set of interactions in the international capital market. They therefore claim that it is highly probable that a country-wide increase in Canadian property taxes will be borne by property owners in Canada.

To the extent that the supply of savings available for investment is sensitive to the rate of return, the property tax will discourage new investment in total and thus reduce the supply of new structures. The prices of services produced by these buildings will rise and the tax will be borne partially by the consumers of these services and partially by the owners.

A further assumption, which frequently has been attacked, is that of perfectly competitive markets. Critics have suggested that property owners may have sufficient power to set property prices and to increase them when property taxes are raised. The weight of this claim, however, is somewhat uncertain in that the real estate market is reasonably competitive throughout the country. On the other hand, the introduction of rent controls in much of Canada has provided a legitimate justification for increasing rents when property taxes rise.

Finally, the existence of a number of product and factor market imperfections suggests that these factors are unlikely to receive a payment equal to the value of their marginal product. As well, labour and reproducible capital may not be as completely mobile as assumed in the original model. If this is true, then workers, consumers, and property owners may have higher real incomes in lower-taxed areas than in higher-taxed areas.

Empirical Evidence on Regressivity of the Residential Property Tax

Depending on the assumptions chosen, each view arrives at different theoretical conclusions on the incidence of the property tax. What is needed, therefore, is an empirical examination of the incidence of this tax based on the different assumptions outlined in the two views presented above.

Table 8.4 presents seven different estimates of the incidence of property taxation. The first five cases are reproductions of a study by Bird and Slack.[49] Cases 6 and 7 are based on information drawn from a study by Ballentine and Thirsk.[50] Case 1 assumes that taxes on residential owner-occupied buildings are borne by homeowners and that taxes on the land portion of rental residential properties fall on the owner. In addition, it assumes that taxes on the improvements part of rented residential properties are fully shifted onto tenants. Case 2 accepts the first two assumptions of Case 1 but changes the third assumption so that taxes on the improvements portion of rented residential property are divided evenly between renters and owners. Case 3 is similar to Case 1 except that owners bear all of the taxes on rented residential property. Case 4's assumptions include homeowners bearing all of the taxes on the land portion of owner-occupied residential properties, while owners of capital, in general, bear all of the taxes on the improvements portion of owner-occupied property. Taxes on the land portion of rented properties are borne by owners and taxes on the improvements part of rented properties are assumed to be borne by owners of capital in general. Case 5 assumes all taxes are borne by owners of capital in general.

---

[49]Supra footnote 25, at 62.

[50]Supra footnote 48, at 203.

Table 8.4   Alternative Estimates of the Incidence of the Residential Property Tax

	Income class								
Case	Under 3,000	3,000 3,999	4,000 4,999	5,000 5,999	6,000 6,999	7,000 9,999	10,000 14,999	Over 15,000	All classes
	taxes as a percentage of income								
1.........	6.9	5.3	3.8	3.1	3.3	3.1	2.4	2.1	2.8
2.........	6.7	5.3	4.2	3.0	3.1	2.9	2.3	2.3	2.8
3.........	6.6	5.4	4.6	2.8	2.9	2.8	2.1	2.6	2.8
4.........	6.1	5.2	4.8	3.3	3.6	2.1	1.7	3.7	2.8
5.........	5.9	5.1	4.9	3.5	3.8	1.8	1.5	4.0	2.8
6.........	7.1	4.7	3.4	2.4	2.4	2.1	2.4	3.4	2.8
7.........	6.3	5.5	3.9	2.8	2.6	2.3	2.4	3.2	2.8

Source: Reproduced from Wayne R. Thirsk, "Political Sensitivity Versus Economic Sensibility: A Tale of Two Property Taxes," in Wayne R. Thirsk and John Whalley, eds., *Tax Policy Options in the 1980s* (Toronto: Canadian Tax Foundation, 1982), at 392.

Obviously, Cases 1 to 3 are variants of the traditional view of property tax incidence with Case 1 representing the purest version of traditional incidence theory. Cases 4 and 5, on the other hand, represent two views of the new approach to incidence analysis with Case 5 illustrating the purest form of the new approach. In each of the cases (Table 8.4), the results presented are for the province of Ontario. Nevertheless, it can be reasonably assumed that a similar pattern prevails for the rest of the country. Cases 6 and 7 undertaken by Ballentine and Thirsk use a general equilibrium model of the Canadian economy in order to estimate property tax incidence in Canada. The basic difference in each of these latter two models lies in the different assumptions made about the elasticity of the supply of capital in the Canadian economy.

A comparison of the results of the different models generates some useful observations. Regardless of the model chosen, each suggests that the property tax is regressive at the lowest end of the income scale. Under the strictest traditional assumptions (Case 1), the tax is viewed as being regressive for all income classes. If one observes the modified traditional models (Cases 2 and 3), however, the tax is seen to be roughly proportional or slightly progressive when moving into the middle- and upper-income ranges.

By way of comparison, results from the new view (Cases 4 and 5) and the general equilibrium models (Cases 6 and 7) suggest that the property tax becomes more progressive at the upper end of the income scale. The U-shaped incidence profile depicted in each of the models 4 to 7, arises because individuals in the higher- and lower-income strata, when compared with the middle-income groups, receive proportionately more of their income in the form of capital income. The basic difference in the results generated by the models based on the new view of property tax incidence (Cases 4 and 5) and those based on a general equilibrium approach (Cases 6 and 7) exists in the depth of the trough of the U-shaped incidence profile and not on the shape of the profile itself.[51]

[51]For further elaboration on the material in this paragraph, see Wayne R. Thirsk, "Political Sensitivity Versus Economic Sensibility: A Tale of Two Property Taxes," in Wayne R. Thirsk and John Whalley, eds., *Tax Policy Options in the 1980s* (Toronto: Canadian Tax Foundation, 1982), 384-403.

What conclusions can be drawn from the evidence on the regressivity of the residential property tax? Unfortunately, there is no simple or obvious answer to this question; especially in view of the numerous conceptual and statistical problems haunting all quantitative incidence exercises.[52] Perhaps the safest and best observation that can be made as a result of these studies is that the new view indicates that the property tax is not as regressive as the traditional view claims nor is it likely to be as progressive as some of the advocates of the new view have suggested. Empirically and theoretically, the incidence question is in an embryonic state. Further research and analysis is required before any semblance of a definitive and conclusive position can be taken.

An assessment of the incidence profile across income groups, as illustrated in Table 8.4 and discussed in the preceding paragraphs, concerns itself solely with the question of vertical equity or a fair distribution of the residential property tax burden across income strata. Of equal and perhaps more importance is the issue of horizontal equity, that is, equal treatment of all taxpayers deemed to be in similar or identical circumstances. Clearly, the tax seems to be deficient in this instance. Uneven assessment procedures combined with the fact that individuals with similar incomes spend proportionately different amounts on housing services both work to generate horizontal inequities (that is, individuals with identical incomes frequently pay proportionately different amounts of their identical incomes in property taxes).

On the other hand, it is highly questionable whether income should be used as a basis for addressing the equity issue at all. To judge the equity of the property tax on the basis of how closely it resembles the income tax is sure to make the property tax look inferior. No other tax resembles the income tax as much as the income tax itself. It has been argued[53] that the property tax has a very different rationale. It is a levy on particular forms of nonhuman wealth and its fairness should be judged on how closely it fits that rationale and not the income tax rationale.

Property Tax Relief

As was observed in the preceding section, the extent to which the property tax is actually regressive is a subject of considerable controversy. What is more important, however, is the fact that a number of provincial and municipal governments have assumed it is either regressive or not progressive enough, and consequently they have introduced certain measures to alleviate part of the burden. Relief, either by statute or option, has been granted in municipalities in Ontario, Manitoba, Alberta, New Brunswick, Prince Edward Island, Nova Scotia, and British Columbia through the implementation of differential mill rates so that rates imposed on residential properties are lower than those imposed on business properties. In other instances, specific types of property are exempt from assessment or taxation, are assessed at less than normal rates, or are taxed on statutory rates of assessment that may or may not represent a

---

[52]For an excellent review of these weaknesses, see supra footnote 25, at Chapter 5.

[53]M. Mason Gaffney, "The Property Tax is a Progressive Tax," in *Proceedings of the Sixty-Fourth Annual Conference on Taxation,* September 26-30, 1971 (Columbus, Ohio: National Tax Association, 1972), 423.

level of revenue comparable to other assessments. Again federal and provincial governments and Crown agencies may or may not pay the equivalent of full or partial taxes on Crown properties. The situation varies greatly among the provinces.

Partial exemptions, determents, or more generous provisions of relief programs available to all taxpayers are provided for the elderly and the impoverished in most of the provinces. Saskatchewan provides a grant to businessmen conducting business from their places of residence. Nova Scotia has implemented a tax allowance to be applied against the business assessment of small businesses. In all provinces, some property tax relief is provided to farmers whose land is assessed in relation to its value in farming rather than by its market value. This is particularly important for those farmers located near urban areas.[54]

Two of the more popular forms of tax relief, which have captured the interest of provincial and municipal politicians and administrators, include homeowner grants and tax credits. Homeowner grants, although not as widely used as they once were,[55] still play an important role in Saskatchewan and British Columbia. While these programs differ in their specific details, they do provide owner-occupiers with grants that will vary depending on the specific circumstances of the recipient. For example, in British Columbia in 1983, taxpayers under the age of 65 were eligible to receive up to $380 per year with a minimum tax payable of $125 (increased to $150 in 1984). Taxpayers over the age of 65 could receive up to $630 with a minimum tax payable of $1. A similar situation prevails in Saskatchewan where homeowners (excluding farmers) receive grants in respect of their principal residences equal to the lesser of $230 or 50 per cent of their property taxes. For farmers, the grant is the lesser of $375 or the equivalent of a 25 mill levy on eligible assessment. For business, the grant is the lesser of $250 or the equivalent of a 25 mill levy on eligible assessment.[56] In neither of these provinces is relief provided to the tenant through the homeowner grants program.

Property tax credits against provincial personal income taxes exist in Quebec, Ontario, and Manitoba.[57] In each of these instances, the objective is to remove part of the alleged regressivity of the property tax. In fact, in one specific study of residential real estate in London, Ontario, the author[58] concluded that the impact of the property tax credit in Ontario converted what was felt to be a regressive tax into one that is roughly proportional.

---

[54]For a fuller explanation of property tax relief in each of the provinces, see supra footnote 6, at Chapter 7, and Finnis, supra footnote 9.

[55]For a discussion of homeowner grants in the mid-1960s, see Harry Kitchen, "Home-Owner Grants" (January-February 1967), 15 *Canadian Tax Journal* 63-67.

[56]Canadian Tax Foundation, *Provincial and Municipal Finances, 1983* (Toronto: the Foundation, 1983), Chapter 7.

[57]New Brunswick has a tax credit scheme, but it is not a tax credit against income; rather it is a property tax credit against property assessment.

[58]Peter Chinloy, "Effective Property Taxes and Tax Capitalization" (November 1978), 11 *The Canadian Journal of Economics* 740-50.

In Quebec, personal income tax liability is reduced or cash refunds are paid to property owners or tenants. For property owners, the credit equals 40 per cent of property taxes paid less 2 per cent of the household's taxable income with a maximum credit of $400. For tenants, the same rules apply except that property taxes are limited to the portion of the dwelling occupied. In Ontario, "the property tax credit formula is $180 or 'occupancy cost' (property taxes or 20 per cent of rent), whichever is the lesser amount, plus 10 per cent of 'occupancy cost' less 2 per cent of taxable income."[59] This is not available to senior citizens; instead they receive a flat grant of $500 per person. In Manitoba, the credit is the lesser of $375 (minus $150 or 1 per cent of taxable income whichever is lower) or the amount of property taxes or rent paid on the principal residence.

Alberta has implemented a property tax credit scheme just for renters. Renters there are allowed to deduct from provincial income taxes payable an amount equal to $80 plus 5 per cent of rent paid, up to a maximum of $250, reduced by 1 per cent of taxable income. The minimum tax credit is $50. Homeowners, on the other hand, are allowed a property tax reduction equal only to the lesser of $200 or total taxes on the owner's principal residence.

Although this section has not covered, in detail, the full range of property tax relief programs available in the different provinces, it has served to outline the types of schemes available. Knowing that the magnitude and form of direct relief from property taxation varies from province to province, one must still be cautious in making interprovincial comparisons without some knowledge of the responsibility for financing local expenditures. For example, in Newfoundland and Prince Edward Island, all or most of the educational services and some of the other traditionally local services are financed by the provincial government. This is not the case in many of the remaining provinces. Similarly, provincial grants may vary from one province to another and affect the level of property taxes required to finance local expenditures. In those provinces where provincial grants are relatively more important or where the responsibility for funding local services rests with the provincial government, there will not be as much importance placed on the property tax, and consequently, there will be less incentive to provide relief from property taxation.

EVALUATION OF LOCAL PROPERTY TAXES

An evaluation of local property taxation will inevitably involve suggestions for reform. The extent to which these suggestions are implemented will depend on a number of considerations including economic, political, and administrative factors. While most analysts accept the position that local governments should not be concerned with income redistribution programs (these can be more effectively and efficiently handled by provincial or federal governments), there is less consensus on the extent to which local property taxes should be used to finance many local services.

At one extreme is the view that property taxation ought to be designed as a collection of user charges.[60] The advantages arising from such benefit-based

---

[59]Supra footnote 6, at 191.

[60]For a thorough discussion of the design and implications of basing property taxes on the "benefit-received principal" (user charges), see supra footnote 36.

taxation cannot be denied (for a discussion of the advantages of using user charges to finance local services, see Chapter 10). Adoption of this reform would involve the separation of local services into those that are property-related and those that are people-related. Property-related services (water supply, sewage, roads, and fire protection) would be financed from property tax revenue. This does not mean that effective property tax rates need be constant across all classifications of property within and among municipalities. Indeed, effective property tax rates could differ for a number of reasons. First, differentials are justified where the costs of servicing different properties vary either because of type or location within the municipal boundary. Second, higher rates should be imposed on properties that generate negative externalities, that is, where the use of the property generates higher costs for others who do not directly use the property.

People-related services (health, education, and welfare), on the other hand, generally would be financed through taxes based on the ability-to-pay principle (personal income tax). Since local governments do not have access to personal income taxation, these functions ought to be funded by provincial or federal governments. The one exception to this principle may occur in financing local public services (people- or property-related) for which the demand is higher in certain localities or for certain property types. In this instance, higher effective property tax rates would be required to finance this increased demand.

Finally, variations in effective property tax rates assigned to different classifications of property may be desirable and acceptable in instances where particular land use or development is to be encouraged or discouraged.

While the existing property tax system tends to be considerably removed from the principles outlined here, there is at least one instance where property taxes may conform partially to benefit-based levies for specific services. In residential properties there is some evidence suggesting that front footage and lot size are positively correlated with the ratio of property taxes to market values (that is, the larger the area, the higher the effective tax rate).[61] This is justifiable for property-related services as long as the cost of providing local services is dependent on lot size, as may be true for fire and police protection, or front footage as in the case of water and sewage connections or street construction and maintenance.[62]

Unfortunately, the reform of property taxation along the lines of separating the funding responsibility for property- and people-related services will be difficult, if not impossible, to achieve. First, it will be impossible to make a clear distinction between services that benefit property and those that benefit people. For instance, are such services as protection, general government, and environmental expenditures people- or property-related? Second, even if a clear delineation of local services into one of these two categories were possible, all

---

[61]M. Denny and P. Grainger, *An Imputed Property Tax Decision Rule,* Working Paper no. 7409 (Toronto: University of Toronto, Institute for Policy Analysis, 1974), Table IV.

[62]For a discussion of financing a number of local services through benefit-based levies, each of which conforms to a component of the assessment base, see William W. Vickrey, "General and Specific Financing of Urban Services," in Howard G. Schaller, ed., *Public Expenditure Decisions in the Urban Community* (Washington, D.C.: Resources for the Future, 1963), 62-90, at 64-86.

services accruing to property including water provision, sewage disposal, roads, and fire protection are ultimately for the benefit of people. A service that did not benefit the local residents would not get the necessary political support for its provision.[63] Third, the construction of effective tax rates, or differentials in effective tax rates to capture differences in the costs of providing local services, or differences in the demand for these services, or to provide incentives for certain types of land use is considerably more difficult in practice than in theory. Seldom do local governments collect appropriate unit cost data on the cost of providing specific services to the different properties. Similarly, data on the cost of externalities are never collected. Information on the extent to which effective tax rates must differ if certain development incentives are to be provided is virtually non-existent. Fourth, reforming the property tax system to conform with the user charge principle "would in all likelihood be as difficult to sell politically as market-value assessment itself."[64]

The combination of difficulties associated with the separation of services into property- versus people-related categories along with the actual measurement of benefits received from these services and the costs of financing them, plus the political difficulties of implementing a property tax system designed on the basis of user charges suggests that a benefit-based property tax structure is not likely to be considered as a possible reform in the near future.

Realizing that local property taxation is not likely to be altered so as to conform to the pure benefits received principle, it, nevertheless, remains that, whenever possible, the property tax should be designed to capture as closely as possible the benefits arising from the services provided by local governments. With this in mind, the rest of this section will concentrate on an evaluation of the existing property tax systems and changes that might be made to improve their distribution and efficiency.

Most of the criticism levelled against the property tax has been predicated on the belief that it is regressive. This tax allegedly absorbs a larger proportion of the personal income of lower-income individuals than of higher-income individuals. While this measure of fairness (equity) may be inappropriate for a benefit-based tax, it must be addressed on two fronts: extant property taxes are not pure benefit-based taxes and the assertion that they are regressive may not be supported by the available evidence. The emphasis on personal income as the best index by which to judge the fairness of a tax does not present a complete picture. An individual's ability to command goods and services is not only a function of one's income but also of one's wealth, part of which is frequently held in the form of real property. Since high-income earners are more likely (through one device or another) to escape income taxes and since a larger percentage of this income frequently is converted into property, a more extensive use of property tax would capture some of the untaxed income, a large portion of which consists of net imputed rent and is, therefore, nontaxable. Furthermore, as stated above, a review of the recent literature challenges the claim that property taxes are as regressive as traditionally stated. In fact, the more

---

[63]Ontario, *Report of the Royal Commission on Metropolitan Toronto: Detailed Findings and Recommendations*, Vol. 2 (Toronto: the Commission, 1977), 186.

[64]Supra footnote 30, at 481.

recent interpretation and evidence suggests that the impact on taxpayers may be proportional and even somewhat progressive in the higher-income groups. The magnitude and strength of the traditional criticism of regressivity that has been levied against the property tax can no longer be upheld. This is not to suggest, however, that the property tax cannot be improved. Indeed it can and should be. For example, a move to market value assessment on all properties (residential, commercial, and industrial) in all provinces would eliminate a number of inconsistencies that exist particularly within but even among municipalities. In addition, the inclusion of all tax-exempt property in the tax base would eliminate the favourable treatment these properties currently enjoy and would very likely lead to an overall improvement in the allocation of resources. The extent to which social policy dictates that certain relief should be provided to organizations currently owning tax-exempt property, should be supplied in the form of cash grants. As such, taxpayers would be more fully aware of the value of the assistance and better able to judge whether it was acceptable or worthwhile.

Further progress toward improving the efficiency of this tax could be gained by eliminating the current discrimination against nonresidential property vis-à-vis residential property. Such discrimination takes different forms. It may involve the imposition of higher nominal tax rates on nonresidential property as exists in Ontario, Manitoba, Alberta, New Brunswick, Prince Edward Island, Nova Scotia, and British Columbia where split mill rates favour residential property. Alternatively, nonresidential properties in Ontario and British Columbia are subject to higher assessment/market value ratios than residential properties. Table 8.5 illustrates the variation in the effective tax rates (tax as a percentage of market values) between residential and industrial properties across Canada. In each case cited, industrial property appears to bear a substantially higher tax burden than residential property. Similar results were obtained in another study[65] that compared the effective property tax rates for residential and nonresidential property located in the larger municipalities of Ontario and western Canada. The results here approached those reported in Table 8.5 for cities in the same provinces. Effective residential property tax rates tended to be in the range of 1 or 2 per cent while effective nonresidential property rates, with very few exceptions, tended to be one-half to one percentage point higher.

Discrimination against nonresidential property is difficult to support. Local governments engage in expenditures for a number of services, some of which primarily accrue to property while others primarily accrue to people. For residential property, the demand for the consumption of housing services will cause ownership and/or the rental values of residential property to be related to the household's ability to pay, although the degree to which this relationship holds may not be close. For nonresidential property owners, there is no basis for assuming any rough approximation between the owner's ability to pay and the market value of the property.[66]

Since the tax rate imposed on the nonresidential sector is established on the basis of supplying both people- and property-related services and since the

---

[65]Supra footnote 51, at 388. Business taxes are included as part of the property tax burden on nonresidential property.

[66]Supra footnote 36, at 34-35.

Table 8.5   Residential and Industrial Property Taxes as a Per Cent of Market Value, 1978

Province and municipality	Residential	Industrial
	per cent	*per cent*
Newfoundland		
St. John's	.99	1.84
Prince Edward Island		
Charlottetown	1.82	3.64
Nova Scotia		
Halifax	1.69	6.45
Dartmouth	1.51	4.57
New Brunswick		
Saint John	1.15	4.32
Quebec		
Montreal		
Pierrefonds	3.45	—
Dollard des Ormeaux	2.40	—
Pointe Claire	—	4.33
Quebec City[a]	1.97	3.06
Ontario		
Metro Toronto		
Scarborough	1.41	4.18
Manitoba		
Winnipeg	1.67	3.30
Saskatchewan		
Regina	1.59	1.97
Alberta		
Calgary..............................	.86	2.30
Edmonton	.86	2.04
British Columbia		
Vancouver (Burnaby)	1.16	2.90
Victoria (Saanich)	1.03	2.81

[a]Industrial property is in Ste. Foy.

Source: F.H. Finnis, "The Weight of Property Taxation in Canada—Single-Family Dwellings and Light Industrial Property" (May-June 1980), 28 *Canadian Tax Journal* 311.

benefits accruing to the nonresidential sector are primarily those accruing to property alone, it follows that nonresidential property bears a heavier tax than can be justified. In fact, the limited evidence which is available suggests that business receives only about 60 per cent of the benefits received by the residential sector.[67] Based on this information, it may be argued that the current treatment overtaxes nonresidential property and undertaxes residential property. Clearly, a shift in the relative tax burdens would be fairer and would lead to an improvement in the allocation of capital resources. Indeed, one could go so far as to suggest that, whenever possible, a system of user fees should be implemented (at the local level) for the purpose of financing many local services going to the nonresidential sector.

---

[67]Frank A. Clayton, "An Assessment of Proposals Affecting Property Tax Burdens," in *Report of Proceedings of the Special Tax Conference,* January 12-13, 1968 (Toronto: Canadian Tax Foundation, 1968), 47-64. Clayton suggested that his results indicated that a form of reverse discrimination was needed; that is, lower taxes on nonresidential vis-à-vis residential property.

While the preceding comments provide little, if any, justification for the imposition of equal effective property tax rates on both residential and nonresidential property, they clearly provide no justification, whatsoever, for higher rates on nonresidential property. The existence of higher rates on nonresidential property has been defended and supported by local politicians, administrators, and taxpayers alike. In essence, these groups have argued that higher nonresidential rates are essential if residential rates are to be restrained. Their attempt to argue openly in favour of shifting the local tax burden onto the nonresidential sector has been widely accepted and seldom challenged. Unfortunately, this position has had more political appeal than sound economic and analytical support.

A further issue in the taxation of nonresidential property surrounds the incidence of this tax. There is nothing wrong with it as long as it rests on local residents and is used to finance local services. However, the extent to which the nonresidential tax burden is exported to residents of other municipalities in order to finance services whose benefits are restricted to the taxing jurisdiction raises other inequities.[68] Politically, the exportation of local taxes is readily accepted, that is, it is accepted as long as the local community is able to export more taxes to other jurisdictions than it imports from those jurisdictions.

Tax exportation can exist if one community is able to export more goods to other communities than it imports from those communities; for example, if a higher effective tax rate on nonresidential property induces a relatively higher price charged on the sale of that community's exports (to other communities) or a relatively lower price for its imports (from other communities), it will have effectively shifted part of its tax burden to residents in other municipalities.[69] The limited evidence that exists on tax exportation in Canada covers a sample of the larger municipalities in Ontario.[70] The results suggest that the degree of tax exportation ranged from a low of 16 per cent of the nonresidential tax burden (Ottawa) to a high of roughly 100 per cent (Hamilton and Sault Ste. Marie). The unweighted average for all municipalities was 56 per cent of the nonresidential property tax burden. Although this burden is partially borne by workers in the form of lower wages and salaries, a larger portion of it is borne by consumers inside and outside the taxing community. Unfortunately, an accurate depiction of the precise effects upon the pattern of the income distribution in each municipality is impossible to obtain.[71]

Finally, in the absence of greater reliance on user charges at the local level or the failure of provincial governments to assume more responsibility for people-related local expenditures, a case can be made for designing a two-part property tax system.[72] One part applies to both residential and nonresidential property and is based on an estimation of benefits from services primarily going to

---

[68]For evidence supporting this position, see supra footnote 51, at 398.

[69]For a more detailed discussion of this, see ibid., at 396-400.

[70]J. G. Ballentine and W. R. Thirsk, "Representation Without Taxation: The Nonresidential Property Tax" (mimeograph, 1980). For a summary of this material, see supra footnote 51, at 384-403.

[71]For a lengthier discussion of this, see supra footnote 51, at 397-99.

[72]For support of this position, see supra footnote 36, and supra footnote 51.

property. In fact, an ideal tax structure would use differential rates reflecting the differential costs or benefits from those local services accruing to different classifications of property. The second part, designed to cover services whose benefits are primarily available to people would be imposed on residential property only. In this latter instance, greater reliance on the residential property tax may create severe hardships for some individuals in specific circumstances, namely, the elderly or other homeowners whose current income is insufficient to allow them to meet their property tax commitments. If this occurs, greater reliance on tax credits applied against provincial income tax liability (as in the case of Ontario) or outright cash grants to worthy recipients should alleviate the problem.[73]

MUNICIPAL BUSINESS TAX

The municipal business tax is included in this chapter because it is added to the nonresidential property tax as applied to most commercial and industrial properties. The business tax is the second most important source of tax revenue for local governments. Although not extremely productive in terms of revenue yield, it generates around 11 per cent or 12 per cent of the total revenue obtained from taxes on real property or roughly 4 per cent to 5 per cent of local government revenues from all sources.

> Wherever a business tax is imposed in Canada, the statutory liability for payment is on the occupant (whether the owner or tenant) except in British Columbia where the final responsibility rests with the owner of the premises and in St. John's where, if the occupant is also the owner, the tax becomes a lien on the property. Some form of business taxation, additional to the real property tax, is levied in all provinces except Prince Edward Island, where the province levies a tax on business properties at double the rate imposed on noncommercial properties. Most municipalities in Prince Edward Island also levy an optional tax on commercial realty at double their residential rates. The business tax is mandatory upon all municipalities in Newfoundland, Nova Scotia, New Brunswick, Ontario, and Saskatchewan and optional under general legislation in all others (except Prince Edward Island, where the tax as such is not levied).[74]

Although the business tax is employed in most municipalities in Canada, the basis for this tax is far less uniform.[75] There are no less than eight bases in current use and these include:

1) The assessment and taxation of stock-in-trade which may be used in Newfoundland and in some instances in Manitoba.
2) Rental value, which need not be the "actual rent but is more likely to be the one which, in the opinion of the assessor, is fair and comparable to other

---

[73]For a critical assessment of a number of tax relief measures, including the tax credit scheme in Ontario, see supra footnote 25, at Chapters 6 and 7, and supra footnote 15, at 343-45.

[74]Supra footnote 6, at 139-40.

[75]For a more detailed description of the alternative bases, see ibid., at 139-42, and Finnis, supra footnote 9, at Chapter 1.

similar properties,"[76] has been authorized (but not always used) by provincial legislation in all municipalities in British Columbia, Alberta, Manitoba, Quebec, cities in Saskatchewan, and the city of St. John's, Newfoundland.

3) The square footage occupied for business purposes is the usual basis of business assessment in Saskatchewan and an alternative to the annual rental system authorized in Alberta.

4) Storage capacity is an optional basis in Alberta for grain and coal dealers, gasoline and oil distribution, and in Saskatchewan it is used as the basis for business assessment on grain elevators and oil storage tanks.

5) The use of real property assessment is authorized as the business tax base in Newfoundland, New Brunswick, and Ontario. Prince Edward Island achieves a similar result by applying a provincial property tax rate that is twice as high as the residential rate.

6) A percentage of gross revenue may serve as the basis of business taxation in Newfoundland when the real property tax is not imposed and in Manitoba, municipalities can impose this tax on Cable TV operators leasing from a Crown agency.

7) Licensing of businesses at flat rates is common in all provinces.

8) The taxable value of personal property used for business purposes may be employed as an alternative to the gross annual rental value in British Columbia.[77]

EVALUATION OF THE BUSINESS TAX

Although there are arguments made in favour of a municipal tax on business property, there appears to be no sound economic rationale for the general imposition of this tax. Those who favour it argue that businesses create additional municipal costs such as police and fire protection and, therefore, must pay for these costs. The weakness in this argument, however, is similar to that presented for the taxation of nonresidential property. First, as was mentioned earlier, the limited empirical evidence available suggests that in Ontario, businesses receive benefits from municipal services that are substantially lower than those going to residential properties. Consequently, effective tax rates on nonresidential properties should be lower and not higher than similar rates on residential properties.[78] Second, even if the cost of supplying services to business properties is higher, the imposition of an additional tax (which is likely to be unrelated to the actual cost of the services supplied) is clearly an inefficient way of charging for these services. Surely, a more efficient approach involves, as was suggested in the preceding section, the implementation of user charges as a means of financing these property-related services. Since businesses can deduct all expenses incurred in earning income (including business taxes) and since

---

[76]Supra footnote 6, at 140.

[77]For a detailed description of the business tax in each province, see Finnis, supra footnote 9.

[78]Supra footnote 67, at 57.

owner-occupiers of residential dwellings are not allowed the same deductions, it has been suggested that an extra tax on business is legitimate in that this tax attempts to even out the disparities in taxes that would otherwise exist on these two different categories of taxable property. While it is true that owner-occupiers are not able to deduct property taxes, it is also the case that owner-occupiers are not required to include either their imputed income from their owner-occupied dwellings or the capital gains earned on the disposal of their principal residences in their income tax bases.[79] Such an exclusion is similar to a deduction from income for tax purposes (as in the case of the business tax) in that both reduce the taxable economic income of the taxpaying unit. On this basis, it is difficult to make a case for a special local tax on commercial and industrial properties.

Finally, the extent to which the business tax is not uniform among municipalities in Canada and the United States creates a number of distortions. For example, capital used in financing most businesses tends to be fairly mobile and this provides an incentive for businesses to locate where lower tax rates prevail. It has also been argued that "on efficiency grounds taxes should be heavier on those components of the tax base which are least elastic in supply."[80] Since capital tends to be more mobile than people, it can generally be argued (although there may be some exceptions)[81] that lower taxes should be imposed on businesses than on residential properties. Once again, when combined with the arguments against the current treatment of nonresidential properties (as outlined under property taxation), a strong case for adjusting the overall tax structure on nonresidential properties is evident.

AN ALTERNATIVE FORM OF PROPERTY TAXATION: SITE-VALUE TAXATION[82]

Problems with the current system of taxing real property have moved a number of critics to suggest site-value taxation as a feasible alternative. Site-value taxation is a tax that is based on a site's capacity to serve rather than on its current use.

The arguments in favour of site-value taxation are generally couched in terms of improved equity and allocation of resources. Critics have attacked such a tax because of the enormous administrative problems that would arise in changing from the current system of taxing real property. For example, it has been "argued that assessors find it difficult to separate the value of land from total

---

[79]For a discussion of this, see supra footnote 1, at 57.

[80]For elaboration on this point, see supra footnote 25, at 30.

[81]Two exceptions that have been suggested by Bird and Slack in ibid., at 31, include downtown commercial property and businesses operating in a national market with some degree of market power, for they may be able to "export" much of their tax burden.

[82]For a detailed analysis of the elements of site-value taxation, see M. Mason Gaffney, "The Many Faces of Site-Value Taxation," in *Report of Proceedings of the Twenty-Seventh Tax Conference,* November 10-12, 1975 (Toronto: Canadian Tax Foundation, 1976), 749-63.

value of a given piece of property because the use to which land is put often determines the value of the property."[83]

Proponents of the site-value tax claim it would improve the overall equity of the local tax system now in place. A large share of the value of land is determined by activities other than those of the individual landlord including the growth of government expenditures. Since much of the value of land represents an unearned increment, the overall equity could be improved by taxing this surplus.

A stronger argument for site-value taxation revolves around the improvements in the allocation of resources that such a tax would foster. The current system of real property taxation distorts the use to which resources are put. Because of its relatively heavy impact on buildings and improvements in property, it reduces the quantity and quality of housing that would otherwise exist. In addition, it discriminates against industries that use large physical structures in their production process. A change to site-value taxation would not lead to such distortions, since the impact would be the same regardless of the use of the property.

Although the equity and efficiency of site-value taxation may be superior to the present system of real property taxation, any conversion to such a scheme for local taxation in Canada would undoubtedly impose severe transitional costs for certain groups or individuals. For this reason and because "there are no reliable estimates regarding the value of either the benefits of site taxation or the costs of making this change,"[84] it would be quite unwise to consider such a transition.[85]

SUMMARY

On the whole, the residential property tax is a satisfactory tax. Admittedly, there are problems, particularly with respect to uneven assessment practices and a less than comprehensive tax base. These problems, however, are mainly of a administrative nature and can be overcome. In addition, the residential property tax suffers from a number of misconceptions, the most glaring is that it is extremely regressive. By comparison, the existing nonresidential property and business tax cannot be supported on the basis of any sound economic rationale for it is discriminatory and generates incidence patterns that are highly questionable.

Given the uncertainty of the effects of property taxes on vertical equity or the distribution of the tax across taxpayers in different classes (or the benefits it

---

[83]Supra footnote 15, at 340. For a more detailed analysis of the administration problem, see Dick Netzer, *Economics of the Property Tax,* Studies of Government Finance (Washington, D.C.: Brookings Institution, 1966), Chapter 8.

[84]Supra footnote 15, at 341.

[85]For further support of this conclusion, see Finnis, supra footnote 9, at 17.

finances) and perhaps too, the distortions that it creates,[86] the major concern of local policy makers should be the achievement of horizontal equity within each class of property taxpayers. This can be attained by establishing a set of uniform effective tax rates via uniform assessment policies and appropriate tax rates. Any attempt by local authorities to alter the base or rate structures to reflect income redistribution goals is likely to generate increased distortions, reduce revenues and create a general misallocation in the provision of local public goods. Income redistribution issues (the achievement of vertical equity) must be undertaken by a more senior level of government (either federal or provincial) for it is only at this level that a successful redistribution policy can deal with the population at large.

---

[86]While this chapter has outlined a number of distortions created by the existing property tax, these distortions may not be as serious as suggested in some cases. For example, higher nonresidential property taxes may result in lower prices for such property, leaving the net returns to capital and the size of that sector no different than if a lower rate were used. Unfortunately, evidence on the extent to which differentials in the assessment practice, the tax base, and rate structures, have been capitalized into property prices in Canada, simply does not exist. Given this lack of evidence, this chapter has concentrated on the more noticeable distortions that do exist and should be corrected if inconsistencies in the application of property taxes are to be eliminated.

9
Intergovernmental Transfers

INTRODUCTION

An important development in the financing of local government expenditures over the past three decades has been the substantial increase in both the number[1] and value of intergovernmental grants[2] received by local governments. These transfers from both the federal and provincial governments are used for operating as well as for capital purposes. In some instances, they are awarded directly to the municipal governments, while in other instances they are awarded to one or more of the various boards, agencies, or commissions operating in a municipality.

Grants fall into two categories: unconditional and conditional. Unconditional grants may be used for any purpose including the reduction of local taxes. The term "unconditional," it must be emphasized, refers to the use of the grant, not necessarily to the conditions for its receipt. For example, the per capita police grant in Ontario is available to those municipalities supporting their own police forces. While the size of this grant depends on population size, the funds can be spent in any manner desired by the recipient municipality. The resource equalization grant in Ontario is also an unconditional transfer. It is given to any municipality whose fiscal capacity (ability to raise revenue to finance its expenditures without having exorbitant rates relative to other jurisdictions) is below the provincial average. In this instance, the grant is awarded on the basis of need with the size of the grant determined by a formula that measures the extent to which per capita assessment in a particular municipality falls below the provincial average.

Conditional grants must be spent on specific services or facilities such as education, roads, libraries, homes for the aged, or social welfare services. Conditional grants, moreover, may be matching or nonmatching. A matching grant is given only if the municipality agrees to cover a specified percentage of expenditures on a specific service or facility. This may require the municipality to pay 50 per cent of the cost as long as the donor government provides the other 50 per cent. Nonmatching grants carry no restrictions of this sort but do have some upper support limit. Matching grants may be open-ended or closed-ended. Open-ended grants do not specify upper limits on available funds; whereas, closed-ended grants place a restriction on the maximum amount of funds the donor government will provide. Finally, conditional grants may be used for operating or capital purposes.

---

[1] For a listing of provincial-municipal grant programs in all provinces, see Ontario, *Report of the Provincial-Municipal Grants Reform Committee,* Vol. II (Toronto: the Committee, 1977), 427-572.

[2] For an indication of the rising value of per capita grants, see the data in Appendix Tables C.1 and C.2.

Although a categorization of the many municipal grants according to the characteristics outlined here has been done only in Ontario,[3] the limited available evidence[4] suggests that a similar classification scheme applied to municipal grants in the other provinces would reveal a corresponding array of grants employed. Most grants have conditional features attached to them. They tend to be matching and closed-ended but not in the sense that the upper limit of available grant funding is fixed necessarily, rather that regulations or controls (such as ministerial restrictions or alterations in the approval process for certain expenditures) effectively limit the extent to which municipalities have access to total grants.[5]

DISTRIBUTION OF PER CAPITA GRANTS

FEDERAL VERSUS PROVINCIAL

Total grants for both capital and current expenditures, on average, accounted for almost 48 per cent of all municipal expenditures in 1978. This figure represented an increase of 12 percentage points from 1968, thus indicating that local governments have become increasingly more dependent on grants. Unlike Australia,[6] for example, almost all grants to local governments come from and are established by the provincial rather than federal authorities.[7] The bulk of these grants are for conditional purposes with, by far, the largest proportion coming from provincial governments (Table 9.1). In addition, all unconditional grants are distributed by provincial governments with the total per capita size of these grants being considerably lower total per capita levels of conditional transfers.

While federal grants (conditional) accounted for slightly more than 2 per cent of all municipal grants or slightly more than 1 per cent of all local revenue in 1978 (Table 9.1), some interprovincial variation in their relative dependence on grants was noted (see Appendix Tables C.1 and C.2). With the exception of local governments in Newfoundland and Prince Edward Island, where the dependence on federal grants in 1978 accounted for almost 9 per cent and 20 per cent of all revenues respectively, federal contributions to the remaining provinces marginally deviated above or below 1 per cent (Appendix Tables C.1 and C.2).

---

[3]Enid Slack, "Provincial-Municipal Grant Reform in Ontario," in John Bossons, Michael Denny and Enid Slack, *Municipal Fiscal Reform in Ontario: Property Taxes and Provincial Grants* (Toronto: Ontario Economic Council, 1981), 129-62, at 136-49.

[4]For a listing, but not a classification, of the grants according to the characteristics mentioned here, see supra footnote 1.

[5]For a discussion of this in Ontario, see supra footnote 3, at 146-47.

[6]Melville L. McMillan, *Local Intergovernmental Fiscal Relations in Australia and Canada,* Occasional Paper no. 23 (Canberra: Centre for Research on Federal Financial Relations, Australian National University, 1981), 41.

[7]Some federal transfers are given initially to provincial governments through unconditional and conditional transfers (for example, health and welfare) and subsequently to municipal governments. These are recorded in this book as provincial transfers as the provincial governments are the last donors involved in the transfers.

Table 9.1   Per Capita Grants to Local Governments
by Donor Government, 1968 and 1978

Donor government	1968			1978		
	Per capita dollars	Per cent of total grants	Per cent of total revenue	Per capita dollars	Per cent of total grants	Per cent of total revenue
Conditional:						
Federal	2	1.9	.7	10	2.3	1.1
Provincial	100	97.1	34.7	372	84.9	40.5
Total	102	99.0	35.4	382	87.2	41.6
Unconditional:						
Provincial-general purpose	1	1.0	.3	56	12.8	6.1
Total grants	103	100.0	35.7	438	100.0	47.7

Source: Appendix Tables C.1 and C.2.

While provincial transfers to local governments were considerably larger than federal ones[8] over the period studied, the types of grants were also of a different nature.[9] Federal assistance to local governments tended to support capital projects rather than operating expenses (Table 9.2). Support for capital projects was concentrated primarily in the areas of environmental facilities and/or transportation and communication services in 1978. Exceptions to this were observed in Manitoba and Saskatchewan where relatively large grants were received for regional planning and industrial development and in Prince Edward Island where the federal government provided a large grant for educational facilities. By comparison, in almost every province (Newfoundland and Prince Edward Island were the exceptions), provincial grants for capital projects exceeded federal grants for similar kinds of projects. With the exception of housing services and resource conservation and industrial development where no provincial capital grants were available and only small sums provided for protection, regional planning and development, and social welfare facilities, provincial support, in most provinces, was spread across the remaining functions.

During this period, federal grants for operating purposes ranged from 1 per cent to 2 per cent of all grants received by local governments, while provincial support for similar services ranged from 32 per cent of all grants received by municipalities in New Brunswick to 92 per cent in Nova Scotia (Table 9.2). On average, provincial support for operating purposes accounted for 89 per cent of all grants, while federal support for the same services averaged less than 1 per cent. Federal support across Canada tended to concentrate almost entirely on recreation and regional planning and development services. Small sums,

[8]Canadian Tax Foundation, *Provincial and Municipal Finances, 1981* (Toronto: the Foundation, 1981), 180.

[9]For a brief discussion of this, see Dale E. Richmond, "Some Common Issues in Provincial-Municipal Transfer Systems" (Summer 1980), 23 *Canadian Public Administration* 252-68, at 252-54.

Table 9.2 Municipal Distribution of Per Capita Conditional Capital and Operating Grants by Province and by Donor Government, 1978

Province	Federal						Provincial						Total of provincial and federal per capita grants
	Per capita operating	Per cent of total grants	Per capita capital	Per cent of total grants	Total per capita	Per cent of total grants	Per capita operating	Per cent of total grants	Per capita capital	Per cent of total grants	Total per capita	Per cent of total grants	
	$	%	$	%	$	%	$	%	$	%	$	%	$
Newfoundland	1.63	2.5	14.33	22.2	15.96	24.8	40.26	62.5	8.21	12.7	48.47	75.2	64.43
Prince Edward Island	5.68	1.2	109.71	22.7	115.39	23.9	342.30	70.9	25.11	5.2	367.41	76.1	482.80
Nova Scotia	3.86	1.1	8.61	2.4	12.47	3.4	337.20	92.1	16.51	4.5	353.71	96.6	366.18
New Brunswick	.41	1.3	6.56	20.7	6.97	22.0	10.10	31.9	14.61	46.1	24.71	78.0	31.68
Quebec	9.31	2.1	2.32	.5	11.63	2.7	395.09	90.3	30.66	7.0	425.75	97.3	437.38
Ontario	1.42	.4	5.67	1.4	7.09	1.8	351.55	88.9	36.87	9.3	388.42	98.2	395.51
Manitoba	1.47	.4	5.61	1.7	7.08	2.1	296.42	88.2	32.59	9.7	329.01	97.9	336.09
Saskatchewan	2.76	.6	5.49	1.3	15.33	3.6	374.69	88.1	35.32	8.3	410.01	96.4	425.34
Alberta	1.52	.3	12.49	2.2	14.01	2.5	494.92	88.1	53.08	9.4	548.00	97.5	562.01
British Columbia	3.57	1.5	6.23	2.7	9.80	4.2	205.64	87.9	18.59	7.9	224.23	95.8	234.03
All provinces	3.62	.9	5.81	1.5	9.01	2.4	339.99	89.1	32.63	8.6	372.62	97.6	381.63

Source: From unpublished data provided by Statistics Canada, Public Finance Division, Local Government Section.

however, were given to support transportation and communication, general government, protection of persons and property, and environment functions. Provincial support for operating purposes went primarily to education (in those provinces where this was not the responsibility of provincial governments), health, social welfare, and transportation and communication.

UNCONDITIONAL GRANTS

From 1968 to 1978, unconditional grants to municipal governments increased in every province, both in absolute value and in the proportion of total local revenues obtained from this source. The largest absolute increases occurred in Quebec ($77 per capita), Nova Scotia ($73 per capita), and New Brunswick ($71 per capita), while the smallest increases were witnessed in Newfoundland ($13 per capita), Manitoba ($15 per capita), and Prince Edward Island ($16 per capita). The relative dependence on this source of revenue rose by almost 6 percentage points over all provinces during the period under study. Larger increases than this were observed in New Brunswick (from 0 per cent to 31.7 per cent of total revenue), Nova Scotia (2.1 per cent to 10.5 per cent), Quebec (0 per cent to 8.1 per cent), and Newfoundland (0 per cent to 6.9 per cent), while smaller increases were recorded elsewhere (see Table 9.3). While these figures reflect the significant changes that occurred over the 11-year period under observation, recent developments in the provincial-municipal grant systems in Newfoundland (effective April 1, 1980), Nova Scotia (effective January 1, 1980), and Quebec (effective January 1, 1980) suggest that unconditional grants may be assuming an even more important role. This is true especially in Nova Scotia where all grants—with the exception of capital grants—are now unconditional.

Similar interprovincial variations also can be noted in the structure of these grants.[10] A new municipal grants program came into operation on April 1, 1980 in Newfoundland. This program provides (1) a general municipal assistance grant based on population, social assistance, and road mileage and (2) a tax incentive grant based on actual property taxes collected. In this latter instance, an equalization factor is introduced. For example, the ratio of grant-per-dollar value of property taxes collected is highest for municipalities whose total property tax collection is low and lowest for municipalities with high property tax yields. Both St. John's and Cornerbrook receive additional general-purpose grants from the province based on this formula.

An equalization grant based on a formula designed to reflect the ability of local governments to finance local services is provided to all municipalities in Prince Edward Island. In addition, the municipalities of Charlottetown and Summerside along with all incorporated towns and villages receive per capita entitlements from the provincial government. This payment is highest for Charlottetown and lowest for the incorporated villages.

Because of significant changes implemented on January 1, 1980, the relative importance of unconditional grants for municipalities in Nova Scotia is understated in the figures recorded in Table 9.3. In essence, this new system of unconditional operating grants replaced a number of conditional grants that

---

[10]For further detail on municipal unconditional grants, see supra footnote 8, at Chapter 7.

Table 9.3   Per Capita Unconditional and Conditional Municipal Grants by Province, 1968 and 1978

Province	1968				1978			
	Conditional	Per cent of total revenue	Unconditional	Per cent of total revenue	Conditional	Per cent of total revenue	Unconditional	Per cent of total revenue
	$	%	$	%	$	%	$	%
Newfoundland	6	12.5	0	0	64	35.3	13	6.9
Prince Edward Island	95	57.2	0	0	482	82.5	16	2.8
Nova Scotia	81	41.9	4	2.1	366	49.6	77	10.5
New Brunswick	2	3.4	0	0	32	14.1	71	31.7
Quebec	93	34.2	0	0	438	46.6	77	8.1
Ontario	124	36.4	1	.3	396	40.0	54	5.5
Manitoba	99	35.6	3	1.1	336	37.7	18	2.0
Saskatchewan	94	32.7	2	.7	418	44.0	48	5.0
Alberta	111	33.4	1	.3	562	47.2	37	3.1
British Columbia	110	37.8	1	.3	234	27.6	48	5.6
All provinces	102	35.4	1	.3	382	41.6	56	6.1

Source: Appendix Tables C.1 and C.2.

were felt to be unfair and excessively regulatory. The new system of grants is based on a formula that takes into consideration each municipality's expenditure needs, fiscal capacity, size, and type. As well, unconditional grants are indexed to reflect any growth in provincial revenues.

In New Brunswick,[11] unconditional grants are based on three factors: (1) any municipality whose per capita assessment is below that for all municipalities in the province is eligible for funds; (2) any municipality whose population density, as measured by the assessment per road mile, is lower than the provincial average is entitled to funds; and (3) in order to recognize the additional costs of providing services to more heavily populated areas, unconditional grants are higher for all communities with more than 5,000 people. Yearly grant increases in New Brunswick correspond to forecasted percentage changes in provincial net revenues.

Quebec also introduced a new provincial-municipal unconditional grant system in 1980. This new system includes an equalization transfer based on a formula designed to reflect the size and fiscal capacity of each municipality.

There are six unconditional grant programs potentially available to local governments in the province of Ontario.[12] First, general per capita grants are based on population size and are payable to every municipality with the rates varying depending on the size of the population centre—higher rates exist for large centres and lower rates for smaller centres. This differential rate structure is designed to compensate for the differential costs associated with the provision of local services in communities of different sizes. In 1981, for example, the rate ranged "from $7 per capita on population up to 4,000 to $9 per capita on population in excess of 200,000. In regions, the general per capita grant at a rate of $10 per capita is paid to regional governments on the basis of constituent area municipalities" population.[13] Second, per capita police grants are paid to every municipality operating its own police force. The rate for 1981 was $12 per capita for all municipalities with the exception of regional governments where it was $17 per capita. Third, density per capita grants, which vary inversely with the number of households per acre, are designed to reflect the high costs of servicing sparsely populated areas. Fourth, general support grants are paid to all municipalities. They equal 6 per cent of the previous year's net general dollar levy. Fifth, special support grants are available only to northern municipalities. The value of this grant is equal to 18 per cent of the previous year's net general dollar levy. The justification for this kind of grant is based on the fact that services to northern parts of the province are more expensive to provide. Sixth, resource equalization grants are paid to all lower-tier municipalities (regional governments are excluded) with below-average assessment bases. In 1981, all municipalities with an equalized assessment base of less than $18,600 per capita

[11]Any interprovincial comparison of municipal dependency on unconditional grants must be treated and interpreted with extreme caution because, while Table 9.3 suggests that the municipal sector in New Brunswick was relatively more dependent upon conditional grants in 1978, different municipal expenditure responsibilities (no conditional school grants, for example) exist in New Brunswick, vis-à-vis other provinces. Note as well the figures for New Brunswick in Table 9.2.

[12]See David Siegel, "Provincial-Municipal Relations in Canada: An Overview," supra footnote 9, 281-317, at 310-11.

[13]Supra footnote 8, at 191.

qualified for this kind of grant. The amount of this grant is determined by a formula that estimates the value as being equal to the lesser of 60 per cent of the relative assessment deficiency multiplied by the net general dollar levy or 25 per cent of the net general dollar levy.

The value of unconditional grants in Manitoba is determined by the provincial government's allocation of 2.2 percentage points of provincial personal income tax revenue and 1 percentage point of provincial corporate taxable income to the municipalities. In 1981, the distribution of this revenue amounted to $21 per capita plus an urban services supplement ($5.25 per capita when population exceeds 5,000 and $3.75 when population is below 5,000). As for the city of Winnipeg, one unconditional block grant ($38.5 million in 1981) has replaced nine conditional grant programs that previously existed.

A provincial-municipal revenue-sharing scheme is utilized in Saskatchewan.[14] A portion of provincial revenue (which grows according to the tax base of four provincial taxes: corporate income tax, personal income tax, gasoline and fuel taxes, and sales tax), is allocated to municipalities through conditional and unconditional grants according to specified conditions. The unconditional grant consists of (1) a per capita amount ($45 in 1981); (2) a basic grant (ranging from $1,650 to $2,420 in 1981) that is paid to every community to compensate for the limited funds received under the per capita grant by the smaller municipalities; and (3) a foundation grant whose formula recognizes that expenditures tend to increase with the size of the municipality and outstrip revenue potential.

In the province of Alberta for grant purposes,[15] the municipal sector is divided into four categories based on population size. Within each municipal classification an equalization formula is used to calculate the per capita assessment deficiency (determined as the amount by which the municipal assessment falls below the average for all municipalities in that category) and the provincial government allocates funds accordingly. A per capita grant (which has the same value regardless of the size of the community), is paid to all municipalities. Rural communities receive an unconditional grant, the amount of which is determined by the number of miles of roads contained in each community. Finally, in 1979 a one-shot grant of up to $500 per capita was allocated to each municipality for the purpose of retiring municipal debt.

British Columbia is one of two provinces where a tax-sharing[16] provincial-municipal program exists (the other is Manitoba). Revenues for this program

---

[14]For a description and evaluation of revenue sharing in Saskatchewan, see O. Yul Kwon, "Revenue Sharing as an Improvement in Provincial-Municipal Relations in Canada: An Evaluation of Saskatchewan Revenue Sharing" (September-October 1979), 27 *Canadian Tax Journal* 576-87.

[15]For a description and evaluation of unconditional grants in Alberta, see Melville L. McMillan, "Local Fiscal Reform in Alberta?—A Review and Assessment of the Report of Alberta's Provincial-Municipal Finance Council" (March-April 1980), 28 *Canadian Tax Journal* 164-79; and Melville L. McMillan and Deryk G. Norton, "The Distribution of Unconditional Transfers to Alberta Municipalities: Existing and Alternative Methods" (March-April 1981), 29 *Canadian Tax Journal* 171-83.

[16]Tax sharing is distinguished from revenue sharing because the former refers to a specific and limited number of tax sources while the latter refers to a larger revenue base.

are generated from the proceeds of 1 percentage point of individual income tax; 1 per cent of corporation taxable income; and 6 per cent of the sales tax revenue from renewable and nonrenewable resources. These revenues are distributed through conditional and unconditional grants. Unconditional grants are allocated to municipalities on the basis of population, municipal expenditures, and relative assessment deficiency.

GRANTS IN-LIEU-OF TAXES[17]

In every province[18] (with the exception of Prince Edward Island), provincially owned property and Crown corporations are exempt from municipal taxes. In place of local taxes, provincial governments and Crown corporations pay unconditional grants to the municipalities in which these properties are located.

Determination of the size of these grants depends on two factors, each of which displays considerable variation across provinces. First, the number of provincial properties or crown corporations located within any municipality will determine the size of the grant. Second, the extent to which these grants reflect the value of property taxes that would have been paid had their properties been owned by the private sector will dictate the size of grant per piece of property. In some provinces including Nova Scotia, New Brunswick, Manitoba, and Alberta, grants in-lieu-of taxes on provincial properties are equal to full property taxation. In others, such as British Columbia, revenues from these grants are equal to revenues which would have been generated from the application of local general municipal mill rates. In Ontario, the commercial mill rate for general municipal purposes plus a fixed sum for prescribed hospitals ($50 per rated bed), provincial penal institutions ($50 per resident place), and qualifying post secondary institutions ($50 per full-time student) combine to establish the value of the grant. In Quebec, the maximum rate that may be paid to municipalities is equal to 50¢ per $100 of assessment subject to certain conditions. For social welfare and non-elementary or secondary educational properties, the grant is fixed at 80 per cent of the overall tax rate in effect in each municipality. For secondary and elementary properties, this rate is 40 per cent. In Saskatchewan, the province does not pay grants in-lieu-of municipal or school taxes but does pay local improvement taxes on government-owned land.

Not only are grants in-lieu-of taxes paid on provincial properties, they are also paid by Crown corporations and agencies. The determination of the grant to be paid by the Crown corporation or agency, however, may differ from the grant paid on provincial property. In Ontario, for example, the grant is equal to the property tax which would have been payable under the commercial mill rate for general and school purposes. In Saskatchewan, most Crown corporations pay grants equal to full taxation (a few pay grants equal to partial taxation only). In Nova Scotia, all Crown corporations and agencies establish their own arrangements with local governments.

---

[17]The above discussion on unconditional grants did not include unconditional grants provided in lieu of taxes.

[18]For a more detailed description of grants in-lieu-of taxes as they exist across provinces, see supra footnote 8, at 183-97.

While this summary is not complete, it does reflect the diversity and variety that exist in the determination and calculation of grants municipalities receive for properties on which local property taxes have not been levied directly. Although not terribly significant as revenue generators, these grants do provide some necessary funds. In fact, in 1978 grants in-lieu-of taxes accounted for almost 5 per cent of all local revenue in Manitoba, slightly more than 1 per cent in Saskatchewan, Alberta, and British Columbia, and between 2 per cent and 3 per cent in Nova Scotia, Newfoundland, Quebec, and Ontario (see Appendix Table C.2).

CONDITIONAL GRANTS

From 1968 to 1978, the importance of conditional grants as a revenue yielder, for all provinces combined, grew by slightly more than 6 percentage points (from 35.4 per cent to 41.6 per cent of local revenues). This increase can be compared roughly to the increase in the dependence on unconditional grants (Table 9.3). While the relative dependence on conditional grants for local governments increased in all provinces but one (British Columbia), this increase displayed considerable interprovincial variation with Prince Edward Island and Newfoundland recording the largest increase (25 and 23 percentage points respectively), Manitoba and Ontario the smallest increase (2 and 4 percentage points respectively), and British Columbia a decrease of 10 percentage points (calculated from data in Table 9.3).

Conditional grants are provided for a wide range of municipal activities— both operating and capital. Because the majority of all transfers to municipalities come from and are determined by provincial governments (see Table 9.2), the system of conditional provincial-municipal grants is necessarily unique to each province. A cursory examination of Table 9.3 reveals the magnitude of the variation among provinces in the late 1970s. Conditional (federal and provincial combined) per capita grants, in total, ranged from $32 in New Brunswick (the lowest) to $562 in Alberta (the highest) with the overall average being $382 in 1978. This variation in assistance can be correlated with the levels of local service responsibility assumed—that is, local governments receiving the lowest assistance had the least responsibility.

Overall, in 1978, conditional grants for operating purposes accounted for almost 90 per cent of total grant assistance to local governments. In fact, in 7 of the 10 provinces, conditional grants for operating purposes accounted for between 88 per cent and 93 per cent of capital and current conditional grants combined (Table 9.4). Only in the province of New Brunswick did the importance of capital grants exceed that of operating grants. The explanation for this is obvious in that the bulk of the services for which local governments are traditionally responsible in the rest of Canada are in the domain of the provincial government in this province.

Operating Conditional Grants

Considerable variation in the per capita level of conditional grants distributed for the various operating purposes is displayed in Table 9.5. Part of this variation is attributed to differences in the volume and level of services funded across Canada, while part is attributed to the specific government responsible for

Table 9.4   Per Capita Capital and Operating Conditional Grants to Local Governments, 1968 and 1978

| | 1968 | | | | 1978 | | | |
| | Operating | | Capital | | Operating | | Capital | |
Province	Per capita dollars	Per cent of total conditional grants	Per capita dollars	Per cent of total conditional grants	Per capita dollars	Per cent of total conditional grants	Per capita dollars	Per cent of total conditional grants
Newfoundland	4.31	66.5	2.17	33.5	41.89	65.0	22.54	35.0
Prince Edward Island	69.43	73.2	25.39	26.8	347.98	72.1	134.82	27.9
Nova Scotia	82.23	88.5	10.64	11.5	341.06	93.1	25.12	6.9
New Brunswick	.35	14.9	2.00	85.1	10.51	33.2	21.17	66.8
Quebec	69.49	74.5	23.75	25.5	404.40	92.5	32.98	7.5
Ontario	113.18	83.5	22.34	16.5	352.97	89.2	42.54	10.8
Manitoba	88.67	78.7	24.00	21.3	297.89	88.6	38.20	11.4
Saskatchewan	112.66	90.9	11.24	9.1	377.45	90.2	40.81	9.8
Alberta	132.28	91.0	13.10	9.0	496.44	88.3	65.57	11.7
British Columbia	97.95	89.1	11.96	10.9	209.21	89.4	24.82	10.6
All provinces	91.99	82.8	19.10	17.2	343.61	89.9	38.44	10.1

Source: Appendix Table C.3.

delivering the service; that is, if the provincial or federal governments are responsible for providing a specific service, then conditional grants will not be distributed to local authorities for this purpose.

Without repeating a discussion of the level of government responsible for providing the different services in the various provinces (this was done in Chapters 4 and 5), and without attempting to measure the volumes or levels of local services supplied on an interprovincial basis (for this requires more detailed information and analysis than is possible here), this section will attempt to highlight four important features of conditional grants: (1) the actual variation in per capita conditional grants for operating purposes in 1978; (2) the distribution of these grants by function in each province for the same year; (3) the per cent of all local expenditures on each major function for which the specific grants accounted in 1978; and (4) a very brief interprovincial comparison of the types of conditional grants in actual existence.

When reviewing the functional distribution of conditional operating grants for 1978, education is by far the most important in absolute terms ($244 per capita overall) and as a proportion of total operating conditional grants (71 per cent). With the exception of Newfoundland and New Brunswick (where elementary and secondary education is provided by the provincial governments), the remaining provinces allocated the largest percentage of their conditional operating grants to this function with these grants absorbing between 94 per cent of all grants in Prince Edward Island (highest) and 56 per cent in Alberta (lowest) in 1978. Perhaps of more significance is the extent to which these grants fund all educational expenditures for which the local sectors are responsible. At one extreme these grants funded almost 100 per cent of all expenditures in Prince Edward Island in 1978, while at the other extreme similar funds supported less than 40 per cent of all expenditures in British Columbia (Table 9.5). Overall, conditional grants funded almost 63 per cent of all local expenditures on educational services.

The only function for which conditional grants accounted for a higher proportion of local expenditures was health services (including hospitals). In 1978, 88 per cent of all local expenditures on this service were financed from grants. A similar pattern was witnessed in Nova Scotia, Ontario, Manitoba, Saskatchewan, and Alberta but not in British Columbia where this grant accounted for 43 per cent of all local expenditures. Health care was not a responsibility of local governments in Newfoundland, Prince Edward Island, New Brunswick, and only minimally so in Quebec. In each of these provinces, the provincial government assumed direct responsibility and, therefore, conditional grants were not awarded to local governments for the provision of health services.

Per capita grants for health services provided by local governments were wide ranging with Alberta leading the way at $166, followed by Saskatchewan at $117, ranging down to $4 in British Columbia, and zero in those provinces listed earlier (Table 9.5). In Ontario, Manitoba, Saskatchewan, and Alberta, grants for health services accounted for the second largest proportion of all conditional grants received by local governments. Elsewhere, the relative importance was less noticeable.

Table 9.5   Per Capita Operating Conditional Grants, Distribution and Relative Importance^a by Province and Major Function, 1978

Province	Gen. govt.	Protection	Trans-port. & com.	Health	Social serv.	Education	Environment	Rec. & cult.	Other	Total
Nfld.										
Per capita $	.02	—	12.66	.21	—	—	22.10	4.05	2.85	41.89
% total cond. grants	0	—	30.2	.5	—	—	52.8	9.7	6.9	100.0
% total local expend.	.1	—	54.1	100.0	—	—	94.0	36.3	—	30.3
P.E.I.										
Per capita $	.08	.02	.50	—	—	326.37	.06	2.25	18.71	347.98
% total cond. grants	0	0	.1	—	—	93.8	0	.6	5.4	100.0
% total local expend.	.6	.1	3.5	—	—	99.0	.3	16.3	48.5	77.9
N.S.										
Per capita $	.31	8.91	6.04	30.67	37.06	230.87	6.22	5.22	15.74	341.06
% total cond. grants	.1	2.6	1.8	9.0	10.9	67.7	1.8	1.5	4.6	100.0
% total local expend.	1.2	16.4	20.0	80.0	49.8	67.1	27.0	23.4	23.9	50.3
N.B.										
Per capita $	—	—	1.33	—	—	—	4.26	4.10	.81	10.51
% total cond. grants	—	—	12.7	—	—	—	40.6	39.0	7.8	100.0
% total local expend.	—	—	3.3	—	—	—	18.2	20.2	2.3	5.9
Que.										
Per capita $	2.90	.57	6.12	.01	.05	345.39	5.34	4.40	39.61	404.40
% total cond. grants	.7	.1	1.5	0	0	85.4	1.3	1.1	9.8	100.0
% total local expend.	4.3	.8	11.5	.8	1.9	75.9	16.7	11.1	31.2	47.5

(Table concluded on next page.)

Table 9.5   Concluded

Province	Gen. govt.	Protec-tion	Trans-port. & com.	Health	Social serv.	Educa-tion	Envi-ron-ment	Rec. & cult.	Other	Total
Ont.										
Per capita $	.33	.22	31.63	45.29	35.15	231.12	.49	3.76	4.98	352.97
% total cond. grants	.1	.1	9.0	12.8	10.0	65.5	.1	1.1	1.4	100.0
% total local expend.	.9	.3	53.2	86.2	61.1	56.9	1.1	7.8	5.3	40.3
Man.										
Per capita $	.98	1.63	5.42	70.31	8.59	188.11	1.01	4.84	16.99	297.89
% total cond. grants	.3	.6	1.8	23.6	2.9	63.2	.3	1.6	5.7	100.0
% total local expend.	3.5	2.5	9.2	93.9	82.1	53.4	2.5	12.2	17.2	38.9
Sask.										
Per capita $	.58	1.69	16.75	116.80	4.38	228.30	.79	5.43	2.73	377.45
% total cond. grants	.2	.5	4.4	30.9	1.2	60.5	.2	1.4	.7	100.0
% total local expend.	1.6	3.2	24.7	89.9	54.3	62.3	2.2	15.2	3.7	46.9
Alta.										
Per capita $	.43	9.74	13.67	165.97	4.78	280.36	9.78	6.24	5.97	496.44
% total cond. grants	.1	2.0	2.8	33.4	1.0	56.4	2.0	13.	1.3	100.0
% total local expend.	1.2	12.9	14.2	93.8	34.8	70.8	21.1	10.2	4.1	47.3
B.C.										
Per capita $	6.04	.33	1.09	3.50	.27	156.76	11.75	3.38	26.09	209.21
% total cond. grants	2.9	.2	.5	1.7	.1	74.9	5.6	1.6	12.4	100.0
% total local expend.	19.5	.5	2.6	43.3	2.4	39.0	33.9	18.9	19.7	26.8
All prov.										
Per capita $	1.66	1.54	15.79	39.48	15.00	243.85	4.66	4.27	17.36	343.61
% total cond. grants	.5	.5	4.6	11.5	4.4	70.9	1.4	1.2	5.0	100.0
% total local expend.	3.9	2.2	27.9	88.0	55.0	62.6	12.4	9.9	16.3	42.0

aRow 2 under each province records conditional operating grants for each function as a per cent of total conditional grants. Row 3 under each province records conditional grants on each function as a per cent of total local expenditures on each specific function.

Source: Calculated or recorded from data in Appendix Tables B.2 and C.3.

Social welfare is a third function of which conditional grants fund a large portion of local expenditures—55 per cent of per capita expenditures on this function was funded through grants in 1978. Provincial governments in Newfoundland, Prince Edward Island, New Brunswick, and Quebec assumed virtually all responsibility for social services; whereas, local governments in the remaining provinces displayed varying proportions of local funding requirements (see Table 9.5). As with the previous functions, per capita grants ranged widely from $37 and $35 per capita in Nova Scotia and Ontario respectively to almost $9 in Manitoba, $5 in Alberta, and $4 in Saskatchewan, with Quebec and British Columbia reporting infinitely small amounts. When conditional grants on social services are calculated as a percentage of total conditional grants, only two provinces recorded percentages in excess of the overall average of slightly more than 4 per cent (Ontario at 10 per cent and Nova Scotia at 11 per cent).

The final local expenditure category to be a major recipient of conditional transfers is transportation and communication. In 1978, the average per capita grant of almost $16 accounted for nearly 28 per cent of all local expenditures on this function. Only in the provinces of Newfoundland (54 per cent of all expenditures) and Ontario (53 per cent of all expenditures) did local governments receive more than 25 per cent of local expenditures from grants. Funding support in the remaining provinces tended to be lower than the national average (Table 9.5).

The per capita grant in Ontario ($32) was twice as high as the average per capita grant in Canada ($16). Saskatchewan ($17) was the only other province in which local governments' per capita conditional grants for this service exceeded the national average. As a proportion of all conditional operating grants, these transfers were higher than the national average of 4.4 per cent in only three provinces: Newfoundland (30 per cent), New Brunswick (13 per cent), and Ontario (9 per cent). The relative size of this grant for all other provinces was rather insignificant (Table 9.5).

Table 9.5 lists the remaining functions (each of which is relatively insignificant) for which per capita grants were received in 1978.

Finally, total per capita conditional grants ranged from a low of $11 in New Brunswick and $42 in Newfoundland to a high of $496 in Alberta and $404 in Quebec, with the overall average being $344. A large part of the variation in grant levels is obviously a result of differences in the level of government supplying the services. For example, health, education, and social services are provided almost entirely and thus directly financed by provincial governments in Newfoundland and New Brunswick, while this is not true for one or more of these services in the remaining provinces. In fact, the provinces responsible for providing one or more of these important people-related services almost always funded a proportionately higher percentage of local expenditures through the use of conditional grants (see Table 9.5).

A note of caution must be used in transposing these 1978 figures to the present. Changes in the grant systems (1980) in Newfoundland, Nova Scotia, and Quebec may have led to changes in the per capita level of conditional grants and the relative importance of these in funding specific local services. Unfortunately, at the time of writing, data were not available to indicate such changes.

It does seem, however, that operating conditional grants for services provided by local governments in Nova Scotia, for example, are likely to be lower as a result of a substantial move to the deconditionalization of this province's provincial-municipal grant program.

Provincial conditional grant programs have taken long periods of time to develop and this development has occurred mostly in a unilateral way (that is, dictated by the provinces). Seldom are these grants systematically or regularly reviewed. Once in place, they tend to remain although their matching provisions or requirements for receipt may change. As provincial governments scramble for revenue in depressed times, they tend to reduce provincially funded portions of grants or to tighten regulations for receipt, while at the same time expecting the municipalities to continue with the levels of service that existed prior to reduced funding.[19]

While the number of conditional grants available to local governments is larger in some provinces than others (over 90 in Ontario, roughly 70 in Alberta, and very few in Prince Edward Island, for example), many of these transfers are distributed under different rules and procedures. This lack of uniformity and consistency can be noted in the variation reported in the corresponding acts and often lengthy regulations produced by the dispensing ministries or departments. As well, there are various instances where the grants provided by one department vary depending on the characteristics of the recipient local government. Grants vary according to the formulas applied, the criteria imposed on local governments, and the various rules or regulations attached to the different conditional transfers.[20]

As suggested earlier, this variation in the requirements attached to conditional grants makes any categorization of them according to matching provisions (open-ended as opposed to closed-ended, etc.) virtually impossible.[21] Without listing or attempting to categorize all of the conditional grants in the remaining provinces,[22] there are a few similarities and differences that should be cited. For example, in Nova Scotia all operating grants are now completely unconditional. Municipalities no longer have to expend on certain services to be eligible for grant support.[23] Similarly, conditional grants play a limited role in the financing of local operating expenditures in New Brunswick and British Columbia (Table 9.3). In Winnipeg, the provincial-municipal transfer system has been deconditionalized.[24]

---

[19]For examples of this, see Harry M. Kitchen, *Public Finance in Metropolitan Toronto,* A Study for The Royal Commission on Metropolitan Toronto (Toronto: the Commission, 1977), 76-77.

[20]Supra footnote 3, at 136-37.

[21]The study by Enid Slack, supra footnote 3, is the only Canadian publication attempting to classify conditional grants according to these characteristics and it was done for the province of Ontario alone.

[22]For a partial listing of conditional grants available to local governments, agencies and commissions in each province, see supra footnote 1, at 427-572.

[23]Supra footnote 8, at 186.

[24]Dale E. Richmond, "Provincial-Municipal Tax and Revenue Sharing: Reforms Accomplished, 1978 Compared with 1971," in L.D. Feldman, ed., *Politics and Government of Urban Canada: Selected Readings,* 4th ed. (Toronto: Methuen, 1981), at 199.

The bulk of the existing conditional operating transfers go to various p. grams included under the social service, health, and education functions. some cases, these grants are awarded on a per pupil (education) or per bed (hospitals) basis, while in others they amount to a specific percentage of eligible budgetary costs (social services and health).

In those provinces with a large number of conditional grants transfer systems involve a complex mixture of rules, regulations, and requirements. Most grants have strings attached, thus suggesting that provincial governments still retain considerable control over the types and often levels of expenditures undertaken by local governments and their associated agencies or commissions.

Capital Conditional Grants

With the exception of Newfoundland (35 per cent), Prince Edward Island (28 per cent), and New Brunswick (67 per cent), capital grants in the remaining provinces accounted for only 4 per cent to 12 per cent of all conditional grants received by local governments in 1978 (Table 9.4). While the absolute size of these grants is not large in comparison with conditional operating grants and while the lumpy nature of capital investment projects suggests that grants in any particular year or province may be considerably higher than in adjacent years or provinces, any interprovincial comparison of municipal capital grants over time and across provinces must be treated with care. With this cautioning note in mind, the following will discuss briefly the relative overall importance of grants in financing local capital projects.[25]

Per capita grant support for capital expenditures on transportation and communication, education and environmental facilities was noticeably higher than for other functions in 1978 (Table 9.6). In fact, with very few exceptions (see Appendix Table C.3), these three functions accounted for most conditional capital grants in every province. At the same time, grants for capital expenditures on these projects did not always fund the largest proportion of total local expenditures. Only 24 per cent of all transportation and communication capital expenditures and 12 per cent of similar expenditures on environmental facilities were funded by grants; whereas 43 per cent of general government expenditures and 39 per cent of expenditures on health facilities were paid for with grants (Table 9.6). (For variations on a province by province basis, see Appendix Table C.3).

Capital grants (through one type of allocating formula or another) are consistently provided to local governments across Canada for the partial financing of public transit systems, roads, sewage and water plants, libraries, parks, and recreational facilities. Provincial funding of the remaining capital projects has been less consistent because these projects and their funding are in the provincial domain or because provincial authorities are not willing to aid in the financing of them.[26]

---

[25]For a more detailed description of the importance of grants and their use in financing capital projects, see Chapter 6.

[26]For a brief listing of conditional grants, see supra footnote 24, at 173-96.

Table 9.6   Per Capita Conditional Grants for All Provinces
by Major Function, 1978

Function	Per capita dollars	Per cent of total conditional capital grants	Conditional capital grants as a per cent of local capital expenditures on each function
General government	1.24	3.2	43.1
Protection	.22	.6	5.7
Transportation and communication	13.82	36.0	23.9
Health	1.31	3.4	38.6
Social services	.12	.3	6.7
Education	9.85	25.6	39.1
Environment	5.45	14.2	11.6
Recreation and culture	3.29	8.6	21.5
Total	38.44	100.0	23.0

Source: Calculated from data in Appendix Tables B.2 and C.3.

GRANTS BY SIZE OF MUNICIPALITY

It was observed earlier that per capita local expenditures and revenues tended to be higher in larger urban areas than elsewhere. Table 9.7 notes that unconditional grants to urban regions were considerably higher than those to the average municipality in Nova Scotia, New Brunswick, and Quebec in 1978. Roughly comparable (if not slightly higher) per capita unconditional grants were distributed to larger urban areas in Ontario, Manitoba, Saskatchewan, and British Columbia. Relatively lower per capita unconditional grants for large urban regions were recorded in Newfoundland and Alberta.[27]

With the exception of urban regions in Nova Scotia and New Brunswick, per capita conditional grants tended to be lower for larger urban areas than for all municipalities combined in the remaining provinces. This differential is not easy (and perhaps impossible without a thoroughly detailed description) to explain, for a comparative assessment of conditional grants to all municipalities vis-à-vis large urban areas arranged by function (Appendix Table C.4) does not display a uniform pattern. Consistently higher grants for all functions for all municipalities combined as opposed to urban regions is not observed except in St. John's, Newfoundland. In the remaining provinces, the larger urban regions received higher per capita conditional grants for some functions and lower for others—no common thread can be noted (Appendix Table C.4). Similar variation exists in the size of the per capita conditional grant support given to different-sized communities. In no instance did one specific function receive consistently higher or lower grant support for certain sizes of communities across all provinces (Appendix Table C.4).

---

[27]For an assessment of the reasons why larger municipalities receive less per capita unconditional grant assistance in Alberta, and the implications associated therewith, see McMillan and Norton, supra footnote 15.

Table 9.7   Comparison of Per Capita Unconditional and Conditional (Operating and Capital) Grants by Urban Size and by Province, 1978a

Province	Unconditional grants		Conditional grants			
			Per capita level		Per cent of all expenditures financed by conditional grants	
	All municipalities	Urban regions	All municipalities	Urban regions	All municipalities	Urban regions
	dollars	dollars	dollars	dollars	per cent	per cent
Newfoundland	13	—	64	21	31.7	6.4
Nova Scotia	77	125	366	381	49.4	34.3
New Brunswick	71	159	32	38	12.2	10.9
Quebec	77	99	437	429	43.0	42.1
Ontario	54	53	396	369	38.3	41.4
Manitoba	18	19	336	309	37.6	31.0
Saskatchewan	48	56	418	371	42.2	35.9
Alberta	37	26	562	497	40.9	35.8
British Columbia	48	52	234	212	24.9	23.4

aPrince Edward Island is excluded because there are no urban regions as defined by Statistics Canada.
—Negligible.

Source: Calculated or obtained from data in Table 9.3, Appendix Table C.3, and Statistics Canada, *Local Government Finance, Preliminary 1978—Estimates 1979*, Catalogue no. 68-203.

Finally, in every province except for Ontario, conditional grants accounted for a higher proportion of local expenditures (total local capital and operating expenditures) for all municipalities combined vis-à-vis larger urban areas (Table 9.7). Larger urban areas were generally more dependent on their own revenue sources as a means of meeting their local expenditure commitments.

ECONOMIC RATIONALE FOR GRANT SUPPORT

While the absolute value and relative importance of both conditional and unconditional grants as revenue generators for local governments was outlined in the previous section, nothing has yet been mentioned about the basic rationale underlying the provision of such grants as a means of funding local expenditures. In this regard, there are two areas that should be examined: (1) the justification for grant support and (2) what types of grants best fit the legitimate needs of municipalities.

The existing literature on the rationale for grant support is vast and well-known.[28] Briefly, intergovernmental transfers are justified on economic grounds when a better allocation of resources or an improved redistribution of income within and among communities is achieved through them. Unconditional transfers are used to redistribute or to equalize fiscal capacity across municipalities. "The objective is to allow each jurisdiction to provide some 'average' level of services by exerting an 'average' fiscal effort."[29] If local communities are left on their own to finance necessary public services, differences in local governments' revenue bases would lead to noticeably different tax rates or other charges to finance a specific quantity and quality of services. Alternatively, similar tax rates and charges could bring noticeably different levels in the quantity and/or quality of local services. To avoid these disparities in local services or local charges, it has been argued that resource augmenting transfers of an unconditional nature should be available. Their purpose is simply to provide additional revenues to local governments without any conditions on how the money is to be spent.

The rapid increase in the demand for local services and the relatively slow growth in local revenues at given rates (taxes and charges) also has created a mismatch of local revenues and expenditures that, it has been argued, should be offset by the granting of unconditional funds from the provincial government.[30]

The nature of unconditional grants is such that they expand local revenues without altering the relative prices of providing the various local services. No incentive is provided, therefore, to spend on some services and not on others. Conditional grants are defended on the basis of providing subsidies designed to cover the extra costs (at the margin) associated with the external benefits (spillovers) inherent in the provision of many local public services. In most cases, the benefits of publicly provided services, such as health or education, are

---

[28]For a detailed examination of the arguments, see Robin W. Boadway, *Intergovernmental Transfers in Canada* (Toronto: Canadian Tax Foundation, 1980), and W. Oates, *Fiscal Federalism* (New York: Harcourt, Brace, 1972).

[29]Supra footnote 3, at 134.

[30]For a critical evaluation of whether this is the best way to offset the fiscal gap, see Richard M. Bird and N. Enid Slack, *Urban Public Finance in Canada* (Toronto: Butterworths, 1983), 102.

not confined to the residents of the jurisdiction, but rather "spillover" to accrue to the residents of neighbouring communities. In such instances, conditional grants allow provincial governments to direct their assistance to services that generate these externalities, by inducing a greater provision of the service, or simply ensuring the achievement of a specific level or quality. In short, subsidies are necessary to ensure that municipalities do not neglect projects where important spillover effects exist, since the jurisdiction providing the service is likely to consider only the benefits accruing to its own residents. The absence of a conditional grant program provides an incentive for municipalities to finance only those projects that benefit its own residents directly, leading to a less than optimal allocation of resources and the ensuing result that all residents (both in that community and adjacent communities) are left with a level of service lower than is deemed desirable from society's point of view.

While the spillover rationale is useful in identifying services that require conditional grant support, it does not provide any guidance on the rate of subsidization that ought to exist. This would necessitate a precise measure of the value of the externality at the margin. Obviously such a measure of what is essentially an intangible benefit is impossible. If externalities, however, could be measured, even crudely, the considerable diversity among municipalities within any province and the existence of such a large number of communities (approximately 835 in Ontario and 1,600 in Quebec to list only two provinces), each of which deals directly with the provincial government, suggests that any attempted policy involving explicitly the spillover criterion on a community-by-community basis would be totally unmanageable. Instead, conditional grants have been used by provincial governments to promote specific projects in which the province has a distinct interest, even though these grants frequently distort local priorities. In Ontario, Wintario grants have served this purpose. These grants are popular because of their political visibility rather than their attempt to cover the spillovers generated by the provision of selected local services.

Conditional grants may take different forms; for example, matching, open-ended grants are similar to unconditional grants in that they expand the revenue available for financing local public services. They do, however, differ from unconditional grants in that they alter the relative prices (in terms of the demands on locally raised revenues) of providing the various services. For example, the provision of grants for "selected" services creates an incentive for increased output of these funded services as compared to those that are not grant-supported. (Different grant rates for different services may display similar incentives.)

This shift in the relative prices of providing the various services is likely to alter the expenditure priorities of local governments. The extent to which specific services are provided or expanded, however, will depend on the extent to which the demand for these services is sensitive to changes in the relative costs of their provision. If the grant is open-ended, there will be some stimulative effect. On the other hand, if the grant is closed-ended, the stimulative effect may be blunted considerably.[31] If the upper limit is binding on the recipient government, the price of undertaking further expenditures at the margin is borne

---

[31]Boadway, supra footnote 28, at 52.

entirely by the municipality. This may cause the government to ignore the spillover benefits since it selects a level of expenditures consistent with marginal cost pricing (that is, the perceived marginal gain to its citizens equals the marginal cost of the expenditures). If, however, the upper limit is not binding, then the effect is similar to that generated by an open-ended grant and an incentive to increase the level of output is provided.

Nonmatching conditional grants are identical to unconditional grants in that they expand local revenues without altering the relative cost of the provision of the various local services. They do, however, differ from conditional grants in that their receipt is dependent on the provision of specified services. The effect of this kind of grant can be demonstrated easily. If the service to be supported by the grant was deemed previously to be worthy of support by the local government, then the subsequent transferral of the lump-sum funding might be sufficient to cover the desired expenditure without the use of locally allocated funds. The freed-up local funds could then be applied against other local expenditures, without necessarily stimulating increased provision of the service for which the grant was intended. Consequently, a lump-sum grant may improve the community's overall fiscal position without creating the desired stimulative effect.

The most effective conditional grant in terms of output-per-dollar of grant is, therefore, an unrestricted matching grant designed to cover the costs of interjurisdictional spillovers. Such a grant will alter the relative costs of providing local services and provide an incentive for the provision of the subsidized service. Nonmatching grants, by comparison, are provided to municipalities who agree to meet certain conditions. These grants expand the pool of local revenues without distorting the relative price of providing local services. Finally, unconditional grants serve to correct intermunicipal differences in the capacities of local governments to finance many of their services.

EVALUATION

As with the theoretical literature, there exists a vast body of empirical literature documenting the economic impact and budgetary effects of intergovernmental grants on recipient municipalities. Unfortunately, the bulk of this literature is based on experiences in the United States, and only a limited number of Canadian studies exist. This is particularly surprising given the growing importance of intergovernmental transfers in financing local government services in Canada. With few exceptions, the documented Canadian case studies are based on doctoral dissertations[32] dealing with either determinants of provin-

---

[32]The interested reader is directed to the following sources: Nicholas A. Michas, "Variations in the Level of Provincial-Municipal Expenditures in Canada: An Econometric Analysis" (1969), 24 *Public Finance,* no. 4, 597-613; Jean-Yves Rivard, "Determinants of City Expenditures in Canada" (Ph.D. dissertation, University of Michigan, 1967); J.M. Maley, "The Impact of Federal Grants on Provincial Budgets: Canada" (Ph.D. dissertation, University of Rochester, 1971); Helen M. Hardy, "The Effects of Federal Grants on Provincial Expenditure and Revenue Decisions: Ontario and New Brunswick Compared" (Ph.D. dissertation, McMaster University, 1973); H.M. Hardy, "Some Aspects of Federal Grants in Canada" (May-June 1974), 22 *Canadian Tax Journal* 285-94; H.M. Hardy, "Budgetary Responses of Individual Government Units to Federal Grants" (July 1976), 4 *Public Finance Quarterly* 173-86; Enid Slack, "Local Fiscal Response to Intergovernmental Transfers" (August 1980), 62 *Review of Economics and Statistics* 364-70; D.A.L. Auld, "Provincial Grants and Local Government Expenditure" (July 1976), 4 *Public Finance Quarterly* 295-306.

cial/local expenditures or the budgetary responses of recipient governments to federal grants and usually are modelled after their American counterparts.

Some of the early determinant studies (especially in the United States[33]) attempted to measure the impact of a number of independent variables including income, population, population density, urbanization, and intergovernmental transfers on the level of local government expenditures. In some instances, it was observed that an increase of a fixed amount in grants led to an increase in local government expenditures of a greater amount. In other cases, the opposite was observed, that is, an increase in grants led to a proportionately smaller increase in expenditures. This inconsistency in the empirical results, when combined with the conceptual difficulties of properly formulating a theoretical model, cast considerable suspicion on the usefulness of these studies as predictors of the impact grants have on local expenditure levels.

Consequently, recent theoretical and empirical studies have directed their attention toward the formulation and testing of a more sophisticated and rigorous model of utility maximization. This model is drawn from consumer behaviour theory and assumes that an individual will select those options (from all available) that will maximize his/her satisfaction subject to a budget constraint and fixed relative prices of the various options available. When applied to government behaviour, the different types of grants are assumed to exert different effects on the budget constraint and the relative prices of providing the various local services (for a review of these effects, see the previous section).

The only published Canadian study employing a utility maximization model analyzed the budgetary response from the distribution of provincial grants to local governments (upper-tier local governments as distinct from lower-tier) in Ontario in 1973 and 1974 (pooled cross-section data).[34] This study distinguished between grants that affect municipal expenditures though an expansion of the community's income without altering the relative prices of the locally provided services (unconditional), and those that both expand the income and alter the relative prices of providing the various services (conditional matching). Employing two different functional forms for the utility function, the author found that unconditional grants exhibited only a slight positive effect on local expenditures; for example, a $1 increase in unconditional grants led to a reduction in property taxes of $0.95 or $0.99 depending on the utility function selected.[35] Considerable substitution of grant funds for property tax revenue, therefore, seems to exist.

By comparison, the impact of conditional grants is unclear. Under one form of utility function, an increase in conditional grants (open-ended matching) of $1 generated an expenditure increase of over $2, implying that other revenues are required to meet expenditure needs. Under the alternative utility function, a $1 grant increase was accompanied by an increase in expenditure of only

---

[33]See, for example, Ernest Kurnow, "Determinants of State and Local Expenditures Reexamined" (September 1963), 16 *National Tax Journal* 252-55, at 252-53; and Seymour Sacks and Robert Harris, "The Determinants of State and Local Government Expenditures and Intergovernmental Flows of Funds" (March 1964), 17 *National Tax Journal* 75-85.

[34]Slack, supra footnote 32.

[35]Ibid., at 368-69.

$0.43, thus showing some substitution of grant revenue for property tax revenue.[36] This uncertainty of the impact of conditional grants suggests, therefore, that one must be very cautious in making statements about their stimulative or nonstimulative effects.

Finally, utility maximization models are based on the assumption that local politicians and administrators maximize the satisfaction of their constituents. While this may be possible, it is just as plausible to assume that local officials are more interested in maximizing the size of their budgets and bureaucracies.[37] Although there is no empirical basis for accepting or rejecting this hypothesis, it does suggest that the "expenditure response to grants would be different from that predicted by the theory of utility maximization."[38]

POLITICAL EVALUATION OF THE GRANT STRUCTURE

A ranking of grants based solely on an economic analysis does not take into consideration some important political factors in Canadian government. It does not look at the motivation behind the choice of grants (other than those based on economic analysis), thus giving an incomplete assessment of the grant picture. The choice of the type of grant used by a provincial government is influenced a great deal by its political objectives. In particular, a provincial government's extensive use of conditional grants is a result of varying political motives—such as a desire to keep as much control over the funds it disperses as possible. This perhaps represents a lack of faith in a local government's ability to conduct its own activities or it may be the result of the prevalent belief that separation of the expenditure and financing functions leads to excessive and wasteful spending because the recipient looks upon the funds as being "free money." It also may be motivated by a desire to use local governments as agents to produce amounts and kinds of public goods and services that are deemed to be in the provincial government's interest. These goods and services may only be produced by changing the local government's priorities through the leverage of a matching conditional grant, and the donor government may feel a responsibility in encouraging the provision of these services. (If this is the case it must be argued that the provincial government should provide the service, but in order to reduce the likelihood of duplication and to take advantage of local expertise in various areas, it may be more appropriate to designate production to local governments.) Conditional grants may be motivated by a desire to spread innovations in the provisions of public goods or to control the quality of technology used by various local governments. Finally, they may be used to change jurisdictional or service area boundaries by promoting intermunicipal cooperation in order to achieve economies of scale in the provision of certain services.

The desirability of these political motives and in turn the conditional grants based on them, really depends on whether they are viewed from the provincial

---

[36]Ibid., at 369.

[37]Martin McGuire, "Notes on Grants-in-Aid and Economic Interactions Among Governments" (May 1973), 6 *Canadian Journal of Economics* 207-21.

[38]Supra footnote 3, at 152.

government's or the local government's perspective. Local governments prefer unconditional grants because they provide the greatest flexibility in the expenditure patterns of local governments. Donor governments, by contrast, often strive for control of expenditure programs through the use of conditional grants. Since both donors and recipients frequently support different types of grants, an evaluation of each grant must involve the establishment of an objective to be achieved. Once this objective is adopted, a set of criteria or factors are necessary for indicating whether a specific grant type actually achieves the desired goal.

While there is some debate over the appropriate objective, it is generally accepted that governments (regardless of the level) are established to serve their constituents. To best serve local residents, it is important that local services be supplied by the level of government that is best able to recognize and respond to the needs and preferences of the local citizens. To meet this objective, it has been suggested that there are three criteria that play a role in the satisfaction of local needs and preferences. First, a considerable degree of local autonomy will aid in the selection of local services to be provided. Second, simplicity in the grant structure and a clear definition of the jurisdictional responsibility for providing the various services is necessary. Third, local governments must be accountable to the taxpayers for their actions.[39] The greater the levels of autonomy, clarity, and accountability, the greater the chances of providing sound local government.

The type of grant employed will have a direct effect on the level of local autonomy. Unconditional grants with their inherent flexibility impinge less on local autonomy than do conditional grants. They have virtually no distortive effects on local priorities. They allow local decision makers to select the services on which the grant will be spent. Conditional grants, on the other hand, can have an undermining effect on the ability of a local government to respond to local priorities. Matching grants whether they are open- or closed-ended exert more financial leverage on local councils than do lump-sum grants. The degree of distortion and infringement on local autonomy depends on the specificity of a grant, and the relative priority the project was given by the local government before the grant was received. It can be concluded that the fewer strings attached to grants, the less local autonomy is undermined.

It should be clearly stated which government has the jurisdictional responsibility for providing the services for which each grant is provided. The grant formula should be simple to comprehend so that it is readily understood by legislators and taxpayers. Again, unconditional grants score well on both points. Such grants clearly give the expenditure responsibility to local governments and their formulae are generally simpler to understand. On the other hand, conditional transfers by their very nature blur the jurisdictional boundaries. By stating where and how the funds are to be spent, donor governments are staking a claim to responsibility in the area where the grant is aimed. Meanwhile, local governments by virtue of the fact that they must at least provide the service, if not put up some funds of their own (under matching grants), must

---

[39]Ontario, *Report of the Provincial-Municipal Grants Reform Committee,* Vol. I (Toronto: the Commission, 1977), 33-57.

also take some of the responsibility. In such a situation, it is frequently difficult to tell where the jurisdictional responsibility lies.

Conditional grants can also become very complex. Their use can leave smaller municipalities at a disadvantage because the municipality may not be able to afford the expertise required to cope with the auditing procedures and administration connected with these grant programs, let alone understand them. This situation is compounded when the grant system includes many conditional grants from different sources, using varying formulae and criteria to operate each program, as is found in many of the provinces. The aggregate result is a maze of programs and bureaucracies that waste time and money. Jurisdictional confusion and operational complexities are major drawbacks for the use of such grant programs.

It is important that local governments be held accountable for their actions. Under an intergovernmental transfer program, as outlined in the previous paragraph, it becomes difficult to see who has jurisdictional responsibility in various program areas. As a result, "taxpayers are not sure to whom their dollars go; they are not sure to whom to turn when they want information or assistance; they are not sure whom they should hold accountable."[40] Unconditional grants leave local governments accountable for their actions. Conditional grants, on the other hand, leave the taxpayer in a weakened position in terms of expressing his/her own preferences. With conditional grants it is important to stipulate who is responsible for providing the service and, in turn, who becomes accountable in the implementation of that service. Clearly, unconditional grants appear to be superior to conditional ones in preserving sound local government. There is little that can be said about the relative political desirability of the different types of conditional grants. It would require a detailed examination of each conditional program in order to make any general conclusions as to their comparative effects on autonomy, clarity, and accountability.

In the final analysis it is hard to say what weight should be put on each criterion, whether economic or political. It would seem that there is no getting around the fact that unconditional and conditional grants are designed to cope with very distinct and often opposing purposes. Unfortunately, grantors often confuse the situation and claim one objective and then use the wrong instrument to achieve it. For example, a major problem with conditional grants is that they are often justified on the basis of helping financially pressed local governments rather than on the basis of spillovers.

REFORM OF GRANT STRUCTURE

ROYAL COMMISSION REPORTS

From the mid-1960s to the late 1970s, a number of provincial royal commissions studied, among other things, the role of provincial and local governments in the provision of local services.[41] In all cases, these reports recommended the retention and strengthening of local governments with specific emphasis placed on the provincial government's role in assisting in the provision of local services.

---

[40]Ibid., at 40.

[41]See New Brunswick, *Royal Commission on Finance and Municipal Taxation Report*
(Continued on next page.)

Seldom was there much emphasis placed on "the importance of the role of local government as a device for expressing and fulfilling the needs and wishes of the citizens it serves."[42] To achieve this objective, local governments need more control over their revenue bases, either through increased use of property taxes, grants with fewer strings attached, reduced expenditure responsibilities, or access to new tax sources such as those currently in the domain of the provincial governments.[43] In many of the reports there was some emphasis placed on substantial shifts away from conditional and onto unconditional grants as a means of funding local services. In one report (New Brunswick), an attempt was made to alleviate local revenue shortfalls by moving many local services to the provincial level. While this partially eliminated some revenue problems, it did little to satisfy the needs and preferences of local citizens, an objective that is felt to be important in providing the appropriate level and mix of public services.

SUGGESTIONS FOR REFORM

One of the major criticisms levied by local politicians and administrators against existing grant programs in a number of provinces is the inadequacy of grant revenues in meeting local expenditure commitments. Much of this criticism has evolved as a result of difficulties in finding enough locally raised funds to meet the local public service requirements. The consequent mismatching of local revenues and expenditures has led to demands for increased grant support. Whether or not this claim for increased grant funding is justified is far from obvious. Other means of solving the revenue shortfall may be more desirable;[44] for example, increased access to new tax revenues (as is done through tax sharing in Manitoba and British Columbia) or revenue-sharing (Saskatchewan), the shifting of local responsibilities to the provincial level (as in New Brunswick), or greater utilization of local property taxes or user charges (Chapters 10) may be more appropriate in correcting this deficiency.

A second and more contentious issue facing local authorities is the increase in grants that municipalities can expect in future years. Knowledge of the expected level of future grants or the base used for calculating annual increases is essential if local authorities are to estimate the impact of jointly funded (provincial and local) programs on future budgets effectively. All too frequently, one hears about provincial withdrawal or partial withdrawal of grant support for a number of established local programs, thus leaving municipalities with the responsibility for assuming a larger share of the funding responsibility for these programs if they are to continue.[45] This has tended to be more of a problem in

---

[41]Continued
(Fredericton: the Commission, 1963); Manitoba, *Royal Commission on Local Government Organization and Finance Report* (Winnipeg: Queen's Printer, 1964); Quebec, *The Quebec Royal Commission on Taxation* (Quebec: the Commission, 1965); Ontario, *Report of the Ontario Committee on Taxation* (Toronto: Queen's Printer, 1967); Nova Scotia, *Report of the Royal Commission on Education, Public Services and Provincial-Municipal Relations* (Halifax: Queen's Printer, 1974); Alberta, *Report of the Provincial-Municipal Finance Council on the Responsibilities and Financing of Local Government in Alberta* (Edmonton: the Council, 1979).

[42]Supra footnote 9, at 255.

[43]For a fuller discussion of three of these options (grants excluded), see Chapter 15.

[44]See supra footnote 30, at 103.

[45]See supra footnote 9, at 258-59.

some provinces (Ontario, for example) than others. By and large, this problem has disappeared where the provincial-municipal transfers have been indexed to increase in a specific manner. Indexation has taken the form of following the increase in provincial revenues in New Brunswick and Nova Scotia, the growth in the yield of selected provincial taxes in Manitoba and British Columbia, or the growth in the tax bases for selected provincial taxes in Saskatchewan. In most of the remaining provinces, there is no similar mechanism for determining future grants. It tends to depend "on the largesse of the province."[46]

In addition, legislated provincial-municipal transfer agreements have evolved in those provinces displaying a form of indexation. This legislation has introduced some certainty and continuity, features that are essential if one is to avoid a complex set of rules and regulations. Unfortunately, in those provinces where decisions on the level of transfers and annual increases are dictated by provincial administration, the transfer system is susceptible to the desires and preferences of provincial authorities and this can be potentially detrimental to municipal interests. To avoid these potentially damaging consequences, legislated provincial-municipal transfer programs, along with an appropriate indexation scheme, ought to be introduced in every province. These measures will assist local governments in their budgetary operations. Unfortunately, most provincial authorities view such a scheme with distinct concern, for it limits the provincial government's control over the distribution of transfers and leaves them with less control over local programs. This concern over erosion of control reflects the view of some provincial officials that municipal authorities are incapable of effectively managing their own activities and must be directed by their provincial counterparts.

In those provinces where a substantial deconditionalization of their transfer programs has emerged (Nova Scotia and Prince Edward Island) or where many of the local responsibilities have been shifted to the provincial government (New Brunswick), the actual distribution of the remaining grants has not generated serious difficulties. In the remaining provinces, however, the multitude of conditional grants with their separate rules, provisions, and formulae have created complex and confusing transfer systems (perhaps nowhere as confusing as in Ontario). This complexity has led to higher than necessary administration costs. For example, provincial authorities must devote considerable time to assessing eligibility, allocating the funds, and monitoring their use. Local officials devote an inordinate amount of time deciphering eligibility rules and making applications for funds. This complexity also generates uncertainty in the calculation of future grants, and thus creates serious forecasting problems and the concomitant future budgetary requirements. It has been argued that the larger and wealthier municipalities have been the real beneficiaries from such a complex grant structure, for they are the communities who can afford the cost and time of hiring employees who are responsible for keeping up to date on changes in the rules and regulations, so as not to miss out on potential funds.[47]

It is difficult to eradicate the complex nature of transfer systems. Many grants were introduced years ago when specific needs or preferences dictated

---

[46]Supra footnote 24, at 201.

[47]Supra footnote 39, at 17.

their implementation. Since then, needs and preferences have changed but initial grant structures have remained. Concern has tended to centre on annual changes in grant support rather than on a general rationalization of the system's existence.[48] Rationalization of the existing transfer system has led to greater deconditionalization of the grant structure in some provinces (Nova Scotia, for example) and virtually no changes at all in others. The recommendation by the Grants Reform Commission in Ontario (1977), for example, involved an amalgamation of a large number of conditional grants into a few grants and an elimination of others; however, these recommendations were ultimately rejected.

While an increased emphasis on unconditional grants may generate greater local autonomy, it may also create a few unwanted and unexpected consequences. For example, if unconditional grants are less stimulative in their effect on local expenditures than are conditional grants, then certain services that are provided under conditional grants may not be supplied if these grants are deconditionalized. It is also possible that some local governments prefer to have their expenditure decisions dictated by provincial authorities and thus prefer conditional grants.[49]

Finally, unconditional grants containing an equalization factor and designed to improve the fiscal capacities[50] of the poorer regions are essential if equity in local taxes or charges and similarities in the minimum levels and quality of required local services are to be achieved across the many communities within and among the 10 provinces.

SUMMARY

While grants are awarded to municipalities by both federal and provincial governments, the federal government's primary role in providing assistance to local governments has been in the area of capital grants for selected facilities even though provincial capital grants often exceed, in absolute value, the size of federal grants. The provincial role, on the other hand, has been to provide substantial assistance toward the operating costs of many local services.

Over the past two decades, the relative importance of conditional and unconditional grants has increased significantly as a revenue yielder for local governments. The increased emphasis on unconditional grants allocated on the basis of some sort of equalization formula stressing revenue raising capacity, servicing needs and costs of providing local services, still does not exceed the dependence on conditional grants in most provinces. The fact that considerable use of conditional grants with some type of matching basis exists, suggests that the donor governments are attempting to dictate or control the provision of services that are felt to be important from the donor's perspective, either because of the political impact they will create or because of the spillovers they will bring

---

[48]J. Stefan Dupré, *Intergovernmental Finance in Ontario: A Provincial-Local Perspective,* A Study prepared for The Ontario Committee on Taxation (Toronto: Queen's Printer, 1967).

[49]Supra footnote 3, at 157.

[50]For a discussion of the practical difficulties associated with the resource equalization grant in Ontario, see supra footnote 3, at 157-58.

about. Internalizing the spillovers through the adoption of conditional grants is the strongest theoretical argument in favour of their use; however, measuring the magnitude of these externalities (spillovers) is extremely difficult and virtually impossible in actual practice. Since the matching provisions are unlikely to reflect the ratio of external benefits to total benefits, these grants frequently distort (in an economically inefficient manner) the expenditure patterns of the recipient governments.

Continued emphasis on a multitude of conditional grants, each with its own set of rules, regulations, and allocating formulae, has created a highly complex and generally confusing grant structure. Attempts at reform have suggested that conditional grants be simplified and reduced with considerable emphasis placed on deconditionalizing the system of provincial-local intergovernmental transfers. Greater dependence on unconditional grants would erase many of the existing distortions and leave local governments with greater accountability to their constituents and more autonomy in allocating their funds among those services and programs that best reflect the needs and preferences of the local citizenry.

Finally, the noticeable difference between the federal-provincial intergovernmental transfer system (cooperative federalism) and the provincial-local intergovernmental transfer system (multi-level finance) may be the source for much of the concern expressed by local officials about the inadequacies of the current provincial-local grant system structure. For example, with few exceptions, the lack of a cooperative provincial-local tax or revenue sharing program and the unilateral determination by provincial officials on both the size of grants and the services to be funded have created considerable uncertainty and extreme difficulty in properly forecasting and budgeting for future expenditures and corresponding revenues. By comparison, many of these problems are non-existent in federal-provincial transfer programs where both governments share in the same tax base.

Furthermore, the chaotic and complex nature of the local grant system structure can be attributed largely to two features that are peculiar to this transfer system. The absence of any periodic and systematic review of provincial-local grants (federal-provincial transfer programs are reviewed every five years) and the large number of local governments, their separate agencies, boards and commissions, each of which receive grants on their own (federal government transfers almost always go to provincial governments alone), have contributed to grant structures that seldom change, are difficult to comprehend, and defy any serious rationale.

Clearly, what is needed is greater acceptance, by provincial and local authorities, of a careful and thoroughly presented review of the existing grant structures. This review should outline the role of local government and, with this in mind, design a more simplified and rational system of local grants.

10
Other Local Revenue Sources

INTRODUCTION

Although local governments are dependent to a large extent on revenues from local property taxes and grants, they are becoming increasingly more dependent on revenues from other local sources. In 1968, the average Canadian municipality received slightly more than 9 per cent of its total revenue from local nontax sources. By 1978, this figure had increased significantly to almost 15 per cent of total revenues (Table 7.1). Clearly, resistance on the part of local politicians and administrators to raise property taxes suggests that nonproperty tax revenues and specifically user fees or charges will play an increasingly important role in financing local expenditures in the future. This chapter will outline and evaluate the major sources of local nonproperty tax revenues as well as local revenues derived from other-than-tax sources.

NONPROPERTY TAX REVENUES[1]

Nonproperty taxes at the local level (excluding realty, special assessment and business taxes) do not generate significant sums of revenue for local governments. In fact, in 1978, municipalities in Newfoundland, on average, displayed the greatest dependence on this revenue source by collecting from these miscellaneous taxes, slightly more than 3 per cent of total revenues (Appendix Table C.1). By comparison, municipalities in the remaining provinces collected 1 per cent or less of all revenue from nonproperty local taxes. Specifically, municipalities in Prince Edward Island, New Brunswick, Alberta, and British Columbia either recorded negligible sums of revenue from this source or did not utilize other local taxes at all.

Included here are a number of small and seemingly insignificant taxes such as the land transfer taxes collected in municipalities in Nova Scotia and Quebec.[2] In Nova Scotia, almost one-third of all municipalities levy this tax at a rate of ½ per cent to 1 per cent of the value of property transferred. In Quebec, municipalities are authorized to levy taxes on most immovables situated in a municipality at the rate of $\frac{3}{10}$ of 1 per cent on the first $50,000 of sale price and $\frac{6}{10}$ of 1 per cent on the excess. Municipalities in Manitoba can also collect this tax but no municipality has done so and, consequently, no rates have been set.

While most municipalities in all provinces generate some revenue from amusements in the form of issuing licences, municipalities in Newfoundland, Quebec, and Saskatchewan also collect revenue from this source in the form of amusement taxes.[3] Local governments in Newfoundland can impose an enter-

---

[1]For more detail, see Canadian Tax Foundation, *Provincial and Municipal Finances, 1981* (Toronto: the Foundation, 1981), Chapter 6.

[2]This is a provincial tax in Ontario.

[3]This tax is a provincial source of revenue for general purposes in Prince Edward Island, Nova Scotia, New Brunswick, and Ontario.

tainment tax with a rate that varies depending on the type of entertainment and whether it is performed by a resident or nonresident. In Quebec, the tax can be as high as 10 per cent of the admission price but is collected under the supervision of the provincial government. All local governments in Saskatchewan have the authority to establish and determine the rate structure (percentage of admission price) of all taxes imposed on amusement activities. As in the case of land transfer taxes, municipalities in Manitoba are entitled to impose an amusement tax at rates established by local councils, but at the time of writing no municipality had implemented this tax. In each of these four provinces where this tax can be used to collect revenue, local governments have the right to grant tax exemptions.

In general, municipal governments in Canada must adhere to statutory rates applied to pipe and power lines passing through their respective municipalities. Obviously, the revenue generated from this tax is small and generally insignificant except in some rural areas where total municipal revenues are small to begin with.

Poll taxes are authorized in municipalities in Newfoundland and Saskatchewan but only employed in Newfoundland.

Retail sales taxes are collected by every provincial government with the exception of Alberta. In British Columbia, legislation provides that the province share retail sales tax revenues with the municipalities. In Manitoba, on the other hand, municipalities are authorized, at their own discretion, to apply sales tax on liquor, hotel accommodations, and restaurant meals exceeding a specified amount. The province must approve this municipal decision and may collect revenues on behalf of the municipalities.

In British Columbia, municipalities are authorized to impose a special tax on holders of provincial liquor licences with the value of the tax not to exceed the value of the licence.

Fuel in the form of coal, fuel oil, and propane gas may be taxed at legislated rates by municipalities in Newfoundland.

Provincial income taxes are large revenue yielders in all provinces. In Manitoba the entire revenue from 2.2 percentage points of the provincial personal income tax and 1 percentage point of provincial corporate taxable income is passed over to municipalities for their use. Similarly, the provincial government in British Columbia transfers to municipalities the revenue generated from 1 percentage point of personal income taxes, 1 per cent of corporate taxable income, and 6 per cent of the sum of a number of provincial taxes and other revenues.[4] Finally, municipalities in Saskatchewan, through a revenue sharing scheme, share in the revenues generated by provincial taxes. These revenues grow annually according to an escalator index designed to follow the growth in provincial revenues.

Various miscellaneous municipal taxes exist, each of which is small in magnitude and importance. Such taxes include a tax of $1 for every subscriber on the main line telephone in communities in Newfoundland. As well, water and sewage taxes may be levied at rates established by local councils on owners

---

[4]Supra footnote 1, at 197.

or occupiers of premises not connected to local water or sewage systems. A fire protection tax levied at a uniform rate on the value of real taxable property is part of the municipal tax picture in Halifax. A water tax is part of the local tax structure in many Quebec municipalities. This, however, is not always imposed on water consumption, but is determined instead as a percentage of the rental value of property and levied on the occupant whether renter or owner.

Needless to say, not all local taxes have been presented here. Instead, the more obvious ones have been selected since they provide a general flavour of the type and variety of local taxes collected in different municipalities in Canada.

EVALUATION

It is difficult to evaluate all local taxes in a few short paragraphs. Such an exercise, however, is undoubtedly all that can be justified given the relatively limited sums of revenue generated by each of these sources. Most local taxes reviewed in this chapter are unknown to the general public and, as such, generate limited criticism and are thus more palatable to local officials. They are, however, analytically distasteful to most analysts. A good tax or tax system, it can be argued, is one that is explicit, is easy to administer, is understood by the taxpayer, is fair, and does not distort the allocation of society's resources.

Local taxes, unfortunately, typically fail to meet most of these criteria. The existence of so many different taxes creates a system that is much more complicated and difficult to understand than is generally thought to be desirable. Many of these taxes are hidden and hence, either unknown or not understood by local taxpayers; for example, the municipal fuel tax in Newfoundland, local amusement taxes in Newfoundland, Quebec, and Saskatchewan, alcoholic beverage taxation imposed at the local level in British Columbia to name only a few. Furthermore, a number of these taxes are assumed to be unfair in that they do not treat individuals in similar circumstances in the same way, that is, they do not conform to either the ability to pay criterion or benefits received criterion of fairness. This inequity exists both within and among municipalities. Similarly, distortions are created as long as taxes are imposed at less than uniform rates on all forms of economic activity. To be more specific, the exemption of amusement taxes[5] on activities organized for charitable, religious, and educational purposes discriminates in favour of these activities and against the non-exempt ones. The existence of land transfer taxes[6] in only some municipalities creates similar unwanted distortions both within and among municipalities.

Perhaps the strongest and most rational defence that can be made for the utilization of these taxes is that they are relatively easy and inexpensive to administer and that they can be designed to capture the additional costs to the locality of certain activities such as extra police or fire protection for specific events.

---

[5]For a discussion of this, see Harry M. Kitchen, *Public Finance in Metropolitan Toronto,* A Study for the Royal Commission on Metropolitan Toronto (Toronto: the Commission, 1977), 157-60.

[6]Ibid., at 160-64.

Because the rates applied to nonproperty taxes do not reflect either the benefits the taxpayers receive from the local services consumed or the abilities of the recipients of these services to pay local taxes, they are likely to generate distributional impacts on local taxpayers that are both uncertain and distorting. Indeed, a careful analysis of the actual distributional impact and distortions created by these taxes may very well exhibit results that are completely unacceptable to the local citizenry. One of the serious problems with "ad hoc" local tax systems is that virtually no careful economic analysis on the effects of the "other tax" category has been undertaken. Ease of administration and political acceptance have dictated their use.

In essence, greater use of local taxes or explicit user charges that reflect actual benefits received should be adopted, while local taxes not capturing specific benefits should be eliminated.

LOCAL NONTAX REVENUES

Unlike nonproperty local taxes, "local nontax revenues" generate significant sums in every province. In 1978, per capita local nontax revenues for the average Canadian municipality amounted to $114 or almost 24 per cent of total own-source revenues (Table 10.1). Although the local per capita average on a province-by-province basis varied across the country, it exceeded $100 in Ontario and the four western provinces with Alberta's level ($223) being slightly less than twice as high as that for the other four provinces. In the East, the level ranged from $24 to $72 per capita in Atlantic Canada and $89 in Quebec.

Interestingly, the range in the percentage of total own-source revenues for which local nontax revenues accounted does not display the same regional variation. For instance, the average municipality in Alberta and Prince Edward Island placed the greatest reliance on this revenue source where 46 per cent and 38 per cent respectively of their total own-source revenues were contributed by this category. Other provinces in which municipalities displayed higher-than-average (national) reliance on this source included New Brunswick (33 per cent), Nova Scotia (24 per cent), and Saskatchewan (28 per cent). Quebec and Manitoba recorded the least relative dependence (21 per cent) on local nontax revenues, while Ontario, Newfoundland, and British Columbia all collected between 21 per cent and 22 per cent of their locally raised revenues from this source in 1978 (Table 10.1).

Part of the variation in the relative dependence can be attributed to differences in expenditure responsibility and hence local revenue sources. For example, property taxes in Prince Edward Island and New Brunswick are limited mainly to the provincial government, therefore it is not surprising that nontax revenues as a per cent of total own-source revenues are high for local governments in these two provinces. (The data in Table 7.1 indicate that own-source revenues are substantially lower in these provinces than elsewhere.) The rest of the variation in many provinces, however, can be attributed to differences in the usage of certain charges. This is especially true in Ontario and the four western provinces — provinces with similar fiscal structures.

In reviewing the individual sources listed in Table 10.1, it becomes apparent that with the exception of Manitoba, local revenues from the sale of goods and

Table 10.1   Local Per Capita Nonproperty Tax Revenue by Source and as a Per Cent of Total Own-Source Revenue by Province, 1978

Revenue source	Newfoundland		Prince Edward Island		Nova Scotia		New Brunswick		Quebec		Ontario	
	$a	%b	$a	%b	$a	%b	$a	%b	$a	%b	$a	%b
Sales of goods and services												
Water	8.38	7.9	11.07	12.8	15.15	5.1	14.98	12.4	35.48	8.3	24.21	4.5
Rentals	1.93	1.8	2.36	2.7	1.93	0.7	2.77	2.3	0.06	0.0	5.42	1.0
Other	9.10	8.6	14.45	16.8	34.22	11.6	15.88	13.1	23.35	5.5	53.84	10.0
Privileges, licences, and permits												
Concessions and functions	0.04	0.0	0.05	0.0	0.03	0.0	—	—	0.36	0.1	1.72	0.3
Licences and permits	1.31	1.2	0.51	0.6	1.41	0.5	1.37	1.1	1.82	0.4	3.86	0.7
Return on investments												
Own enterprises	0.05	0.0	2.51	2.9	0.29	0.1	0.76	0.6	2.45	0.6	2.15	0.4
Other	0.55	0.5	4.25	3.5	3.90	1.3	1.71	1.4	7.72	1.8	14.28	2.6
Other revenues												
Interest and penalty on taxes	0.90	0.9	0.05	0.0	4.25	1.4	0.45	0.4	2.47	0.6	3.09	0.6
Other fines and penalties	0.04	0.0	2.52	2.9	2.19	0.7	0.71	0.6	5.83	1.4	2.32	0.4
Miscellaneous	1.40	1.3	2.12	2.5	8.37	2.8	0.85	0.7	9.59	2.2	7.47	1.4
Total	23.68	22.4	39.90	46.3	71.73	24.3	39.48	32.6	89.14	20.9	118.36	21.9

(Table concluded on next page.)

Table 10.1 Concluded

Revenue source	Manitoba		Saskatchewan		Alberta		British Columbia		All provinces	
	$a	%b	$a	%b	$a	%b	$a	%b	$a	%b
Sales of goods and services										
Water	23.39	4.4	22.91	4.7	33.50	5.6	23.13	4.1	26.74	5.6
Rentals	3.09	0.6	3.18	0.7	9.09	1.5	20.07	3.5	5.37	1.1
Other	32.63	6.1	64.09	13.2	100.59	17.0	46.15	8.1	45.08	9.4
Privileges, licences, and permits										
Concessions and functions	0.31	0.1	2.83	0.6	7.96	1.3	1.35	0.2	1.66	0.3
Licences and permits	5.41	1.0	4.70	1.0	10.63	1.8	9.79	1.7	4.38	0.9
Return on investments										
Own enterprises	13.42	2.5	6.92	1.4	30.52	5.1	0.93	0.2	5.00	1.0
Other	17.05	3.2	13.45	2.8	13.12	2.2	14.64	2.6	11.42	2.4
Other revenues										
Interest and penalty on taxes	4.37	0.8	1.59	0.3	5.81	1.0	2.99	0.5	3.03	0.6
Other fines and penalties	2.92	0.5	5.33	1.1	4.78	0.8	1.19	0.2	3.38	0.7
Miscellaneous	9.33	1.7	12.82	2.6	7.11	1.2	3.48	0.6	7.53	1.6
Total	111.92	20.8	137.83	28.4	223.12	37.6	123.70	21.8	113.59	23.7

aPer capita dollars. bPer cent of total own-source revenue.

Source: Calculated from data in Statistics Canada, *Local Government Finance: Revenue and Expenditures, 1978*, Catalogue no. 68-202.

services accounts for over 65 per cent of all local nontax revenues. Average per capita revenue from water sales alone varied from between $8 and $15 per capita in the provinces in Atlantic Canada to around $23 or $24 per capita in Ontario, Manitoba, Saskatchewan, and British Columbia with Alberta's and Quebec's level being substantially higher at $37 and $35 respectively. Greater variation in the local government's dependence on rental revenue and other revenue from sales of goods and services was quite evident.[7] Almost every municipality collects some revenue from the rental of real property. Included in this are charges for arena rentals, rental of recreational facilities owned by local governments, and rentals of municipally owned land, buildings, and machinery. Other local revenue from the sale of goods and services (and this tends to be larger than either rental or water income in most provinces), arises from fees charged for the sale of specific services regardless of whether these services are sold to other governments, private businesses, local residents, or nonresidents. Such services sold to other governments and occasionally to larger businesses include snowploughing and fire and police protection. Services sold to individuals cover a wide range of items including public transit fares, greens fees, and admission prices for the use of municipally owned golf courses and swimming pools.

There are a number of other local government fees and charges including licences, permits, and concessions (taxi licences, business licences, and building permits) that frequently are included in the user fee category. For purposes of this discussion, however, these are not defined as user charges. Instead, user fees are defined as charges imposed on local services that are available to all citizens. In the absence of user charges, these services would likely be provided and financed from alternative revenue sources. Licences, permits, and concessions, by comparison, represent examples of municipalities charging individuals for the right to undertake particular activities designed to benefit specific groups of individuals or to allow individuals to engage in money-making operations.

USER FEES

Table 10.2 lists the types of municipal charges that currently are used or may be used. Table 10.3 displays the extent to which local governments depend on user fees as a base for financing a number of local services in Ontario. Similar observations would be drawn if data were available for all of Canada. Some services, particularly water provision, sewage treatment, and public transit, exhibit greater dependence on user charges than do others. This difference in the proportion of total costs that are financed by user charges partially reflects differences in the costs to be recovered by user fees. For example, some municipalities only attempt to cover operating costs, while others attempt to cover both operating and capital costs. A further explanation for greater dependence on user charges in the three services cited here arises from tradition (that is, these services have almost always carried user fees) and/or expectations (that is, consumers expect to pay for services whose benefits are assumed to accrue directly to the user). Library services and police protection generally collect very little revenue from user fees, while parks, recreation facilities, and

---

[7]The coefficient of variation across provinces ranged from .42 for water to .76 for other revenue from sales of goods and services to 1.17 for rental income.

Table 10.2   Types of Municipal User Charges

Parks and recreation		Fire
Arenas	— skating admissions	Alarm connection fees
	— hourly ice rentals	Inspection fees
	— instruction	Charges for services to
Pools	— swimming admissions	neighbouring municipalities
	— memberships	Police
	— instruction	Special events charges
Tennis	— court fees	
	— membership	Daycare
	— instruction	Per diem charges
Camps/	— campground fees	Weekly charges
Camping	— day camp charges	"After 4" program charges
Golf course	— greens fees	Other fees and charges
	— membership	Senior citizens' homes per diem fees
	— instruction	Entrance fees to museums, zoos, etc.
		Animal control fees
Nonresident fees		Parking lot and meter charges
		Fire hydrant inspection fees
Libraries		Room and hall rentals
Memberships		
Nonresident borrowers fees		Utilities
Interlibrary loan fees		Water connection fees
A.V. equipment rentals		Water service charges
Overdue fines		Sewer surcharge
Rental fees		Industrial waste fees
		Garbage collection levy
Public transit		
Cash fares		
Passes		

Source: Bureau of Municipal Research, *Municipal Services: Who Should Pay?* (Toronto: the Bureau, 1980), 3.

daycare services are slightly more dependent on this source of revenue (Table 10.3).

The rates charged for using the different services vary depending on the service. All municipalities charge for water, either through the imposition of a flat-rate charge (relating to the number of taps, bathrooms, other rooms, toilets) or by charging for the volume of water consumed (by metering). Regardless of the pricing policy adopted, the tendency has been to set the rate at a level that will provide for recovery of most, if not all, of the costs of providing this service.

Greater variation in the extent to which sewage costs were recovered in 1977 is evident in Table 10.3, ranging from a low of .02 per cent in Peterborough to a high of 98 per cent in the region of Hamilton/Wentworth. With few exceptions (Metro Toronto and Kingston where flat fees were levied) the sewage charge was generally established as a fixed percentage of the water consumption bill. These percentages fluctuated from 6 per cent of the water rate in Sarnia to 100 per cent of the rate in Hamilton/Wentworth. This exercise of tying sewage rates to the water rates is a recognition that water is used for sewage collection.

Most municipalities have, for various social and economic reasons, conscientiously decided not to attempt to recover all of the costs of transit services from user charges. In 1977, between 45 per cent and 72 per cent of all transit budgets in Ontario were covered by user charges with fares per trip varying considerably. For example, adult fares ranged from a low of 30 cents per trip to a high of 55 cents per trip (Table 10.4). Similar variations can be observed in the charges imposed on students, children, and senior citizens. At the same time, there is little correlation in the relationship between fares and the proportion of the budget covered by these fares. Some municipalities had relatively low fares (London and St. Catharines at 40 cents per adult trip) and high recovery rates (72 per cent and 61 per cent of transit budgets respectively), while other municipalities had relatively higher fares (Windsor and the region of Ottawa/Carleton at 50 cents per adult trip) and lower recovery rates (56 per cent of the transit budget). In other municipalities, moreover, the fares varied directly with the recovery rates. This lack of consistency between fares and recovery rates may be attributed to a number of factors including the size of the municipality, service levels, patronage of the system, the size of operating and capital grants,[8] and the definition of costs that are to be recovered — that is, operating alone or a combination of operating and capital.

In the last few years, increased leisure time accompanied by a greater desire to use recreational facilities has led to an increase in the proportion of local budgets absorbed by expenditures on parks and recreational services. Consequently, this budgetary claim has led to attempts to charge users for a higher proportion of the costs of supplying these services. Along with considerable variation in the proportion of budgets recovered from user charges (Table 10.3) is a similar variation in the charges for services (Table 10.5). For example, in 1977 tennis memberships, court fees, and instruction showed considerable variation (Table 10.5) with memberships ranging from $0.00 to $50.00 per family, court fees ranging from $0.00 to $1.00 per hour, and instruction from $10.00 to $40.00 per week. Similarly, wide discrepancies existed in camp ground fees ($3.00 to $6.00 per night), skating admissions ($0.00 to $1.25 per time), ice-time rentals ($10.00 to $50.00 per hour), swimming pool admissions ($0.00 to $1.00 per visit), pool rentals ($10.00 to $35.00 per hour), golf memberships ($0.00 to $280.00 per year), and green fees ($2.25 to $7.00 per time).

All public libraries collect fines on overdue books with the rate of fine varying from one municipality to another (Table 10.6). Many municipalities also impose annual nonresident borrower fees and collect revenues from a number of miscellaneous sources including film and projection rentals, photocopy services, and lecture hall rentals. In total this revenue covered between .5 per cent and 6 per cent of public library budgets in 1977 (Table 10.3).

The provision of police services generated relatively small sums of money in virtually every municipality surveyed (Table 10.3). The bulk of this revenue still comes from the hiring of off-duty policemen for special events and from parking ticket revenue.

---

[8]Bureau of Municipal Research, *Municipal Services: Who Should Pay?*, Topic no. 13 (Toronto: BMR, 1980), 14.

Table 10.3   Proportion and Amount of Department Budgets from User Charges, 1977

Government	Parks and recreation		Libraries		Water		Sewage	
	%	$	%	$	%	$	%	$
Upper tier								
Hamilton/Wentworth..	n/a	n/a	1.9	11,626	86.0	10,503,182	98.7	10,009,133
Metro Toronto.......	14.5	1,472,863	.5	54,900	100.0	41,732,500	29.0	10,178,100
Niagara............	n/a	n/a	n/a	n/a	n/a	n/a	n/a	n/a
Ottawa/Carleton.....	n/a	n/a	n/a	n/a	51.1	10,457,607	n/a	n/a
Peel...............	n/a	n/a	n/a	n/a	96.0	9,951,000	85.0	9,027,698
One tier								
Kingston...........	n/r	n/r	5.4	32,072	n/a	n/a	17.1	985,560
London............	40.0	2,368,000	n/r	n/r	88.8	5,180,000	n/r	n/r
Peterborough.......	36.4	669,000	4.7	18,000	100.0	1,778,000	.02	60,000
Sarnia.............	28.0	508,000	5.7	37,697	100.0	n/r	7.1	126,575
Windsor	13.2	755,339	1.0	26,365	100.0	5,268,000	n/a	n/a
Lower tier								
Burlington	20.4	977,856	4.8	59,558	n/a	n/a	n/a	n/a
Etobicoke	2.0	1,903,200	2.0	81,000	100.0	9,346,936	general tax levy	
Gloucester	22.0	2,216,723	2.3	409,094	n/a	n/a	n/a	n/a
Nepean	n/r	2,029,000	n/r	5,000	n/a	n/a	89.0	948,000
Ottawa	18.0	700,000	2.5	111,999	n/a	n/a	56.8	4,669,486
St. Catharines......	25.0	660,727	3.3	43,305	100.0	3,359,553	nominal amount	
Toronto	n/a	n/a	1.0	112,222	100.0	26,103,993	80.0	9,839,757

(Table concluded on next page.)

Table 10.3   Concluded

Government	Transit		Daycare		Police	
	%	$	%	$	%	$
Upper tier						
Hamilton/Wentworth	61.0	12,814.078	19.7	21,806	.1	224,327
Metro Toronto	69.0	132,500,000	9.0	1,516,000	.7	1,083,300
Niagara	n/a	n/a	5.6	50,000	1.1	196,000
Ottawa/Carleton	56.1	20,841,323	16.7	233,740	n/a	n/a
Peel	n/a	n/a	26.0	364,391	.8	141,000
One tier						
Kingston	54.0	887,122	17.0	177,948	8.0	218,445
London	72.2	7,322,000	2.2	15,000	n/r	n/r
Peterborough	45.0	887,000	23.7	43,000	.01	30,000
Sarnia	51.0	625,505	20.2	37,970	23.0	598,702
Windsor	56.0	3,100,000	22.7	140,641	n/a	n/a
Lower tier						
Burlington	45.7	660,710	n/a	n/a	n/a	n/a
Etobicoke	n/a	n/a	n/a	n/a	n/a	n/a
Gloucester	n/a	n/a	n/a	n/a	13.0	22,673
Nepean	n/a	n/a	n/a	n/a	.1	24,000
Ottawa	n/a	n/a	*	*	10.0	1,761,077
St. Catharines	60.8	2,353,713	No program		n/a	n/a
Toronto	n/a	n/a	n/a	n/a	n/a	n/a

*—purchase services from region.   n/a—not applicable, function carried out at a different level.   n/r—no response given on questionnaire.

Source: Bureau of Municipal Research, *Municipal Services: Who Should Pay?* (Toronto, the Bureau, 1980), 12-13.

Table 10.4   Public Transit User Charges, 1977

Government	Adult	Student	Children	Seniors	Comments
Upper tier					
Hamilton/Wentworth	$.55	6/$1	6/$1	6/$1 or pass for $12.50	
Metro Toronto	$.55	$.30	$.20	$.30	Discounts available for multiple purchases
Niagara	n/a	n/a	n/a	n/a	
Ottawa/Carleton	$.50	n/a	$.25	n/a	Discounts available for multiple purchases
Peel	n/a	n/a	n/a	n/a	
One tier					
Kingston	$.35	$.25	$.25	$.15	
London	$.40	$.20	$.20	$.40	
Peterborough	$.30	$.25	$.25	$.30	
Sarnia	$.35	$.20	$.15	$.35	
Windsor	$.50	$.35	$.25	$.35	
Lower tier					
Burlington	$.40	$.30	$.15	$.15	
Etobicoke	n/a	n/a	n/a	n/a	
Gloucester	n/a	n/a	n/a	n/a	
Nepean	n/a	n/a	n/a	n/a	
Ottawa	n/a	n/a	n/a	n/a	
St. Catharines	$.40	$.30	$.20	$.40	Discounts available for multiple purchases

n/a—not applicable, function carried out at a different level.

Source: Bureau of Municipal Research, *Municipal Services: Who Should Pay?* (Toronto: the Bureau, 1980), 16.

Table 10.5   Parks and Recreation Charges, 1977

Government	Arenas			Swimming		Golf	
	Skating admissions	Ice rentals	General admissions	Memberships	Pool rentals	Memberships	Greens fees
Upper tier							
Hamilton/Wentworth	n/a	n/a	n/a	n/a	n/a	n/a	n/a
Metro Toronto	—	—	—	—	—	—	$2.25-$4.45
Niagara	n/a	n/a	n/a	n/a	n/a	n/a	n/a
Ottawa/Carleton	n/a	n/a	n/a	n/a	n/a	n/a	n/a
Peel	n/a	n/a	n/a	n/a	n/a	n/a	n/a
One tier							
Kingston	$.25-$.50	$18-$28/hr.	$.30-$.50	—	$12/hr.	$40-$110	$3.00-$5.00
London	$.25-$.60	$22/hr.	$.10-$.50	—	—	$70-$110	$2.50-$6.00
Peterborough	$.50-$1.25	$33-$43/hr.	$.50-$1.00	—	—	—	—
Sarnia	*	*	—	—	—	—	—
Windsor	$.50-$1.00	$21-$50/hr.	up to $.50	—	$15/hr.	$185-$280	$2.25-$7.00
Lower tier							
Burlington	$1.00	$40/hr.	$.75	$12	$20/hr.	$200	$5.00-$7.00
Etobicoke	*	$20-$45/hr.	*	—	*	—	—
Gloucester	*	*	*	—	*	—	—
Nepean	$.35-$.60	$27/hr.	$.35-$.60	—	$35/hr.	—	—
Ottawa	—	$10-$30/hr.	—	—	$10-$20	—	—
St. Catharines	$.35-$.75	$11-$42/hr.	—	$25/season/fam.	—	—	$2.50-$5.00
Toronto	n/a	n/a	n/a	n/a	n/a	n/a	n/a

(Table concluded on next page.)

Table 10.5   Concluded

Government	Tennis			Camps/camping		Other
	Memberships	Court fees	Instructions	Day camps	Campground fees	
Upper tier						
Hamilton/Wentworth	n/a	n/a	n/a	n/a	n/a	—
Metro Toronto	—	—	—	—	$4.00-$4.50	Moorings—$100-$110/season
Niagara	n/a	n/a	n/a	n/a	n/a	
Ottawa/Carleton	n/a	n/a	n/a	n/a	n/a	
Peel	n/a	n/a	n/a	n/a	n/a	
One tier						
Kingston	—	$.40-$1.00	—	—	$3.00-$5.50/day	Moorings—varies
London	$50/family	—	—	$32/2 wks	—	
Peterborough	—	—	—	$20/wk	$4.50-$6.00/night	
Sarnia	—	—	*	*	*	
Windsor	—	up to $1/hr	$5.00-$15.00	—	—	
Lower tier						
Burlington	$15	$1/hr	$10/lesson	$38/wk	—	Ski and fencing lessons $20/lesson; garden plots; community centres; community centres rental.
Etobicoke	—	—	*	*	—	
Gloucester	—	—	—	—	—	
Nepean	$12-$28	$.50-$1.00	—	$25-$40/wk	—	
Ottawa	—	—	$5 for 5 hrs	$10/wk	—	School of art—$30
St. Catharines	$12-$20	—	$20/season	$15/wk	—	
Toronto	n/a	n/a	n/a	n/a	n/a	

n/a—not applicable.   ——no charge.   *charge for these but did not list the rate.

Source: Bureau of Municipal Research, *Municipal Services: Who Should Pay?* (Toronto: the Bureau, 1980), 17-18.

Table 10.6 Public Library Charges, 1977

Government	Nonresident borrowers fees	Overdue fines	Miscellaneous services
Upper tier			
Hamilton/Wentworth	No charge	$.05-$.25 per day	Rent projectors—$2-$3/day
Metro Toronto	$5.00/person	$.01-$.05 per day	
Niagara	Not applicable		
Ottawa/Carleton	Not applicable		
Peel	Not applicable		
One tier			
Kingston	$15/family; $10/single	$.02-$.05 per day	Photocopying—$.10; Film—$.50-$4.00/day
London	Not applicable		
Peterborough	$7/family; $5/adult	$.02 per day	Photocopying—$.10
Sarnia	No charge	*	
Windsor	$5/person	No charge	Equipment rentals—$1-$4/day
Lower tier			
Burlington	No charge	*	
Etobicoke	$5/person	$.10 per day	Films—$1/day *
Gloucester	*	*	
Nepean	$5/person	$.03 per day	
Ottawa	*	*	
St. Catharines	No charge	$.05 per day	Film rentals and lecture hall rentals
Toronto	$5/person	$.01-$.05 per day	

*Indicates that the municipality charges some fee for this service but did not indicate the rate at which it charges.

Source: Bureau of Municipal Research, *Municipal Services: Who Should Pay?* (Toronto: the Bureau, 1980), 21.

Table 10.7   Daycare Charges, 1977

	Charges per day	
Government	Unassisted	Assisted minimum
Upper tier		
Hamilton/Wentworth	$7.00-$8.00	—
Metro Toronto	$10.50	—
Niagara	$10.00	$0.50
Ottawa/Carleton	$10.50	—
Peel	$10.00	$1.50
One tier		
Kingston	$ 7.00	—
London	$ 0.60	—
Peterborough	$ 9.00	$1.00
Sarnia	$ 8.90	—
Windsor..............................	$10.00	—
Lower tier		
Burlington...........................	Not applicable (regional function)	
Etobicoke	Not applicable (regional function)	
Gloucester	Not applicable (regional function)	
Nepean	Not applicable (regional function)	
Ottawa..............................	Not applicable (regional function)	
St. Catharines	No program	
Toronto.............................	Not applicable (regional function)	

Source: Bureau of Municipal Research, *Municipal Services: Who Should Pay?* (Toronto: the Bureau, 1980), 20.

Table 10.7 lists the charges for daycare services in 1977. From this, it is obvious that daycare is highly subsidized for needy users (compare figures in assisted column with figures in unassisted column), although a subsidy exists for all daycare users. Some municipalities simply waive the daycare fee for low income parents. Regardless of the rates charged, municipalities tended to recover less than 25 per cent of their budgets on this function in 1977 (Table 10.3), a fact that reflects the social and essentially income-redistributive nature of this service.

Evaluation of User Fees

In Theory
Theoretically, one can make a case affirming user charges[9] as an appropriate device for aiding in the achievement of a more efficient allocation of society's resources. In reality, however, practical difficulties and administration costs may prevent the imposition of such charges.

The economic principle underlying the efficient allocation of resources suggests that the level of output should be produced up to the point where the price charged for an additional unit equals the extra cost of producing that same

---

[9]It is assumed that user charges are established on a charge-per-unit basis and not on a flat-rate basis, regardless of the quantity consumed.

unit.[10] In this instance, the price or user charge is a measurement of the monetary value of the additional benefit received from consuming the last unit. The extra cost (marginal cost) refers to the opportunity cost of producing the last unit. To be more precise, this states that the true economic cost of producing an extra unit is measured by the value of the output that could have been produced had these resources been devoted to their next best use. If the price (user charge) charged for the service exceeds its marginal cost, then the service will be under supplied and economic inefficiency will result. Economic inefficiency arises because resources have been diverted to the production of less valuable goods or services at the expense of more valuable goods or services. Similarly, if the price is below marginal cost, an oversupply and hence economic inefficiency exists once again. Here, a less valuable good or service has attracted resources away from a more valuable good or service. Ideally, therefore, the efficient pricing policy states that services must be produced up to the point where the price (user charge) of the last unit produced is equal to the marginal cost of the last unit produced.

The achievement of economic efficiency at the local level involves the implementation of a proper and correct pricing policy for local goods and services. The application of user charges to cover the entire marginal cost is warranted as long as the benefits from the good or service accrue solely to the recipients of the good or service provided. By comparison, in those instances where some of the benefits spill over onto residents who are not involved directly in partaking of the local good or service, a case can be made for not using user fees to recover the entire marginal cost of supplying the optimum level of output. In this instance, partial use of user fees along with alternative sources of funds may be desirable as a means of funding these outputs.

The advantages of properly established user charges as opposed to alternative revenue sources as a basis for supporting local goods and services are fairly clearcut. User charges, where they can be applied, have the important advantage of providing correct signals in terms of indicating the quantity and quality of things that local residents desire. In the absence of user charges, there is no appropriate mechanism for signalling the proper demand for the local government's output. When consumers are forced to pay a price for each unit consumed, their actions signal the quantity and quality of output desired. Alternatively, if these same outputs were financed from local tax revenues, correct signals would not exist. Local residents not being required to pay each time for each unit consumed, would perceive the price imposed as being essentially zero and, therefore, create a greater than optimal demand for the local output. The resultant misallocation of resources would arise because too many resources were being devoted to the provision of these local government goods and services.

Despite the inherent problems of establishing correct user charges, "a strong case can be made that more use of pricing in the public sector would lessen the number of occasions on which the wrong product is produced, in the wrong

---

[10]For an elaboration on the principle of public prices, see supra footnote 8, at 33-42, and Selma J. Mushkin and Richard M. Bird, "Public Prices: An Overview," in Selma J. Mushkin, ed., *Public Prices for Public Products* (Washington, D.C.: Urban Institute, 1972), 3-25, at 11 and 18-25.

quantity, and with inappropriate quality differentiation.''[11] The local government provision of what can be classified as private goods (those whose benefits accrue to individuals who directly consume them) could be handled, in almost every instance, more efficiently under a system of user charges. This policy would provide for a relatively efficient way of raising local revenue. In addition, it would generate more efficient levels of local government output. If individuals were required to pay a price that covered the extra cost of resources used up in producing this good, there would be less of a tendency to under or over supply. Finally, for those who argue that local taxation ought to be structured on the basis of benefits received, user charges form an important complement to local taxes.

While the equating of marginal cost with price is relatively straightforward in theory, it is significantly more difficult to achieve in practice. First, the inability or difficulty of being able to define units of output for many public goods combined with the inability or excessive difficulty in collecting cost data and/or the problems of assigning costs to outputs creates situations where neither output nor cost per unit of output can be measured or where collection of the charge is prohibitively expensive.

Second, if other sectors of the economy are producing levels of output where price is not equal to marginal cost, then there may be no reason to insist on local provision at the point where the two are equal. Instead, efficiency may be improved by supplying the output at the point where the divergency between marginal cost and price at the local government level is similar to the divergence in the rest of the economy.[12]

Third, in instances where external benefits exist, it is unlikely that local officials will be able to achieve the efficient level of output. To do so would require a proper measure of the monetary value of the marginal external benefits along with the proper user charge for direct beneficiaries of the public service. If the former cannot be calculated, then the user charge is almost certain to be at a level too high or too low for optimum efficiency.

Fourth, provision of a local government service at the level where price equals marginal cost may not generate enough revenue to cover the cost of supplying this service, that is, where price is equal to marginal cost but less than average cost. In this instance, if certain conditions are met (that is, efficient markets exist elsewhere), then a case can be made for producing where price equals marginal cost and subsidizing the losses from those tax revenues that are nondistorting.[13] Unfortunately, all local taxes currently in use tend to be distorting and, therefore, a subsidization of local service provision may lead to a more efficient level of output of the subsidized service at the expense of creating greater inefficiencies in the areas from which taxes have been extracted.

---

[11]Richard M. Bird, *Charging for Public Services: A New Look at an Old Idea* (Toronto: Canadian Tax Foundation, 1976), 34.

[12]R.G. Lipsey and Kelvin Lancaster, "The General Theory of Second Best" (1956), 24 *Review of Economic Studies* 11-32.

[13]For a further discussion of this, see John F. Due and Ann F. Friedlaender, *Government Finance: Economics of the Public Sector*, 7th ed. (Homewood, Illinois: Richard D. Irwin, 1981), 93-98.

Whether or not overall efficiency is improved will depend on the relative gains and losses in the different sectors.

A strong case can be made for marginal cost pricing in the following instances: (1) where externalities do not exist, (2) where individuals can be excluded from consuming the good, (3) where efficiency prevails in all other areas of the economy, (4) where precise measurements of output and cost can be calculated, and (5) where collection and administrative costs are low. Clearly, these conditions will never be met entirely. The fact that a precise calculation of marginal cost applicable to those individuals or properties partaking of the service directly cannot be calculated is, however, an inadequate justification for ignoring the marginal cost pricing approach altogether. To disregard this principle is tantamount to claiming that the alternatives are superior—that is, financing from local taxes or employing user charges based on the average cost of provision. Realizing that the alternatives may have more intuitive and political appeal for local politicians and administrators, a case can and must continue to be made for greater use of marginal cost pricing. After all, if the case is not argued by those who are concerned with efficiency in the allocation of public services, then it will rarely be made by local officials or residents in an organized or consistent fashion.

The lack of public acceptence of charges for government activities has led many politicians to advocate financing through local taxes rather than through user charges. The notion that governments should not charge for services provided has somehow become engrained in the attitudes of local residents. Their anathema for charges has been witnessed in the substantial outcrys that have arisen when governments have tried to raise, for example, transit prices or fees for admission to parks and recreational areas. In the relatively few instances where user charges have been accepted, the major concern has been with setting the price equal to average cost in order to cover all costs incurred with revenues received from the services supplied.

On efficiency grounds, none of the alternatives is likely to provide more efficiency and hence, a better allocation of resources than exists under the marginal cost pricing rule. For instance, the imposition of local taxes themselves, tends to create distortions and inefficiencies. When combined with the fact that these taxes seldom bear a close or significant relationship to the marginal cost of supplying services to the properties taxed, one is left with the impression that a crude and rough approximation of the marginal cost pricing principle is better than dependence on taxes for funding many local goods and services. Surely what is important here is not the fact that an ideal and accurate marginal cost pricing policy must be ensured before it can be adopted, but rather that actions be taken to place greater reliance on the pricing of local outputs. Not only would this make consumers much more aware of the costs of local government activities, but it would also improve the allocative efficiency of providing local services in addition to generating revenues in a more efficient and equitable manner (providing the benefits-received principle is assumed to be the appropriate criterion for assessing equity at the local level).

Continuing with the efficiency arguments, the equating of user charges with average cost rather than marginal cost often violates the efficiency condition outlined above. Under the average cost pricing rule, the marginal cost of providing the last unit of output (as measured by the value of output foregone if these resources were employed in their next best use) will almost certainly not be equal to the monetary value of the benefits that the consumer perceives he or she is getting from the consumption of that unit.

Accepting the fact that theory dictates greater inefficiency under the average rather than the marginal cost pricing principle, there has been a suggestion that, in practice, allocative inefficiency may not be all that bad under average cost pricing, especially when one observes the problem facing the establishment of a correct and proper marginal cost pricing policy.[14] On the other hand, it has been claimed that that conclusion is erroneous and that under no circumstances can it be stated that average cost pricing is superior to marginal cost pricing as a principle on which to finance and allocate public resources.[15] Given these contradictory conclusions, one is left with considerable uncertainty as to which of the previous observations is correct. Perhaps the best that can be concluded is that each service should be considered on the basis of its respective merits and the constraints it faces. A more appropriate conclusion that can be drawn, however, is that either pricing principle is certain to be more allocatively efficient than local taxes.

In light of the practical problems of employing marginal cost pricing, one variant that has been suggested is the multi-part tariff. Here, the consumer pays a fixed charge for the privilege of using or gaining access to the facility and then pays a charge equal to the marginal cost of each unit consumed. In spite of some difficulty in achieving an optimal allocation of resources under this approach,[16] it "might produce results superior to the prices which would otherwise be set."[17] Overall, this pricing policy looks rather attractive as a means of financing many local public services. Clearly, it should be encouraged and its use extended in a number of areas where local services currently are not priced in an appropriate manner.

A common criticism levelled against the pricing of public outputs is the impact that such schemes will have on the distribution of income. Clearly, income distribution questions are important; however, as was argued earlier in this book, they should not be of prime concern to local governments. Rather, local officials should be more concerned with the provision of services in the most efficient manner. Greater dependence on the pricing of public services (rather than local taxes) would undoubtedly assist in the achievement of a more allocatively efficient and desirable level of local public services. Clearly, prices have the advantage of acting as a signal for correctly determining the quantity and quality of services desired and only prices can lead to a proper rationing of public outputs. For those who argue that local governments should have some responsibility for income redistribution questions, greater use of the pricing

---

[14]Peter Dixon, "The Costs of Average Cost Pricing" (1972), 1 *Journal of Public Economics* 245-56.

[15]Richard T. Gustely, "Public Service Pricing and the Urban Housing Market: An Analysis of Land Use Impacts" (July 1978), 45 *Southern Economic Journal* 75-89.

[16]For a more detailed and analytical discussion of the conditions necessary for optimal allocation, see supra footnote 13, at 76.

[17]Supra footnote 11, at 40.

system does not preclude subsidies to deserving individuals (transit passes for the poor and assistance for daycare), while expecting those who are able, to pay their own way.

In Practice

In pricing local government services, a number of schemes are currently in use. These range from fixed charges that are completely unrelated to the volume of service consumed, to charges that vary directly with the quantity consumed. A mixture of charges with both fixed and variable components lies in between. In addition, revenue from the various pricing structures is designed to cover somewhere between a very high and a very low proportion of all costs. Clearly, the decision as to the type of user charge structure and proportion of costs to be recovered cannot be related to a single or specific factor. Local tradition, the type of service, the tastes or preferences of the residents, and the desire or lack of desire of local politicians to substitute revenue from user fees for local taxes all contribute to the policy adopted. Perhaps a quick review of local practices and their inherent implications will aid in assessing the specific pricing policies for the diverse local services.

Water.—Having mentioned earlier that local governments should be concerned primarily with the allocation of resources in the most efficient possible manner, it remains to be stated that the establishment of an efficient pricing policy (marginal cost equalling price) can best be achieved for publicly provided outputs with private good properties. The most obvious example of a local public good with these characteristics (benefits from consumption accrue almost exclusively to those directly consuming the good) exists in the provision of residential and commerical/industrial water. Given this, it is somewhat surprising to note the variation in pricing schemes actually employed and the extent to which these schemes deviate from any attempt at achieving economic efficiency. In fact, economic efficiency appears to be of little concern to those responsible for establishing water charges. Instead, the primary objective almost always consists of setting prices so that they will cover all costs of production and distribution.

There are, at least, two issues that must be addressed in the evaluation of local water pricing schemes. First, the extent to which fixed-rate charges are inferior to metered charges and second, the extent to which the existing metering schemes could be improved. Fixed charges that are unrelated to the quantity consumed create the same problems as those that exist in any instance where the consumer can control the quantity used up and where he or she is not required to pay a price for each unit consumed. This lack of a proper pricing policy dictates that there is no correct mechanism for rationing water nor is there any effective means of determining the desirable quantity and quality of the good to be provided.

In light of obvious deficiencies with fixed charges, it is surprising to note that 26 out of 57 Canadian municipalities surveyed in 1971 actually employed water charges that were unrelated to the quantity consumed.[18] As well, data collected

---

[18]Harry M. Kitchen, *A Statistical Estimation of a Demand Function for Residential Water,* Social Science Series no. 11 (Ottawa: Inland Waters Directorate, Water Planning and Management Branch, Environment Canada, 1975).

in this same survey indicated that average yearly consumption per dwelling unit was roughly twice as high in centres using flat rates as those communities using metered rates. Since many municipalities have expanded their water systems to meet excessively high demands, considerable over-investment has been created in most flat-rate centres. In fact, in more than one of the municipalities surveyed, local officials originally employing flat-rate charges for water consumption and operating with a system at full capacity were faced with the problem of either expanding the facility to meet the demand or attempting to reduce the demand. In each case, a decision was taken to introduce metered rates with the consequent result that demand fell drastically. What had been a fully utilized system became a system with excess capacity. Given the evidence, it is difficult to understand why the remaining flat-rate centres have not converted to metered charges.

In most Canadian municipalities with metered systems, the tendency is to use a declining block rate schedule with a fixed minimum charge. While this charge varies from muncipality to municipality, the following hypothetical example will serve to illustrate a typical rate structure. It is very likely to involve a fixed charge of something in the order of $6.00 per month plus a charge, let us say, of 30¢ per 1,000 gallons for the first 50,000 gallons of water consumed per month with subsequent charges of 26¢ for the next 50,000 gallons and 22¢ for a further 50,000 gallons, and so on.[19] Unfortunately, such a pricing policy may lead to undesirable consequences. Consumers without dishwashers, multiple cars to wash, and large lawns to sprinkle subsidize those individuals with dishwashers, large lawns, and many cars. As well, residential users subsidize commercial and industrial users.

Perhaps one justification for a pricing policy of this type would exist if it closely resembled the true marginal cost of supplying the good. Some evidence suggests, however, that the average and marginal costs are not falling continuously as quantities consumed increase.[20] Indeed, the outcome of pricing water below marginal cost has resulted in an over-investment in the capacity of most municipal systems, a result that also occurs under fixed rates.

Recognizing the distinct advantages inherent in a proper pricing policy for water consumption, at least two Canadian authors[21] have suggested that it is not metering that is important in controlling demand and hence reducing the degree of over-investment in water facilities, rather it is the price charged that matters. In principle this is certainly true; however, in practice metering also has had considerable effect on controlling the demand. For example, a number of local officials have suggested that consumers perceive metered rates as being higher than fixed charges when, in fact, this may not be true. In this instance it is the customer's perception of the charge that is important in controlling quantities demanded. Furthermore, the fact that water prices are so low and that water expenditures, in total, absorb such a small fraction of consumers' total expend-

---

[19]For evidence on rate structures in Ontario a few years ago, see Angelo P. Grima, *Residential Water Demand Alternative Choices for Management,* Research Publication no. 7 (Toronto: University of Toronto, Department of Geography, 1972), 30.

[20]Harry M. Kitchen, "A Statistical Estimation of an Operating Cost Function for Municipal Water Provision" (1977), 4 *Journal of Urban Analysis* 119-33.

[21]Supra footnote 19, at 189, and supra footnote 11, at 120.

itures suggest that many customers ignore this charge when making water-consumption decisions. Once again, the exercise of metering is likely to be more important than frequently has been recognized by most writers on this topic.

Current emphasis on a pricing structure that declines as quantities consumed increase can be justified on efficiency grounds only if the marginal cost of providing water continuously declines. Clearly, marginal costs do not continuously fall and furthermore, "the marginal price charged for water. . .is almost always less than its marginal cost."[22] If, as is true in many instances in metered centres, users do not consume enough to raise the amount they pay above the minimum bill, then the true marginal price is effectively zero, exactly the same as in centres with flat rate charges. This type of pricing policy readily leads to excessive demand and over-investment in the water plant. As will be obvious, over-investment in one sector uses resources that could more optimally be employed elsewhere.

In the case of water provision as with most other local services, the distance from the source of supply clearly affects the marginal cost of providing the good. Residents on the perimeter pay the same price per unit as those near the source, yet the marginal cost of providing the good to those further away is noticeably higher.[23] Optimal efficiency dictates that the pricing structure be altered to reflect the marginal cost of providing water. Failure to do this leads to users with lower marginal costs subsidizing those with higher marginal costs and to a subsequent capitalization of these subsidies into land values with the land value at the fringe or on the outskirts being priced higher than would otherwise be the case.[24]

The lack of an appropriate pricing policy has created excessive demands for water in certain months (summer) and at certain times of the day (late afternoon or evening). Unfortunately, local officials have been concerned more frequently with building facilities large enough to accommodate this consumption rather than adopting a pricing policy, issuing warnings, or establishing controls to reduce the demand.[25] Seasonal or peak-load pricing has proven to be effective in allocating resources in the private sector and there seems to be little reason why it could not be effective in the pricing of water.

The current pricing structures adopted in the provision of water for residential and commercial/industrial purposes substantially deviate from the principle of marginal cost pricing. While realizing that there may be difficulties in accurately recording incremental costs and then assigning prices to cover them, there is, nevertheless, a case to be made for closely approximating the marginal cost pricing principle. This could consist of the adoption of multi-part tariff systems discussed earlier. Briefly, this kind of system would involve fixed charges for on-site capital expenditures and any required connection charges plus further charges reflecting approximations of the variable costs of actually

---

[22]Supra footnote 11, at 120.

[23]Paul B. Downing, "User Charges and the Development of Urban Land" (December 1973), 26 *National Tax Journal* 631-37, at 632.

[24]Ibid., at 634-37.

[25]The issuance of warnings or imposition of controls has proven to be fairly effective in some municipalities. See supra footnote 18, at 5.

providing the water to each user. Since the marginal cost of supplying water varies directly with the distance from the source, users would be required to pay prices that reflect the operating and maintenance costs.[26]

Sewage.—As was suggested above, any charge (price) that does not attempt to cover the true marginal social cost is deemed to be inefficient because it encourages users, be they residential or commercial and industrial, to produce a greater than desirable output of sewage and waste and hence to cause an over-investment in sewage treatment facilities. The proper design of an optional pricing scheme for sewage, however, involves detailed knowledge of the incremental cost of collecting and treating it. Unfortunately, administrative or practical difficulties in correctly determining the strength of the sewage that must be treated and that, therefore, becomes an important determinant of marginal cost is impossible to obtain. Consequently, the best that can be hoped for is to achieve an approximation of marginal cost pricing. In this case, as in the case of water, a multi-part tariff probably best approaches the efficient pricing principle, "with, for example, a connection fee to cover per unit average costs for transmission and treatment capacity, a front footage charge to cover collection costs, and a monthly fee, preferably related to water usage, to cover out-of-pocket operating charges."[27] In fact, differential connection fees could handle the situation where there are higher costs of servicing areas far away from the sewage treatment plant.

In practice, however, the existing pricing schemes are far from ideal. In no instance has there been an attempt to separate the costs associated with treatment, collection, and transmission of sewage. Sewage charges are set to cover a portion, if not all, of total disposal costs and as such have not been designed to aid in the achievement of an optimal allocation of resources. Flat rate levies as a means of covering total costs do not lead to any economizing on the generation of waste nor do they lead to an efficient means of charging for this service. Charges prorated on the basis of the water bill, which are by far the most common in use, are likewise deficient in that they fail to reflect accurately the true cost of sewage disposal for each user; for example, the assumption underlying this approach is that water consumption is directly and positively correlated with sewage generation and, therefore, the required costs of disposal. Unfortunately, this positive correlation is frequently not significant because a large component of water consumption may be used for lawn sprinkling, car washing, and many other household uses, a number of which may be quite independent of sewage generated. Perhaps the overcharging for sewage treatment, collection, and disposal under this kind of scheme partially offsets the underpricing of water cited earlier.[28]

In essence, failure to construct a pricing policy reflecting differentials in costs attributed to collection of waste from the source, transmission of it to the treatment plant, and the actual treatment itself has led to an undesirable level of

---

[26]For a discussion of this approach, see J. E. Dickey, "A Guide for Analyzing Local Government Service Pricing Policies" (memorandum) (Blacksbury, Va.: Centre for Urban and Regional Studies, Virginia Polytechnic Institute and State University, 1975).

[27]Supra footnote 11, at 125.

[28]Ibid.

sewage generated and very likely to an over-investment in the plant capacity. In no Canadian municipality known to this author are charges assigned on the basis of collection and transmission costs and in only a few communities (larger ones) are they varied according to treatment costs. In this latter case, industrial users are charged a surcharge on the assumption that industrial waste is more dense and, therefore, more costly to treat than residential waste.

Obviously, better and more carefully worked-out pricing policies would assist in the achievement of better uses of local governments' scarce resources and more desirable means of financing this public service.

Public Transit.—While there are considerable variations in the proportion of local transit budgets covered by user fees, considerable subsidization from other revenue sources still exists. As to whether or not local authorities are recovering the correct proportion of their local budgets in this way is a question that is beyond the scope of this book. Clearly, the answer depends on the extent to which local municipalities wish to encourage public as compared to private transport. This, in turn, is related to such issues as local development, use of downtown areas for parking lots, and urban sprawl.

In the absence of practical alternatives, the earlier discussion of water and sewage suggested that local governments move toward an approximation of the marginal cost pricing approach. In the case of local public transit, however, a different position may be taken. To advocate that public transit users pay a price equal to the full marginal social cost would be acceptable only if private transit (automobiles) users were levied a charge that reflected their full marginal social cost. Since the latter is clearly not followed, the former ought not to be attempted. Indeed, a rational and strong case can be made for subsidizing local public transit and the question then becomes one of establishing the correct subsidy.[29]

Basic fare structures in Canadian municipalities tend to be similar, although the absolute levels charged vary. Fixed fares are set for adults, with lower rates established for senior citizens, students, and children and discounts are available for quantity purchases. This current fare structure creates some economic problems both in terms of what it does and what it does not do. The failure to charge higher prices in peak hours in order to reduce the demand at this time and to encourage usage during off-peak hours has often been noted. This emphasis on the same fare structure regardless of the time used has led to over-investment and greater capacity than can be justified efficiently. On the other hand, higher peak-load fares can lead to a greater use of private autos, a result that for other socio-economic reasons may be undesirable. To prevent excessive auto use, a more effective and direct policy might involve higher charges in the form of licences, parking fees, or simple regulations preventing their use.

The problems generated by the lack of peak-load charges are further complicated by the availability of quantity discounts. These discounts are used primarily by rush-hour travellers, effectively lowering their per trip charge, and precisely at a time when higher fares make more economic sense.

---

[29]For a discussion of the correct subsidy, see ibid., at 64-68.

Since the marginal cost of carrying a rider tends to vary with distance travelled, the failure to use zone charges, as is frequently the case in many municipalities, in order to cover the added cost makes little economic sense.

Finally, the lower rates for senior citizens and students are difficult to justify especially at times when transit systems are over-used (peak hours). Subsidies supplied on the basis of age or status and completely unrelated to income are difficult to support on analytical grounds of any sort.

Public Recreation.—Increasing amounts of leisure time combined with a growing emphasis on recreational activities have led to substantial demands for local public and private recreational facilities. In fact, many private facilities serve as substitutes, and in some cases, perfect substitutes, for public facilities. Given the availability of private facilities, the emphasis on public facilities has arisen, at least partially, in an attempt to provide recreational services to people who cannot afford to pay the charge for private services. Unfortunately, this subsidization is neither efficient nor fair. First, a case can and has been made for suggesting that local governments ought not to be concerned with income distribution questions. Second, if income distribution were a local responsibility, it should be provided through relief based on income or some other measure of ability to pay and not by reducing prices for everyone regardless of their ability to pay. Probably the soundest basis for subsidization arises where significant positive externalities exist. These externalities may take the form of a more physically fit and healthier society and hence lower medical costs for everyone. In reality, this is a questionable supposition for the externalities are unlikely to be significant. Indeed, they would probably be greater under an alternative and equally subsidized scheme of improved health and educational programs.

Clearly, the largest portion of the benefits accrue directly to the users and as such, it seems appropriate to price the services so as to extract sufficient revenues to cover the costs. Unfortunately, the public sector has not adopted many aspects of private pricing for similar services. Private suppliers, faced with the prospect of recovering all costs through their pricing structures, have recognized the advantages of such things as an annual fixed levy plus an admission charge for each time the facility is used. Municipalities virtually never follow this approach and, as such, neither cover costs nor efficiently utilize their scarce resources.

With the exception of a few local public services such as arena rentals and golf courses, access to municipally provided facilities is generally rationed by queuing rather than prices. Failure to adopt a peak-load pricing policy so as to even out the demand over a day and a week has led to over-investment in many local facilities. This has been aggravated further by reduced charges for children and students (lower rates for skating, swimming, etc.) at all times. Lower fares for specific groups might be justified if a further restriction (as is frequently the case for private facilities but not public facilities), limiting them to use of the facility in off-peak hours were imposed. Such a policy approximates the use of a peak-load pricing structure.

To advocate greater dependence on user charges for the financing of recreational facilities without proper promotional and carefully articulated arguments undoubtedly will generate significant outcries and general hostility, especially from local citizens who have become accustomed to a number of services previously provided at little cost to the individual user. On the other hand, continued use of the extant user charge structure will create further demands on local budgets, demands that are difficult to justify given the private characteristics of the specific services under consideration. Current charges generate insufficient revenue, encourage over-investment in local public facilities, and are inequitable in their overall impact on the distribution of income. Greater dependence on user charges is essential if each of these deficiencies is to be overcome or partially overcome.

Library Charges.—The current structure of user fees employed by most local public libraries is in need of reorganization. Local public libraries collect money from rentals, overdue books, and occasionally nonresident fees (fixed charge), but never from local residents on a usage basis. Consequently, an extremely high percentage of funding for local public libraries comes out of general revenue (Table 10.3). Support for this high degree of subsidization may be warranted if it can be proven that significant and positive externalities arise from the existence of public libraries. Clearly, some positive externalities do exist, both in terms of easy accessibility to a vast collection of library resources and because a better and more educated society creates a better environment in which to live. However, substantial private benefits also accrue directly to the users of these services. In fact, it is likely to be the case that private benefits noticeably outweigh the external benefits. As such, it is difficult to justify the degree of general funding currently provided. A better policy and one that would lead to a more ideal level of library services and hence a better mix of scarce local resources involves a usage charge that would approximate the marginal private cost of each visit plus a subsidy from the local government to cover the rest.

The availability of alternatives (such as books for purchase by individuals or groups or borrowing from private clubs or organizations for which there is a charge), suggests that private benefits do exist. Failure to price local public library services on a per usage basis leads to a number of consequences, some of which would be unwanted if the local citizenry were aware of their existence. For example, failure to charge for local library usage means that both users and non-users share in the cost of the library system. Since a higher proportion of the users tend to come from high income rather than low-income families, it is questionable whether this form of effective income redistribution would be tolerated under a direct and open scheme specifically designed to alter the distribution of income. Once again, local governments ought to pay more attention to designing a pricing scheme to ration and control the local demand for scarce resources.

Police Services.—Police services, which consist of numerous functions, are financed almost entirely from general local revenues. The only services for which special charges are levied are those that involve the policing of special events. In fact, in the occasional municipality, higher rates are charged at certain times of the year, such as Christmas and New Year's. Obviously, the emphasis here is on general revenue funding and this creates some allocational problems, problems that could be eliminated under a more sophisticated or extensive user pricing system. As long as police services generate positive externalities (and indeed many of their diverse services do generate such externalities), a case can be made for general funding. To the extent that some police services have private-good characteristics, efficiency (and perhaps equity) in the allocation of resources suggests, however, greater emphasis ought to be placed on charges imposed on the direct users. Evidence of the "privateness" exists because protection services are or can be purchased from private protection agencies. As well, individuals can and do purchase burglar alarms, guard dogs, and firearms. The fact that these activities are priced in the private sector suggests that similar protection services provided by police could be priced through the public sector. Indeed, such pricing might very well generate a better or more ideal level of police services than currently exists.

Where private-good characteristics for police services actually prevail, the difficulty of precisely or even closely approximating the price equals marginal social cost principle for each individual suggests that individuals separately should not be forced to pay a charge, but that all individuals who benefit from the same service ought to pay a price that is identical for all members of that group. For example, special municipal vehicle or operator licence fees or a transfer from provincial to local governments of provincially collected revenue from road user taxes (gasoline) would assist in covering part of the police costs associated with traffic control and safety.

In addition, fines or charges may be instituted for people who fail to lock their autos or premises, be they residential, commercial or industrial dwellings. Failure to protect private property adequately only creates an incentive for criminal behaviour with the inherently higher cost of police protection. At least one author has gone so far as to suggest that special fees or charges ought to be imposed on all enterprises with a high incidence of crime, while reduced rates should rest on those dwellings where the incidence of criminal behaviour is substantially lower.[30]

As long as the administrative costs of imposing an expanded system of user charges for police services is not prohibitive, a strong case can be made for greater use of such charges in funding these services.

Daycare[31].—On efficiency grounds, it is difficult to justify the current pricing of publicly provided daycare services. Clearly, these services are supplied at less than their marginal social cost and, consequently, are heavily subsidized to all users regardless of their ability to pay. Local public support for this subsidization would be enhanced if it could be proven that positive externalities exist; however, such externalities are unlikely to be observed. Basically, daycare services are characterized by traits associated with private goods (that is, the benefits from the services accrue entirely, or almost entirely, to the direct users).

Local politicians have often argued that subsidized daycare services reduce welfare costs. Subsidized daycare, they claim, is necessary in order to avoid higher welfare costs by allowing women to obtain employment. This emphasis on redistributing income through the local sector is neither efficient nor adequately handled. Clearly, a more senior level of government ought to assume

[30]For the rationale behind this suggestion, along with a description of how it might be adopted, see ibid., at 129-33.

[31]For a thorough discussion of daycare policies and their implications in Ontario, see Michael Krashinsky, *Day Care and Public Policy in Ontario,* Ontario Economic Council Research Studies (Toronto: University of Toronto Press, 1977).

greater responsibility for the provision of any service that is justified primarily on the basis of redistributing income.

PRIVILEGES, LICENCES, PERMITS, AND CONCESSIONS

Privileges, licences, and permits generate very small sums of revenue (less than 2 per cent of total own-source revenue in each province), yet they are used primarily as a means of controlling certain activities. Licences and permits accord authorization or grant a right or privilege to undertake a particular activity, the right for which would otherwise be withheld. These include licences to carry out a profession or trade (examples include accountants, lawyers, auditors, contractors, carpenters, and plumbers), business licences (generally required in most municipalities for manufacturers, wholesalers, retailers, and service-providing establishments), amusement licences and permits, taxi and delivery-vehicle licences, animal licences, building demolition permits, bicycle licences, and permits for billboards.

Concession and franchise revenue accounts for slightly more revenue in municipalities in all provinces except for New Brunswick (where they appear to be non-existent), with local governments in Saskatchewan and Alberta recording the greatest use of this revenue source. Concessions and franchises grant privileges or rights to undertake specific municipal functions, activities, or responsibilities including public transit systems operated by private concerns; fees from parking-lot concessions granted to the private sector; fees from private individuals or corporations who have been granted the concession to collect and dispose of garbage; fees collected from privately owned producers and distributors of gas and electricity; and street vendors, circuses, and private fairs.

Evaluation

The imposition of licences, permits, concessions, and franchises[32] is supported primarily on the basis of their potential to control or restrict a number of activities that are deemed not to contribute to the public's best interest if left on their own. Whether or not the current rates are effective in controlling these activities will depend upon one's view of the acceptable level of these controlled activities.

Ideally, an optimal pricing or charging policy (where the price or charge per unit of service equals the real cost to society of producing the last unit) could assist in the achievement of a better allocation of society's resources. In practice, however, most licences, permits, and concessions vary. Fee structures were set so long ago that they bear no current relationship to the real cost of resources used up in providing the service. As well, these prices are not really prices because they are lump sum charges "which are independent of usage and hence do not affect cost, as they would have to do for efficiency purposes. In many instances, then, such charges afford an example of inept pricing."[33] Unfortunately, the actual implementation of licences, permits, and fees falls short of

---

[32]For a discussion of fees and licences, see supra footnote 11, at 140-48.

[33]Ibid., at 142.

the optimal pricing policy that could be implemented if careful consideration and analysis were devoted to both the allocative and regulatory powers along with the revenue yields of these local revenue sources.

OTHER

Municipal revenue from the return on investments is more prevalent and noticeable in Quebec, Ontario, and the western provinces. This covers all revenues resulting from investments including interest earned on securities, loans and advances; profits on the sale of investments; profits arising from foreign exchange transactions or related to the sale or redemption of debentures; royalty revenues from natural resources (Alberta); and other investment income such as dividends and interest on bank deposits.

Other local revenue tends to be relatively, although not significantly, more important in Quebec and Atlantic Canada than elsewhere. This includes a wide range of sources extending from fines to penalties and interest on delinquent or late tax payments. Finally, contributions from individuals or other governments, commissions, and other sundry revenues are included under miscellaneous.

SUMMARY

In total, local per capita nonproperty tax revenues accounted for somewhere between 21 per cent and 46 per cent of all revenues raised from own-revenue sources in 1978. Of this revenue source, the bulk of the funds came from revenues generated by sales of goods and services (water, rentals, etc.).

The utilization of so many disparate local taxes and charges is difficult to support on analytical or economic grounds yet may be highly plausible on political grounds. Unfortunately, the bulk of these taxes or charges have been imposed on an "ad hoc" basis without any clear analysis of their ultimate effects. Retention of some of these taxes can be justified if the levy or tax-price charged per unit of service approximates the value of the marginal benefit accruing to the property. Obviously, a precise measurement of the benefits received may not be forthcoming yet this should not negate the "benefits received" principle as a basis for raising revenues for a number of services. In fact, wherever possible, the introduction of a properly designed user charge should be encouraged. This has the ultimate advantage of generating a better allocation of local resources. This charge would perform the role of a rationing device in the sense that users would consist of only those people who actually pay for the goods plus it would act as a signalling mechanism by indicating whether local services ought to be expanded, contracted, or otherwise remain the same. In addition, if properly presented to the local citizenry, user charges could provide a useful and more politically acceptable source of revenue for local expenditures.

Obviously, the implementation of an expanded system of user charges may create severe hardships for low-income individuals who will find that the charges imposed may absorb a relatively high percentage of their disposable incomes. Clearly, if this exists, it is a serious problem; however, it ought not to be the major responsibility of local governments to engage in income redistribution programs for these could be handled, more efficiently and fairly, by more senior levels of government. Nevertheless, income distribution is and will continue to be an issue with the local politicians and electorate. The efficiency benefits of user fees may appear faint to many if they imply severely "adverse" distributional effects. Consequently, there may be a need, wherever possible, to integrate widely accepted distributional norms with proposals for user fees to make the total package palatable. This might take the form of special concessions to selected groups, while expecting others to pay their way. In these instances, both the allocation and distribution objectives may be approached simultaneously.

Finally, the current use of user charges is inadequate. Clearly, the charges that currently exist could be expanded or altered to achieve greater efficiency in the provision of local goods and services. As well, these charges could be extended to cover a number of other services including residential refuse collection where, surprisingly, municipalities tend to finance this service through the local tax system rather than through a price for the service. Fire protection[34] is a further local service that could make greater use of user charges. In fact, some municipalities have said that they are investigating the possibility of levying charges that would vary with the fire risk associated with the property in question.

---

[34]A case can be made for greater dependence on user fees for fire protection. See supra footnote 11, at 135-39.

Part IV

Issues in Municipal Finance

11
Local Government Employment and Compensation Issues

INTRODUCTION

It is unfortunate that public employment issues are comparatively new subjects for those whose primary interests are in the area of local budget management. One of the most significant developments in the area of municipal government since the early 1960s has been the explosive growth of public-sector employment[1] and unionism, and their concomitant impact on local budgets. As one labour analyst wrote:

> Given the obvious policy importance of public sector wage determination, it is surprising that so little analytical work, either theoretical or empirical, has been devoted [sic] this subject. . . .industrial relations analysts have examined the collective bargaining process and its outcomes, but labour market economists apparently have been less willing to examine the public sector as a labour *market*.[2]

It is clear then that public employment, which accounts for the largest single operating expenditure in most general-purpose governments, no longer can be ignored by public finance specialists. Policymakers cannot be expected (or be allowed) to make decisions, which carry critical fiscal implications, concerning the public work force without having a sound theoretical or empirical basis for their actions.

Recent attention focussed on the magnitude of wage settlements and compensation in the public sector often has been based on limited and sometimes contradictory evidence. The consequence has been a plethora of often impressionistic popular commentary. Not surprisingly, the emergent conclusions have been competing, and worse, mythological.[3] Key issues that seem to have generated considerable controversy are those related to the number of municipal employees in Canada, and those related to the growth of Canadian municipal wage and compensation levels, as a consequence of rapid public-sector unionization. Because each of these items is tied intimately to the local budget, it is essential that accurate magnitudes and impacts be known. Though it would seem there could be no simpler task than to enumerate government employees in Canada, and to determine their level of compensation, a consensus on methodology and, therefore results, does not exist. In this chapter, a number of issues will be discussed and illustrated including the difficulties in determining the number of local workers employed by municipal governments

---

[1]Morley Gunderson, "Data on Public Sector Wages in Canada," in David K. Foot, ed., *Public Employment and Compensation in Canada: Myths and Realities,* published for the Institute for Research on Public Policy (Toronto: Butterworth, 1978), 107-25, at 108.

[2]Morley Gunderson, "Public Sector Wage Determination: A Review of the Literature," ibid., 167-88, at 168.

[3]Foot, in supra footnote 1, at 1-8, identified 12 such popular propositions that are by no means exhaustive but rather illustrative of the breadth of conclusions possible from existing data, and analyzed the legitimacy of each.

in Canada. Once employment levels are known, such issues as local government unionization, collective bargaining, and pensions will be discussed. Later, emphasis will be placed on both the determination of current employment and compensation levels along with the impact that public sector employment and wages have on the management of local government budgets.

GROWTH IN LOCAL GOVERNMENT EMPLOYMENT

To be able to say that the number of Canadian government employees at the local level has increased substantially over the past 25 years depends on the source of data and whether one refers to relative or absolute increases. Table 11.1 illustrates the degree of variation possible when employment in any one of the government sectors is tabulated. Since each source bases its calculation on a very different interpretation of what constitutes a government employee in the various sectors, it is not surprising to discover one figure exceeding another in the same category by as much as 50 per cent. This situation is exacerbated at the municipal level, where some sources include teachers and hospital workers as local employees, where others attempt to include urban transit employees, and still others exclude workers in municipal enterprises.[4] Given this variability in definition, it is easy to understand how conflicting statements about the size and growth of local government have arisen on the basis of existing data. Nonetheless, it may be useful to cite one or two of the more notable sources in order to obtain approximate magnitudes of public employment in the various subsectors, so that the growth trends may be identified. Table 11.2 shows that employees in the local government sector numbered 273,735 in 1980, representing just over one-fifth of all public-sector workers. In 1980, the provinces were and still are the largest single government employer. At that time, just over 40 per cent of the public work force was employed by the provinces, while municipalities employed about 23 per cent, and the federal government roughly 37 per cent.

In absolute terms, there was a fairly large growth in public-sector employment from 1947 to 1961. Notwithstanding this increase, the public sector's share of total employment has remained relatively stable, despite popular perceptions, and has declined slightly in recent years.[5] There is no doubt, however, that the public sector is a large employer, since it annually accounts for approximately one-quarter of total employment in Canada.

According to Statistics Canada records, total government employment increased by 50 per cent between 1961 and 1975, with an annual growth rate of 4.29 per cent. The provincial sector grew the fastest at 5.82 per cent, the federal sector the slowest at 2.02 per cent, and the local sector at 4.64 per cent. Within the local sector, however, employment growth has been faster for municipalities under 10,000 (5.32 per cent) and slower for those over 10,000 (3.96 per cent) for the same period.[6] More recent data contained in Table 11.3 indicates that over

---

[4]David K. Foot and Percy Thadaney, "The Growth of Public Employment in Canada: The Evidence From Taxation Statistics 1946-1975," in Foot, *supra* footnote 1, 45-62, at 48.

[5]Richard M. Bird, "The Growth of the Public Service in Canada," in Foot, *supra* footnote 1, 19-44, at 32.

[6]David K. Foot, Edward Scicluna, and Percy Thadaney, "The Growth and Distribution of Federal, Provincial and Local Government Employment in Canada," in Foot, *supra* footnote 1, 63-92, at 68, Table 4.2.

Table 11.1   Comparison of Public Employment Data, 1971

Source	Total	Federal	Provincial	Municipal
Census	609,840	299,025	161,465	147,025
Labour force statistics	601,000	—	—	—
Taxation statistics	1,077,207	321,050	394,431	361,726
Statistics Canada	716,970	266,805	245,023	205,142
Civil service reports	427,589	216,488	211,101	—
Federal estimates	—	245,731	—	—
Pay Research Bureau	—	212,632	—	—

Source: Richard M. Bird, "The Growth of the Public Service in Canada," David K. Foot, ed., *Public Employment and Compensation in Canada: Myths and Realities,* published for the Institute for Research on Public Policy (Toronto: Butterworth, 1978), 22, Table 2.1.

Table 11.2   Public Sector Employment, 1980

Level of government	Number	Per cent
Federal	441,696	36.8
Provincial	483,677	40.4
Municipal	273,735	22.8
Total	1,199,108	100.0

Source: Canadian Tax Foundation, *Provincial and Municipal Finances, 1981* (Toronto: the Foundation, 1981) and Canadian Tax Foundation, *The National Finances, 1981-82* (Toronto: the Foundation, 1982).

the period 1970 to 1980, growth in municipal employment has trailed only slightly that of the provincial level.

In relative terms, the local sector has not risen rapidly. It has, in fact, continued to employ approximately one-fifth of all government employees since 1961. This stability is in direct contrast to an increasing provincial employment trend (30.4 per cent to 40.3 per cent of the total over the 1961 to 1975 period) and a decreasing federal employment trend (49.6 per cent to 38.8 per cent of total over the same period).[7] Generally, local government employment is concentrated in the two largest provinces (over 70 per cent in Ontario and Quebec) and in the largest municipalities (over 50 per cent of each province's total is in municipalities with populations of over 50,000). If any trend exists, however, it is toward a growth in the number of local employees in smaller municipalities (under 10,000 residents).[8] But according to Table 11.4, even this trend is barely noticeable, since the proportion has risen from 23.2 per cent to only 25.6 per cent over the nine-year period.

Another measure of employment growth is the number of government employees per capita. Table 11.3 illustrates that over the period 1970 to 1980, municipal workers per 1,000 residents increased from 9.3 to 11.4, a somewhat smaller increase than that recorded for the provinces, but one that still represents an increase of more than 20 per cent. Table 11.5, however, reveals significant interprovincial variation with above-average levels of municipal

---

[7]Calculated from ibid., at 66, Table 4.1.

[8]Ibid., at 64.

Table 11.3 Provincial and Municipal Employment for
Selected Years, 1970 to 1980

	Provincial employment		Municipal employment	
Year	Number	Per 1,000 residents	Number	Per 1,000 residents
1970	345,175	17.7	201,425	9.3
1972	383,705	19.7	210,160	9.4
1974	418,448	20.8	236,531	10.5
1976	447,230	21.5	253,305	10.9
1978	469,816	22.4	266,237	11.3
1980	483,677	22.6	273,735	11.4
1970-80...........................	28.6%		26.4%	

Source: Canadian Tax Foundation, *Provincial and Municipal Finances, 1971* and *1973, 1975, 1977, 1979* and *1981* (Toronto: the Foundation, various years).

Table 11.4 Distribution of Local Government Employees by
Municipality Size for Selected Years

Municipality size	1967	1971	1975	Average annual growth rate[a]
		per cent		
Over 50,000	59.3	58.0	58.5	4.32
10,000-50,000	17.4	15.9	15.9	3.84
Under 10,000...........................	23.2	26.1	25.6	4.90
Total	100.0	100.0	100.0	4.37

[a]March 1967 to December 1976.

Source: Statistics Canada, *Local Government Employment,* Catalogue no. 72-009.

employees per 1,000 residents existing in Alberta and Ontario in each of the years observed. Quebec's level of local employees was higher than the national average in 1970 and lower in every other year. The municipal sectors in Atlantic Canada recorded the lowest level of local public employees per 1,000 residents over the decade of the 1970s.

Finally, a comparison of municipal and provincial government employment (Table 11.6) across the country reveals approximately equal growth overall for the period between 1960 and 1976, but considerable provincial variation is evident. In fact, in three of the eight provinces (Ontario, Manitoba, and Saskatchewan) for which comparisons are possible, the growth in municipal employment exceeds that of provincial, and in all cases it exceeds the population growth in each province.

WAGE ISSUES

As long as local government employment represents a growing component of the public-sector work force, attention must be paid to the wage expenditures required and their concomitant impact on municipal budgets. Prior to the last decade, the magnitude of such compensation was not regarded as a serious issue, since employment levels were reasonably stable and wage settlements not

Table 11.5   Local Government Employment[a] per 1,000 Residents by Province for Selected Years

Province	1970	1972	1974	1976	1978	1980
Newfoundland	3.0	3.4	3.6	4.4	4.3	4.0
Prince Edward Island	2.2	2.1	2.3	2.4	2.7	2.9
Nova Scotia	5.7	5.5	6.1	6.3	7.2	7.3
New Brunswick	4.4	4.4	5.0	5.0	5.0	5.5
Quebec	9.7	9.0	10.2	10.2	10.4	10.0
Ontario	10.8	11.8	12.6	13.1	13.8	14.0
Manitoba	8.2	8.3	9.1	9.5	9.6	9.6
Saskatchewan	7.7	7.3	8.1	9.2	10.6	10.6
Alberta	9.8	10.5	11.5	12.3	12.2	13.4
British Columbia	8.9	9.0	9.7	10.5	10.5	10.4
All provinces	9.3	9.4	10.5	10.9	11.3	11.4

[a]Includes employees classified as general service employees working in the following areas: police, fire, sanitation, public works, health, welfare, waterworks, administration, libraries, exhibitions, arenas, and golf courses. It excludes employees in municipal enterprises, transit, utilities, municipally-owned hospitals, and school boards.

Source: Supra Table 11.3.

Table 11.6   Municipal and Provincial Employment Annual Growth Rates by Province for Selected Years

Province	Municipal[a]	Provincial[b]	Population[c]
	per cent		
Newfoundland	1.7	4.8	1.3
Prince Edward Island	n.a.	0.6	0.7
Nova Scotia	3.7	5.1	0.7
New Brunswick	0.9	3.4	0.7
Quebec	1.2	3.1	1.1
Ontario	5.9	4.6	2.0
Manitoba	6.8	5.6	0.6
Saskatchewan	2.0	1.6	0.0
Alberta	4.5	5.7	1.9
British Columbia	4.9	n.a.	3.3
Total	4.4	4.3	1.6

[a]1967-1976. [b]1960-1976. [c]1961-1975. n.a.—not available.

Source: Provincial and municipal figures from Foot, Scicluna and Thadaney, supra footnote 6, at 81-87. Population growth rates from David K. Foot and Percy Thadaney, "The Growth of Public Employment in Canada: The Evidence from Taxation Statistics 1946-1975," in Foot, supra footnote 1, 45-62, at 62.

unusually large. In fact, traditional low pay in the public sector generally was thought to be the necessary burden that civil servants had to bear. Indeed, it was conventional wisdom that jobs in the public sector paid less than similar jobs in the private sector, but this was considered a fair exchange for job security, better fringe benefits, and less competitive pressure.[9] Throughout the early and

---

[9]A. M. Rufolo, "Local Government Wages and Services: How Much Should Citizens Pay?" (January-February 1977), *Business Review: Federal Reserve Bank of Philadelphia* 13.

mid-1970s not only was the municipal worker able to maintain his/her nonwage compensation standard, but he/she was able to secure an edge in wages. Initially, these public-sector wage gains were justified by many people as reflecting a catch-up process.[10]

While there are obvious data limitations in the measurement of total compensation, evidence from the available sources do indicate that wages of public-sector employees in Canada exceeded their private-sector counterparts by between 5 per cent and 15 per cent throughout the early and mid-1970s.[11] While some critics would like to attribute such a trend to the advent of widespread collective bargaining in the public sector, there are some fundamental institutional reasons why the determination of wages in this sector is different, and why the potential for an upward wage bias exists. First, however, it may be useful to identify the patterns and trends in municipal earnings and to compare these with earning patterns in other sectors of the economy.

PUBLIC-SECTOR AND PRIVATE-SECTOR WAGE DIFFERENTIALS

While no single Canadian data source exists for the sole purpose of providing a comprehensive comparison of local public-sector wages with similar wages for other levels of government or with the private sector, some information does exist from which data can be extracted and arranged in order to facilitate this comparison. For example, *Taxation Statistics* provide some indication of the emergence of wage differentials between the public and business sectors, but only on a composite scale. That is, earnings figures used to compute the following chart are not separable by labour type, therefore, the differential can be identified only for broad categories. Specifically, Table 11.7 shows the ratio of annual earnings per taxable return for each of the three levels of government to annual earnings per taxable return in the business sector.

The last column indicates that the ratio of all public to business earnings has increased steadily since the post-war period, with public earnings not exceeding business earnings until the mid-1960s (1966 to be precise). This was generally true for both the federal and provincial levels of government; however, the data reveal that municipal earnings have been at par with business earnings as far back as the late 1940s. While the municipal sector vis-à-vis the private sector has experienced a relative increase in its earnings, this increase is smaller than that recorded for both the federal and provincial sectors. In fact, this is further illustrated in the earnings figures themselves. These show the percentage increase in earnings between 1946 and 1975 for each sector as follows: federal —581 per cent, provincial—561 per cent, and municipal—522 per cent. Business earnings rose only 465 per cent for the same period.[12]

On such an aggregate scale it is difficult to identify precise causes for this differential. The gains in earnings are legitimate if they can be attributed to relative

---

[10]See for example: supra footnote 2, at 185; A.J.H. Dean, "Earnings in the Public and Private Sectors 1950-1975" (November 1975), 74 *National Institute Economic Review* 60-70, at 61; and supra footnote 9, at 14.

[11]Morley Gunderson, "Public-Private Wage and Non-Wage Differentials in Canada: Some Calculations From Published Tabulations," in Foot, supra footnote 1, 127-66, at 127.

[12]Ibid., at 130.

Table 11.7   Ratio of Public to Business Earnings, Taxation Statistics for Selected Years

Year	Federal	Provincial	Local	All government[a]	All public[b]
1946	.97	.98	1.01	.98	.95
1950	.96	.96	1.00	.97	.94
1955	.99	.97	1.01	.99	.94
1960	1.02	.97	1.04	1.01	.96
1965	1.08	1.04	1.04	1.05	.98
1970	1.25	1.15	1.12	1.17	1.10
1975	1.16	1.14	1.11	1.14	1.09

[a]Weighted average of federal, provincial, and municipal. [b]Weighted average of federal, provincial, municipal and teachers, professors, and employees in institutions.

Source: Supra footnote 11, at 129.

improvements in human capital endowments (education), productivity increases (efficiency), or relative reductions in nonwage benefits (pensions).[13] No one can deny that many such improvements have occurred in the public sector; for example, the increase in formal qualifications of teachers since 1946. It is difficult, however, to prove that such changes justify the entire earnings increases. Furthermore, the higher increase in federal and provincial employee earnings, relative to municipal earnings, is more consistent with the hypothesis that tax and political constraints are less restrictive at the senior levels of government.[14]

An attempt to list the array of possible ad hoc explanations to explain the differential in the increase in relative earnings in the public sector is both tedious and potentially dangerous. The safest conclusion that can be reached from these data appear to be that local earnings have increased relative to private sector earnings, but the causes of these increases are not entirely obvious.

Further attempts at identifying the public-sector and private-sector wage differential is evident in data that can be disaggregated. At the municipal level this can be accomplished, with limited success, by either comparing "like" workers in similar occupations or by "controlling" for the influence of wage determining variables through econometric estimations of wage equations.[15] Labour Canada uses the former approach through an occupational wage rate survey in which it records data on the wages of both municipal and private-sector labourers in a variety of communities across Canada. Table 11.8 records the ratio of these data sets (public to private) for selected years between 1950 and 1980. The last row suggests that municipal wages were, up until the 1960s when the situation reversed, marginally lower in most instances than comparable private-sector wages. From 1969 to 1973, municipal wages exceeded private-sector wages by an (unweighted) average of approximately 8 per cent. Relatively recent data, however, indicate that this upward trend may have reached its peak, since the 1975 to 1980 period shows a gradual reduction in the municipal/

[13]Ibid.

[14]Ibid.

[15]Morley Gunderson, "Wage Determination in the Public Sector: Canada and the U.S." (January 1979), 4 *Labour and Society* 49-70, at 56.

Table 11.8   Ratio of Municipal to Private Average Wages of Labourers in Various Communities for Selected Years, 1953 to 1980

Municipality	1953	1955	1957	1959	1961	1963	1965	1967	1969	1971	1973	1975[a]	1977[a]	1979[a]	1980[a]
Halifax	1.13	1.12	.98	.93	1.09	.95	.94	.96	1.06	1.05	1.04	1.05	1.01	1.05	1.04
St. John	1.18	1.14	1.17	1.12	1.03	1.03	1.10	1.11	1.05	.99	.99	1.02	.99	1.00	n.a.
Montreal	.88	.97	.94	n.a.	1.09	1.09	1.14	1.27	1.19	1.18	1.12	1.07	1.06	1.05	.85
Quebec	.86	.86	.86	.81	.92	.98	1.21	1.07	1.06	1.11	1.07	1.02	1.08	.92	1.06
Hamilton	n.a.	.93	.89	.94	.96	.94	.90	1.10	1.07	1.03	1.12	.95	.95	.95	.96
Kitchener	.93	1.00	1.01	1.12	1.01	1.01	1.00	1.05	1.07	1.05	1.16	1.03	.92	.98	1.01
London	.90	.99	.98	n.a.	1.09	1.05	1.08	1.12	1.14	1.11	1.14	1.06	1.00	.98	n.a.
Ottawa	1.03	1.16	1.02	1.16	1.11	1.11	1.01	1.04	1.15	1.14	1.21	1.05	1.01	1.01	.97
St. Catharines	.95	.87	.95	1.02	.96	.96	.94	.99	1.18	1.04	.99	1.08	.99	1.02	.94
Thunder Bay	.85	.94	.87	.98	.96	.95	.99	1.04	1.01	1.10	1.07	.95	.97	.90	.90
Toronto	1.08	1.11	1.03	n.a.	1.14	1.16	1.16	1.19	1.19	1.22	1.13	1.11	1.04	.98	1.04
Winnipeg	1.00	.96	1.05	n.a.	1.03	1.05	1.06	1.08	1.10	1.05	1.10	.98	.99	.85	1.05
Regina	1.05	.98	1.06	.94	.91	.96	.95	.97	1.07	1.02	1.08	.94	1.00	.96	n.a.
Calgary	.95	.97	.94	1.04	1.04	1.02	1.07	1.10	1.06	1.08	1.10	1.02	.95	1.05	n.a.
Edmonton	1.04	1.02	1.01	.99	1.13	1.12	1.11	1.09	1.11	1.11	1.04	1.07	1.04	1.06	.87
Vancouver	1.03	1.02	1.04	n.a.	1.04	1.03	1.02	1.04	1.01	1.03	1.00	1.02	1.00	.92	.99
Victoria	.89	.89	.87	.87	1.01	.97	.96	.96	.99	.99	1.04	1.00	1.01	1.02	1.01
Average	.98	1.00	.98	.99	1.03	1.02	1.04	1.07	1.08	1.08	1.08	1.02	1.00	.98	.98

[a]1975, 1977, 1979, and 1980 actually include wages for labourers in the federal, provincial, and municipal sectors, aggregated under the title "public administration." n.a.—not available.

Source: 1953-1973 data from supra footnote 11, at 138-39, Table 7.4. 1975-1980 data from Canada, *Wage Rates, Salaries and Hours of Labour* (Ottawa: Information Canada, appropriate years).

private-sector ratio. Interpretation of this latest trend, however, is cautioned since the 1975 to 1980 calculations, because of data limitations, are based on a composite of municipal, provincial, and federal wage rates, rather than simply on municipal figures as is the case in all previous years.[16] As well, it is not yet possible to determine whether this movement has been sustained in the early 1980s. Consequently, until more conclusive data are available, the emergence of this downward trend merits careful scrutiny and should not be considered as sufficient proof that a reversal in the wage differential is permanent.

Additional evidence on public and private wage settlements can be extracted from collective agreement data published by Labour Canada.[17] While data limitations, such as the use of a base rate (the lowest paid classification) and omission of fringe-benefit values are apparent, the focus on large bargaining units, which are most likely to gain real wage increases, makes the sample useful as a benchmark from which to compare public and private wage settlements.

Table 11.9 illustrates annual percentage base increases for the public and private sectors for the 15-year period between 1967 and 1981. Contrary to popular belief, the first two columns indicate that the overall increase in both public and private collective agreements has been approximately equal, with an average of 9.5 per cent in the private sector and 9.9 per cent in the public sector. Nonetheless, a simple trend analysis reveals that public-sector settlements slightly trailed those in the private sector prior to the early 1970s, but for the most part since then, have exceeded them. The exceptions are the years of 1977 and 1978; the final years of a three-year wage-control program begun in 1975, and partly triggered by the unusually high settlements in all sectors in the year previous to that. It is of particular interest to note that since removal of the controls, wage increases in both the private and public sectors have exceeded those in the controls-on period, and that those in the public sector have continued to exceed those in the private sector.

When the unweighted average annual percentage increases are compared, the local government sector ranks ahead of other sectors of the government and ahead of increases in private-sector settlements. The local sector has, however, experienced a sporadic series of base-wage increases, with much of the unevenness being attributed to short-run compensating effects. That is to say, unusually high settlements in 1967, and again in 1975, were immediately followed by much lower increases in the following years. This pattern tends to support the hypothesis that political forces exerted constraining influences of a long-term rather than short-term nature, with the result that neither unusually large nor small increases were sustained. Recent data reveal, however, that local sector settlements have been highly successful in their achievement of higher-than-average base increases: 10.0 per cent compared to 9.5 per cent in the private sector in 1980, and 13.0 per cent compared to 11.5 per cent in 1981 (Table 11.9). With the exception of the federal government, all other government sectors achieved higher base rate increases than those in the private sector. This has

---

[16]In addition, evidence for a reversal of the differential is based on a very limited sample in which only 7 of the 13 private-sector wages exceeded those of municipal labourers in 1980.

[17]For all industries except construction covering 500 or more employees, see Canada, *Wage Developments Annual Review* (Ottawa: Labour Canada, 1980).

Table 11.9   Annual Percentage Base Wage Increases in Canada,[a] 1967 to 1981

	Sector						
Year	Private	Public	Federal	Provincial	Local	Health, education, and welfare	Utilities[b]
1967	7.8	9.6	n.a.	8.5	12.5	9.4	7.7
1968	8.1	7.6	7.0	8.3	7.0	10.0	6.5
1969	8.6	7.2	6.3	8.5	11.4	6.9	7.2
1970	8.6	8.4	8.4	7.2	9.9	8.9	7.7
1971	8.0	7.6	6.6	7.9	9.4	8.4	6.7
1972	9.2	7.2	8.9	8.0	7.6	6.5	7.9
1973	10.1	10.6	12.3	10.1	9.9	10.2	10.4
1974	14.4	14.8	11.3	15.1	12.6	17.8	18.0
1975	14.4	18.6	14.3	20.0	17.8	21.3	17.2
1976	9.4	11.1	11.5	11.3	10.6	10.7	12.3
1977	7.4	7.8	9.5	7.8	7.7	6.7	7.1
1978	7.0	6.8	6.8	7.3	6.5	6.6	6.7
1979	8.5	8.1	7.6	8.7	8.4	7.9	7.8
1980	9.9	10.2	10.3	11.1	10.2	10.0	10.6
1981	11.5	12.7	11.5	13.2	13.0	13.3	13.3
Average	9.5	9.9	9.5[c]	10.2	10.3	10.2	9.8

[a]For collective agreements covering 500 or more employees. [b]Telephone, electrical, and water. [c]1968-1981 average only.

Source: Supra footnote 11, at 134 (for the years 1967-1976); and for the years 1977-1981, Canada, *Wage Developments Annual Review* (Ottawa: Labour Canada, 1981), 77.

caused some people to conclude that the public sector has resumed its role as the wage leader, a reputation that it first acquired in the mid-1970s.[18] Such a concern, when coupled with ongoing inflationary trends partially is responsible for many attempts by local governments to institute wage guidelines corresponding to federal legislation (6 per cent in 1982-83 and 5 per cent in 1983-84).

THE LOCAL PUBLIC-SECTOR LABOUR MARKET

Since the data tend to confirm the existence of a local public-sector/private-sector wage differential, it may be useful to mention briefly why this differential has emerged.[19] Among the most obvious explanations is the relatively inelastic demand for labour used in providing many local services that tend, as well, to be price inelastic (for example, hospitals, fire and police protection, and education). When such a service is distributed in a market influenced not by a profit constraint but by a political constraint, the traditional pressures that influence wages are frequently absent. Recent concern over escalating costs and subsequent criticism by the local electorate, however, have combined to place a partial check on the increase in local-sector wage settlements.

[18]Ronald Anderson, in "Report on Business," *The Globe and Mail,* May 7 and 11, 1982.

[19]For a more thorough discussion of this, see Jean-Michel Cousineau and Robert Lacroix, *Wage Determination in Major Collective Agreements in the Private and Public Sectors* (Ottawa: Economic Council of Canada, 1977), 43; supra footnote 15; and David Lewin, "Aspects of Wage Determination in Local Government Employment" (March/April 1974), 34 *Public Administration Review* 149-55.

The lack of a profit constraint when coupled with a relatively inelastic demand for most local public services suggest that the determination of wages in the local public sector may differ significantly from that in the private sector. For example, most local services are financed or partially financed by grants and local taxes, hence there is no unique relationship between the selling price of local services and the nominal wage paid to municipal employees. Consequently, wage rates are not determined simply by relating the demand for labour to anticipated prices for the final services produced by this labour. To the extent that local governments are in a competitive position to recruit labour, there are forces operating, however, that ensure that a wage floor, roughly equal to the floor in the private sector, exists. These same competitive forces, nonetheless, need not provide an effective ceiling on wages and may even create the need to offer wages above the floor in order to reduce turnover and improve morale.[20] Hence, a potential upward bias for wages exists since an effective floor, but not ceiling, exists in the absence of a profit constraint.

Since local governments usually have virtual monopoly power over the services they provide, there is no need to compete for sales. But even where private institutions—such as schools—do compete with government, the local citizen still is required to support the public school system through local taxes, so that government provision of such services rarely is put to a full-market test.

Because of the absence of private-sector equivalents in the provision of many local services, municipalities will often tie the salaries of professions such as police and firefighters to a fixed formula rather than to wages paid in similar occupations elsewhere.[21] Such a practice easily can result in overpayment of the more unique public-sector positions thereby contributing to the local public-sector/private-sector wage differential.[22]

The policy of wage increases in the public sector can be partially dangerous if the wage payments are granted but not justified on productivity grounds. In the private sector, at least part of higher wage costs can be recovered through productivity gains. Unfortunately, the nature of most local government services is such that improvements in labour productivity are frequently not evident. This is partially explained by an inability to measure productivity improvements for a number of local services including education, health and welfare, and police and fire protection and partially explained by the fact that productivity gains, if they could be measured, have simply not occurred in any significant fashion.[23] In short, the end result of higher wages without offsetting productivity improvements has led to higher local-sector wage bills and an ensuing strain on the fiscal position of local governments.

It is clear from the above that the absence of a profit constraint, the inelastic demand for many local services, and the determination of wages on the basis of wage levels elsewhere rather than on some basis of productivity improvements,

---

[20]Morley Gunderson, *Labour Market Economics: Theory, Evidence and Policy in Canada* (Toronto: McGraw-Hill Ryerson, 1980), 332.

[21]See, for example, H. A. Julis and P. Feuille, *Police Unionism* (Lexington, Mass.: Lexington Books, 1973), 121.

[22]Lewin, supra footnote 19.

[23]See the section on "Productivity" in Chapter 14.

all contribute to a difference in the determination of wages paid in the local public and private sectors.[24] Finally, one further factor that has had considerable impact on the wage differential and has been the focus of much recent discussion and controversy is the unionization of public employees.

THE UNIONIZATION OF PUBLIC-SECTOR EMPLOYEES

Public-sector unionism is an important and recent phenomenon, since as little as 20 years ago it was illegal for several government sectors to even form unions. Municipal employees, however, have enjoyed varying degrees of organization for many years. The teacher, nurse, hospital worker, and municipal labourer associations were transformed into certified unions when unionization came to the local public sector in the 1960s.[25] To the extent that collective bargaining had become an accepted practice of labour relations in the private sector, it seemed only a matter of time before government employees would argue for its adoption in the public sector.[26]

GROWTH OF UNIONISM IN LOCAL GOVERNMENTS

Historical resistance to the unionization of the civil servant was based largely on the principle of sovereignty of the state. Quite simply, collective bargaining and its corollary the strike were considered incompatible with the obligation of the public service to provide essential services.[27] Consequently, it was not until the late 1960s that most provinces passed legislation that granted qualified bargaining rights to public employees.[28] Since that time, however, the rise in public-sector unionism has been substantial: between the years 1967 and 1975, the number of public-sector employees protected by major collective agreements

---

[24]William J. Baumol, "Macroeconomics of Unbalanced Growth: The Anatomy of Urban Crisis" (June 1967), 57 *American Economic Review* 415-26.

[25]J. K. Keaton, *Growth of Unionism in the Sixties* (Ottawa: Labour Canada, 1976).

[26]It is not the purpose of this section to review in any detail the copious research into the reasons for the unionization of the public sector. The interested reader is instead directed to Jean Boivin, "Collective Bargaining in the Public Sector: Some Propositions on the Cause of Public Employee Unrest," in Morley Gunderson, ed., *Collective Bargaining in the Essential and Public Service Sectors* (Toronto: University of Toronto Press, 1975), 3-17.

[27]Shirley B. Goldenberg, *Public Service Bargaining: Implications for White Collar Unionism* (Kingston, Ontario: Industrial Relations Centre, Queen's University, 1973), 2. See also Shirley B. Goldenberg, "Collective Bargaining in the Provincial Public Services," in Institute of Public Administration of Canada, *Collective Bargaining in the Public Service* (Toronto: the Institute, 1973), 11-43. It should be noted that, although the terms "unionization" and "collective bargaining" will be used interchangeably here, they are not one and the same. Unionization usually refers to the portion of the work force that belongs to a union, while collective bargaining is the formal structure of negotiations between management and labour.

[28]Goldenberg, *Public Service Bargaining,* supra, at 3. Traditional resistance of public employers in the United States also weakened around this time; see Robert J. Thornton, "Collective Bargaining and Local Finance," in J. Richard Aronson and Eli Schwartz, eds., *Management Policies in Local Government Finance,* Municipal Management Series, published for the Institute for Training in Municipal Administration (Washington, D.C.: International City Management Association, 1981), 346-66, at 347. For a summary of the U.S. trend in public employee unionism, see N. R. Pierce, "Employment Report: Public Employees Unions Show Rise in Membership, Militancy" (August 1975), 1 *National Journal* 1239-49.

**Table 11.10   Percentage Increase in the Number of Employees
Covered by Collective Agreements, 1968 to 1975**

Sector	1968	1969	1970	1971	1972	1973	1974	1975
Total public	128.7	35.0	18.3	12.7	14.9	11.0	8.7	15.0
Local government	6.9	3.5	11.5	15.3	10.7	3.7	8.3	3.5
Education	58.0	94.9	290.8	29.5	27.8	25.1	10.0	7.1
Health	23.8	55.7	9.9	14.7	26.3	5.3	3.1	8.9
Private sector	11.7	5.7	5.3	14.1	12.0	8.0	8.2	6.3

Source: Infra footnote 32, at 8, Table 2-1.

**Table 11.11   Percentage Distribution of Collective Agreements
and of Number of Employees Covered, 1968 to 1975**

Sector	1968	1969	1970	1971	1972	1973	1974	1975
Number of agreements								
Public	15.3	20.3	23.6	26.7	29.0	29.5	29.6	31.1
Private	84.7	79.7	76.4	73.3	71.0	70.5	70.4	68.9
Number of employees								
Public	18.3	30.3	36.4	38.3	40.4	43.4	44.8	45.7
Private	81.7	69.7	63.6	61.7	59.6	56.6	55.2	54.3

Source: Cousineau and Lacroix, supra footnote 19, at 6.

increased sevenfold (a rather impressive showing beside the comparable figure
of only 1.2 for the private sector).[29] Table 11.10 provides a breakdown of the
percentage increases in membership levels for the local, education, and health
sectors and Table 11.11 illustrates the compositional changes collective
agreements have undergone since 1968. There is little doubt that both measures
reveal significant gains in union representation for the public sector (in 1968
only one in five employees covered by collective agreements were from the
public sector, whereas by 1975 this had risen to one in two). Similarly, public-
sector agreements represented only 15 per cent of total agreements in Canada in
1968, but more than doubled this percentage by 1975. This rapid growth in
union membership and the number of public-sector agreements paralleled the
unprecedented growth of the public-sector labour force.[30] It has been argued,
in fact, that the dramatic rise in government employment, coupled with low
employer resistance, provided active union organizers with perfect conditions
under which to bolster union membership levels in the public sector.[31] The field
of education for example, experienced almost a 300 per cent increase in the

---

[29]Cousineau and Lacroix, supra footnote 19, at 7, Table 1-3. "Major collective agreements"
refers to those that govern bargaining units of 500 members or more. "Public sector" in this context refers to the pure public sector (federal, provincial, and local levels of government) and what
the authors refer to as the "quasi-public sector" (education and health).

[30]Ibid., at 7.

[31]Bernard Jump, Jr., "Public Employment, Collective Bargaining, and Employee Wages and
Pensions," in John E. Petersen and Catherine Lavigne Spain, eds., *Essays in Public Finance and
Financial Management: State and Local Perspectives* (Chatham, N.J.: Chatham House, 1980),
74-85, at 77.

number of employees covered by collective agreements in the early 1970s.[32] It is little wonder that there were widespread fears at this time that the public sector was somehow out of control. Union membership growth at the local level, by comparison, was not quite as substantial, but at least parallelled (and in some years even surpassed) the rate of increase for the private sector.

Today, the public sector forms a relatively homogeneous critical mass, much more centralized in terms of bargaining units than the private sector.[33] In fact, the merger of the Trade and Labour Congress (TLC) and the rival Canadian Congress of Labour (CCL) created a very large and powerful Canadian Union of Public Employees (CUPE) that, by the 1970s, had gained sufficient strength and numbers to make it the largest union in Canada, a position it maintains today.[34] In addition, the degree of unionization (that is, the percentage of workers unionized in a particular sector) is higher for public administration than for any other sector in Canada (in 1979, 67.8 per cent of the public work force was organized, Table 11.12). The only other sector that comes close to this degree of representation is transportation, communication, and utilities, with approximately half of its employees unionized by 1979.

To find comparable figures for the municipal sector is not an easy task, since several occupations, mainly police and firefighters, are unionized under independent locals. Admitting obvious data inadequacies, estimates show that in 1978 almost 42 per cent of all municipal employees across Canada were unionized, varying from a high of 72 per cent in New Brunswick to a low of 31 per cent in Ontario (Table 11.13). The main reason for what appears to be a large interprovincial variation in the percentage of unionized employees may be attributed directly to the use of Labour Canada classification codes that do not provide for the identification of all relevant municipal unions.[35] In fact, it has been estimated recently that virtually all eligible municipal employees are covered by collective agreements. Most of these are organized under CUPE locals (column 3, Table 11.13).[36] The exceptions are primarily police and firefighters who, in most provinces, are prohibited from joining unions not consisting exclusively of their own professional members.[37] As Table 11.13 displays, virtually all municipal firefighters across the country belong to an International Association

---

[32]D.A.L. Auld, *Wage Behaviour and Wage Control in the Public Service,* Study no. 137, for the Centre for the Study of Inflation and Productivity (Ottawa: Economic Council of Canada, 1979), 6. It must be noted that these figures tend to be erratic because there is no normalization for the length of contract and hence the renewal dates for several contracts may coincide in one calendar year.

[33]Cousineau and Lacroix, supra footnote 19, at 8. Canadian public employees, furthermore (in contrast with private employees), are almost always represented en masse by an indigenous rather than international union. The Canadian Union of Public Employees, for example, almost has a monopoly on civilian municipal workers. See Peter Feuille and John C. Anderson, "Public Sector Bargaining: Policy and Practice" (Fall 1980), 19 *Industrial Relations* 309-24, at 311.

[34]D. Morton, "The History of Canadian Labour," in John Anderson and Morley Gunderson, eds., *Union-Management Relations in Canada* (Toronto: Addison-Wesley, 1982), 110.

[35]A point identified in conversations with officials from Labour Canada.

[36]J. Fryer, "Public vs Private Wage Comparison" (January-February 1979), *Business Review: Federal Reserve Bank of Philadelphia* 17.

[37]Quebec and Alberta have, in fact, passed specific acts to this effect—see T. J. Plunkett, "Municipal Collective Bargaining," in Institute, supra footnote 27, 1-10, at 3.

Table 11.12 Degree of Unionization Within the Public and Private Sectors, 1979

Sector	Percentage of unionized workers
Public administration[a]	67.8
Transportation, communication, and utilities	48.3
Construction	43.9
Manufacturing	40.9
Fisheries	39.0
Forestry	34.1
Mining	32.8
Service	22.5
Trade	7.8
Agriculture	0.4
Average	33.8

[a]Includes federal, provincial, and municipal governments.

Source: Canada, *Corporations and Labour Unions Returns Act Report for 1979,* Part 2—Labour Unions (Ottawa: Labour Canada), 60.

of Firefighters, and New Brunswick is the only province where police are not organized independently of CUPE.

In addition to police and firefighters, two other principle bargaining units have evolved in municipal governments: inside and outside workers.[38] It is easy to discern from Table 11.13, however, that a great deal of variability exists across the country in terms of the number of additional bargaining units that may be formed. In any case, all are subject to labour legislation characterized by diversity. Table 11.14 illustrates the degree of intrajurisdictional and interjurisdictional statutory differentiation. At one extreme is Ontario, where virtually every major public-sector group is subject to a different piece of legislation: general municipal employees are governed by the general private-sector statutes under the Labour Relations Act, police by the Police Act, and firefighters by the Fire Department Act. Conversely, Quebec has but one statute (the Quebec Labour Code) that governs all public employees with only a minimal number of special provisions. The remaining jurisdictions fall somewhere between the Quebec and Ontario extremes, but the multiplicity of statutes illustrates the variety of approaches taken for various public-sector groups.[39] Municipal employees, police, and hospital workers in Manitoba can strike, but teachers and firefighters must submit to arbitration. Police and firemen in Quebec are subject to arbitration, but all other public employees legally may withdraw their services. In Alberta, Ontario, Quebec, and Newfoundland, police are prohibited from association with general labour organizations, but such restrictions for police do not exist anywhere else.

---

[38]According to Plunkett, ibid., at 4, inside workers include all staff engaged in clerical, accounting, or stenographic duties, as well as technical duties related, for example, to engineering, building inspection, and property valuation, while outside workers generally include all employees engaged in maintenance and operational activities relating to municipal services and facilities.

[39]The following text material is a description of legislation taken from A. Ponak, "Public Sector Collective Bargaining," in Anderson and Gunderson, supra footnote 34, at 361.

Table 11.13   Union Membership in Local Government Administration, 1978[a]

Province	Locals	Membership	All province total	Employees unionized
		no.	*per cent*	
Newfoundland				
Firefighters	3	275		
Nfld. Associates of Public Employees	3	71		
CUPE[b]	10	767		
Total[c].....................	16	1,113	1.0	44.9
Prince Edward Island				
CUPE.........................	3	121		
Total........................	3	121	0.1	36.7
Nova Scotia				
International Brotherhood of Electrical Workers	1	30		
International Union of Operating Engineers	1	35		
Firefighters	6	431		
CUPE..........................	27	1,558		
Total........................	35	2,054	1.8	33.6
New Brunswick				
Firefighters	4	413		
CUPE[d]	30	2,114		
Total........................	34	2,527	2.3	72.3
Quebec				
Service Employees International	1	3,784		
Firefighters	36	1,900		
Machinists	1	85		
Office employees..................	2	102		
Steel workers	4	214		
Professional salaried	2	122		
Public service employees	101	3,820		
CUPE..........................	67	11,197		
Municipal and school employees	71	4,933		
Directly chartered	4	248		
Independent local[e]	1	2,400		
Total........................	290	28,805	25.8	43.9
Ontario				
Service Employees International	1	138		
United electrical	1	98		
IBEW	3	96		
Firefighters	75	7,360		
Labourers	1	80		
Office employees..................	1	71		
Service employees	1	62		
CUPE..........................	147	28,944		
Total........................	230	36,849	33.0	31.4

(Table concluded on next page.)

Table 11.13   Concluded

Province	Locals	Membership	All province total	Employees unionized
	no.		*per cent*	
Manitoba				
Firefighters	4	930		
Steel workers	2	107		
CUPE...........................	9	5,660		
Independent local	1	48		
Total.......................	16	6,745	6.0	67.9
Saskatchewan				
Service Employees International	1	13		
Firefighters	7	549		
CUPE...........................	24	2,635		
Independent	4	600		
Total.......................	36	3,797	3.4	37.5
Alberta				
Firefighters	8	1,701		
Alberta Civil Service[f]	1	46		
CUPE...........................	26	9,296		
Total.......................	35	11,043	9.9	45.6
British Columbia				
Firefighters	35	2,097		
Steel workers	1	45		
B.C. Peace Officers	12	1,470		
CUPE...........................	50	9,507		
Independent	6	5,475		
Total.......................	104	18,594	16.6	69.5
All provinces	799	111,648	100.0	41.9

[a]As listed under the Standard Industrial Classification (SIC), Local Administration 951 does not include police departments which are classified under SIC-850, Independent Union Locals. (See Note d.) [b]Canadian Union of Public Employees—this is by far the largest union for government employees, accounting for just over 60 per cent of all unionized public employees. [c]Each provincial total is only for selected major municipal unions and may omit some smaller independent locals. [d]This is the only province in which police are unionized under CUPE. [e]Contains transit commission union members. [f]In 1980, name changed to Alberta Union of Provincial Employees.

Source: Compiled from Canada, *Labour Data* (Ottawa: Labour Unions Section, Business Finance Division, Labour Canada, 1982).

Clearly such a spectrum of legislative practice creates inequities for municipal collective bargaining that are far in excess of those found in the private sector.

A unique aspect of public labour relations is the curious position of the government. It is both an employer of a significant number of unionized employees and a key player in the formulation of the labour legislation under which as an employer it must operate. Clearly this dual role creates problems: self-interest conflicts with the need to set equitable labour relations legislation.[40] However, this is not as severe a problem at the municipal level, since rarely do local governments have legislative powers. The entire process can still be

---

[40]Goldenberg, "Collective Bargaining. . .," supra footnote 27, at 36, explains that the government, by virtue of its legislative and executive functions, its obligation to protect the public purse and to ensure the provision of essential services, is clearly a different kind of employer than is found in the private sector.

Table 11.14   Private and Municipal Government Labour Legislation

Province	Private sector	Municipal sector	Police	Fire
Newfoundland	Labour Relations Act	Labour Relations Act	Labour Relations Act	Labour Relations Act and St. John's Fire Dept. Act
Prince Edward Island	Labour Relations Act	Labour Relations Act	Labour Relations Act	Labour Relations Act
Nova Scotia	Trade Union Act	Trade Union Act	Trade Union Act	Trade Union Act
New Brunswick	Industrial Relations Act	Industrial Relations Act	Industrial Relations Act	Industrial Relations Act
Quebec	Labour Code	Labour Code	Labour Code	Labour Code
Ontario	Labour Relations Act	Labour Relations Act	Police Act	Fire Dept. Act
Manitoba	Labour Relations Act	Labour Relations Act	Labour Relations Act	Fire Dept.'s Arbitration Act
Saskatchewan	Trade Union Act	Trade Union Act	Police Act	Fire Dept. Platoon Act
Alberta	Alta. Labour Act	Alta. Labour Act	Firefighter's and Policeman's Labour Relations Act	Firefighter's and Policeman's Labour Relations Act
British Columbia	B.C. Labour Code	B.C. Labour Code	B.C. Labour Code	B.C. Labour Code

Source: W. D. Wood and Pradeep Kumar, eds., *The Current Industrial Relations Scene in Canada 1980* (Kingston, Ontario: Queen's University, Industrial Relations Centre, 1980).

frustrated, though, by a very fragmented management structure designed somewhat deliberately to strike a balance between political and nonpolitical decision making.[41] Many provinces, for example, divide the responsibility for managing municipal police forces among a police chief, municipal officials, and a police board, and education decisions are apportioned among locally elected school boards, provincially appointed superintendents, and ministries of education. Public-sector funding arrangements also contribute to shared authority, since a multiplicity of sources invariably seek to influence the way in which money is spent.[42] Urban transit authorities, for example, are often financed through a combination of user charges, municipal subsidies, and provincial grants, with each source wanting some role in the negotiation process. The end result is to disperse decision-making authority and to frustrate collective bargaining with additional and often opposing participants. Rarely is the private-sector process so exacerbated by structural disunity and political competition.[43]

COLLECTIVE BARGAINING

Amidst this rather disparate system of legislation and management, municipal collective bargaining has managed to produce somewhat attractive wage and nonwage settlements for local employees. This has emerged largely because of a public-sector labour relations policy in Canada that is among the most liberal in the world.[44] In fact, Canadian bargaining systems seem to exhibit greater maturity, stability, and scope than do those in either the United States or Great Britain, where the sovereignty doctrine is still used to resist collective bargaining and strike rights.[45] In Canada, however, debate has shifted from whether public employees should be allowed to bargain collectively to much more specific issues—such as the scope of bargaining, the right to strike, and impasse procedures.[46] In fact, at the municipal level, workers have been enjoying explicit bargaining rights for several decades, since under provincial labour relations legislation local governments were included in the definition of "employer" and

---

[41]According to David Lewin and Shirley B. Goldenberg, in "Public Sector Unionism in the U.S. and Canada" (Fall 1980), 19 *Industrial Relations* 239-56, at 249, the organizational responsibility for public sector bargaining in Canada is not highly centralized at the municipal level. In some jurisdictions responsibility for collective bargaining has been added to the other personnel functions of existing civil service commissions, but in most cases the negotiating function is assigned to a staff relations division of another governmental agency.

[42]Milton Derber, "Management Organization for Collective Bargaining in the Public Sector," in Benjamin Aaron, Joseph R. Grodin, and James L. Stern, eds., *Public-Sector Bargaining*, Industrial Relations Research Association Series (Washington, D.C.: Bureau of National Affairs, 1979), 80-117.

[43]All the ensuing ramifications are described in supra footnote 39, at 354-57. In addition, the rather frustrating impact created by the existence of a multiplicity of municipal jurisdictions with varying resource capacities, both fiscal and managerial, is also noted in supra footnote 37, at 8-10.

[44]Sandra Christensen, "Pay Boards Versus Collective Bargaining in the Public Sector" (Autumn 1980), 6 *Canadian Public Policy* 605-13, at 605.

[45]It is not clear, however, if these characteristics are the result of longer bargaining histories, the specific shape of public policies, socioeconomic environmental constraints, union and management strategies and tactics, or any other factors. See Feuille and Anderson, supra footnote 33, at 332.

[46]Ibid., at 310. It should be noted that these achievements were greatest for the federal and provincial governments, as there has been substantial organization at the municipal level for several decades.

members of the municipal service as "employees." Consequently, there are few, if any, restrictions on the scope of bargaining, because the governing statutes are within the general framework applicable to the private sector in each province.[47]

Because the range of negotiable issues is so broad at the municipal level, strong local unions have been able to secure rather attractive compensation packages for their members. While these settlements represent significant gains for municipal workers, they also represent explicit and hidden costs for local governments and the supporting taxpayers. Explicit costs, such as wage increases, are those that materially raise the level of municipal expenditures as soon as wage agreements are negotiated. Hidden costs are those that do not appear immediately, but either manifest themselves in future budgets (fringe benefits and pensions) or alter the nature of the service provided (cutbacks on expenditure levels, reduced levels of service, and layoffs of non-essential workers). In short, collective bargaining exerts an impact on municipal expenditures on a scale that is much broader than initially might appear.

COLLECTIVE BARGAINING AND WAGES

It is generally accepted that an important reason to bargain collectively is to raise the level of wages.[48] In fact, the premise that unionization leads to wage increases that would not occur in the absence of collective action has a theoretical foundation that has been recognized for some time.[49] The available data seem to support this hypothesis. Table 11.15 indicates that since the introduction of widespread public-sector collective bargaining, the public sector collectively has achieved higher base rate increases for agreements in force than the private sector. By 1981, this spread was almost 22 points. The total public-sector index of base rates had increased to 277.1 compared to only 255.6 in the private sector. These gains appear to be greatest for the more senior levels of government (provincial first, then federal) as well as for the education and the telephone and utilities sectors. The local government sector has, however, steadily achieved settlements with base rate increases 1 to 3 points higher than the private sector in all but 4 years since 1970. The data do suggest, therefore, that the public sector has been able to enhance the special nature of its labour market through collective action. At least one very recent study illustrates that in the education field, a 10 per cent increase in the ratio of unionized to total employees led to a 1.4 per cent increase in wages that would not otherwise have occurred.[50] For municipal employees, a similar explanatory factor was small, but evident.

---

[47]John Crispo, "Collective Bargaining in the Public Service: Seminar Report," in Institute, supra footnote 27, 95-105, at 98.

[48]See supra footnote 32, at 23; Cousineau and Lacroix, supra footnote 19, at 45; and D.A.L. Auld, L. N. Christofides, R. Swidinsky, and D. A. Wilton, *The Determinants of Negotiated Wage Settlements in Canada (1966-1975): A Microeconometric Analysis* (Ottawa: Supply and Services, 1979).

[49]Albert Rees, *The Economics of Trade Unions* (Chicago: University of Chicago Press, 1962); and H. Gregg Lewis, *Unionism and Relative Wages in the United States: An Empirical Inquiry* (Chicago: University of Chicago Press, 1963).

[50]D.A.L. Auld, *The Impact of Unionization and Government Growth on Public Sector Wages,* Discussion Paper no. 1982-3 (Guelph, Ontario: University of Guelph, Department of Economics, 1982), 8.

Table 11.15   Index of Base Rate Increases for All Agreements in Force—Bargaining Units of 500 or More Employees, Excluding Construction Industry (1971 = 100)

Sector	1971	1972	1973	1974	1975	1976	1977	1978	1979	1980	1981
Public sector	100.0	106.6	116.4	129.6	149.3	174.7	196.6	210.3	225.9	247.2	277.1
Federal[a]	100.0	106.7	113.7	130.5	149.1	172.0	186.7	197.9	216.8	233.6	262.5
Provincial[b]	100.0	106.6	117.5	132.4	157.6	180.3	203.5	217.1	232.6	257.7	291.6
Education[c]	100.0	105.2	116.5	127.1	143.3	172.8	199.2	213.5	227.3	249.2	278.4
Utilities[d]	100.0	109.0	117.5	138.0	169.3	196.4	212.6	229.6	246.0	269.6	300.9
Local[e]	100.0	108.8	118.1	130.2	150.2	168.0	182.5	195.7	211.8	230.8	258.3
Private sector	100.0	108.0	116.1	131.5	149.1	166.3	182.5	194.5	210.9	231.4	255.6

[a]Settlements covered by Public Service Staff Relations Act. [b]Includes provincial liquor, wine, and beer stores. [c]Excludes settlements covered by Public Service Staff Relations Act. [d]Excludes Bell Canada, Quebec and B.C. Telephone, Ontario and Quebec Hydro. [e]Includes urban transit systems.

Source: Canada, *Wage Developments* (Ottawa: Labour Canada, 1981), 73, Table G-2.

The nature of the bargaining process at the local level is thought to be a critical factor in the impact on wage settlements insofar as the use of either intercity- or intracity-pattern bargaining occurs. With intercity bargaining, CUPE, for example, establishes national bargaining goals. These are then negotiated in key municipalities so as to establish a pattern that will be followed in other municipalities.[51] Given that over 70 per cent of all municipal agreements in Canada today are negotiated in highly urbanized centres (populations of 50,000 or more), it follows that unions will demand at least parity with the settlements of other strong trade unions existing in these communities (Table 11.16). Similarly with intracity-pattern bargaining, unions representing city employees (usually police or firefighters) formally meet to plan bargaining strategies and generally agree to undertake negotiations with one union for the purpose of establishing the wage pattern for others.[52] As a result, some unions will stall their negotiations until the chosen union has settled with the city, then all groups are likely to be granted the same or similar percentage wage increases. Thus, no matter what form pattern bargaining takes, the consequence is to expand the range of employees who are affected. The more important effect, however, is that regardless of the approach used, the presence of an aforementioned diffused managerial authority with little real focus on wage negotiations, places considerable power in the hands of local unions that are able to attack a relatively weak employer.[53] Insofar as collective bargaining is a relatively new phenomenon in the public sector, managerial bargainers with limited bargaining experience can easily be led to higher settlements as they are "beaten" by more experienced labour representatives.[54] Further, the argument has been made that since the public sector is not faced with the profit constraint existing in the private sector, government-employee unions are in a better position to press wage claims than are their private-sector counterparts.[55] This may be especially true when combined with the suggestion that the public-sector labour market does not face the same check on wage demands imposed in the normal trade-off between employment and wages.[56] Finally, a number of studies have suggested that collective bargaining increases the share of the municipal budget that goes toward the cost of labour.[57]

COLLECTIVE BARGAINING, FRINGE BENEFITS, AND TOTAL COMPENSATION

The price of labour is not the only input in a total compensation package and not the only factor affected by collective bargaining. In fact fringe benefits,[58]

---

[51] John Anderson, "The Structure of Collective Bargaining," in Anderson and Gunderson, supra footnote 34, at 176.

[52] Ibid.

[53] Ibid.

[54] Supra footnote 15, at 55.

[55] Dean, supra footnote 10.

[56] Supra footnote 9, at 16-17.

[57] J. Batterschneider, "The Impact of Collective Bargaining Laws Covering Police and Firefighters on Municipal Budgeting" (unpublished Ph.D. dissertation, Cornell University, Ithaca, New York, 1979); supra footnote 50; Thornton, supra footnote 28, at 361; and supra footnote 9, at 18.

[58] The term was first used around 1943 by the U.S. War Labor Board when direct wage increases were not feasible. Fringe benefits are generally defined as "pay for time not worked." The increasing

(Continued on next page.)

Table 11.16   Municipal Collective Agreements and Employee Coverage in Cities with Population of 10,000 or More[a] by Province, 1980

| Province | All agreements | | City size | | | | | | | | | |
| | Number of agreements | Number of employees | 10,000-24,999 | | 25,000-49,999 | | 50,000-99,999 | | 100,000-499,999 | | 500,000 + | |
			Number of agreements	Number of employees	Number of agreements	Number of employees	Number of agreements	Number of employees	Number of agreements	Number of employees	Number of agreements	Number of employees
Newfoundland	1	450	—	—	—	—	1	450	—	—	—	—
Nova Scotia	4	870	—	—	1	110	1	155	2	605	—	—
New Brunswick	5	1,025	2	110	—	—	3	915	—	—	—	—
Quebec	34	21,595	1	200	7	695	14	2,745	6	2,490	6	15,465
Ontario	56	27,160	—	—	—	—	13	2,230	33	11,365	10	13,565
Manitoba	7	5,220	—	—	2	175	—	—	—	—	5	5,045
Saskatchewan	8	2,770	2	100	2	300	—	—	4	2,300	—	—
Alberta	10	9,960	—	—	4	835	—	—	6	9,125	—	—
British Columbia	58	11,085	16	985	14	1,360	18	3,680	8	2,260	2	2,800
All provinces	183	80,065	21	1,345	30	3,475	50	10,175	59	28,145	23	36,875

[a]Does not include police or firefighters, for agreements covering at least 100 employees.

Source: Calculated from data in Canada, *Provisions in Collective Agreements in Canada Covering 200 and More Employees* (Ottawa: Labour Canada, 1980).

which presently account for up to one-third of total annual employee compensation in Canada, are emerging quickly as the centre of a controversy whose resolution could have far-reaching repercussions not only for local government budgets, but also for the Canadian economy.[59] Since nonwage compensation is an important component of the entire compensation package, some evidence on both its size and relative importance is necessary.

Limited evidence in Canada indicates that in the early 1970s, several important changes in fringe benefits and working conditions came about as a result of widespread collective bargaining in the public sector.[60] These included significant improvements in sick leave and severance pay, as well as dramatic changes in the payment of premiums and pay guarantees.[61]

Table 11.17 suggests that the municipal labour sector, by 1980, had secured a number of provisions that were more generous than similar provisions in the manufacturing sector. At least one-half of all municipal workers had secured some protection against loss of jobs due to technological change, whereas, only one-third of all manufacturing workers had secured similar protection (section A, Table 11.17). Through collective bargaining, contracting out the provision of local services to the private sector is prohibited in over 50 per cent of all municipal agreements if it leads to lay-offs, but only one-quarter of all manufacturing contracts have the same provision (section B, Table 11.17). Almost 99 per cent of all contracts in the municipal sector provide for at least 10

---

[58]Continued

number and variety of fringe benefits today, however, defy simple definition. One source lists no less than 113 items that could be classified as fringe benefits—see Bill Megalli, "The Fringe Benefit Debate" (July 1978), 78 *Labour Gazette* 311-15, at 311-13.

[59]Ibid., at 311.

[60]Similar evidence is also available for the United States, although conclusive evidence is not abundant. Since 1970, the Labor Management Relations Service (LMRS) of the National League of Cities (NLC) in the U.S. has conducted several surveys of benefits paid to municipal employees. See Labor-Management Relations Service of the United States Conference of Mayors, *National Survey of Employee Benefits for Full-Time Personnel of U.S. Municipalities,* Special Report (Washington, D.C.: L-MRS, 1970, 1973 and 1975). Thornton, supra footnote 28, at 359, has also found that in 1970 municipal employees received benefits equal to an average of 31.0 per cent of pay for hours worked, while the comparable figure for private-sector employees was only 27.4 per cent. The value of fringe benefits to uniformed personnel, such as police and firefighters, was even higher at 33.8 per cent of straight time pay to cover special items such as uniforms, death benefits, non-production bonuses, and educational expenses, in addition to regular benefits such as pensions, social security, vacations, holidays, paid sick leave, and worker's compensation. Over the period 1970 to 1975, the rate of growth of fringe benefits was found to be rapid for both the private and public sectors. Municipalities, however, continued to spend a larger percentage of pay for fringe benefits than did private employers. By 1977, police and firefighters were receiving $46 in fringe benefits for every $100 in salary, while the comparable figure for all industry personnel averaged only $41. The fact, however, that the average level of fringe benefits paid to municipal employees exceeded that paid to private-sector employees was not considered unusual because, even before wide-scale unionization, local governments were known to be relatively generous with fringe benefits. It was noted, however, that this edge could no longer be considered as a compensatory measure for low public-sector wages, since the wage differential had been reduced, and recently reversed.

[61]T. J. Wilkins, "Wage and Benefit Determination in the Public Service of Canada," in Institute, supra footnote 27, at 66.

or more paid holidays, while approximately 25 per cent of all manufacturing workers receive 9 days or less (section C, Table 11.17). Over 80 per cent of all municipal contracts have bargained for relatively generous paid sick-leave benefits, the same proportion in the manufacturing sector has no provision for sick-leave compensation whatsoever (section D, Table 11.17). Finally, various paid leaves of absence are more generously provided in municipal than in manufacturing collective bargaining contracts (sections E-1 and E-2, Table 11.17).

Some interesting trends have emerged in the bargaining successes of various municipal union locals across the country.[62] Table 11.18 reveals that contracts in Quebec provide for substantially more paid holidays than in any other province (section A, Table 11.18). Almost 70 per cent of all contracts provide for 18 days of paid sick leave, but the majority of these are found in Ontario (section B, Table 11.18). Almost all contracts in Ontario require a 100 per cent major medical employer contribution, while in the Prairies and Quebec, approximately 70 per cent have no similar provision (section C, Table 11.18). Employers in British Columbia contribute to approximately one-half of the cost of hospital insurance premiums, while none of the municipal agreements in Quebec and Atlantic Canada have any provision for the payment of premiums by the municipal employer (section D, Table 11.18). With the exception of municipal agreements in Ontario where the entire cost of dental-plan premiums is absorbed by more than 70 per cent of local government employers, local government employer contributions range from nothing in Quebec and Atlantic Canada to a mix of employer-employee contributions in British Columbia and the Prairies (section E, Table 11.18). Finally, municipal contracts in Ontario tend to be the most generous in the portion for long-term disability premiums paid by the employer (section F, Table 11.18).

To cost out the value of fringe benefits is not an easy task nor are the values obtained likely to be conclusively accurate. Nevertheless, the available data allow us to obtain an approximation of the value of fringe benefits. Table 11.19 compares the dollars spent per employer in the private and public sectors for two selected years.[63] In 1976, the value of fringe benefits, expressed either as a per cent of payroll or as dollar expenditures per employee per year, were roughly

---

[62]The sample is based on major municipal agreements in 1980, divided among the provinces in the following way:

	Local	Members	Per cent of total
British Columbia	10	6,030	9.5
Prairies	12	18,437	29.0
Ontario	57	24,161	38.0
Quebec	10	13,314	20.9
Atlantic	6	1,689	2.6
	95	63,631	100.0

Source: System for the Analysis of Labour Agreement Data (SALAD) Research Department, Canadian Union of Public Employees, *Major Municipal Agreements, November 1980.*

[63]Municipal figures for 1980 have been collected by the Pay Research Bureau in Ottawa; however, the data are unfortunately confidential and not available for presentation in Table 11.19.

Table 11.17   Comparison of Some Provisions in Major Collective Agreements in the Municipal and Manufacturing Sectors, 1980

A. Percentage of Wage Guarantees in the Case of Technological Change

Sector	No provision exists	Some form of guarantee exists	Other
Municipal	49.6	50.3	—
Manufacturing	65.3	33.7	9

B. Percentage of Contracting Out Rules

Sector	No provision exists	Permitted	Prohibited	Prohibited if leads to layoffs
Municipal.	33.8	14.6	0.2	51.4
Manufacturing	30.6	39.2	2.4	24.3

C. Percentage of Paid Holiday Provisions

Sector	Eight to nine days	Ten to twelve days	Thirteen to sixteen days
Municipal.	1.6	69.7	28.1
Manufacturing	25.9	48.6	27.8

D. Percentage of Sick Leave Provisions

Sector	No provision	Five days	Six to twelve days	Fourteen to twenty days	Other
Municipal	17.0	0.5	3.8	68.7	17.5
Manufacturing	78.9	1.9	3.6	1.3	14.3

E. Percentage of Paid Leave of Absence

(1) For death in family

Sector	No provision	Three days	Four days	Five days
Municipal	1.4	79.4	4.0	15.2
Manufacturing	1.2	86.6	1.5	10.8

(2) For death of relative

Sector	No provision	One day	Two days	Three days
Municipal	47.1	31.0	2.8	11.0
Manufacturing	66.6	26.0	1.9	5.5

(3) For childbirth

Sector	No provision	One day	Two days	Other
Municipal	68.3	19.1	1.6	10.9
Manufacturing	97.5	2.3	0.3	0.0

(4) For jury duty

Sector	No provision exists	Paid difference between jury pay and regular wage	Regular wage
Municipal	9.0	81.5	9.5
Manufacturing	14.7	71.1	14.2

Source: Calculated from data in Canada, *Provisions in Collective Agreements in Canada Covering 200 and More Employees* (Ottawa: Labour Canada, 1980).

Table 11.18 Regional Variations[a] in Selected Local Government Nonwage Benefits, 1980

A. Days of Nonvacation Paid Holidays

Region	11	11.5	12	12.5	13	14	14.5	15.5	Total
British Columbia	8	—	2	—	—	—	—	—	10
Prairies	7	5	—	—	—	—	—	—	12
Ontario	22	16	15	2	2	—	—	—	57
Quebec	—	—	—	4	2	2	1	1	10
Atlantic	4	—	—	—	—	—	—	—	4
Total	41	21	17	6	4	2	1	1	91

B. Paid Sick Leave

Region	5 days	15 days	18 days	20 days	Weekly	Varies	Other	Total
British Columbia	—	—	2	1	5	2	—	10
Prairies	—	4	—	—	2	3	3	12
Ontario	—	—	50	—	7	—	—	57
Quebec	2	5	—	—	—	—	—	7
Atlantic	—	—	5	1	—	—	—	6
Total	2	9	57	2	14	5	3	92

C. Major Medical Plans: Percentage of Employer Contribution

Region	No provision	50	70	75	90	100	Combined with other benefits	Total
British Columbia	2	5	—	—	—	3	—	10
Prairies	7	2	3	—	—	—	—	12
Ontario	2	—	—	—	2	53	1	57
Quebec	7	2	—	—	—	—	1	10
Atlantic	1	1	—	2	—	2	6	12
Total	19	10	3	2	2	58	8	101

D. Hospital Insurance: Percentage of Employer Contribution

Region	50	70	90	100	None required by provincial plan	Total
British Columbia	7	—	—	3	—	10
Prairies	2	3	—	—	7	12
Ontario	—	—	2	55	—	57
Quebec	—	—	—	—	10	10
Atlantic	—	—	—	—	6	6
Total	9	3	2	58	23	95

E. Dental Plans: Percentage of Employer Contribution

Region	No provision	50	65	75	80	90	100	Employee pay all	Total
British Columbia	—	7	—	—	—	—	3	—	10
Prairies	5	1	1	—	—	—	5	—	12
Ontario	4	—	—	8	3	2	40	—	57
Quebec	10	—	—	—	—	—	—	—	10
Atlantic	4	—	—	—	—	—	—	2	6
Total	23	8	1	8	3	2	48	2	95

(Table concluded on next page.)

Table 11.8   Concluded

F. Long-Term Disability Plans: Percentage of Employer Contribution

Region	No provision	50	75	90	100	Employee pay all	Sick leave bank	Not specified	Total
British Columbia ..	3	—	—	—	3	—	2	2	10
Prairies	1	2	—	—	3	1	3	2	12
Ontario	21	1	2	2	24	7	—	—	57
Quebec...........	8	1	—	—	—	1	—	—	10
Atlantic	1	—	—	—	—	1	4	—	06
Total	34	4	2	2	30	10	9	4	95

ªFor the distribution of local agreements, see infra footnote 62.

Source: Data collected from infra footnote 62.

comparable in the local, provincial, and private sectors. This similarity was greatest if both office and non-office employees (comparable to inside and outside municipal workers) were combined, since employers in each sector spent approximately $3,000 per employee for the fringe benefits listed.[64] An analysis of the individual benefit plans illustrates that only two of the six benefits listed vary significantly from one another in each of these sectors. Both the municipal and provincial sectors appear to have the edge in sick-leave benefits, since local governments contributed $457 per employee for this cause, provincial governments contributed $406, and private employers contributed only $267 per employee. Conversely, private-sector employers contributed just over $900 toward each employee's pension plan, while the comparable contributions by the provincial and municipal sectors were lower by $37 and $202 respectively. Because of the importance of municipal pensions in the overall benefit package and their impact on government budgets in the future, they will be discussed in Chapter 12.

While figures for the mid-1970s suggest approximate parity between private and municipal fringe benefits, more recent data in unpublished form suggest that in addition to higher wage gains in the local sector (Table 11.9), this sector has surfaced as a leader in the value and size of fringe benefits. By 1980, for example, this unpublished data suggest that municipal and provincial employees received better health benefits and salary continuation plans (sick leave and long-term disability) than did the private sector.[65] The gains were particularly impressive in the area of health, since over the four-year period (1976 to 1980) public-sector employer contributions came from behind to exceed those in the private sector by between 50 per cent (municipal) and 100 per cent (provincial).[66] The municipal sector also enjoyed increases in the areas of vacation and holiday pay, substantially widening the slight advantage they previously held over the private sector. Such gains probably represent successful attempts to circumvent anti-inflation guidelines imposed between 1975 and 1978 and thus are not of an ad hoc nature. The number of benefits that may be devised for such reasons is potentially limited only by the ingenuity of the

[64]The figures in the Table are simply arithmetic totals of the expenditures on the benefits.

[65]Conversations with provincial and municipal officials.

[66]See ibid. Paid sick leave for local administrative employees was also documented.

Table 11.19 Value of Fringe Benefits, Private, Private, Provincial, and Municipal Sectors, 1976 and Private Sector, 1980

Benefits	1976						1980	
	Private[a]	Per cent of payroll[b]	Provincial[a]	Per cent of payroll[b]	Municipal[a]	Per cent of payroll[b]	Private[a]	Per cent of payroll[b]
All employees								
Life insurance	86	0.7	43	0.4	60	0.5	96	0.5
Health plans	146	1.2	146	1.3	128	1.1	212	1.2
Sick leave	267	2.3	406	3.8	457	3.9	401	2.2
Legislated benefits	390	3.3	298	2.7	420	3.7	645	3.9
Vacations	1,278	10.3	1,164	10.5	1,211	10.3	2,686	15.5
Pensions[c]	917	7.4	880	8.4	715	6.0	1,417	7.9
Total	3,084	25.2	2,937	27.1	2,991	25.5	5,457	31.2
Office employees								
Life insurance	104	0.8	43	0.4	80	0.6	107	0.5
Health plans	153	1.2	140	1.2	140	1.0	218	1.3
Sick leave	283	2.3	413	3.8	535	4.1	497	2.6
Legislated benefits	342	2.7	288	2.5	421	3.3	559	3.0
Vacations	1,278	10.1	1,881	10.5	1,418	10.8	2,855	15.0
Pensions[c]	1,011	7.7	901	8.4	898	6.8	1,517	7.8
Total	3,171	24.8	2,966	26.8	3,492	26.6	5,753	30.2
Non-office employees								
Life insurance	64	0.6	45	0.4	44	0.4	82	0.5
Health plans	137	1.3	160	1.5	117	1.1	207	1.3
Sick leave	245	2.3	389	3.8	393	3.8	305	2.0
Legislated benefits	441	4.0	322	3.1	419	3.1	742	5.0
Vacations	1,175	10.6	1,119	10.7	1,052	10.7	2,488	16.1
Pensions[c]	809	7.1	827	8.4	560	8.4	1,296	7.8
Total	2,871	25.9	2,862	27.8	2,564	27.8	5,120	32.7

[a]Dollars per employee per year. [b]Percentage of straight time payroll.
[c]Includes retirement allowances and severance pay.

Source: 1976 figures are from supra footnote 11, at 151, Table 7.8. 1980 figures are from Canada, *Employee Benefits and Conditions of Employment in Canada* (Ottawa: Pay Research Bureau, 1980), 145-61).

negotiating parties.[67] In any case, there is some evidence to suggest that the Canadian municipal sector has pulled significantly ahead of the private sector in fringe benefits compensation, from an approximately equal position in 1976.

These results corroborate the conclusion that because of the political nature of unionism, which makes unions more representative of average than marginal workers, and because of the role of unions as stable market institutions, unions can be expected to raise the fringe benefits share of the compensation package.[68] More importantly, the results suggest that the relative position of local government employees in terms of total compensation might be re-evaluated. That is, if one considers base wage increases alone (Table 11.9), the figures understate the advantage the local sector employees are currently enjoying. If the fringe-benefit figures just mentioned were added to base rate increases, as they should be to reflect the entire compensation package, then the total compensation package may be as much as 10 per cent higher than similar compensation packages in the private sector. Municipal employers all too often appear to have ignored both the full impact and implications that fringe benefits have on the total compensation package and the ensuing impact that these costs will have on future local budgets.

COLLECTIVE BARGAINING AND LOCAL BUDGETS

While collective bargaining has not basically altered the budget and financial processes of the city, it has added considerable stress to the already difficult financial situations of most municipal governments.[69] In the days before unions acquired bargaining rights, the budget process could readily accommodate the previously discussed changes in pay and benefits. Modifications were simply kept within anticipated financial resources and timed to start with the next fiscal year.[70] Today, however, the budget-execution process is much less controllable, because unions, with greater strength and higher visibility, have a major impact on both the content and process of budgets.[71] In fact, it has been illustrated that under conditions of fiscal adversity, collective bargaining in the public sector is tied much more closely to the budget-making process. The bargaining process is a time consuming venture. A union's strategy, however, may involve extending settlements past budget deadlines in order to force employers to yield to demands.[72] As a result, further legislative action may be necessary if additional financial measures are required. Limited evidence suggests it is possible to incorporate bargaining results after the budget goes to the legislature, but this forces

---

[67]Supra footnote 58, at 312.

[68]Richard B. Freeman, "The Effect of Unionism on Fringe Benefits" (July 1981), 34 *Industrial & Labour Relations Review* 489-509.

[69]Thornton, supra footnote 28, at 361.

[70]David T. Stanley, "Managing Local Government Under Union Pressure (excerpts)," in W. Patrick Beaton, ed., *Municipal Needs, Services and Financing: Readings on Municipal Expenditures* (New Brunswick, N.J.: Centre for Urban Policy Research, Rutgers University, 1974), 311-34, at 316.

[71]Milton Derber and Martin Wagner, "Public Sector Bargaining and Budget Making Under Fiscal Adversity" (October 1979), 33 *Industrial & Labour Relations Review* 18-23.

[72]A. E. Bent and T. Z. Rewes, *Collective Bargaining in the Private Sector* (Menlo Park, California: Benjamin-Cummings, 1978), 128.

the budgetary process to become more protracted, less formal, and less controllable from a management viewpoint.[73] Collective bargaining, thus becomes one more item on the long list of unexpected or hard-to-plan-for items, especially if settlements cost more than budgets provide.[74] Budget managers can, however, protect themselves from such an impact if they use contingency funds, or simply "hide" money in the budget in anticipation of high settlements. The former method (use of an ear-marked fund) is risky insofar as it may represent a "sitting duck" for other legislators who wish to eliminate it for another purpose, or it may become a target for bargaining demands.[75] The latter method, on the other hand, gives some bargaining leeway to the city if it is difficult for unions to learn the exact amount committed.[76] Regardless of the approach taken, it is apparent that just the anticipated results of collective bargaining, let alone the actual settlements, can cause municipal governments to devote more of their local budgets to wages and salaries than is otherwise justified. Insofar as more than 75 per cent of the typical municipal operating budget tends to be allocated to personnel, the importance of the effect of collective bargaining on local budgets cannot be overlooked.

COLLECTIVE BARGAINING AND THE DELIVERY OF LOCAL SERVICES—STRIKES

While union tactics can severely frustrate the local budgetary process, a much more political and emotional effect of collective bargaining occurs when the negotiating parties cannot reach an agreement. The use of strikes and lockouts by public-sector employees and employers as an ultimate strategy has been a contentious issue for years.[77] In fact, the potentially disruptive impact of strikes in the provision of many local government services has equipped municipal unions with what many consider to be "excessive" bargaining power. Police, fire-fighters, and sanitation workers are prime examples of local government employees who offer essential services to communities for which there exist relatively few, if any, substitutes.[78] The unavailability of viable alternatives places municipal politicians in rather precarious negotiating positions, especially since service disruption in the more essential areas, such as school closings or transit stoppages, tend to capture a disproportionate amount of citizen and media attention. When strikes do persist, they serve as visible reminders that tax dollars must finance eventual bargaining outcomes. The mere threat of a strike,

---

[73]Ibid., at 317.

[74]In some parts of the United States, however, provisions in public employee bargaining statutes have been enacted to ensure that the negotiation process and the budgetary process occur simultaneously. See Thornton, supra footnote 28, at 362-63.

[75]Supra footnote 70, at 318.

[76]Ibid., at 319.

[77]"Strike" is defined as a stoppage of work by a group of employees to press for settlement of a demand or a grievance. "Lockout" is defined as a suspension of work initiated by an employer as a result of failure to reach agreement in the course of a dispute over terms of employment.

[78]Recent trends, however, in some occupations (such as teaching) suggest that this competitive edge of municipal employee unions may be losing ground. Changes in technology have made the threat of public service strikes less effective since automation in areas such as utilities has enabled a small supervisory crew to maintain effective service for months. See Gilbert Levine, "The Inevitability of Public-Sector Strikes in Canada" (March 1977), 77 *Labour Gazette* 117-20, at 118.

however, may be just as damaging to local governments as the strike itself; for example, the municipal employer's efforts to successfully thwart a potential strike may lead to unnecessarily high compensation settlements. The revenues necessary to fund these settlements, often come from a variety of unidentifiable sources or may not emerge until future budgets are tabled.[79]

There have been fewer restrictions on the right to strike for public employees in Canada as compared with the United States. This undoubtedly has led to an increase in strike activity over the past few years. Government employees and unions, in fact, have come to regard the strike as a normal part of the bargaining process.[80] Indeed, since the advent of public-sector unionism, strikes and lockouts by government employees and employers have grown at a rate considerably faster than those by all employees and employers combined in Canada. They have also accounted for an increasing proportion of person-days lost, rising from .2 per cent of total days lost in 1957 to almost 8 per cent in 1980 (Table 11.20).

Because municipal employees have been organized for a longer period of time (when compared with federal or provincial employees), the growth in municipal strike activity has been fairly steady. From 1957 to 1973, almost all public-sector strikes occurred at the municipal level. Since 1973, the number of strikes occurring in the municipal sector has risen, but these have accounted for a smaller percentage of all strikes by government employees (in 1980 the local sector accounted for 72 per cent of public-sector strikes, Table 11.20). In short, the municipal sector continues to be more strike prone than either the federal or provincial sector. Strikes can be expected to increase as budgets become tighter and unions more demanding. They may even seem less horrendous, since continued exposure tends to build a public tolerance for them.[81] Their impacts, unfortunately, become particularly significant for local governments attempting to negotiate under rather tight fiscal conditions.

COLLECTIVE BARGAINING AND THE LEVEL AND QUALITY OF SERVICE

Not only can collective bargaining result in strikes, which aggrevate the delivery of local services, but it also can alter the level and quality of services being delivered. In fact, a much more hidden cost of collective bargaining is the loss of the budget as an efficient instrument of rational choice among program priorities. If alternative revenues cannot be found to finance increased compensation packages, as is often the case with a finite tax base, some programs or services are likely to be reduced if not eliminated.[82] Indeed, there is a growing consensus that collective bargaining has driven municipal expenditures upward

---

[79]Supra footnote 44, at 607.

[80]Supra footnote 41, at 252. Since the mid-1960s, federal and provincial labour legislation in Canada has made the strike legally available to many public service workers. This contrasts sharply with policy in the United States where most federal and state workers are prohibited from striking. See supra footnote 44, at 605.

[81]H. Rubin, "Labour Relations in State and Local Governments" (no. 2, 1970/1972), 30 *Academy of Political Science Proceedings* 27.

[82]Supra footnote 70, at 320.

Table 11.20   Strikes and Lockouts in Canada for Selected Years

Year	Total strikes and lockouts		Total public		Municipal		Provincial		Federal	
	Number	Person-days lost	Number	Person-days lost	Number	Person-days lost	Number	Person-days lost	Number	Person-days lost
1957	249	1,634,881	4	3,488	4	3,488	—	—	—	—
1960	274	738,700	—	—	—	—	—	—	—	—
1962	311	1,417,900	4	950	3	840	1	110	—	—
1964	343	1,580,550	4	20,130	4	20,130	—	—	—	—
1966	617	5,178,170	16	169,300	14	76,670	1	91,200	1	1,430
1968	582	3,974,760	16	67,540	16	67,540	—	—	—	—
1970	542	6,539,560	13	30,660	12	29,950	—	—	1	710
1973	724	5,776,080	23	99,020	20	95,160	3	3,860	—	—
1974	1,218	9,221,890	59	109,580	54	13,269	5	96,311	—	—
1976	1,039	11,609,890	59	62,680	46	49,450	11	12,450	2	780
1978	1,058	7,392,820	55	257,140	45	167,740	8	89,120	2	280
1980	1,028	8,975,390	58	700,090	42	229,120	12	140,880	4	330,090

Source: Canada, Department of Labour, Economics and Research Branch, *Strikes and Lockouts in Canada* (Ottawa: Supply and Services, appropriate years).

and has forced a reduction in the level of services provided.[83] Of the few studies undertaken, most have found that local governments in large centres more frequently resort to such a response because of the existence of numerous, varied, and often peripheral programs that easily can be eliminated in times of fiscal adversity.[84] It is more difficult to cut local programs and services for municipal governments in small centres offering a basic core of municipal services. Nevertheless, some cuts have been made.

SUMMARY

Since the early 1960s, the growth in public-sector employment at the local level has exceeded the growth in population; however, it has not always exceeded the growth in provincial government employment. The expanding size of the local public sector has contributed to an increased attention being devoted to wage and nonwage benefits received by local government employees. This attention has revolved, in many instances, around the notion that local wage and compensation packages, which have been negotiated through various collective agreements, have been financially more attractive than similar settlements in the private sector. Indeed, in the very late 1970s and very early 1980s, the limited available evidence supports this view.

A large part of the explanation for the emergence of differentials in local public-sector and private-sector compensation packages (wages and fringe benefits) has been directed toward the increase in local public-sector unionization and the effects that this has had on the increases in wages and fringe benefits. Local unions, in many instances, have extracted concessions designed to create a virtual monopoly over the provision of local services (for example, clauses such as those prohibiting the "contracting out" for the provision of local services to the private sector if this leads to layoffs of local public employees). This and other clauses of a similar nature have served to solidify the bargaining strength of local unions. When combined with a number of other features including the absence of a profit constraint, which serves to restrict the behaviour of management in private-sector negotiations, the relatively inelastic demand for local service and the lack of, or inability to measure, productivity levels that could serve as a benchmark against which local wage and fringe benefits could be established, the local public-sector labour market has developed a strong and cohesive bargaining unit.

Strengthening of local public-sector unions has led to increased demands for higher wages, improved fringe benefits, and greater protection from layoffs. The combination of these factors has created some difficulties in the management of local budgets including the inability to control and finance the growth in local expenditures. Perhaps the current legislation restricting wage increases to 6 per cent in 1982/83 and 5 per cent in 1983/84 will serve to control, at least partially, some of the growth in local government expenditures.

---

[83]See Thornton, supra footnote 28, at 363; David T. Methé and James L. Perry, "The Impacts of Collective Bargaining in Local Government Services: A Review of Research" (July/August 1980), 40 *Public Administration Review* 359-71, at 367.

[84]A. H. Pascal, "The Hidden Costs of Collective Bargaining in Local Government" (no. 2, 1980), 3 *Taxing and Spending* 39.

In spite of the fact that unionization and collective bargaining have created financial difficulties for local management, it must not be concluded that all of the effects of unionization and collective bargaining are necessarily bad. Indeed, freedom for local managers to hire and fire at will, particularly in local monopoly activities, such as police, fire, and education, could create a situation where society might be worse off. Collective bargaining in the local public sector is, obviously, here to stay, and is likely to continue altering union-management relations, local administration, and the operation of traditional local-service systems. Clearly, much more empirical research is needed to assess fully the impact of municipal collective bargaining on both the inputs and outputs of local government services. While some issues such as wages and fringe benefits now receive regular attention in both the literature and media, it is essential that local governments monitor the rate of growth of these wage and nonwage aspects of compensation. Still other issues, such as the influence that collective bargaining has exerted on labour productivity and the quantity or quality of service need to be properly addressed before the complete impact of unionization can be assessed. In any case, it is becoming evident that municipal governments must seriously assess the current and future budgetary impacts of each negotiated settlement. Until such informed assessment occurs, the true impact of unionism and its corollary, collective bargaining, will continue to be surrounded by mystery and controversy.

12
Pension Issues

INTRODUCTION

Pensions, traditionally included in compensation packages of public employees, today represent one of the largest single nonwage benefits (see Table 11.19 in Chapter 11). Historically, employment pensions were viewed as rewards for long and faithful service—instruments of personnel policy. Currently, however, they are an integral part of the total compensation package and are responsible for much more than simply removing disabled or superannuated personnel from the labour force.[1] For a relatively long period of time when the work force, benefit levels, and retirement age remained fairly stable, the fiscal implications of public-sector pension benefits did not pose a problem for local jurisdictions. Recent and rather abrupt changes in a variety of economic, social, and demographic conditions, however, have altered significantly the otherwise stable environment in which pension plans were devised.[2] Longevity coupled with earlier retirement in an inflationary economic climate have put in question the adequacy of promised pension funds. While this concern is not limited strictly to the public sector, it is less severe in the private sector where employers are motivated to design pension benefits within the bounds of profit constraints. Conversely, plan features and actuarial soundness of public-sector pension plans (PSPPs) easily are camouflaged behind a governmental taxing authority assumed to be both sufficient and non-exhaustible.

Within this framework, institutional factors such as favourable income tax treatment, pressures from unions, and promotion of pension plans by actuaries specializing in their management have stimulated the growth in pension systems to what many believe approach unmanageable proportions.[3] In addition, anti-inflation controls in the 1970s placed ceilings on wages and effectively converted pensions, along with a wide variety of other fringe benefits into ostensible forms of deferred wages.[4] Few municipalities, unfortunately, realize the magnitude of the long-term fiscal commitment associated with pension obliga-

---

[1]Michael S. March, "Pensions for Public Employees: Present Nationwide Problems" (July/August 1980), 40 *Public Administration Review* 382-89, at 382-83.

[2]These changing conditions will be discussed at length later in this section. See also, Bernard Jump, Jr., "Public Employment, Collective Bargaining, and Employee Wages and Pensions," in John E. Petersen and Catherine Lavigne Spain, eds., *Essays in Public Finance and Financial Management: State and Local Perspectives* (Chairman, N.J.: Chatham House, 1980), 74-85, at 78.

[3]See Ontario, *Report of the Royal Commission on the Status of Pensions in Ontario,* Vol. II (Toronto: the Commission, 1980), 48.

[4]The argument that pension benefits represent a form of deferred wages is considered self apparent. Congress of the United States, *The Labor Market Impacts of the Private Retirement System*, a Study prepared for the use of the Subcommittee on Fiscal Policy of the Joint Economic Committee, Studies in Public Welfare, Paper no. 11 (Washington, D.C.: USGPO, 1973). It is argued also that, to the extent labour negotiators are willing to trade off current wages for higher pension benefits, the deferred wage theory is supported. See J. E. Pesando and S. A. Rea, Jr., *Public and Private Pensions in Canada: An Economic Analysis*, Ontario Economic Council Research Studies (Toronto: University of Toronto Press, 1977), 10.

tions. By promising benefits that will not come due until a future government is in power, municipalities effectively can ignore the true cost of local labour services, creating what many critics refer to as "financial time bombs."[5] Recent evidence, furthermore, suggests that local taxpayers are unaware of the magnitude of this deferred wage payment, and thus, support higher levels of employment and local services than they would support if the full costs of employment were known to them.[6] Clearly, municipal residents have a right to question the solvency of the PSPPs their tax dollars support.[7]

Throughout this chapter, where possible, the management of local government pension funds will be compared to that of the private sector. If it can be illustrated that benefit levels and plan features are more generous and funding constraints less binding in the public sector, a case for more effective control of government employment pensions can be made. To the extent that current payments to retired municipal employees place additional pressure on an already difficult budgetary situation faced by most local governments, this issue is critical.

HISTORICAL AND CONSTITUTIONAL PERSPECTIVE

In order to assess adequately the management of local government pension funds, it is useful first to place pension design, financing, and administration in their historical perspective, and to identify constitutional authorities. Pensions, whether for social security or employment purposes, were not referred to specifically in the BNA Act of 1867. The Old Age Pensions Act of 1927 authorized the federal government to enter into an agreement with the provinces to pay one-half of the pensions paid under provincial legislation.[8] This was replaced by the Old Age Security Act in 1957 that provided universal pensions at age 70.[9] Since 1965, the responsibility for providing social security on a public scale has been assumed by the federal government under the Canada Pension Plan.[10]

Conversely, employment pensions (that is, those awarded by employers on the basis of services rendered) have remained essentially a matter of provincial jurisdiction, though the federal government exercises considerable control through the enactment of detailed guidelines set by Revenue Canada, under the

---

[5]See Jump, supra footnote 2, at 75.

[6]D. Epple and K. Schripper, "Municipal Pension Funding: A Theory and Some Evidence" (1981), 37, no. 1 *Public Choice* 141.

[7]See supra footnote 3, Summary Report, at 55.

[8]The 50-50 cost-sharing arrangement was first passed by British Columbia in 1927, followed by Saskatchewan and Manitoba in 1928, Alberta, Northwest Territories, and Ontario in 1929, Prince Edward Island, New Brunswick, Nova Scotia, and Quebec in the 1930s, and Newfoundland after joining Confederation. See Canada, *Report of the Joint Committee of the Senate and House of Commons on Old Age Security* (Ottawa: Queen's Printer, 1950), 24.

[9]The first old age security law to be placed on the statute books in Canada was to cover "deserving indigent persons of 70 years and upwards." Ibid.

[10]B. Watson, "Government Pensions: An Analysis of the Benefit Structure of the Canadian System" (thesis on microfilm, McGill University, Department of Economics, Montreal, 1972). Provision of old age pensions currently ranks among the costliest items on the social security budget in Canada.

Income Tax Act.[11] Unfortunately, for a very long time, government supervision and inspection of pension plans, be they public or private, was extremely uneven and it was not until the mid-1960s that the provinces began to pass appropriate legislation.[12] Ontario was the first province to introduce such legislation with its Pension Benefits Act, 1965.[13] It was followed closely by Quebec, Alberta, and Saskatchewan. In 1967 the federal government passed the Pension Benefits Standards Act for all plans under federal jurisdiction. Finally, New Brunswick, Nova Scotia, and Manitoba introduced pension legislation in the mid- to late-1970s, but as of 1980, Newfoundland, Prince Edward Island, and British Columbia were still outside of legislative supervision.

To the extent that these acts require plans to be registered with a provincial authority and to comply with standards of vesting, solvency, investment, and disclosure,[14] their regulation appears somewhat more orderly than that devised for the separately administered public employee retirement systems in the United States.[15] Unfortunately, compliance with such reporting standards alone does not ensure parity between public- and private-sector plans, nor that benefit levels supported by present or future tax dollars can be supported by municipal residents.

PENSION MEMBERSHIP

The first formal pension plan appeared in the public sector in 1870 for employees of the government. By 1918, there were some 172 formal pension arrangements across Canada, and by 1936, just over 600 public and private pension plans were in existence.[16] By 1980, there were more than 14,500 pension plans in the country, covering almost 4.5 million employees, or about half of the

---

[11]All plans must register with the Department in order to qualify for substantial tax advantages and exemption of retirement income under the Act. See supra footnote 3, Vol. III, at 175.

[12]Ontario, *Committee on Portable Pensions, Second Report* (Toronto: the Committee, 1961), 2. Supervision of pension plans has long been viewed as a provincial and not a federal responsibility. By the 1950s the partial regulation that had been exercised by the federal government by way of income tax policy was relaxed completely.

[13]The Pension Benefits Act in Ontario is the provincial statute under which plans in both the private and public sectors are regulated. It requires registration of all employment plans having members in Ontario, excluding those financed entirely by employees. See supra footnote 3, Vol. III, at 4.

[14]For a sample of the specific requirements for the Pension Benefits Act in Ontario, see supra footnote 3, Vol. III, at 4-8. With the introduction of such provincial and federal legislation regulating pension plans, there emerged the first opportunity to collect and maintain complete, computerized records of the characteristics of most pension plans in Canada.

[15]Clearly, the Canadian situation is not as severe as that identified in the New York fiscal crisis, and more recently in Cleveland, where disclosure principles and state regulation were virtually absent. Guidelines relating to what should be reported about a jurisdiction's pension obligations are contained in Municipal Finance Officers Association of the United States and Canada, *Disclosure Guidelines for Offerings of Securities by State and Local Governments* (Chicago: the Association, 1976). See also, Anthony M. Mandolini, "Accounting and Reporting for Public Employee Retirement Systems" (February 1978), *Governmental Finance* 10-15, for a description of recent U.S. activity in this area.

[16]Supra footnote 12, at 18.

full-time labour force.[17] Of this number, some of the largest employer-sponsored plans in the country are in the public sector representing just under one-half of all pension plan members (Table 12.1). Throughout the last decade, when the public sector made significant gains in pension plan coverage, membership in PSPPs increased from 87 per cent of full-time workers to 100 per cent by 1980. Over the same period, private-sector coverage increased only 4 percentage points, from just under 30 per cent to approximately 34 per cent.[18] Pension coverage is, therefore, far more extensive in the public sector, and it is unlikely that the private sector will ever obtain a comparable rate of coverage.

Many PSPPs cover employees in a variety of subsectors. This is especially true for municipal pension plans, since eligible members are drawn from school boards, hospitals, and municipalities. In fact, most PSPPs appear liberal in their eligibility criteria since 96 per cent of their members are in plans that permit unrestricted participation, while only 45 per cent of private-sector members are in similar plans.[19] Municipal employees, in 1980, represented almost 18 per cent of public-sector pension plan membership, and less than 8 per cent of the membership in all plans in Canada (Table 12.1). In 6 of the 10 provinces, municipal pension plans are province-wide, with their membership encompassing not only strictly defined municipal employees (such as, office and non-office staff and inside and outside workers), but also employees in some hospitals and libraries, as well as police and firefighters (Table 12.2). In most of these provinces, the area-wide plans provide pensions for close to the entire municipal employee population.

Unlike the private sector, which has developed specialized pension plans to meet a wide variety of job descriptions, salaries, and conditions across various industries, the public sector has provided retirement pensions to a relatively homogenous work force. This is true particularly within the municipal system, where one plan has proven to be satisfactory for a large number of local workers. In the province of Ontario, for example, the Ontario Municipal Employees' Retirement System (OMERS) is one large integrated unit that combines plans for 1,200 municipalities and local boards; a simple three-option supplemental package is sufficient to cover all workers adequately.[20]

---

[17]The following table indicates the percentage of the total labour force, and the percentage of paid workers in the labour force, who were covered by pension plans for the years indicated:

	1970	1978	1980
Number in pension plans	2,822,336	4,193,244	4,475,429
Per cent of total labour force	34.1	39.6	39.7
Per cent of full-time paid workers	42.0	43.7	54.0

Source: Statistics Canada, *Pension Plans in Canada*, 1980, Table III, Catalogue no. 74-401.

[18]Ibid., at 17.

[19]"Unrestricted" means not excluded from membership by type (part-time) or category (non-office) of employment. See supra footnote 17, at 25-26. In addition, most members are granted immediate coverage; that is, no probationary period is required before employers will make vested contributions on behalf of employees. See supra footnote 3, Vol. VI, at 28.

[20]Only 365 small villages and townships did not participate in OMERS. In addition, some rather large regions (such as Metro Toronto) opted to develop their own closed municipal plans—supra footnote 3, Vol. VI, at 2. For a detailed description of the Type 1, Type 2, and Type 3 supplements

(Continued on next page.)

**Table 12.1   Pension Plans and Members
by Type of Employer, 1980**

Public sector	Plans	Per cent of total	Members	Per cent of total	Per cent of Subsector
Municipal	534	3.7	349,956	7.8	17.8
Provincial	109	0.7	1,071,265	23.9	54.3
Federal.....................	43	0.3	548,517	12.3	28.0
Non-Canadian	4	—	193	—	—
Total	690	4.7	1,969,931	44.0	100.1
Private sector					
Incorporated companies	11,829	81.1	1,696,285	37.9	67.7
Partnerships	301	2.1	12,683	13.0	0.5
Cooperatives................	279	1.9	36,701	0.8	1.5
Associations	663	4.6	25,070	0.6	1.0
Multi-economies	250	1.7	632,853	14.1	25.3
Other	574	3.9	101,806	2.3	4.1
Total	13,856	95.3	2,505,498	56.0	100.1
Grand total	14,586	100.0	4,475,429	100.0	—

Source: Statistics Canada, *Pension Plans in Canada,* 1980, Catalogue no. 74-401.

PENSION FUND MANAGEMENT

FUNDAMENTAL SOCIOECONOMIC FORCES

Until recently, municipal pension fund administration has required little more than perfunctory attention.[21] As long as the size of the work force, benefit levels, and the number of retirees did not grow too rapidly, and the jurisdiction's financial condition remained stable, the need for strict management and cost control seemed unimportant. Now, however, a wide variety of external and internal forces have been operating to alter significantly an otherwise relatively stable pension environment, and to draw considerable attention to the management of public-sector pensions. Among the most important of the external forces are demographic trends, retirement preferences, and economic conditions. Internal forces include public employment trends, budgetary limits, and disclosure principles. Each will be discussed in turn.

Demographic Trends

It has become apparent to pension fund administrators that the decline in the birth rate during the late 1960s coupled with the aging demographic bulge

[20]Continued

available to OMERS participants, the interested reader is directed to CUPE Research Department, *OMERS Supplementary Agreements*, as of February 4, 1982 (Ottawa: CUPE, 1982), 2-4. Briefly, Type 1 offers a pension based on the basic formula for credited past service; Type 2 offers a fixed amount of pension for credited past service based on earnings before the date of the supplementary agreement; and Type 3 offers an unreduced pension on early retirement.

[21]Jump, supra footnote 2, at 78.

Table 12.2   Province-Wide Pension Plans for Local Government Employees

Province	Name of plan	Type of benefit	Coverage
British Columbia	B.C. Municipal Superannuation Plan	Defined benefit—highest five-year average earnings	Employees of cities, districts, towns, villages, regional district hospitals, school districts, regional colleges, or other employers covered by the Pension (Municipal) Act
Alberta	Local Authorities Pension Plan (LAPP)	Defined benefit—highest five consecutive years earnings	Employees of cities, towns, villages, counties, municipalities, school districts or divisions, hospitals, or public service bodies
Saskatchewan	Municipal Employees' Superannuation Plan	Defined benefit—highest five-year average earnings	Employees of participating municipalities, town, villages, school board, telephone boards, health region boards, and community colleges
Manitoba	Municipal Employees' Benefit Plan	Defined benefit—highest seven-year average earnings	Employees of all municipalities in Manitoba and many quasi-municipal employees
Ontario	Ontario Municipal Employees' Retirement System (OMERS)	Defined benefit—best five-year average earnings	Employees of municipalities, school boards, public utility commissions, children's aid societies, libraries
New Brunswick	New Brunswick Municipal Employees' Pension Plan	Defined benefit— highest five-year average earnings	Employees of participating municipalities

Source: CUPE, *Brief to the Royal Commission for the Status of Pensions in Nova Scotia* (Halifax: CUPE, 1981), 26, Table 3.

Table 12.3   Canada's Aging Population, 1921 to 2021

Year	Age category		
	0-14	*15-64*	*65 +*
1921[a]	34.4	60.8	4.8
1931	31.6	62.8	5.5
1941	26.9	66.4	6.7
1951	30.3	61.9	7.8
1961	34.0	58.4	7.6
1971	29.6	62.3	8.1
1981	23.8	66.9	9.3
2001[b]	22.8	66.4	10.9
2011	22.1	66.6	11.3
2021	22.0	64.2	13.9

[a] 1921-81   Statistics Canada - actual. [b] 2001-21   Statistics Canada - projected with medium fertility rate and net migration of 60,000.

Source: Ontario, *Issues in Pension Policy*, Treasury Studies, Staff Paper no. 16 (Toronto: Ministry of Treasury and Economics, 1979), 23-25.

known as the baby boom will lead to a shrinking work force required to support an expanding retired population.[22] Table 12.3 illustrates the potential magnitude of this change: in 1921, less than 5 per cent of Canada's population was over 65; whereas by 2021, the figure is expected to reach 14 per cent. Obviously, this problem of supporting pensioners has been created by the failure of the public sector to fund their pension plans fully and simply to pay pensions out of current revenues.

Retirement Preferences

A trend toward earlier retirement, as evidenced by the normal retiring age of 60 in the public sector, coupled with advanced medical technology that promotes longevity, certainly will require municipalities to provide pensionable benefits for longer-than-past-average retirement spans. The rise in union militancy, furthermore, has created a demand for improved pensions and municipalities may soon be under pressure to index fully their local pension plans.[23]

Economic Conditions

Close to double digit inflation in recessionary times placed added strain on the already stretched pension dollar, encouraging local government employees to

[22]See Ontario, Ministry of Treasury and Economics, *Demographic and Economic Aspects of Canada's Aging Population in Issues in Pension Policy*, staff paper (Toronto: the Ministry, 1979). See also, Economic Council of Canada, *One in Three: Pensions for Canadians to 2030* (Ottawa: Supply and Services, 1979).

[23]The federal pension fund has been established in almost total disregard for its total cost, notes Geoffrey N. Calvert, in *Pensions and Survival: the Coming Crisis of Money and Retirement* (Toronto: Maclean-Hunter, 1977), 130. He states that the cumulative effect of allowing contributions to cease after 35 years, with early retirement at the age of 55 after 30 years of service, and no-limit indexing, is to produce a situation in which there can be a staggering increase in costs over which management would have little effective control.

demand even more secure inflation-proof measures in the overall pension design. No longer will ad hoc adjustments do. Automatic escalation with the consumer price index may soon be the minimally acceptable method to insulate pension systems from prolonged inflationary effects.[24]

Public Employment Trends

Given the growth in municipal employment and the mandatory nature of pension membership, too few municipalities have carefully assessed the growth in pensions and the impact that this will have on local governments' budgets in the not too distant future.

Budgetary Limits

Many municipalities facing tight budget constraints have chosen to defer current wage payments to labour to future time periods through the use of more extensive pension provisions. While this strategy may circumvent financial constraints in the short run, it only serves to escalate the cost of future commitments. In fact, few municipalities keep sight of the true cost of the labour services they employ, simply because they notice only current payments as they come due.[25]

Disclosure Principles

Until recently, actuarial soundness and the principles designed to disclose such information were left, by and large, to the discretion of the municipality. Most local governments fund their pensions on a pay-as-you-go principle, ignoring any total asset and liability calculations. Recent legislation has tightened reporting and disclosure measures, but the ambiguous nature of many forecasting methods currently utilized enables municipalities to keep future total costs indeterminate.[26]

The above forces suggest that municipal pension plans are under considerable pressure. This raises two important questions: are the programs managed in the most efficient and economical manner?—and most crucial—will benefits promised today be affordable by the contributing governments tomorrow? Owing to the absence of extensive research and an easily accessible data base, much of the research to date has been of the case-study variety, heavily descriptive and inventory-like.[27] This ground-work, though perhaps mundane, actually lays the basis on which to assess the more complex questions of cost and actuarial soundness, since it is often the type of benefit provided that explains why pension costs are rising so rapidly. Some of the most generous benefit packages available are to be found in PSPPs and these will serve to escalate pension costs.

---

[24]Supra footnote 1, at 386.

[25]For a further discussion, the interested reader is directed to Roy W. Bahl and Bernard Jump, "The Budgetary Implications of Rising Employee Retirements System Costs" (September 1974), 27 *National Tax Journal* 479-90.

[26]Bernard Jump, Jr., "Evaluating the Financial Condition of Public Employee Pension Plans: Some Guidelines for the Unwary" (February 1978), *Governmental Finance* 3-9.

[27]Gene E. Mumy, "The Economics of Local Government Pensions and Pension Funding" (June 1978), 86 *Journal of Political Economy* 517-27.

PENSION COSTS: A SURVEY OF PLAN FEATURES

The question of cost is much more critical for public-sector pension plans than for those in the private sector, for in the latter the cost is ultimately a market decision and a matter strictly between the employer and employee. In the public sector, however, similar constraints do not exist and the cost is of interest to the taxpayer who ultimately must pay the bill. The public, therefore, has a valid interest in determining whether such costs are reasonable and whether proper administration has assured the orderly accounting of funds. Cost is of central concern here for it indicates how much must be paid for promised benefits and whether such benefits are affordable.[28] There is some evidence to support the contention that the costs of public-sector pension plans exceed those of the private sector. At least one study identified a distinct trend in the public sector toward increased pension costs as a percentage of payroll, and concluded that increased unfunded actuarial liabilities meant insufficient control was being exercised by the public sector.[29] Recent data from a Statistics Canada (discussed below) report, *Pension Plans in Canada* (1980), corroborate these results.

In attempting to compare the costs of private- and public-sector pensions, it may be useful to assess plan features from a "cost-rating" perspective.[30] The majority of plans will not be able to afford many, if any, costly items (such as, final average formula, indexation, early retirement without actuarial reduction, survivor benefits, and reciprocal transfer rights). Detailed analysis of the public and private plan features, however, reveals a definite advantage in most of these more lucrative provisions for the public sector. There are, in fact, some rather striking differences in benefits ranging from provisions as simple as retirement age to provisions as complex as indexing for inflation. Each will be discussed in turn.

As Table 12.4 suggests one of the more curious differences is that of normal age of retirement. Over one-quarter of all public-sector employees normally retire at age 60, whereas less than 5 per cent of private-sector plan members are permitted this option.[31] Only the provinces of Quebec and Saskatchewan still require public servants to attain an age of 65 with 10 years of service before retirement benefits commence, while Alberta and New Brunswick require a retirement age of 65 with 5 years of service. In all other provinces, 60 is the normal retirement age, provided a minimum of 10 years of service has passed.[32]

---

[28]The difference between costs for accounting purposes and costs for funding purposes is set out in detail in Accountants International Study Group, no. 18, *Accounting for Pension Costs: Current Practices in Canada, the United Kingdom and the United States* (New York: AISG, 1977), paragraph 12. Cost determination is concerned solely with accounting, whereas funding is a cash-flow matter. According to the accounting firm of Clarkson Gordon, the pension cost accounting problem involves estimating the ultimate costs for which the employer will become obligated under the plan, and allocating those costs in a rational way to preretirement years so as to provide a fair measure of deferred wage expenses year-by-year. See Ross M. Skinner, *Pension Accounting: A Research Report* (Toronto: Clarkson Gordon, 1980), 12.

[29]Supra footnote 3, Vol. VI, at 121.

[30]This replicates the method adopted by supra footnote 3, Vol. VI.

[31]Furthermore, it was found that the likelihood of early retirement is much greater for those with high retirement income plans. See Economic Council of Canada, supra footnote 22, at 66.

[32]Supra footnote 3, Vol. VI, at 60.

Table 12.4   Normal Retirement Age, 1980

Age	Male		Female	
	Public	Private	Public	Private
	per cent			
60	25.7	2.3	24.4	4.8
65	60.1	92.9	63.8	85.9

Source: Supra Table 12.1, at 82-83, Table 18.

Necessarily, therefore, less than two-thirds of public servants actually retire at age 65, while virtually all (90 per cent) private plan members must attain the age of 65 before they can collect pension benefits. At the municipal level, the pensionable benefit period is further increased for those plans that provide a past service option. In the province of Ontario, for example, employees in the OMERS plan are credited with service prior to the date of joining the plan.[33] Although the lower retirement age in a number of public plans may be viewed as a significant gain by members, it more importantly represents a substantial increase in the area of cost. In addition to the obvious extension of the payable retirement income period, an early retirement age means a shorter period for pension fund accruals, so pension accumulations actually may be lower. Under such circumstances, the pressures on government programs to subsidize incomes are increased, while the tax base is reduced.[34] While these concerns may not yet present a serious threat to pension fund management, early retirement coupled with an increasing life span will force future governments to provide pensions for an even longer-than-average retirement period. Since the trend toward earlier retirement is expected to continue for at least another decade, municipal pension plans must make the proper adjustments now if they are to be actuarially sound in the future.[35]

Related to retirement age are the issues of early retirement and special retirement. Both items appear to be more liberally provided in the public rather than private sector. For example, early retirement (that is, retirement before the normal age requirement with a reduced pension) is permitted more frequently at the employee's option in the public sector (20.5 per cent as compared to 13.9 per cent in the private sector). Furthermore, Table 12.5 illustrates that only two-thirds of public-sector plans require mutual consent for an early retirement request to be valid; whereas in the private sector, over three-quarters of the plans require both employer and employee consent.

In the case of special retirement, where the right to retire before normal retirement age is accompanied by a fully accrued pension with no reduction, public pension plan members need only attain an age of between 55 and 60 to be eligible—much lower than the 60 to 62 age range requirement in the private

[33]This is known as the Type 1 option, chosen most often by police, fire, and management groups. See CUPE, supra footnote 20, at 2.

[34]Supra footnote 3, Vol. III, at 109.

[35]J.E. Pesando, *The Elimination of Mandatory Retirement: An Economic Perspective*, Discussion Paper Series (Toronto: Ontario Economic Council, 1979).

Table 12.5 ˙ Early Retirement, 1980

	Public	Private
	per cent	
Employee's option	20.5	13.9
Employer's option	5.9	4.9
Mutual consent	66.5	77.7

Source: Supra Table 12.1, at 84, Table 19.

Table 12.6   Special Retirement, 1980

	Public	Private
Conditions		
Age	55-60	60-62
Service	30	10-35
No reduction in benefits		
percentage of plans	58%	30%

Source: Supra Table 12.1, at 45-46.

sector (Table 12.6).[36] As of 1980, an overwhelming 58 per cent of all public-sector plans provided for special retirement with unreduced pension privileges, compared to only 30 per cent in the private sector (Table 12.6). Such liberal provisions as unreduced retirement income, when years of service (and therefore contributions) have been lowered substantially, place additional demands on existing pension funds that cannot continue unabated forever. This is especially true at the municipal level, where special retirement privileges are granted to almost all police and firefighters who seek consideration on the grounds that stress-related work and loss of physical requirements endanger the public after the working age of 60.[37] In Ontario, almost all of the 12 per cent of OMERS members who chose this option in 1982 were from police or firefighting groups. Furthermore, since this particular option permits retirement 10 years before normal retirement, employees with the supplementary package may retire as early as the age of 50 on full pension, assuming 30 years of service has been attained.[38] Clearly, such groups have coverage far superior to that of other municipal employees, let alone the private sector. While special circumstances may be evident, this full-pension option creates demands for at least equal treatment from other local government workers.[39] Such preferential benefit schemes, because they are so widely subscribed, place additional pressures on municipal budgets.

A further provision that increases pension costs arises in the area of death benefits. While most pension plans provide some form of benefit on death,

---

[36]Supra footnote 17, at 45.

[37]Supra footnote 3, Vol. VI, at 68.

[38]CUPE, supra footnote 20, at 4.

[39]Supra footnote 3, Summary Report, at 68.

Table 12.7   Pension Benefits on Death Before Retirement, 1980

	Public	Private
	per cent	
No death benefit..	0.2	29.8
Widow's pension	70.9	23.9
Some form of refund of		
employee contribution	28.7	42.6

Source: Supra Table 12.1, at 85, Table 20.

Table 12.8   Pension Benefits on Death After Retirement, 1980

	Public	Private
	per cent	
No death benefit..	0.9	22.4
Widow's pension	69.6	21.8

Source: Supra Table 12.1, at 86, Table 21.

public-sector pensions appear more liberal in their provisions. For over 70 per cent of the members in public-sector pension plans, death prior to the retirement age brings a pension for the widow (Table 12.7). In private-sector plans, equivalent benefits are provided for only 24 per cent of plan members. Private-sector plans, more often, tend to provide a return of contributions (some combination of employee and employer) in a single lump-sum payment. The tendency to provide a continuous pension for widows in the public sector is indeed a costly venture for local governments.

Differences between death benefits provided by both sectors is also apparent in instances where death occurs after retirement. Again, approximately 70 per cent of all public-sector plan members are entitled to the widow's pension; whereas, fewer than 22 per cent of private-sector plans provide this benefit (Table 12.8). Furthermore, an additional 22 per cent of all private-sector plans are devoid of any death benefits. Although some interprovincial variation is found in the size of the pension and in the number of members that constitutes a family (spouse or spouse and children) to whom death benefits are paid in public-sector pension plans, fewer than 1 per cent of all plan members have no provision for death benefits.[40] Such universal coverage coupled with the extensive widow's pension provisions, certainly render this feature far more costly in the public than in the private-sector pension system.

Perhaps the most contentious and expensive pension issue is that which relates to the indexing of future retirement income. Some private-sector plans attempt to inflation-proof their pensions through the use of final earnings or best-average earnings when calculating the pension, since few can afford to provide contractually for the escalation of pensions after the employee retires.[41]

---

[40]Supra footnote 3, Vol. VI, at 61.

[41]Supra footnote 17, at 61. Even in this respect, however, private-sector employees are disadvantaged, since only 31 per cent of plan members are in a final earnings plan compared to almost 96 per cent of all public-sector plan members.

Table 12.9   Automatic Escalation of Pension Benefits, 1980

	Membership			
	Public		Private	
	members	*per cent*	*members*	*per cent*
Full indexing (CPI)	940,811	47.8	2,280	0.1
Partial indexing	347,579	17.6	119,598	4.8
Total	1,288,390	65.4	121,878	4.9
No indexing	681,541	34.6	383,620	95.1
Grand total	1,969,931	100.0	505,498	100.0

Source: Supra Table 12.1, at 58, Table XXV.

The public sector, however, provides a glaring exception to this rule. Over two-thirds of its pension plan members receive some type of automatic escalation in pension income. For almost 50 per cent of all pension plan members, this comes in the form of full indexing based on the upward movement of the Consumer Price Index (CPI).[42] As Table 12.9 indicates, the private sector, in direct contrast, provides similar indexing for less than 1 per cent (.1 per cent) of its plan members, and partial indexing for under 5 per cent of all eligible members.[43]

The actuarial implications of such promised benefits along with insufficient compensatory increases in pension contributions are worth noting. *The Report of the Royal Commission on the Status of Pensions in Ontario* (RRCSP) estimates that the nominal dollar cost of indexing public-sector pensions in the province of Ontario (taken as 4 per cent of payroll, rising to 5.3 per cent of payroll) will increase almost 14-fold by 2005, rising from $305 million in 1980 to $4.2 billion.[44] In an inflationary environment, however, the failure to index may be unjust. The contribution of the employee or those on his behalf (or the benefits promised if the plan is unfunded) provides a given level of real income on retirement that should be maintained. If this is not the case, then someone—taxpayer, local government, or the company providing the plan—is benefitting because they acquired past services that will be paid for eventually with inflation-eroded dollars. Even fully funded plans properly invested and operated in the absence of unanticipated inflation provide inflation adjusted (indexed) returns. Hence, fully and accurately indexed pension plans, by themselves, do not increase the real cost of resources used up. Increases in real costs arise when pension plans are broadened to include a wider group of

[42]Exceptions to the rule include Alberta (which makes annual increases with CPI, but not automatically), Saskatchewan (where ad hoc increases are legislatively possible), and British Columbia (where automatic adjustments are made quarterly). See supra footnote 3, Vol. VI, at 60 for details.

[43]An indeterminate amount of private sector plans occasionally do provide ad hoc adjustments to the current monthly pension payments but with no guarantee that the practice will continue in the future. In such cases, the additional cost is at least partially borne by current employee contributions, depending on the needs of the retirees and the financial situation of the employer. Supra footnote 17, at 59.

[44]Supra footnote 3, Vol. VI, at 187, based on a pay-as-you-go contribution basis until 2005, but if inflation is greater or retirement age lower than the assumptions used, cost estimates rise.

employees or expanded in terms of benefits per employee so that the cost of providing these additional benefits (in total) absorbs a greater share of society's real resources.

In the municipal sector, few plans provide the full and automatic escalation found in federal and provincial public-service pension plans. Exceptions to this occur in British Columbia where local pension plans are adjusted in line with the CPI up to a maximum of 8 per cent.[45] Many municipal plans, however, currently allow for some form of ad hoc indexing adjustment as is the case in Ontario.

A final plan feature, and one that appears to be unique to the public sector is that of transferring rights for pensions. Reciprocal transfer agreements are considered advantageous since they increase portability.[46] The ability to transfer pension service credits from one plan to another through such agreements is, in both theory and practice, much easier in the public than in the private sector because of homogeneity of the employer. In fact, reciprocal transfer agreements are virtually non-existent in the private sector. Agreements exist among most municipalities in almost all provinces, permitting the transfer of double contributions (that is, both the employer and employee portion) with a nominal rate of interest.

Before concluding that the more attractive features of most public-service pension plans are supported financially by employer contributions alone, it may be useful to review the limited evidence on the breakdown between employer and employee contributions to pension plans in Canada. In all pension plans, it has been estimated that the average employee contribution rate in Canada is 4.2 per cent of salary, and the average employer cost, 9.9 per cent for a total of 14.1 per cent.[47] A provincial breakdown for public-sector plans is difficult to ascertain, since few provinces publish such information on a disaggregated scale. The Province of Ontario, however, has estimated figures for its major PSPPs and these are reproduced in Table 12.10.[48]

On the basis of the percentages in Table 12.10, the RRCSP concluded that the public sector was providing better benefits than many private-sector plans for larger employers, and was paying a higher percentage of payroll costs toward the provision of these pension benefits.[49] A forecast of the extent to which these costs could be expected to change over the next few decades also was undertaken. Based on the projections that the total number of Ontario public-sector employees will more than double in the next 25 years, that the municipal sector will experience greater growth than others (almost 3-fold in size), that prices will

---

[45]Conversation with CUPE official.

[46]See supra footnote 3, Chapter 8, for a description of portability.

[47]Supra footnote 3, Vol. VI, at 146.

[48]Supra footnote 3, Vol. VI, is devoted entirely to pension plans of public employees in Ontario and provides extensive detail on descriptions of plan benefits, plan memberships, funded status, and cost methods. While it does cover most of the 127 Ontario public sector plans, it deals mainly with the 6 largest plans which contain more than 84 per cent of all plan members in Ontario. Two notable exceptions to the cost figures listed were the Toronto Firefighters' Plan at 21.6 per cent and the City of Toronto Civic Employees' Plan at 26.5 per cent. Both incurred large deficiency payments as a result of past service costs that came due through benefit improvements.

[49]Supra footnote 3, Vol. VI, at 146.

Table 12.10   Total Payments into PSPPs by the Province of Ontario
as a Percentage of Pensionable Payroll, 1977[a]

Pension plan	Per cent of payroll
Public Service Superannuation Fund (PSSF)	16.9
Teachers Superannuation Fund (TSF)	20.8
Hospitals of Ontario Pension Plan (HOPP)	13.7
Ontario Hydro Pension Plan (OHPP)	20.5
Workman's Compensation Board (WCB)	15.1

[a]See supra footnote 49.

Source: Supra footnote 3, Vol. VI.

rise to 3 times their present level, and that payroll costs will multiply by 5 times in the next 25 years, the commission concluded that pension contributions will increase from an average of 13.7 per cent to 14.8 per cent of the public sector's pensionable payroll.[50]

Recent concern over the problems faced by municipalities in meeting their budgetary commitments has generated additional concern over the proportion of local budgets devoted to pension plan obligations. The costs of pension plans must be controlled if they are to be kept within manageable limits. If not, undue burdens will be placed on local taxpayers. Unfortunately, to exercise effective cost control is not an easy task since few (almost none) public-sector plans come under direct government control.[51] Most employees and provincial governments are separated by school boards, special purpose commissions, municipalities, and hospitals. At the local level in Ontario, the cost of the basic OMERS plan is determined by the OMERS board and a set percentage of payroll is charged to each member municipality. Consequently, such pension costs are borne directly by each participating municipality, and they appear as expenditures that must be financed out of municipal tax levies or provincial grants.[52] Finally, additional costs of any supplementary program, such as early retirement, are charged directly to the individual municipality receiving that benefit, therefore each municipality in fact bears the burden of each expensive option chosen (selected) by its employees.[53]

In the case of many municipal plans, however, administration responsibility does not lie with the employer. In the case of OMERS, an 11-member board, consisting of 7 employees, 2 elected representatives, and 2 civil servants administer the plan. This separation of responsibility from the employer creates special problems for the control of pension costs. In an attempt to remedy this problem, most provinces in Canada recently have established central coordinating and control mechanisms for public employee pension funds. In the last four or five years steps have been taken to strengthen the existing control

[50]These projections are exclusive of CPP contributions but include indexing. See supra footnote 3, Vol. VI, at 149.

[51]In addition, at least 9 factors were identified which present formidable difficulties when an attempt is made to determine the costs of PSPP. See supra footnote 3, Summary Report, at 62-63.

[52]Supra footnote 3, Vol. VI, at 148.

[53]Ibid.

mechanisms in Quebec, where consolidation of many small PSPPs has produced the appropriate measure of financial awareness and responsibility; in British Columbia where the establishment of a central board has been the mechanism through which legislative changes and cost controls are initiated; and in Ontario where a management board provides the appropriate channel through which public service pension guidelines have been established.[54]

PENSION FUNDING

The financing of the above-mentioned costs is one of the more difficult areas in the management of municipal retirement systems. In fact, pension funding (that is, the setting aside of monies now for payment of promised benefits in the future), is one of the more contentious issues, since there exists no one correct method of financing.[55] At one extreme are the advocates of pay-as-you-go (pay-go) funding who argue that the ongoing governmental tax base is sufficient to generate the necessary revenues for promised benefits. At the other end of the spectrum are those concerned about the future ability of the government to meet pension obligations unless a disciplined approach to prefunding has been undertaken. Pay-go proponents question the need to stock large reserves when such assets could be put to better use.[56] Accountants respond with the claim that good accounting practices represent security and real assets provide the base on which to rely should cash flow difficulties arise. Oddly enough, if the solvency of funds or security of promise were the only point at issue, pay-as-you-go funding probably would be an acceptable method for financing public-service pension plans. Full funding, rather than pay-go financing, however, is necessary to ensure effective cost control. To many municipalities, the basic appeal of the pay-as-you-go approach is that it permits generous commitments to be made to local employees with low visibility to the taxpayers.[57] Thus, one of the strongest arguments in favour of fully funding PSPPs is that such funding imposes a discipline on local authorities who are then forced to assess accurately the cost of their promised benefits.

The type of pension plan that is utilized, quite often, will determine its funded status. A defined-contribution plan is a promise for a contribution rather than a pension (that is, whatever the contribution with interest will purchase at retirement) and is always fully funded. A retirement system that recognizes accrued liabilities falls under the general heading of reserve funding, and sets the employer free of all future liability once its contribution has been made. With this method, the risk is borne by the employee whose benefits depend only on how much has accumulated in his or her account and how wisely the contributions have been invested.[58] Defined-benefit plans, on the other

---

[54]Ibid., at 216. As of November 1976, disparities in funding methods and actuarial assumptions were to be reduced through adherence to guidelines by a management board in Ontario.

[55]John E. Petersen, ''Pension Fund Management,'' in J. Richard Aronson and Eli Schwartz, eds., *Management Policies in Local Government Finance* (Washington, D.C.: International City Management Association, 1981), 367-88, at 381.

[56]For a fuller discussion of the controversy, see supra footnote 3, Vol. VI, at 69.

[57]Supra footnote 23, at 135.

[58]Supra footnote 55, at 379.

Table 12.11   Ontario Public Sector Pension Plans: Assets and Liabilities by Subsector, 1977

Subsector	Assets	Liabilities	Ratio (a/l)
	millions of $		
Provincial government	1,347.2	1,866.5	.72
Municipal government	1,684.6	1,909.9	.88
Health	659.7	757.2	.87
Provincial utility	957.7	1,158.3	.83
Education	2,960.2	4,747.0	.62
Total	7,609.4	10,438.9	.73

Source: Supra footnote 3, Vol. VI, at 90, Table 3.

hand, run the risk of becoming actuarially unsound at any time because pension credits are determined at the outset, while contributions are determined later through extensive actuarial formulae. Under a defined benefit plan, rarely do the calculations accurately match employee contribution rates with the true costs of the defined benefits.

In the municipal sector most pension plans are of the defined-benefit variety, with pension credits based on a latest career earnings average. This is advantageous to the municipal employee particularly in years of rapid inflation where the latest years of earnings generally will be the highest years of earnings. This, however, also becomes the more expensive plan from the viewpoint of the employer (in this case the government), who must pay pension benefits that are much higher than they would be otherwise.[59] The result is the accumulation of liabilities not offset fully by contributions normally set aside to help pay promised future benefits. In fact, in recent years, many analysts have become alarmed by the large and unexpected increases in unfunded liabilities revealed in the actuarial valuations of PSPPs.[60] Table 12.11 indicates that Ontario public-sector plans overall were only 73 per cent funded, ranging from less than two-thirds funding in the education sector to just over 85 per cent in the municipal and health sectors. While the municipal sector appears to be reasonably well funded, Table 12.12 illustrates the wide variation in the assets-to-liabilities ratio across various plans: the province-wide OMERS plan is more than fully funded, but the two closed Metropolitan Toronto plans (Metro Toronto Police and Metro Toronto Civic) are at best only one-half funded. Comparative ratios of assets to liabilities for municipal plans in other provinces are not readily available. The under-funded status of plans in Saskatchewan, however, was sufficient to warrant conversion from defined-benefit to defined-contribution pension plans.[61]

---

[59]Ibid., at 360.

[60]It should be remembered that estimated actuarial soundness and other financial aspects of PSPP have been seriously restricted by data inadequacies. At best, therefore, the figures listed below should not be considered actual statements of funded status but rather indications of relative funded positions. For the host of associated problems, see ibid., at 381.

[61]Supra footnote 3, Vol. VI, at 65.

**Table 12.12   Ontario Provincial and Municipal Sector Pension Plans:
Assets to Liabilities Ratio, 1977**

Plan	Ratio of assets/liabilities
Teacher's superannuation	.66
OMERS	1.17
Ontario Hydro	.99
Hospital Workers of Ontario	.91
Toronto Transit Commission	.81
Metro Toronto civic	.47
Metro Toronto police	.50
City of Ottawa	.97

Source: Supra footnote 3, Vol. VI, at 88-89, Table 2.

The economic implications of underfunding can be significant. On the most direct level, underfunding threatens the credibility of promised pensions. Potential recipients are harmed to the benefit of past taxpayers who received labour services but who now default on the promised labour compensation. Further inequities arise if mandatory payment shifts the pension burden onto current taxpayers in order to pay for past underfundings. In such cases past taxpayers become the beneficiaries at the expense of future taxpayers who are required to produce sufficient monies to cover all unfunded liabilities.[62]

SUMMARY

By any set of standards, public-sector pension plans including those at the local level tend to be more comprehensive than similar plans in the private sector. For example, when compared with the private sector, a higher proportion of all public-sector employees are members of a pension plan. Similarly, the extent of benefits and coverage tends to be greater in public than in private pension plans.

Currently, municipal retirement schemes represent one of the largest and fastest-growing budgetary expenses of local governments. Given the impact that rapidly changing demographic and socioeconomic factors have had on membership levels, retirement patterns, and benefit levels, it is highly unlikely that this trend will be reversed. This is especially true since too many municipal governments, in light of the multi-generational nature of pension systems, approach their pension commitments without regard for long-range implications. The current underfunded status of many local plans permits the true value or cost of pension obligations to be concealed too easily and deferred from present to future generations of taxpayers.[63] If municipal pension liabilities do represent to the taxpayers an invisible means of financing municipal expenditures, or if municipalities assume that underfunded pension plans ultimately will be bailed out by higher levels of government, then imposition of funding restrictions by higher levels of government may increase the welfare of

---

[62]R.P. Inman, "Municipal Pension Funding: A Theory and Some Evidence. A Comment," supra footnote 6, at 179.

[63]A statement made by the Council of the Canadian Institute of Actuaries, in supra footnote 23, at 141.

municipal residents.[64] At the most direct level, more care must be exercised in the determination of contribution rates in defined-benefit plans so that both employers and employees are obliged to face the true cost of plan features, and all parties can judge their affordability. While statements such as "it is the high cost of public employee pensions which is bankrupting municipalities"[65] are probably extreme, a more systematic approach to pension fund management is essential to ensure that plans are costed out accurately and that financial responsibility is apportioned equitably.

---

[64]Supra footnote 6, at 169.

[65]Robert H. Edelstein, *An Economic Analysis of the Public Sector Funding of Large City Pension Systems*, Draft Final Report prepared for the National Science Foundation (Philadelphia: Winklevoss, 1978), V.2.

13

Accounting and Budgeting Issues

LOCAL GOVERNMENT ACCOUNTING

Because of the rapid increase in local government expenditures over the past decade and the ensuing increase in the concern over sources of revenue for financing these expenditures, financial accounting and budgeting at the local level have assumed a new degree of importance. Local politicians, in their attempt to placate angry constituents or to provide information of an understandable and meaningful nature to enquiring citizens, have demanded frequently that local officials provide basic accounting information in a careful, clear, and intelligible fashion. Unfortunately, this demand almost never has been satisfied. Many municipal accounting statements remain unintelligible to the vast majority of local taxpayers. As such, local residents are unable to determine whether they are receiving an adequate level, quality, and range of services. Not only are the local citizenry unable to evaluate local statements, but the more professional and sophisticated of our accounting experts also experience difficulties. For instance, the general lack of any clearly defined set of accepted accounting principles (including the unevenness displayed in the inclusion of fixed assets in the balance sheet and in the application of depreciation rules) and the impossibility of understanding how reserves and reserve funds are covered or accounted for from a reading of most of the published financial statements reflect a few of the issues that permeate the field. Before pursuing these issues and others in detail, one must remember that the ultimate criterion for success in communicating financial information is the usefulness of the information provided and not the reporting process itself.[1]

DEVELOPMENT OF LOCAL ACCOUNTING SYSTEMS

The development of local government accounting systems in Canada has fallen behind the development of similar systems in both the private sector and senior levels of government. This development has revolved around the publication of manuals or handbooks on the practice of municipal financial accounting or reporting[2] "rather than on an examination of the underlying principles and objectives."[3] The whole question of what "ought to be" or what is theoretically desirable seldom has been pursued. Instead, attention at the local level has been devoted entirely to the practice or application of certain procedures or rules as they relate to local governments. As a result, there appears to be very little in the

---

[1]William W. Holder, "Local Government Accounting," in J. Richard Aronson and Eli Schwartz, eds., *Management Policies in Local Government Finance* (Washington, D.C.: International City Management Association, 1981), 414-32, at 416.

[2]See Ontario, Municipal Finance Branch, Ministry of Municipal Affairs and Housing, *Municipal Financial Reporting Handbook* (Toronto: the Ministry, 1981).

[3]A. Beedle, *Accounting for Local Government in Canada: The State of the Art* (Vancouver: Canadian Certified General Accountants Research Foundation, 1981), 11.

way of "generally accepted accounting principles" (GAAP) for local governments in Canada. Any principles that have evolved, as a result of the intergovernmental conferences dealing with this topic, tend to be incomplete and lacking authority.[4]

A perusal of local audited financial statements indicates that these financial statements have indeed complied with generally accepted accounting principles. For most readers or users, this suggests that local governments have been responsible, honest, and complied with specific statutory or legal requirements in conducting their financial affairs. To most of these same readers (professionals and laymen), however, this statement is meaningless—what are generally accepted accounting principles and what are the basic objectives of a local government accounting system? Who is the authoritative body responsible for establishing proper accounting procedures? Unfortunately, there are no clear-cut or positive answers to these questions, answers that must be available if one is to articulate a carefully planned and delineated accounting system. Perhaps the best that can be concluded is that local government accounting has developed in a haphazard manner adopting standards or concepts primarily established for use in the profit-oriented private sector. Local government accounting standards, moreover, have shown considerable variation both within and among provinces.

OBJECTIVES OF ACCOUNTING SYSTEMS

The basic objective of any accounting system is to provide financial information in a form that allows users to make informed and intelligent decisions. This objective is achieved for investors and creditors in the private sector; however, the "needs of users of financial information for local governments are different from those of commercial enterprises,"[5] and, therefore, the accounting principles employed in the private sector are frequently inappropriate for local governments.

The potential users of local government accounting information are more wide ranging and diversified than are those in the private sector. These include investment creditors and bond raters, other creditors, suppliers, granting agencies, constituents, employees, legislators, and managers.[6] Unfortunately, the current presentation of financial information is geared to those who directly use it; namely, internal users, provincial overseeing bodies, and statistics gathering agencies. Local officials will argue that the provision of data in a form understandable to other users is largely a waste of time, for these individuals are not interested enough to justify either the time or cost of collecting, compiling, and diseminating the information. While there may be some truth in this statement, it is likely to be equally true that many potential users have not shown an interest previously because they have been unable to decipher the available financial information. Consequently, if the data were improved, its usefulness would be extended. The fact that local governments are ultimately accountable

---

[4]Ibid.

[5]Allan R. Drebin, "Governmental vs. Commercial Accounting: The Issues" (November 1979), 8 *Governmental Finance* 3-8, at 4.

[6]For a more detailed description, see supra footnote 3, at 51-54.

to the voters also suggests that the data should be provided in a form that will allow individuals to make informed and intelligent decisions on a number of local issues. In other words, local governments have an obligation to alter the financial information that is provided in order to meet the needs of the potential users, particularly the local citizens who directly fund a large portion of the expenditures.

To facilitate the discussion of users and their respective financial information needs, it may be useful to categorize these users into the following groups: external users, internal users, and senior governments. Each of these will be considered separately.

External Users

This category of users (which includes constituents, creditors, suppliers, and others engaged in business transactions with the government) is external to the government and generally lacks any effective control over the type of financial information it receives. Their need for financial information is obvious for these users have either provided financial support for government services or have engaged in or are contemplating engaging in business transactions with the local government unit.

Since these individuals or organizations have no authority to specify the information they require, some generally accepted accounting principles need to be established (see discussion below). These principles are essential if users are to make intermunicipal comparisons over time and among communities. These principles, unfortunately, are often either loosely or poorly defined or do not provide information in an appropriate manner; for example, seldom is anything provided on performance budgeting[7]—a necessity if external users are to assess intelligently the unit cost, efficiency, and effectiveness of local programs or services. Many of these users are concerned with the maintenance of a financially healthy and viable community. Solvency and liquidity ratios do not provide this information alone. What is needed is some indication of the impact of current capital projects on future operating budgets; the ability of local governments to be able to draw on future resources (taxes, grants, and user charges) and the extent to which these revenue sources may be substituted for each other; and the impact of inflation on future expenditures and hence revenues needed to be collected. The list could go on and on but this brief recitation suffices in providing the reader with an indication of the deficiencies in this area.

Internal Users

This category includes all individuals engaged in the managerial and administrative functions of local government. Specifically, it includes policymakers, managers, and administrators. Their functions involve the planning, organization, execution, and evaluation of the diverse programs and services provided by local governments.

---

[7]For a thorough presentation of performance measures and how they might be derived for local governments, see Ontario, Municipal Budgets and Accounts Branch, Ministry of Municipal Affairs and Housing, *Performance Measurement for Municipalities* (Toronto: the Ministry, 1981).

The financial information needs of these users are more comprehensive than those of external users. Not only do policymakers and administrators require the same information as is available or should be available to the external users, in addition, they require cost estimates for alternative ways of achieving specific goals: cost/benefit analyses of proposed and existing programs, forecasts of current and capital expenditures, and the impact these will have on local revenue sources both in terms of the effect on rates or charges and their distributional impact on local residents. With the exception of a few larger urban or regional municipalities, impact studies, cost/benefit analyses, and careful forecasts are relatively new and virtually unexplored. As pressures mount for more account-ability and cost-efficient programs, it can only be hoped that a greater emphasis will be placed on more useful and relevant financial information—information that will assist in making local administrators and policymakers more respon-sive to users' desires and needs.

Provincial and Federal Governments

Since local governments are creatures of the provinces and since local govern-ments receive considerable grant support from their senior counterparts, there is both an expectation and a requirement that senior governments collect finan-cial, economic, and statistical information from their local underlings in a-consistent and uniform manner. Much of this information may be of little use to external users. Indeed, in its initial stages it may be of limited use even to the municipality actually supplying it. Once collected and compiled by a senior level of government, however, it may be very useful in indicating different trends in expenditure and revenue categories over time; differences in the extent to which municipalities support different expenditure programs; and differences in the dependence of municipalities on their various sources of revenue. Such inter-municipal comparisons on a uniform basis will allow municipalities, provincial analysts, and others to assess the feasibility, cost, level, and quality of current programs. If specific expenditures, costs, or dependence on a particular revenue source, tend to be out of line for one or some municipalities vis-à-vis other municipalities, this information may provide a base for pursuing a more in-depth analysis of the reasons for this difference—reasons that may generate improvements in the quantity and/or quality of local services or programs or improvements in the funding of these services or programs.

Provincial governments, in exercising their legal and statutory respon-sibilities also require information that will allow them to oversee and control certain activities of local governments. Provincial governments, for instance, require detailed information on capital budgets and debt capacities in order to ensure that local governments do not commit themselves to future excessive financial burdens. As well, other information is required as a basis for deter-mining the recipients of many grant programs. Equalization grants, for exam-ple, are established only after economic, financial, and statistical data have been supplied, compiled, and evaluated.

While much of this financial information may be necessary to control and protect the financial health and viability of local governments, some of it is unnecessary and even out-dated. Unfortunately, provincial or federal requests seldom change or when they do, the request is generally for additional information and not for a deletion of past information that no longer may be relevant. As such, the information format becomes institutionalized, creating costly and time-consuming paperwork that is difficult to justify and no longer useful.

Summary of Users

Given the wide-ranging needs of existing and potential users and the consequent costs of attempting to provide the financial information required to satisfy all of these needs, it may be reasonable to assume that local governments should be responsible only for serving the primary users. Unfortunately, there is no authoritative source that clearly defines the primary users nor are there any authoritative guidelines that can be followed in local government accounting.[8] Without these guidelines, "present Canadian practice. . .seems to stab at satisfying an undefined range of users and their needs without (with exceptions) specifically defining those users, their needs, or the objectives"[9] of the accounting information and reports.

Financial information provided through general-purpose financial statements is expected to meet the needs of internal users, external users, senior levels of governments, and statistics collecting agencies. As such, these statements attempt to serve many purposes simultaneously, including the separation of capital and operating funds; an indication of transfers between funds; a comparison of actual revenues and expenditures with budgeted revenues and expenditures; funds earmarked for future expenditures; information on expenditures by service or program; and the local government's financial position.[10] This diverse information frequently is provided in a general-purpose statement with the result that the information and published reports are generally incomprehensible to all but those with some knowledge of local government accounting. In reality, internal users and senior levels of government and their statistics collection agencies, all of whom can prescribe the financial information they require, have been able to comprehend most of the available information. External users, on the other hand, cannot prescribe the information they want and frequently are unable to comprehend in any meaningful way, the extant financial information provided. If one assumes, as a number of individuals do, that external users are or ought to be in the category of primary users, then one can argue that current financial information and statements are deficient.

In essence, what seems to be required is a clearly defined set of users and their primary needs. Once this has been established, a clearly defined set of objectives will follow. Finally, a clear presentation of objectives will allow local administrators and managers to establish some generally accepted accounting principles as they apply to general-purpose financial statements.[11]

---

[8]The closest authoritative source in Canada is Canadian Institute of Chartered Accountants, *Financial Reporting by Governments: A Research Study* (Toronto: CICA, 1980). This publication discusses, among other things, accounting objectives as they apply to the public sector and to the federal and provincial levels specifically. The local sector per se is excluded.

[9]Supra footnote 3, at 73.

[10]For a more detailed description of the information provided, see ibid.

[11]Specific purpose statements, as opposed to general purpose statements, have little difficulty with generally accepted accounting principles.

GENERALLY ACCEPTED ACCOUNTING PRINCIPLES (GAAP)

One definition of generally accepted accounting principles suggests that "certain rules, conventions or practices have gained general acceptance as appropriate methods of applying these concepts in particular circumstances."[12] Although these principles almost always have been applied to the commercial sector,[13] there is a question as to whether or not they should be applied to the government sector. If, as a few but increasing number of individuals believe, the government sector is or can be operated as a commercial enterprise, then the private-sector principles should apply and there need be no concern over the way in which local governments handle certain accounting transactions—they merely follow the standards already set. On the other hand, if different concepts are to apply to different organizations, and there is still a widespread belief that this applies to the public sector, then the public sector ought to know what rules or concepts govern its operation. In the case of local governments, there is considerable diversity among municipalities within a province and even greater diversity across provinces. This variation still exists even though a set of principles was reached after a series of long, drawn-out discussions by the various intergovernmental conferences on local government information development. Unfortunately, in the eyes of at least one expert,[14] these principles were not rigorously or comprehensively developed nor were they developed by a representative group.

To overcome the existing difficulties of establishing a set of GAAP, it seems reasonable to suggest that Canada set up an independent, fully funded, and adequately staffed body whose intent is to resolve local government accounting issues. Similar organizations currently exist in both the United States and the United Kingdom.[15] In each of these countries, local governments have a clearly defined set of standards to follow in handling the numerous and varied accounting transactions.

Only recently has there emerged in Canada an organization whose intent involves the establishment of GAAP for the various levels of government including the local level. This group, called the Public Sector Accounting and Auditing Committee, is sponsored by the Canadian Institute of Chartered Accountants (CICA). The acceptance of this responsibility by the CICA, however, has not gone without criticism. It has been suggested, for example, that the current sponsorship will not represent adequately the interests of local governments; that there will be insufficient participation by non-accountants in setting standards; and that one particular group of accountants may

---

[12]Committee on Accounting and Auditing Research, *The Auditors Report,* Bulletin no. 17 (Toronto: CICA, 1969), paragraph 6.

[13]For a description of these principles, see Canadian Institute of Chartered Accountants, *CICA Handbook*, annual edition (Toronto: CICA).

[14]For a discussion of this, see A. Beedle, "Generally Accepted Accounting Principles (GAAP) for Local Government Accounting and Research Needs Concerning Local Government Financial Statements," paper presented to the Canadian Certified General Accountants Association Sponsored Conference at Queen's University, January 22, 1982 (Vancouver: CCGAA, 1982), 2.

[15]The National Council on Governmental Accounting in the United States, and the Chartered Institute of Public Finance and Accountancy in the United Kingdom, each ensures adequate representation of local government interests in setting standards in its respective country.

dominate the standard-setting process.[16] Recognizing the legitimacy of these criticisms, one must also applaud the CICA for initiating this worthwhile and potentially useful venture. If this body can assume many of the characteristics of the independent bodies in both the United States and United Kingdom, then it will be possible to more clearly identify the primary users, their needs, and hence objectives of local government accounting and financial information. Once this has been completed, a set of generally accepted accounting principles can be developed.

Local government accounting practice currently differs from that of the private sector in a number of ways, the most important of which will be presented and discussed below.

Fund Accounting

Perhaps the most consistent difference between accounting information provided by municipalities, school boards, and most hospitals,[17] and similar information provided by commercial enterprises in Canada exists in the use of fund accounting. Fund accounting involves the establishment of a set of accounts to ensure that revenues collected or appropriated for a specific purpose are used only for that purpose(s). As such these separate funds and reporting entities are designed to demonstate compliance with the various legal and budgetary constraints facing local governments.

Despite the prevailing practice of fund accounting used by local governments in Canada, (indeed it is legally required in many provinces including British Columbia, Ontario, Quebec, and Manitoba) there is growing support for its elimination as a basis for financial reporting for general-purpose statements. Those in favour of eliminating the fund basis because of its unnecessary detail and extreme complexity have suggested that it be replaced by a simpler, concise, and yet comprehensive overview of the municipal financial picture. Where fund accounting is still appropriate or required, as for internal use or legal compliance, a series of specific and detailed reports can be made available to the requesting individuals or bodies. In support of this point, some cities in Canada (Edmonton and Halifax to name only two) have responded by presenting combined or consolidated statements eliminating the detailed fund information; however, for interested users, the fund information is available in separate published statements.[18]

The establishment of funds by municipal governments in Canada shows a considerable amount of uniformity[19] in a number of areas including revenue

---

[16]See supra footnote 3, for a more detailed discussion of these and other issues relating to CICA sponsorship.

[17]In Canada, hospitals have a choice of using a fund basis corresponding to that used for municipal purposes plus funds to cover special activities or endowments, or alternatively they may choose an integrated basis for presenting their financial information. This latter approach includes all assets in one place and minimizes the number of funds that must be set up.

[18]For more detail on fund accounting, see supra footnote 3, at Chapter 5.

[19]Suggestions for funds in Canadian municipalities were originally made in Canada, *Municipal Finance Reporting Manual*, 3rd ed. (Ottawa: Dominion Bureau of Statistics, 1960), and updated in "principles" endorsed at the Intergovernmental Conference on Local Government Information Development, in Winnipeg, 1980.

funds for general municipal activities, revenue funds for special activities, utility operations, sinking funds, reserves, trusts, and agency funds where desired or required. There is, however, some diversity in the treatment of fixed assets and long-term indebtedness. Briefly, municipalities in Quebec tend to follow the American approach by utilizing a loan bylaw fund (similar to the Capital Projects Fund in the United States) rather than a capital and loan fund as is used for general municipal activities, utilities, and other special activities in municipalities in the rest of Canada. In essence, the Quebec approach establishes a fund for capital activities that outlines the net financial resources available for future use. This includes the funds designated (including long-term borrowing) for financing capital projects, but excludes fixed assets because they are not available for meeting current or future expenditures and it excludes long-term liabilities because they do not represent a drain on current revenue sources. To provide information on both long-term indebtedness and fixed assets, two separate statements are published along with information on the fund. By contrast, the capital and loan fund used in the remaining provinces includes information on assets acquired and still existing plus long-term liabilities and the equity of local taxpayers in the municipal operation.

In summary, the use of complex multiple funds for municipal activities has led to incomprehensible financial accounting information provided to all but the more knowledgeable and professional of the external users. What is desired is an approach adopted by at least two Canadian cities cited earlier and that is to provide a simpler, more concise set of financial statements outlining the overall financial position of the municipal operation. This would involve the abandonment of fund accounting as the basis for these financial statements. For internal management use and control or where compliance with certain legal or stipulated requests must be ensured, however, statements based on fund accounting could be retained and made available as requested.

Reserves and Reserve Funds

The accounting treatment of reserves and reserve funds has been inconsistent over time and has lacked uniformity among municipalities in Canada at any given time. These problems have arisen because "the terms, their definitions and the suggested accounting procedures that relate to them, are not synonymous."[20] In addition to the conceptual problem of not having a clearly defined and unanimously endorsed set of principles or rules to follow, there is the practical problem of not being able to understand, from published financial statements, the numerous transfers into and out of the many reserves and reserve funds and the resultant impact these transfers have on the overall financial position of the local government. Municipal treasurers, in virtually every municipality at some time, have used reserves and reserve funds as hiding places. Their defence for this action rests on the argument that local councils occasionally vote for certain expenditures without careful planning, thus forcing local officials to supply the necessary funds. The problem with this approach is that it makes it virtually impossible for users (even the more sophisticated) to comprehend the true meaning of reserves and reserve funds

---

[20]Supra footnote 3, at 91. Beedle draws upon four sources to support this point and fully outlines the nature of the problem created by the many reserves and reserve funds used by local governments.

and their real impact. What is required is a set of clearly defined, easily understood, and uniformly accepted guidelines for the many transactions that arise with respect to these funds or accounts.

Accounting Bases

Cash, accrual, and modified accrual accounting form the three possible accounting bases that can be used for municipalities and their enterprises. Cash accounting involves the recording of expenditures and revenues when funds are actually disbursed or received. Accrual accounting records transactions when they occur regardless of when expenditures are made or funds received. Exceptions to this arise when it may be impossible to measure the value of the disbursement or receipt until the cash actually is dispensed or received. Modified accrual accounting adopts the same principles and approach as accrual accounting with the exception that interest on long-term debt is not accrued. This exclusion is justified because these amounts are not current liabilities and their payments will not require expenditures from current revenues. The adoption of accrual or modified accrual accounting does not suggest that absolutely every revenue source or expenditure item be accrued. Indeed, for very small revenue and expenditure items, a simple recording on a cash basis along with proper notation of the approach followed is sufficient.

While the accrual basis is universal for commercial enterprises, such uniformity does not exist for municipalities and their enterprises. Canadian practice, in fact, displays considerable variation with the modified accrual accounting base being the most dominant. This different manner of handling a number of accounting transactions makes intermunicipal comparisons involving accounting entries and their implications considerably more difficult to assess than if complete uniformity were followed. If one were to follow the municipal accounting principles established by the Intergovernmental Conference on Local Government Information Development in 1979 and modified in 1980, one would argue that modified accrual accounting be adopted by all municipalities and their enterprises.

Operating Fund Statement—Selected Items

In addition to differences in the accounting base used in the private sector (accrual) and that used by local governments and their enterprises (modified accrual and occasionally cash), a number of specific items also receive different treatment.

Expense versus Expenditure

In arriving at net income figures, commercial enterprises concentrate on recording the actual expenses (labour costs, interest payments, rental charges, and depreciation) involved in earning their gross incomes. This emphasis on expired costs allows enterprises to calculate their annual operating costs including per unit costs. Unfortunately, for general government functions at the local level, this interest in per unit costs seldom exists and if it does exist, often it is impossible to calculate from accounting information available in published statements. Instead of recording expenses, local governments often record expenditures.

Indeed, even the authoritative accounting bodies[21] support the recording of expenditures rather than expenses. This emphasis on expenditures generates a final figure on the statement of operation for the revenue fund that is different from that which would have been derived if the cost of operation (expenses) had been recorded. Under expenses, for example, one would have recorded depreciation (the value of the asset used up during the current accounting period); however, under expenditures, one records the actual outlays for capital assets acquired during the current accounting period, regardless of whether this asset is used up in the current accounting period or is to last for a number of accounting periods. Other expenditures that are listed include the repayment of the principal portion of long-term debt and contributions to various funds.

The emphasis, therefore, is on accounting for the use of current funds in meeting a number of commitments. The final figure on the general operating fund statement will reflect the municipal financial position after accounting for a number of long-term liabilities and capital outlays rather than the actual resources used during the period.

While the authoritative bodies have not clearly stated whether municipal utilities or enterprise should record expenditures or expenses and while the practice tends to be varied, considerable opinion exists in favour of recording expenses on the premise that these operations are more akin to commercial enterprises and hence should follow commercial accounting principles.

Depreciation

Where the recording of expenditures rather than expenses prevails, depreciation figures are not entered in the general fund operating statement; however, if expenses are listed, as in the case of some municipal utilities and enterprises, then depreciation figures must be included in the operating fund statement. While the calculation of depreciation figures, on the surface, appears fairly straightforward, such is not the case in actual practice. For example, how does one correctly measure the depreciation charge for fixed assets including roads, sidewalks, and buildings? In practice, municipalities tend to charge both the original outlay and any expenditures for renewing roads and sidewalks against the revenue fund. Because the asset on which the original expenditure is made generally is not recorded in the capital and loan fund, the value of the asset and the equity fund both tend to be understated.[22] The method of recording the expenditure on renewal may be reasonable as a proxy for measuring depreciation as long as these renewal expenditures occur in a consistent and relatively uniform manner over time. If, however, these expenditures are erratic and subject to the whims of local councils, then these expenditures will not reflect the use of fixed assets consumed in a particular accounting period. In any case, there still remains the question of how the original outlay is to be treated. Obviously, if the asset is to last for a number of years, then it can be argued that future generations ought to pay for the value of the assets they consume. Under current policies, it is frequently the current taxpayers who absorb the cost for future generations, thus creating a situation that may be challenged on equity grounds.

---

[21]See supra footnote 3, at 124.

[22]Ibid., at 108-9.

Finally, there is the more fundamental and conceptual problem of whether or not the recording of depreciation of local government fixed assets is meaningful. The listing of depreciation for private enterprises leads to a reduction in taxable income. Since net income for local governments (their utilities and enterprises) is not taxable, depreciation figures have not been recorded nor have local officials felt them to be important. It can be argued, however, that depreciation correctly calculated is necessary because it represents an estimation of the flow of capital services used up by residents in each year. If depreciation were accepted, then a further issue would involve the base on which it should be calculated—that is, should it be calculated on historic costs or replacement costs? Obviously, depreciation accounting based on replacement cost would serve as a guide to an optimal replacement policy.

Capital Expenditures from Current Revenue

Whereas commercial enterprises seldom deduct from current revenues the portion of capital expenditures that generate benefits for residents in future accounting periods, local general government operations, their utilities and enterprises, all too frequently, deduct from current revenues, the value of total capital disbursements regardless of the period over which the benefits accrue. As such, the measurement of the accounting period expenses or expired costs is non-existent. In its place is an indication of how the capital expenditures are funded.

Miscellaneous[23]

When comparing the local government sector with the private sector or when comparing one local government and its related utilities or enterprises with a similar operation in another local sector, a distinct lack of uniformity or consistency in the accounting treatment of a number of items often is evident. Variations exist, for example, (1) in the accounting treatment of inventories; (2) in the practice of recording repayment of long-term debt; (3) in the treatment of surpluses or deficits from a previous year; and (4) especially in the multitude of funds and the inherent interfund transfers and contributions that ensue. Arising from this variety of accounting approaches and procedures is the opinion that local government published financial statements in their current form are simply incomprehensible and therefore meaningless to the majority of users or potential users.

Balance Sheet—Fixed Assets

Although the inclusion of fixed assets on a balance sheet has never been an issue in the private sector, this is not the case in local government operations. Local governments, their utilities, and enterprises have displayed different approaches[24] toward the treatment of fixed assets. These approaches include: (1) not recording fixed assets on balance sheets as is the case for general municipal operations at the local level in Ontario (this is also an option for local

---

[23]For a fuller discussion of these, see ibid., at 110-16.

[24]For a presentation of the rationale and explanation of the various approaches, see supra footnote 3, at 117-20.

government enterprises in Ontario); (2) not recording fixed assets as part of a fund but rather disclosing them in a separate statement as is done in municipalities in Quebec; (3) listing fixed assets and any long-term debt incurred in their acquisition in a balance sheet for a capital (and loan) fund as is done for general municipal operations in the remaining eight provinces with one of the eight, Alberta, employing it as an alternative (this approach is used solely as the basis for municipal enterprise operations in British Columbia and Saskatchewan and as an alternative in Alberta, Manitoba, Ontario, and Nova Scotia); and (4) recording fixed assets in a combined revenue and capital fund (this is the only approach for municipal enterprises in Nova Scotia, is an alternative for municipal enterprises in Alberta, Manitoba, and Nova Scotia, and is an alternative for general municipal activities in Alberta).

While there is substantial variation in the practice of recording fixed assets, there is also wide variation[25] in the accounting treatment of a number of issues directly related to fixed assets. First, where the assets are recorded on balance sheets, there is considerable variation in the value that is to be assigned to their initial recording. Cost tends to be the most frequent base although a number of exceptions do exist both within and among municipal operations, utilities, and enterprises. Alternative bases for recording fixed assets include the amount of debenture debt created for the purchase of the asset, assessed or appraised value for land acquired, appraised or market value for gifts from other governments, and the value of outstanding liabilities.

Second, where fixed assets are purchased out of reserves or current revenues, there is considerable discrepancy in the portion of these capital expenditures recorded as fixed assets. In some municipalities, capital expenditures out of revenue funds are capitalized, while in other municipalities similar expenditures are not capitalized. As well, not only are fixed assets of general operations, utilities, enterprises, and school boards treated differently from one municipality to the next, but similar variations in accounting for these assets exist among these different entities within one municipality.

Third, where depreciation of fixed assets is recorded on balance sheets, noticeable variation exists in the basis used for recording this figure. It may include an estimation based on allocating the cost of the fixed asset over the useful life of the asset, a figure based on the current repayment of debt principal, or a mixture of these two approaches. As well, in certain municipalities, there have been instances where some assets are depreciated while others are not.

COST DETERMINATION

Cost determination for most commercial activities of local governments (utilities and enterprises) is relatively straightforward and primarily involves collecting and classifying existing expense (expired cost) data according to a set of prescribed accounting standards. Cost determination for most municipal general operations, however, is readily available but, as was stated above, the figures recorded may vary depending on the particular accounting principle (or lack of principle) adopted. Problems frequently arise in the attempt to appor-

---

[25]Ibid., at 120-23.

tion these general costs to the different programs or services provided through general revenue funds. How are, for example, overhead costs such as those associated with personnel or purchasing departments or those associated with general office building expenses to be assigned to the different activities? How are some direct costs such as labour costs or the cost of materials purchased to be apportioned if employees to whom these wages are paid or for whom the supplies are provided are responsible for assisting in the provision of more than one service or program? In many municipalities, particularly the smaller ones, there are few attempts and limited interest in the apportionment of these general costs to the proper function. In some of the larger urban areas, fairly sophisticated procedures have been developed to assign direct and indirect costs accurately to the different general programs or activities of municipal governments. The City of Calgary, in fact, has set up a reasonably sophisticated set of accounts for each of the diverse services or programs provided by it. Each of these service operations, although provided by the same local government, is set up as though it were a separate business entity, with indirect and direct costs being apportioned on a fee-for-service basis. This treatment (if all costs are properly recorded) provides a better framework for evaluating the actual costs of the various programs and allows the various users (taxpayers, councillors, and local administrators) to assess more effectively the usefulness and importance of each of the separate programs and services. The full cost accounting method charges various programs or agencies for resources they directly consume. This provides a greater incentive for these operations to be more efficient or cost conscious in providing their many services or programs. Too few municipalities, unfortunately, have fully and effectively adopted this full cost accounting approach.

Coincident with cost determination is an evaluation of the operating costs associated with the provision of the various municipal activities. The traditional line item listing of expenditures for particular activities effectively sets a limit beyond which expenditures cannot rise unless they can be strongly supported. This particular procedure is fairly effective in controlling expenditures but is unsatisfactory for evaluating the quality, level, and general efficiency of service provision. What is required, therefore, is an effective procedure for evaluating local services or programs based on the various criteria associated with measuring performance (see discussion under local budgeting). Once these criteria have been established, any deviation from the norm must be subject to investigation. Such an investigation may indicate that overexpenditure is a result of a higher-than-expected rate of inflation, it may indicate that a municipality is providing a level of service higher or lower than anticipated, or it may simply display an excessive and unnecessary level of spending. Regardless of the explanation, this variance analysis is fundamental if a municipality hopes to improve the efficiency of providing local services.

FINANCIAL REPORTS

Not only is local government accounting information recorded in a variety of ways for a specific operation or report, but it is also presented in numerous and different reports. Starting with the wide variety that exists in the presentation of similar information, balance sheets are universally used but frequently in different ways. Some municipalities, for example, provide balance sheets for specific funds and separate accounts alone, while other municipalities (those in

Ontario) are required to present a balance sheet for all capital and revenue fund statements combined. As well, headings and subheadings adopted in balance sheets differ across the country. In Ontario, municipalities are required to use the subheadings of current assets, fixed assets, current liabilities, and long-term liabilities for general government activities. Such subheadings seldom are adopted elsewhere, except for utility operations and hospitals.

Operating statements reflect similar diversity. Depending on the municipality or location, these may be referred to as "statements of operations," "statements of income," "statements of revenue and expenditures," "statements of revenue and expenses," "statements of earnings," "statements of operation and retained earnings," "statements of income and equity," "statements of revenue, expenditures and surplus," or "statements of revenue."[26] Further variation is reflected in the actual recording of local government financial information. Some municipalities record expenditures rather than expenses; some report gross revenue and expenditures of all activities, while others simply list the net revenue or expenditure; some record revenue collected for and directly dispersed to other levels of government (school boards, conservation authorities, upper-tier governments), while others make no mention of this activity since it is a straight transfer of funds from one authority to another; and some list budget figures with actual figures, while others do not. Indeed, the list could continue but these examples provide a flavour of the extent of the variation that exists at the local level.

The number of financial reports prepared by local governments has been increasing over the past few years. These reports include annual reports and general purpose financial statements provided for external users, a series of information reports submitted to federal and provincial governments and their statistics collecting agencies and routine and special management reports for internal use. Without providing a detailed outline of the many financial statements produced, the following is a partial description of the more important reports[27] based on special funds or activities established by local governments. General funds, which provide data for general purpose financial statements, account for all resources devoted to the general operation of municipalities (activities such as administration and police services). Special revenue funds are the basis for generating special fund reports. They account for the receipt of revenues designated for specific purposes—an example might include the receipt of a special local tax levy for an arena or civic centre. Similar funds and the resultant reports arise in instances where capital project funds are established for the acquisition and financing of capital assets. Special assessment funds have been prominent in areas where local improvement projects have been initiated to benefit a specific group of properties—examples include sewer installation, sidewalk construction, and street paving. In each of these cases, the abutting property owners are levied a special assessment and hence property tax in order to finance the specific project. Debt service funds are established to account for the financing of all long-term debt. Municipal utilities, swimming pools, and golf courses, which cover their operating costs

---

[26]See ibid., at 179, for a listing of these.

[27]For a more detailed description of these reports, see Holder, supra footnote 1, at 418-19.

from revenues received, provide financial statements similar to those of a business or commercial enterprise.

While all of the reports listed in the preceding paragraph are published in order to accommodate external users, or to comply with legal or statutory requirements, or both, there are a number of additional financial reports that may be provided as the need dictates. These include special reports for investors that are issued when the municipality is interested in borrowing long-term funds for capital projects or brief reports issued by the mayor, chief administrator, or board of education, on the activities (financial and otherwise) for which each of these individuals or groups are responsible.

Reports for local councils, administrators, or other internal users display the same kind of variety as those for external users. These may include special reports (in some cases, numerous reports) on a regular or occasional basis on a particular activity or specific topic or they may include more regular reports on an annual, quarterly, or monthly basis for a number of budgetary revenue and expenditure activities (for example, the preparation of estimates), the comparison of estimates with the previous year's figures, and the comparison of actual with estimated figures. Further reports on cash flows and comparisons of these flows with forecasted flows are also necessary.

Finally, to comply with the monitoring and statistical requirements of senior governments and their statistics collection agencies, municipalities are required to complete a series of information returns. These returns show some variation across provinces, both in terms of the requirements for information and the extent to which provincial governments tend to monitor the operation of local governments. Local budgets must be submitted along with the required financial information in some provinces. These provinces closely and frequently scrutinize the financial statements of their municipalities (an example is Manitoba where monthly statements of municipal revenues and expenditures along with balance sheets of revenue and capital funds must be submitted to the provincial ministry). Budgets need not be submitted in other provinces and in these provinces a more relaxed approach to monitoring local activities tends to be the norm.

As distinct from the reports prepared for internal and external users where some use seems to be obvious, many municipalities view the financial reports prepared for senior governments and their agencies as time-consuming, expensive, and of little use in the day-to-day operation of their municipalities. However, these municipal reports may be necessary to allow senior levels of government to treat all municipalities within their borders in a consistent and uniform manner.

SUMMARY

Perhaps the greatest deficiency in local government accounting in Canadian municipalities is the lack of any generally accepted set of accounting principles. This lack of a uniform set of standards has not been deliberate and has arisen because of the absence of any clear definition of users of local accounting information and their requirements. Fortunately, interest in the issue of identifying users and their needs has emerged recently. Once this identification is achieved, a set of principles can be established. With these principles, a number of perplexing issues, hopefully, can be resolved; for example, is fund accounting the appropriate accounting approach for municipal governments? should expenditures or expenses be listed in operating statements? how are reserves and reserve funds to be treated? is accrual, cash or modified accrual accounting the appropriate base to employ? how should fixed assets be recorded in financial statements? how should depreciation be calculated and recorded for fixed assets listed in the balance sheets? how are inter- and intra-fund transfers to be recorded? Indeed, this list is lengthy but serves to suggest the magnitude of the current problem associated with local government accounting.

Finally, some consideration should be given to improving both the base for determining the costs of providing the diverse range of local services and the ways of reducing and making more comprehensible and useful the number of financial reports currently prepared by local governments.

LOCAL GOVERNMENT BUDGETING

INTRODUCTION

In times of financial restraint, local government budgeting becomes a more important component of accounting for local government activities. The impact of inflation, rising interest rates, collective bargaining decisions, and rising energy prices have contributed substantially to the increasing costs of providing local programs and services. Simultaneously, political pressure to restrict tax increases, a declining or slow-growing economic base, and access to predominantly inelastic revenue sources have all combined to exert pressures on local officials in their planning and provision of local programs and services.

Since municipalities in Canada are not allowed, by statute, to budget for operating deficits, careful trimming and reconsideration of all activities undertaken by local governments must be attempted. Unfortunately, such careful planning is often lacking. Many municipalities, particularly the smaller ones, continue to emphasize the coordination and control of expenditures on a line-by-line basis. This emphasis on controlling expenditures on inputs is important, but it does ignore the more important and necessary role of local budgets—to determine the relative worth of the various services or programs provided. Only when the relative worth of each of the separate outputs is determined can local officials efficiently allocate their scarce resources among the many competing programs and services.

As an alternative to the line-by-line approach to local budgeting, at least two approaches have been recommended on the basis that either would lead to a more carefully planned and integrated output-oriented approach. These include the planning-programming budget system (PPB) and zero-based budgeting (ZBB), each of which will be referred to below. An integral part of each of these approaches also involves the extensive and accurate use of benefit/cost analysis to ensure that proper decisions are being made.

BUDGETS AND THEIR FORMATION

Although annual budgets consisting of projected revenues and expenditures plus the relevant capital asset transactions component are prepared by all local governments in Canada, the actual format and legal or statutory requirements in preparing and presenting these budgets differ from province to province. Local governments in most provinces are required to complete standard budget forms designed and provided by the relevant provincial ministries. In some provinces, including Prince Edward Island, Quebec, Saskatchewan, and Alberta, local governments need not submit their budgets to provincial authorities. Submission but not approval is required in Nova Scotia. In provinces such as British Columbia and Manitoba, a preliminary budget is required and must be approved by the provincial authorities to encompass all budgetary transactions occurring between the beginning of the fiscal year and the actual passing and approval of the final budget for the year. Further requirements in British Columbia dictate that any amendments to a budget must be submitted to the provincial authorities for approval as well. In Prince Edward Island, the annual budgets for all villages must be approved on an item-by-item basis at a meeting of local residents.

While the above examples illustrate the statutory differences that exist in the submission and approval of local budgets, similar differences exist in the preparation of the budget itself. The bulk of this variation, however, can be attributed to the size of the municipality not its location. For example, in large centres with large budgets, there are simply more actors, each playing a different role in the preparation of the annual budget. By comparison, more than one role is often assumed by the same person in smaller communities with smaller budgets. What tends to be similar though, is the number of stages through which the budget cycle passes and it is this cycle along with the roles played by the various participants that will be addressed in the following few paragraphs.

The first stage of the budgetary cycle[28] involves the preparation of the initial requests for funds on a department-by-department basis. The preparation of these budgetary requests depends on a number of factors including the size of the municipality's budget, the degree of sophistication involved in operating and evaluating local programs or services, the importance attached to budgeting, the size of the department, and even the style of the department head. If departments are reasonably large, there may be an identifiable department budget staff. In those instances where municipalities are relatively small, the budget requests may be made by department heads or staff members on an ad hoc or a part-time basis. The adoption of performance measures and cost/benefit techniques as a basis for making budgetary decisions tends to be correlated positively with the size of the municipal budget. Seldom, if ever, are performance measures and cost/benefit analyses employed in smaller centres; whereas, these techniques have been gaining popularity as a budgetary tool in larger centres. Unfortunately, the larger centres have not been moving in this direction as quickly as one might like.

During the second stage of the budget cycle, the various departments or individuals responsible for administering the local programs and services submit their budgetary requests to the chief administrative or financial officer. This officer and his staff (if one exists) compile, combine, and coordinate all requests for funds. Since local governments are required by law to approve a balanced

---

[28]The stages of the budgetary cycle for local governments in the United States are discussed by Lewis Friedman, in "Budgeting," Aronson and Schwartz, supra footnote 1, 91-119, at 91-93.

budget for the general activities of the municipality for the up-coming year, it is the responsibility of the chief financial officer and his staff to estimate revenue yields and acceptable increases. Once this revenue constraint has been established, the objective becomes one of considering the alternative requests and selecting those (often after some trimming) that are felt to be most important. Inevitably, conflicts arise and protests abound. After frantic pleading by department heads or their delegates, requests are occasionally rearranged or the financial constraint expanded. Ultimately, the chief financial officer arrives at a budget that is then presented to the budget committee of the local or municipal council.

The third stage is the adoption of the budget. At the local level, and particularly for smaller communities, this exercise is much less sophisticated than at the provincial level or federal level. Local politicians are almost always part-time and hence, have insufficient time to assess and evaluate critically the budgetary recommendations presented by the chief financial or administrative officer or a person acting in this capacity. As well, the nature of the political system is such that local staff have sufficient contact and familiarity with the local councillors so that most (if not all) decisions as to appropriate expenditure or revenue changes have been agreed upon prior to the submission of the budget. In essence, the budget submitted generally has been agreed upon beforehand. Council receives the budget, perhaps debates it or portions of it in a public forum, and ultimately approves it. In a few instances (villages in Prince Edward Island), legislation requires that local budgets be approved by the local residents.

The execution and monitoring of the adopted budget throughout the fiscal year constitutes the fourth stage of the budget cycle. The responsibility for these activities along with the presentation of an updated picture of the municipality's financial position to the local council rests with the chief financial officer and/or his staff.

Finally, legislation requires that all municipalities have their financial records audited by an independent auditor after the completion of the fiscal year. This ensures that the municipality has adhered to legal requirements regarding local expenditures and that local officials have not misappropriated (deliberately or accidently) local funds.

Throughout the budgetary process, there are a number of actors, each performing different roles. The departments through their respective heads or delegates almost always request more funds than they really need on the assumption that their requests will be trimmed. The chief financial officer and his staff act as economizers—trimming requests and selecting from the many alternatives given their financial constraints. Finally, council scrutinizes the budgetary requests, sometimes debates them, and ultimately approves them. Local taxpayers exert their pressure through requests made to local councillors and, in this instance, their ultimate power is simply to not re-elect any member or members who fail to serve them in a responsible manner.

ROLE OF LOCAL BUDGETS

Local government budgets should be designed to achieve the following objectives: (1) to provide for the maintenance of financial control; (2) to provide information essential for useful and efficient management decisions; and (3) to improve program and financial planning. Local government budgets, with few exceptions, are used for control purposes only. All too frequently, information that could be of some use in improving management decisions or in assisting in future planning is simply not collected and, therefore, not reported. Recently, there has been increasing emphasis (although not as much action as is desirable) placed on the necessity of collecting more relevant data that will allow local officials to make better informed and more intelligent decisions.

The following will outline the extent to which local governments actually achieve the objectives suggested above and how they might alter their budgetary process in order to achieve a more "ideal" role for local budgets.

Financial Control

Historically, financial control has been the primary and sole concern of local government budgets. The fact that local officials have control over local funds has necessitated the implementation of certain controls (statutory or otherwise) so as to regulate and monitor expenditures on particular functions and at particular times throughout the year.

Control budgeting tends to be input oriented, as opposed to goal or output oriented, and is frequently negative in its approach. Emphasis is placed on restricting expenditure increases with very little attention, if any, being devoted to the benefits accruing as a result of the progams or services affected. While this may be a laudable objective, especially in times of restraint, it is far from obvious that it is in fact the most desirable or effective approach. A line-by-line or item-by-item assessment of expenditures usually ensues when inputs are identified and budgeted figures established on an incremental basis.[29]

Incrementalism in the budgeting process has been, and still is, fairly common, particularly in smaller communities with a less specialized and relatively small managerial staff. Although there are some noticeable problems with using one year's expenditures as a base on which to add an incremental value in determining the budgeted figures for the following year, it is defended by many local officials because of the lack of any other information relevant to the budgetary decision-making process. Their argument suggests that in the absence of useful "other information" (see discussion below) on extant programs and services, there is no basis for reducing or eliminating on-going expenditures since costs alone do not provide a sufficient rationale for that exercise.

In addition, the incrementalist approach creates some further problems; for example, it provides no mechanism for assessing the benefits from existing expenditures and, therefore, no rationale for encouraging local officials to allocate their resources in an efficient manner. As well, the information provided (as discussed under "Local Government Accounting") is frequently incomprehensible to all but the most sophisticated readers. Finally, the problem of a lack of any information that would improve the managerial efficiency and planning function of local officials is especially serious.

---

[29]For a discussion of incremental budgeting, see Aaron B. Wildavsky, *The Politics of the Budgetary Process* (Boston: Little, Brown, 1964).

In essence, control budgeting is important but it often creates "a narrow and cumbersome financial management system, characterized by paperwork, detail, duplication, complexity, and inflexibility."[30] It also lacks the truly relevant information necessary for proper planning and efficient management of local government activities.

Operational Management

Unfortunately, budgeting for managerial purposes has seldom been an integral part of the budget process in Canadian municipalities. Part of the explanation for this rests with the traditional format of local budgets themselves;[31] that is, budgets presented on a line-by-line basis emphasize the cost of inputs purchased rather than the objectives to be achieved. The lack of managerial budgeting also rests in the unwillingness or inability of local budgeters to collect and compile data of the kind necessary to provide relevant background for efficient management decisions.

To improve managerial decision making at the local level, budgets should be designed to reflect both past and projected expenditures on outputs or goals achieved or to be achieved rather than on the cost of inputs as has been accepted traditionally. To achieve this may be a rather tall order, yet one that is necessary in the current economic climate of restraint. Such identification involves the establishment of workloads or targets; for example, a council may set as one of its targets a 5 per cent reduction in crime rates at an average cost of X man-hours per investigation or it may state that all garbage must be collected with a minimum amount of inconvenience to all residents at an average cost of $X per ton. Similar targets may involve a reduction in per capita fire losses of a fixed percentage at an average cost of $X per alarm or the completion of road maintenance that ensures smooth riding at a cost of $X per kilometre.[32] Once such targets, or objectives have been established, the task of achieving these objectives must begin. Workloads or targets must be defined in quantifiable terms. Such quantification requires data on both inputs and outputs for it is the measurement of the ratio of inputs to outputs that defines the target to be achieved.

For most municipal performance measurement purposes, figures on inputs include the total cost of an activity or employee time, although other measures such as floor space, machine time, amount of land, and units of energy, have been recorded as inputs in specific circumstances. When inflationary pressures are noticeable, it may be desirable to use employee time as the input measure so as to avoid the distortions created by inflation. Alternatively, it has been suggested that in instances where year-to-year comparisons are to be made, and cost figures used, the cost figure should be adjusted by an appropriate price

[30]Friedman, supra footnote 28, at 103.

[31]Edward A. Lehan, "Public Budgeting," in John E. Petersen and Catherine Lavigne Spain, eds., *Essays in Public Finance and Financial Management: State and Local Perspectives* (Chatham, N.J.: Chatham House, 1980), 34-41, at 37.

[32]These examples are drawn from supra footnote 7, at 22-26. Numerous other examples of performance measures can be obtained from City of Thunder Bay, *Performance Measurement Manual and Catalogue* (Thunder Bay: Corporate Planning and Development Division, 1980).

index to reflect constant dollar costs.[33] Finally, a uniform measurement of inputs across municipalities must exist in order to facilitate intermunicipal comparisons.

While the measurement of output, which is the denominator of the unit cost ratio, is relatively straightforward for services such as sewage disposal, garbage collection, snow removal, and water provision (services in which the unit of output subject to quality standards can be measured), it is considerably more difficult for the provision of services such as education, health, welfare, and crime prevention where the unit of output is not clearly defined. For example, what is the unit of output for education?—the number of students taught annually or the number of students who passed? Indeed, this is a difficult question to answer and these examples point out the measurement problems associated not only with education but with all "soft" services. The recognition of measurement problems is important but in spite of these problems, attempts should be made to establish output measures subject to quality standards. Recognizing the subjectivity inherent in defining output measures for services of this nature, these are essential, nevertheless, if one is to establish targets or goals as benchmarks against which comparisons of actual performance are to be measured in order to assess the technical efficiency and effectiveness[34] of providing local service.

Technical efficiency measures the relationship between inputs and outputs. While this can be measured by the ratio of outputs to inputs (productivity ratio) or inputs to outputs (unit cost ratio), the latter tends to be used more commonly as an indicator of technical efficiency. An activity is defined as being more technically efficient if the output to input ratio rises or the input to output ratio declines.

By way of contrast, the term effectiveness measures the extent to which an activity contributes to the achievement of the stated goals, objectives, or targets. For example, an activity such as building a road may be very efficient in terms of cost per kilometer, but its effectiveness will depend on the usefulness of the road in providing convenience, safety, and economy for vehicular transportation. Difficulties may arise in the extent to which effectiveness can be measured, yet in spite of these difficulties attempts must be made at such measurement. When a direct evaluation of the benefits arising from local services is not possible, the demand for services subject to quality standards might be measured through "citizen surveys, studies of local economic conditions, reports on the number of applications, requests or complaints received, expert evaluations"[35], etc., of specific needs. In this way, a measure of the value of the service provided can be estimated. Thus, effectiveness will measure the success of not only doing things, but of doing them to the citizens' satisfaction.

The establishment of targets or workloads allows local budgetary officials to make decisions on budgeted expenditures not solely on the basis of costs but

---

[33]Supra Footnote 7, at 5-6.

[34]For a discussion of the measures which might be used in measuring effectiveness and efficiency of local services, see Allan R. Drebin, "Criteria for Performance Measurement in State and Local Government" (December 1980), 9 *Governmental Finance* 3-7.

[35]Supra footnote 7, at 4.

rather on the basis of costs (efficiency) with some notion of returns (effectiveness). Budgets, therefore, should be built around the kind of work to be undertaken in the next fiscal year. These workload targets dictate the programming part of budget preparation, which involves scheduling work, developing an organizational structure, and establishing procedures to reach the proposed plans. Alternative methods of achieving the volume of work to be undertaken should also be considered. This arrangement of budgeting expenditures allows local budgeters faced with scarce resources to allocate their funds among the various services in a managerially efficient and effective manner.

Estimates of workload and other performance indicators ought to be measured, established, and monitored periodically to make certain that targets are adhered to or that actual changes of a justifiable nature are being incorporated into the budget. Such periodic reporting also provides a basis for evaluating improvements or discovering deviations that must be corrected. These deviations might exist because of unplanned inflationary cost pressures, inadequate financial control, unrealistic revenue or expenditure estimates, and/or simply because of foolish management decisions. Once the basis for the deviation has been determined, local officials must either alter the targets or adjust their operation to achieve the previously stated objective. Finally, an independent audit by an individual not employed directly by the municipality is necessary in order to guarantee that the objectives or goals have been achieved in an effective and efficient manner.

Budgeting to facilitate managerial decisions of the type outlined in this section is a relatively new idea. Because of tradition, bureaucratic inertia, or an inability or unwillingness to change, municipalities, by and large, have concentrated on budgeting for control purposes alone. The objectives of control budgeting are understood and generally pose no threat to local officials who may view the exercise of performance budgeting as something beyond their comprehension and expertise. Performance budgeting, therefore, is almost non-existent with the possible exception of a few larger municipalities. In centres such as Halifax, Thunder Bay, Scarborough, and the Region of Ottawa-Carleton, the adoption and implementation of performance measures has been established for the purpose of improving efficiency and productivity in the provision of local services. In very few instances, however, have there been any systematic and formal attempts to link these performance measures with the budgetary process. The tighter financial constraints facing local authorities along with greater pressure for public accountability probably will force more municipalities to outline clearly their targets, goals or objectives; to establish performance measures; to evaluate alternative means of achieving the same objectives; to employ cost-benefit analysis in assessing the various alternatives; and to provide those services yielding the greatest return given revenue constraints. Assistance in the initiation and implementation of performance budgeting along with the evaluation of the various alternatives may be provided by provincial authorities. (Ontario provides assistance to municipalities interested in developing and implementing performance measures.) This will be of particular importance to those communities lacking both the manpower and expertise to conduct such exercises. Once this is achieved, greater efficiency can be introduced into the budgetary process.

Financial Planning

Although budgeting for financial planning has not been given a great deal of consideration in most municipalities, the decade of the 1980s with its emphasis on expenditure limitations and inelastic revenue sources will undoubtedly place greater emphasis on the importance of careful financial planning, particularly when current expenditure decisions exert funding commitments from future revenues.

As distinct from incremental budgeting, which is based on the premise that budgets are built from the bottom up, budgeting for adequate and useful financial planning necessitates a clear delineation of objectives (this is also true for managerial budgeting outlined above). By identifying the goals at an early stage and ranking them, a criterion for spending is actually established. Over time, the needs or desires of local citizens change and programs or services that were important and valuable in the past may no longer be desirable, thus necessitating a reallocation of local commitments. Once the program or service is in place, an evaluation of its effectiveness and efficiency must be undertaken and continuously monitored.

Planning in the budgetary sense has two meanings—forecasting and assessment. First, it is an attempt to shape the future; to forecast the type of expenditures that will be made and the revenue sources that will be tapped. Each annual budget represents a one-year instalment in a longer-range plan with the goal ultimately being reached sometime in the future. Second, it is an attempt to assess the impact of current expenditure decisions on future revenue sources. To achieve this, impact studies are an invaluable input into the budgetary allocation process. All too often, local governments commit themselves to current programs without any accurate indication of the drain of these programs on future revenue sources. Metro Toronto is one of the few municipalities where detailed and sophisticated fiscal impact studies have been undertaken.[36]

REFORM OF LOCAL BUDGETS

Budgetary accounting primarily emphasizes financial control through systems that traditionally have ensured public accountability and compliance. This occurred through the use of the line-by-line approach to local budgeting. Historically, there has been very little real interest in using the budget as a tool for improving local decision making or financial planning. This situation, fortunately, appears to be shifting, although at a very slow pace. This change is evidenced in the implementation of two new systems—planning-programming budget system, (PPB) and zero-based budgeting (ZBB). These two approaches concentrate on budgeting according to outputs or goals to be achieved rather than inputs or funds allocated to particular programs or services. This output-oriented approach leads to budgetary systems that help local officials make more intelligent and informed decisions about current programs or services as well as those planned for the future. Each of these approaches will be outlined below.

---

[36]Harry M. Kitchen, *Public Finance in Metropolitan Toronto*, a Study for The Royal Commission on Metropolitan Toronto (Toronto: the Commission, 1977), 74-75.

Table 13.1   Use of PPB and ZBB by Municipalities in Canada

Alberta	
Edmonton	On PPB since 1974; pilot project 1978-9 testing ZBB; adopted, June 1979, a modification of PPB to incorporate ZBB techniques.
Calgary	On PPB since 1973.
British Columbia	—
Manitoba	
Winnipeg	On PPB.
New Brunswick	
St. John	Uses program budgeting but not performance.
Newfoundland	—
Nova Scotia	
Halifax	Uses programs and relates to production achievement reports.
Ontario	A number of Ontario municipalities have moved in the direction of program budgeting by undertaking a modest type of budgetary reform. London is developing a program approach that includes performance monitoring features. The following municipalities have espoused ZBB: Cambridge, Guelph, Hamilton,[a] Peterborough, Sudbury, Thunder Bay, and York (recommended for adoption). Ottawa and Scarborough have program budgeting coupled with modified ZBB. Several other municipalities are considering ZBB but had not made final decisions.
Prince Edward Island	—
Quebec	—
Saskatchewan	
Regina	Some PPB evaluation criteria developed in public works.

[a]First Canadian city to adopt ZBB.

Source: A. Beedle, *Accounting for Local Government In Canada: The State of the Art* (Vancouver: The Canadian Certified General Accountants' Research Foundation, 1981), 219.

Planning-Programming Budget System (PPB)

The budgeting system known as the planning-programming budget (PPB) gained prominence as early as 1961 when it was introduced into the United States Department of Defense. Since then, a number of national governments in various countries and a few local governments in Canada have followed suit (see Table 13.1).

The structure of the PPB[37] system can be outlined under four headings. First, an overall plan of the community's needs must be established. This involves an assessment of community needs, the establishment of objectives, and the choice

---

[37]For a brief discussion of the PPB system at the local government level in Canada, see supra footnote 3, at 215-23. For further detail, see A.J. Robinson, *Economic Evaluation of Municipal Expenditures: PPB* (Toronto: Canadian Tax Foundation, 1971).

of the appropriate means of reaching the desired objectives. This planning function involves an assessment of long-term as well as annual goals. Second, an overall program designed to achieve the stated objectives must be devised. This involves the organization, implementation, and constant monitoring of the prescribed program so as to guarantee that the desired objectives are being approached. Use of performance measures and cost-benefit analyses are essential if the programs or services are to be supervised and presented in an efficient and effective way. Third, all planning and programming decisions must be converted into specific financial plans for the upcoming fiscal year. In addition, information on the impact of current expenditures on future revenue sources must be presented. Finally, a careful interpretation of all budgetary decisions must be completed. Beyond this, continuous reviewing, checking, and monitoring must be undertaken. If the objectives change as the community's desires or needs change, then adjustments to expenditure commitments for the disparate services or programs must be initiated.

The adoption of PPB grew out of and incorporated many of the components of performance budgeting and program budgeting. Performance budgeting emphasizes the achievement of specific targets or workloads, while program budgeting tends to emphasize a program structure without the inclusion of the impact of current decisions on future budgets or the use of analytical techniques such as cost-benefit analysis.

The advantages of PPB, it is alleged, are many. This system emphasizes proper planning including the establishment of objectives and priorities that reflect the community's needs or desires. It requires the establishment of performance measures and provides for the use of reasonably sophisticated analytical tools such as operations and cost-benefit analyses. It concentrates on a multi-year approach to budgeting, while, at the same time, emphasizing that services or programs must be provided in an efficient and effective manner. In essence, a budgetary system designed under PPB "becomes an integral part of the total management system."[38]

In principle, the advantages of PPB are beyond reproach; however, in practice, there have been some problems with the implementation of this budgetary system. Practical difficulties have emerged in the establishment of objectives; for instance, councils and local officials have considerable difficulties in agreeing on a common set of objectives. In addition, the establishment of performance measures is difficult for a number of services, although the Ontario government has attempted to establish many of these measures or to provide assistance for their establishment in interested Ontario communities. Furthermore, local officials are often resistant to change and sometimes view the introduction of a new budgeting approach as a threat to their positions. Finally, and this is especially true for smaller communities, local governments lack both the manpower and the proper levels of managerial sophistication. Despite these difficulties, a few Canadian municipalities (Table 13.1) have employed PPB successfully over the past few years.

---

[38]Supra footnote 3, at 216.

ZERO-BASED BUDGETING (ZBB)

The history of zero-based budgeting (ZBB) is relatively short. It was adopted initially in the private sector in the United States (Texas Instruments Incorporated) in 1969. Since then, its adoption has spread to a number of private firms and other governmental units in different countries. At the local level, the City of Hamilton was the first Canadian municipality to adopt ZBB (for the fiscal year 1978). Since then, a number of other municipalities including Edmonton, Cambridge, Guelph, Peterborough, Thunder Bay, and Sudbury have followed suit. Although the adoption of ZBB has been more noticeable in larger Ontario municipalities, currently it is being considered by a number of communities across Canada.

The basic elements of ZBB are not unique. It emphasizes a goal-oriented, priority-setting approach with the appropriate adoption of proper evaluative techniques and this suggests that substantial improvements in local decision making and planning are possible from the adoption of ZBB.

Briefly, ZBB involves a number of stages.[39] First, decision units must be identified. While there is no uniform or consistent method for identifying each unit, each must be "self-contained and susceptible to budget decisions."[40] Such units may include such cost centres as water treatment plants, sewage disposal plants, or garbage collection operations. Alternatively, they may relate to a subset of employees within a department such as the "non-uniform staff in the fire department."[41] The key ingredient in establishing a decision unit is the ability to define a measurable output (perhaps defined according to a performance measure discussed earlier) resulting from the funds supplied to the unit providing this output. The number of decision units will vary from municipality to municipality but will be related to the size of the local budget and the extent to which an activity can be defined as being independent of other activities.

Second, "a decision package is a form or document that presents a comprehensive picture of one way of performing an activity (defined decision unit)."[42] In fact, there may be several decision packages for each decision unit with each package reflecting an alternative level of expenditure and service. These packages may range from one illustrating the consequences of not funding the activity to one that assesses the impact of funding legal or statutory levels to one reflecting funding at 75 per cent of the previous year's level to one exhibiting an increase in the level of service and the funds required. Each package contains detailed and documented information describing the activity, outlining the objectives to be achieved, establishing performance and workload measures, evaluating alternative methods of achieving each goal, presenting the benefits and costs of the various alternatives, and a recitation of other relevant nonmonetary and financial information.

---

[39]For a detailed discussion of zero-based budgeting, see Ontario, *Zero-Base Budgeting,* Financial Procedures Bulletin no. 4 (Toronto: Ministry of Intergovernmental Affairs, Local Government Division, Municipal Budget and Accounts Branch, 1979).

[40]Supra footnote 28, at 112.

[41]Supra footnote 39, at 13.

[42]Ibid., at 16.

The third stage involves the sequential ranking of all decision packages with those given the greatest or highest priority being ranked at the top and those with the lowest priority appearing at the bottom. The acceptance or rejection of any given package will depend ultimately on the combined ranking efforts of local officials and councillors. Once this prioritization has been completed, council must decide where to draw the line in terms of packages accepted. This will depend on the local budgetary revenue constraint. In instances where councillors are hesitant to raise or introduce new taxes or changes in order to generate additional revenue, the number of packages selected will be different than in those instances where revenues tend to be more plentiful.

In principle, ZBB states that each person responsible for a particular activity (decision unit) must justify, in detail, the entire budgetary request each year and not the incremental increase alone. Such a requirement means that every activity must be examined to ensure that it, effectively and efficiently, continues to meet the stated objectives. In practice, however, it is unrealistic to expect that the annual budget will be formulated from a zero dollar amount. Instead, for the majority of local government activities, it is necessary to define a critical dollar limit below which an activity becomes worthless. Once this critical limit has been established, it may be necessary to justify only those budgetary requests above this stated level. The term "zero-based", therefore, is employed not to suggest that all requests start from a zero dollar level, but rather to emphasize the fact that expenditure requests are not granted automatically.

Because ZBB is output oriented rather than input oriented and because it uses a series of evaluative techniques such as peformance measures and cost-benefit analyses, it is similar to PPBS. However, it differs from PPBS in two ways—first, it employs decision packages and second, each decision package is ranked against all other packages.

All of the advantages[43] arising from an output-oriented approach to local budgeting, and listed earlier under PPB, apply here. In addition, ZBB encourages local managers to construct and evaluate creative alternatives in reaching the same objectives. The ranking of all decision packages forces local officials to work toward a more integrated approach to local budgeting and management. The emphasis on justifying annual increases, the importance of local officials (at all levels) in evaluating all activities from the bottom up, the fact that it can be employed on a selective basis, and the opportunity to re-allocate resources as the objectives change all support the notion that ZBB can assist local officials in improving their managerial decision making and planning.

There are, however, a number of disadvantages in the application of ZBB. There is the concern that existing staff members will feel threatened by any attempt to introduce a new budgeting system. In order to devise a system that will be practical and include the orderly development and valuation of alternative decision packages, considerable time is needed—time some local governments cannot spare. It also has been suggested that the adoption of reasonable output measures and proper evaluation techniques may be difficult and this makes it impossible to construct a ZBB system. Fortunately, none of these criticisms is impossible to overcome. In fact, with a properly and carefully

---

[43]For a detailed listing of benefits and limitations of zero-based budgeting, see ibid., at 25-27.

presented case for ZBB and with the assistance of provincial authorities where requested, these difficulties can be overcome. One, therefore, is left to conclude that the advantages of ZBB far outweigh the disadvantages and local governments should give serious consideration to implementing ZBB either for all services or for selected ones.

SUMMARY

The degree of sophistication in the formulation and structure of local budgets tends to vary directly with the size of the municipality. Smaller communities, with their limited expertise and smaller budgets, generally emphasize the line-by-line input-oriented approach to local budgeting. Some of the larger Canadian municipalities, although fewer than is desirable, recently have placed a greater emphasis on the output-oriented approach followed under either the planning-programming budget or zero-based budgeting model. The advantages of the output-oriented approach to local budgeting include greater financial control over local budgets, the determination of output measures that are then used to establish local objectives, and the determination of the financial impact the achievement of these goals will have on current and future budgets.

14
Productivity, Cash Management Policies, and Other Issues

INTRODUCTION

This chapter will discuss a number of unrelated issues that have a direct bearing on the costs of providing local programs or services. These issues include productivity at the local government level, cash management of local revenues, purchasing and pooling arrangements, boards, commissions and special purpose bodies, provincial/municipal funding of jointly sponsored programs, and local government forecasting. Under each of these topics, an attempt will be made to outline the extent to which changes could be made to reduce the costs and improve the efficiency of providing local programs and services. This emphasis on cost reduction or improved efficiency in the delivery of local programs or services is extremely important.

PRODUCTIVITY

INTRODUCTION

The concept of productivity in an economic sense "identifies the *quantity* of goods or services which can be produced from a specific *quantity* of resources—manpower, capital, energy, and raw materials."[1] As an absolute ratio, the productivity rate measures the level of output per unit of input supplied at a specific point in time. Over time, or among similar operations, changes in the productivity ratio measure the increase or decrease in the level of output per unit of input while maintaining the quality of the output supplied. Increases in productivity levels reflect improvements in the efficiency of supplying local services. Obviously, improvements in productivity are desirable for it is these improvements that can lead to a reduction in the per unit cost of supplying local services; for example, if an increased level of output can be produced with the same quantity of resources and if the costs of employing these resources remain fixed, then the per unit cost of supplying the final output can decline. Such a decrease in costs is a goal that is being pursued more and more vigorously by virtually every municipality for it is precisely this achievement that will avoid either the elimination or the reduction of local services or, alternatively, the necessity of raising additional revenues from local sources.

Local governments, historically, have not been as interested in productivity improvements as they are now. Part of the explanation for this rests with the difficulty in defining a unit of output for many local services; for example, how does one measure the output associated with education or police expenditures. For other services such as sewage disposal, garbage collection, and water pro-

---

[1]Nancy S. Hayward, "Productivity Improvement in the Public Sector," in John E. Petersen and Catherine Lavigne Spain, eds., *Essays in Public Finance and Financial Management: State and Local Perspectives* (Chatham, N.J.: Chatham House, 1980), 165-76, at 165.

vision, a unit of output can be defined more clearly. Part of the explanation also can be attributed to an unwillingness or inability on the part of local government to collect the information required to measure outputs and the costs associated with these. Fortunately, some provincial governments have offered considerable assistance in the establishment of a number of performance measures[2] and with this kind of aid, municipalities are moving into a position where output measures, even though many are of a proxy nature, are becoming available.

Productivity, in reference to a particular service, is the technical efficiency of providing that service; however, in any society where both public and private goods and services are supplied, efficiency takes on a more encompassing meaning. Not only is it defined in the technical manner described above, but it also refers to the proper allocation of society's resources among both public and private goods in the first instance, and laterally among the diverse goods and services in each of the private and public sectors separately. To achieve this broader objective of efficiency, some measure is needed in order to determine whether local governments ought to devote their limited resources to roads, to parks, or to education. Similarly, choices must be made as to the proper allocation of resources between local public goods and private goods. Obviously, these choices may be difficult.

For private goods and services, the price system serves the role of rationing the goods and services to these people who are willing to pay for them. As well, it acts as a signal in the sense that it indicates which goods are desirable and at what price different quantities will be purchased. For the provision of public goods, however, the price system performs neither the rationing nor signalling function.

Determination of the proper mix of local public and private goods or the trade-off between local public goods and services themselves must be made in alternative ways. Questionnaires, local citizen surveys, or pressure on local politicians have been used in indicating the different services and the appropriate level of each that ought to be provided. Indeed, a growing number of Canadian municipalities have been relying on questionnaires or survey information to provide them with inputs into the allocation process.

Productivity improvements, which have been interpreted as cost saving innovations by local officials, have arisen in many areas. Table 14.1 lists 161 improvements that were reported by 30 cities (100 were sent questionnaires) that completed and returned questionnaires distributed by the Bureau of Municipal Research.[3] Such a large number of improvements reported by a relatively small number of cities is indicative of the interest displayed by local governments, particularly in a climate of fiscal restraint.

While the sources of productivity improvements and hence cost savings may vary, they result from using fewer inputs or varying the mix of inputs in order to achieve a more optimal allocation of society's resources. Fewer resources

---

[2]Ontario, Municipal Budgets and Accounts Branch, Ministry of Municipal Affairs and Housing, *Performance Measurement for Municipalities* (Toronto: the Ministry, 1981).

[3]For a description of the questionnaire and a summary of the findings, see Bureau of Municipal Research, *Civic Affairs: Cost Saving Innovations in Canadian Local Governments* (Toronto: the Bureau, 1979).

Table 14.1   Productivity Improvements by Function in
Canadian Municipalities

General administration (25)[a]
Planning and development	2
Personnel	3
Clerk's office	5
Building department	6
Management and computer services	6
Supply and services	2
Telecommunications	1

Public works (56)
Engineering	17
Works	27
Utilities	2
Sanitation	10

Finance (22)
Treasury department	16
Comptroller	4
Assessment	2

Community and social services (8)
Social services	7
Community services	1

Public safety (19)
Fire	11
Police	6
Health	2

Transportation (16)
Roads and traffic	6
Transit	10

Parks, recreation, and libraries (13)
Parks and recreation	12
Libraries	1

Economic development (1)

[a]The numbers in parentheses represent the number of cost saving innovations in each area.

Source: Bureau of Municipal Research, *Civic Affairs: Cost Saving Innovations in Canadian Local Government* (Toronto: the Bureau, 1979), 26-27.

may be necessary when technological improvements arise. The transferral of certain services from the public to the private sector may bring a substantial reduction in costs without any deterioration in quality. The redeployment of local employees from one area to another, the provision of greater incentives, or the use of techniques that lead to greater motivation of local employees may generate greater output from the same number of employees. To categorize all improvements in productivity as falling specifically in one or the other of these areas is simply impossible. Indeed, many improvements arise from changes in a combination of factors including technology, redeployment, incentives, and motivation. With these qualifications in mind, productivity improvements will be discussed under each of the three headings suggested here.

TECHNOLOGICAL IMPROVEMENTS: EXAMPLES

The rapidly rising costs of providing many services have prompted a number of technological changes, each of which is designed to generate cost savings in both the present and the future. Some of these improvements such as more efficient nozzles on fire hoses or the adoption of breakaway light standards have led to relatively small, yet important savings. Others have generated much larger savings; for example, a significant improvement has arisen in the area of bridge inspection and repair in the Municipality of Metropolitan Toronto.[4] In the past, inspection and repair of bridges required the expensive and time-consuming construction of scaffolding with the added problem that frequently only a small portion of the underside of the bridge could be inspected. To overcome this problem and expense, Metro Toronto purchased a bridge crane truck (a flat bed heavy duty truck with a hydraulic arm mounted on the back) to handle this operation. Both the quality and coverage of inspection and repairs have been improved and when not used for this purpose, the truck has served as an additional unit for servicing light standards. As well, the number of personnel required to perform this task has been reduced and man-days lost due to injuries arising from scaffold construction have fallen significantly. Estimates suggest that in the first five years of operation of the bridge crane truck, Metro Toronto saved at least $138,000.[5] Given the high purchase price of this piece of equipment, there seems to be considerable potential for a joint purchase agreement among municipalities located near each other.

A second example of technological innovation is in the area of refuse collection. In the district of Burnaby, British Columbia and the city of Guelph in Ontario, to name two, the introduction of new refuse collection vehicles requiring fewer men per truck have led to fewer resources being devoted to this service without any deterioration in quality.[6] In the city of Windsor, an experiment involving the use of a mechanical arm, which was attached to the garbage truck, allowed the driver to pick up and dump refuse without leaving the cab of the truck. The Ministry of the Environment's cost-benefit assessment[7] of this mechanical collection device suggested that costs would considerably outweigh the benefits over a ten-year period; hence, the project was terminated. The results of this study, however, have been challenged by the Bureau of Municipal Research.[8] This institution, on the basis of its own statistical analysis, suggests that the mechanical collection device is superior to the manual collection method and does not generate costs in excess of benefits. These conflicting results leave one in a quandary but do indicate that perhaps the experiment ought to have been continued with greater emphasis being placed on an accurate recording of the respective benefits and costs.

---

[4]For a description of this, see Bureau of Municipal Research, *Civic Affairs: Cost Saving Innovations in Canadian Local Governments—A More In-Depth Look* (Toronto: the Bureau, 1980), 5-9.

[5]Ibid., at 8.

[6]Thomas J. Plunkett, *Some Approaches to Productivity Improvements by Municipal Governments* (Kingston, Ontario: Institute of Local Government, Queen's University, 1981), 8-9.

[7]B. I. Boyko and A. J. Burnham, *Innovative Refuse Collection: Municipality of Windsor* (Toronto: Ontario Ministry of the Environment, Waste Management Branch, 1978), 26.

[8]Supra footnote 4, at 17-29.

Technological improvements have occurred in the area of administrative services. In the city of Winnipeg, for instance, the local government introduced a computerized building-monitoring system that controls simultaneously the heating, ventilating, air conditioning, security, fire alarm, lighting, and maintenance function for a number of municipal buildings including libraries, swimming pools, arenas, car parks, and administration buildings.[9] The savings here were derived from a reduction in required staff and energy and have been estimated at $150,000 annually.[10]

Similarly, computerization of all documentation necessary for city council and its committees has led to an estimated savings of $150,000 annually in the City of Toronto.[11] As well, Burnaby, British Columbia has realized significant savings by utilizing a computer-assisted mapping system for map production and up-dating.[12] In addition, a number of municipalities have introduced or are considering the introduction of word processors to reduce secretarial staff and thus generate significant savings.

The consumption of raw materials contributes to productivity improvements; for example, the substantial increase in the cost of energy has caused a number of municipalities to undertake energy conservation policies ranging from an increase in the level of insulation in municipal buildings to a conversion of gas-driven vehicles to propane driven. As well, in the city of Windsor, Ontario, the introduction of new control equipment and chemicals in the pollution control plant resulted in estimated annual savings of $25,000 and $85,000 in chemicals and manpower respectively. This happened at the same time as the capacity of the plant grew by 50 per cent.[13]

CONTRACTING OUT: EXAMPLES

Municipalities have had a long history of contracting a number of construction projects including buildings, water, and sewage lines and certain professional services such as engineering design and legal advice, from the private sector. Indeed, given the haphazard occurrence of these expenditures, it can be argued that private-sector provision is less costly since these inputs are simply purchased for the duration of time required to complete the project and, therefore, are not funded when not required.

For municipal services providing a final output (refuse collection, snow removal, police and fire protection), definitive statements on the body or organization responsible for delivering the service in the most efficient manner are difficult to obtain. Some evidence, nevertheless, has been emerging on both the utilization and efficiency of private-sector provision of a number of local services. For example, in a study on municipal refuse collection in Canada,[14] it was observed, after the elimination of virtually all other variables affecting per

---

[9]Ibid., at 30-37.

[10]Ibid., at 33-34.

[11]Supra footnote 6, at 10.

[12]Ibid.

[13]Ibid., at 9.

[14]Harry M. Kitchen, "A Statistical Estimation of an Operating Cost Function for Municipal Refuse Collection" (No. 1, 1976), 4 *Public Finance Quarterly* 56-76.

unit costs, that a refuse collection system operated directly by the municipal government was significantly more expensive than a private operation (contracted out by the local government) providing the same quality and quantity of service. In reality, this tends to occur because local governments, lacking competition, seldom have any index by which to measure efficiency and performance. In fact, even if this index were available, there is seldom little desire to improve on, let alone maintain, efficiency. All of this, when combined with the fact that revenues are not keyed to output, undoubtedly makes the municipal operation a more costly venture.[15]

The extension of similar contracting out operations to other municipalities in the case of refuse collection and to other urban services in all municipalities may very well generate lower per unit costs of providing urban services with absolutely no loss in quantity and quality of the services supplied. A recent study[16] attempted to determine which local services were frequently contracted out by Canadian municipalities and whether municipalities were intending to expand this practice. Eighty-four cities were contacted and forty-seven (ranging in size from 35,000 to 500,000 people) responded. The survey showed that 55 per cent contracted out refuse collection and/or disposal; 47 per cent contracted out street construction and maintenance, and 30 per cent contracted out snow removal. Other services that are contracted-out, although less frequently, include utility construction, street lighting, public health and welfare, street cleaning, equipment maintenance, park maintenance, public protection, parking-meter collection, animal control, and landfill maintenance. Six of the responding municipalities did not contract out any services.[17] This same survey revealed that a number of the respondents were seriously considering contracting-out arrangements for a number of services currently supplied by local governments. In fact, one can argue that contracting-out operations could be expanded to include the general areas of police protection, fire protection, and recreational services to name only a few. While such a suggestion may generate considerable controversy and concern over whether these services would be supplied at a proper level, this concern should not be exaggerated for both the level and quality of service could be dictated and monitored by local officials. In addition, periodic checks on the quality of the service provided would be enforced effectively through the annual tendering or bidding on the various services to be supplied by the private sector. Such an approach could provide a greater incentive to minimize per unit costs and a more effective way of forcing municipal officials to evaluate clearly the demands for each service and the local tax price that residents must pay for these services. In essence, a more optimal level of output may be achieved.

EMPLOYEE PRODUCTIVITY: EXAMPLES

Since most local government services are labour intensive, improvements in productivity, regardless of source, will depend inevitably on the extent to which

---

[15]For an excellent discussion of the potential and actual shortcomings of municipally-run operations, see Dennis Young, *How Shall We Collect the Garbage? A Study in Economic Organization* (Washington, D.C.: Urban Institute, 1972).

[16]Bureau of Municipal Research, *Civic Affairs: Providing Municipal Services—Methods, Costs and Trade-Offs* (Toronto: the Bureau, 1981).

[17]Ibid., at 2.

labour is efficiently and effectively utilized in the delivery of local services. Among the noticeable "influences on employee productivity are factors such as skill level, scheduling of work, availability of necessary tools and equipment, absenteeism and tardiness, health and safety, working conditions, career development opportunities, and supervision."[18] Some of these influences have been handled more easily than others; for instance, improvements in the technical skills of employees, provision of necessary tools and equipment, improvements in the general working conditions, and devotion of more attention to on-the-job safety have all contributed to an improved and more efficient work force.

Unfortunately, a number of other influences including health problems, work schedules, career development opportunities, absenteeism and tardiness have been more difficult to solve. In the recent past, however, a few municipalities have initiated some changes in these areas in order to improve the output per employee. For instance, in the late 1970s, municipal officials in the city of Winnipeg became concerned with the reduction in output and its corresponding costs attributed to factors such as intoxication on the job, extensive use of sick leave, increasing absenteeism, and unnecessary accidents.[19] As a result, city council initiated a project designed to solve these problems. This involved the introduction of an occupational health program operated by a medical doctor and a nurse on a contractual basis. While statistical findings arising from this program are only preliminary, it does appear as if this program has led to a partial reduction in many of the influences that created the problem.

Reorganizations of work schedules have been effective in leading to reductions in downtime and cost savings. In the maintenance division of the Public Works Department of the City of Windsor, the introduction of four ten-hour days in place of five eight-hour days was estimated to save the city $155,000 in 1980.[20] This saving arose because more jobs were started and finished with less time lost through starting up and winding down operations on a daily basis. A similar shift to a four-day ten-hour per day work week has been introduced in the maintenance division of the Physical Environment Department of the City of Ottawa.[21] Scheduling of jobs so as to avoid unnecessary duplication of activities has led to cost reductions in virtually every municipality.

The available evidence suggests that efforts aimed at introducing innovation in local governments must deal with the question of how local employees are affected. Indeed, the labour-intensive nature of most local public services suggests that any innovation designed to cut costs must obtain the cooperation of the local public-sector work force if it is to be implemented successfully. The degree of this cooperation will depend, at least partially, on the extent to which local employees are given an incentive or are motivated to aid in productivity improvements.

Although much more attention, both in terms of research and municipal application, has been devoted to programs designed to improve employee

---

[18]Hayward, supra footnote 1, at 166.

[19]Supra footnote 6, at 15-16.

[20]Ibid., at 12.

[21]Ibid.

motivation in the United States,[22] interest in this topic has been growing in some Canadian municipalities. Improvements in motivation may take the form of providing monetary incentives. This has been instituted in the service of refuse collection in Burnaby, British Columbia where the introduction of new vehicles and a reduced labour force (accepted by the union) resulted in less time lost due to illness, higher morale, and increased productivity. This increased workload with fewer employees has led to the implementation of a bonus pay system plus a nonfinancial incentive system that allows all refuse workers to leave work as soon as pre-set tasks are completed on all routes.[23] Similarly, the City of Sudbury provides a financial incentive in the form of bonus payments to employees who suggest innovations that ultimately generate productivity improvements. To date, several large bonus payments have been made for technologically innovative ideas.[24]

The setting and appraisal of performance targets—explicit, quantitative statements of the desired performance of an individual or group—is a management device that can serve as a motivator. Periodic appraisals of performance targets and the extent to which they are being achieved should serve as a motivational force in generating improvements. Fortunately, as was pointed out earlier,[25] a number of Canadian municipalities have been introducing performance targets in order to improve their levels of productivity and hence reduce costs or at least hold them at a level that is lower than would be the case otherwise.

Job enrichment programs are designed to improve employee motivation and job satisfaction, thus reducing absenteeism and tardiness. The content of the job is altered through increasing the employee's autonomy, varying the skills used and/or adjusting the task performed. In the public sector, these enrichment programs may involve the use of teams, job redesign, participative decision making, and job rotation.[26] By comparison with the private sector where job enrichment programs have been documented, there is virtually no readily available documentation of similar programs in the local public sector in Canada. One example that is available exists in the City Clerk's Department in the City of Windsor[27] where experimentation with job rotation has existed for a number of years. The staff performs work other than their regular job for three months out of every twelve. Greater job satisfaction and suggestions for improving productivity have emerged from this exercise. Obviously, greater consideration and implementation of programs such as this would lead to a reduction in absenteeism and tardiness and create a situation where productivity improvements could be observed.

---

[22]For a thorough discussion of this, see H. H. Greiner, H. P. Hatry, M. P. Koss, A. P. Millar, and J. P. Woodward, *Productivity and Motivation: A Review of State and Local Government Initiatives* (Washington, D.C.: Urban Institute, 1981).

[23]Supra footnote 6, at 8-9.

[24]Supra footnote 4, at 65.

[25]For an assessment of this in Canadian municipalities, see the discussion in the chapter on local government budgeting.

[26]Supra footnote 22, at 398.

[27]Supra footnote 4, at 64-65.

SUMMARY

Given the constraints on tax increases and demands for improved delivery of local services or improved working conditions for local government employees, local governments have become increasingly more interested in productivity improvements designed to hold down per unit costs or to improve the quality and/or quantity of local services. The majority of productivity improvements can be attributed to the implementation of a number of technological innovations in the production or delivery of local services. In addition, some improvement in efficiency has arisen from altering the mix of inputs used in supplying the various services. Regardless of the basis for increased productivity, one must remember that the labour-intensive nature of most local services suggests that improvements of any kind only will be efficient and effective if they are fully accepted and supported by employees (and hence the local unions where they exist), department heads, local politicians, and the general public.

The key to employee acceptance and cooperation resides in the extent to which employees can be motivated to assist in the achievement of maximum benefits from the innovative processes. Increasing an employee's desire to complete a task or improve the quality of the task completed may take various forms including the provision of monetary incentives, job enrichment schemes, or the establishment of performance targets.

With the exception of establishing performance targets (which are gaining in popularity at the local level in Canada), very little has been done in the area of financial and nonfinancial incentives and in the field of job enrichment. These are areas that should be pursued more actively in the interest of productivity improvements. At the same time, considerable progress appears to have been made and is continuing to be made in the implementation of technological innovations. Obviously, further progress in this area should be encouraged.

CASH MANAGEMENT

INTRODUCTION

In a financial environment of growing inflation and high interest rates, the accumulation of excess cash balances will result in losses in forgone interest income if these balances are not invested in marketable securities. Surprisingly, this loss in earnings forgone is not insignificant and perhaps of greater surprise is the fact that many municipalities have never attempted to seek an optimal level of investment for income purposes. While the reasons for this are not documented fully, they appear to revolve around inertia, a lack of time (financial officials frequently are too involved with other administrative details to concentrate on a detailed cash planning system), tradition (excess cash historically has been deposited in existing bank accounts without any consideration being given to alternative forms of investment), and the difficulty of forecasting cash resources because of an absence of effective controls over receipts and disbursements. To overcome this problem and to assist municipalities in their attempts to generate greater incomes from excess cash balances, at least one provincial government (Ontario) has published two

374 LOCAL GOVERNMENT FINANCE IN CANADA

bulletins dealing with this problem.[28] As a result, a number of municipalities have been moving toward a more efficient strategy for handling idle funds.

OBJECTIVES

Cash balances emerge at times when municipalities have received more funds than they have disbursed. If this excess cash is not invested wisely and carefully, earning interest, and hence generating additional revenues, then the municipality has handled public funds inefficiently. Such inefficiency, it may be argued, is similar to that associated with unnecessary and wasteful government expenditures. The primary objective of any cash management system, therefore, should be to provide the necessary amount of cash to meet the requirements of the municipality as they arise while maintaining the rest in secure investments with attractive yields.

CASH MANAGEMENT SYSTEMS

The implementation of a cash management system requires a thorough review of all cash receipt and disbursement procedures. This might begin with a review of all existing bank accounts on the assumption that a number of accounts could be consolidated into one or very few. At the same time, the package of services offered by the various banks (where more than one exists) should be evaluated with the intention of choosing the specific bank providing maximum net benefits to the municipality. Provision should be made for hasty deposits (in a banking institution) of all receipts. This might include, where possible, the use of banks as the direct collector of tax or utility revenues. Similarly, cash disbursements must be reviewed with the ultimate intention of paying all invoices when they are due and not before. Early payments result in forgone interest income.

Once the system has been established, a set of formal procedures outlining the steps to be followed must be drawn up and carefully explained to all of the actors at the various stages. These formal procedures with accurate and current data will allow the municipal treasurer or chief financial officer to receive, on a daily basis, a cash management report. This report will provide the information required to make daily decisions on the cash position of the municipality. This information will allow the municipality to maximize its interest income as well as providing data to be used in preparing a cash budget—an instrument that is essential in a smoothly and efficiently functioning cash management system.

The formulation of a cash budget[29] is designed to forecast the need for cash balances. Although this budget can be drawn up for any interval, monthly forecasts are the most common. A cash budget differs from operating and capital budgets in that it displays only the total of all disbursements and receipts in a specific time period. As well, cash budgets for municipal governments are frequently more accurate than for the commercial or business sector. This is

---

[28]Ontario, Ministry of Intergovernmental Affairs, Municipal Budgets and Accounts Branch, Local Government Division, *Cash Management in Municipalities*, Financial Bulletin F.1 (Toronto: the Ministry, 1978) and also *Municipal Investments*, Financial Bulletin F.3 (1979).

[29]For illustrations of potential cash budgets, see *Cash Management. . .*, supra, at 13-14.

primarily a function of greater reliability in the estimation of both expenditures and receipts for governments vis-à-vis the private sector.

Finally, the presentation of a cash budget will illustrate the timing and magnitude of expected cash requirements and receipts. A shortfall in cash may dictate changes in the due dates of tax notices or alter the scheduling of certain expenditures of a flexible nature. An excess of cash will provide local officials with information that is necessary for wise and efficient investment decisions.

OPTIMUM CASH BALANCES

If one of the objectives of a cash management system is to maximize the return from the municipality's holdings of all liquid funds including cash and marketable securities, then the next step is to establish how much of each kind of asset to hold given that the combined total of the two is established.

The simplest guideline to follow falls under the rubric of "rule of thumb."[30] There is no sophisticated analysis or theoretical underpinning for this approach, yet some type of "rule of thumb" guideline has been adopted in the majority of Canadian municipalities operating with a cash management system. For example, one variation of this approach might state that a municipality must hold, as cash balances, a sum equal to its average weekly estimated expenditures. If cash balances exceed this level, they are invested in short-term marketable securities. If they fall below this level, then the deficiency must be covered from revenues earned in disposing of similar securities. Because local revenues and expenditures can be estimated fairly accurately, this approach has worked quite well, particularly for smaller communities. Indeed, its noticeable simplicity and low administrative costs suggest that for many municipalities, a "rule of thumb" approach is preferable to a more analytically technical, computer-based optimal cash balance model. In essence, the additional benefits gained from the more sophisticated models may not be sufficient to justify the additional cost of these approaches. Having mentioned that analytical models may not be worthwhile in many communities, it must also be mentioned that for a few larger centres with significant liquid funds, a more sophisticated modelling approach would be desirable if the local government is to optimize its holdings of cash balances. While the complexity of these models vary, two of the simpler formats are outlined below.[31] These models, fortunately, display almost all of the variables that are contained in the more sophisticated approaches.

Perhaps the simplest of all cash models is that which is derived from the economic ordering quantity formula used in inventory management.[32] Briefly, this approach suggests that if a municipality is in receipt of a predictable and certain stream of cash payments and faces a predictable and certain stream of disbursements then it is possible to indicate the optimal level of cash balances to

---

[30]James C. Van Horne, "Cash Management," in J. Richard Aronson and Eli Schwartz, eds., *Management Policies in Local Government Finance* (Washington, D.C.: International City Management Association, 1981), 328-45, at 331.

[31]For a reasonably thorough description of each of these models, see ibid., at 332-37.

[32]For the initial application of this model to cash management, see W. J. Baumol, "The Transaction Demand for Cash: An Inventory Theoretic Approach" (November 1951), 66 *Quarterly Journal of Economics* 543.

hold at any particular time. In arriving at the optimal level, one must weigh the carrying cost of holding cash balances if they were invested in marketable securities against the estimated cost per transaction of transferring funds from cash to marketable securities or vice versa. The carrying cost of holding cash balances varies directly with the average cash balances held; for example, the higher the average cash balance, the larger the interest income forgone. By comparison, the transaction cost moves in the opposite direction; the higher the average cash balances, the lower the number of transactions and the lower the cost of transferring cash to securities or securities to cash. The optimum level of cash balances, then, will involve a trade-off between these two costs.[33]

If receipts and disbursements are predictable and certain, then the model outlined in the preceding paragraph will provide a basis for determining the optimal level of cash balances. Indeed, this model, by incorporating some precautionary cash balance (cash held for unforeseen expenditures), could be modified to account for a small degree of uncertainty. On the other hand, if there is a strong element of uncertainty and an inability to predict the demand for cash with any degree of precision, then a different model based on control theory[34] could be adopted. In this case, upper and lower limits on the level of cash held are set. When the cash balances reach the upper limit, an automatic transfer of cash to marketable securities takes place. When the lower limit is reached, the opposite type of transaction (securities to cash) occurs. For cash balances between these limits, no such transaction occurs. The establishment of the limits, therefore, plays an integral role in this model. These will depend on the fixed costs associated with each security transaction plus the forgone interest income from holding idle cash. Since these two costs are known or can be estimated, it follows that the demand for cash must be obtained at the lowest possible total cost.[35]

MARKETABLE SECURITIES

Once the optimum level of cash balances has been established for a particular municipality, the rest of its cash may be used to purchase marketable securities. Provincial statutes stipulate the types of securities that may be purchased. While these restrictions are designed to protect local governments from risky purchases and the possibility of default and loss of funds, they also prevent them from buying securities yielding a return in excess of that earned on the stipulated securities. This restriction has generated criticism in those municipalities that now have both the expertise and time to seek out safe purchases and that would appreciate the opportunity of earning greater interest income.

Purchases of securities[36] are generally restricted to (1) those from reserve funds of the municipality itself; (2) those from funds made available by other

[33]For a discussion of the formula employed in choosing the optimum level and some numerical illustrations, see Van Horne, supra footnote 30, at 332-35.

[34]For a discussion of control theory, see M. H. Miller and D. Orr, "A Model of the Demand for Money by Firms" (August 1966), 80 *Quarterly Journal of Economics* 431-35.

[35]For a presentation of the formula and the use of a numerical illustration, see Van Horne, supra footnote 30, at 335-37.

[36]For a more thorough listing of allowable securities in Ontario, see *Municipal Investments,* supra footnote 28, at 2-6.

municipalities; (3) bonds, debentures, and other securities guaranteed by the federal or provincial governments; (4) certain securities or deposit certificates endorsed and guaranteed by chartered banks or trust and loan companies; and (5) various other minor securities stipulated by the provincial statutes.

Given that security sources are restricted, it may be useful to list the more common types of instruments that municipalities use. The most preferred[37] are term deposits (deposit receipts, term notes, or certificates of deposit obtained from chartered banks and trust and loan companies), intermunicipal loans, bearer deposit notes (issued periodically by chartered banks for large sums of money), bankers' acceptances, Canada treasury bills, provincial treasury bills, municipal notes, and provincial and Canada bonds.

Because the legally required securities tend to be of high quality, the risk of default is not a problem for the municipal investor. Consequently, the municipal investor can concentrate on purchasing securities so that maturity dates coincide, as closely as possible, with the need for funds. Short-term needs or holding cash for liquidity or emergency purposes may be best served by the acquisition of treasury bills and deposit certificates. For cash requirements of a long-term nature, it may be desirable, given the higher rate of return, to acquire securities that are not marketable prior to maturity. In any case, the wise municipal investor will allocate his portfolio of securities so as to minimize the amount of idle cash balances and to maximize the rate of return.

SUMMARY

A carefully designed and well-managed cash management system is an integral and important component of any local government management scheme. Idle cash funds represent a waste and a cost in the sense that interest income that could have been earned has been forgone. To avoid this cost, time and effort must be devoted to the establishment of an optional level of cash balances. Although there are some sophisticated and highly complex models available for determining the ideal level of cash balances, most municipalities rely on a more simplistic, yet fairly effective, "rule of thumb" approach. Once this ideal level of cash balances has been determined, the municipality is left with the exercise of arranging its portfolio so as to secure the greatest return given the constraints it faces. The most important and significant constraints include provincial restrictions on the sources from which securities can be purchased and the dates when securities must be converted into cash to meet expenditure obligations.

PURCHASING AND POOLING ARRANGEMENTS

All municipalities are interested in ways of reducing costs and in this regard one area that has been receiving increasing support is that of centralized purchasing and pooling arrangements. Centralized purchasing may involve the institution of a person or department whose objective is to be familiar with sources of supply, prices, the process of bidding, market conditions, quality of materials, and availability of discounts. This department or individual may do the purchasing for all departments in city hall and perhaps for hospitals and boards of

---

[37]Ibid., at 9-13.

education as well, or it may do all the purchasing for a geographically concentrated group of communities, particularly if these centres are reasonably small in size and financially cannot justify a purchasing agent if left on their own.

While statistical documentation of the number of municipalities employing purchasing officers is not available, there are a considerable number of instances where public institutions (municipal governments, boards of education, universities, and occasionally hospitals) have banded together to benefit from bulk purchases and quantity discounts. Through quality checks, quantity discounts, and competitive bidding, purchasing officers have generated substantial savings in the purchase of various materials.

Closely associated with centralized purchasing is or should be adequate controls over the levels of inventories. Inventories consist of many things including paper products, books, food, chemicals, and hardware. In order to avoid the costs associated with excessive or insufficient inventories, consideration should be given to the establishment of an optimum inventory policy. This should be designed to "(1) minimize the total of ordering and holding costs, and (2) control the frequency of stockouts or shortages relative to holding and storing costs."[38]

Holding or carrying costs include costs related to deterioration, obsolescence, storage, unaccounted losses, insurance, and imputed financing costs. These costs are generally estimated as a percentage (20 per cent or 25 per cent for example) of the purchase price of the items placed in inventory.

Stockout or shortage costs may arise from losses directly attributed to a loss in service resulting from a lack of parts in inventories or they may consist of political or social costs generated by the resentment of the local citizens who are faced with interruptions in local services. These costs may be calculated fairly simply on the basis of costs associated with acquiring needed items quickly or they may be much more difficult to calculate as in the case of citizen resentment. An implicit cost, nevertheless, should be included.

As in the case of cash management policies, there are also fairly sophisticated inventory control models. Briefly, these computer-based models[39] establish a point at which the level of inventory is optimum. For example, a large inventory is desirable to avoid stockout or shortage costs (that is, the cost in citizen resentment or the cost of acquiring materials in an emergency decreases as the size of the inventory increases). By comparison, the cost of carrying an inventory (insurance, spoilage, storage, and obsolescence) increases directly with the size of the inventory. Once these two cost functions have been estimated, one decreasing with the size of the inventory and the other increasing, an inventory holding total cost function can be obtained. The optimum inventory level, therefore, is determined when the total of the two costs is minimum.

While the theoretical model is useful in providing the ideal solution, it is virtually never precisely employed in practice. In its place are a number of "rules-of-thumb" approaches that tend to approximate the optimum solution. Such

---

[38]Eli Schwartz, "Inventory, Purchasing, and Risk Management," in Aronson and Schwartz, supra footnote 30, 389-413, at 390.

[39]For a discussion of these models, see ibid., at 390-97.

rules suggest that inventories must be rolled over at least four or five times per year or inventories must be sufficient to meet one month's usage. Obviously, these rules will be designed to minimize the costs outlined above. The important advantage of linking inventory control with the purchasing function rests in the notion that the same individual or department can exercise the purchase option at the moment inventories begin to fall below their desirable levels.

Pooling arrangements, which are interpreted here to be much more comprehensive than centralized purchasing or inventory control, refer to those instances where cost savings are available in the sharing of equipment or other resources used by a number of departments or municipal operations within and among municipalities, to the provision by one common supplier of specific local services to a number of municipalities. Perhaps a few examples will illustrate this point. In one study on the organizational implications of providing an urban service,[40] it was observed that considerable inefficiencies and hence higher costs often prevail in instances where different departments or municipal operations acquire a separate complement of labour and capital equipment for their respective operations. When this happens, economies are not realized through the utilization of a common pool of resources that are rented out to the various areas as the need arises. Obviously, greater emphasis on pooling of this sort would avoid a considerable amount of duplication and unnecessary costs. Similarly, improvements in productivity and reductions in costs could arise from various joint purchase agreements entered into by a number of municipalities in a given area for large pieces of capital equipment. An example of this exists in the acquisition of a bridge crane truck for inspecting and repairing bridges. Very few municipalities could justify the purchase of this piece of equipment on an individual basis. The improvement in service and savings in maintenance costs, however, could justify its acquisition for a group of municipalities.[41]

The formation of municipal insurance pools in the United States[42] has generated considerable interest for similar policies in Canadian municipalities. This procedure allows units of local government to join together to obtain benefits collectively that would not be available individually. While these pools originally concentrated on workers' compensation coverage, many have now broadened their coverage to include comprehensive and automotive liability and, in a few instances, property insurance.[43] The guidelines for a typical American pool consist of three parts: (1) the municipality agrees to cover small losses on their own (generally the first $1,000); (2) losses above those assumed individually and up to an upper limit (perhaps $100,000) are covered by the pool; and (3) the individual municipality or in some instances the pool will obtain insurance to cover losses greater than the pool limit. Assuming that legal problems (which currently prevent insurance pools in Canada) with respect to the construction of insurance pools can be overcome, the pool offers benefits,

[40]Harry M. Kitchen, "Some Organizational Implications of Providing an Urban Service: The Case of Water" (Summer 1975), 18 *Canadian Public Administration* 297-308, at 302-3.

[41]Supra footnote 4, at 8.

[42]New York State Legislature Assembly Ways and Means Committee, "Municipal Insurance Pools: An Appropriate Alternative for Local Governments?" (April 1981), 10 *Local Finance* 9-12.

[43]Schwartz, supra footnote 38, at 411-12.

especially to smaller communities who are unable to diversify their risk, through risk diversification and the cost reduction associated with this.

Empirical evidence in the United States suggests that substantial savings in insurance costs have occurred as a result of municipal insurance pools.[44] This is clearly an area that is untapped in Canada and one that offers potential savings for local governments.

Pooling arrangements in the provision of some local services offer a potential for cost savings. This potential arises particularly for those services that incur reasonably high annual charges before service can be supplied at all. In most instances, this is likely to apply to smaller communities where it would be best to spread these initial costs over a number of communities so as to make it financially feasible for the recipients to obtain the services at a reasonable charge. Fortunately, a number of services currently are supplied on this basis—police protection for rural villages and very small towns in Ontario, is provided by the provincial government. Certain portions of the water provision operations are supplied by one community and sold to other communities in order to reduce costs. The joint operation of refuse collection and disposal, and fire protection have generated cost reductions for municipalities within the same geographic proximity. Indeed, there are further examples and it is to be hoped that municipalities will continue to devote their attention to further pooling arrangements designed to generate existing or improved quantities and qualities of service at lower costs.

There are obvious savings to be generated from improved purchasing and inventory policies. As has been witnessed by the growth in the number of municipal purchasing individuals or departments over the past few years, these savings can be quite significant. Similarly, greater savings still could be realized in the pooling of local inputs used for the provision of various municipal services. The delivery of many local services also could be conducted more efficiently through an arrangement where the municipalities receive the same service from the same body (one municipality or provincial government supplying to more than one community). Finally, the use of joint purchasing agreements for the acquisition of large items of capital equipment could assist in the achievement of greater productivity and lower costs.

BOARDS, COMMISSIONS, AND SPECIAL-PURPOSE BODIES

Local boards, commissions, and special-purpose bodies responsible for undertaking or overseeing a wide range of activities currently exist in Canada, but are more noticeable in Ontario than in the other provinces. While these bodies have been established for a number of reasons, some of them pre-date the structure of municipal institutions themselves. For example, the election of school trustees and school boards in Ontario began in 1816. In the same province, police commissions were authorized as early as 1866, library boards and utility commissions began in 1882, parks boards in 1885, and children's aid societies in 1893. By the turn of the century, interest in reforming municipal structures began to emerge. This led to an upsurge in the creation of local special-purpose

---

[44]Supra footnote 42, at 11-12.

bodies, the rationale for which arose from a belief that appointed experts rather than politicians and local government officials could administer more efficiently the operation and provision of a number of local services. For example, by the mid-1970s, Metropolitan Toronto and its constituent municipalities listed over 100 special-purpose bodies[45] responsible for a wide range of services including boards óf education, boards of management for recreational and sports facilities, library boards, boards of health, utility commissions, and transit commissions. The growth in the size and level of expertise of the municipal staff over the past few decades plus the technical expertise made available by provincial governments, however, suggest that this rationale no longer carries much weight.

A second argument in favour of continued dependence on boards, commissions, and special-purpose bodies arises in those instances where councillors are part time. It is alleged in such instances that councillors have insufficient time to handle the workload required to plan, administer, and oversee all municipal functions. The appointment or election of a number of interested citizens to these independent boards or commissions, therefore, allows the community to benefit from citizen involvement and assists in removing part of the workload placed on the local council itself. The recent growth and/or restructuring of municipal government, however, now provides the expertise necessary to engage in these diverse activities. In addition, the citizens who previously contributed through independent special bodies could still make their contribution as a member of a committee directly responsible to the local council.

A further argument in support of independent boards and commissions has arisen in instances where special bodies (district health councils, regional conservation authorities, and transport commissions) have been structured to oversee the provision of certain services provided on an intermunicipal basis. Their purpose is to pool financial resources and provide a larger area over which a less costly administration of these activities can take place.[46] Once again their current usefulness is drawn into question. Surely, a committee made up of council representatives drawn from the separate area municipalities would be more accountable to local taxpayers and equally able to draw on both local and provincial expertise in carrying out their mandate.

Of the many boards and commissions currently in existence at the local level, a large number enjoy considerable autonomy and financial independence. In fact, most of these bodies are little governments in themselves with the inherent characteristic that they are legally independent and in no way subordinate to the municipal council. Although this structure may offer certain advantages, the effect of this proliferation of decision-making bodies has been to "create a diffuseness of municipal organization that is inevitably more difficult for the citizens to understand, much less to control."[47] With responsibilities divided

[45]Ontario, *Report of the Royal Commission on Metropolitan Toronto,* Vol. 2 (Toronto: the Commission, 1977), 96-99.

[46]For an outline of other less significant arguments in favour of boards and commissions, see Association of Municipalities of Ontario, *Special Purpose Boards and Commissions,* AMO Reports no. 9 (Toronto: the Association, 1980), 3-5.

[47]Thomas J. Plunkett, *Urban Canada and Its Government: A Study of Municipal Organization* (Toronto: Macmillan, 1968), 60.

among such a large number of separate local bodies, coordination of inter-related activities is difficult and, in many instances, impossible to achieve. All too frequently, attempts by local councils to undertake particular programs or services are thwarted or made more difficult because of decisions made by special-purpose boards or commissions. For example, a coordinated approach by council to administer effectively and to provide community and social services is complicated because the relevant programs may fall under the juris-diction of such separate bodies as the children's aid society, the housing author-ity, the library board, or the health unit and council. Similarly, actions taken by utility commissions, parks boards, conservation authorities, industrial commis-sions, or planning boards may conflict with local council's overall planning efforts.[48]

From the financial perspective of a municipality, the most serious problem encountered with local boards and commissions is the extent to which these bodies appropriate significant portions of local revenues. For example, an examination of the net expenditures of Metropolitan Toronto on special-purpose bodies for each of the years 1968, 1971, and 1974 indicated that these expenditures accounted for approximately 60 per cent of the total net expend-itures financed from own-source revenue.[49] Although it was impossible to obtain detailed data for most other municipalities, a cursory review of the figures, crude as they may be, suggests that a lower, although highly significant, percentage of total expenditures were directed toward these special groups. Perhaps the most outstanding example of a board that lays claim to local tax revenues are the school boards in Ontario. These boards claim a substantial portion of locally raised revenues, yet local councils have no legal right to restrict the sums of money they are asked to contribute to the funding of the local education budget. Similar problems are created by other bodies including those who face council restrictions on the money they may receive and those who face no such restrictions. Regardless of the level of autonomy exercised by these bodies, the existence of so many separate agencies, each determining its financial needs independently, often results in either greater than desirable demands being placed on the municipal treasury or undesirable cost cutting in areas where the councils have effective control. "Because the municipal council cannot, in many cases, interfere with the policy decisions of an independent board or commission, it is denied the most effective means of exercising proper and effective budgetary control."[50] Consequently, financial decisions are not undertaken in a manner that is responsible and accountable to the citizens of the community.

Of considerable importance in evaluating local expenditures by boards and commissions is the question of whether expenditures by these agencies could be handled more efficiently and effectively if placed under the direct control of

---

[48]These examples and others describing the potential for conflicts between local councils and special boards or commissions are drawn from C. R. Tindal and S. Nobes Tindal, *Local Govern-ment in Canada* (Toronto: McGraw-Hill Ryerson, 1979), Chapter 5.

[49]These figures were calculated from Municipality of Metropolitan Toronto, *Annual Report of the Commissioner of Finance,* for the years 1968, 1971, and 1974 (Toronto: the Municipality). The actual percentages were: 1968—60 per cent; 1971—59 per cent; and 1974—62 per cent.

[50]Supra footnote 47, at 62.

local councils. In some cases, the answer to this question is not obvious; however, the limited evidence that is available does suggest that a less costly and more efficient means of providing some services could be undertaken by local councils rather than local boards, commissions, or special-purpose bodies. For example, the only published Canadian study addressing this issue dealt with the organizational implication of providing water in urban municipalities in Canada.[51] The author of that study observed that the cost of supplying water through a separate water or utilities commission was significantly greater than the costs of supplying it by a department directly responsible to city council.[52] Since the technique employed in comparing the costs netted out the influence of a number of variables affecting water supply costs, it was evident that the organizational structure itself had significantly influenced the cost. For instance, the main factors generating higher costs under a separate commission seem to be the result of weaker pressures toward public accountability and an inability to benefit from integration with other functions currently performed by municipal officials directly responsible to municipal council. Furthermore, the cost differential is not justified by a higher quality of service from commissions since service levels in all municipalities tend to be standardized. Finally, it must be noted that the fragmentation of authority that occurs in the case of providing water through a separate utilities commission is unnecessary and unwise. There is little this authority can do that could not be done by a regular government unit. Similar comments could be made about many other local services supplied by special-purpose bodies where their functions or programs could be carried out by or be subject to the direction of municipal councils. Such a transfer of responsibility would eliminate the current morass of local government organizations and would allow local councils to set overall priorities and to weigh and consider the trade-offs necessary in making decisions on the relative merits of spending on education versus health versus conservation versus local transit, etc. This overall improvement in the allocation of scarce municipal financial resources would produce a council more directly responsible for all municipal functions. As such, it would lead to an improvement in the co-ordination of all municipal services and functions (at present, the policies of these local agencies sometimes run counter to the policies of local councils) and would assist in the provision of central budgeting control and establish the basis for long-range financial planning. Unfortunately, the present system, where council has no effective or only limited control, often generates conflicts between certain boards and commissions seeking to promote their own special interests and the municipality attempting to hold the line on tax rates or restricting expenditures over which it does have substantial control. To overcome these conflicts and to assist in the provision of a better allocation of local resources, local councils must be given sole responsibility for making decisions on the appropriate trade-offs to be made among expenditures on the various programs provided at the local level.

Finally, the great diversity of special-purpose bodies weakens the thrust of local government accountability and responsibility. With the exception of very

---

[51]Supra footnote 40, at 297-308.

[52]Harry M. Kitchen, "A Statistical Estimation of an Operating Cost Function for Municipal Water Provision" (January 1977), *Journal of Urban Analysis* 119-33.

few boards and commissions (school boards and utility commissions in Ontario, for example), the membership of local special-purpose bodies is appointed rather than elected. This "so-called" sheltered position has been defended on the grounds that sensitive issues should be "protected from politics." It can be counter-claimed more legitimately, however, that sensitive political issues should be placed directly under council control so as to ensure maximum accountability and responsiveness to the local tax-paying public.

In essence, it can be argued that the function and role of all boards and commissions should be reviewed seriously with the objective of eliminating those agencies for which an extremely strong case cannot be made for their retention. Such elimination would lead to greater political control, financial accountability, and efficiency of operation.

PROVINCIAL-MUNICIPAL FUNDING ARRANGEMENTS

Of particular concern to local governments considering the possibility of initiating new programs or services jointly funded by the municipality and the provincial government are the long-term claims these programs make on local budgetary revenues. Such claims, just as in the case of certain boards and commissions, may be beyond the control of local politicians and administrators. In each province there is a history of projects or programs that have been implemented under the influence and financial support of the provincial government. Guidelines have been established, commitments have been made and once the program has been functioning, the province (which had instigated the project) either financially withdraws or substantially reduces the percentage of the costs that it is prepared to fund. In those instances where the municipality, for one reason or another, is unable to terminate the service or program, it is left with its funding responsibility even though it had little if anything to do with its actual introduction. The original cost to the local government may have been minimal whereas the long-term commitment has become substantial. The examples[53] below will illustrate this problem.

Until 1971, the Ontario government contributed 25 per cent of the costs of capital projects for public transit systems and 50 per cent toward the capital costs associated with road construction. In 1971, the province increased its support for transit projects to 75 per cent and, in addition, agreed to pay 50 per cent of the operating deficit for transit systems. Because of this, some municipalities expanded their transit facilities. In 1975, however, the province placed a ceiling on the amount it would contribute to the systems' operating deficits. Then in 1976, the province decided that its maximum contribution would be only 5 per cent more than the previous year, leaving each municipality to absorb the remainder. At a time when operating costs were rising much faster than 5 per cent annually, each community was faced with a significant increase in expenditures over which it had little or no control.

Similar financial problems arose with respect to the provision of daycare services. The province of Ontario and its municipalities initially funded these on

---

[53]Harry M. Kitchen, *Public Finance in Metropolitan Toronto,* A Study for The Royal Commission on Metropolitan Toronto (Toronto: the Commission, 1977), 76-77.

an 80/20 basis. The demand for daycare was substantial and the level of provincial assistance in the field was relatively high. Consequently, many municipalities greatly expanded their daycare programs. In 1976, the province announced that its annual increases in funds for supporting this service would only rise by 5.5 per cent. Once again, many local governments became locked into escalating expenditures over which they seemed to have minimal control.

To avoid such significant drains on local budgets, one might suggest that the programs or projects be reduced accordingly. Unfortunately, the solution is not that easy. The expansion of many programs has established a set of expectations in the minds of the local citizenry and these expectations tend not to diminish when funding support is reduced. Furthermore, some of these programs are mandatory and it is impossible to eliminate or significantly restrict them in an attempt to cut expenditures.

These examples, which represent only two cases out of a reasonably large number, illustrate the way in which a municipality's expenditures can be skewed by changes in external funding support. Two possible solutions to this problem should be explored. First, a provincial commitment should be made to ensure that a municipality will not be saddled with a long-term responsibility for specific programs unless it is clearly aware of the future financial implications of such programs and accepts them. Second, and alternatively, a provincial revenue or grant commitment could be established to finance the necessary long-term expenditures.

FORECASTING

INTRODUCTION

Earlier discussions in this chapter emphasized the importance of financial planning in order to improve local budget decision-making and overall operational efficiency. Of extreme importance in facilitating good financial planning is the requirement of accurate and comprehensive forecasts of all facets of the municipal financial picture.

While the importance of forecasting has generally been recognized in the private sector for some time and has become an integral component of managerial decision-making, its use and importance, unfortunately, has not been recognized in the local public sector to any great extent. In reality, forecasting has consisted generally of nothing more than a projection of revenues and expenditures for the upcoming fiscal year. Unfortunately, very few municipalities have used forecasting techniques to estimate cash requirements for the next few years, to assess the fiscal impact on future budgets arising from current decisions to implement new programs or services, to expand existing programs and services, or to evaluate alternative means of achieving specific municipal goals or objectives.

METHODS AND USES OF FORECASTS

Because forecasting is such an important managerial tool, it is absolutely essential that each municipality devise a means of forecasting that is appropriate for its own use. In a world without a constraint such as the cost of undertaking the forecast, each rational municipality will aim for the highest degree of accuracy that it can possibly achieve. Given that the cost of generating a forecast depends upon the availability of data, however, the level of expertise required, and the degree of sophistication involved in constructing and running the forecast model, each municipality must make a trade-off between the cost of operating the forecasting system and the degree of accuracy and availability of information required. In making this trade-off, one must be aware of the positive correlation between accuracy, availability of information, and the cost associated with forecasting. For many communities, particularly small and medium-sized centres, the lack of available data, technical expertise, and time suggests that simpler, potentially less accurate forecasts may be acceptable, primarily because the cost of collecting additional data and/or raising the level of expertise is too high. For other larger communities, the improvement in accuracy and availability of information very well may justify the costs of a more fully developed and sophisticated forecasting model.

The forecasting methods[54] that have been suggested range from a "best guess" forecast involving calculations that may be nothing more than "back of the envelope" guestimates to fairly sophisticated forecasts based on highly analytical and extremely technical econometric models. Generally, the level of accuracy will depend on the degree of sophistication; however, there are instances (usually in smaller urban and rural areas) where a forecaster, because of his/her experience and familiarity with all aspects of the municipal operation is able to guess reasonably accurately what the expenditures and revenues will be in the future. The advantage of this simple approach is that it is inexpensive; however, there are a number of disadvantages that stem from the lack of a formal model. When the estimates are wrong, for example, the lack of a formal model may prevent an assessment of why the forecasts are wrong. As well, this approach to forecasting exists only as long as the forecaster is employed by the community. When he/she leaves, the forecast disappears and the community has no reliable technique or approach on which it can rely. Finally, the lack of a more formal forecasting model limits the ability to predict the effect of a number of shocks that may arise from discretionary policy changes or external factors.

Fortunately, the emphasis on long-range planning and the difficulties inherent in the informal guestimate approach to forecasting have forced a number of communities (albeit not as many as might be desirable) to adopt models or approaches based on information rather than on intuition as a basis for forecasting revenues and expenditures.[55] The importance placed on information systems has generated a body of scientific and analytical techniques including those assimilated under the heading of trend techniques, deterministic techniques, and econometric forecasting.[56]

---

[54]For a discussion of forecasting methods suggested for the local public sector in the United States, see Larry D. Schroeder, "Forecasting Revenues and Expenditures," in Aronson and Schwartz, supra footnote 30, 66-90, at 69-83.

[55]Robert M. Cramer, "Local Government Expenditure Forecasting" (November 1978), *Governmental Finance* 3-9.

[56]For a discussion of these techniques, see Schroeder, supra footnote 54, at 70-76.

Trend techniques include the general category of forecasts that are based on projecting past events; for example, expenditures for the next few years will increase annually by the same absolute amount as in the past few years or the growth rate may be projected as an extension of the growth rates in the recent past. The use of an "elasticity of local public expenditures coefficient"[57] has been adopted as a basis for possible future expenditure trends. In essence, the percentage change in the level of public expenditures over the past few years is divided by the percentage change in the level of national income or provincial income or municipal income over the same period. The resultant coefficient, which is referred to as the elasticity coefficient, is then used to predict the change in local public expenditures given that one can predict the change in national, provincial, or municipal incomes[58] in the future.

Where this technique has been employed, it has generally been found that local governmental expenditures are quite income elastic, having elasticity coefficients well in excess of 1.0.[59] What this suggests is that a 1 per cent increase in the income base will generate more than a 1 per cent increase in local government expenditures. Perhaps this is not surprising given the rising costs of inputs required to provide the ultimate programs or services.

Although trend techniques may be useful in deriving short-range forecasts, they suffer from the weakness that they will never be able to predict a turning point. Their entire basis of projection depends on the trend of past events. As well, to argue that changes in income generate changes in local public expenditures may be conceptually meaningless for what is important is the real explanation as to why expenditures increase proportionately or more than proportionately as the income base grows.[60] Clearly, this will involve a careful assessment of why expenditures (individually and collectively) change in the predicted fashion.

Deterministic techniques are similar to trend techniques with the exception that past changes in income do not provide the basis for estimating future expenditures or revenues. In this instance, some variable such as the projected changes in school-aged population will be used to estimate changes in expenditures on education or changes in grant support from the provincial government. For example, knowledge of changes in the number of school-aged students will indicate changes in the minimum demands for education resources (supplies, teachers, and buildings) and the costs associated with the changes. Similarly, changes in grant revenue for educational purposes can be estimated from knowledge of changes in the primary and secondary school-aged population along with the per capita level of grant support.

A major weakness of this approach revolves around the assumptions implicit in the estimation procedure. To predict that an additional level of educational resources will be required if the school-aged population increases suggests that

---

[57]For a presentation and discussion of this method of calculation, see Alan Water Steiss, *Local Government Finance* (Toronto: D. C. Heath, 1975).

[58]For an application of elasticity coefficients in projecting local public sector expenditures, see supra footnote 53, at 59-71.

[59]Ibid., at 59.

[60]Richard M. Bird, *The Growth of Government Spending in Canada* (Toronto: Canadian Tax Foundation, 1970), 90-91.

an assumption must be made about the level of service supplied. For instance, if the current student to teacher ratio is 25:1, then an increase of 100 additional students will require 4 additional teachers if this ratio is to be maintained. It may be feasible or possible, however, to alter the student to teacher ratio so that the required increase in additional resources need not be as suggested. Indeed, utilization of this method requires an explicit statement or statements about the assumptions employed.

While documentation of the forecasting techniques used by the different municipalities is difficult to catalogue, the available evidence suggests that deterministic methods are growing in popularity and becoming quite useful. Obviously, as the above example suggests, they are often used for projecting educational expenditures. They also are applied in the projections of expenditures and revenues associated with property-related services. If reasonably accurate projections on the number of additional residential and commercial/industrial dwellings can be made, then projection of property-related expenditures will follow. At the same time, knowledge of mill rates provides for projected increases in additional property tax revenues arising from the expanded assessment base. Finally, considerable scope exists for imaginatively employing this method as a basis for projecting expenditures on additional resources required for providing people-related services of a specified level and quality.

Econometric forecasting is a fairly sophisticated and more complex method of prediction than either the trend or deterministic techniques described above. In essence, this approach is capable of estimating the effects on local expenditures or revenues arising from simultaneous changes in a number of independent variables that are hypothesized to have some effect on municipal expenditures and revenues. Or, alternatively, it can be used to estimate the effect on local expenditures or revenues coming from a change in only one of the independent variables while holding all other variables constant.[61] The potential for accurate estimates and information on the importance of the various causal (independent) factors suggests that this approach is far superior to either trend or deterministic techniques that almost always measure the effect of only one causal factor (income, population, or time) on local expenditures or revenues. The econometric approach, for example, will allow a municipality to measure the effect of population density on the average unit cost of collecting refuse from residential units while holding output, pickup location, annual snowfall, collection frequency, number of multi-unit dwellings, labour costs, type of collection vehicles, size of family per dwelling unit, and private versus public collection constant. It also will allow the municipality to estimate the effect on average cost from simultaneously changing all or a number of these variables.[62] Similar exercises could be conducted on other local expenditures or revenues in order to estimate the importance of the various independent factors on the expenditures or revenues to be forecast.

---

[61]Econometric forecasting is discussed in a number of statistics or econometric books. One particularly useful description is included in T. H. Wonnocatt and R. J. Wonnocatt, *Introductory Statistics for Business and Economics* (New York: John Wiley, 1977).

[62]For an application of the econometric technique to municipal refuse collection, see Kitchen, supra footnote 14, at 56-76.

A further and relatively important advantage of this forecasting approach is that it is based on "behavioral relationships that contain a theoretical foundation and that can be evaluated by the user of the forecast."[63] This attribute is missing from the other forecasting techniques. As well, this approach allows for changes in direction of expenditures or revenues, a characteristic that is not available in any forecast dependent on past trends. Finally, the econometric approach can be used to identify whether the observed relationship between each causal factor and the level of local revenues or expenditures (dependent variable) is statistically significant, a feature that is not available in the other approaches.

Given the distinct advantages of this forecasting approach over the available alternatives, one may be left wondering why it is seldom, if ever, used. The explanation for this rests in the cost of implementation. Data collection can be expensive, especially since much of it is not likely to be readily available. In addition, the specification of the forecasting equation requires a level of expertise and skill that may not be available, at a reasonable cost, to many local governments. Finally, the econometric approach may contain errors due to improper specifications of the forecasting equation or misuse of available data.

SUMMARY

While there are a number of techniques that may be used for forecasting local expenditures and revenues, each may differ in the degree of accuracy achieved and the cost of the forecast. The more sophisticated and complex the forecast model, the more expensive it is to operate. Each municipality, therefore, must weigh carefully the accuracy desired and the costs involved.

Econometric forecasting models are seldom used by local governments; whereas, combinations of trend or deterministic techniques have become popular in most municipalities engaging in forecasting activities. While it is impossible to assign specific forecasting techniques to particular communities or specific revenue or expenditure functions, most local governments use techniques that are a combination of the most commonly used approaches. One noticeable constraint that may interfere in achieving the most desirable level of expenditures, however, is the political constraint; that is, elected councillors, concerned with the prospect of satisfying their constituents, may dictate the maximum increase in local tax rates they view as being tolerable in the next year or two. Most municipalities, for example, are able to estimate with reasonable precision the level of provincial grant (conditional and unconditional) revenues available. Given this, council then dictates the maximum percentage tax increase that can be imposed. Once determined, the revenue constraint is established and it is this constraint that must be adhered to in approving expenditure increases or choosing among alternative expenditure programs or services.

As well, the attitudes and perceptions of local officials and councillors toward effective forecasting will contribute significantly to the approach taken and the costs incurred. In any case, local forecasting in Canada tends not to be sophisticated and faces a number of constraints (cost, attitude of those respon-

---

[63]Schroeder, supra footnote 54, at 75.

sible for forecasting, availability of data, and expertise) that may be difficult to remove. Every effort, however, should be made to eliminate constraints that currently impede any approach designed to generate more accuracy in forecasting and long-range planning.

CHAPTER SUMMARY

This chapter has outlined a number of areas in which improvements at the local level could lead to increased services for the same expenditures, additional revenues without corresponding increases in tax rates or charges, or increased levels of services without higher expenditures and revenues being increased. Productivity improvements, for example, may lead to lower costs of providing existing services or to an expansion in local services for the same costs. Similarly, purchasing and pooling arrangements may reduce the costs of buying a number of inputs. Improvements in the management of cash balances will generate additional revenues for local governments. Restrictions or more effective controls over the powers and activities of local boards, commissions, and special-purpose bodies will eliminate many financial problems for locally elected councils. Greater provincial/local cooperation in the initiation, implementation, and funding of jointly sponsored programs and services will remove a lot of the uncertainty with respect to the impact on local budgets in future years. Finally, a more sophisticated approach to the forecasting of local revenues and expenditures will serve as an aid in improving the financial planning and management of local government activities.

15
The Future of Municipal Finance

INTRODUCTION

For some time, local politicians and administrators have been concerned with problems of financing local expenditures. Recently, this concern has heightened, particularly in the presence of rapid increases in the costs of maintaining local services and less than corresponding increases in the local own-source revenue base. This growing discrepency between local expenditures and local own-source revenues has been offset partially by grant increases from senior governments, by increases in existing local tax rates or user charges, and to a lesser extent, by increases in the levels of borrowing for capital projects. Whether or not past trends will continue is is a matter of some conjecture. The existence of provincial deficits, however, has prompted some significant "belt tightening" by provincial governments. This has generated and will continue to generate slower rates of growth in provincial/municipal grants. In addition, the American experience with local tax limitations, such as Proposition 13 in California, has served to create an environment in which property tax increases will almost certainly be restricted somewhat, in order to avoid similar actions in Canada. Finally, recent developments in a number of municipalities suggest that continued expansion of user charges, as a means of financing local services, will ensue throughout the next decade.

Since perfect foresight is not possible, any discussion of the future of municipal finance must be necessarily speculative. Such a discussion may revolve around minor changes in the provision or funding of local services. This would, for example, consist of potential productivity improvements or innovative cost saving techniques that could be introduced in the provision of specific services or it might involve an increased emphasis on user fees rather than property tax revenues as a means of funding certain services. Indeed, a number of comments of this nature have already been made throughout this book. Alternatively, the discussion might be directed at a few major changes that could assist local governments in supplying or funding local services. This is, in fact, the approach followed in this chapter. Here, it is assumed that local governments must collect local revenues in order to continue financing many local services and programs. This chapter, then, will explore some of the financial consequences or potential consequences arising from the implementation or introduction of a number of alternatives designed to bring locally funded expenditures into line with own-source revenues. These include a more extensive use of property taxes; the financial implications of transferring some local expenditure responsibilities onto provincial governments; and the introduction of additional or new tax sources. In each instance, an estimation of the financial implications arising from the proposed changes will be conducted on the 1968 to 1978 or 1980 data base. The choice of this time period is necessitated by the absence of any post-1980 data. The financial implications arising from the period studied will form the basis for comments on the possibility of future changes that may take place. Before launching into a discussion of each of these potential changes, however, a few comments will be made on the "alleged" mismatch between local expenditure responsibilities and locally raised revenues.

LOCAL EXPENDITURE RESPONSIBILITY AND REVENUE CAPACITY

While much has been written on the growing differential between local government expenditures and the ability or capacity these governments have to continue financing local services at adequate levels through the use of acceptable property tax rates and/or user charges, much of this writing has revolved around the measurement and assessment of the existing and future fiscal imbalance. This imbalance at the local level has been measured in two ways. The first measure[1] involves a comparison of total local government expenditures and total local government revenues from all sources except borrowing. Following this, the differential (fiscal imbalance) between local expenditures and revenues records the level of government borrowing. Any change in fiscal imbalance merely reflects a corresponding change in the level of borrowing. Using this measure, the emphasis is on the size of local government deficits and the cost of servicing them.

The second measure[2] records the imbalance between total local government expenditures and own-source revenues. Own-source revenue excludes grants (federal and provincial) and borrowings. Utilization of this approach indicates the degree to which local governments could finance their own expenditures without relying on borrowing for capital projects or transfers from other governments. In both instances, total municipal expenditures include capital and current items.

Although both measures have been employed in studies of local government fiscal imbalance,[3] neither are very useful in the context of what is being attempted in this book. Any presentation of fiscal imbalance figures that records the level of government borrowing, for example, is somewhat meaningless at the local level, because local governments in Canada are forbidden by law from budgeting for deficits in their operating budgets. The only allowable municipal government borrowing is that which is done for financing capital projects or for some short-term borrowing to finance an unexpected shortfall in current revenues. This short-term borrowing must be covered by budgeting for sufficient revenues in the ensuing year. Furthermore, interprovincial and intertemporal comparisons of fiscal imbalance figures for local governments

---

[1]For a discussion of fiscal imbalance in Canada, using total local government expenditures minus local government revenue except for borrowing, see W. Irwin Gillespie, *The Urban Public Economy,* Research Monograph no. 4 (Ottawa: CMHC, 1971); and W. Irwin Gillespie, "An Examination and Analysis of Municipal Financial Problems," in *Report of Proceedings of the Twenty-fifth Tax Conference,* November 19-21, 1973 (Toronto: Canadian Tax Foundation, 1974), 561-90.

[2]For Canadian studies employing this alternative, namely total local government expenditures minus local own-source revenues, which excludes transfers and borrowings, see Gillespie, ibid.; D.A.L. Auld, "Financing Canadian Municipal Government" (mimeograph, Department of Economics, University of Guelph, November 1971); and Harry M. Kitchen, *Public Finance in Metropolitan Toronto,* A Study for The Royal Commission on Metropolitan Toronto (Toronto: the Commission, 1977), 170-78.

[3]See the sources listed in supra footnotes 1 and 2.

may be difficult to make because of different provincial/municipal responsibilities in each of the provinces and changes that have occurred in this division
of responsibility over time.

In essence, fiscal imbalance figures are not presented here because it is
unlikely that their inclusion would shed any light on this study. The presentation of fiscal imbalance figures for ex post own-source expenditures and own-
source revenues are almost always equal. Discrepancies may exist but these are
fairly small and thus insignificant. Any fiscal imbalance discussion on these
revenue and expenditure totals, therefore, would be of limited use. Similarly, a
discussion of borrowing and capital expenditures has already been covered in
Chapter 6.

While a presentation of fiscal imbalance figures would be fruitless at this
time, it must be stated that municipalities continuously are concerned about
various ways of financing their local commitments. This concern has led to suggestions ranging from a more extensive use of existing revenue sources, to
shifting some expenditure responsibilities away from local governments and
onto the provincial level, to the adoption of new revenue sources. These will be
discussed below.

EXPANSION OF EXISTING PROPERTY TAXES

In Chapter 10, a strong argument was made in favour of placing greater
dependence on user fees as a means of financing those local services that carry
a number of private good characteristics; that is, where the benefits are divisi-
ble and essentially accrue to the direct users. Such an approach would lead to a
better allocation of society's resources. Individuals who consume these services
would pay for them and the fees paid would reflect the user's benefits.

Without constructing a detailed assessment of the advantages and disadvantages of property taxes (this was done in Chapter 8), a case can be made for a
fuller use of property taxes in many municipalities in Canada. Much of local
governments' concern with property taxation revolves around the assumption
that it is and must, by the nature of the tax, be an inelastic source of revenue.
This view has arisen because of a reluctance or unwillingness on the part of local
politicians and administrators to raise tax rates or expand the tax base as fully
as might be justified otherwise. The high visibility of the property tax and constant concern over political repercussions such as those witnessed in some areas
of the United States (Proposition 13 in California, for example) have discouraged many local governments from using this form of taxation as a greater
source of revenue. Unfortunately, much of this criticism has taken on a tone of
hysteria and emotion. Local residents in their quest for lower taxes seldom, if
ever, consider the benefits derived from local expenditures; for example, streets
are available for use at any time, fire and police protection are always available,
garbage collection and disposal occur at regular intervals, and the list continues.
Since a charge (price) or a fee is not assessed each time the services are used,
taxpayers perceive them as free goods and generally forget that they must
be financed. Consequently, in the minds of many citizens, local expenditures,
and hence revenues necessary to finance them, appear to be excessive.

Recognizing the political constraints of increasing the use of property taxation and leaving aside the legitimate argument that a structural change in property taxation designed to place relatively more emphasis on residential versus nonresidential property would be desirable (see Chapter 8), it may be useful to comment on the issue of whether property taxes could have been utilized more extensively in the period from 1968 to 1980. If one discovers that there was a case for greater utilization throughout this period, then an argument can be presented for greater utilization of property taxes in the future. To address this issue, the existing property tax base and structure is accepted. Tax utilization,[4] is measured by taking per capita tax yield as a per cent of the per capita tax base. Obviously, this measure of tax utilization may be challenged; however, given the data limitations and various difficulties associated with all other alternatives, this measure is deemed acceptable.

While per capita property tax data are easy to obtain, an accurate measure of the tax base is considerably more difficult to acquire. Assessment data frequently are outdated and almost never reported in a uniform manner within or across provinces. Perhaps the best available proxy for reflecting the property tax base in a uniform and consistent manner across provinces is per capita gross domestic provincial product (GDPP) (see Chapter 2 for use of this measure in other contexts). Even though this total is derived from the combined output of all factors of production (land, labour, and capital), this need not create a problem as long as the contribution of property (land and buildings) in each province reflects approximately the same proportion of GDPP in each year. Indeed, the limited available evidence suggests that this may be an understatement, for the rapid appreciation in property values supports the contention that this component has risen. Nevertheless, operating on the assumption that the contribution of property is constant will lead to an understatement rather than an overstatement of the results.

Table 15.1 records per capita taxes (tax yield) as a per cent of per capita GDPP (tax base) for each of the years 1968 to 1980 and for each province. Where the percentages are constant from one year to the next, per capita property taxes have increased at the same rate as the tax base. Where the percentages have increased in value, the growth in taxes exceeded the growth in the tax base. Where the percentages fell, the tax yield grew more slowly than the tax base.

Since the pattern displayed for the average Canadian (last row of Table 15.1) was not the same as in all provinces and for all years, a perusal of the individual provincial figures suggests a basis for some interprovincial comparisons. Every province exhibited cyclical swings, although the peaks, troughs, and rates of change varied substantially. For example, with 1968 as the base year, three provinces (Newfoundland, Nova Scotia, and New Brunswick) initially reported a decrease in the extent to which property taxes were utilized, while the remainder exhibited an increase.

Utilization of property taxes in Newfoundland and Manitoba, while displaying a cyclical pattern around an increasing trend over the 13-year period, absorbed a larger proportion of the tax base in 1980 than in 1968. In the case of

---

[4] For a discussion of this, see Harry M. Kitchen, "Property Taxation: Overutilized or Underutilized?" (July-August 1982), 30 *Canadian Tax Journal* 610-17.

Table 15.1   Per Capita Property Tax Collected as a Per Cent of Per Capita GDPP, 1968 to 1980

Province	Year												
	1968	1969	1970	1971	1972	1973	1974	1975	1976	1977	1978	1979	1980
							per cent						
Newfoundland	0.67	0.63	0.70	0.68	0.80	0.75	0.74	1.03	1.00	1.14	1.07	1.06	1.13
Prince Edward Island	3.23	3.45	2.69	2.96	2.81	2.63	2.24	2.09	2.26	2.53	2.44	2.42	2.31
Nova Scotia	3.65	3.39	3.69	4.04	3.99	3.52	3.18	3.20	3.20	3.01	2.73	2.69	2.69
New Brunswick	2.81	2.77	2.91	2.91	2.92	2.66	2.63	2.40	2.50	2.85	2.78	2.65	2.77
Quebec	3.87	3.97	4.69	4.17	4.07	3.80	3.36	3.25	3.30	3.21	3.31	2.92	2.91
Ontario	4.19	4.24	4.44	4.25	4.01	3.54	3.37	3.46	3.71	3.80	3.59	3.54	3.54
Manitoba	4.00	4.09	4.25	4.15	4.21	3.77	3.89	4.20	4.42	4.26	4.19	4.18	4.32
Saskatchewan	4.88	4.96	5.48	4.88	4.94	3.89	3.08	2.94	3.15	3.39	3.16	2.94	2.90
Alberta	3.43	3.46	3.57	3.59	3.55	3.03	2.37	2.32	2.31	2.24	2.21	1.99	1.95
British Columbia	4.07	4.09	4.85	4.61	4.48	3.98	4.11	4.65	4.55	4.24	4.28	3.98	3.90
Average	3.94	3.99	4.37	4.13	3.99	3.56	3.33	3.34	3.46	3.42	3.35	3.17	3.15

Source: Supra footnote 4, at 614.

Newfoundland, this can be largely explained by the extremely low level of property taxes in the first year under study. In fact, per capita property taxes (in absolute values) were roughly one-fifth of the next lowest province and slightly more than one-tenth of the Canadian average in 1968, thus supporting the contention that on a comparative basis property taxes were relatively low. Indeed, by comparison with other provinces, they were low throughout the 13 years. Manitoba, on the other hand, displayed property taxes that were slightly below the Canadian average from 1968 to 1973 and considerably higher from 1974 to 1980, thus suggesting that municipalities in this province utilized the property tax much more fully than the other provinces in 1980 when compared with 1968.

In New Brunswick and British Columbia, the proportion of the tax base absorbed by property taxes in 1980 was very close to the proportion in 1968, although this ratio displayed cyclical swings over the entire period. For the remaining six provinces, similar swings were evident but the pattern was one of a substantially smaller proportion of the tax base being absorbed by property taxes in 1980 when compared with 1968.

Finally, in making intertemporal comparisons on a regional basis, it is worth noting that property taxes in Saskatchewan and Alberta, when compared with the neighbouring provinces of Manitoba and British Columbia, absorbed a considerably smaller proportion of the tax base for each of the years from the early 1970s to 1980. In central Canada, Quebec, when compared with Ontario, placed noticeably less emphasis on property taxes as a source of revenue from the mid-1970s to 1980. As well, over the entire period, both provinces were relatively more dependent on this source of revenue than were the four provinces in Atlantic Canada. Finally, as was suggested above, Newfoundland, when compared with the other provinces, placed considerably less weight on property taxation as a source of revenue.

To help judge whether property taxes have been over-utilized or under-utilized, the utilization of property taxes and other major taxes must be compared. In this exercise, a benchmark has been established using per capita personal income taxes expressed as a percentage of the same tax base (per capita GDPP). As illustrated in Table 15.2, the utilization of personal income taxes has risen in every province from 1968 to 1980, whereas the use of property taxes has grown in only two provinces (Newfoundland and Manitoba). Per capita property taxes on average declined from 3.94 per cent of the tax base in 1968 to 3.15 per cent in 1980, while per capita personal income taxes rose from 8.94 per cent to 12.68 per cent over the same period. As well, similar increases (although differing in magnitude) in the use of the income tax prevailed in each of the provinces. On this basis, it might be argued that property taxes could have been used more intensively as other major taxes were.[5]

It must be noted, however, that the argument in favour of a greater usage of property taxes may depend on two important assumptions. First, the choice of the base year used in making projections and second, the choice of the tax rate that is applied to the tax base. In this study, the year 1968 was chosen as the base

---

[5]For evidence supporting this suggestion, although using a different tax base, see David B. Perry, "Fiscal Figures: Changes in the Canadian Tax Structure" (July-August 1977), 25 *Canadian Tax Journal* 441-45.

Table 15.2 Utilization of Property Taxes Compared with Utilization
of Personal Income Taxes for Selected Years by Province

	1968		1971		1975		1980	
Province	Property[a] tax	Personal[b] income tax	Property[a] tax	Personal[b] income tax	Property[a] tax	Personal[b] income tax	Property[a] tax	Personal[b] income tax
				per cent				
Newfoundland	0.67	6.46	0.68	8.76	1.04	12.08	1.13	11.92
Prince Edward Island	3.23	5.36	2.96	8.33	2.09	9.68	2.31	10.12
Nova Scotia	3.65	7.21	4.04	10.22	3.20	11.98	2.69	12.23
New Brunswick	2.81	6.79	2.91	10.36	2.40	11.43	2.77	11.17
Quebec	3.87	9.38	4.17	12.39	3.25	12.00	2.91	16.54
Ontario	4.19	9.59	4.25	10.81	3.46	12.20	3.54	12.37
Manitoba	4.00	8.16	4.15	10.79	4.20	11.48	4.32	11.33
Saskatchewan	4.88	6.93	4.88	7.61	2.94	9.91	2.90	9.19
Alberta	3.43	6.59	3.59	9.41	2.32	8.62	1.95	8.94
British Columbia	4.07	9.39	4.61	12.11	4.65	12.97	3.90	12.84
Average	3.94	8.94	4.13	11.50	3.34	11.67	3.15	12.68

[a]Recorded from Table 15.1. [b]Per capita personal income taxes collected (federal and provincial) as a per cent of per capita GDPP.

Table 15.3   Potential Change in Property Tax Revenue, 1980

Province	Millions of dollars[a]			Per cent of existing property tax revenue[a]		
Newfoundland	− 16,501	to	− 15,410	− 40.4	to	− 37.7
Prince Edward Island	7,323	to	3,030	39.9	to	16.5
Nova Scotia	61,304	to	63,865	35.6	to	37.1
New Brunswick	4,126	to	9,232	3.0	to	6.6
Quebec	584,567	to	1,085,751	32.8	to	61.0
Ontario	633,871	to	878,686	18.3	to	25.3
Manitoba	− 34,318	to	− 9,348	− 7.9	to	− 2.2
Saskatchewan	225,726	to	294,288	68.0	to	88.7
Alberta	558,367	to	611,073	76.2	to	83.4
British Columbia..........	57,932	to	317,867	4.5	to	24.5
Total....................	2,106,785	to	3,256,479	25.0	to	38.6

[a]The first figure is projected on the assumption that the relationship between per capita property taxes and the tax base (in per capita values) was the same in 1980 as in 1968, while the second figure accepts, as the assumption, the relationship that existed in 1970.

because it was the first year for which property tax data were recorded in a uniform and consistent manner intertemporally and interprovincially. The choice of 1968 may not be without criticism, however, for this was around the time when property taxes relative to personal disposable incomes were at a post-war high.[6] In fact, it might be argued that increased emphasis on property taxation from the mid-1950s to the late-1960s led to political forces yielding increased provincial assistance and lower property tax burdens in the 1970s. To claim that the relatively lower property tax burden in the mid-1950s when compared with the late-1960s, is a more appropriate base year against which to measure the extent to which property taxes could have been utilized is to imply that the relationship between property taxes and the tax base in the earlier period was more appropriate or accurate. Given that there is no theoretical or empirical base for supporting this suggestion and given the data limitations for the earlier period, 1968 was chosen as the base year.

Table 15.3 shows the range of additional revenue that might have been generated in 1980 on the assumption that the relationship between per capita tax yields and the tax base was the same as in 1968 or, alternatively, as in 1970. Obviously, the choice of year will reflect the outcome—1968 was chosen because it was the first year used for comparative purposes while 1970 was the year in which the overall dependence on this revenue source was greatest. In addition, earlier rather than later years seemed more appropriate as a base because they represented a time when the emotional criticism of property taxation tended to be less noticeable.

[6]See Melville L. McMillan, *Local Intergovernmental Fiscal Relations in Australia and Canada,* Occasional Paper no. 23 (Canberra: Australian National University, Centre for Research on Federal Financial Relations, 1981), 11.

If the dependence on property taxes in 1980 had corresponded to that in 1968 or 1970, total tax revenues would have been between \$2.1 and \$3.3 billion more than the amount that actually was collected. These figures represent between 25 per cent and 39 per cent of total property taxes collected in 1980 (the last row of Table 15.3), although there are substantial variations in the extent to which tax revenues might have been altered in each province. Alberta and Saskatchewan exhibited the greatest capacity to raise additional revenue from property taxation. The estimates in Table 15.3 show that, depending on the year selected as the base for projections, Alberta could have raised between 76 per cent and 83 per cent more from property taxes, while Saskatchewan could have earned between 68 per cent and 89 per cent more. At the other extreme, the evidence for Newfoundland and Manitoba suggests that property taxes collected grew faster than the tax base. Figures for the remaining provinces are recorded in Table 15.3.

TRANSFERRAL OF EXPENDITURE FUNDING

An alternative means of assisting local governments in meeting their financial constraint might consist of the transfer of certain expenditures to the provincial government or the provision of additional grant revenues to local governments in order to finance the entire cost of certain local services. Expenditures that rank as prime candidates for this treatment are those that are made to finance programs or services of a people-related rather than property-related nature. Obvious examples include education, health, and social welfare expenditures. Support for the exclusion of these services from the property tax base revolves around the argument that property taxes should be treated as user charges for services accruing specifically to property.[7] Such a tax price would generate greater allocative efficiency in the provision of local services, leaving the important issue of fairness in the distribution of the tax burden to the income tax system and the various tax-relief measures administered by either or both of the federal and provincial governments.

To shed some light on the magnitude of the reduction in local per capita property taxes arising from a policy that either provides additional grant revenue to local governments to continue with existing health, education, and social welfare services or shifts the responsibility and hence financing of these services to the provincial level, the reader is referred to Table 15.4. From these data, one observes the significant and noticeable reduction in local property taxes that could have arisen if the provincial government had financed these local services completely in each of the years 1968 and 1978. For the average Canadian, local property taxes would have been reduced by approximately 64 per cent and 51 per cent in 1968 and 1978 respectively. The transferral of the funding burden onto the provincial authorities would have generated significant reductions in per capita local property taxes in all but two provinces in each year (the exceptions being Newfoundland and New Brunswick in 1968 and Prince Edward Island and New Brunswick in 1978). The largest absolute and per-

---

[7]For arguments in support of this use of property taxes, see John Bossons, "Property Tax Reform: What is Desirable?" in John Bossons, Michael Denny, and Enid Slack, eds., *Municipal Fiscal Reform in Ontario: Property Taxes and Provincial Grants* (Toronto: Ontario Economic Council, 1981), 9-88, at 14.

Table 15.4   The Reduction in Local Real Property Taxes Arising from a Transfer of Education, Health, and Social Welfare Expenditures Financed from Own-Source Revenues to the Provincial Level, 1968 and 1978

Province	1968		1978	
	Per capita reduction[a]	Percentage reduction in extant property tax[b]	Per capita reduction[a]	Percentage reduction in extant property tax[b]
	dollars	*per cent*	*dollars*	*per cent*
Newfoundland	1.21	10.1	16.12	30.4
Prince Edward Island	31.22	62.4	4.88	11.6
Nova Scotia	64.95	83.3	147.40	87.7
New Brunswick	1.24	6.9	.03	0.0
Quebec	49.99	48.5	65.02	29.0
Ontario	109.46	72.5	186.46	56.5
Manitoba	56.77	48.9	158.81	51.6
Saskatchewan	86.66	65.2	162.74	58.8
Alberta	101.50	81.2	157.97	59.2
British Columbia	86.51	65.5	234.67	64.3
Average	76.94	63.6	139.70	51.0

[a]From data in Appendix Tables B.1 and B.2. [b]Figures in previous column as a per cent of actual property taxes collected.

centage reduction would have occurred in Nova Scotia, Ontario, and the four western provinces. In each case, the reduction in 1978 would have amounted to more than 50 per cent of the existing per capita property tax levels (Table 15.4). In the remaining provinces, the majority of these services currently are funded by the provincial government and, therefore, there would not be significant tax savings to be gained by local taxpayers in the transfer of responsibility for the funding of such people-related services.

ALTERNATIVE TAX SOURCES

While a case may be made for increased utilization of property taxes, with greater weight being placed on the residential as opposed to the nonresidential portion, the public outcry and general criticism that would follow such a move has created a general reluctance on the part of local officials to adopt such a policy. As a result, local officials have been casting around for alternative sources of revenue. The most recent claim for new revenue sources came from the President of the Federation of Canadian Municipalities who stated that local governments will be making a "definite thrust to get a better share of national tax resources and this could mean a direct portion of income-tax revenue."[8]

To assess the various alternatives that may be available to local governments and to provide a rough estimate of the revenue impact, the following few pages set out the criteria on which an evaluation should take place followed with an assessment of the different alternatives along with an estimate of potential revenue yields wherever possible.

[8]Reported in *The Globe and Mail,* June 7, 1982, 5.

CRITERIA

In evaluating the desirability of alternative tax sources, the criteria employed will be those of equity, efficiency, and ease of administration.[9] While these three criteria exist in virtually every assessment of taxation, perhaps a note of explanation is in order. In our earlier discussion of user fees (Chapter 10) and property taxes as they represent a charge for benefits received (Chapter 8), it was argued that local governments should not be concerned primarily with the distributional effects (equity) of these charges. Instead, the prime objective of local officials should be an achievement of an efficient (nondistorting) tax or charge leaving the broader question of the distributional impact on income earners to a more senior level of government better equipped to deal with equity issues. Indeed, this position still holds. Once local governments decide to tap revenue sources that bear no relationship between the tax price and the benefits received, however, local governments should be concerned with the distributional effects of their new levies. A discussion of equity as a criterion for local governments thus becomes important.

Leaving aside those taxes designed to capture the benefits received (user fees and a portion of property taxes), there is no scientific basis for establishing an equitable tax. Any statement claiming that a tax is equitable involves a value judgment and a situation that may lead to the choice of any tax as representing a justifiable index of equality. Fortunately, such variation in the potential choice of indices of equality does not exist. Most individuals tend to accept income, after allowance for the various deductions and exemptions, as being the most acceptable base for measuring fairness or equity in the distribution of the tax burden.

Once income has been chosen (as the index for measuring fairness) and after appropriate deductions and exemptions to reflect the specific circumstances of the local taxpayers, it is essential to tax all individuals in similar circumstances at the same level (horizontal equity) and those in different circumstances at different levels (vertical equity). For example, all individuals left with $20,000 of income per year after the appropriate deductions and exemptions would pay the same level of tax, while individuals left with more or less income would pay appropriately more or less in taxes with the amount by which taxes would be more or less determined by political decision-makers. In short, income is the measure that will be used in assessing the fairness or equity of the potential tax sources discussed below.

A second criterion upon which each potential tax source should be assessed is that of efficiency (neutrality). If we assume for the moment that there are no other distortions or imperfections in the local economy, then the imposition of a tax that creates a distortion in favour of or against certain types of activities will be inefficient (not neutral). To generate efficiency in this instance requires the imposition of a tax that is uniform in its application and, therefore, does not lead to favourable treatment of certain types of consumption or production

---

[9]While the criteria of growth and stabilization are also important, they are not employed as criteria for local governments. For a more complete discussion of the various criteria and the conflicts created by attempting to simultaneously achieve more than one, see Robin W. Boadway and Harry M. Kitchen, *Canadian Tax Policy* (Toronto: Canadian Tax Foundation, 1980), 7-24.

activities vis-à-vis others. On the other hand, if distortions or imperfections in economic activity currently exist, the imposition of a tax that is not applied in a uniform manner may correct some of the extant distortions, and thus create a more efficient overall allocation of society's resources. Since it is impossible to measure the distortions or imperfections currently existing in the local economy, our evaluation of each of the following taxes on efficiency grounds will revolve around whether their imposition will create a situation that encourages or discourages certain types of economic behaviour.

Ease of administration is an important criterion to consider in the evaluation of introducing a new tax. A tax should not be costly to administer and it should be understood clearly by the taxpaying public and, thus, accepted by them. While these three criteria are important bases on which to evaluate a municipal tax, the simultaneous achievement of all three may create serious conflicts. For example, a tax that is designed to be equitable is likely to be inefficient or it may be necessary to make a tax less equitable or less efficient in order to facilitate its administration.

A final point to consider, although not stated as a criterion on which to base a tax, is the revenue yield that would be generated by its implementation. A tax that fulfills the criterion of equity or efficiency but yields little revenue in relation to its collection costs is unlikely to be considered seriously; whereas, a tax generating significant revenues may be readily accepted and widely used even though it creates more inefficiencies or inequities than are thought to be desirable. From the perspective of the local policymaker, the revenue generating capacity of potential new tax sources is extremely important and, wherever possible, estimates of the revenue yields from these taxes will be supplied.

MUNICIPAL INCOME TAX[10]

Although the federal income tax was not levied in Canada until 1917, both the provinces and municipalities had introduced a tax on income more than 80 years earlier.[11] In fact, the revenue importance of this tax at the local level was proven by the observation that municipal income tax revenues exceeded provincial income tax revenues in every year up to and including 1930. By the early 1940s, some form of municipal income tax (although the rates and structures varied) had been accepted by some cities in every province in Canada. In 1941, however, the provinces entered into the Wartime Tax Rental Agreement with the federal government and since that date no municipality in Canada has levied a municipal income tax.[12] Indeed, local governments in Canada now are legally forbidden to introduce such a tax.

---

[10]For a discussion of municipal income taxation in Canada, see Harry M. Kitchen, "Municipal Income Taxation—A Revenue Alternative?" (September-October 1982), 30 *Canadian Tax Journal* 781-86; and Enid Slack, "The Potential Use of PIT for Municipal/Fiscal Government Financing" (mimeograph) (Toronto: Ontario Economic Council, 1983).

[11]For a very brief review of the historical development of municipal income taxes, see Sheldon Silver, "The Feasibility of a Municipal Income Tax in Canada" (September-October 1968), 16 *Canadian Tax Journal* 398-406, at 398-99.

[12]Ibid.

Around the time municipal income taxes were disappearing in Canada, they began to emerge in the United States. Philadelphia was the first city to adopt a local income tax and did so in 1938. By the late 1970s, local income taxes had been authorized by localities in 15 states and were actually being used in 13.[13]

Increasing concern over revenue shortages combined with the expected and unwanted political reprisals arising from higher property taxes and user fees have renewed the interest of local politicians and administrators in gaining access to income tax revenues.[14] An evaluation of the possible implications of municipal income taxation, therefore, should be undertaken. Since the revenue generated by the personal income tax has been roughly three times greater than that generated by the corporate income tax,[15] and since the overwhelming efficiency and administrative arguments against local corporate income taxes rule them out, the following evaluation of income taxation will be confined to the personal income tax alone.

While the two most important criteria on which to evaluate the personal income tax may be those of equity and efficiency, it is not this author's intention to review these criteria as they apply to personal income taxes in this chapter, for they have been discussed comprehensively in numerous other sources.[16] Indeed, the imposition of a personal income tax at the local level would generate efficiency and equity effects similar to those arising from an increase in the provincial income tax rates applied to an identical tax base with one or two possible exceptions. These exceptions are created by the proximity of one local income tax jurisdiction to an adjacent non-income tax jurisdiction. For example, if every community implemented a local income tax on the same tax base (that is, similar to the provincial income tax base) and at the same rate, then differential treatment among neighbouring communities would not exist. When one community imposes a municipal income tax while an adjacent community does not, however, the potential for encouraging certain types of behaviour is created. People and businesses will tend to locate in those areas that are not taxed. Minimization of this migratory effect may necessitate extremely low tax rates. As well, the imposition of an income tax in selected communities might generate effects that would strike nonresidents as well. To the extent that a local income tax on individuals forces up local wages and/or raises the prices of locally produced goods and services, part of this tax may be passed on to nonresidents in the form of higher prices for goods and services purchased from the taxed areas.

If municipalities can secure the legal right to adopt local income taxes, the question that is then raised is whether these municipalities should piggyback onto the existing provincial income tax base[17] or whether they should administer their own income tax systems as is done in all but one of the states (Maryland)

[13]James D. Rodgers, "Sales Taxes, Income Taxes, and Other Revenues," in J. Richard Aronson and Eli Schwartz, eds., *Management Policies in Local Government Finance* (Washington, D.C.: International City Management, 1981), 152-83, at 166-67.

[14]See the Federation of Canadian Municipalities' proposal referred to in supra footnote 8.

[15]Supra footnote 9, at 3.

[16]For example, see ibid., at Chapter 2.

[17]For a discussion of this, see Slack, supra footnote 10.

using this tax in the United States.[18] Clearly, the least costly means of administering and collecting local income taxes is to adopt the existing provincial tax system. In addition, the efficiency and distributional effects (equity) of the tax system would be similar to those that currently exist.

On the other hand, if local governments in their quest for more local autonomy and greater control over their tax bases decide to implement and administer their own income tax system, the equity and efficiency implications will differ as long as the tax bases and tax rates differ. The administration costs also will rise. Assessing the effects of a local income tax on the distribution of income and the distortions that are created or corrected will depend on the tax base and rate structure employed. If one chooses the local income tax structure as it exists in the United States as a guide,[19] then one realizes that there are a number of issues that must be resolved including decisions on applicable tax rates, allowable exemptions and deductions, treatment of commuters versus residents, and collection and administration policies.

Variations in the solutions accepted for each of the potential problems are wide ranging. The local tax base, for example, is identical to the federal base in very few instances, while it is significantly different in a number of states. Differences arise in that nonlabour income almost always is excluded from total income, while personal exemptions and nonbusiness deductions frequently are not allowed either. The exclusion of nonlabour income creates more inequities than exist under a federal tax base for it leads to different tax burdens on two individuals with identical net incomes (after deductions and exemptions) but earned in different ways (that is, from nonlabour (property) as opposed to labour sources). This treatment also creates an incentive for individuals to earn their incomes from nonlabour rather than labour-related sources. Similar inequities are created by disallowing the deduction from gross income of personal exemptions and deductions. Two individuals with identical gross labour incomes will be taxed at the same level yet their ability-to-pay taxes may vary substantially due to differences in their legitimate exemptions and deductions.

Many of these inequities, particularly in the types of income taxed, have arisen from an attempt to reduce the administration and collection costs. Local income tax systems administered by local governments, for example, have enacted legislation that requires employers to withhold taxes on income earned by their employees. Since employers have no information on nonlabour income received by their employees, this nonlabour income has escaped local income taxation. This taxation of income at the source rather than at the place of residence raises a question of the appropriate treatment of residents as opposed to commuters. Should commuters be taxed and if so, at what rate? A case clearly can be made for taxing commuters. They derive benefits from the community in which they work and as such, should be expected to contribute toward the cost of providing the services that generate these benefits. The more difficult question, however, involves the establishment of the appropriate rates of tax for

---

[18]For a more detailed discussion of local income taxes in the United States, see Rodgers, supra footnote 13, at 167-73.

[19]Christopher H. Gadsden and Roger W. Schmenner, "Municipal Income Taxation," in John R. Meyer and John M. Quigley, eds., *Local Public Finance and the Fiscal Squeeze: A Case Study* (Cambridge, Mass.: Ballinger, 1977), 69-98.

nonresidents. One study for the City of Detroit estimated that a 0.5 per cent tax on commuters (one-half the rate on residents) represented full compensation for benefits received by nonresidents.[20] Benefit estimation, unfortunately, frequently is based on best guesses rather than on solid facts. Because of the inability to measure correctly benefits and because of the increased cost of applying different tax rates to residents as opposed to nonresidents, most locally administered income taxes tax nonresidents at the same rate as residents.

As long as all neighbouring communities impose taxes either at source or at place of residence, double taxation from municipal income taxes does not exist. Where some municipalities tax at source while adjacent communities tax on the basis of residence, however, taxpayers working in the former community and living in the latter will be taxed twice. To eliminate this problem, there is virtually universal provision for crediting the tax paid to one local government against that payable to a second local government.

Further variation exists in applicable tax rates, with the most frequently accepted rate being in the order of a 1 per cent flat rate applied to the tax base, although at least one city (Philadelphia) has a rate in excess of 4 per cent. Local governments in New York and Maryland are the only ones employing graduated rates.

It appears as if the Americans have created unnecessary administration and collection costs and produced unwarranted inequities and inefficiencies. The income tax as applied at the provincial or federal levels in Canada, is certain to be more equitable and less distorting. "Piggybacking" onto an extant provincial tax base through the application of a surtax would significantly lower collection and administration costs without creating further inequities and distortions. "Piggybacking," however, would be a form of provincial/municipal revenue sharing and would provide very little additional local autonomy, accountability, or responsibility. To achieve these objectives, locally determined tax rates would be necessary. In this way, there is an incentive for local decision-makers to answer local residents, otherwise the incentive would be to push the provincial government for an increasing share of the revenue base and let it bear the political burden.[21]

Although local income taxes per se do not exist in Canada, there are a few schemes in some provinces that allow local governments to tap the revenue generated by the provincial income tax. The province of Manitoba, for example, currently distributes 2.2 percentage points of personal federal basic tax and 1 percentage point of corporate taxable income to municipal governments (this program began in 1976). The allocation of these revenues to the various municipalities is conducted on a per capita grant basis and has replaced the former unconditional per capita grant program.[22] In addition, munici-

---

[20]Rodgers, supra footnote 13, at 172.

[21]For arguments in favour of a municipal income tax with locally determined rates, see Richard H. M. Plain and Melville L. McMillan, *The New Partnership: Policies for Reforming Municipal/Provincial Fiscal Relations in Alberta,* a report prepared for the Alberta Urban Municipalities Association (Edmonton: the Association, 1979), 23-33.

[22]Canadian Tax Foundation, *Provincial and Municipal Finances 1981* (Toronto: the Foundation, 1981), 192.

pal/provincial revenue sharing schemes have been introduced in British Columbia (1977)[23] and Saskatchewan (1978).[24] These schemes give local governments access to growth taxes. When the economy is buoyant, municipal revenues rise; when the economy is flat, municipal revenues fall. In both provinces, the revenue base includes more than income taxes; however, the income tax represents the largest proportion of the tax base. The allocation of the appropriated municipal revenue to the respective communities is provided through both conditional and unconditional grants.

Finally, local governments' renewed interest in growth taxes and, more specifically the income tax, suggests that some indication of potential revenue yields is in order if local administrators and politicians are to become seriously interested in considering the implementation of this tax. The yield estimated obviously will depend on both the tax bases and rates applied. To minimize the cost of administering the tax, the estimates in Table 15.5 accept the existing base and rate structure. The yield is obtained by applying an additional 1 percentage point to the basic federal tax payable on personal incomes and to corporate taxable income. The acceptance of this base is premised on the fact that it does not distort either the existing base or marginal rates and it is currently the base used in calculating the portion of provincial income tax revenues allocated to local governments in British Columbia and Manitoba.[25]

As long as this additional tax revenue does not lead to an offsetting or partially offsetting reduction in other own-source revenues, then local access to income taxes would have generated an increase in local revenues ranging from almost 3 per cent to slightly more than 9 per cent (depending on the province) of local own-source revenue in 1980 (Table 15.5, last column). Given that local governments in Newfoundland, Prince Edward Island, and New Brunswick have fewer expenditure responsibilities than in other provinces and collect relatively smaller sums of own-source revenue, it is not surprising to observe that income tax revenue as a per cent of own-source revenue was higher in these provinces than elsewhere in Canada. In any case, the simple addition of one extra percentage point could have generated increases in local revenues for each of the years included in the table. As well, for every province, income tax as a percentage of own-source revenue was higher in 1980 than in 1968, suggesting that if access to local income tax revenues had existed under the rate structure outlined above, the revenues generated would have grown at a faster rate than the actual increase in own-source revenues over the same period.

MUNICIPAL SALES TAX

As distinct from the United States where local sales taxes exist in a number of municipalities, local sales taxes do not exist in Canada. This, however, has not always been the case. Montreal levied the first municipal sales tax in 1935. By 1964, 353 of the approximately 1,700 municipalities in the province of Quebec

---

[23]Ibid., at 197.

[24]Saskatchewan Municipal Affairs, *Annual Report 1978-79* (Regina: the Ministry, 1979), 39.

[25]It is implicitly assumed in these estimates that the additional percentage point would not have led to a reduction in taxable income earned by individuals and corporations for each of the years recorded in Table 15.5.

Table 15.5 Estimated Local Income Tax Revenues Arising from a One Percentage Point Tax on Both Corporate Taxable Income and the Federal Basic Tax Payable on Personal Income[a] for Selected Years by Province

Province	1968 $million[b]	1968 Per cent of own-source revenue[c]	1971 $million[b]	1971 Per cent of own-source revenue[c]	1975 $million[b]	1975 Per cent of own-source revenue[c]	1980 $million[b]	1980 Per cent of own-source revenue[c]
Newfoundland	1,205.9	5.7	1,653.3	9.0	3,554.5	8.8	5,994	7.0
Prince Edward Island	186.8	2.4	300.3	3.2	693.4	9.9	1,157	9.1
Nova Scotia	2,065.4	2.5	3,171.2	2.7	6,871.6	3.8	11,401	4.0
New Brunswick	1,534.3	4.4	2,318.7	9.3	5,292.6	10.7	9,219	8.7
Quebec	25,238.9	2.4	34,370.5	2.9	68,715.7	4.0	112,979	3.9
Ontario	48,142.2	3.0	66,922.0	3.4	126,039.6	4.2	194,363	3.6
Manitoba	4,136.3	2.4	5,468.3	2.4	11,907.0	3.0	16,913	2.6
Saskatchewan	2,969.3	1.6	3,423.3	1.5	11,190.6	3.9	17,836	3.3
Alberta	7,934.6	2.4	12,024.1	2.9	47,655.5	7.0	87,356	5.6
British Columbia	12,496.5	3.5	17,012.9	3.3	35,749.2	3.6	66,760	3.8

[a]This base was chosen because it is currently the base for calculating the municipal portion of income tax revenues in British Columbia and Manitoba. [b]Estimated by applying 1 per cent to corporate taxable income (obtained from Statistics Canada, *Corporate Taxation Statistics* for selected years, Catalogue no. 61–208), and to federal basic tax (obtained from Revenue Canada, *Taxation Statistics* (Ottawa: Supply and Services, for selected years)). [c]Previous column as a per cent of own-source revenue figures for local governments in Statistics Canada, *Local Government Finance: Revenue and Expenditures, Assets and Liabilities, Actual*, for selected years, Catalogue no. 68–204.

levied a sales tax at a rate of 1 per cent or 2 per cent. Problems of tax evasion and difficulties in agreeing on the proper distribution of the tax revenues collected led to that province assuming complete responsibility for the administration and operation of the sales tax beginning in 1964.[26] While there may be little reason to believe that Canadian municipalities will obtain retail sales tax revenues in the near future, recent concern over insufficient revenues has created an environment in which local politicians and administrators have expressed interest in gaining access to revenues generated by new or additional taxes, one of which is the retail sales tax. Perhaps a brief review of some of the more salient features arising from access to retail sales tax revenue is in order.

While an evaluation of this revenue source should be based on the criteria of equity, efficiency, and ease of administration, such an evaluation may vary depending on whether the tax is administered locally or provincially. If the tax were administered provincially, administration and compliance costs would be substantially lower than if local governments attempted to duplicate the provincial retail sales tax machinery. As well, the application by a local government of a tax rate to a tax base that differs from the existing provincial sales tax base will create equity and efficiency implications that differ from those currently arising from provincial sales tax legislation.

Regardless of the level at which the tax is administered, there are some equity and efficiency implications that are general in their effect.[27] The retail sales tax, which is defined as a percentage of the selling price of specific items, is not progressive in its impact on taxpayers. The principle of vertical equity (as adopted in our evaluation) is violated because this tax absorbs a higher percentage of the income of a poor taxpayer than of a rich taxpayer. This tax also does not achieve horizontal equity because equal-income earners have different preferences for taxed and nontaxed items. This tax discriminates against those consumers who, for one reason or another, spend a larger percentage of their incomes on taxable items. To eliminate some of the inequities associated with the burden that the tax imposes on low-income earners, a number of exemptions or exclusions have been introduced into provincial tax legislation. These include many essential items such as prescription drugs, shelter, food, and children's clothing. These exemptions or exclusions have removed some regressivity associated with the application of a provincial sales tax system; however, the extent to which regressivity has been eliminated is far from clear. On balance, most authors suggest that provincial retail sales taxes are still regressive, with one or two authors suggesting that they may be proportional at best. No one has suggested that their impact on the distribution of income is progressive.[28]

In addition to the equity implications of provincial sales taxes in Canada, there are a number of potential distortions (inefficiencies) created by current tax legislation. First, the less than comprehensive inclusion of all goods and services in the tax base creates inefficiencies in that consumers are encouraged to buy nontaxed items in preference to taxed items. If this treatment is justifiable, it

---

[26]See James A. Johnson, "New Tax Sources and Tax-Sharing for Canadian Municipalities," in supra footnote 1, 591-612, at 602.

[27]For a fuller discussion of this, see supra footnote 9, at 196-201.

[28]See ibid., for a review of these studies.

must be supported on other than efficiency grounds. With the exception of Ontario's recent attempt to expand the sales tax coverage,[29] most provinces have tended to increase exemptions with the consequence that the sales tax has moved away from being a broadly based consumption levy. Second, the differential base and rate structure among provinces or between Canada and the United States, provides an incentive for consumers to purchase items in non-taxed or lower-taxed regions. Similarly, the extent to which production or industrial machinery is subject to tax in some provinces and not others may encourage industries to alter their production or distribution methods or to move to lower-taxed areas. Whether or not this latter point is significant is a matter of some speculation. Consumers who purchase items out of province and bring them into the province where they live are required to pay a tax at the rate existing in their home province.

The retail sales tax is generally recognized as being relatively simple and inexpensive to administer. Government auditors are dealing with relatively few taxpayers (vendors), most of whom have consistent and accurate financial records and statements. If local governments were given access to retail sales tax revenue, it would be difficult to support a system where they were responsible for administering their own retail sales tax (as is done frequently in American municipalities).[30] The obvious savings in "piggy backing" onto the provincial tax system through the application of one or two additional percentage points to the existing provincial tax base would more than offset the extra flexibility and local autonomy gained from having access to a locally designed and administered tax source. In addition, locally administered sales taxes would create further problems if each municipality's tax rate or base differed from that in adjacent communities. Failure to coordinate neighbouring tax systems could create distortions and inequities over and above those currently existing. For example, some American studies have attempted to measure the magnitude of sales tax losses due to local sales tax differentials. In New York city, one study indicated that an increase in that city's sales tax rate of 1 percentage point led to a loss in sales of 6 per cent.[31] A further study on the same city concluded that the increased tax in New York led to an increase in the sales of untaxed goods and a loss in the sales of taxed goods.[32] Finally, a more general assessment of city-suburb sales tax differentials concluded that a 1 per cent increase in the ratio of city to suburb sales tax resulted in a reduction in per capita retail sales ranging from 1.69 per cent to 10.97 per cent.[33] Avoidance of problems such as these under a locally administered sales tax would require the careful, time-consuming, and administratively expensive coordination of activities.

---

[29]The Honourable Frank S. Miller, Treasurer of Ontario, *1982 Ontario Budget* (Toronto: Ministry of Treasury and Economics, 1982).

[30]For a discussion of the U.S. system, see Rodgers, supra footnote 13, at 154-65.

[31]William Hamovitch, "Effects of Increases in Sales Tax Rates on Taxable Sales in New York City," in Graduate School of Public Administration, New York University, *Financing Government in New York City* (New York: NYU, 1966), 619-34.

[32]Harry Levin, "An Analysis of the Economic Effects of the New York City Sales Tax," in ibid., at 634-91.

[33]John L. Mikesell, "Central Cities and Sales Tax Rule Differentials: The Border City Problem" (June 1970), 23 *National Tax Journal* 206-13.

While the minimization of administrative and compliance costs and the avoidance of unnecessary distortions and inequities are important in evaluating any local tax, the concern foremost in the minds of most local administrators is the potential revenue yield that might be generated from a tax imposed on retail sales. To estimate the tax yield, Table 15.6 records the additional revenues that would have been generated by the application of a sales tax of one additional percentage point to the existing retail sales tax base in each province (with the exception of Alberta where provincial retail sales taxes are non-existent), for selected years.[34] In addition, this revenue is recorded as a percentage of total own-source revenues so as to exhibit the relative importance that it might have had as a revenue generator.

Because of a lack of more accurate information, these estimates are based on the assumption that the value of taxed purchases would not have declined as a result of an additional percentage point in the sales tax rate being applied to the provincial tax base. If one wishes to assume that the value of sales would have declined by a specific percentage, then one could quickly recalculate the potential revenue that could have been generated.[35] That exercise, however, will be left up to the reader who can then apply his or her own assumptions.

The estimates in Table 15.6 suggest that an additional percentage point of sales tax revenue would have generated larger sums of money for local governments than would an additional percentage point of income tax revenue applied to taxable corporate income and personal basic federal taxes payable. The reason for this, of course, lies in the size of the base to which the tax rate was applied.

For the provinces of Newfoundland, Prince Edward Island, and New Brunswick where the estimated absolute yields were lower than the other provinces, these yields represented a much larger proportion of existing own-source revenues. This, of course, can be attributed to the fact that the provincial/local mix in funding and the provision of many local services were concentrated more heavily in the provincial sector. For 1980 (Table 15.6, last column) in the remaining provinces, the potential yields were estimated to range from almost 7 per cent to slightly more than 11 per cent of actual own-source revenues, figures that are significant in terms of potential additional revenues for local governments.

MISCELLANEOUS POTENTIAL TAX SOURCES

While the bulk of interest in new tax sources has revolved around municipal access to income and retail sales taxes, some interest has been expressed in additional local taxes being imposed on such items as alcoholic beverages, tobacco, fuel, motor vehicle gasoline and licences, amusement taxes, and hotel

---

[34]In these estimates, it is assumed that one additional percentage point in the rate of sales taxation applied uniformly across each province (Alberta excluded) would not have altered existing sales or created additional distortions.

[35]Unfortunately, there are no available and accurate elasticity coefficients that could be used in estimating potential yields.

Table 15.6   Estimated Local Sales Tax Revenue from an Additional One Percentage Point Applied to the Existing Provincial Sales Tax Base[a] for Selected Years by Province

Province	1968		1971		1975		1980	
	$ millions[b]	Per cent of own-source revenue	$ millions[b]	Per cent of own-source revenue	$ millions[b]	Per cent of own-source revenue	$ millions[b]	Per cent of own-source revenue
Newfoundland	5,043	23.9	7,332	40.0	15,311	38.0	21,626	25.3
Prince Edward Island ...	670	8.6	1,302	13.8	2,279	32.5	3,910	30.8
Nova Scotia	4,095	5.0	10,577	9.1	16,391	9.1	25,508	8.9
New Brunswick	4,758	13.6	7,460	30.0	13,507	27.3	24,030	22.7
Quebec	61,162	5.8	80,402	6.7	150,445	8.7	208,138	7.2
Ontario	98,617	6.2	153,766	7.8	266,835	8.9	370,119	6.9
Manitoba	12,280	7.2	14,953	6.6	32,390	8.3	48,639	7.5
Saskatchewan	13,094	7.1	15,545	7.0	29,995	10.3	60,939	11.3
Alberta	—		—		—		—	
British Columbia	35,853	9.9	49,812	9.8	90,127	9.1	184,577	10.5

[a]See supra footnote 34 for assumptions. [b]Calculated from Statistics Canada, *Provincial Government Finance: Revenue and Expenditure*, for selected years, Catalogue no. 68-207.

taxes, all of which tend to be in the provincial domain.[36] Adoption of any of these consumption-based taxes would generate equity and efficiency implications similar (but possibly more severe because of the narrower base) to those of the retail sales tax. By way of comparison with local income or sales taxes, introduction of these taxes at low tax rates would generate relatively small sums of revenue.

SUMMARY

While one can make a case for using the property tax as a user charge to finance only those services that generate benefits for property, it was not the intention in this chapter to do so. Instead, the property tax structure was accepted as a base for financing both property and people-related services. Given this, the limited evidence suggests that property taxes have grown less quickly than the tax base or less quickly than the extent to which personal income taxes have been used over the past decade. In fact, if property taxes had grown at a rate that corresponded to the increase in the estimated tax base, most local governments could have increased their own revenues significantly.

As an alternative to an increased use of property taxation, it has been suggested that provincial governments assume responsibility (where they have not already done so) for most of the people-related services. This would shift some of the more costly expenditure functions away from the local level and, therefore, reduce the requirements for local revenue.

Finally, civic leaders recently have claimed that local governments should be given greater access to new tax sources with the two most commonly mentioned being the provincial income and retail sales tax. The revenue yield from the application of a low rate in either case would generate noticeable sums of revenue. The choice of one tax as opposed to another or as opposed to an increased use of property taxes obviously would generate different effects on both the distribution of income and the extent to which certain production or consumption activities are encouraged over other activities.

Of these three alternatives for improving the financial position of local governments, it is highly unlikely that local governments will increase their use of property taxes or that provincial governments will agree to fund, in total, a number of programs or services that are currently supported or partially supported by locally generated revenues. This leaves municipalities with the option of attempting to gain access to one or more of the so-called "growth taxes" currently in the domain of the provinces. Perhaps the fact that British Columbia and Manitoba have given municipalities access to the growth taxes will serve to provide the impetus for similar revenue arrangements in some or all of the remaining provinces.

---

[36]There are a few instances where municipalities currently have access to one or more of these taxes. Although they have not done so, municipalities in Manitoba, for example, may, on a local decision basis, levy sales taxes on liquor, hotel accommodation, and restaurant meals. In Newfoundland, local governments may tax fuels such as coal, fuel oil, and propane gas. In British Columbia, under the Urban Transit Authority Act, the Greater Vancouver Region currently levies a tax of .66 of a cent per litre on gasoline, the resulting revenue being used to finance urban transportation. Most municipalities in all provinces obtain some revenue from amusements, although generally through licences. Municipalities in Quebec, Manitoba, and Saskatchewan have the right to levy an amusement tax.

Appendix A

Table A.1   Government Sector as a Percentage of
Gross National Expenditure, [a] 1947-1980

Year	Federal	Provincial	Local	Total[b]
1947	14.1	5.2	4.4	23.7
1948	11.6	5.5	4.6	21.8
1949	12.1	5.9	4.8	22.8
1950	11.5	5.7	4.9	22.1
1951	13.6	5.6	5.0	24.2
1952	16.8	5.0	5.1	26.9
1953	16.4	4.8	5.1	26.4
1954	16.3	5.2	5.9	27.4
1955	15.3	5.2	5.8	26.3
1956	14.4	5.5	5.8	25.7
1957	14.6	5.7	6.2	26.6
1958	15.9	6.1	6.6	28.6
1959	15.2	6.8	6.9	28.9
1960	15.0	7.3	7.3	29.7
1961	15.3	6.1	7.4	30.8
1962	14.8	6.1	7.8	30.7
1963	14.0	6.3	7.9	30.3
1964	13.4	6.5	7.7	29.6
1965	12.9	6.8	8.1	29.9
1966	13.1	7.3	8.2	30.9
1967	13.5	8.3	8.6	32.9
1968	13.6	8.7	8.8	33.7
1969	13.5	9.0	8.9	34.1
1970	13.8	10.2	9.4	36.4
1971	13.8	11.1	9.3	37.3
1972	14.8	11.0	8.9	37.8
1973	14.3	10.7	8.5	36.5
1974	15.4	11.1	8.3	37.9
1975	16.8	12.2	8.8	41.3
1976	15.8	12.1	8.8	40.2
1977	16.2	12.6	9.0	41.3
1978	16.6	12.6	8.9	41.7
1979	15.7	12.2	8.6	40.2
1980	16.7	12.5	8.6	41.7

[a]Excludes intergovernmental transfers. [b]From 1947 to 1960, figures in the total column equal the sum of the figures in the federal, provincial, and local columns. From 1961 to 1980, the figures in the total column exceed the sum of those in the federal, provincial, and local columns. This difference is attributed to expenditures on hospitals from 1961 onward and to expenditures on the Canada and Quebec Pension Plans from 1966 to the present.

Source: Calculated from data in Canada, Department of Finance, *Economic Review,* April 1981 (Ottawa: Supply and Services, 1981), Tables 7, 50, 52, 57, and 61.

Table A.2   Per Capita Total Federal, Provincial, and Local Expenditures, 1947-1980[a]
(Current and Constant 1971 Dollars)

Year	Federal Current	Federal Constant[c]	Provincial Current	Provincial Constant[c]	Local Current	Local Constant[c]	Total government[b] Current	Total government[b] Constant[c]	Total per capita GNE excluding gov. sector Current	Total per capita GNE excluding gov. sector Constant[d]	Total per capita GNE Current	Total per capita GNE Constant[d]
1947	147.19	520.11	54.55	194.82	46.40	163.96	248.14	876.82	797.25	1,411.82	1,045.39	2,288.64
1948	136.86	423.72	65.16	201.73	54.53	168.82	256.55	794.27	921.32	1,501.70	1,177.87	2,295.97
1949	150.81	435.87	73.10	211.27	60.46	174.74	284.38	821.91	964.97	1,512.29	1,249.35	2,334.20
1950	154.54	430.47	77.23	215.13	65.78	183.23	297.55	828.83	1,050.98	1,633.39	1,348.53	2,462.22
1951	209.51	521.17	86.44	215.02	77.16	191.94	373.11	928.13	1,171.61	1,602.39	1,544.72	2,530.52
1952	285.22	679.10	84.86	202.05	86.73	206.50	456.81	1,087.64	1,243.72	1,583.15	1,700.53	2,670.79
1953	286.02	665.16	83.46	194.09	89.39	207.88	458.88	1,067.16	1,281.30	1,668.10	1,740.18	2,735.26
1954	276.31	618.14	88.18	197.27	99.37	222.30	463.86	1,037.72	1,231.57	1,585.82	1,695.43	2,623.54
1955	277.49	600.63	94.73	205.04	105.43	228.20	477.64	1,033.85	1,339.66	1,762.11	1,817.30	2,795.96
1956	286.98	580.93	109.07	220.79	115.35	233.50	511.41	1,035.24	1,482.12	1,924.71	1,993.53	2,959.96
1957	295.06	568.52	115.77	223.06	125.35	241.52	536.18	1,033.10	1,481.46	1,899.95	2,017.64	2,933.05
1958	322.78	603.33	124.82	233.31	134.72	251.81	582.32	1,088.45	1,453.80	1,829.82	2,036.12	2,918.27
1959	320.20	579.02	142.54	257.76	146.26	264.48	608.99	1,101.25	1,498.54	1,858.02	2,107.53	2,959.27
1960	321.88	561.75	157.69	275.20	157.25	274.43	636.82	1,111.38	1,509.74	1,867.41	2,146.56	2,978.79
1961	332.33	562.32	132.14	223.59	161.75	273.69	668.93	1,131.86	1,504.88	1,869.62	2,173.81	3,001.48
1962	341.82	564.06	141.63	233.71	180.60	298.02	710.17	1,171.90	1,599.84	1,974.79	2,310.01	3,146.69
1963	340.18	539.11	152.55	241.76	192.86	305.64	735.94	1,166.31	1,692.77	2,081.64	2,428.71	3,247.95
1964	350.34	537.33	168.22	258.01	199.48	305.95	772.68	1,185.09	1,833.85	2,216.15	2,606.53	3,401.24
1965	362.45	531.45	191.81	281.25	228.57	335.15	842.70	1,235.63	1,975.67	2,326.83	2,818.37	3,562.46
1966	404.15	555.15	225.23	309.38	254.81	350.01	954.33	1,310.89	2,134.75	2,428.51	3,089.08	3,739.40
1967	441.55	567.54	270.93	348.24	279.08	358.71	1,071.16	1,376.81	2,187.70	2,418.66	3,258.86	3,795.47
1968	476.16	579.27	305.78	372.00	308.39	375.17	1,182.17	1,438.16	2,324.23	2,516.43	3,506.40	3,954.59
1969	511.55	574.78	340.79	382.91	339.89	381.90	1,296.41	1,456.64	2,504.12	2,649.12	3,800.53	4,105.76
1970	557.12	591.42	409.35	434.55	377.33	400.56	1,462.55	1,552.60	2,560.79	2,597.75	4,023.34	4,150.35
1971	605.64	605.64	486.30	486.30	407.16	407.16	1,632.20	1,632.20	2,746.77	2,746.77	4,378.97	4,378.97
1972	714.10	666.14	530.71	495.07	430.48	401.57	1,822.76	1,700.34	3,004.27	2,897.98	4,827.03	4,598.32
1973	799.12	686.53	597.74	513.52	476.70	409.54	2,043.51	1,755.59	3,561.90	3,135.40	5,605.41	4,890.99
1974	1,015.20	751.44	729.25	539.79	550.57	407.53	2,502.28	1,852.17	4,067.39	3,141.48	6,596.67	4,993.65
1975	1,225.62	786.66	891.44	572.17	639.16	410.24	3,006.96	1,930.01	4,281.58	3,054.48	7,288.54	4,984.49
1976	1,315.31	738.52	1,010.57	567.42	723.70	406.34	3,354.11	1,883.27	4,974.16	3,309.35	8,328.27	5,192.62
1977	1,453.99	745.64	1,123.01	575.90	800.71	410.62	3,715.11	1,905.18	5,319.72	3,364.45	9,034.83	5,269.63
1978	1,618.12	766.52	1,241.22	587.98	870.79	412.50	4,106.09	1,945.09	5,767.21	3,449.74	9,873.30	5,394.83
1979	1,727.26	755.58	1,338.47	585.51	947.57	414.51	4,417.01	1,932.20	6,579.78	3,536.12	10,996.79	5,468.32
1980	2,006.52	788.11	1,505.35	591.26	1,035.59	406.75	5,071.65	1,992.01	6,977.19	3,428.07	12,048.84	5,420.08

[a]Excludes intergovernmental grants. [b]See footnote (b) in Table A.1. [c]The current dollars were deflated by the gross national expenditure implicit price index for current expenditures on goods and services. [d]Deflated by the gross national expenditure implicit price index.

Source: Calculated from data in Canada, Department of Finance, *Economic Review*, April 1981 (Ottawa: Supply and Services, 1981), Tables 1, 43, 50, 52, 57 and 61.

**Table A.3   Property Taxes and Government Transfers as a Percentage
of Local Government Revenue, 1947-78**

Year	Real and personal property tax	Government transfers	Other
1947	51.5	17.2	31.3
1948	50.1	19.3	30.6
1949	49.9	21.2	28.9
1950	49.6	21.0	29.4
1951	54.6	21.1	24.3
1952	55.3	20.4	24.3
1953	54.9	21.0	24.1
1954	55.8	20.8	23.4
1955	53.4	23.7	22.9
1956	54.6	23.3	22.1
1957	53.6	25.6	20.8
1958	52.0	27.6	20.4
1959	52.6	27.7	19.7
1960	52.4	28.7	18.9
1961	52.1	30.6	17.3
1962	49.9	34.1	16.0
1963	49.1	34.4	16.5
1964	48.8	35.9	15.3
1965	48.5	36.4	15.1
1966	46.4	38.7	14.9
1967	45.3	39.2	15.5
1968	45.6	39.2	15.2
1969	45.9	39.0	15.1
1970	43.1	41.8	15.1
1971	42.3	43.0	14.7
1972	41.7	43.8	14.5
1973	40.6	44.6	14.8
1974	38.9	45.9	15.2
1975	37.2	47.9	14.9
1976	39.6	46.8	13.6
1977	37.4	48.9	13.7
1978	37.0	47.6	15.4

Source: Calculated from data in Statistics Canada, *National Income and Expenditure Accounts,*
Vol. 1—1926-1974, Catalogue no. 13-531, and for 1964-1978, Catalogue no. 13-201.

Table A.4 Calculation of Factors Affecting Local/Provincial Expenditure Increases, 1968-1978

Province	(1) Change in total current expenditures[a] $000,000	(2) Change in total constant expenditures[b] $000,000	(3) Percentage of total expenditure increase due to inflationary increases[c] %	(4) Population change from 1968-1978[d] $000	(5) Dollar volume change[e] $000,000	(6) Percentage change in volume of service[f] %	(7) Percentage of total expenditure increase attributed to volume change[g] %	(8) Change in levels of service[h] $	(9) Increased expenditure attributed to an increase in the levels of service[i] $000,000	(10) Percentage change in the levels of service[j] %	(11) Percentage of total expenditure increase attributed to increase in the levels of service[k] %
Newfoundland	1,218.5	251.2	79.4	63	41.0	16.3	3.4	369.40	210.2	83.7	17.2
Prince Edward Island	245.6	60.5	75.4	12	6.6	10.9	2.7	441.71	53.9	89.1	21.9
Nova Scotia	1,480.0	316.5	78.6	74	43.9	13.9	3.0	324.23	272.7	86.2	18.4
New Brunswick	1,094.9	205.9	81.2	70	41.1	20.0	3.8	237.05	164.7	80.0	15.0
Quebec	13,994.9	3,167.5	77.4	345	230.8	7.3	1.6	468.16	2,936.8	92.7	21.0
Ontario	15,017.2	2,786.0	81.4	1,182	841.0	30.2	5.6	223.81	1,889.9	67.8	12.6
Manitoba	1,817.0	350.2	80.7	63	37.8	10.8	2.1	302.14	312.4	89.2	17.2
Saskatchewan	1,828.2	342.4	81.3	-12	-7.8	-2.3	-0.4	369.49	350.3	102.3	19.1
Alberta	5,139.0	1,302.4	74.7	430	328.6	25.2	6.4	498.36	973.8	74.8	18.9
British Columbia	5,259.9	1,255.2	76.1	527	334.1	26.6	6.4	364.05	921.0	73.4	17.5
All provinces	47,095.3	9,928.7	78.9	2,762	1,870.4	18.8	4.0	344.11	8,058.4	81.2	17.1

[a]Calculated from Table 2.1. [b]Current expenditures deflated by the implicit price index for government current expenditures adjusted for regional differences. [c]Calculated by subtracting the change in total constant expenditures (column 2) from the change in total current expenditures (column 1) and dividing by the change in total current expenditures (column 2). [d]Obtained from Canada, Department of Finance, *Economic Review*, April 1981 (Ottawa: Supply and Services, 1981). [e]Volume increase was obtained by multiplying the change in population (column 4) by the 1968 per capita level of expenditure). [f]Column 5 as a percentage of column 2. [g]Calculated by taking the figures in

column 6 as a percent of the total increase not attributed to inflationary increases that are recorded in column 3. [h]Obtained by subtracting 1978 per capita constant dollar expenditures (column 3 of Table 2.3) from the 1968 per capita constant dollar expenditures (column 2 of Table 2.3). [i]Calculated by multiplying the figures in column 8 by the population level in 1978. [j]Column 9 as a per cent of column 2. [k]Calculated by taking the figures in column 9 as a per cent of the total increase not attributed to inflationary increases that are recorded in column 3.

Source: Figures in columns 1 and 2 were calculated from the data in Table 2.1.

Table A.5 Total Local Expenditures, Total Local Fixed Capital Expenditures, and Fixed Expenditures as a Proportion of Total Expenditures, 1968 and 1978

	1968			1978		
	Total local expenditures	Local Fixed capital expenditures	Fixed expenditures as a per cent of total expenditures	Total local expenditures	Local Fixed capital expenditures	Fixed expenditures as a per cent of total expenditures
	$000	*$000*	%	*$000*	*$000*	%
Newfoundland	30,757	14,195	46.2	114,727	36,005	31.4
Prince Edward Island	18,499	3,087	16.7	80,301	25,807	32.1
Nova Scotia	158,232	31,744	20.1	648,777	78,409	12.1
New Brunswick	41,738	10,608	25.4	181,588	57,994	31.9
Quebec	1,780,519	501,616	28.2	6,382,196	1,037,969	16.3
Ontario	2,758,372	702,204	25.5	8,739,167	1,334,402	15.3
Manitoba	271,492	47,185	17.4	923,852	128,431	13.9
Saskatchewan	292,860	57,819	19.7	938,790	175,702	18.7
Alberta	580,921	151,332	26.1	2,681,285	634,651	23.7
British Columbia	627,540	126,934	20.2	2,382,372	404,321	17.0
All provinces	6,560,930	1,646,724	25.1	23,073,055	3,913,691	17.0

Source: Data obtained from Statistics Canada, *Local Government Finance, 1968*, and *1978*, Catalogue no. 68-204.

Table A.6 Total and Per Capita Consolidated Provincial and Local Government Expenditures by Major Function and by Province Including and Excluding Federal Grants, 1968

Function	Newfoundland						Prince Edward Island					
	Total expenditures	Per capita including federal grants	Per cent of total[a]	Per capita excluding federal conditional grants	Per cent of total[a]	Per capita excluding federal conditional and unconditional grants[b]	Total expenditures	Per capita including federal grants	Per cent of total[a]	Per capita excluding federal conditional grants	Per cent of total[a]	Per capita excluding federal conditional and unconditional grants[b]
	$000	$	%	$	%	$	$000	$	%	$	%	$
General government	12,838	25.37	3.9	24.50	5.5	15.44	2,941	26.74	4.9	26.74	6.3	18.03
Protection of persons and property	9,308	18.40	2.8	17.60	4.0	11.09	1,622	14.75	2.7	14.58	3.4	9.83
Transportation and communication	63,526	125.55	19.3	51.96	11.7	32.75	11,942	108.56	19.7	77.56	18.2	52.29
Health	52,922	104.59	16.1	59.13	13.3	37.28	8,657	78.70	14.3	37.71	8.9	25.42
Social services	44,222	87.40	13.4	47.24	10.6	29.78	6,600	60.00	10.9	34.75	8.2	23.43
Education	74,782	147.79	22.7	139.84	31.4	88.15	17,918	162.89	29.6	140.22	33.0	94.53
Resource conservation & industrial development	15,200	30.04	4.6	26.40	5.9	16.64	3,041	27.65	5.0	23.45	5.5	15.81
Environment	10,264	20.28	3.1	2.06	0.5	1.30	328	2.98	0.5	2.56	0.6	1.73
Recreation and culture	3,246	6.42	1.0	5.76	1.3	3.63	904	8.22	1.5	7.82	1.8	5.27
Housing, regional planning, and development	4,258	8.42	1.3	3.55	0.8	2.24	31	0.28	0.1	0.28	0.1	0.19
Debt charges	28,031	55.40	8.5	55.40	12.5	34.92	6,476	58.87	10.7	58.87	13.8	39.69
Other	11,058	21.85	3.4	11.56	2.6	7.29	80	.73	0.1	0.60	0.1	0.40
Total	329,655	651.49	100.0	444.99	100.0	280.51	60,540	550.36	100.0	425.14	100.0	286.62

(Table continued on next page.)

Table A.6   Continued

Function	Nova Scotia						New Brunswick					
	Total expenditures	Per capita including federal grants	Per cent of total[a]	Per capita excluding federal conditional grants	Per cent of total[a]	Per capita excluding federal conditional and unconditional grants[b]	Total expenditures	Per capita including federal grants	Per cent of total[a]	Per capita excluding federal conditional grants	Per cent of total[a]	Per capita excluding federal conditional and unconditional grants[b]
	$000	$	%	$	%	$	$000	$	%	$	%	$
General government	18,347	23.92	4.0	23.92	5.0	17.98	15,305	24.49	4.2	24.49	5.1	17.90
Protection of persons and property	19,432	25.34	4.3	25.09	5.3	18.86	16,131	25.81	4.4	25.74	5.4	18.81
Transportation and communications	76,175	99.32	16.8	74.14	15.6	55.72	57,214	91.54	15.6	77.15	16.2	56.39
Health	82,769	107.91	18.2	67.42	14.1	50.67	62,942	100.71	17.1	59.01	12.4	43.13
Social services	30,012	39.13	6.6	21.35	4.5	16.04	26,046	41.67	7.1	22.76	4.8	16.64
Education	150,397	196.08	33.08	171.70	36.0	129.04	123,346	197.35	33.6	172.48	36.2	126.08
Resource conservation & industrial development	22,560	29.41	5.0	26.41	5.5	19.84	18,926	30.28	5.2	20.85	4.4	15.24
Environment	10,796	14.08	2.4	13.97	2.9	10.50	10,635	17.02	2.9	16.98	3.6	12.41
Recreation and culture	5,694	7.42	1.3	7.35	1.5	5.53	5,046	8.07	1.4	7.25	1.5	5.30
Housing, regional planning, and development	2,265	2.95	0.5	2.95	0.6	2.22	3,349	5.36	0.9	3.66	0.8	2.67
Debt charges	30,366	39.59	6.7	39.59	8.3	29.75	26,354	42.17	7.2	42.17	8.9	30.82
Other	5,729	7.47	1.3	2.81	0.6	2.11	1,974	3.16	0.5	3.16	0.7	2.31
Total	454,542	592.62	100.0	476.70	100.0	358.26	367,268	587.63	100.0	476.48	100.0	347.70

(Table continued on next page.)

Table A.6 Continued

Function	Quebec						Ontario					
	Total expenditures	Per capita including federal grants	Per cent of total[a]	Per capita excluding federal conditional grants	Per cent of total[a]	Per capita excluding federal conditional and unconditional grants[b]	Total expenditures	Per capita including federal grants	Per cent of total[a]	Per capita excluding federal conditional grants	Per cent of total[a]	Per capita excluding federal conditional and unconditional grants[b]
	$000	*$*	*%*	*$*	*%*	*$*	*$000*	*$*	*%*	*$*	*%*	*$*
General government	199,312	33.62	5.0	33.57	5.3	29.38	237,590	32.72	4.6	32.70	5.2	32.31
Protection of persons and property	234,676	39.59	5.9	39.39	6.2	34.48	351,781	48.44	6.8	48.26	7.7	47.69
Transportation and communication	471,407	79.52	11.9	77.44	12.1	67.79	660,759	90.99	12.8	87.59	14.0	86.55
Health	667,664	112.63	16.8	110.68	17.3	96.88	942,965	129.85	18.3	87.22	13.9	86.19
Social services	470,672	79.40	11.9	76.85	12.0	67.27	285,034	39.25	5.5	22.45	3.6	22.18
Education	1,119,332	188.82	28.2	167.85	26.3	146.92	1,891,458	260.46	36.6	241.64	38.5	238.78
Resource conservation & industrial development	142,033	23.96	3.6	23.80	3.7	20.84	130,627	17.99	2.5	17.00	2.7	16.80
Environment	178,875	30.17	4.5	29.82	4.7	26.10	197,996	27.26	3.8	26.50	4.2	26.19
Recreation and culture	94,949	16.02	2.4	15.57	2.4	13.62	129,617	17.85	2.5	17.69	2.8	17.48
Housing, regional planning, and development	11,914	2.01	0.3	1.92	0.3	1.68	15,171	2.09	0.3	2.09	0.3	2.06
Debt charges	291,217	49.13	7.3	49.13	7.7	43.00	245,303	33.78	4.7	33.78	5.4	33.38
Other	83,069	14.01	2.1	14.01	2.2	12.26	78,429	10.80	1.5	10.35	1.6	10.22
Total	3,965,120	668.88	100.0	638.71	100.0	560.22	5,166,730	711.47	100.0	627.26	100.0	619.82

(Table continued on next page.)

Table A.6 Continued

Function	Manitoba Total expenditures ($000)	Per capita including federal grants ($)	Per cent of total[a] (%)	Per capita excluding federal conditional grants ($)	Per cent of total[a] (%)	Per capita excluding federal conditional and unconditional grants[b] ($)	Saskatchewan Total expenditures ($000)	Per capita including federal grants ($)	Per cent of total[a] (%)	Per capita excluding federal conditional grants ($)	Per cent of total[a] (%)	Per capita excluding federal conditional and unconditional grants[b] ($)
General government	25,538	26.30	4.4	26.30	5.1	23.64	27,125	28.26	4.3	28.26	5.1	27.12
Protection of persons and property	33,129	34.12	5.7	33.95	6.6	30.52	28,493	29.68	4.5	29.60	5.3	28.41
Transportation and communication	82,167	84.62	14.1	81.16	15.8	72.95	106,751	111.20	17.0	109.24	19.6	104.85
Health	94,106	96.92	16.2	58.36	11.3	52.46	137,550	143.28	21.9	90.68	16.3	87.03
Social services	38,544	39.70	6.6	22.91	4.4	20.59	33,944	35.36	5.4	21.11	3.8	20.26
Education	185,864	191.42	31.9	173.92	33.8	156.33	188,977	196.85	30.1	175.40	31.5	168.35
Resource conservation & industrial development	37,840	38.97	6.5	30.72	6.0	27.61	32,102	33.44	5.1	25.09	4.5	24.08
Environment	26,060	26.84	4.5	26.67	5.2	23.98	18,210	18.97	2.9	18.81	3.4	18.05
Recreation and culture	19,050	19.62	3.3	19.57	3.8	17.59	24,204	25.21	3.9	24.08	4.3	23.11
Housing, regional planning, and development	3,371	3.47	0.6	3.47	0.7	3.12	2,073	2.16	0.3	1.99	0.4	1.91
Debt Charges	21,520	22.16	3.7	22.16	4.3	19.92	12,165	12.67	1.9	12.67	2.3	12.16
Other	15,105	15.56	2.6	15.56	3.0	13.99	15,794	16.45	2.5	16.16	2.9	15.51
Total	582,294	599.68	100.0	514.74	100.0	462.70	627,388	653.53	100.0	556.93	100.0	530.84

(Table continued on next page.)

Table A.6 Continued

Function	Alberta						British Columbia					
	Total expenditures	Per capita including federal grants	Per cent of total[a]	Per capita excluding federal conditional grants	Per cent of total[a]	Per capita excluding federal conditional and unconditional grants[b]	Total expenditures	Per capita including federal grants	Per cent of total[a]	Per capita excluding federal conditional grants	Per cent of total[a]	Per capita excluding federal conditional and unconditional grants[b]
	$000	$	%	$	%	$	$000	$	%	$	%	$
General government	37,142	24.37	3.2	24.37	3.6	23.88	66,836	33.37	5.3	33.32	6.0	33.18
Protection of persons and property	72,275	47.42	6.2	47.25	7.0	46.30	78,910	39.40	6.2	39.18	7.1	39.03
Transportation and communication	150,576	98.80	12.9	98.52	14.7	96.53	153,753	76.76	12.1	75.77	13.8	75.47
Health	214,331	140.64	18.4	95.47	14.2	93.54	245,421	122.53	19.3	71.77	13.0	71.49
Social services	71,678	47.09	6.2	25.79	3.8	25.27	106,616	53.23	8.4	32.45	5.9	32.33
Education	433,878	284.70	37.2	258.98	38.5	253.75	425,624	212.49	33.5	201.41	36.6	200.62
Resource conservation & industrial development	55,357	36.32	4.8	33.47	5.0	32.80	42,261	21.10	3.3	19.89	3.6	19.81
Environment	41,703	27.36	3.6	27.05	4.0	26.50	51,713	25.82	4.1	25.51	4.6	25.24
Recreation and culture	32,484	21.31	2.8	21.12	3.1	20.69	39,134	19.54	3.1	19.37	3.5	19.29
Housing, regional planning, and development	5,041	3.31	0.4	3.31	0.5	3.24	10,130	5.06	0.8	5.06	0.9	5.04
Debt charges	18,055	11.85	1.6	11.85	1.8	11.61	23,190	11.58	1.8	11.58	2.1	11.54
Other	32,299	21.19	2.8	21.13	3.1	20.70	26,313	13.14	2.1	13.05	2.4	13.00
Total	1,164,819	764.32	100.0	672.24	100.0	654.81	1,269,901	634.00	100.0	548.36	100.0	546.04

(Table concluded on next page.)

Table A.6   Concluded

Function	Total expenditures	All provinces				
		Per capita including federal grants	Per cent of total[a]	Per capita excluding federal conditional grants	Per cent of total[a]	Per capita excluding federal conditional and unconditional grants[b]
	$000	$	%	$	%	$
General government	642,974	31.13	4.6	31.10	5.1	28.87
Protection of persons and property	845,758	40.94	6.0	40.75	6.7	37.84
Transportation and communication	1,834,270	88.80	13.1	84.49	14.0	78.45
Health	2,509,327	121.48	17.9	89.62	14.8	83.21
Social services	1,113,368	53.90	8.0	39.88	6.6	37.02
Education	4,611,576	223.26	33.0	203.86	33.7	189.28
Resource conservation & industrial development	499,947	24.20	3.6	21.99	3.6	20.42
Environment	546,580	26.46	3.9	26.01	4.3	24.15
Recreation and culture	354,328	17.15	2.5	16.85	2.8	15.64
Housing, regional planning, and development	57,603	2.79	0.4	2.58	0.4	2.40
Debt charges	702,677	34.02	5.0	34.02	5.6	31.59
Other	269,850	13.06	1.9	12.71	2.1	11.80
Total	13,988,257	677.20	100.0	604.10	100.0	560.67

aMay not add to 100 due to rounding. bPer capita unconditional grants were applied to each function according to the proportion of per capita expenditures excluding conditional grants on each function.

Source: Calculated from data in Statistics Canada: *Consolidated Government Finance: Revenue, Expenditure, Assets and Liabilities: Fiscal year ended nearest to December 31, 1968,* Catalogue no. 68-202; *Provincial Government Finance: Revenue and Expenditure, Fiscal Year Ended March 31, 1968,* Catalogue no. 68-207; and *Local Government Finance, 1968,* Catalogue no. 68-204.

Table A.7   Total and Per Capita Consolidated Provincial and Local Government Expenditure by Major Function and by Province Including and Excluding Federal Grants, 1978

Function	Newfoundland						Prince Edward Island					
	Total expenditures $000	Per capita including federal grants $	Per cent of total[a] %	Per capita excluding federal conditional grants $	Per cent of total[a] %	Per capita excluding federal conditional and unconditional grants[b] $	Total expenditures $000	Per capita including federal grants $	Per cent of total[a] %	Per capita excluding federal conditional grants $	Per cent of total[a] %	Per capita excluding federal conditional and unconditional grants[b] $
General government	60,977	107.17	3.9	106.72	4.6	77.11	20,160	165.25	6.5	163.76	8.9	112.82
Protection of persons and property	48,163	84.64	3.1	84.52	3.7	62.02	10,015	82.09	3.3	81.70	4.5	56.29
Transportation and communication	144,358	253.70	9.3	186.13	8.1	135.77	33,221	272.30	10.9	226.98	12.4	156.37
Health	231,453	406.77	14.9	237.75	10.3	172.65	49,078	402.28	16.0	251.48	13.7	173.25
Social services	119,647	210.28	7.7	143.79	6.3	105.60	27,290	223.69	8.9	138.16	7.5	95.18
Education	306,603	538.85	19.8	469.38	20.4	341.95	83,138	681.46	27.2	524.16	28.6	361.11
Resource conservation & industrial development	298,059	523.83	19.3	500.76	21.8	365.41	38,232	313.38	12.5	176.66	9.6	121.71
Environment	44,892	78.90	2.9	60.55	2.6	43.58	6,015	49.30	2.0	40.01	2.2	27.56
Recreation and culture	30,290	53.23	2.0	47.44	2.1	35.20	7,769	63.68	2.5	49.48	2.7	34.09
Housing, regional planning, and development	13,695	24.07	0.9	12.01	0.5	8.38	5,943	48.71	1.9	4.51	0.2	3.11
Debt charges	216,406	380.33	14.0	380.33	16.5	276.57	21,186	173.66	6.7	173.66	9.5	119.64
Other	33,642	59.12	2.2	55.29	2.4	40.23	4,013	32.89	1.3	0.26	0.0	0.18
Total	1,548,185	2,720.89	100.0	2,300.62	100.0	1,664.47	306,060	2,508.69	100.0	1,830.82	100.0	1,261.30

(Table continued on next page.)

Table A.7 Continued

Function	Nova Scotia						New Brunswick					
	Total expenditures	Per capita including federal grants	Per cent of total[a]	Per capita excluding federal conditional grants	Per cent of total[a]	Per capita excluding federal conditional and unconditional grants[b]	Total expenditures	Per capita including federal grants	Per cent of total[a]	Per capita excluding federal conditional grants	Per cent of total[a]	Per capita excluding federal conditional and unconditional grants[b]
	$000	$	%	$	%	$	$000	$	%	$	%	$
General government	94,868	112.80	4.9	112.80	5.9	85.51	81,792	117.69	5.6	117.27	6.9	84.14
Protection of persons and property	93,766	111.49	4.8	108.71	5.7	82.41	63,726	91.69	4.4	90.82	5.3	65.16
Transportation and communication	195,580	232.56	10.1	214.61	11.2	162.69	202,711	291.67	13.9	260.46	15.2	186.87
Health	374,951	445.84	19.4	284.26	14.8	215.49	280,861	404.12	19.2	243.11	14.2	174.42
Social services	176,303	209.63	9.1	151.48	7.9	114.83	167,684	241.27	11.5	156.41	9.1	112.22
Education	463,649	551.31	24.0	479.99	25.0	363.86	340,777	490.33	23.3	403.11	23.6	289.21
Resource conservation & industrial development	122,632	145.82	6.3	100.81	5.3	76.42	83,221	119.74	5.7	117.97	6.9	84.64
Environment	56,303	66.95	2.9	62.34	3.3	47.26	41,219	59.31	2.8	54.35	3.2	38.99
Recreation and culture	35,804	42.57	1.9	40.63	2.1	30.80	29,466	42.40	2.0	41.06	2.4	29.46
Housing, regional planning, and development	50,943	60.57	2.6	42.57	2.2	32.27	14,317	20.60	1.0	0.00	0.0	0.00
Debt charges	171,665	204.12	8.9	204.12	10.6	154.74	136,208	195.98	9.3	195.98	11.5	140.61
Other	98,082	116.63	5.1	114.86	6.0	87.07	20,244	29.13	1.4	29.13	1.7	20.90
Total	1,934,546	2,300.29	100.0	1,917.18	100.0	1,453.34	1,462,226	2,103.92	100.0	1,709.67	100.0	1,226.60

(Table continued on next page.)

Table A.7 Continued

	Quebec						Ontario					
Function	Total expenditures	Per capita including federal grants	Per cent of total[a]	Per capita excluding federal conditional grants	Per cent of total[a]	Per capita excluding federal conditional and unconditional grants[b]	Total expenditures	Per capita including federal grants	Per cent of total[a]	Per capita excluding federal conditional grants	Per cent of total[a]	Per capita excluding federal conditional and unconditional grants[b]
	$000	$	%	$	%	$	*$000*	$	%	$	%	$
General government	1,526,160	243.29	8.5	241.82	9.5	221.58	1,028,708	121.83	5.1	121.65	5.8	121.25
Protection of persons and property	905,438	144.34	5.0	143.05	5.6	131.08	1,186,695	140.54	5.9	138.42	6.6	137.97
Transportation and communication	1,474,118	234.99	8.2	222.53	8.7	203.91	1,567,351	185.62	7.8	183.22	8.7	182.63
Health	3,226,952	514.42	18.0	380.67	14.9	348.81	4,132,427	489.39	20.5	333.18	15.8	332.11
Social services	2,558,485	407.86	14.2	343.62	13.5	314.86	2,392,121	283.29	11.9	234.62	11.1	233.86
Education	4,528,746	721.94	25.3	645.38	25.3	591.37	5,081,826	601.83	25.2	533.84	25.4	532.12
Resource conservation & industrial development	621,586	99.09	3.5	86.65	3.4	79.39	465,453	55.12	2.3	53.13	2.5	52.96
Environment	604,460	96.36	3.4	89.83	3.5	82.32	895,636	106.06	4.4	103.49	4.9	103.16
Recreation and culture	493,320	78.64	2.7	76.33	3.0	69.94	754,389	89.34	3.7	88.55	4.2	88.26
Housing, regional planning, and development	215,300	34.32	1.2	33.81	1.3	30.98	544,359	64.47	2.7	62.54	3.0	62.34
Debt charges	1,533,658	249.49	8.5	244.49	9.6	224.03	1,794,219	212.48	8.9	212.48	10.1	211.79
Other	271,794	43.33	1.5	41.41	1.6	37.94	340,736	40.35	1.7	40.16	1.9	40.03
Total	17,960,017	2,863.07	100.0	2,549.48	100.0	2,336.11	20,183,920	2,390.33	100.0	2,105.28	100.0	2,098.49

(Table continued on next page.)

Table A.7   Continued

Function	Manitoba						Saskatchewan					
	Total expenditures	Per capita including federal grants	Per cent of total[a]	Per capita excluding federal conditional grants	Per cent of total[a]	Per capita excluding federal conditional and unconditional grants[b]	Total expenditures	Per capita including federal grants	Per cent of total[a]	Per capita excluding federal conditional grants	Per cent of total[a]	Per capita excluding federal conditional and unconditional grants[b]
	$000	$	%	$	%	$	$000	$	%	$	%	$
General government	105,492	102.01	4.4	101.23	5.1	88.78	167,770	176.97	6.8	176.73	8.0	173.62
Protection of persons and property	138,277	133.73	5.8	132.12	6.7	115.87	117,190	123.62	4.8	120.53	5.4	118.40
Transportation and communication	217,374	210.23	9.1	190.81	9.7	167.34	291,599	307.59	11.9	293.34	13.2	288.17
Health	517,357	500.35	21.6	337.12	17.1	295.66	431,793	455.48	17.6	298.61	13.5	293.36
Social services	302,237	292.30	12.6	225.93	11.5	198.14	287,909	303.70	11.7	237.19	10.7	233.01
Education	535,813	518.19	22.3	424.48	22.5	388.07	532,411	561.61	21.7	481.35	21.7	472.88
Resource conservation & industrial development	77,929	75.37	3.2	58.88	3.0	51.64	181,454	191.41	7.4	159.90	7.2	157.09
Environment	68,626	66.37	2.9	65.67	3.3	57.60	70,788	74.67	2.9	72.04	3.2	70.77
Recreation and culture	80,508	77.86	3.4	77.39	3.9	67.87	79,800	84.18	3.2	84.07	3.8	82.59
Housing, regional planning, and development	31,540	30.50	1.3	26.09	1.3	22.89	34,667	36.57	1.4	23.25	1.0	22.84
Debt charges	267,658	258.86	11.2	258.86	13.1	227.03	194,190	204.84	7.9	204.84	9.2	201.24
Other	56,449	54.59	2.4	54.04	2.7	47.40	65,985	69.60	2.7	67.32	3.0	66.13
Total	2,399,260	2,320.37	100.0	1,970.61	100.0	1,728.28	2,455,556	2,590.25	100.0	2,219.16	100.0	2,180.11

(Table continued on next page.)

Table A.7 Continued

Function	Alberta						British Columbia					
	Total expenditures	Per capita including federal grants	Per cent of total[a]	Per capita excluding federal conditional grants	Per cent of total[a]	Per capita excluding federal conditional and unconditional grants[b]	Total expenditures	Per capita including federal grants	Per cent of total[a]	Per capita excluding federal conditional grants	Per cent of total[a]	Per capita excluding federal conditional and unconditional grants[b]
	$000	$	%	$	%	$	$000	$	%	$	%	$
General government	482,632	247.00	7.7	243.19	8.4	239.94	523,268	206.83	8.0	206.54	9.1	204.65
Protection of persons and property	329,733	168.75	5.2	167.98	5.8	165.74	381,548	150.81	5.8	149.10	6.6	147.73
Transportation and communication	659,323	337.42	10.5	330.23	11.4	325.82	663,414	262.22	10.2	255.30	11.2	252.96
Health	1,081,618	553.54	17.2	402.27	13.9	396.89	1,371,641	542.15	21.0	400.70	17.6	397.03
Social services	464,328	237.63	7.4	173.45	6.0	171.13	846,724	334.67	13.0	252.40	11.1	250.09
Education	1,314,715	672.83	20.9	616.11	21.3	607.87	1,402,402	554.31	21.5	493.24	21.7	488.72
Resource conservation & industrial development	751,679	384.69	11.9	347.78	12.0	343.12	229,332	90.65	3.5	84.76	3.7	83.98
Environment	327,768	167.74	5.2	162.66	5.6	160.49	257,149	101.64	3.9	97.73	4.3	96.84
Recreation and culture	249,528	127.70	4.0	126.22	4.4	124.54	227,802	90.04	3.5	87.28	3.8	86.48
Housing, regional planning, and development	125,522	64.24	2.0	62.80	2.2	61.96	77,055	30.46	1.2	29.27	1.3	29.00
Debt charges	398,895	204.14	6.3	204.14	7.1	201.41	401,353	158.64	6.1	158.64	7.0	157.19
Other	118,062	60.42	1.9	55.46	1.9	54.72	148,171	58.57	2.3	56.79	2.5	56.27
Total	6,303,803	3,226.10	100.0	2,892.31	100.0	2,853.63	6,529,860	2,580.97	100.0	2,271.75	100.0	2,250.92

(Table concluded on next page.)

Table A.7   Concluded

		All Provinces				
Function	Total expenditures	Per capita including federal grants	Per cent of total[a]	Per capita excluding federal conditional grants	Per cent of total[a]	Per capita excluding federal conditional and unconditional grants[b]
	$000	*$*	*%*	*$*	*%*	*$*
General government	4,091,827	174.73	6.7	173.85	7.6	164.23
Protection of persons and property	3,274,551	139.83	5.4	138.15	6.0	130.50
Transportation and communication	5,449,049	232.69	8.9	222.25	9.7	209.95
Health	11,698,131	499.54	19.2	350.45	15.3	331.05
Social services	7,342,728	313.55	12.0	252.26	11.0	238.29
Education	14,590,080	623.03	23.9	552.43	24.1	521.85
Resource conservation & industrial development	2,869,577	122.54	4.7	109.82	4.8	103.74
Environment	2,372,856	101.33	3.9	96.86	4.2	91.50
Recreation and culture	1,988,676	84.92	3.3	83.25	3.6	78.64
Housing, regional planning, and development	1,113,342	47.54	1.8	43.25	1.9	40.86
Debt charges	5,135,438	219.29	8.4	219.29	9.6	207.15
Other	1,157,178	49.41	1.9	47.75	2.1	45.11
Total	61,083,433	2,608.40	100.0	2,289.61	100.0	2,162.88

aMay not add to 100 due to rounding. bPer capita unconditional grants were applied to each function according to the proportion of per capita expenditures excluding conditional grants on each function.

Source: Calculated from data in Statistics Canada, *Consolidated Government Finance: Revenue, Expenditure, Assets and Liabilities: Fiscal year ended nearest December 31, 1978*, Catalogue no. 68-202; *Provincial Government Finance: Revenue and Expenditure, Fiscal Year Ended March 31, 1978*, Catalogue no. 68-207; and *Local Government Finance, 1978*, Catalogue no. 68-204.

Table A.8 Total and Per Capita Consolidated Provincial/Local Government Revenue by Major Revenue Source and by Province, 1968

Revenue source	Newfoundland Total $000	Per capita $	Per cent of total[a] %	Prince Edward Island Total $000	Per capita $	Per cent of total[a] %	Nova Scotia Total $000	Per capita $	Per cent of total[a] %
1. Personal income tax	13,829	27.33	4.9	2,668	24.25	4.3	29,335	38.25	7.0
2. Corporation income tax	8,267	16.34	2.9	1,054	9.58	1.7	11,197	14.60	2.7
3. Property taxes	8,609	17.01	3.1	5,953	54.12	9.5	62,589	81.60	14.9
4. Consumption taxes	58,899	116.40	20.9	11,490	104.45	18.4	61,595	80.31	14.6
5. Other taxes	2,353	4.65	0.8	461	4.19	0.7	4,320	5.63	1.0
6. Total taxes	91,957	181.73	32.7	21,626	196.60	34.6	169,036	220.39	40.2
7. Sale of goods and services	11,202	22.14	4.0	5,363	48.75	8.6	16,262	21.20	3.9
8. Privileges, licences, and permits	11,544	22.81	4.1	1,575	14.32	2.5	11,097	14.47	2.6
9. Natural resource revenue	3,531	6.98	1.3	47	0.43	0.1	1,530	1.99	0.4
10. Payments-in-lieu-of taxes	2	0.0	0.0	5	0.05	0.0	2,743	3.58	0.7
11. Other revenue	14,644	28.94	5.2	4,953	45.03	7.9	40,662	52.96	9.7
12. Total own-source revenue	132,880	262.61	47.2	33,569	305.17	53.7	241,300	314.60	57.3
13. Federal unconditional grants	83,229	164.48	29.6	15,237	138.52	24.4	90,844	118.44	21.6
14. Federal conditional grants	65,173	128.80	23.2	13,737	124.88	22.0	88,913	115.92	21.1
15. Total[b]	281,282	555.89	100.0	62,543	568.57	100.0	421,087	549.01	100.0

(Table continued on next page.)

Table A.8 Continued

Revenue source	New Brunswick			Quebec			Ontario		
	Total	Per capita	Per cent of total[a]	Total	Per capita	Per cent of total[a]	Total	Per capita	Per cent of total[a]
	$000	$	%	$000	$	%	$000	$	%
1. Personal income tax	21,253	34.00	6.4	696,983	117.57	18.5	620,476	85.44	12.3
2. Corporation income tax	8,170	13.07	2.4	184,512	31.13	4.9	304,679	41.96	6.0
3. Property taxes	34,770	55.63	10.4	796,482	134.36	21.2	1,288,608	177.45	25.5
4. Consumption taxes	67,664	108.26	20.2	882,807	148.92	23.5	944,808	130.10	18.7
5. Other taxes	1,365	2.18	0.4	118,283	19.95	3.2	117,691	16.21	2.3
6. Total taxes	133,222	213.16	39.8	2,679,067	451.93	71.2	3,276,262	451.15	64.9
7. Sale of goods and services	14,323	22.92	4.3	93,985	15.85	2.5	164,254	22.62	3.3
8. Privileges, licences, and permits	9,426	15.08	2.8	148,285	25.01	4.0	220,781	30.40	4.4
9. Natural resource revenue	4,766	7.63	1.4	65,948	11.12	1.8	54,130	7.45	1.1
10. Payments in-lieu-of taxes	0	0.00	0.0	2,007	0.34	0.1	8,413	1.16	0.2
11. Other revenue	23,587	37.74	7.1	122,282	20.63	3.3	657,305	90.51	13.0
12. Total own-source revenue	185,324	296.52	55.3	3,111,574	524.89	82.7	4,381,145	603.30	86.8
13. Federal unconditional grants	80,119	128.19	23.9	472,126	79.64	12.6	54,002	7.44	1.1
14. Federal conditional grants	69,466	111.15	20.8	178,856	30.17	4.8	611,541	84.21	12.1
15. Total[b]	334,909	535.85	100.0	3,762,556	634.71	100.0	5,046,688	694.94	100.0

(Table continued on next page.)

Table A.8   Continued

Revenue source	Manitoba			Saskatchewan			Alberta		
	Total	Per capita	Per cent of total[a]	Total	Per capita	Per cent of total[a]	Total	Per capita	Per cent of total[a]
	$000	$	%	$000	$	%	$000	$	%
1. Personal income tax	64,655	66.59	10.7	54,978	57.27	8.3	98,334	64.52	8.5
2. Corporation income tax	24,830	25.57	4.1	19,596	20.41	3.0	49,858	32.72	4.3
3. Property taxes	128,806	132.65	21.4	143,918	149.91	21.7	217,501	142.72	18.8
4. Consumption taxes	118,344	121.88	19.6	122,222	127.31	18.4	71,685	47.04	6.2
5. Other taxes	4,520	4.66	0.8	4,426	4.61	0.7	7,422	4.87	0.7
6. Total taxes	341,155	351.34	56.6	345,140	359.52	52.1	444,800	291.86	38.4
7. Sale of goods and services	30,867	31.79	5.1	33,435	34.83	5.1	57,439	37.69	5.0
8. Privileges, licences, and permits	20,032	20.63	3.3	19,022	19.81	2.9	39,808	26.12	3.4
9. Natural resource revenue	6,221	6.41	1.0	38,376	39.98	5.8	294,353	193.15	25.4
10. Payments in-lieu-of taxes	2,652	2.73	0.4	2,182	2.27	0.3	168	0.11	0.0
11. Other revenue	69,110	71.17	11.5	109,429	113.99	16.5	158,796	104.20	13.7
12. Total own-source revenue	470,037	484.08	78.0	547,584	570.40	82.6	995,364	653.13	86.0
13. Federal unconditional grants	50,543	52.05	8.4	21,501	22.40	3.3	20,682	13.57	1.8
14. Federal conditional grants	82,485	84.95	13.7	93,737	97.64	14.2	141,214	92.66	12.2
15. Total[b]	603,065	621.08	100.0	662,822	690.44	100.0	1,157,260	759.36	100.0

(Table concluded on next page.)

Table A.8   Concluded

Revenue source	British Columbia			All provinces		
	Total	Per capita	Per cent of total[a]	Total	Per capita	Per cent of total[a]
	$000	$	%	$000	$	%
1. Personal income tax	161,791	80.77	11.7	1,764,302	85.41	12.8
2. Corporation income tax	48,163	24.05	3.5	660,326	31.97	4.8
3. Property taxes	307,040	153.29	22.1	2,994,276	144.96	21.8
4. Consumption taxes	255,162	127.39	18.4	2,594,676	125.61	18.9
5. Other taxes	20,276	10.12	1.5	281,117	13.61	2.1
6. Total taxes	792,432	395.62	57.0	8,294,697	401.56	60.5
7. Sale of goods and services	89,053	44.46	6.4	516,183	24.99	3.8
8. Privileges, licences, and permits	51,363	25.64	3.7	532,852	25.80	3.9
9. Natural resource revenue	126,952	63.38	9.1	595,854	28.85	4.4
10. Payments in-lieu-of taxes	3,160	1.58	0.2	21,302	1.03	0.2
11. Other revenue	155,234	77.50	11.2	1,356,083	65.65	9.9
12. Total own-source revenue	1,218,194	608.18	87.7	11,316,921	547.88	82.5
13. Federal unconditional grants	4,313	2.15	0.3	892,596	43.21	6.5
14. Federal conditional grants	166,752	83.25	12.0	1,511,874	73.19	11.0
15. Total[b]	1,389,259	693.59	100.0	13,721,441	664.28	100.0

Source: Calculated from data in Statistics Canada, *Consolidated Government Finance: Revenue, Expenditure, Assets and Liabilities: Fiscal year ended nearest to December 31, 1968*, Catalogue no. 68-202.

aMay not add to 100 due to rounding.
bAdd only rows 12, 13, 14 for column totals.

Table A.9   Total and Per Capita Consolidated Provincial/Local Government Revenue
by Major Revenue Source and by Province, 1978

Revenue source	Newfoundland			Prince Edward Island			Nova Scotia		
	Total	Per capita	Per cent of total[a]	Total	Per capita	Per cent of total[a]	Total	Per capita	Per cent of total[a]
	$000	$	%	$000	$	%	$000	$	%
1. Personal income tax	153,650	270.04	11.7	29,145	238.89	10.1	264,645	314.68	15.1
2. Corporate income tax	18,102	31.81	1.4	3,631	29.76	1.3	37,994	45.18	2.2
3. Property taxes	40,547	71.26	3.1	15,306	125.46	5.3	166,337	197.78	9.5
4. Consumption taxes	217,582	382.39	16.6	36,558	299.66	12.7	228,979	272.27	13.1
5. Other taxes	13,284	23.35	1.0	1,210	9.92	0.4	10,901	12.96	0.6
6. Total taxes	443,165	778.85	33.8	85,850	703.69	29.8	708,856	842.87	40.5
7. Sale of goods and services	55,135	96.90	4.2	17,962	147.23	6.2	89,844	106.83	5.1
8. Privileges, licences, and permits .	29,945	52.63	2.3	3,099	25.40	1.1	30,731	36.54	1.8
9. Natural resource revenue	16,958	29.80	1.3	434	3.56	0.2	7,733	9.20	0.4
10. Payments in-lieu-of taxes	828	1.46	0.1	31	0.25	0.0	10,998	13.08	0.6
11. Other revenue	162,416	285.44	12.4	23,091	189.27	8.0	185,003	219.98	10.6
12. Total own-source revenue	708,447	1,245.07	54.0	130,467	1,069.40	45.3	1,033,165	1,228.50	59.0
13. Federal unconditional grants ...	356,044	625.74	27.1	74,972	614.52	26.0	396,648	471.64	22.6
14. Federal conditional grants	248,217	436.23	18.9	82,699	677.86	28.7	322,197	383.11	18.4
15. Total[b]	1,312,708	2,307.04	100.0	288,138	2,361.79	100.0	1,752,010	2,083.25	100.0

(Table continued on next page.)

Table A.9   Continued

Revenue source	New Brunswick			Quebec			Ontario		
	Total	Per capita	Per cent of total[a]	Total	Per capita	Per cent of total[a]	Total	Per capita	Per cent of total[a]
	$000	$	%	$000	$	%	$000	$	%
1. Personal income tax	205,862	296.20	14.7	4,095,289	652.84	24.2	3,514,692	416.24	18.9
2. Corporate income tax	35,652	51.30	2.5	460,029	73.33	2.7	957,728	113.42	5.1
3. Property taxes	113,706	163.61	8.1	1,916,754	305.56	11.3	3,323,539	393.60	17.9
4. Consumption taxes	207,723	298.88	14.8	2,260,870	360.41	13.3	2,670,508	316.26	14.4
5. Other taxes	5,324	7.66	0.4	236,723	37.74	1.4	530,309	62.80	2.9
6. Total taxes	568,267	817.65	40.6	8,969,663	1,429.88	53.0	10,996,776	1,302.32	59.1
7. Sale of goods and services	47,384	68.18	3.4	601,293	95.85	3.6	1,164,576	137.92	6.3
8. Privileges, licences, and permits .	24,250	34.89	1.7	588,170	93.76	3.5	528,245	62.56	2.8
9. Natural resource revenue	11,598	16.69	0.8	113,632	18.11	0.7	130,195	15.42	0.7
10. Payments-in-lieu-of taxes	242	0.35	0.0	51,160	8.16	0.3	95,348	11.29	0.5
11. Other revenue	123,557	177.78	8.8	3,143,977	501.19	18.6	3,169,998	375.41	17.0
12. Total own-source revenue	775,298	1,115.54	55.3	13,467,895	2,146.96	79.5	16,085,138	1,904.92	86.5
13. Federal unconditional grants ...	335,736	483.07	24.0	1,501,841	239.41	8.9	112,642	13.34	0.6
14. Federal conditional grants	290,222	417.59	20.7	1,967,136	313.59	11.6	2,406,975	285.05	12.9
15. Total[b]	1,401,256	2,016.20	100.0	16,936,872	2,699.96	100.0	18,604,755	2,203.31	100.0

(Table continued on next page.)

Table A.9   Continued

Revenue source	Manitoba			Saskatchewan			Alberta		
	Total	Per capita	Per cent of total[a]	Total	Per capita	Per cent of total[a]	Total	Per capita	Per cent of total[a]
	$000	$	%	$000	$	%	$000	$	%
1. Personal income tax	391,354	378.49	16.9	309,954	326.96	12.2	686,884	351.53	7.8
2. Corporate income tax	103,971	100.55	4.5	98,836	104.26	3.9	529,824	271.15	6.0
3. Property taxes	384,915	372.26	16.6	309,269	326.23	12.1	692,128	354.21	7.9
4. Consumption taxes	278,117	268.97	12.0	274,429	289.48	10.8	43,853	22.44	0.5
5. Other taxes	40,482	39.15	1.7	42,732	45.08	1.7	44,790	22.92	0.5
6. Total taxes	1,198,839	1,159.42	51.7	1,035,220	1,092.00	40.6	1,997,479	1,022.25	22.7
7. Sale of goods and services	102,346	98.98	4.4	145,943	153.95	5.7	450,206	230.40	5.1
8. Privileges, licences, and permits	44,818	43.34	1.9	42,991	45.35	1.7	112,892	57.77	1.3
9. Natural resource revenue	34,612	33.47	1.5	522,095	550.73	20.5	4,052,748	2,074.08	46.0
10. Payments in-lieu-of taxes	6,929	6.70	0.3	8,321	8.78	0.3	6,464	3.31	0.1
11. Other revenue	308,208	298.07	13.3	402,732	424.82	15.8	1,454,198	744.22	16.5
12. Total own-source revenue	1,695,752	1,639.99	73.2	2,157,302	2,275.64	84.7	8,073,987	4,132.03	91.6
13. Federal unconditional grants	259,378	250.85	11.2	39,176	41.32	1.5	84,439	43.21	1.0
14. Federal conditional grants	361,646	349.75	15.6	351,794	371.09	13.8	652,230	333.79	7.4
15. Total[b]	2,316,776	2,240.60	100.0	2,548,272	2,688.05	100.0	8,810,656	4,509.04	100.0

(Table concluded on next page.)

Table A.9   Concluded

Revenue source	British Columbia			All provinces		
	Total	Per capita	Per cent of total[a]	Total	Per capita	Per cent of total[a]
	$000	$	%	$000	$	%
1. Personal income tax	1,176,531	465.03	17.9	10,828,004	462.38	17.9
2. Corporate income tax	294,697	116.48	4.5	2,540,464	108.48	4.2
3. Property taxes	1,128,514	446.05	17.1	8,091,015	345.50	13.4
4. Consumption taxes	947,609	374.55	14.4	7,166,228	306.01	11.8
5. Other taxes	73,390	29.01	1.1	999,145	42.67	1.6
6. Total taxes	3,620,741	1,431.12	54.9	29,624,856	1,265.05	48.9
7. Sale of goods and services	358,351	141.64	5.4	3,033,040	129.52	5.0
8. Privileges, licences, and permits	133,349	52.71	2.0	1,538,490	65.70	2.5
9. Natural resource revenue	556,967	220.15	8.5	5,446,972	232.60	9.0
10. Payments in-lieu-of taxes	11,963	4.73	0.2	192,284	8.21	0.3
11. Other revenue	1,067,049	421.76	16.2	10,040,229	428.74	16.6
12. Total own-source revenue	5,748,420	2,272.10	87.2	49,875,871	2,129.81	82.4
13. Federal unconditional grants	60,171	23.78	0.9	3,221,047	137.55	5.3
14. Federal conditional grants	782,345	309.23	11.9	7,465,461	318.79	12.3
15. Total[b]	6,590,936	2,605.11	100.0	60,562,379	2,586.15	100.0

aMay not add to 100 due to rounding. bAdd 12, 13 & 14 for column totals.

Source: Calculated from data in Statistics Canada, *Consolidated Government Finance: Revenue, Expenditure, Assets and Liabilities: Fiscal year ended nearest to December 31, 1978*, Catalogue no 68-202.

Appendix B

Table B.1   Current and Capital Local Expenditures by Major Function and Province, Including and Excluding Grants, 1968

Newfoundland

Function	Current						Capital				
	Total including grants	Per capita including grants	Per cent of total	Per capita excluding conditional grants	Per cent of total	Per capita excluding conditional and unconditional grants	Total including grants	Per capita including grants	Per cent of total	Per capita excluding conditional grants	Per cent of total
	$000	$	%	$	%	$	$000	$	%	$	%
General government	2,137	4.21	12.9	4.21	14.9	3.53	1,033	2.04	7.3	2.04	7.9
Protection	1,359	2.68	8.2	2.66	9.4	2.23	—	—	—	—	—
Transportation and communication	4,022	7.93	24.3	6.68	23.6	5.60	2,893	5.71	20.4	4.22	16.4
Health	5	0.01	—	0.01	—	—	—	—	—	—	—
Social services	2	0.01	—	0.01	—	—	—	—	—	—	—
Education	742	1.46	4.5	1.46	5.1	1.21	—	—	—	—	—
Resources conservation and industrial development	—	—	—	—	—	—	—	—	—	—	—
Environment	2,664	5.25	16.1	2.33	8.2	1.94	7,600	14.99	53.5	14.87	57.6
Recreation and culture	800	1.58	4.8	1.49	5.3	1.26	392	0.77	2.8	0.68	2.6
Housing, regional planning, and development	—	—	—	—	—	—	—	—	—	—	—
Other	4,831	9.53	29.2	9.50	33.5	7.94	2,277	4.49	16.0	4.01	15.5
Total	16,562	32.66	100.0	28.35	100.0	23.71	14,195	28.00	100.0	25.83	100.0

(Table continued on next page.)

Table B.1 Continued

Prince Edward Island

Function	Current						Capital				
	Total including grants	Per capita including grants	Per cent of total	Per capita excluding conditional grants	Per cent of total	Per capita excluding conditional and unconditional grants	Total including grants	Per capita including grants	Per cent of total	Per capita excluding conditional grants	Per cent of total
	$000	$	%	$	%	$	$000	$	%	$	%
General government	387	3.52	2.5	3.31	4.7	3.10	—	—	—	—	—
Protection	665	6.05	4.3	5.83	8.2	5.41	2	0.02	0.1	0.02	0.7
Transportation and communication	594	5.40	3.9	4.90	6.9	4.55	302	2.75	9.8	2.56	83.4
Health	—	—	—	—	—	—	—	—	—	—	—
Social services	45	0.41	0.3	0.41	0.6	0.40	2,710	24.64	87.8	φ	φ
Education	11,163	101.48	72.4	33.04	46.7	30.82	—	—	—	—	—
Resources conservation and industrial development	—	—	—	—	—	—	—	—	—	—	—
Environment	585	5.32	3.8	5.32	7.5	4.95	15	0.14	0.5	φ	φ
Recreation and culture	193	1.75	1.2	1.69	2.5	1.65	8	0.07	0.2	0.04	1.3
Housing, regional planning, and development	—	—	—	—	—	—	—	—	—	—	—
Other	1,781	16.18	11.6	16.18	22.9	15.11	49	0.45	1.6	0.45	14.6
Total	15,412	140.11	100.0	70.68	100.0	66.00	3,087	28.07	100.0	3.07	100.0

(Table continued on next page.)

Table B.1 Continued

Nova Scotia

Function	Current						Capital				
	Total including grants	Per capita including grants	Per cent of total	Per capita excluding conditional grants	Per cent of total	Per capita excluding conditional and unconditional grants	Total including grants	Per capita including grants	Per cent of total	Per capita excluding conditional grants	Per cent of total
	$000	$	%	$	%	$	$000	$	%	$	%
General government	6,041	7.95	4.8	7.93	8.5	7.70	20.7	2.65	6.3	2.65	8.4
Protection	10,382	13.66	8.2	11.03	11.8	10.71	5.3	0.74	1.8	0.74	2.3
Transportation and communication	3,921	5.16	3.1	4.49	4.8	4.36	4,915	6.47	15.5	φ	φ
Health	2,157	2.84	1.7	φ	φ	0	963	1.27	3.0	1.27	4.0
Social services	9,369	12.33	7.4	4.68	5.0	4.55	26	0.03	0.1	φ	φ
Education	73,721	97.00	58.3	38.81	41.5	37.68	16,300	21.45	51.0	21.45	67.8
Resources conservation and industrial development	—	—	—	—	—	—	—	—	—	—	—
Environment	6,461	8.50	5.1	8.23	8.8	7.99	4,335	5.70	13.7	4.21	13.3
Recreation and culture	2,653	3.49	2.1	2.92	3.1	2.84	852	1.12	2.7	1.03	3.3
Housing, regional planning, and development	—	—	—	—	—	—	—	—	—	—	—
Other	11,783	15.50	9.3	15.36	16.4	14.91	1,773	2.34	5.6	0.29	0.9
Total	126,488	166.43	100.0	93.45	100.0	90.72	31,744	41.77	100.0	31.64	100.0

(Table continued on next page.)

Table B.1   Continued

New Brunswick

	Current						Capital				
Function	Total including grants	Per capita including grants	Per cent of total	Per capita excluding conditional grants	Per cent of total	Per capita excluding conditional and uncondi- tional grants	Total including grants	Per capita including grants	Per cent of total	Per capita excluding conditional grants	Per cent of total
	$000	$	%	$	%	$	$000	$	%	$	%
General government	2,795	4.48	9.0	4.31	8.7	2.30	470	0.75	4.4	0.75	5.0
Protection	8,333	13.35	26.8	13.34	26.9	7.12	1,043	1.67	9.8	1.67	11.0
Transportation and communication	5,116	8.20	16.4	8.20	16.6	4.39	3,013	4.83	28.4	4.56	30.1
Health	87	0.14	0.3	0.12	0.2	0.05	—	—	—	—	—
Social services	34	0.05	0.1	0.05	0.1	0.03	—	—	—	—	—
Education	1,358	2.18	4.4	2.18	4.4	1.16	—	—	—	—	—
Resources conservation and industrial development	—	—	—	—	—	—	—	—	—	—	—
Environment	6,457	10.35	20.7	10.35	20.9	5.53	4,077	6.53	38.4	6.50	43.0
Recreation and culture	2,246	3.60	7.2	3.57	7.2	1.91	1,031	1.65	9.7	1.65	10.9
Housing, regional planning, and development	—	—	—	—	—	—	—	—	—	—	—
Other	4,704	7.54	15.1	7.42	15.0	3.97	974	1.57	9.3	φ	φ
Total	31,130	49.89	100.0	49.54	100.0	26.47	10,608	17.00	100.0	15.13	100.0

(Table continued on next page.)

Table B.1 Continued

Quebec

	Current						Capital				
Function	Total including grants	Per capita including grants	Per cent of total	Per capita excluding conditional grants	Per cent of total	Per capita excluding conditional and unconditional grants	Total including grants	Per capita including grants	Per cent of total	Per capita excluding conditional grants	Per cent of total
	$000	$	%	$	%	$	$000	$	%	$	%
General government	97,906	16.52	7.7	16.52	11.3	14.02	8,147	1.37	1.6	1.31	2.2
Protection	128,578	21.69	10.1	21.54	14.7	18.24	2,525	0.43	0.5	0.40	0.7
Transportation and communication	108,255	18.26	8.5	14.53	9.9	12.29	35,152	14.37	17.0	13.16	21.6
Health	8,579	1.45	0.7	1.45	1.0	1.24	—	—	—	—	—
Social services	5,947	1.00	0.5	1.00	0.7	0.87	—	—	—	—	—
Education	616,719	104.05	48.2	39.44	27.0	33.51	210,750	35.56	42.0	14.37	23.6
Resources conservation and industrial development	—	—					—	—			
Environment	63,724	10.75	4.9	9.84	6.7	8.31	115,151	19.43	23.0	18.18	29.8
Recreation and culture	47,389	8.00	3.7	8.00	5.5	6.83	15,927	2.69	3.2	2.69	4.4
Housing, regional planning, and development											
Other	201,806	34.06	15.7	33.97	23.2	28.79	63,964	10.78	12.7	10.78	17.7
Total	1,278,903	215.78	100.0	146.29	100.0	124.09	501,616	84.64	100.0	60.89	100.0

(Table continued on next page.)

Table B.1 Continued

	Ontario										
	Current						Capital				
Function	Total including grants	Per capita including grants	Per cent of total	Per capita excluding conditional grants	Per cent of total	Per capita excluding conditional and unconditional grants	Total including grants	Per capita including grants	Per cent of total	Per capita excluding conditional grants	Per cent of total
	$000	$	%	$	%	$	$000	$	%	$	%
General government	92,090	12.60	4.5	12.60	7.1	12.12	33,171	4.54	5.3	4.54	6.2
Protection	174,553	23.89	8.5	23.89	13.5	22.96	8,337	1.14	1.3	1.14	1.5
Transportation and communication	218,903	29.96	10.6	15.61	8.9	15.01	179,145	24.52	28.8	13.29	18.0
Health	27,093	3.71	1.3	φ	φ	φ	15,256	2.09	2.5	2.09	2.8
Social services	91,691	12.55	4.5	5.72	3.2	5.50	9,770	1.34	1.6	1.34	1.8
Education	1,056,895	144.66	51.4	66.49	37.5	63.90	332,704	36.63	43.1	36.63	49.7
Resources conservation and industrial development	—	—	—	—	—	—	—	—	—	—	—
Environment	114,912	15.73	5.6	15.73	8.9	15.11	19,392	9.54	11.2	9.54	12.9
Recreation and culture	70,438	9.65	3.4	9.45	5.3	9.09	23,166	3.17	3.7	3.17	4.3
Housing, regional planning, and development	—	—	—	—	—	—	—	—	—	—	—
Other	209,593	28.69	10.2	27.65	15.6	26.57	21,263	2.03	2.4	2.03	2.8
Total	2,056,168	281.44	100.0	177.14	100.0	170.21	7,022	85.00	100.0	73.77	100.0

(Table continued on next page.)

Table B.1   Continued

Manitoba

Function	Current						Capital				
	Total including grants	Per capita including grants	Per cent of total	Per capita excluding conditional grants	Per cent of total	Per capita excluding conditional and uncondi-tional grants	Total including grants	Per capita including grants	Per cent of total	Per capita excluding conditional grants	Per cent of total
	$000	$	%	$	%	$	$000	$	%	$	%
General government	11,249	11.58	5.0	11.58	7.6	11.36	147	0.15	0.3	0.15	0.6
Protection	18,965	19.53	8.5	19.51	12.7	19.14	948	0.98	2.0	0.91	3.6
Transportation and communication	15,347	15.81	6.8	15.50	10.1	15.20	15,221	15.68	32.3	11.08	43.4
Health	2,206	2.27	1.0	φ	φ	φ	1,364	1.40	2.9	1.40	5.5
Social services	4,515	4.65	2.0	2.09	1.4	2.05	—	—	—	φ	φ
Education	123,286	126.97	55.0	54.36	35.5	53.32	17,011	17.52	36.0	φ	φ
Resources conservation and industrial development	—	—	—	—	—	—	—	—	—	—	—
Environment	12,084	12.44	5.4	12.44	8.1	12.20	8,825	9.09	18.7	8.92	34.9
Recreation and culture	8,633	8.89	3.8	8.84	5.8	8.67	1,722	1.77	3.6	1.77	6.9
Housing, regional planning, and development	—	—	—	—	—	—	—	—	—	—	—
Other	28,022	28.86	12.5	28.84	18.8	28.29	1,947	2.01	4.2	1.30	5.1
Total	224,307	231.00	100.0	153.17	100.0	150.47	47,185	48.60	100.0	25.53	100.0

(Table continued on next page.)

Table B.1 Continued

Saskatchewan

Function	Current — Total including grants ($000)	Current — Per capita including grants ($)	Current — Per cent of total (%)	Current — Per capita excluding conditional grants ($)	Current — Per cent of total (%)	Current — Per capita excluding conditional and unconditional grants ($)	Capital — Total including grants ($000)	Capital — Per capita including grants ($)	Capital — Per cent of total (%)	Capital — Per capita excluding conditional grants ($)	Capital — Per cent of total (%)
General government	10,865	11.32	4.6	11.26	7.2	11.26	934	0.97	1.6	0.97	2.0
Protection	14,867	15.49	6.3	15.40	9.8	15.40	715	0.74	1.2	0.74	1.5
Transportation and communication	34,351	35.78	14.6	18.90	12.0	18.90	14,574	15.18	25.2	15.17	31.0
Health	5,036	5.25	2.1	φ	φ	φ	8,541	8.90	14.8	8.90	18.2
Social services	2,789	2.91	1.2	1.82	1.2	1.82	14	0.01	—	0.01	—
Education	125,101	130.31	53.2	68.89	43.8	68.89	17,357	18.08	30.0	7.15	14.6
Resources conservation and industrial development	—	—	—	—	—	—	—	—	—	—	—
Environment	10,684	11.13	4.5	10.15	6.5	10.15	7,326	7.84	13.0	7.55	15.4
Recreation and culture	7,937	8.28	3.5	7.51	4.8	7.51	7,994	8.33	13.8	8.31	17.0
Housing, regional planning, and development	—	—	—	—	—	—	—	—	—	—	—
Other	23,411	24.38	10.0	23.40	14.9	23.40	164	0.18	0.4	0.18	0.3
Total	235,041	244.84	100.0	157.33	100.0	157.33	57,819	60.23	100.0	48.99	100.0

(Table continued on next page.)

Table B.1   Continued

	Alberta										
	Current						Capital				
Function	Total including grants ($000)	Per capita including grants ($)	Per cent of total (%)	Per capita excluding conditional grants ($)	Per cent of total (%)	Per capita excluding conditional and unconditional grants ($)	Total including grants ($000)	Per capita including grants ($)	Per cent of total (%)	Per capita excluding conditional grants ($)	Per cent of total (%)
General government	17,242	11.30	4.0	11.26	6.5	10.00	1,590	1.04	1.0	1.04	1.2
Protection	36,159	23.70	8.4	23.57	13.7	20.93	2,146	1.41	1.4	1.33	1.5
Transportation and communication	38,312	25.11	8.9	20.20	11.7	17.93	42,448	27.82	28.1	20.37	23.7
Health	17,668	11.58	4.1	φ	φ	φ	10,287	6.74	6.8	6.10	7.1
Social services	8,248	5.40	1.9	3.07	1.8	2.72	196	0.13	0.1	0.13	0.2
Education	226,771	148.60	52.8	59.74	34.6	53.01	66,600	43.64	44.0	39.54	45.9
Resources conservation and industrial development	—	—	—	—	—	—	—	—	—	—	—
Environment	24,526	16.07	5.7	15.88	9.2	14.10	17,177	11.26	11.4	10.56	12.3
Recreation and culture	17,334	11.36	4.0	11.13	6.5	9.89	7,600	4.98	5.0	4.92	5.7
Housing, regional planning, and development	—	—	—	—	—	—	—	—	—	—	—
Other	43,325	28.39	10.2	27.67	16.0	24.55	3,288	2.15	2.2	2.08	2.4
Total	429,589	281.51	100.0	172.51	100.0	153.08	151,332	99.17	100.0	86.07	100.0

(Table continued on next page.)

Table B.1 Continued

British Columbia

Function	Current						Capital				
	Total including grants ($000)	Per capita including grants ($)	Per cent of total (%)	Per capita excluding conditional grants ($)	Per cent of total (%)	Per capita excluding conditional and unconditional grants ($)	Total including grants ($000)	Per capita including grants ($)	Per cent of total (%)	Per capita excluding conditional grants ($)	Per cent of total (%)
General government	17,242	11.30	4.0	11.26	6.5	11.26	3,811	1.90	3.0	1.81	3.5
Protection	50,270	25.05	10.1	21.45	14.0	21.45	3,083	1.54	2.4	1.48	2.9
Transportation and communication	24,993	12.45	5.0	φ	φ	φ	29,650	14.77	23.4	13.93	27.2
Health	4,127	2.07	0.8	1.77	1.2	1.77	175	0.09	0.1	0.09	0.2
Social services	49,958	24.89	10.0	7.28	4.8	7.28	4	– –	–	– –	– –
Education	248,412	123.77	49.6	63.98	41.7	63.98	51,381	25.60	40.5	15.39	30.0
Resources conservation and industrial development	–	–	–	–	–	–	–	–	–	–	–
Environment	26,157	13.03	5.2	11.19	9.3	11.19	25,556	12.73	20.1	12.29	24.0
Recreation and culture	21,938	10.89	4.4	10.64	6.9	10.64	8,864	4.42	7.0	4.22	8.2
Housing, regional planning, and development	–	–	–	–	–	–	–	–	–	–	–
Other	53,120	26.47	10.6	26.32	17.2	26.32	4,410	2.20	3.5	2.10	4.0
Total	500,606	249.44	100.0	153.40	100.0	153.89	126,934	63.25	100.0	51.29	100.0

(Table concluded on next page.)

Table B.1 Concluded

Function	All provinces										
	Current						Capital				
	Total including grants	Per capita including grants	Per cent of total	Per capita excluding conditional grants	Per cent of total	Per capita excluding conditional and unconditional grants	Total including grants	Per capita including grants	Per cent of total	Per capita excluding conditional grants	Per cent of total
	$000	$	%	$	%		$000	$	%	$	%
General government	262,341	12.67	5.3	12.66	8.4	11.72	51,320	2.48	3.1	2.46	4.1
Protection	444,131	21.46	9.0	20.95	13.8	19.39	19,362	0.94	1.2	.92	1.5
Transportation and communication	453,816	21.93	9.2	13.19	8.7	12.21	377,313	18.23	22.9	12.77	21.1
Health	66,958	3.23	1.4	φ	φ	φ	36,586	1.77	2.2	1.72	2.8
Social services	172,597	8.34	3.5	3.60	2.4	3.34	10,011	0.48	0.6	0.47	0.8
Education	2,484,168	120.02	50.6	52.82	34.8	48.88	714,813	34.54	43.4	22.53	37.3
Resources conservation and industrial development	—	—	—	—	—	—	—	—	—	—	—
Environment	268,254	12.96	5.5	12.38	8.2	11.46	269,654	13.03	16.4	12.02	19.9
Recreation and culture	179,561	8.68	3.7	8.50	5.8	7.88	67,556	3.26	4.1	3.23	5.3
Housing, regional planning, and development	—	—	—	—	—	—	—	—	—	—	—
Other	582,380	28.13	11.8	27.61	18.2	25.59	100,109	4.83	6.1	4.34	7.2
Total	4,914,206	237.42	100.0	151.71	100.0	140.43	1,646,724	79.56	100.0	60.46	100.0

— no expenditure. – –under .1. φ grant exceeds expenditure.

Source: Calculated from data in Statistics Canada, *Local Government Finance, 1968*, Catalogue no. 68-204, and from unpublished data provided by the Local Government Section, Public Finance Division, Statistics Canada.

Table B.2 Current and Capital Local Expenditures by Major Function and Province, Including and Excluding Grants, 1978

| | Newfoundland | | | | | | | | | | |
| | Current | | | | | | Capital | | | | |
Function	Total including grants	Per capita including grants	Per cent of total	Per capita excluding conditional grants	Per cent of total	Per capita excluding conditional and unconditional grants	Total including grants	Per capita including grants	Per cent of total	Per capita excluding conditional grants	Per cent of total
	$000	*$*	*%*	*$*	*%*	*$*	*$000*	*$*	*%*	*$*	*%*
General government	9,984	17.55	12.7	17.53	18.1	15.22	1,656	2.91	4.6	2.69	5.7
Protection	5,391	9.47	6.8	9.47	9.8	8.22	32	0.06	0.1	φ	φ
Transportation and communication	13,327	23.42	16.9	10.76	11.1	9.34	11,330	19.91	31.5	12.69	27.1
Health	54	0.09	φ	φ	φ	φ	—	—	—	—	—
Social services	—	—	—	—	—	—	—	—	—	—	—
Education	8,724	15.33	11.1	15.33	15.8	13.31	—	—	—	—	—
Resources conservation and industrial development	148	0.26	0.2	0.26	0.3	0.23	103	0.18	0.3	0.18	0.4
Environment	13,372	23.50	17.0	1.40	1.4	1.22	19,467	34.21	54.1	27.08	57.7
Recreation and culture	6,344	11.15	8.1	7.10	7.3	6.17	2,533	4.45	7.0	3.85	8.2
Housing, regional planning, and development	456	0.80	0.6	φ	φ	φ	884	1.55	2.4	0.41	0.9
Other	20,922	36.77	26.6	34.79	35.9	30.21	—	—	—	—	—
Total	78,722	138.35	100.0	96.88	100.0	84.13	36,005	63.28	100.0	46.90	100.0

(Table continued on next page.)

Table B.2 Continued

Prince Edward Island

Function	Current						Capital				
	Total including grants	Per capita including grants	Per cent of total	Per capita excluding conditional grants	Per cent of total	Per capita excluding conditional and unconditional grants	Total including grants	Per capita including grants	Per cent of total	Per capita excluding conditional grants	Per cent of total
	$000	$	%	$	%	$	$000	$	%	$	%
General government	1,547	12.68	2.8	12.60	12.8	10.55	4	0.03	– –	0.02	– –
Protection	2,037	16.70	3.7	16.68	16.9	13.93	403	3.30	1.6	0.86	0.5
Transportation and communication	1,752	14.36	3.2	13.86	14.0	11.54	893	7.32	3.5	φ	φ
Health	8	0.07	– –	0.07	0.1	– –	–	–	–	–	–
Social services	6	0.05	– –	0.05	0.1	– –	–	–	–	–	–
Education	40,205	329.55	73.8	3.18	3.2	2.64	18,152	148.79	70.3	130.44	72.4
Resources conservation and industrial development	2	0.02	– –	0.02	– –	– –	–	–	–	–	–
Environment	2,547	20.88	4.7	20.82	21.1	17.40	1,752	14.36	6.8	14.36	8.0
Recreation and culture	1,687	13.83	3.1	11.58	11.7	9.65	612	5.01	2.0	1.94	1.1
Housing, regional planning, and development	625	5.12	1.2	1.78	1.8	1.48	3,991	32.71	15.5	32.51	18.0
Other	4,078	33.43	7.5	18.06	18.3	15.09	–	–	–	–	–
Total	54,494	446.67	100.0	98.70	100.0	82.28	25,807	211.53	100.0	180.13	100.0

(Table continued on next page.)

Table B.2   Continued

Nova Scotia

Function	Current — Total including grants ($000)	Current — Per capita including grants ($)	Current — Per cent of total (%)	Current — Per capita excluding conditional grants ($)	Current — Per cent of total (%)	Current — Per capita excluding conditional and unconditional grants ($)	Capital — Total including grants ($000)	Capital — Per capita including grants ($)	Capital — Per cent of total (%)	Capital — Per capita excluding conditional grants ($)	Capital — Per cent of total (%)
General government	21,561	25.64	3.8	25.33	7.5	19.48	4,134	4.92	5.3	3.73	5.5
Protection	45,617	54.24	8.0	45.33	13.5	35.07	936	1.11	1.2	0.84	1.2
Transportation and communication	25,395	30.20	4.5	24.16	7.2	18.70	15,898	18.90	20.3	11.17	16.4
Health	32,251	38.35	5.7	7.68	2.3	5.97	537	0.64	0.7	0.52	0.8
Social services	62,544	74.37	11.0	37.31	11.1	28.83	35	0.04	–	0.04	0.1
Education	289,556	344.30	50.8	113.43	33.6	87.28	23,631	28.10	30.1	24.92	36.6
Resources conservation and industrial development	1,012	1.20	0.2	1.20	0.4	1.04	403	0.48	0.5	0.48	0.7
Environment	19,374	23.04	3.4	16.82	5.0	12.99	29,035	34.52	37.0	23.35	34.3
Recreation and culture	18,771	22.32	3.3	17.10	5.1	13.25	1,668	1.98	2.1	1.39	2.0
Housing, regional planning, and development	5,224	6.22	0.9	2.91	0.8	2.08	1,053	1.25	1.3	0.64	0.9
Other	49,061	58.34	8.6	45.91	13.6	35.32	1,079	1.28	1.4	1.03	1.5
Total	570,368	678.20	100.0	337.14	100.0	260.00	78,409	93.23	100.0	68.11	100.0

(Table continued on next page.)

Table B.2   Continued

New Brunswick

Function	Current						Capital				
	Total including grants	Per capita including grants	Per cent of total	Per capita excluding conditional grants	Per cent of total	Per capita excluding conditional and unconditional grants	Total including grants	Per capita including grants	Per cent of total	Per capita excluding conditional grants	Per cent of total
	$000	$	%	$	%	$	$000	$	%	$	%
General government	9,474	13.63	7.7	13.63	8.1	7.80	1,237	1.78	2.1	1.48	2.4
Protection	31,109	44.76	25.2	44.76	26.7	25.72	3,082	4.43	5.3	3.86	6.2
Transportation and communication	27,626	39.75	22.4	38.42	23.0	22.16	25,852	37.20	44.6	30.34	48.7
Health	26	0.04	—	0.04	—	—	—	—	—	—	—
Social services	—	—	—	—	—	—	—	—	—	—	—
Education	—	—	—	—	—	—	—	—	—	—	—
Resources conservation and industrial development	1,282	1.84	1.0	1.84	1.1	1.06	267	0.38	0.5	0.38	0.6
Environment	16,275	23.42	13.3	19.16	11.5	11.08	21,953	32.59	39.1	20.95	33.6
Recreation and culture	14,117	20.31	11.4	16.21	9.7	9.34	4,167	6.00	7.2	4.83	7.7
Housing, regional planning, and development	1,332	1.91	1.1	1.67	1.0	1.25	444	0.63	0.8	0.25	0.4
Other	21,964	31.60	17.8	31.03	18.6	17.92	232	0.33	0.4	0.26	0.4
Total	123,594	177.83	100.0	166.74	100.0	96.33	57,994	83.44	100.0	62.35	100.0

(Table continued on next page.)

Table B.2 Continued

Quebec

Function	Current					Per capita excluding conditional and unconditional grants	Capital				
	Total including grants	Per capita including grants	Per cent of total	Per capita excluding conditional grants	Per cent of total		Total including grants	Per capita including grants	Per cent of total	Per capita excluding conditional grants	Per cent of total
	$000	$	%	$	%	$	$000	$	%	$	%
General government	423,919	67.47	7.9	64.57	14.5	53.61	14,591	2.32	1.4	2.32	1.8
Protection	456,139	72.60	8.5	72.03	16.1	59.23	14,429	2.30	1.4	2.30	1.7
Transportation and communication	333,986	53.15	6.2	47.03	10.5	38.22	378,200	60.19	36.4	56.50	42.7
Health	7,506	1.19	0.1	1.18	0.3	1.11	—	—	—	—	—
Social services	16,625	2.65	0.3	2.60	0.6	2.22	—	—	—	—	—
Education	2,859,570	455.13	53.5	109.74	24.6	90.96	167,347	26.63	16.1	—	—
Resources conservation and industrial development	10,606	1.69	0.2	1.69	0.4	1.48	—	—	—	—	—
Environment	201,014	31.99	3.8	26.65	6.0	22.18	384,291	61.16	37.0	58.90	44.6
Recreation and culture	248,801	39.60	4.7	35.20	7.9	29.21	71,608	11.40	6.9	11.00	8.3
Housing, regional planning, and development	36,607	5.80	0.7	5.54	1.2	4.62	7,503	1.19	0.7	1.19	0.9
Other	749,494	119.29	14.0	79.94	17.8	65.81	—	—	—	—	—
Total	5,344,227	850.59	100.0	446.19	100.0	369.58	1,037,969	165.20	100.0	132.21	100.0

(Table continued on next page.)

Table B.2 Continued

Ontario

Function	Current						Capital				
	Total including grants	Per capita including grants	Per cent of total	Per capita excluding conditional grants	Per cent of total	Per capita excluding conditional and unconditional grants	Total including grants	Per capita including grants	Per cent of total	Per capita excluding conditional grants	Per cent of total
	$000	$	%	$	%	$	$000	$	%	$	%
General government	314,114	37.20	4.2	36.87	7.0	32.86	22,294	2.64	1.7	2.51	2.2
Protection	856,072	77.69	8.9	77.47	14.8	69.47	36,390	4.31	2.7	4.18	3.6
Transportation and communication	502,516	59.50	6.8	27.87	5.3	24.88	510,768	60.48	38.3	33.49	28.7
Health	443,786	52.55	6.0	7.26	1.4	6.57	14,345	1.70	1.1	0.81	0.7
Social services	486,110	57.56	6.6	22.41	4.3	20.18	41,468	4.91	3.1	4.76	4.1
Education	3,428,883	406.03	46.3	174.91	33.4	156.78	175,831	20.82	13.2	20.82	17.9
Resources conservation and industrial development	54,641	6.47	0.7	6.47	1.2	5.63	56,961	6.74	4.3	6.74	5.8
Environment	372,540	44.12	5.0	43.63	8.3	38.96	288,911	34.21	21.7	27.34	23.4
Recreation and culture	404,957	47.95	5.5	44.19	8.4	39.43	138,235	16.37	10.4	11.68	10.0
Housing, regional planning, and development	61,108	7.23	0.8	6.45	1.2	5.63	49,199	5.83	3.7	4.28	3.7
Other	680,038	80.53	9.2	76.33	14.7	69.00	—	—	—	—	—
Total	7,404,765	876.82	100.0	523.85	100.0	469.39	1,334,402	158.01	100.0	116.61	100.0

(Table continued on next page.)

Table B.2 Continued

Manitoba

Function	Current						Capital				
	Total including grants	Per capita including grants	Per cent of total	Per capita excluding conditional grants	Per cent of total	Per capita excluding conditional and unconditional grants	Total including grants	Per capita including grants	Per cent of total	Per capita excluding conditional grants	Per cent of total
	$000	$	%	$	%	$	$000	$	%	$	%
General government	28,705	27.79	3.6	26.81	5.7	25.87	1,153	1.12	0.9	0.96	1.1
Protection	68,674	66.48	8.6	64.85	13.7	62.18	4,602	4.46	3.6	4.40	5.0
Transportation and communication	60,646	58.71	7.6	53.29	11.3	51.29	52,100	50.44	40.6	39.28	45.0
Health	77,321	74.85	9.7	4.54	1.0	4.54	4,675	4.53	3.6	4.35	5.0
Social services	10,803	10.46	1.4	1.87	0.4	1.82	144	0.14	0.1	0.14	0.2
Education	364,131	352.50	45.9	164.39	34.8	157.94	30,460	29.49	23.7	10.06	11.5
Resources conservation and industrial development	3,625	3.51	0.5	3.51	0.7	3.17	598	0.58	0.5	0.58	0.7
Environment	42,148	40.80	5.3	39.79	8.4	38.12	20,616	19.96	16.1	18.22	20.9
Recreation and culture	41,120	39.81	5.2	34.97	7.4	33.58	10,190	9.86	7.9	9.22	10.6
Housing, regional planning, and development	8,950	8.66	1.0	8.60	1.8	8.17	3,893	3.77	3.0	—	—
Other	89,302	86.45	11.2	69.52	14.8	67.17	—	—	—	—	—
Total	795,421	770.01	100.0	472.12	100.0	453.87	128,431	124.33	100.0	87.21	100.0

(Table continued on next page.)

Table B.2   Continued

Saskatchewan

	Current						Capital				
Function	Total including grants	Per capita including grants	Per cent of total	Per capita excluding conditional grants	Per cent of total	Per capita excluding conditional and unconditional grants	Total including grants	Per capita including grants	Per cent of total	Per capita excluding conditional grants	Per cent of total
	$000	$	%	$	%	$	$000	$	%	$	%
General government	33,798	35.65	4.4	35.07	8.2	31.25	1,690	1.78	1.0	1.55	1.0
Protection	49,650	52.37	6.5	50.68	11.8	44.96	7,406	7.81	4.2	5.33	3.6
Transportation and communication	64,189	67.71	8.4	50.96	11.9	45.34	65,783	69.39	37.4	63.56	43.0
Health	123,125	129.88	16.1	13.08	3.1	11.81	4,613	4.87	2.6	φ	φ
Social services	7,650	8.07	1.0	3.69	0.9	3.43	116	0.12	0.2	0.12	0.1
Education	345,748	364.71	45.3	136.41	31.8	121.17	38,698	40.82	22.0	30.13	20.4
Resources conservation and industrial development	1,008	1.06	0.2	1.06	0.3	1.04	699	0.74	0.4	0.74	0.5
Environment	34,256	36.14	4.5	35.35	8.2	31.25	27,979	29.51	15.9	23.58	15.9
Recreation and culture	33,929	35.79	4.4	30.36	7.1	27.06	25,158	26.54	14.3	19.49	13.2
Housing, regional planning, and development	3,543	3.74	0.5	1.14	0.3	1.14	3,560	3.76	2.0	3.39	2.3
Other	66,200	69.83	8.7	69.20	16.4	62.49	—	—	—	—	—
Total	763,088	804.95	100.0	428.82	100.0	381.04	175,702	185.34	100.0	147.89	100.0

(Table continued on next page.)

Table B.2   Continued

Alberta

Function	Current Total including grants ($000)	Current Per capita including grants ($)	Current Per cent of total (%)	Current Per capita excluding conditional grants ($)	Current Per cent of total (%)	Current Per capita excluding conditional and unconditional grants ($)	Capital Total including grants ($000)	Capital Per capita including grants ($)	Capital Per cent of total (%)	Capital Per capita excluding conditional grants ($)	Capital Per cent of total (%)
General government	71,264	36.51	3.5	36.08	6.5	33.46	12,935	6.63	2.0	φ	φ
Protection	147,309	75.47	7.2	65.73	11.9	61.26	9,188	4.71	1.4	4.58	1.6
Transportation and communication	188,041	96.33	9.2	82.66	15.0	77.22	185,471	95.02	29.2	79.66	28.6
Health	345,460	176.98	16.9	11.01	2.0	10.30	54,807	28.08	8.6	19.39	7.0
Social services	26,844	13.75	1.3	8.97	1.6	8.24	141	0.07	– –	φ	φ
Education	773,347	396.18	37.8	115.82	21.0	108.11	42,018	21.53	6.6	21.25	7.6
Resources conservation and industrial development	11,521	5.90	0.6	5.90	1.1	5.67	43,129	22.09	6.8	22.09	7.9
Environment	90,642	46.44	4.4	36.66	6.7	34.49	184,954	94.75	29.2	87.79	31.6
Recreation and culture	119,591	61.27	5.8	55.03	10.0	51.48	57,983	29.70	9.2	21.79	7.8
Housing, regional planning, and development	28,350	14.53	1.4	13.18	2.5	12.87	43,580	22.33	6.9	21.64	7.8
Other	244,265	125.14	11.9	119.92	21.7	111.72	445	0.23	0.1	φ	φ
Total	2,046,634	1,048.48	100.0	551.54	100.0	514.82	634,651	325.13	100.0	278.19	100.0

(Table continued on next page.)

Table B.2   Continued

British Columbia

Function	Current						Capital				
	Total including grants	Per capita including grants	Per cent of total	Per capita excluding conditional grants	Per cent of total	Per capita excluding conditional and unconditional grants	Total including grants	Per capita including grants	Per cent of total	Per capita excluding conditional grants	Per cent of total
	$000	$	%	$	%	$	$000	$	%	$	%
General government	78,545	31.05	4.0	25.01	4.4	23.10	7,693	3.24	2.0	3.24	2.4
Protection	182,735	72.23	9.2	71.90	12.6	66.15	13,825	5.46	3.4	5.13	3.8
Transportation and communication	105,860	41.84	5.4	40.75	7.1	37.27	105,278	41.61	26.0	37.78	27.9
Health	20,478	8.09	-1.0	4.59	0.8	4.20	426	0.17	0.1	0.13	0.1
Social services	28,319	11.19	1.4	10.92	1.9	9.97	231	0.09	0.1	0.07	—
Education	1,015,843	401.52	51.4	244.76	42.7	224.17	94,167	37.22	23.3	26.26	19.4
Resources conservation and industrial development	4,147	1.64	0.2	1.64	0.3	1.57	1,234	0.49	0.3	0.49	0.4
Environment	87,690	34.66	4.4	22.91	4.0	21.00	118,881	46.99	29.4	42.21	31.2
Recreation and culture	123,942	48.99	6.3	45.61	7.8	40.95	45,329	17.92	11.2	13.89	10.3
Housing, regional planning, and development	21,484	8.49	1.1	6.97	1.2	6.30	17,257	6.83	4.3	6.03	4.5
Other	309,008	122.14	15.6	97.57	17.2	90.30	—	—	—	—	—
Total	1,978,051	781.84	100.0	572.63	100.0	524.98	404,321	159.81	100.0	135.23	100.0

(Table concluded on next page.)

Table B.2   Concluded

	All provinces										
	Current						Capital				
Function	Total including grants	Per capita including grants	Per cent of total	Per capita excluding conditional grants	Per cent of total	Per capita excluding conditional and unconditional grants	Total including grants	Per capita including grants	Per cent of total	Per capita excluding conditional grants	Per cent of total
	$000	$	%	$	%	$	*$000*	$	%	$	%
General government	992,911	42.40	5.2	40.74	8.6	35.96	67,387	2.88	1.7	1.64	1.3
Protection	1,644,733	70.23	8.6	68.69	14.5	60.64	90,293	3.86	2.3	3.64	2.8
Transportation and communication	1,323,282	56.51	6.9	40.72	8.6	35.93	1,351,573	57.72	34.5	43.90	33.6
Health	1,050,015	44.84	5.5	5.36	1.1	4.60	79,403	3.39	2.0	2.08	1.6
Social services	63,890	27.28	3.3	12.28	2.6	10.87	42,135	1.80	1.1	1.68	1.3
Education	9,126,007	389.70	47.6	145.85	30.7	128.38	590,304	25.21	15.1	15.36	11.7
Resources conservation and industrial development	87,992	3.76	0.5	3.76	0.8	3.36	103,394	4.42	2.6	4.42	3.4
Environment	879,858	37.57	4.6	32.91	6.9	28.86	1,097,839	46.88	28.1	41.43	31.7
Recreation and culture	1,013,261	43.27	5.3	39.00	8.2	34.29	357,483	15.27	9.1	11.98	9.2
Housing, regional planning, and development	168,072	7.18	0.9	6.33	1.4	5.86	132,124	5.65	3.4	4.62	3.5
Other	2,234,332	95.41	11.7	78.90	16.6	69.43	1,756	0.08	– –	φ	φ
Total	19,159,364	818.15	100.0	474.54	100.0	418.18	3,913,691	167.12	100.0	130.75	100.0

—no expenditure.   – –under .1.   φ grant exceeds expenditure.

Source: Calculated from data in Statistics Canada, *Local Government Finance, 1978*, Catalogue no. 68-204, and from unpublished data provided by the Local Government Section, Public Finance Division, Statistics Canada.

Table B.3   Local Debenture Debt, by Purpose and Province, 1978

	Newfoundland				Prince Edward Island				Nova Scotia			
	Serial		Sinking fund		Serial		Sinking fund		Serial		Sinking fund	
Purpose	Total	Per capita	Total	Per capita	Total	Per capita	Total	Per capita	Total	Per capita	Total	Per capita
	$000	$	$000	$	$000	$	$000	$	$000	$	$000	$
General	172,215	302.66	31,063	54.59	18,932	155.18	8,069	66.14	194,500	231.27	8,413	10.00
Schools	N.A.	N.A.	N.A.	N.A.	16,630	136.31	2,878	23.59	122,169	145.27	1,671	1.99
Utilities												
Electric power and light	N.A.	N.A.	N.A.	N.A.	960	7.87	—	N.A.	648	0.77	—	N.A.
Gas supply systems	N.A.	N.A.	N.A.	N.A.	N.A.	N.A.	N.A.	N.A.	N.A.	N.A.	N.A.	N.A.
Transit systems	—	—	—	—	—	—	—	—	420	0.50	750	0.89
Telephone systems	N.A.	N.A.	N.A.	N.A.	N.A.	N.A.	N.A.	N.A.	N.A.	N.A.	N.A.	N.A.
Central heating	N.A.	N.A.	N.A.	N.A.	N.A.	N.A.	N.A.	N.A.	N.A.	N.A.	N.A.	N.A.
Airports	N.A.	N.A.	N.A.	N.A.	N.A.	N.A.	N.A.	N.A.	N.A.	N.A.	N.A.	N.A.
Total debenture debt	172,515	302.66	31,063	54.59	36,522	299.36	10,947	89.73	317,737	377.81	10,843	12.89

(Table continued on next page.)

Table B.3 Continued

Purpose	New Brunswick				Quebec				Ontario			
	Serial		Sinking fund		Serial		Sinking fund		Serial		Sinking fund	
	Total	Per capita	Total	Per capita	Total	Per capita	Total	Per capita	Total	Per capita	Total	Per capita
	$000	$	$000	$	$000	$	$000	$	$000	$	$000	$
General	219,378	315.65	4,690	6.75	4,592,087	732.04	493,223	78.63	3,093,292	366.33	n.a.	n.a.
Schools	N.A.	N.A.	N.A.	N.A.	1,390,361	221.64	n.a	n.a.	1,394,003	165.09	161,197	19.09
Utilities												
Electric power and light	6,555	9.43	52	0.07	13,262	2.11	—	—	130,202a	15.42	n.a.	n.a.
Gas supply systems	N.A.	N.A.	N.A.	N.A.	N.A.	N.A.	N.A.	N.A.	n.a.	n.a.	n.a.	n.a.
Transit systems	—	—	—	—	—	—	—	—	143,586	17.00	n.a.	n.a.
Telephone systems	N.A.	N.A.	N.A.	N.A.	N.A.	N.A.	N.A.	N.A.	n.a.	n.a.	n.a.	n.a.
Central heating	N.A.	N.A.	N.A.	N.A.	N.A.	N.A.	N.A.	N.A.	N.A.	N.A.	N.A.	N.A.
Airports	N.A.	N.A.	N.A.	N.A.	N.A.	N.A.	N.A.	N.A.	N.A.	N.A.	N.A.	N.A.
Total debenture debt	225,933	325.08	4,742	6.82	5,995,710	955.80	493,223	78.63	4,761,083	563.84	161,197	19.09

(Table continued on next page.)

Table B.3 Continued

Purpose	Manitoba Serial		Manitoba Sinking fund		Saskatchewan Serial		Saskatchewan Sinking fund		Alberta Serial		Alberta Sinking fund	
	Total	Per capita	Total	Per capita	Total	Per capita	Total	Per capita	Total	Per capita	Total	Per capita
	$000	$	$000	$	$000	$	$000	$	$000	$	$000	$
General	134,452	130.03	227,842	220.35	107,124	113.00	61,621	65.00	1,351,894	691.86	19,650	10.06
Schools	188,660	182.46	5,797	5.61	93,816	98.96	14,974	15.80	366,986	187.81	n.a	n.a.
Utilities												
Electric power and light	1,248	1.21	46,808	45.27	179	0.19	3,664	3.86	216,777	110.94	15,250	7.80
Gas supply systems	N.A.	N.A.	N.A.	N.A.	N.A.	N.A.	N.A.	N.A.	12,587	6.44	—	—
Transit systems	3,093	2.99	8,400	8.12	—	—	—	—	66,919	34.25	—	—
Telephone systems	N.A.	N.A.	N.A.	N.A.	38	0.04	—	—	208,104	106.50	11,250	5.76
Central heating	287	0.28	—	—	N.A.	N.A.	N.A.	N.A.	N.A.	N.A.	N.A.	N.A.
Airports	N.A.	N.A.	N.A.	N.A.	N.A.	N.A.	N.A.	N.A.	1,601	0.82	—	—
Total debenture debt	327,740	316.96	288,847	279.35	201,157	212.19	80,259	84.66	2,224,868	1,138.62	46,150	23.62

(Table concluded on next page.)

Table B.3 Concluded

Purpose	British Columbia				All provinces			
	Serial		Sinking fund		Serial		Sinking fund	
	Total	Per capita	Total	Per capita	Total	Per capita	Total	Per capita
	$000	$	$000	$	$000	$	$000	$
General	634,702	250.87	818,100	323.36	10,518,546	449.17	1,672,671	71.43
Schools	31,686	12.52	910,123	359.73	2,404,311	102.67	1,096,640	46.83
Utilities								
Electric power and light	562	0.22	—	—	370,393	15.82	65,774	2.81
Gas supply systems	N.A.	N.A.	N.A.	N.A.	12,587	0.54	—	—
Transit systems	—	—	—	—	214,018	9.14	9,150	0.39
Telephone systems	—	—	—	—	208,142	8.89	11,250	0.48
Central heating	N.A.	N.A.	N.A.	N.A.	287	0.01	—	—
Airports	N.A.	N.A.	N.A.	N.A.	1,601	0.07	—	—
Total debenture debt	666,950	263.62	1,728,223	683.09	13,729,885	586.30	2,855,485	121.94

n.a.—not available. N.A.—not applicable. —nil or zero. aIncludes electric light and power, gas supply, and telephone.

Source: Calculated from data in Statistics Canada, *Local Government Finance, 1978*, Catalogue no. 68-204, Table 17.

Table B.4   Local Per Capita Operating Expenditures Financed from Own-Source Revenue, by Province, 1968 and 1978

Province	1968			1978						Rate of growth 1968-1978					
				Operating		Capital		Total		Operating		Capital		Total	
	Operating	Capital	Total	Current	Constant[a]	Current	Constant[a]	Current	Constant[a]	Current	Constant[a]	Current	Constant[a]	Current	Constant[a]
	dollars									*per cent*					
Newfoundland	23.71	25.83	49.54	79.93	29.99	46.90	20.97	126.83	50.96	237.1	26.5	81.6	−18.8	156.0	2.9
Prince Edward Island	66.00	3.07	69.07	82.28	32.52	180.13	84.57	262.41	117.09	24.7	−50.7	5767.1	2,654.7	280.0	69.5
Nova Scotia	90.72	31.64	122.36	260.00	103.63	68.11	32.22	328.11	135.85	186.6	14.2	115.3	1.8	168.2	11.0
New Brunswick	26.47	15.13	41.60	96.33	37.76	62.35	29.07	158.68	66.83	263.9	42.7	312.1	92.1	281.4	60.6
Quebec	124.09	60.89	184.98	369.58	146.78	132.21	62.51	501.79	209.29	197.8	18.3	117.1	2.7	171.3	13.1
Ontario	170.21	73.77	243.98	469.39	184.94	116.61	54.75	586.00	239.69	275.8	8.7	58.1	−25.8	140.2	−1.8
Manitoba	150.47	25.53	176.00	453.87	176.40	87.21	32.30	541.08	208.70	201.6	17.2	241.6	26.5	207.4	18.6
Saskatchewan	157.33	48.99	206.32	381.04	150.49	147.89	69.46	528.93	219.95	142.2	−4.3	201.9	41.8	156.4	6.6
Alberta	153.08	86.01	239.09	514.82	201.50	278.19	130.00	793.01	331.50	236.3	31.6	223.4	51.1	231.7	38.7
British Columbia	153.40	51.29	204.69	524.98	203.09	135.23	62.12	660.21	265.21	242.2	32.4	163.7	21.1	222.5	29.6
All provinces	140.43	60.46	200.89	418.18	163.74	130.75	60.23	548.93	223.97	197.8	16.6	116.3	−0.4	173.2	11.5

[a]To obtain constant dollar figures, the current dollar figures were deflated by adjusting the implicit price index on government expenditures on goods and services and on fixed capital formation. For a description of this adjustment, see footnote 4 in Chapter 2.

Source: Calculated from Tables B.1 and B.2, and Canada Department of Finance, *Economic Review*, April 1981 (Ottawa: Supply and Services, 1981).

Appendix C

Table C.1   Distribution of Local General Revenues by Province, 1968

Revenue source	Newfoundland			Prince Edward Island			Nova Scotia		
	Total	Per capita	Per cent of total	Total	Per capita	Per cent of total	Total	Per capita	Per cent of total
	$000	$	%	$000	$	%	$000	$	%
1. Own-source revenue (total of 2,3,4,5,6,7)	21,111	42	87.5	7,773	71	42.8	82,442	108	56.0
2. Total taxes	10,573	21	43.8	6,122	55	33.1	65,173	86	44.6
Real property	5,951	12	25.0	5,474	50	30.1	59,079	78	40.4
Special assessment	274	0	0.0	70	0	0.0	1,023	1	0.5
Business	2,384	5	10.4	421	4	2.4	2,381	3	1.6
Other	1,964	4	8.3	157	1	0.6	2,690	4	2.1
3. Grants in-lieu-of taxes	2,564	5	10.4	615	6	3.6	6,164	8	4.1
4. Sales of goods and services	2,133	4	8.3	643	6	3.6	6,546	9	4.7
5. Privileges, licences, and permits	601	1	2.1	84	1	0.6	996	1	0.5
6. Return on investment	67	0	0.0	125	1	0.6	1,498	2	1.0
7. Other own-source revenue	5,173	11	22.9	184	2	1.2	1,865	2	1.0
8. Transfers—total	3,285	6	12.5	10,435	95	57.2	64,460	85	44.0
Unconditional—provincial	2	0	0.0	5	0	0.0	2,713	4	2.1
Conditional—total	3,283	6	12.5	10,430	95	57.2	61,747	81	41.9
—federal	65	0	0.0	27	0	0.0	3,976	5	2.6
—provincial	3,218	6	12.5	10,457	95	57.2	57,771	76	39.3
9. Total gross revenue	24,396	48	100.0	18,208	166	100.0	146,702	193	100.0

(Table continued on next page.)

Table C.1   Continued

Revenue source	New Brunswick			Quebec			Ontario		
	Total	Per capita	Per cent of total	Total	Per capita	Per cent of total	Total	Per capita	Per cent of total
	$000	$	%	$000	$	%	$000	$	%
1. Own-source revenue (total of 2,3,4,5,6,7)	34,865	56	96.6	1,061,868	179	65.8	1,581,094	216	63.3
2. Total taxes	11,424	18	31.0	813,177	137	50.4	1,286,854	176	51.6
Real property	11,361	18	31.0	611,647	103	37.9	1,104,895	151	44.3
Special assessment	63	0	0.0	137,428	23	8.4	33,052	5	1.5
Business	–	–	–	47,407	8	2.9	149,903	20	5.9
Other	–	–	–	16,695	3	1.1	–	–	–
3. Grants in-lieu-of taxes	14,397	23	39.7	136,007	23	8.5	80,446	11	3.2
4. Sales of goods and services	6,773	12	20.7	44,147	7	2.6	100,155	14	4.1
5. Privileges, licences, and permits	643	1	1.7	16,158	3	1.1	18,001	2	0.6
6. Return on investment	205	0	0.0	9,533	2	0.7	11,537	1	0.3
7. Other own-source revenue	1,423	2	3.4	42,846	7	2.6	84,101	12	3.5
8. Transfers—total	1,466	2	3.4	554,633	93	34.2	912,646	125	36.7
Unconditional—provincial	–	–	–	2,007	0	0.0	8,413	1	0.3
Conditional—total	1,466	2	3.4	552,626	93	34.2	904,233	124	36.4
—federal	21	0	0.0	2,904	0	0.0	27,693	4	1.2
—provincial	1,445	2	3.4	549,722	93	34.2	876,540	120	35.2
9. Total gross revenue	36,331	58	100.0	1,616,491	272	100.0	2,493,740	341	100.0

(Table continued on next page.)

Table C.1 Continued

Revenue source	Manitoba			Saskatchewan			Alberta		
	Total	Per capita	Per cent of total	Total	Per capita	Per cent of total	Total	Per capita	Per cent of total
	$000	$	%	$000	$	%	$000	$	%
1. Own-source revenue (total of 2,3,4,5,6,7)	170,422	176	63.3	183,507	191	66.6	335,864	220	66.3
2. Total taxes	129,461	133	47.8	147,613	154	53.7	217,501	143	43.1
Real property	112,322	116	41.7	127,256	133	46.3	190,451	125	37.7
Special assessment	8,044	8	2.9	7,545	8	2.8	16,252	11	3.3
Business	8,440	9	3.2	8,916	9	3.1	10,798	7	2.1
Other	655	0	0.0	3,896	4	1.4	—	—	—
3. Grants in-lieu-of taxes	8,025	8	2.9	1,958	2	0.7	35,679	23	6.9
4. Sales of goods and services	15,156	16	5.8	17,092	18	6.3	32,216	21	6.3
5. Privileges, licences, and permits	2,582	3	1.1	3,386	4	1.4	11,291	8	2.4
6. Return on investment	6,779	7	2.5	5,636	6	2.1	23,238	15	4.5
7. Other own-source revenue	8,419	9	3.2	7,822	8	2.8	15,939	10	3.0
8. Transfers—total	99,321	102	36.7	92,171	96	33.4	170,992	112	33.7
Unconditional—provincial	2,652	3	1.1	2,182	2	0.7	1,824	1	0.3
Conditional—total	96,669	99	35.6	89,989	94	32.7	169,168	111	33.4
—federal	608	0	0.0	876	1	0.3	832	1	0.3
—provincial	96,061	99	35.6	89,113	93	32.4	168,336	110	33.1
9. Total gross revenue	269,743	278	100.0	275,678	287	100.0	506,856	332	100.0

(Table concluded on next page.)

Table C.1 Concluded

Revenue source	British Columbia			All provinces		
	Total	Per capita	Per cent of total	Total	Per capita	Per cent of total
	$000	$	%	$000	$	%
1. Own-source revenue (total of 2,3,4,5,6,7)	360,484	180	61.9	3,839,230	185	64.2
2. Total taxes	296,564	148	50.9	2,984,462	144	50.0
Real property	265,344	132	45.4	2,493,784	121	42.0
Special assessment	23,779	12	4.1	227,530	11	3.8
Business	7,405	4	1.4	237,055	11	3.8
Other	36	0	0.0	26,093	1	0.3
3. Grants in-lieu-of taxes	3,428	2	0.7	289,283	14	4.9
4. Sales of goods and services	28,265	14	4.8	253,126	12	4.2
5. Privileges, licences, and permits	13,955	7	2.4	67,697	3	1.0
6. Return on investment	5,747	3	1.0	64,365	3	1.0
7. Other own-source revenue	12,525	6	2.1	180,297	9	3.1
8. Transfers—total	223,637	111	38.1	2,133,046	103	35.7
Unconditional—provincial	3,160	1	0.3	22,958	1	0.3
Conditional—total	220,477	110	37.8	2,110,088	102	35.4
—federal	2,340	1	0.3	39,342	2	0.7
—provincial	218,137	109	37.5	2,070,746	100	34.7
9. Total gross revenue	584,121	291	100.0	5,972,276	288	100.0

Source: Statistics Canada, *Local Government Finance, 1968*, Catalogue no. 68-204, Table 1.

Totals may not add precisely because of rounding. — — nil or zero. 0 denotes very small sums.

Table C.2 Distribution of General Revenue by Province, 1978

Revenue source	Newfoundland			Prince Edward Island			Nova Scotia		
	Total	Per capita	Per cent of total	Total	Per capita	Per cent of total	Total	Per capita	Per cent of total
	$000	$	%	$000	$	%	$000	$	%
1. Own-source revenue (total of 2,3,4,5,6,7)	60,050	106	57.8	10,509	86	14.7	248,283	295	40.0
2. Total taxes	43,907	77	42.3	5,641	46	7.9	168,813	202	27.3
Real property	30,402	53	29.3	5,533	45	7.7	141,622	168	22.8
Special assessment	871	2	0.8	108	1	0.2	3,587	4	0.6
Business	9,274	16	8.9	n.a.	n.a.	n.a.	20,823	25	3.4
Other	3,360	6	3.2	—	—	—	3,781	4	0.6
3. Grants in-lieu-of taxes	2,668	5	2.6	—	—	—	18,142	22	2.9
4. Sales of goods and services	11,035	19	10.6	3,401	28	4.8	43,144	51	6.9
5. Privileges, licences, and permits	769	1	0.7	69	1	0.1	1,204	1	0.2
6. Return on investment	338	1	0.3	825	7	1.2	3,522	4	0.6
7. Other own-source revenue	1,333	2	1.3	573	5	0.8	12,458	15	2.0
8. Transfers—total	43,796	77	42.2	60,885	499	85.3	373,036	444	60.0
Unconditional—provincial	7,134	13	6.9	1,983	16	2.8	65,073	77	10.5
Conditional—total	36,662	64	35.3	58,902	482	82.5	307,963	366	49.6
—federal	9,083	16	8.7	14,077	115	19.7	10,490	12	1.7
—provincial	27,579	48	26.6	44,825	367	62.8	297,473	354	47.9
9. Total gross revenue	103,846	183	100.0	71,394	585	100.0	621,319	739	100.0

(Table continued on next page.)

Table C.2 Continued

Revenue source	New Brunswick			Quebec			Ontario		
	Total	Per capita	Per cent of total	Total	Per capita	Per cent of total	Total	Per capita	Per cent of total
	$000	$	%	$000	$	%	$000	$	%
1. Own-source revenue (total of 2,3,4,5,6,7)	84,280	121	54.2	2,674,312	426	45.3	4,560,523	540	54.5
2. Total taxes	56,840	82	36.5	1,973,994	315	33.4	3,394,333	402	40.6
Real property	56,638	81	36.4	1,605,008	256	27.2	2,850,380	338	34.1
Special assessment	202	0	0.0	171,502	27	2.9	40,273	5	0.5
Business	n.a.	n.a.	n.a.	140,244	22	2.4	430,625	51	5.2
Other	n.a.	n.a.	n.a.	57,240	9	1.0	73,055	9	0.9
3. Grants in-lieu-of taxes	n.a.	n.a.	n.a.	141,157	23	2.4	166,763	20	2.0
4. Sales of goods and services	23,373	34	15.0	369,454	59	6.3	704,811	83	8.4
5. Privileges, licences, and permits	955	1	0.6	13,648	2	0.2	47,068	6	0.6
6. Return on investment	1,714	2	1.1	63,834	10	1.1	138,740	16	1.7
7. Other own-source revenue	1,398	2	0.9	112,225	18	1.9	108,808	13	1.3
8. Transfers—total	71,337	103	45.8	3,228,361	515	54.7	3,799,755	450	45.5
Unconditional—provincial	49,320	71	31.7	480,320	77	8.1	459,726	54	5.5
Conditional—total	22,017	32	14.1	2,748,041	438	46.6	3,340,029	396	40.0
—federal	4,845	7	3.1	73,021	12	1.2	59,886	7	0.7
—provincial	17,172	25	11.0	2,675,020	426	45.3	3,280,143	388	39.2
9. Total gross revenue	155,617	224	100.0	5,902,673	941	100.0	8,360,278	990	100.0

(Table continued on next page.)

Table C.2   Continued

Revenue source	Manitoba			Saskatchewan			Alberta		
	Total	Per capita	Per cent of total	Total	Per capita	Per cent of total	Total	Per capita	Per cent of total
	$000	$	%	$000	$	%	$000	$	%
1. Own-source revenue (total of 2,3,4,5,6,7)	555,608	537	60.3	460,021	485	51.0	1,158,867	593	49.8
2. Total taxes	395,404	382	42.9	317,120	335	35.2	692,128	354	29.7
Real property	347,893	336	37.7	281,221	297	31.2	590,256	302	25.3
Special assessment	14,384	14	1.6	8,391	9	0.9	25,760	13	1.1
Business	22,171	21	2.4	19,083	20	2.1	76,112	39	3.3
Other	10,956	11	1.2	8,425	9	0.9	—	—	—
3. Grants in-lieu-of taxes	44,477	43	4.8	12,241	13	1.4	30,767	16	1.3
4. Sales of goods and services	61,123	59	6.6	85,497	90	9.5	279,780	143	12.0
5. Privileges, licences, and permits	5,913	6	0.6	7,141	8	0.8	36,326	19	1.6
6. Return on investment	31,503	30	3.4	19,314	20	2.1	85,273	44	3.7
7. Other own-source revenue	17,188	17	1.9	18,708	20	2.1	34,593	18	1.5
8. Transfers—total	366,054	354	39.7	441,806	466	49.0	1,169,659	599	50.2
Unconditional—provincial	18,872	18	2.0	45,291	48	5.0	71,669	37	3.1
Conditional—total	347,182	336	37.7	396,515	418	44.0	1,097,990	562	47.2
—federal	7,317	7	0.8	7,820	8	0.9	27,338	14	1.2
—provincial	339,865	329	36.9	388,695	410	43.1	1,070,652	548	46.0
9. Total gross revenue	921,662	891	100.0	901,827	951	100.0	2,328,526	1,192	100.0

(Table concluded on next page.)

Table C.2 Concluded

Revenue source	British Columbia			All provinces		
	Total	Per capita	Per cent of total	Total	Per capita	Per cent of total
	$000	$	%	$000	$	%
1. Own-source revenue (total of 2,3,4,5,6,7)	1,433,657	567	66.8	11,246,110	480	52.3
2. Total taxes	1,092,689	432	50.9	8,141,869	348	37.8
Real property	1,027,613	406	47.9	6,936,566	296	32.3
Special assessment	39,727	16	1.9	304,805	13	1.4
Business	24,929	10	1.2	743,261	32	3.5
Other	420	0	0.0	157,237	7	0.7
3. Grants in-lieu-of taxes	28,004	11	1.3	444,219	19	2.1
4. Sales of goods and services	226,042	89	10.5	1,807,660	77	8.4
5. Privileges, licences, and permits	28,174	11	1.3	141,267	6	0.7
6. Return on investment	39,377	16	1.8	384,440	16	1.8
7. Other own-source revenue	19,371	8	0.9	326,655	14	1.5
8. Transfers—total	712,628	282	33.2	10,267,317	438	47.7
Unconditional—provincial	120,539	48	5.6	1,319,927	56	6.1
Conditional—total	592,089	234	27.6	8,947,390	382	41.6
—federal	24,800	10	1.2	238,677	10	1.1
—provincial	567,289	224	26.4	8,708,713	372	40.5
9. Total gross revenue	2,146,285	848	100.0	21,513,427	919	100.0

Totals may not add precisely because of rounding.   n.a. not applicable.
- -nil or zero.   0.0 very small sums.

Source: Statistics Canada, *Local Government Finance, 1978*, Catalogue no. 68-204, Table 1.

Table C.3 Municipal Conditional Grants, by Function and Province, 1968 and 1978

Newfoundland

Function	Current 1968			Capital 1968			Current 1978			Capital 1978		
	Total	Per capita	Per cent of total	Total	Per capita	Per cent of total	Total	Per capita	Per cent of total	Total	Per capita	Per cent of total
	$000	$	%	$000	$	%	$000	$	%	$000	$	%
General government	—	—	—	—	—	—	10	0.02	—	126	0.22	1.0
Protection	8	0.02	0.5	—	—	—	118	0.21	0.5	54	0.09	0.4
Transportation and communication	633	1.25	29.0	753	1.49	68.4	7,203	12.66	30.2	4,106	7.22	32.0
Health	—	—	—	—	—	—	—	—	—	—	—	—
Social services	—	—	—	—	—	—	—	—	—	—	—	—
Education	—	—	—	—	—	—	—	—	—	—	—	—
Natural resources	—	—	—	—	—	—	—	—	—	—	—	—
Agriculture, trade, industry, and tourism	—	—	—	—	—	—	—	—	—	—	—	—
Environment	1,481	2.92	67.7	61	0.12	5.5	12,574	22.10	52.8	4,057	7.13	31.6
Recreation and culture	47	0.09	2.1	45	0.09	4.1	2,304	4.05	9.7	339	0.60	2.6
Housing	—	—	—	—	—	—	495	0.87	2.1	650	1.14	5.1
Other	14	0.03	0.7	241	0.48	22.1	1,131	1.98	4.8	3,495	6.14	27.3
Total	2,183	4.31	100.0	1,100	2.17	100.0	23,835	41.89	100.0	12,827	22.54	100.0

(Table continued on next page.)

Table C.3   Continued

Prince Edward Island

Function	Current 1968			Capital 1968			Current 1978			Capital 1978		
	Total $000	Per capita $	Per cent of total %	Total $000	Per capita $	Per cent of total %	Total $000	Per capita $	Per cent of total %	Total $000	Per capita $	Per cent of total %
General government	23	0.21	0.3	—	—	—	10	0.08	—	1	0.01	—
Protection	24	0.22	0.3	—	—	—	2	0.02	—	298	2.44	1.8
Transportation and communication	55	0.50	0.7	21	0.19	0.7	61	0.50	0.1	1,415	11.60	8.6
Health	—	—	—	—	—	—	—	—	—	—	—	—
Social services	—	—	—	—	—	—	—	—	—	—	—	—
Education	7,528	68.44	98.6	2,743	24.94	98.2	39,817	326.37	93.8	2,239	18.35	13.6
Natural resources	—	—	—	—	—	—	—	—	—	—	—	—
Agriculture, trade, industry, and tourism	—	—	—	—	—	—	—	—	—	—	—	—
Environment	—	—	—	26	0.24	0.9	7	0.06	—	—	—	—
Recreation and culture	7	0.06	0.1	3	0.03	0.1	275	2.25	0.6	374	3.07	2.3
Housing	—	—	—	—	—	—	407	3.34	1.0	24	0.20	0.2
Other	—	—	—	—	—	—	1,875	15.37	4.4	12,097	99.16	73.55
Total	7,637	69.43	100.0	2,793	25.39	100.0	42,454	347.98	100.0	16,448	134.82	100.0

(Table continued on next page.)

Table C.3   Continued

Nova Scotia

Function	Current 1968			Capital 1968			Current 1978			Capital 1978		
	Total	Per capita	Per cent of total	Total	Per capita	Per cent of total	Total	Per capita	Per cent of total	Total	Per capita	Per cent of total
	$000	$	%	$000	$	%	$000	$	%	$000	$	%
General government	12	0.02	—	—	—	—	264	0.31	0.1	1,000	1.19	4.7
Protection	1,995	2.63	3.2	—	—	—	7,495	8.91	2.6	231	0.27	1.1
Transportation and communication	506	0.67	0.8	5,219	6.87	64.6	5,082	6.04	1.8	6,501	7.73	30.8
Health	9,185	12.09	14.7	—	—	—	25,797	30.67	9.0	102	0.12	0.5
Social services	5,817	7.65	9.3	107	0.14	1.3	31,166	37.06	10.9	—	—	—
Education	44,225	58.19	70.8	—	—	—	194,163	230.87	67.7	2,675	3.18	12.7
Natural resources	—	—	—	—	—	—	—	—	—	—	—	—
Agriculture, trade, industry, and tourism	—	—	—	—	—	—	—	—	—	—	—	—
Environment	207	0.27	0.3	1,135	1.49	14.0	5,235	6.22	1.8	9,392	11.17	44.5
Recreation and culture	435	0.57	0.7	67	0.09	0.8	4,394	5.22	1.5	497	0.59	2.4
Housing	—	—	—	—	—	—	2,787	3.31	1.0	517	0.61	2.5
Other	110	0.14	0.2	1,556	2.05	19.3	10,451	12.43	3.6	214	0.25	1.0
Total	62,492	82.23	100.0	8,084	10.64	100.0	286,834	341.06	100.0	21,129	25.12	100.0

(Table continued on next page.)

Table C.3   Continued

New Brunswick

Function	Current 1968			Capital 1968			Current 1978			Capital 1978		
	Total	Per capita	Per cent of total	Total	Per capita	Per cent of total	Total	Per capita	Per cent of total	Total	Per capita	Per cent of total
	$000	$	%	$000	$	%	$000	$	%	$000	$	%
General government	104	0.17	48.6	—	—	—	—	—	—	210	0.30	1.4
Protection	8	0.01	2.9	—	—	—	—	—	—	394	0.57	2.7
Transportation and communication	2	--	--	166	0.27	13.5	925	1.33	12.7	4,769	6.86	32.4
Health	13	0.02	5.7	—	—	—	—	—	—	—	—	—
Social services	—	—	—	—	—	—	—	—	—	—	—	—
Education	—	—	—	—	—	—	—	—	—	—	—	—
Natural resources	—	—	—	—	—	—	—	—	—	—	—	—
Agriculture, trade, industry, and tourism	—	—	—	—	—	—	—	—	—	—	—	—
Environment	—	—	—	21	0.03	1.5	2,962	4.26	40.6	7,395	10.64	50.3
Recreation and culture	18	0.03	8.6	—	—	—	2,851	4.10	39.0	812	1.17	5.5
Housing	—	—	—	—	—	—	168	0.24	2.3	1,084	1.56	7.4
Other	76	0.12	34.3	1,058	1.70	85.0	399	0.57	5.5	48	0.01	0.3
Total	221	.35	100.0	1,245	2.00	100.0	7,305	10.51	100.0	14,712	21.17	100.0

(Table continued on next page.)

Table C.3   Continued

Quebec

Function	Current 1968			Capital 1968			Current 1978			Capital 1978		
	Total	Per capita	Per cent of total	Total	Per capita	Per cent of total	Total	Per capita	Per cent of total	Total	Per capita	Per cent of total
	$000	$	%	$000	$	%	$000	$	%	$000	$	%
General government	—	—	—	336	0.06	0.3	18,208	2.90	0.7	—	—	—
Protection	862	0.15	0.2	184	0.03	0.1	3,593	0.57	0.1	—	—	—
Transportation and communication	22,101	3.73	5.4	7,161	1.21	5.1	38,466	6.12	1.5	23,163	3.69	11.2
Health	29	—	—	—	—	—	73	0.01	—	—	—	—
Social services	—	—	—	—	—	—	292	0.05	—	—	—	—
Education	382,944	64.61	93.0	125,600	21.19	89.2	2,170,073	345.39	85.4	167,347	26.63	80.8
Natural resources	—	—	—	—	—	—	—	—	—	—	—	—
Agriculture, trade, industry, and tourism	—	—	—	—	—	—	—	—	—	—	—	—
Environment	5,392	0.91	1.3	7,484	1.26	5.3	33,562	5.34	1.3	14,213	2.26	6.9
Recreation and culture	—	—	—	—	—	—	27,632	4.40	1.1	2,494	0.40	1.2
Housing	—	—	—	—	—	—	1,660	0.26	0.1	—	—	—
Other	562	0.09	0.1	—	—	—	247,265	39.35	9.7	—	—	—
Total	411,890	69.49	100.0	140,765	23.75	100.0	2,540,824	404.40	100.0	207,217	32.98	100.0

(Table continued on next page.)

Table C.3 Continued

Ontario

Function	Current 1968 Total $000	Current 1968 Per capita $	Current 1968 Per cent of total %	Capital 1968 Total $000	Capital 1968 Per capita $	Capital 1968 Per cent of total %	Current 1978 Total $000	Current 1978 Per capita $	Current 1978 Per cent of total %	Capital 1978 Total $000	Capital 1978 Per capita $	Capital 1978 Per cent of total %
General government	—	—	—	—	—	—	2,766	0.33	0.1	1,107	0.13	0.3
Protection	—	—	—	—	—	—	1,861	0.22	0.1	1,077	0.13	0.3
Transportation and communication	104,870	14.35	12.7	82,080	11.23	50.3	267,132	31.63	9.0	227,946	26.99	63.5
Health	91,972	12.59	11.1	—	—	—	382,461	45.29	12.8	7,502	0.89	2.1
Social services	49,955	6.83	6.0	—	—	—	296,883	35.15	10.0	1,248	0.15	0.4
Education	571,099	78.17	69.1	65,091	8.91	39.9	1,951,783	231.12	65.5	—	—	—
Natural resources	—	—	—	—	—	—	—	—	—	—	—	—
Agriculture, trade, industry, and tourism	—	—	—	—	—	—	4,132	0.49	0.1	—	—	—
Environment	1,483	0.20	0.2	9,722	1.33	6.0	31,735	3.76	1.1	58,026	6.87	16.2
Recreation and culture	—	—	—	—	—	—	6,609	0.78	0.2	39,640	4.69	11.0
Housing	—	—	—	—	—	—	—	—	—	13,101	1.55	3.7
Other	7,537	1.03	0.9	6,321	0.87	3.9	35,456	4.20	1.2	9,564	1.13	2.7
Total	826,916	113.18	100.0	163,214	22.34	100.0	2,980,818	352.97	100.0	359,211	42.54	100.0

(Table continued on next page.)

Table C.3   Continued

Manitoba

Function	Current 1968			Capital 1968			Current 1978			Capital 1978		
	Total	Per capita	Per cent of total	Total	Per capita	Per cent of total	Total	Per capita	Per cent of total	Total	Per capita	Per cent of total
	$000	$	%	$000	$	%	$000	$	%	$000	$	%
General government	—	—	—	—	—	—	1,011	0.98	0.3	166	0.16	0.4
Protection	17	0.02	—	70	0.07	0.3	1,684	1.63	0.6	62	0.06	0.2
Transportation and communication	297	0.31	0.3	4,467	4.60	19.2	5,600	5.42	1.8	11,527	11.16	29.2
Health	12,725	13.11	14.8	—	—	—	72,635	70.31	23.6	192	0.18	0.5
Social services	2,485	2.56	2.9	—	—	—	8,872	8.59	2.9	—	—	—
Education	70,506	72.61	81.9	17,910	18.44	76.8	194,321	188.11	63.2	20,076	19.43	50.9
Natural resources	—	—	—	—	—	—	—	—	—	—	—	—
Agriculture, trade, industry, and tourism	—	—	—	—	—	—	—	—	—	—	—	—
Environment	—	—	—	161	0.17	0.7	1,048	1.01	0.3	1,802	1.74	4.6
Recreation and culture	45	0.05	0.1	—	—	—	5,000	4.84	1.6	664	0.64	1.7
Housing	—	—	—	—	—	—	58	0.06	—	4,975	4.82	12.6
Other	19	0.02	—	692	0.71	3.0	17,489	16.93	5.7	—	—	—
Total	86,094	88.67	100.0	23,300	24.00	100.0	307,718	297.89	100.0	39,464	38.20	100.0

(Table continued on next page.)

Table C.3 Continued

Saskatchewan

Function	Current 1968			Capital 1968			Current 1978			Capital 1978		
	Total	Per capita	Per cent of total	Total	Per capita	Per cent of total	Total	Per capita	Per cent of total	Total	Per capita	Per cent of total
	$000	$	%	$000	$	%	$000	$	%	$000	$	%
General government	55	0.06	0.1	—	—	—	551	0.58	0.2	216	0.23	0.6
Protection	85	0.09	0.1	—	—	—	1,602	1.69	0.5	2,347	2.48	6.1
Transportation and communication	16,208	16.88	15.0	5	0.01	0.1	18,878	16.75	4.4	5,531	5.83	14.3
Health	29,183	30.40	27.0	—	—	—	110,726	116.80	30.9	5,866	6.19	15.2
Social services	1,051	1.09	1.0	—	—	—	4,156	4.38	1.2	—	—	—
Education	58,961	61.42	54.5	10,494	10.93	97.2	216,430	228.30	60.5	10,130	10.70	26.2
Natural resources	—	—	—	—	—	—	—	—	—	—	—	—
Agriculture, trade, industry, and tourism	—	—	—	—	—	—	—	—	—	—	—	—
Environment	942	0.98	0.9	275	0.29	2.6	750	0.79	0.2	5,624	5.93	14.5
Recreation and culture	731	0.76	0.7	17	0.02	0.2	5,144	5.43	1.4	6,680	7.05	17.3
Housing	—	—	—	—	—	—	2,461	2.60	0.7	352	0.37	0.9
Other	937	0.98	0.9	—	—	—	125	0.13	—	1,946	2.05	5.03
Total	108,153	112.66	100.0	10,791	11.24	100.0	357,823	377.45	100.0	38,692	40.81	100.0

(Table continued on next page.)

Table C.3 Continued

Alberta

Function	Current 1968			Capital 1968			Current 1978			Capital 1978		
	Total	Per capita	Per cent of total	Total	Per capita	Per cent of total	Total	Per capita	Per cent of total	Total	Per capita	Per cent of total
	$000	$	%	$000	$	%	$000	$	%	$000	$	%
General government	62	0.04	—	—	—	—	839	0.43	0.1	26,234	13.44	20.5
Protection	193	0.13	0.1	115	0.08	0.6	19,012	9.74	2.0	254	0.13	0.2
Transportation and communication	7,497	4.91	3.7	11,366	7.45	56.9	26,684	13.67	2.8	29,983	15.36	23.4
Health	53,203	34.86	26.4	984	0.64	4.9	323,973	165.97	33.4	16,963	8.69	13.3
Social services	3,555	2.33	1.8	—	—	—	9,331	4.78	1.0	1,542	0.79	1.2
Education	135,598	88.86	67.2	6,252	4.10	31.3	547,263	280.36	56.4	547	0.28	0.4
Natural resources	—	—	—	—	—	—	—	—	—	—	—	—
Agriculture, trade, industry, and tourism	—	—	—	—	—	—	—	—	—	—	—	—
Environment	296	0.19	0.1	1,063	0.70	5.3	19,091	9.78	2.0	13,586	6.96	10.6
Recreation and culture	346	0.23	0.2	105	0.07	0.5	12,180	6.24	1.3	15,440	7.91	12.1
Housing	—	—	—	—	—	—	1,464	0.75	0.2	1,347	0.69	1.1
Other	1,104	0.72	0.5	101	0.07	0.5	10,189	5.22	1.1	22,097	11.32	17.3
Total	201,854	132.28	100.0	19,986	13.10	100.0	970,027	496.44	100.0	127,993	65.57	100.0

(Table continued on next page.)

Table C.3   Continued

British Columbia

Function	Current 1968 Total $000	Per capita $	Per cent of total %	Capital 1968 Total $000	Per capita $	Per cent of total %	Current 1978 Total $000	Per capita $	Per cent of total %	Capital 1978 Total $000	Per capita $	Per cent of total %
General government	—	—	—	176	0.09	0.8	15,281	6.04	2.9	—	—	—
Protection	7,227	3.60	3.7	130	0.06	0.5	835	0.33	0.2	835	0.33	1.3
Transportation and communication	28,817	14.36	14.7	1,690	0.84	7.0	2,758	1.09	0.5	9,690	3.83	15.4
Health	606	0.30	0.3	8	– –	– –	8,855	3.50	1.7	101	0.04	0.2
Social services	35,339	17.61	18.0	—	—	—	683	0.27	0.1	51	0.02	0.1
Education	119,998	59.79	61.0	20,500	10.21	85.4	396,603	156.76	74.9	27,729	11.04	44.5
Natural resources	—	—	—	—	—	—	—	—	—	—	—	—
Agriculture, trade, industry, and tourism	—	—	—	—	—	—	—	—	—	—	—	—
Environment	3,700	1.84	1.9	878	0.44	3.7	29,728	11.75	5.6	12,093	4.78	19.3
Recreation and culture	588	0.29	0.3	408	0.20	1.7	8,551	3.38	1.6	10,196	4.03	16.2
Housing	—	—	—	—	—	—	3,846	1.52	0.7	2,075	0.82	3.3
Other	310	0.15	0.2	204	0.10	0.8	62,162	24.57	11.7	25	0.01	– –
Total	196,585	97.95	100.0	23,994	11.96	100.0	529,301	209.21	100.0	62,795	24.82	100.0

(Table concluded on next page.)

Table C.3   Concluded

All provinces

Function	Current 1968			Capital 1968			Current 1978			Capital 1978		
	Total	Per capita	Per cent of total	Total	Per capita	Per cent of total	Total	Per capita	Per cent of total	Total	Per capita	Per cent of total
	$000	$	%	$000	$	%	$000	$	%	$000	$	%
General government	256	0.01	—	512	0.02	0.1	38,874	1.66	0.5	29,038	1.24	3.2
Protection	10,419	0.51	0.6	499	0.02	0.1	36,064	1.54	0.5	5,152	0.22	0.6
Transportation and communication	180,986	8.74	9.5	112,928	5.46	28.6	369,770	15.79	4.6	323,637	13.82	36.0
Health	196,916	9.51	10.4	9	0.05	0.3	924,543	39.48	11.5	30,678	1.31	3.4
Social services	98,202	4.74	5.2	107	0.01	—	351,270	15.00	4.4	2,810	0.12	0.3
Education	1,390,859	67.20	72.9	248,550	12.01	62.9	5,710,479	243.25	70.9	230,667	9.85	25.6
Natural resources	—	—	—	—	—	—	—	—	—	—	—	—
Agriculture, trade, industry, and tourism												
Environment	12,053	0.58	0.6	20,826	1.01	5.2	109,128	4.66	1.4	127,628	5.45	14.2
Recreation and culture	3,700	0.18	0.2	645	0.03	0.2	99,995	4.27	1.2	77,045	3.29	8.6
Housing	—	—	—	—	—	—	19,905	0.85	0.2	24,101	1.03	2.7
Other	10,669	0.52	0.6	10,173	0.49	2.6	386,631	16.51	4.8	49,412	2.11	5.5
Total	1,904,060	91.99	100.0	395,272	19.10	100.0	8,046,654	343.61	100.0	900,188	38.44	100.0

— no grants received.   - - amounts under .1.

Source: Calculated from data in Statistics Canada, *Local Government Finance, 1968* and *1978*, Catalogue no. 68-204, and from unpublished data provided by the Local Government Section, Public Finance Division, Statistics Canada.

Table C.4   Comparison of Per Capita Grant Amounts (Operating and Capital) by Urban Size, [a] by Province

Function	Newfoundland		Nova Scotia		New Brunswick		Quebec	
	All municipalities	Urban regions	All municipalities	Urban regions	All municipalities	Urban regions	All municipalities	Urban regions
General government	0.24	—	1.50	—	0.30	—	2.90	—
Protection	0.09	—	9.18	6.96	0.57	8.51	0.57	0.79
Transportation	19.88	11.27	13.77	19.67	8.19	5.75	9.81	14.63
Environment	29.23	—	17.39	14.15	14.90	12.77	7.60	22.13
Health	0.21	—	30.79	25.46	—	—	0.01	—
Social services	—	—	37.06	49.93	—	—	0.05	—
Regional planning and housing	2.01	0.64	3.92	0.54	1.80	8.59	0.26	2.15
Recreation and culture	4.65	1.74	5.81	4.25	5.27	2.92	4.80	4.28
Education	—	—	234.05	265.05	—	—	372.02	352.72
Total	64.43	21.32	366.18	381.23	31.68	38.46	437.38	428.58

(Table continued on next page.)

Table C.4   Continued

Function	Ontario		Manitoba		Saskatchewan		Alberta	
	All municipalities	Urban regions	All municipalities	Urban regions	All municipalities	Urban regions	All municipalities	Urban regions
General government	0.46	0.41	1.14	—	0.81	0.85	13.87	0.30
Protection	0.35	2.13	1.69	1.09	4.17	0.18	9.87	14.58
Transportation	58.62	37.04	16.58	31.26	22.58	6.98	29.03	40.45
Environment	7.36	6.96	2.75	0.21	6.72	2.72	16.74	6.18
Health.	46.18	28.80	70.49	22.12	122.99	116.23	174.66	121.79
Social services	35.30	34.41	8.59	10.33	4.38	0.96	5.57	12.34
Regional planning and housing . . .	2.33	1.25	4.88	4.25	2.97	1.23	1.44	2.06
Recreation and culture	8.45	6.75	5.48	8.81	12.48	13.97	14.15	2.56
Education.	231.12	240.49	207.54	215.55	239.00	226.89	280.64	282.65
Total	395.51	368.88	336.09	309.22	418.26	371.02	562.01	496.94

(Table concluded on next page.)

Table C.4 Concluded

Function	British Columbia		All provinces	
	All municipalities	Urban regions	All municipalities	Urban regions
General government	6.04	0.06	2.90	0.25
Protection	0.66	0.19	1.76	2.65
Transportation	4.92	1.84	29.61	26.62
Environment	16.53	1.59	10.11	9.50
Health	3.54	3.61	40.79	28.42
Social services	0.29	0.28	15.12	18.70
Regional planning and housing	2.34	2.06	1.88	1.79
Recreation and culture	7.41	4.86	7.56	5.80
Education	167.80	187.61	253.70	259.53
Total	234.03	212.29	382.05	368.39

aPrince Edward Island is excluded because there are no urban regions as defined by Statistics Canada.

Source: Calculated from data in Table C-3 and Statistics Canada, *Local Government Finance, Preliminary 1978-Estimates 1979*, Catalogue no. 68-203.

Index